A DICTIONARY OF

CANADIAN ARTISTS

A DICTIONARY OF CANADIAN ARTISTS

COMPILED BY

COLIN S. MACDONALD

VOLUME SIX

CANADIAN PAPERBACKS PUBLISHING LTD.
17 Gwynne Avenue,
Ottawa, Canada, K1Y 1X1

To

H. Spencer Clark

who made possible the printing of
this volume

I wish to express special acknowledgement to
the Canada Council for research and publication grants.

Colin S. MacDonald

ACKNOWLEDGEMENTS

I wish to express my indebtedness to all who have made possible this compilation:

To Dr. R.H. Hubbard, Chief Curator of The National Gallery of Canada for permission to use material from the National Gallery of Canada publications; the late Alan Jarvis and Paul Arthur for permission to use material from *Canadian Art* magazine; Prof. Melville W. Thistle, School of Journalism, Carleton University, for his vital constructive criticism; J. Russell Harper, author of *Painting in Canada/A History* and *Early Painters and Engravers in Canada* for his key suggestions in the early stages of the manuscript; the late William Colgate, author of *Canadian Art, Its Origin and Development*; the late Graham McInnes, author of *Canadian Art*; the late Robert Ayre of *The Montreal Star*; Robert Fulford, Editor of *Saturday Night* for passages from his writings on Canadian artists; *The Toronto Star*, *The London Free Press*, *The Montreal Gazette*, *Globe & Mail*, for permission to quote passages from their art reviews and columns; W.J. Withrow, author of *Contemporary Canadian Painting* and Director of the Art Gallery of Ontario; Lawrence Sabbath of Montreal, writer and critic; Dr. William S.A. Dale, Chairman and William S. Hart, Associate Professor, Art Department, University of Western Ontario for their vital moral support; Burns and MacEachern Limited for excerpts from Paul Duval's *Canadian Drawings and Prints*, *Canadian Water Colour Painting*, *Group of Seven Drawings*; The MacMillan Company of Canada Limited for excerpts from *Canadian Art*; Clarke, Irwin & Company Limited for excerpts from *A Painter's Country* by A.Y. Jackson and *Growing Pains* by Emily Carr; to Ryerson Press for excerpts from their pubications on Canadian artists too numerous to mention here (acknowledgements to their authors appear in the text); *Maclean's Magazine* for excerpts from articles dealing with Canadian artists (acknowledgements to their authors appear in the text); *Weekend Magazine* for excerpts from their publications (acknowledgements to their authors appear in the text); the Reference Department of the Ottawa Public Library; the following members of the National Gallery of Canada Library: Mrs. Mary N. Balke, former chief Librarian; Deputy Librarian Miss J.E. Hunter also former Librarian Miss Christa Dedering; Reference Services Librarian, Maija Vilcins; Reference Clerk James Kelly; former Art Documentalists, Alexandra Pritz and Isabel Van Lierde (now Serials Librarian) and Art Documentalist Susan Hasbury; Acting Head of Research of the National Postal Museum, James W. Brennan; Evelyn de Rostaing McMann, author of *Royal Canadian Academy of Arts, Exhibitions and Members 1880-1979*: former summer assistants Lucya Yarymowich and Judy Kaminsky; to the following who have supplied information at various times and moral support: Jean-René Ostiguy, National Gallery of Canada, Research Curator, lecturer and author on Canadian art; Dennis Reid, Curator of Canadian Historical Art, Art Gallery of Ontario and author of *A Concise History of Canadian Painting* and numerous other studies on Canadian artists; Charles C. Hill, Curator of Canadian Art, National Gallery of Canada and author of *Canadian Painting in The Thirties*; Paul Duval author of many books and articles on Canadian art and artists; Richard B.Simmins, author, lecturer and critic on art; Miss Norah McCullough, former Western Representative, National Gallery of Canada; J. Stanford Perrot of the Southern Alberta Institute of Technology; to the following art societies: Royal Canadian Academy of Arts; Canadian Group of Painters, Canadian Society of Painters in Water Colour; Sculptors' Society of Canada; Nova Scotia Society of Artists; Ontario Society of Artists; Manitoba Society of Artists, Alberta Society of Artists; British Columbia Society of Artists; Federation of Canadian Wood Carvers; Young Commonwealth of Artists for information on Canadian artists abroad; Raymond Poulin, Mrs. Moy Smith and Michel Champagne for information on Quebec artists; to over 800 Canadian artists from every province in Canada and scores of collectors and art dealers who have contributed information on art and artists in Canada.

Colin S. MacDonald
Author/Editor

PERRIN, Barbara

Born in Detroit, Michigan, she attended the MacKenzie High School and studied life drawing and colour theory at the Cass Technical School in Detroit and later took commercial and fine arts training with the Famous Artists School. For a period she did commercial art for magazines, catalogues and brochures for the Hemsing Advertising Agency in Ferndale, Michigan and drafting for the Michigan Bell Telephone Engineering Department in Detroit. She came to Canada in 1968 when her father and mother, Mr. & Mrs. George Hale retired to Inwood and Barbara set up her studio nearby. She did mainly paintings in water colours for the next five years which she exhibited in fairs at Dresden, Alvinston, Petrolia and Wyoming, winning in the first year numerous prizes. Now working at drafting during the day she continues with her art work in her studio, the Perrin Art Studio at R.R.#1 Inwood. She has worked in a wide variety of mediums including oils, acrylics, conte, silk screen, card and print paintings, pencil and ink. A collection of her sketches, selected from eighty drawings completed over a four year period, was assembled into a book entitled *Lambton County/ A Collection of Ink Drawings* and published by the Bothwell Times Limited. Footnotes were added by Floyd McIntyre, historian from Forest. For several years Barbara Perrin has produced miniature ink drawings of historical interest which have been popular with collectors. She has painted too, scenes of Lambton area in oils, acrylics and water colours incorporating into her work the old buildings and farm utensils of the area.

References

Advertiser-Topic, Petrolia, Ont., Aug. 21, 1969 "Michigan woman seeks art career in Lambton" (article and photo of artist)

Observer, Sarnia, Ont., Jan. 6, 1972 "Inwood Artist Paints District Scenes" (photo of painting with caption)

The North Kent Leader, Dresden, Ont., June 8, 1977 "Lambton artist — Molds profession in public school" (Dresden, Ont. I.O.D.E. crafts show at Lambton-Kent Composite School)

The Windsor Star, Windsor, Ont., Feb. 26, 1977 "Artist Barbara Perrin — The eye of the beholder" by Don Kolfage (with reproductions of Ms. Perrin's drawings)

Lambton Country/A Collection of Ink Drawings by Barbara Perrin, notes by Floyd McIntyre, Bothwell Times Ltd., Bothwell, Ontario/Lambton Historical Society, 1977

PERRIN, Lily

A Courtenay, B.C., artist, she received her basic training at the University of British Columbia and under Shoju Hamada an internationally-known potter and sculptor. She has however been working at various other art forms since the 1940's including shellcraft, candle-making, enamel-on-copper jewellery, ceramics, glass free forms and figurines, leaded stained glass pictures, found objects of wood and stone and painting in oils and water colours. In her pottery she uses local clay whenever possible. She has been experimenting with glass mobiles ornamented with characters from literature. Her exhibits include: Washington State ceramics show, Seattle, Wash., 1958 where she won the Blue Ribbon and Best in Class; Ceramic Spectacular, Long Beach, Calif., 1959, winning a Gold Cup, a "Freddy" Award and Blue Ribbon; Pacific National Exhibition, winning 1st Prize in handicraft, 3rd Prize in pottery and sculpture;

PERRIN, Lily (Cont'd)

Annual Arts and Crafts Fair, Courtenay and elsewhere. Teacher of pottery, candle making and other crafts for Continuing Education classes and local youth groups also hospital extended care units. A member of the American Candle-makers' Society and charter member of the Vancouver Art Gallery.

References

Free Press, Courtenay, B.C., April 15, 1959 "Winner of Ceramics Award" (photo of Lily Perrin, her awards and work)

Nanaimo Free Press, B.C., Mar. 10, 1970 "Gifted Courtenay Woman Triumphs In Ceramic Field" by Ruth McKellar

The Daily Colonist, Vict., B.C., Sunday, Nov. 24, 1974 "Nature's Abstracts. . .in wood and stone" by Doris Farmer Tonkin

PERRIN, Margot Moberly

Born in Toronto, Ontario, she studied at the Ontario College of Art. Married, she received a divorce in 1923 and with her son Peter settled in Connecticut. There she designed costumes, textiles, redecorated antiques, did gold leafing and interior decorating of homes. Planning to go to Europe in 1939 she cancelled her trip when World War II broke out and went to French Morocco instead with her son. Interested in primitive peoples for a number of years she had seen drawings done by a member of the Citroen expedition that crossed the Sahara in the early 1920's. She decided to make sketches of the people of Africa and covered an estimated 160,000 miles sketching natives of many tribes, choosing individuals, architecture and landscapes she felt represented the true character of areas visited including the Gold Coast, Nigeria, Togoland, French Congo, Morocco, Rhodesia, Angola, South Africa, Belgian Congo, Senegal and part of the Sahara Desert. She made a special effort to catch the facial characteristics of each tribe she visited. After eight years she returned with 300 pastel and gouache paintings and drawings. An exhibit of her paintings and drawings was held in Paris in 1948 under the auspices of the Louvre (Colonial Pavilion), Musée de l'Homme, the Colonial Museum and the French Institute for Exchanges of Arts and Techniques. Representatives from six embassies attended her opening. Showings of her work were held in London, England, and in the United States at the American Museum of Natural History (1949).

References

Free Press, London, Ont., Aug. 3, 1948 (AP, Paris, Aug. 2) "Canadian-Born Woman Artist Wins Attention of Paris Salon" by Mel Most

The Gazette, Mtl., P.Q., Aug. 7, 1948 (AP, Paris as above)

The Ottawa Journal, Ont., Nov. 27, 1948 (CP, London, Nov. 26) "Former Toronto Art Student Ends Lengthy African Tour"

PERRIN, Michel
b. 1932

Born in Lyon, France, he studied at the École Nationale des Beaux-Arts de Lyon (1949) under Pierre Pelloux and Robert Rolland and at the École des

PERRIN, Michel (Cont'd)

Arts Décoratifs de Paris. He came to Canada in 1967 and settled in Montreal. A painter of landscapes, especially in winter, his work has been well received. He has held many solo shows including those at: Galerie Troncy, Lyon, France (1955, 1962); Galerie des Temps Heureux, Lyon (1959); Aréna Maurice Richard, Mtl. (1967); Centre d'Art du Mont-Royal, Mtl. (1967); Galerie l'Art Français, Mtl. (1968, 1970, 1972, 1974, 1976); Galerie Emile Walter, New York (1968); Gallery of "World Art", Boston (1968); Hôtel Reine Elizabeth, Mtl. (1971); Galerie d'Art Saint-Jean, Quebec (1972, 1974); Galerie l'Indifferent, Lyon (1973); Galerie 20, Cannes (1974); Galerie Bijou, Bale (1975). His work can be seen in Canada at the Dutch Gallery, Van.; Kar Gallery, Tor.; Galerie l'Art Français, Mtl.; Galerie d'Art Saint-Jean, Quebec and in France at Galerie Loukas, Paris; Galerie l'Indifférent, Lyon. He has won several prizes for his work in France.

References

La Presse, Mtl., Mar. 14, 1970 "Exposition à l'Art Français"

Le Courrier du Sud, Longueuil, P.Q., Feb. 11, 1970 "Pour Michel Perrin, exposition No. 2 à la Galerie l'Art Français" par Thérèse Girouard

Le Devoir, Mtl., P.Q., Dec. 2, 1972 "A la Galerie l'Art Français — Michel Perrin" par J.C. Lalanne Cassou

Le Journal de Montréal, P.Q., Nov. 20, 1974 (note by Lucie Talbot)

Le Soleil, Quebec, P.Q., Nov. 27, 1974 "Servi Froid" par Fernando Lemieux

Info. Form from artist, 1972

Canadian artists in exhibition, 1972-73, Roundstone, Tor., Ont., 1974, P. 169

Le Courrier du Sud, Longueuil, P.Q., 25 Mars, 1970 "Michel Perrin Peintre" (review)

PERRON, Germain

b. 1943

Born in Montreal, P.Q., he studied at the École des Beaux-Arts, Montreal; Centre français du Théâtre à Paris; l'Université du Théâtre des Nations à Paris and stayed in Europe for four years. He was named Lauréat at the Salon of Young Painters and Sculptors in Montreal in 1961. He received a prize for costume design at the National Drama Festival in 1962 and a Quebec Provincial grant for a year's travel in France (1962-63). A painter as well he has been noted for his calligraphic abstracts and has exhibited in solo shows at the following: Centre international de la Jeunesse, Rabaska, Quebec (1960); Centre d'Art de l'Elysée, Mtl. (1961); Galerie Denyse Delrue, Mtl. (1962); Centre d'Art d'Argenteuil (1962); Galerie Paul Fachetti, Paris (1965); Maison du Canada, Paris (1965) and has participated in the following group shows: El Cortijo, Mtl. (1959); 78th Spring Show at the Montreal Museum of Fine Arts (1961); Galerie Namber, Paris (1961); 5th Biennial Exhibition of Canadian Painting (1963); Panorama de la Peinture au Québec 1940-1966 at Musée d'Art Contemporain, Mtl. (1967).

References

NGC Info. Form dated January, 1963

5th Biennial Exhibition of Canadian Painting, 1963, P. 18

École de Montréal par Guy Robert, Editions du Centre de Psychologie et de Pédagogie, Mtl., 1964, P. 19, 47

PERRON, Germain (Cont'd)

Panorama de la Peinture au Québec, 1940-1966, Musée d'Art Contemporain, Mtl., 1967, P. 38-9
L'Art au Québec, depuis 1940 par Guy Robert, La Presse, Mtl., 1973, P. 11, 12, 154

PERRON, Lawrence

Coming to Canada in 1975 he settled in Toronto and set up a studio on Bloor Street East. He is known for his fine pen and ink or pencil cityscapes and is superb in his handling of washes in ink (or water colour). He achieves correct scale and vanishing points of his subjects by using a mechanical projection and this provides paintings or wash drawings that, with the added proposed buildings or structures by architects, show how a site will look when the construction is completed. He creates as well, proposed interiors including shopping malls or other architectural projects which he is commissioned to illustrate. He has completed commissions for designers and architects including: Marcel Breuer, Edward Barnes, Johansen & Behmani, Architects Collaborative (Boston, Mass.); Vincent Kling (Philadelphia); Webb Zerafa, Menkes Housden (Toronto). He has exhibited his work at the Museum of Modern Art (NYC) and the Metropolitan Museum of Art (NYC) and the "O" Gallery, Washington.

Reference

Canadian Interiors, Tor., Ont., July-Aug. 1977 "Lawrence Perron"

PERRON, Louis Paul
b. 1919

Born in Rivière du Loup, Quebec. The Perrons then moved to Quebec City in 1920 and to Montreal in 1929. Louis Perron studied at the Monument Nationale with Adrien Hebert in 1935; Beaux-Arts Montreal as a day student under Joseph St. Charles and evenings under Alfred Laliberté also during this period under James Graham. From 1941 to 1945 he served with the R.C.A.F. and during his service overseas in England took the opportunity to study the masters at the Tate Gallery, The Scottish National Gallery of Modern Art and to take instruction from noted artists. He also studied in New York. By the time he had returned to settle in Canada he had done 200 paintings and murals. In Canada he has filled many commissions for restoration and redecoration of churches including: Notre Dame Church, Mtl.; St. James Basicilica, Mtl.; Cathédrale Marie-Reine-du-Monde, Mtl.; Notre-Dame-de-Lourdes, Mtl. and many others. As an easel painter he has been exhibiting his work in solo shows at L'Art Français and at the Dominion Gallery, Montreal.

References

The Gazette, Mtl., P.Q., Aug. 13, 1949 "Unveiling Tomorrow of Religious Mural"
The Montreal Star, Mtl., P.Q., Sept. 15, 1949 "Mural Pictures At St. Laurent"
La Presse, Mtl., P.Q., Mar. 24, 1961 (photo of Perron at work on a church painting with descriptive caption)
Information from Dominion Gallery, Mtl.

PERRON, Marie L.

A Spaulding, Saskatchewan, artist, the daughter of Mr. & Mrs. Gerard Perron, she received her public and high school education in her hometown and then attended the University of Saskatchewan where she graduated with honours, majoring in Art and French for a B.A. and B.Ed. For a thesis she spent two weeks in France doing research on the life and works of Paul Cézanne. A landscape painter in various media including acrylics and water colours she has exhibited her work at the Centennial Library, Lloydminster (1970) and the Little Gallery Under The Stairs at the Mendel centre, Saskatoon (1975). Nancy Russell writing in the *Star Phoenix* described her work as follows, "She begins with a theme and the series at the Mendel is built around a theme of hills, or more generally nature. Her style is a flowing one, often loose and easy for the eye. Her work borders on being abstract, but does not lose touch with the reality of its original inspiration." A federal field officer for the International Women's Year Secretariat in 1976 she has also taught art and French to high school students in Lloydminster.

References

    Lloydminster Times, Sask., Feb. 18, 1970 "Art Display Now at Library — Works of High School Teacher, Miss Perron"

    Star Phoenix, Saskatoon, Sask., Sept. 12, 1975 "Accent on art with Nancy Russell — Artist handles wide range of media"

    Peterborough Examiner, Ont., Jan. 10, 1976 "Fights Prejudice"

PERRON, Pierrette

A Shawinigan, Quebec, painter she studied at the École des Beaux-Arts, Montreal, under Jean Marie Bastien and Louise-Hélène Ayotte; at the Institut de Technologie de Shawinigan for design under Richard Normandin; at the Centre d'art de Trois-Rivières under Pierre Landry for sculpture, Marcel Bellerive and Jeanne Vanasse in painting. She received her teaching certificate in plastic arts in 1972 from the Université du Québec, Montreal. She has participated in a number of group shows also a solo show of landscapes at the Centre culturel de Trois-Rivières.

Reference

    Le Nouvelliste, Trois-Rivières, P.Q., June 1, 1974 "Exposition Pierrette Perron au Centre culturel de T.-R." par René Lord

PERRON-SYLVER, Lorraine

She studied at the school of drawing in Arvida which is affiliated with the École des Beaux-Arts of Quebec, working under the direction of Laurent Bouchard, Hugh J. Barrett and Gatien Moisan. There she won first prize for drawing in 1962. She held her first solo exhibition at Galerie Jacques Lacroix, Chicoutimi (1967). Subsequently she exhibited her paintings at the Centre Culturel de Jonquière (1968); Coquille, Jonquière (1969). She is particularly

PERRON-SYLVER, Lorraine (Cont'd)

interested in abstract forms which she has been developing in recent years with considerable success. She lives at Arvida.

References

Jonquière-Kenogami Le Réveil, Que., Nov. 13, 1968 "L'une des nôtres, Lorraine Perron-Sylver expose ses dessins à Jonquière"

Ibid, Feb. 19, 1969 "Un élan de peintre qui revient avec le soleil hivernal" par Viviane Simard

PERROTT, J. Stanford
b. 1917

Born in Claresholm, Alberta, he used to watch his relatives at work with their amateur art and became interested himself about the age of twelve. He studied art during his high school years and then at the Banff School of Fine Arts (1935-39); School of Art, Southern Alberta Institute of Technology and Art (1935-39); Pennsylvania Academy of Fine Arts, Philadelphia (1946); Art Students League, New York under Will Barnet (1954-55); Hans Hofmann School of Fine Arts, Provincetown, Mass. (1954); Atelier 17, New York City under Leo Katz (1954-55). In 1940 he attended Calgary Normal School where he received top honours as a student teacher. He started teaching art and music in the Turner Valley. Later he got a job as a draftsman for the Royalite Oil Company. He returned to teaching when he joined the staff of the Provincial Institute of Technology and Art (Art section later became Alberta College of Art) as an art instructor serving in this capacity until 1967 when he was appointed Head of the Alberta College of Art (1967-74). He became a full-time painter in 1974. This same year he was honoured with a merit award from the Alberta government for his service in art education. During his teaching years he had little time for exhibiting his own work and his solo shows were few and far between. He also held many responsible offices in visual arts organizations, clubs and schools. He did show in a three-man exhibit at the Calgary Allied Arts Centre in 1963 when Astrid Twardowski noted, "Stanford Perrott has an almost oriental eye for the small beauties of nature. His 'Seeds at Dusk', with its suggestion of a soft wind blowing over water and its delicate yet warm colours, is completely satisfying. . . . While in 'Rock Through Grass,' Perrott's delicate balance of fantasy and observation is further illustrated." Then in 1974 Lorne E. Render in his book *The Mountains and the Sky* noted Perrott's austere but effective winter landscapes executed in water colours in 1963. In 1977 a solo show of his work was held at the Mount Royal College art gallery during Festival Calgary 77 when a *Calgary Albertan* reviewer noted "In works with fantasy-like titles like 'Rocks Overrun by Snow' Stan Perrott successfully captures the 'childlike spontaneity' that so many seek, yet so few achieve." Perrott's work was of such high caliber that his paintings were selected for showing in the 1961 competition "The Art College Instructor's Exhibition", in New York. There were several hundred entrants from all over North America and Perrott's work received high commendation from George Pietrantonio, director of the exhibition. Praise was also given to fellow instructor George Wood. During his teaching career Perrott lectured to the Engineering Institute of Canada (Calgary); Calgary Sketch Club; Calgary Color Photo Club; Knights of the Round Table; Calgary Medical Society; Home and School Societies; Extension Department of the University of Alberta Fine Arts Faculty. He was

PERROTT, J. Stanford (Cont'd)

Supervisor of Saturday Morning Children's Art Classes which had an attendance of 275 children under 12 teachers. He has adjudicated for Saskatchewan Arts Board (Art Festival, 1958); Edmonton Exhibition (1955-60); Alberta Society of Artists on various occasions; Community Art competitions, Lethbridge, Wetaskiwin and elsewhere; for Order of the Eastern Star and other community groups. Former member of Visual Arts Board of Alberta Government; Visual Arts Committee, Allied Arts Centre, Calgary; former president of Alberta Society of Artists. Lives in Calgary.

References

Herald, Lethbridge, Alta., Feb. 7, 1949 "Makes Good — Stavely Native Successful Artist" (Perrott exhibits 27 oils at Canadian Art Galleries, Calgary)

News clipping, 1952 "Guide Rather Than Painter — Tech Art Instructor Uses Teaching Talent" by Dushan Bresky

Times, Alta., Dec. 20, 1961 "Calgary art in New York" (Instructor's Exhibition, NYC)

Canadian Art, Mar./Apr. 1963 "Clement Greenberg's View of Art on the Prairies" P. 96, 97

Ibid, Sept./Oct. 1963 "Art Reviews — Blodgett, Ungstad, Perrott at the Calgary Allied Arts Centre" by Astrid Twardowski, P. 261

The Mountains and the Sky by Lorne E. Render, Glenbow-Alta. Inst./M&S, Tor., 1974, P. 209, 210, 211

Calgary Herald, Alta., Feb. 23, 1977 (photo of Perrott and his work; caption)

Calgary Albertan, Alta., Mar. 5, 1977 "Back to art"

NGC Info. Forms 1961

Document from artist, 1961

PERRY, Anne

b.(c) 1942

A Prince George, B.C., artist who studied at the Vancouver School of Art and at the Instituto Allende at San Miguel, Mexico. She is known for her oil paintings which include landscapes, garden scenes and other subjects. She held a solo show of her work at the Simon Fraser dining room, Prince George, B.C. (1970). Anne also works as a free lance artist on sign work. Her paintings have been well received and she is represented in a number of private collections in Vancouver and The Montreal Trust Company, Prince George.

References

Prince George Progress, B.C., April 16, 1969 "Office Art By Local Painter"

Prince George Citizen, B.C., August 5, 1970 "Anne paints B.C. interior" by Pat Murphy

PERRY, Art

Born in Ottawa, he attended Nepean High School and Carleton University graduating with his B.A. While attending university he was art editor for the campus newspaper and produced a weekly editorial cartoon. He worked as artist for *Impulse* magazine and contributed cartoons to various student newspapers across Canada. In 1970 he worked for the National Museums designing posters for the Museum and the Arts Centre, also did illustrations for several publications. In 1971 he produced a series of large acrylic canvases based on Byzantine icons. By 1973 he was an education officer with the

PERRY, Art (Cont'd)

National Gallery of Canada where he worked with Saturday morning programmes for children and gave guided tours of the gallery to school groups. He has had a particular interest in contemporary wit. Working at his own art he also had plans for a regional publication about achievements of writers, poets and artists.

Reference

The Ottawa Journal, Ont., Feb. 3, 1973 "Faces of Ottawa — Art Perry" by W.Q. Ketchum

PERRY, Frank
b. 1923

Born in Vancouver, B.C., he became interested in art at the age of thirteen while attending history classes at high school. He then centered his interest on sculpture and studied at the Central School of Arts and Crafts and the Regent Street Polytechnic in London, England, to study wax techniques for bronze under Philip Turner (1954-55). Returning to Canada he received his B.A. from the University of British Columbia in 1956 studying under Archipenko as well and took further study under Cecil Richards (1957). With a Canada Council Fellowship in 1958 he was given leave from his high school teaching job to study in Florence, Italy and elsewhere, working under B.G. Beneduce for practical experience in lost-wax bronze casting at the G. Beneduce Foundary in Florence. He has been influenced by Henry Moore, Constantin Brancusi and the German expressionists. In his sculpture he does small works for the home, and larger works for gardens and architecture, and is known for his anthropomorphic bird forms often bordering on the violent or fearful through his expressionistic style. Viewing his work in 1968 at the Griffiths Galleries, Ann Rosenberg noted, "The greatest strength of Perry's work lies in the fact that he seems able to think well on a small scale and in this format balances off simple smooth-textured shapes with areas of rusticated metal. The size of the sculpture allows a spectator even in a tiny space to see and feel every part. Because bronze has a silky texture and takes on a patina on exposure to air and with handling, direct involvement with these sculptures brings pleasure and mellows their appearance. Although many of the works are entirely without figurative reference, the best works in the show refer to places and figures." While working in bronze, brass, stone and wood Perry has also done work in clay and plaster. His commissions include: granite carving for Burnaby Municipal Hall (1958); bronze fountain, Crescent Apartments, West Vancouver (1967); welded iron sculpture for Department of Public Works, Victoria, B.C. (1966); bronze cast for Playhouse Theatre, Vancouver, B.C. (1967) and sculpture for B.C. Government Buildings (1973). His awards include the Peter B. Curry Award for sculpture, Winnipeg Show (1957); First Prize for sculpture, 75th Annual Spring Show, Mtl. Museum of Fine Arts (1958); Prize, Winnipeg Show (1958); Grand Prize, B.C. Centennial Outdoor Show, Burnaby (1958); Grand Prize, B.C. Centennial Outdoor Sculpture '67 (1967). He has exhibited his work in solo shows at the Griffiths Galleries, Van. B.C. and in many group shows including those of the Royal Canadian Academy. He is a member: Northwest Inst. of Sculpture (1955); B.C. Society of Artists (1957); Sculptors' Society of Canada (1961) and Royal Canadian Academy (1974). Was President N.W.I.S. (1957-58). Taught history at the Carson Graham High

PERRY, Frank (Cont'd)

School. Represented in the Vancouver Art Gallery; Burnaby Municipal Hall, and private collections in Montreal, Toronto, Vancouver and London, England. Lives in North Vancouver.

References

Le Devoir, Mtl., Mar. 31, 1958 (photo & caption about "Bird Form" exhibited at Mtl. Spring Show)

La Presse, Mtl., Apr. 38, 1958 (photo & caption about "Bird Form")

Chatham Daily News, Jan. 23, 1964 (photo & caption of "The Head" at R.C.A. 84th exhibition)

The Ottawa Citizen, Ont., Jan. 25, 1964, ibid

Vancouver Province, B.C., Sept. 20, 1968 (review of solo show at Griffiths Galleries)

Vancouver Sun, B.C., Oct. 1, 1968 "Sculpture — Complexes In Bronze" by Ann Rosenberg

NGC Info. Forms 1958, undated

Document from artist, 1961

Who's Who In American Art, 1976, Jaques Cattell Press, R.R. Bowker, New York & London, 1976, P. 436

PERRY, Jane
b.(c) 1948

A North Bay, Ontario, artist she completed her secondary school studies in North Bay then worked as a Registered Nurse's Assistant which allowed her time to decide what she really wanted to do. She then studied four years at the Ontario College of Art and was awarded the G.A. Reid scholarship and an O.C.A. medal for design. She used her scholarship money to travel to Guatemala where she made a personal study of its culture, its people, architecture and artwork, particularly the crafts of the Mayas which have had a profound influence on her own work. She returned to Canada in 1975 and joined the staff of Canadore College in North Bay as crafts and design instructor in the textile programme. In her free hours she continues to work on her own textile creations described by Bobbi Eberle in 1977 during her solo show at the White Water Gallery in North Bay as follows, "A quick glance about the gallery will impress the viewer with the variety of colors which induce a feeling of motion in a static piece of art. Ms. Perry's work is well designed and lacks nothing in craftsmanship. She believes in doing good durable work which will last on a physical level as well as artistic." She is also experimenting with three-dimensional pieces.

References

North Bay Nugget, Ont., Oct. 15, 1976 "Textile instructor: Design determines quality" by Nancy McGrath

Ibid, Nov. 11, 1977 "Diverse influences make textile show unique" by Bobbi Eberle

PERRY, John
b. 1898

Born in England, he came to Canada in 1913 with the hope of becoming a cowboy. In 1915 he enlisted in the Canadian army and served in the trenches

PERRY, John (Cont'd)

during the First World War and returned to Canada in 1919. Through the soldier's settlement board he started farming. His land turned out to be too stony so when the Depression hit he left farming to work at a variety of jobs. All this time he was working at his painting and in the depth of the Depression was able to find work making portraits for the Sifton newspaper family also portraits of Plains Indians with the help of an Indian Commissioner named Graham. He visited most of the reservations in Western Canada. With the old timers gone he selected his Indian portraits from archive photographs. During the 1940's Perry worked for Willson Stationery which at that time handled art supplies and picture framing. During the Second World War he served in England as a personnel selection officer giving psychometric tests, making recommendations for promotions and other tasks connected with this work. In his off hours he travelled and painted in England. Even though he was not an official war artist four of his works were hung in an exhibition held at the Tate Gallery which featured the work of artists representing all the allied forces. Following the war he spent four years with the Department of Veterans' Affairs as a counsellor for the rehabilitation of ex-servicemen. He opened his own art supply business "Perry's Art Centre" in Regina which he operated until he sold out in 1959 to Mr. & Mrs. D. Barnett. He held a solo show of his work at the Perry Gallery in Regina, that same year when he exhibited 26 pastels, water colours and oils. In 1977 a solo show of his portraits was held at Moose Jaw Art Museum (November) and at the Saskatchewan Power Gallery On The Roof in Regina (December) organized by the Moose Jaw Art Museum and National Exhibition Centre. Viewing his work Lora Burke of *The Leader-Post* noted of his Indian portraits, "These are not prototype calendar Indians, but living pulsing people. One is aware of the bone structure, the flesh and blood reality of the subjects. And though there is a similarity of feature, a kind of family resemblance, each is a distinct individual. While only the heads are portrayed, most seem to stand tall, full of pride and a sense of their own being. In some, there is a certain resignation, a kind of baffled tragedy which perhaps reflects Perry's own feelings for these people who once dominated the plains." His paintings including those described above are in the collections of the Gainsborough Gallery; Dr. Morris Shumiatcher and Mrs. L. Robinson. He is also represented in the Government of Saskatchewan Collection by portraits of Hon. R.J.M. Parker (Lt.-Gov. Sask.); Hon. Thomas Miller (Lt.-Gov., Sask.); and Hon. J.T.M. Anderson (Premier, Sask.). Perry illustrated the book *Songs of the Trenches* and his sketches appeared in *The Bystander*, a London newspaper. Perry has been painting for over sixty years and he lives in his home and studio at Pioneer Village, Regina, with his wife; they have four sons who work in one or another aspects of the arts. In the last few years Perry has turned his interest to landscape painting.

References

Leader-Post, Regina, Sask., July 22, 1959 "One-man show on view in city"

Ibid, Mar. 10, 1977 "Perry still busy painting at 79" by Lora Burke

Moose Jaw Times-Herald, Sask., Nov. 21, 1977 "In Moose Jaw — Regina artist, has first one-man show in 60 years"

Leader Post, Regina Sask., Dec. 24, 1977 "Indian portraits offer visual history" by Lora Burke

Exhibition sheet for Gallery on The Roof, December, 1977

PERRY, Kathleen

A graduate of the Alberta College of Art she twice attended the Banff School of Fine Arts and took credit courses in art at the University of Alberta and Carleton University, Ottawa. She completed a series of seven water colours depicting early posts and forts of the North West Mounted Police. For this series, which was her personal RCMP centennial project, she did research into early writings and photographs in Ottawa and Regina. The wife of Supt. W.F.G. Perry, Officer Commanding Regina Sub-Division (1973) she has taught adult and child art in Calgary, Red Deer and Winnipeg.

Reference

R.C.M.P. Quarterly, Ottawa, Ontario, July, 1973 "Centennial Paintings"

PERVOUCHINE, Nathalie (PERVOUCHINE-LABRECQUE)
b. 1923

Born in Berlin, Germany of Russian refugee parents, she studied art in Paris, France, at the École des Arts Décoratifs, the École des Beaux-Arts and at the St. Serge convent for the study of icons. She arrived in Montreal in 1949. Over the years she has become known for her portraits, landscapes, frescoes, abstract collages and tapestries. She married Canadian sculptor Pierre Labrecque. She has exhibited in Paris, Rome, New York, Houston (Texas), Montreal and Toronto. She was living in Saint-Hilaire Station, Quebec in 1957.

References

Le Canada, Mtl., P.Q., Feb. 24, 1953 (photo of Nathalie Pervouchine and Pierre Labrecque)

The Gazette, Mtl., P.Q., Mar. 27, 1965 "Unexpected Encore" by R.M. (review of her show at Galerie Martin)

Montreal Metro Express, Mar. 29, 1965 (show at Galerie Martin)

L'Art au Québec depuis 1940 par Guy Robert, La Presse, Mtl. 1973, P. 348

NGC Info. Form rec'd Mar. 23, 1957

PERZ, Walter G.
b. 1929

Born in Vienna he studied graphic and fine arts there and following the war founded an experimental avant-garde theatre. He came to Canada in 1954 and lived in the Arctic for two years where his isolation from man and closeness to nature had a profound influence on his outlook towards life and art. He moved south to Toronto where he became a photographic illustrator and continued to work at his art and had a showing of his monochrome acrylics at the Adams and Yves Gallery, Toronto. He is known for his flexibility of imagination which shows up in his work.

Reference

Catalogue sheet from Adams & Yves Gallery, 602 Markham Street, Toronto (undated)

PESTICH, Bruno
b. 1937

Born in Zadar, Yugoslavia, he received his M.A. in Russian and English in 1963 from the University of Zagreb, Yugoslavia and taught foreign languages in Yugoslavia for two years. He took private lessons in drawing and painting from Prof. Alfred Petricic in Zadar (1956-58). He came to Canada in 1966 and settled in London, Ontario, where he studied painting and printmaking at Fanshawe College (1971-72). He has exhibited his work in Yugoslavia and in Canada at the Stratford Festival (1972); Old Theatre, Chatham, Ont. (1972); London Public Library and Art Museum (1972) and the Art Gallery of Windsor (1973). He married Marija Panza (Toronto) and they have two children, Illyrio (1968) and Natasha (1973). Mr. Pestich is an employee of the University of Western Ontario in the Weldon Library and is interested in sports and outdoors. He has a special interest in weightlifting and swimming and is a member of the University of Western Ontario Athletic Club.

Reference

NGC Info. Form rec'd June, 1973

PETCHEY, Winifred Florence (Mrs. Donald Marsh)
b. 1905

Born in London, England, she studied at the Hornsey School of Arts and Crafts, London, and received a scholarship in 1920 from the Board of Education and subsequent scholarships in 1924 (drawing), 1926 (illumination) and the City and Guilds of London Institute Certificate, 1929 (hand embroidery), and an art teachers certificate, 1930. She became a member of The Society of Graphic Art (Eng., 1930) and The National Society of Art Masters (Eng., 1931). She arrived in Canada in 1933 to Eskimo Point, N.W.T. to become the wife of an Archdeacon of Baffin Land, Rev. Donald B. Marsh. There she painted the life of the Eskimo in water colours and exhibited her work in Ottawa at James Wilson and Company galleries (1940); with the Royal Canadian Academy (1942) and the Coste House, Calgary (1951). Viewing her work in 1940 E.W.H. of *The Ottawa Citizen* noted, "Winifred Petchey's water-colors have a dual interest. They are not only remarkably good as paintings, but they are a brilliant account of the ways of the Eskimos of the northern Hudson Bay region. . .Mrs. Marsh can capture the color and atmosphere of the ice and snow of winter and the bright greens and browns of the brief summer. Some of the water-colors will rank, as paintings, with the best work of their kind being done in Canada. Of the life of the Padlemuit Eskimo much is told. We see him fishing, building his igloo, curing his skins and mudding his sleigh runners. We see his wife at work, the interior of the snow house with windows, the ceremonial dance and the caribou hide encampments of spring." Mention was made of Mrs. Marsh spending the winter months at Owen Sound with her two children by the Owen Sound *Sun Times* in 1942.

References

The Ottawa Citizen, Ont., June 24, 1940 "Eskimo Life Seen In Fine Water-Color Show" by E.W.H.

Sun Times, Owen Sound, Ont., Nov. 7, 1942 "Two Paintings Chosen For Academy Exhibit"

PETCHEY, Winifred Florence (Mrs. Donald Marsh) (Cont'd)

The Albertan, Calgary, Alta., Apr. 6, 1951 "Paintings on Display"
NGC Info. Form rec'd Sept. 28, 1939

PÉTEL, Pierre
b. 1920

Born in Montreal, Quebec, he won La Revue Populaire award for plastic arts at the age of twelve. Later he studied at the École des Beaux-Arts and the École du Meuble under Paul Emile Borduas. He exhibited his paintings from time to time including shows at Galerie des Arts, Montreal and in Ottawa at the Duford gallery. He moved to Wrightville, Quebec (near Hull) in 1945 as writer-director for the National Film Board. In 1950 he won the Jessie Dow Award for best realistic painting at the 67th annual Spring Show in Montreal. This particular painting was based on sketches and photographs he made while directing the NFB film "Terre de Cain". He exhibited his work in 1968 at Galerie Libre, Montreal, when Irene Heywood of *The Gazette* noted, "Pierre Petel who shows a combination of painting and collage at Galerie Libre. . . must be a dynamo. . . .His carnival song makes the hit parade each year in Quebec City and his music and lyrics went into our first Canadian full length film, 'Les lumières de ma ville' produced by the National Film Board. Besides all this he has produced two books of poems, one novel and two plays for television. It is presumed that he continues to exercise all of these considerable gifts while he fills a full-time load as director of the light entertainment section of CBC. . .(referring to his show at Libre she went on), there is a great deal of value here, and a great deal of quality. As a vehicle of social comment the combination of paint and collage is excellent." Pétel has won other prizes for his work.

References

The Ottawa Journal, Ont., Mar. 15, 1950 "Pierre Pétel Wins Award For Painting"
The Ottawa Citizen, Ont., Mar. 15, 1950 "Pierre Pétel Wins Art Prize in Montreal"
La Presse, Mtl. P.Q., Mar. 18, 1950 "Le prix Dow"
Canadian Art, Vol. VII, No. 4, 1950 "Artists and Film-Makers" by Donald W. Buchanan P. 142-143
Le Petit Journal, Mtl., Oct. 25, 1959 "Pierre Pétel décroche un prix de peinture"
The Gazette, Mtl., P.Q., June 1, 1968 art column by Irene Heywood
Echos Vedettes, Mtl., P.Q., June 8, 1968 "Pierre Pétel, l'homme aux 1000 talents!"
NGC Info. Forms, July 24, 1940; undated

PETER, Margaret Ann
b. 1943

Born in Leamington, Ontario, she taught school in Burlington and Fergus, Ontario, and in her spare time studied water colour painting with Gery Puley. She married and after her son Toby was born she became a supply teacher and started taking courses at the University of Guelph and graduated from the fine arts department in 1974. She specialized in printmaking and finally was able to acquire her own press in her home studio in Guelph. One of her

PETER, Margaret Ann (Cont'd)

specialty prints which she calls viscosity-collagraph is a multi-level plate capable of holding and printing more than one colour at a time using both oil paint and ink but the plate is limited to between 15 and 20 prints before deteriorating. Ms. Peter has in recent years become interested in weaving under the guidance of Martha Hoey Currie and has been exhibiting this work for several years. Viewing her prints in 1977 Liane Heller noted, "Peter's printmaking is dominated by the colors and images of nature — flowers, leaves, hills — often represented as a circle. Her executions are varied and imaginative, ranging from the soft yellows and greens of her Mother Earth prints, to the detailed patterns of yellow and red roses, to textural richness of Wallflower and Genesis I. Her technique is usually viscosity-collagraph, obtained by three applications of color to a cardboard plate on which collages have been created and then cut at various thicknesses. The prints are referred to as viscosity-collagraphs because of the different stretching properties of the three kinds of ink used in each stage of preparation, Peter said. Especially interesting in Peter's work is the delicate balance between vibrancy and subtlety in her colors and forms. A work such as Expectant Mother Earth, which shows several strata of hills under the outline of a pregnant woman, combines delicacy of color with a gentle, yet wry humor. Peter's ingenuity makes one smile; the symbolism never clouts a viewer on the head, just insinuates itself in one's mind." Her solo shows include: Alice Peck Gallery, Burlington, Ont. (1975); Chimera Gallery, Salem, Ont. (1976); Kitchener Waterloo Art Gallery, Kitchener, Ont. (1977). She participated in group shows in the Gallery Chimera, Salem, an artists' co-operative of which she is a founder-member. She has won many awards in both local and regional art shows including the first prize at Painting-on-the-Green, Guelph (1973); Best Single Print, Thom Thomson Gallery (1975). Her work can be seen at the Alice Peck Gallery, Burlington; The Village Place, Port Carling, Muskoka; Chimera Gallery, Salem and in the permanent collections of: Guelph Campus Co-op; CING-FM Radio Station, Burlington; Dofasco, Hamilton; Norfolk General Hospital, Simcoe and elsewhere including many private collections.

References

Guelph Mercury, Ont., Sept. 29, 1975 "The Poppy Patch"

Kitchener Waterloo Record, Ont., Sept. 12, 1975 "'Spit-biting' is part of Guelph woman's art" by Ruth Thompson

Guelph Mercury, Ont., Oct. 2, 1976 "Sparkling Exhibition Shows City Artist's Prints, Weaving" by Helen Brimmell

Kitchener Waterloo Record, Ont., Oct. 24, 1977 "Guelph Artist's Exhibit — Her prints dominated by circles" by Liane Heller

The Index of Ontario Artists, Ed. Hennie Wolff, Visual Arts Ontario, Tor., 1978, P. 217

PETER, Nori

b.(c) 1935

Born in Hungary, she studied art there until the 1956 revolution when she and her mother left the country spending four days in the countryside before they were able to cross the border. They took only the clothes on their back and a couple of apples. Arriving in Vienna they made their way to a refugee camp where they heard from a German that Canada was a country of great

PETER, Nori (Cont'd)

opportunities. They were accepted by Canada and they were soon on their way by boat to Halifax where upon arrival Nori had to stay in isolation until she was over a bout of German measles. It was on the train to Toronto that she got her first real look at eastern Canada which she found so beautiful and spacious compared to Europe. In Toronto she worked as a filing clerk with the Canadian Imperial Bank of Commerce in a job where English was not essential. Evenings she continued her drawing and painting and watching television in order to learn English. She started doing portraits and found a new job making scale models of interiors for an architectural firm. She had a natural bent for using a hammer and saw and enjoyed doing this type of work. Soon she was painting dolls' faces as part time work. As she made new friends she learned from a Thornhill gift shop owner that most Canadian souvenirs were made outside the country and she took the suggestion that she might try producing something for this market. By using self-drying clay (she had no kiln) she created Eskimo figures after studying such details as customs, clothes, tools, and facial features from her visits to museums and from information found in books. Each piece was an original and no moulds were used. Through an Ojibway Indian couple she spent two months at Lakefield, Quebec, a visit that inspired her to make Indian figures. In 1967 she visited Fort Chimo, Quebec, near Ungava Bay where she fell in love with the Eskimo people and began painting children, mothers and men at work. She returned to settlements all across the Arctic many times and has become known throughout Canada for her paintings of Eskimos. Leaving Hungary with only ten dollars between her mother and herself, she has been so successful that she was able to move from Toronto to a house by Buckhorn Lake north of Peterborough where she enjoys each season, especially winter when she goes cross-country skiing in the company of her two Husky dogs. She has exhibited her work at Graphica 73, Tor.-Dom. Centre, Tor.; St. Laurent Galleries, Ottawa and Eaton's College St. Store, Toronto, and is represented in the Abitibi Paper Collection in the Tor.-Dom. Centre, Tor.

References

Toronto Sun, Ont., May 13, 1974 "Sutton's Place — Artist hopes to help a culture" by Joan Sutton

Pulp & Paper Magazine of Canada, Gardenvale, Que., June, 1974 "What's a nice Eskimo like you..?"

Ottawa Citizen, Ont., May 27, 1975 "Eskimo mothers, children fascinate artist Nori Peter" by Elizabeth Duncan

Toronto Star, Ont., Jan. 28, 1977 column by Robert Sutton

PETERS, Donald Burpee
b. 1919

Born in Saint John, N.B., he studied at the Saint John Vocational School under Violet Gillett, Julia Crawford and Ted Campbell; at the Ontario College of Art under J.W. Beatty; the Montreal Art Association under Edwin Holgate and Will Ogilvie. He served with the Canadian Army Overseas, 1940-45 in Britain, Italy, France, Belgium and Holland and was living in Saint John in 1945.

PETERS, Donald Burpee (Cont'd)

Reference

NGC Info. Form rec'd Sept. 4, 1945

PETERS, Gordon

b. 1920

Born in Edinburgh, Scotland, he was brought to Canada in 1923 to Montreal. His art education was received at the A.C. Valentine School of Art in Montreal and at the New York Phoenix School of Design, NYC, and he then entered the field of commercial art in which he worked for the next twenty years. Retiring around 1968 he turned to landscape painting full time and is known for his fine water colours mainly of Ontario landscapes but also other parts of Canada. Viewing his work in 1972 Hazel Barker of the *Barrie Examiner* noted, "His interest is mainly in the Ontario landscape. He has a smooth sophisticated style. His lines are clean and beautifully drawn. Old barns are a favorite subject which are always carefully drawn and he approaches the subject with sympathy and respect. A painting of the 'Ruins of Osler Castle' not far from Collingwood is a fine example of his style. With trees he seems to have a real affinity. Fallen trees with logs is made a thing of beauty. This feeling for nature is apparent in all of his work." His solo shows include: Pollock Gallery, Tor. (1966); Gallery Ustel, Tor. (1969, 1970); Skelton Gallery, Collingwood (1972); Gustaffon Galleries, Brampton (1976, 1977); Gallery of Fine Arts, Thunder Bay (1976) and he has participated in a number of group shows including a four-man show in 1971 at the Museum and Arts Centre, Laurentian University, Sudbury, Ont. with Adrian Dingle, Hilton Hassel and Osvald Timmas. Member: R.C.A., O.S.A., C.S.P.W.C., A.W.S. He lives at Caledon East, Ontario with his wife Lois.

References

Globe & Mail, Tor., Sept. 3, 1966 (large photo of water colour by Peters)

Oakville Beaver, Ont., Feb. 6, 1969 "Well-known Toronto artist teaches Oakville art class"

Toronto Telegram, Ont., Apr. 2, 1969 (review of Ustel Gal. show)

Globe & Mail, Tor. Ont., May 7, 1970 (review of show at Gal. Ustel)

Barrie Examiner, Ont., Oct. 11, 1972 "Exhibition Of Water Colours Includes 'Ruins of Osler Castle'" by Hazel Barker

Ibid, Oct. 19, 1972 "Now That's Some Water Color!" (photo and caption)

Brampton Daily Times, Mar. 11, 1976 (photo of artist and his work)

The Chronicle Journal, Thunder Bay, Ont., Oct. 19, 1976

Brampton Daily Times, Nov. 15, 1976 "Aims to Create 'Certain Mood'"

Ibid, Oct. 15, 1977 (photo of artist and his work)

NGC Info. Form

The Index of Ontario Artists, Hennie Wolfe, Editor, Visual Arts Ont., 1977, P. 217

PETERS, John P.

b. 1876

Born in England he came to Canada in 1892 and for a few months he worked in a flour mill at Fort Qu'Appelle. The same year he moved to Abernethy where

PETERS, John P. (Cont'd)

he settled on a homestead. For a brief period he helped his father with his business in London, England, but then returned to his farm in Canada. Throughout his life he painted for a hobby as his father had done before him. While still farming he worked at his easel painting first in water colours then around 1947 he switched to oils. He admired the work of the old masters like Leonardo da Vinci. It was estimated in 1957 that John Peters had done about 250 landscapes. One of his paintings of the Leduc oil well fire was hung in the Regina Art Gallery for about two years. Married with two children, a son, Gordon (living at Balcarres in 1957) and a daughter Eileen (a nurse in Victoria in 1957) he was described as a stickler for detail.

Reference

> *Regina Leader-Post*, Sask., Aug. 27, 1957 "At 81 he avoids boredom by farming and painting" by Donna Dilschneider

PETERS, Kenneth
b. 1939

Born in Regina, Saskatchewan, he studied art at the School of Fine Art, Regina Campus at the University of Saskatchewan (1958-1960) and summers at the Emma Lake Artists' Workshop (1960, 62, 64, 65, 67, 69) under such teachers as John Ferren, Clement Greenberg, Jules Olitski, Lawrence Alloway, Frank Stella and Michael Steiner. He had begun to exhibit in group shows in 1959 and by 1963 his work had caught the notice of Clement Greenberg. Greenberg saw in Peter's painting a quality which reminded him of the linearism of Barnett Newman, rendered in Peter's own way of handling paint. His "The Sound of No Sound" was effectively reproduced in Greenberg's article. Known for his abstract experimenting in which he has achieved various effects in his work over the years, he was one of the limited number of artists to exhibit in the Seventh Biennial of Canadian Painting. Andrew Hudson found his work to be, ". . .very fine with a wonderful daring in the use of image, space, and colour." He moved from Regina to Montreal where he continues to be active in painting. He received a number of scholarships and awards which include: Reeves Scholarship (1960); Canada Council travel grant (1962); Saskatchewan Arts Board Travel Grant (1965); Saskatchewan Arts Bursary (1965, 1966); Canada Council Arts Bursary (1967, 1968); Canada Council Travel Grants (1967, 1968, 1969); Canada Council Short-Term Grants (1969, 1972) and received the following prizes: 2nd prize in the Vancouver Sales and Exhibition show (1963); Award, Winnipeg Show (1966); First award Hadassah Art Auction, Winnipeg (1967); Prize, Concours Artistique (1971). His solo shows include: Saskatchewan House, Summer Festival Show (1965); Regina Public Library (1967); Central Library (art gallery), Regina (two-man show, 1968); Galerie d'Art, Mtl. (1969); Galerie Martal, Mtl. (1972, 1973); Optica, Mtl. (1976). From 1964 on he taught drawing and painting at various adult education courses in Regina and Children Art courses for the School of Fine Art, Regina Campus, University of Saskatchewan (1962 to 1968) and courses in drawing, painting and design for the Department of Fine Art, Sir George Williams University, Montreal (1968-69, 1969-70) and was visiting Professor in painting for the Department of Art, University of Calgary. He is represented in the following collections: The

PETERS, Kenneth (Cont'd)

Art Gallery Society, Norman Mackenzie Art Gallery, Regina; Edmonton Art Gallery, Alta.; Canada Council Art Bank, Ottawa; Regina Public Library; Saskatchewan Arts Board and in private collections in Canada, England and the U.S.A.

References

Regina Leader-Post, Sask., Mar. 14, 1959 "Students' work to be displayed" by A.F. McKay

The Vancouver-Sun, B.C., May 24, 1963 "Both Winners and Losers Hang in This Competition"

Canadian Art, Vol. 20, No. 2, Mar./Apr. 1963 "Clement Greenberg's View Of Art On The Prairies" by C.G., P. 90-107

Free Press, Winnipeg, Man., Mar. 1, 1967 "Hadassah Prize Is Awarded To Kenneth Peters"

Leader Post, Regina, Sask., Dec. 7, 1968 "Bold contrast in art works"

Seventh Biennial of Canadian Painting, NGC, 1968, P. 111

Le Campus Estrien, Sherbrooke, P.Q., Feb. 26, 1969 "Art Optique — exposition morris-peters"

Canadian Art Today, Ed. William Townsend, Studio International, London, Eng., 1970 "Memories of Saskatchewan" by Andrew Hudson, P. 49, 51

The Montreal Star, P.Q., Apr. 12, 1972 "Art Galerie Martal..." (review)

The Gazette, Mtl., P.Q., Apr. 14, 1972 "Artist's first show gentle, refined" by Michael White

The Montreal Star, P.Q., 24 Mar., 1973 "Shadows and light" by Catherine Bates

Canadian artists in exhibition, 1972-73, Roundstone Council for the Arts, 1973, P. 170

The Gazette, P.Q., June 26, 1976 "Peters' color fields please despite debt" by Virginia Nixon (review at Optica and his debt to Olitski)

NGC Info. Form rec'd January, 1963, update 1973

Modern Painting in Canada by Terry Fenton & Karen Wilkin, Hurtig Publishers/Edmonton Art Gallery, 1978, P. 113

PETERS, Lawrie
b. 1942

Born at Pioneer Mine, B.C., she was raised on a farm and left home at the age of sixteen. She worked as a maid, a secretary, a model and sales person during her years of schooling and obtained her Bachelor of Education from the University of British Columbia and a master's degree from the Instituto Allende in Mexico. She travelled in Europe, U.S.A. and Mexico and was director of a school on Digby Island on the northern coast of British Columbia and also taught at Woodfibre on the edge of Sechelt Provincial Forest, B.C. and Prince George in the Cariboo District of B.C. She was working on impressionistic frescoes for homes in Montreal in 1970.

References

Vancouver Sun, B.C., Dec. 11, 1969 "Painting of hunger to assuage hunger" by Ann Barling

La Presse, Mtl., P.Q., Aug. 8, 1970 "Des murales pour décorer les maisons?" par Cécile Brosseau

PETERS, Lloyd
b.(c) 1912

Originally from Whitby, Ontario, he was first encouraged by his public school art teacher who gave him his first art lessons as a matter of general education.

PETERS, Lloyd (Cont'd)

He went on to attend several other art classes and to win a scholarship. As a young man he worked as a commercial artist for Eatons while attending evening art classes in painting and etching during the 1930's under teachers who made up the famous Group of Seven painters. He also received considerable help from John (Jack) Martin a fellow member of the Society of Canadian Painter-Etchers and Engravers. Known for his fine water colours he held several one-man shows in Toronto and several large exhibitions in pre-war days throughout Ontario and Montreal. He was a commercial artist until 1963 then worked at the Whitby Psychiatric Hospital. In 1977 he turned to full-time painting with plans to move to a small cabin on the outskirts of Trout Creek which will serve as a studio and vantage point for his trips in a van especially equipped for his needs for painting in all seasons. He paints his scenes on the spot often capturing the mood of the day and in all kinds of weather. He exhibited his paintings at the Upper Level Gallery in North Bay and has an exhibit moving around Ontario on a rotating basis. As paintings are sold from the show new ones are added as he completes them.

Reference
North Bay Nugget, Ont., Sept. 9, 1977 "Group of Seven protege pursues one vocation" story and photos by Karin Caue

PETERSEN, Eric

Born in Denmark he first took art lessons in Copenhagen at the age of ten. He emigrated to Canada in 1920 and worked at the Shawinigan Lake Lumber Company on Vancouver Island. He then farmed on the Prairies for about a year before returning to British Columbia. All during this time he worked at his painting and by 1964 had completed one thousand oil paintings depicting the natural settings in Canada. A number of his paintings are hung in hotels and motels throughout British Columbia including the Travel Lodge Motel at Vernon where forty of his oils hang. He met his wife Marie at Kamloops and they married in 1932 then moved to Vancouver where they lived and raised their two children Mona and Norman. During the Thirties he concentrated on painting the scenic Prairies and the B.C. mountains. He also worked in 1952 for the fish patrol for the Department of Fisheries stationed at Prince Rupert. Living at North Surrey, B.C., in 1964 he was continuing to work at his easel and submit his work for showing at the annual exhibition of the Vancouver Art Gallery. A large painting by him hangs in the hotel at Lumby, B.C.

Reference
The Surrey Leader, Cloverdale, B.C., Dec. 23rd, 1964 "Danish Painter Loves B.C. Scenery"

PETERSMANN, Brigitte
b. 1943
Born in Danzig, Poland, she studied at Kassel, West Germany under Fritz Winter, A. Bode, H. Hillmann and others and received her Master of Fine Arts

PETERSMANN, Brigitte (Cont'd)

in 1967. She came to Canada in 1968 first to Montreal and then to Halifax, N.S., where she became an art specialist for Senior High School (1969-72). In her own work she does figurative compositions in ink drawings, etchings and mixed media paintings and exhibited at the Nova Scotia College of Art and Design in March of 1972.

Reference

    NGC Info. Form rec'd c.1972

PETERSON, Edward

At the age of eighteen he homesteaded in the Yeoford district, west of Pigeon Lake, Alberta, and around the same time was an assistant Wheat Pool agent. He was instrumental in the organization and the work to do with the Canadian Co-Operative Implements Limited and was at one time Secretary of the Board of Directors of the Alberta Co-op Wholesale. For 27 years he was a manager of a local store and in 1957 was representative of the Co-op Insurance Company in Wetaskiwin. He took up painting in 1951 and became a member of the local art club of Wetaskiwin and has since produced many scenes, including landmarks of Wetaskiwin and surrounding district, which were chosen for exhibit in the Historical Art Display at the University of Alberta in 1967. His work has also been exhibited with many provincial groups.

References

    Wetaskiwin Times, Alta., Sept. 11, 1957 "Local Artist Finds Painting Expressive"

    Ibid, July 5, 1967 "Art Display" (paintings by Peterson displayed at Wetaskiwin Pioneer Savings and Credit Union)

PETERSON, Elna (Mrs.)

A Fort Frances, Ontario, painter, she studied two winters with Millie Gladu and briefly with Gene Monahan for portrait. Her landscapes are of the bushy, rocky country where she has spent her life in the Fort Frances and surrounding area. She was winner of a purchase award from the first Great River Road Amateur Art Contest sponsored by the Mississippi River Parkway Commission and Great River Road, with participating artists from ten states and two provinces (actually won Governor's Award for Minnesota but through an error in residence she was disqualified and given the purchase award). Her work was exhibited in the downstairs gallery of the public library in Fort Frances (1968).

References

    The Daily Bulletin, Fort Frances, Ontario, Aug. 24, 1968 "Fort Frances Artists Win Great River Road Contest; Paintings Exhibited"

    Ibid, Oct. 1, 1968 "Exhibit Shows Paintings by Elna Peterson"

PETERSON, Joyce

A New Westminster, B.C. artist who travels with her husband Robert Peterson, owner of the gillnetter "Bergit C" which operates along the coast of B.C. She captures scenes of the coastline including lighthouses also seascapes and fishing crafts. She has been painting for 28 years and has a practised eye for detail. She is a prolific worker who does forty or more paintings a year. The Queen Charlotte Islands are one of her favourite spots to sketch. A painter of portraits as well she has exhibited her work at Fishermen's Hall, Vancouver and elsewhere and her paintings which she does in oil are popular. She has also painted in Mexico during several visits to that country.

Reference

The Fisherman, Van., B.C., Mar. 29, 1974 "Artist on fishing grounds" (photo of artist by Richard Morgan)

PETERSON, Kit

Born in Regina, Saskatchewan she studied life and portrait painting at the Vancouver School of Art; portrait sculpture with Peter Huber and ceramic sculpture with D. Toresdahl. She also studied art and architecture at London University, England. She exhibited her paintings (water colours, acrylics, oils) and some mini sculptures at the New Westminster Public Library in 1972 under the auspices of the Arts Council of New Westminster. She is a poet, musician (A.T.C.M.), swimming and gym instructor as well. She lives in New Westminster with her two daughters where she is an instructor in oil and water colour painting for the New Westminster Recreation Department.

References

New Westminster Columbian, B.C., July 15, 1972 (photo of mini sculptures)

Ibid, July 18, 1972 "Paintings displayed" (photo of paintings)

Biographical notes for New Westminster Public Library show, June 1972

PETERSON, Margaret (Mrs. Howard O'Hagan)
b. 1902

Born in Seattle, Washington, the daughter of Edwin R. and Ellen Charlotte (Larson) Peterson, she attended the Seward Grammar School, Seattle (1908-16); Broadway High School, Seattle (1916-20) and studied under Hans Hofmann and Worth Ryder at the University of California, Berkeley, where she received her A.B. (1923-26) and M.A. (1929-32); with Vaclav Vytlacil and André Lhote in Paris, France (1931-32). She then travelled, researched and worked in Mexico and Central America in 1934 and in British Columbia in 1935 returning to both regions in subsequent years (Mexico & Cent. America 1943, 1949, 1951, 1958; B.C. 1935-39, 1943, 1947-51). She made extensive studies of Indian cultures in the desert, the Guatemala peninsula and remote parts of Mexico and throughout Vancouver Island. She taught at the University of California for 22 years but resigned her post as associate professor of art rather than sign a politically-

PETERSON, Margaret (Mrs. Howard O'Hagan) (Cont'd)

motivated "Oath of Allegiance." She married Canadian author Howard O'Hagan, a writer who was himself attracted to Indian mythology and Indian ways of life. Cowichan Bay, Vancouver Island, was their home from 1953 to 1956. Then they moved to Victoria where Ms. Peterson occupied the studio once owned by Emily Carr. Unlike Emily Carr who painted what she saw of Indian life, Margaret Peterson painted the feelings and sensations derived from the totemic symbolism of the Indians and aboriginal peoples. Various writers have described Ms. Peterson's art as having, "inner vitality", "intensity", "powerfulness" and Arthur Corry noted her paintings as follows, "Her work has a deep mystic quality and a searching for the basic primitive forms in color and in design. Most of the paintings have a spiritual feeling, as though the artist was under a spell or in a trance at the time of conception. One wonders if the hand of a primitive god had not guided the brush. By means of symbols, and with a vivid passion, Miss Peterson depicts fire and water, birth and death, souls and spirits, gods and goddesses. Her expression is singular and her own." Using the ancient medium of egg tempera, and gesso treated panels, she does much of her work on a large scale. She travelled from Sweden to Egypt (1963-68) and did research in Egypt (1967). Throughout her career she has continued to exhibit her paintings in solo shows as follows: California Palace of the Legion of Honor, San Francisco, Calif. (1933, 1960); Biblioteca Nacionale, Mexico (1934); Henry Museum, Seattle, Wash. (1934); Paul Elder Gallery, San Francisco (1934); Raymond & Raymond, San Francisco (1945); San Francisco Art Museum, Civic Center, 1950, 1958, 1973; New Gallery, Algonquin Hotel, NYC (1951); Art Gallery of Greater Victoria (1953, 1959, 1962, retrosp. 1978); Du Casse Studio, San Francisco (1958); Univ. of California, San José (1958); The Point, Victoria (1960); Art Gallery of the Univ. of B.C. (1961); Monterey Peninsula Chapter of American Federation of Arts, Carmel, Calif. (1965). Her work has been exhibited in a number of important group shows including the Fourth and Fifth Biennial Exhibitions of Canadian Art (Painting), 1961, 1963; Sao Paulo Bienniale, Brazil (1963). Her awards include: Tansig travelling fellowship, Univ. Calif. (1931-32); 1st Prize, San Francisco Women Artists (1936); Pur. Awd. San Francisco Art Assoc. (1942); 1st Prize, San F. Art Assoc. (1947); Blue Ribbon, Pacific Artists Festival (1952); 1st Prize, San F. W.A. (1952); Can. Council Senior Grant (1963). Her commissions include: mosaic panel for McPherson Library, Univ. Victoria, B.C. (1964); mural, B.C. Hydro Bldg., Vict., B.C. (1974). She is represented in the following collections: Univ. Victoria, Vict., B.C.; McPherson Lib., Univ. Vict., B.C.; NGC, Ottawa; Confederation Memorial Bldg., Charlottetown, P.E.I.; San Francisco Art Musuem; California Palace of Legion of Honor, San Franc.; San Franc. California Art Inst.; Univ. Calif., Berkeley; Univ. Calif., Santa Cruz; Oakland Art Museum, Calif.

References

Times, Vict., B.C., Aug. 1, 1953 (show at Art Centre Gr. Victoria)

Ibid, May 23, 1959 (note on show at AG Gr. V. May 26 — June 14, 1959)

Colonist, Vict., B.C., May 29, 1959 "At the Art Gallery — How Many Know? Fine U.S. Painter Lives Unnoticed in Victoria" by Ina D.D. Uhthoff

Province, Van., B.C., Feb. 10, 1961 "Realm of art — Harsher kind of interrogation" by The Critic

Newsletter, San Francisco Art Inst., March, 1961 "Notes from Vancouver" by Joan Lowndes

Colonist, Vict., B.C., May 2, 1961 "At the Art Gallery — Victoria's Margaret Peterson Wins

PETERSON, Margaret (Mrs. Howard O'Hagan) (Cont'd)

Place in Famed Show" by Ina D.D. Uhthoff
Globe & Mail, Ont., May 11, 1961 (large photo of artist)
Times, Vict., B.C., May 20, 1961 "Art in Review — Work of Victoria Artist Obscure to Uninitiated" by Arthur Corry
Daily News, Prince Rupert, B.C., May 31, 1961 (Peterson's "The New Star" chosen for exhibit in Canadian Biennial)
Fourth Biennial Exhibition of Canadian Art 1961, NGC, Ott., 1961 No. 67 (see ill. next page)
Times, Vict., B.C., 22 July, 1962 "At the Gallery — Brilliant 'Totemic' Artist Unique Amongst Painters" by Ina D.D. Uhthoff
Ibid, 28 July, 1962 "Art in Review — Artist's Primitive Insight Creates Powerful Style" by Arthur Corry
Ibid, 28 Oct., 1962 "National Gallery Buys Painting by City Woman"
Canadian Art, Vol. 19, No. 6, Nov./Dec. 1962 "Three Centuries of Canadian Painting" by J. Russell Harper P. 450-451
Fifth Biennial Exhibition of Canadian Painting 1963,NGC, Ott. 1963, No. 55
Painting in Canada by J. Russell Harper (1966) 2nd Ed. paper 1977, P. 351
Creative Canada, Vol. 2, McPherson Lib., Univ. Victoria/Univ. Tor. Press, 1972, P. 219-220
Times, Vict., B.C., Dec. 4, 1974 "Hydro Building Art Showpiece" (commission for mural)
Province, Van., B.C., Nov. 22, 1974 "Gov't commissions $137,000 in art"
Times, Vict., B.C., Oct. 14, 1978 "At the Galleries — Margaret Peterson Retrospective"
NGC Info. Forms Mar. 1961, Aug. 1961

PETERSON, Norman

b. 1924

Born in Narol, Manitoba, he studied at the Winnipeg School of Art under B. Pragnall, Prof. McLoy and privately under Clarence Tillenius noted Canadian nature artist. He left his studies to work in advertising and market analysis (package designing, photo retouching and illustration). During his spare time he did carving and moved east and settled in Chippawa, Ontario where he rented a garage next to the old Anglican Church Rectory which he used as a workshop until he moved into a vacant store on Cummington Square. He attracted the attention of many young people who watched him work. Finally Peterson found himself giving them free lessons. His shop became so full of eager students he had to move into larger quarters and was able to obtain the use of the old town hall in Chippawa where he developed a community centre for arts and crafts. He made frequent efforts to enlist the assistance of educational and cultural sources in Ontario to develop the art of crafts in schools and recreation programmes but they could not see that Canadian produced crafts were a valuable thing both for the tourist trade in the area and for the training of children in something that would give them pleasure and a sense of accomplishment for the rest of their lives. Peterson has become noted for the various animals he carves and especially the owl he created from the sumac tree using the grain of the wood to make the ringed eyes of the bird. There are many thousands of his owls throughout the world. Peterson combines the use of power tools and his ability to carve, to create a unique piece he can produce in quantities enough to compete with tourist items which are mass produced in other countries, imported by Canadian dealers to be sold as Canadian souvenirs. After establishing a permanent community centre known as the Peterson Community Workshop Association in Chippawa, he departed

PETERSON, Norman (Cont'd)

with his family to live in his native Winnipeg where he planned to work in schools and appear in T.V. classes to make his craft known to children, shut-ins and senior citizens.

References

Winnipeg Free Press, Man., Jan. 1, 1968 "Whynottas' Inspiration For Wood Carving Artist"

Québec L'Action, Que., Dec. 6, 1968 "Sculpteur sur bois"

Niagara Falls Review, Ont., Jan. 19, 1974 "Carver promotes his craft to the young" by Bill Johnston

Ibid, Feb. 10, 1976 "More than 1,000 visitors attend two-day craft show"

Ibid, July 17, 1976 "Norm Peterson leaves area richer for his talents" by Bernice Huxtable

Ibid, Feb. 24, 1977 "Workshop planning first open house"

NGC Info. Form rec'd Apr. 7, 1952

Winnipeg Tribune, Man., Nov. 16, 1976 "Crafts groups 'dreamy-eyed' — Woodcarver is a salesman" by Patrick McKinley

PETERSON, Roy Eric

b. 1936

Born in Winnipeg, Manitoba, the son of Lawrence and Ethel Peterson, he moved to Vancouver in 1948 where he attended Kitsilano High School. From his earliest years he wanted to be a cartoonist. He worked at display and advertising from 1955 to 1962. He then freelanced for the *Vancouver Sun* and other publications and received the Vancouver Art Directors' Club award in 1962 which was to be the first of a number of other awards. Peterson ranks very high as a gifted and dedicated professional cartoonist. In his work as an editorial cartoonist for the *Sun* he usually sketches three ideas in the morning after reading the newspaper and submits them to the *Sun* editorial page editor who selects one. The afternoon is spent drawing the cartoon in pen, brush and ink. In 1973 he received First Prize in the 10th International Salon of Cartoons at Man and His World exhibition in Montreal. His entry entitled "Le Sommelier Grotesque", a cartoon which reflects Peterson's own personal protest against nuclear testing, depicts French president Georges Pompidou 'selling' the Mururoa atomic test as a fine wine of 'Pacific vintage with a strong bouquet of Strontium 90. . . .' Peterson has also contributed to television shows and designed book covers and done his own book *The Canadian ABC Book* for children and adults alike. Trevor Lautens in a friendly humorous article described Peterson as follows, "He lives in a comfortable, unremarkable house. . .in West Vancouver. . .has a pleasant studio at the back of the garden where he does most of his work. . . .His drawings have hit the most prestigious markets: *Punch*, the *New York Times*, the *Spectator* and the wanted-men posters of the Vancouver Police Department. . . .A love of family, a love of work; pride in both, and a bantering discomfort about explaining either. That, perhaps as well as anyone will ever know, is Roy Peterson." His other awards include: Vancouver International Amateur Film Festival Award for animated film, Life in British Columbia. . .(1964); Graphica Award (1965); Editor & Publisher advertising award (1968); National Newspaper Award (1968). He married Margaret Brand and they have five children.

PETERSON, Roy Eric (Cont'd)

References

The Vancouver Sun, B.C., Sept. 11, 1969 "Meet Mild-Mannered Roy. . .In Reality, Super-Cartoonist" by Robert Sarti

Ibid, June 11, 1971 "Trevor Lautens Talks About Big Daddy Roy" Announcement of winners, Tenth International Salon of Cartoons July 13, 1973

The Vancouver Sun, July 14, 1973 "Sun's Roy Peterson wins international cartoon prize"

The Gazette, Mtl., P.Q., July 14, 1973 "Vancouver cartoonist wins top Salon prize" by Dane Lanken

The Vancouver Sun, B.C., Mar. 14, 1974 (Premier Dave Barrett with Peterson cartoon of himself)

The Canadian ABC Book by Roy Peterson, Hurtig Publishers, Edmonton, Alta., 1977

PETERSON, Warren
b. 1935

Born in Salina, Kansas, he studied at the University of Kansas City and the University of Iowa under Stuart Edie, Robert Knipschild and Mauricio Lasansky. A painter and printmaker he came to Saskatchewan in 1964 and developed a photographic method for making itaglio-reliefs by placing the basic image (photographed or drawn) on a positive transparency, which is the very opposite to a photographic negative. He then prints the image on a photo-sensitized zinc plate and uses acid to cut the image below the surface. He rolls the ink into the depressions and with a flatbed press produces the prints on paper. Peterson was noted by John Noel Chandler, as one of the Canadian artists continuing to work in the representational mode whose etchings are less worked and show a calm spontaneity. He is represented in the Canada Council Art Bank and was one of the exhibiting artists in the annual 1971 show, "Saskatchewan: Art and Artists" sponsored by the Norman Mackenzie Art Gallery and the Regina Public Library Art Gallery. He is a member of the faculty of the University of Saskatchewan, Saskatoon.

References

Artscanada, October/November 1970 No. 148-149 "Drawing reconsidered" by John Noel Chandler P. 31 (column one), ill, P. 53

Saskatchewan: Art and Artists, Norman Mackenzie Art Gal./Regina Pub. Lib. Art Gal., Apr. 2-July 31, 1971 P. 42, 90

Star-Phoenix, Saskatoon, Sask., Oct. 5, 1972 "Canada Council considers prints"

Canada Council Art Bank list of artists in collection

PETHICK, Jerry
b.(c) 1936

Born in London, Ontario, he travelled to England where he attended the Chelsea School of Art and the Royal College of Art and won recognition especially in sculpture. He returned to Canada and in 1970 held a solo show at the 20/20 Gallery in London, Ontario of six traditional works on paper and twenty-two other works in varied media including thermoplastics and holography presentations. A few of these works were described during a review

PETHICK, Jerry (Cont'd)

by Lenore Crawford as follows, "Night Gems, a fine combination of brown and black; Mirrow Towers — a triumph of subtle array of dazzling colors — blood-red, browns, orange, light green, lavender, black for accent or relief; Trilogy of Progression, a skilful laying-on of materials to resemble a mixed-media print; Communications, with its colored dots lighting up the smokey atmosphere of the picture." Crawford went on to note that in most cases the artist kept control of his media rather than the media controlling the artist. Pethick at that time was teaching at the San Francisco Art Institute and kept a studio at Ann Arbor, Michigan, where holography was being studied.

References

Free Press, London, Ont., Feb. 9, 1970 "Pethick art exhibit intrigues, frustrates" by Lenore Crawford

Vancouver Sun, B.C., July 24, 1973 (large photo of Pethick's sculpture Cyclopian Eyes)

PETIT, Gaston (Joseph Gérard Gaston Ignace Petit)
b. 1930

Born in Shawinigan, Quebec, he began painting in oils in 1944 and was mainly self taught. He received his academic training in Philosophy and Theology at the Dominican House of Studies, Ottawa (1952-60) and was ordained a Catholic priest in 1959. Throughout his studies he was active with his art when time permitted. He made silk-screen cards and pictures of all kinds but had little time for painting. After graduation he travelled to a number of countries to learn various art techniques. He volunteered to serve as a missionary in Japan as a result of his interest being kindled by a Japanese classmate. His appointment came through and in 1961 he arrived in Japan where he established the mission and an atelier in the heart of Tokyo. For two years he studied Japanese and in the evenings took instruction in Sumi-é (ink painting) under Furihata, calligraphy under Nankoku Hidai and metal printing under Nakayama. Through a friend, Ronald Robinson, an American author who was researching his book *Seven Contemporary Block Printers* in Japan, Petit met printmaker Tajima who taught him details of the dye-resist technique using oil-based pigment, and chemical and natural dyes. As well Petit elaborated on the "Progressive Linocut" technique used by Picasso and carried out other experiments in his workshop. He worked with lacquer which he often mixed with cement to make a mural sized painting. His murals were done in a variety of materials including: mosaic; coloured paper tubes of equal length inserted between non-reflective glasses thus allowing one to see only the end cut of the paper; murals made of sand casting to obtain huge concrete forms to create a large mosaic; murals made of relief ceramic sections fired in slope type kilns in Kyoto. He made stained-glass windows not by staining the glass but by achieving colours by the use of German antique glass and also slab glass imbedded in concrete. In 1963 he planned the layout of a chapel for a school campus in Kyoto which included stained-glass windows, ceramic mural, concrete wall, glass and paper wall, design for the altar and tabernacle and complete furniture. During 1964-65 he travelled in Asia and Europe visiting Cambodia and India where he studied archeological and traditional art routes which have influenced Japanese art. In Europe he studied contemporary

PETIT, Gaston (Joseph Gérard Gaston Ignace Petit) (Cont'd)

church architecture and liturgical development. He returned to Japan with added knowledge which would prove useful in his work at the atelier. The atelier was enlarged to a staff of four architects and one trained artist working full-time on construction of various buildings and maintenance on others. In deciding a layout for a church Petit travels accompanied by the chief architect to the community requiring the structure and there celebrates the Eucharist with the people, talks with them to find out their needs and observes the setting of the proposed church especially of the surrounding architecture. Sketches of the structure are then made and after common agreement, plans are drawn up including the designing of furniture, vestments, chalice and other objects. In 1967 Petit was named head of the print section at the Junshin University of Art in Hachioji. In his own personal activity he was named member of the Society of Canadian Painter-Etchers and Engravers in 1968 and member of the Japanese Print Association in 1969. In Canada and other countries he is known mainly for his prints although he has exhibited his paintings as well including the 6th Biennial Exhibition of Canadian Painting (1965). His solo shows include: Galerie Beaudet, Trois-Rivières, P.Q. (1960); Koltiska, Tokyo, Japan (1962, 1963); Nihonbashi Gallery, Tokyo (1963); Seido Gallery, Kyoto, Japan (1963); Warren Library, Warren, Penn., U.S.A. (1963); Galerie Libre, Mtl., P.Q. (1963, 1965, 1967, 1968); Kunika Gallery, New Delhi, India (1964); Cultural Centre, Ghent, Belgium (1964); Séminaire St. Joseph, Trois-Rivières (1965); Galerie Houston-Brown, Paris, France (1966); Fran-Nell Gallery, Tokyo (1966, 1967, 1969); Yoseido Gallery, Tokyo, Japan (1967, 1971); Gallery Solidaridad, Manila, Philippines (1968, 1970, 1971); Galerie du Vieux, Trois-Rivières (1968); Gallery Pascal, Tor., Ont. (1968, 1971, 1975); Galerie Champagne, Quebec, P.Q. (1968); Galerie l'Apogée, St. Sauveur, P.Q. (1971, 1972); Artium Orbis, Santa Fe, New Mexico, U.S.A. (1971); Galerie d'Art Les Deux B, Hull, P.Q. (1975). He is represented in the collections of the Cincinnati Art Museum, Ohio, U.S.A.; Musée d'art contemporain, Mtl.; David Rockefeller Collection and in collections of thirty museums in Japan. Lives in Tokyo.

References

Le Nouvelliste, Trois Rivières, P.Q., Nov. 21, 1960 "A la Galerie Beaudet — Gaston Petit, peintre exubérant" by R.L.

Vie des Arts, Mtl., October, 1963

Maintenant, Mtl., October, 1963 "Peinture"

Le Nouvelliste, Oct. 29, 1963 "De L'Image Au Son — Exposition Petit" by G.G.

Ibid, Apr. 18, 1963 "Un peintre trifluvien, le Père Petit, expose au Japon"

La Presse, Mtl., Nov. 2, 1963 "Gaston Petit: un art oriental?"

The Gazette, Mtl., Nov. 2, 1963 "Art Sumi-é" by Dorothy Pfeifer

Le Nouvelliste, May 22, 1965 "Il n'y a pas de demi-mesure pour apprécier les oeuvres du R.P. Petit"

Cité Libre, Mtl., June, 1966

Missionary Bulletin, Tokyo, Japan 1967, 1968

La Presse, Mtl., July 15, 1967 "De la calligraphie à la couleur pénétrante"

Gaston Petit by Jacques de Roussan, Ed. Lidoc, Mtl., 1967

Le Nouvelliste, Sept. 14, 1968 "Touche orientale dans l'oeuvre du Père Petit"

Globe & Mail, Tor., Ont., Sept. 14, 1968 "At the Galleries — Overture to a dozen first shows swells to fortissimo" by Kay Kritzwiser

Québec Le Soleil, P.Q., Oct. 19, 1968 "Gaston Petit et les tonalités"

PETIT, Gaston (Joseph Gérard Gaston Ignace Petit) (Cont'd)

Québec L'Action, Oct. 19, 1968 "Les expositions à Québec — Mémoires du cosmos et de l'éros" par Jean Royer

Québec L'Action, P.Q., Oct. 23, 1968 "Gaston Petit expose à la Galerie Champagne"

La Presse, Mtl., P.Q., Nov. 9, 1968 "Quand le signe est surtout plastique"

Le Nouvelliste, P.Q., Sept. 17, 1968 "Vernissage des oeuvres du Père Gaston Petit" par Robert Lebeuf

Artist's Proof, N.Y., Vol. IX, 1970

Globe & Mail, Tor., Ont., April 3, 1971 (review of Petit & Daudelin at Gallery Pascal)

Winnipeg Free Press, Man., July 14, 1972 "Priest Explores Arts In Japan" by Katie FitzRandolph

Winnipeg Tribune, Man., July 29, 1972 "Just name the art — Father Petit excels at it" by Jan Kamienski

Star Weekly, Tor., Ont., Aug. 26, 1972 "Coals to Tokyo? He teaches printmaking in Japan"

London Evening Free Press, Ont., Mar. 20, 1972 "Art exhibit combines color, message" by Lenore Crawford

Winnipeg Tribune, Jan. 6, 1973 "Priest preaches art in Japan" by John R. Walker

L'Art au Québec depuis 1940 par Guy Robert, La Presse, Mtl., 1973 P. 160, 161, 314, 315, 351

44 Modern Japanese Print Artists (two volumes, 528 pages, 358 colour and black & white illustrations), Kodansha International, Japan, 1973

Le Nouvelliste, P.Q., Feb. 22, 1974 "Gaston Petit publie une imposante étude sur les graveurs japonais"

Vie Des Arts, Printemps, 1974 "lectures", P. 84

Le Nouvelliste, 11 Mai, 1974 "Gaston Petit se sent chez lui à Tokyo"

Globe & Mail, Ont., May 29, 1975 "Petit unfolds new balances as horizons move outward" by James Purdie

Le Nouvelliste, June 3, 1975 "Gaston Petit l'homme des projets monumentaux" par René Lord

Ottawa Citizen, Ottawa, Ont., Sept. 8, 1975 "Canadian makes his mark in Japan" by Kathleen Walker

Ibid, Sept. 19, 1975 "Lifestyle irrelevant"

Le Droit, Ottawa, Ont., Dec. 11, 1976 "Gaston Petit et Pierre Tétreault: deux artistes voués au visible"

Ottawa Citizen, Dec. 24, 1976 "Eastern influence in western frame" by Robert Smythe

Le Nouvelliste, 16 June, 1977 "Le peintre Gaston Petit a dirigé une délégation japonaise à travers sept villes du Canada"

NGC Info. Forms & biographical info deposited in NGC Lib. file

---

PETITJEAN, E.C.

b. 1906

Born in France, he was active in Toronto in the 1950's and had a studio on Severn Street. He did semi-abstract paintings of the construction activity in the building of the Toronto subway.

References

Evening Telegram, Tor., Ont., July 8, 1950 "At The Galleries — Artist Depicts Subway Of Workers And Machines" by Rose MacDonald

Ibid, July 15, 1950 "At The Galleries — Subway Construction Is Artist's Theme" by Rose MacDonald

Ontario Index of Canadian Artists by Jeremy N. Watney, Toronto, 1973

PETITOT, Émile
1837-1917

An Oblate Father who studied art for a short time in Paris and came to Canada in 1861(2) as a missionary to the Canadian north in the Mackenzie River area. When conventional art supplies were not available he ingeniously made his own paint from natural ochres, plants, fruits mixed with fish oils and made his brushes from tufts of hair or fur. In some cases it was thought that he used flour bags for his canvases. He decorated his missions with his own paintings. One of his paintings for the mission at Fort Good Hope was transferred to the museum of the Oblate Fathers at St. Albert, Alberta. Another of his paintings of Fort Edmonton (see Harper's *Painting in Canada/a history*, 1966) is now in the Alberta Legislative Library, Edmonton. He wrote books and illustrated them. He returned to France in 1882 and died at Margueilles-le-Beaux in 1917.

References

Edmonton Journal, Alta., Wed., Aug. 26, 1931 "Oblate Father Paints Picture with Fish Oil" by Clare Ward Farrell

Painting in Canada/a history by J. Russell Harper, Univ. Tor. Press, Tor., 1966, P. 203-5

Early Painters and Engravers in Canada by J. Russell Harper, Univ. Tor. Press, Tor., 1970, P. 249

Painting in Canada/a history by J. Russell Harper, Univ. Tor. Press, 2nd Edition (paperback), 1977, P. 199

PETLEY-JONES, Llewellyn
b. 1908

Born in Edmonton, Alberta, son of Mr. A. Hurdis and Mrs. (née Petley) Jones, he attended public and high school in Edmonton. He began learning his art from magazines, books and other sources and quickly showed an unusual talent for painting and drawing. He worked as a bank clerk for three years then turned to painting. He became a member of the Edmonton Art Club in 1927 and the Alberta Society of Artists in 1931. In the A.S.A. Calgary show in 1931 he received praise from W.J. Phillips. His paintings were also accepted the same year at an annual juried show at the National Gallery of Canada. He established a studio in Edmonton where he also taught a large class of students to help make ends meet. He became known for his landscapes and portraits in oils and water colours of the Edmonton area and the West Coast. He moved to London, England in 1934 then went on to study painting in Paris. Shortly afterwards his painting of Seba Beach was accepted in the (1935) Royal Academy show in London. He had also been accepted for exhibit by the Royal Society of British Artists. He continued to exhibit with these societies and other important ones in the U.K. (see below). In Paris he set up a studio in the Montparnasse section and his "Autumn on the Seine" was exhibited in the Société Nationale des Beaux-Arts, Paris. His success continued with pictures being accepted by the Salon d'Autumne. In 1939 he met and married Nancy Corbet of Calgary who was in London at that time. They went to Italy but had to flee the country a few hours before Mussolini declared war. All his Italian paintings were lost when they made their hasty departure. In London he held his first one-man show at Matthiesen Limited on Bond Street and The Rt. Hon. R.B. Bennett opened the exhibition. Petley-Jones served in the British navy

PETLEY-JONES, Llewellyn (Cont'd)

(mentioned in Tor. Star 15 Aug./42) during World War II. In 1950, fifteen years of his work was shown at the Museum of Arts in Edmonton. Shows were also held at Eaton's College Street store, Toronto, and at the Contemporary Canadian Artists show at the Art Gallery of Toronto and the Western Art Circuit. In 1954 he was commissioned to paint murals for the C.P.R. then with his wife and six children travelled to Paris, France, stopping first in London to exhibit his British Columbia paintings then at Richmond near London then finally Paris to do a series of paintings (between one and two hundred) for Dr. Max Stern of the Dominion Gallery, Montreal. He returned to England and settled with his family at Richmond where he established a studio. In 1955 he was commissioned by the Alberta Government to paint portraits of Queen Elizabeth and the Duke of Edinburgh for the Alberta Legislative Building. The Queen had sat for twenty portraits in four years, was sitting for three more, and was booked for sittings for the next year. It was not possible therefore for Petley-Jones to obtain sittings and still complete the work in the time stipulated by the Alberta Government so he had to work from photographs, masks at Madame Tussaud's waxworks and from occasional public glimpses of the royal couple on special occasions. When the portraits were unveiled at London's Imperial Institute a controversy was sparked by some critics over the portraits' likenesses to the royal couple but members of the Alberta cabinet were quite pleased with the portraits and the paintings were hung in the legislature. By 1958 Petley-Jones was working in the field of abstract painting and held his first show of new work at the Waddington Galleries, London, in 1958. His solo shows during his career are as follows: St. Georges Gallery, Lond. (1941, 1945); Da Vinci Gallery, Lond. (1942-43); Wildenstein, London (1946-48, 1954); Gimpels Fils, Lond. (1949); University of London (1950); U.B.C. Fine Arts Gal., Van. (1951); Art Centre, Vic., B.C.; V.A.G., Van. (1952); Walker Gallery, Lond. (1955); Imperial Inst., Lond. (1956); Dominion Gallery, Mtl. (1957); Waddington Galleries, Lond. (1958); and he participated in a number of group shows including those at the Royal Academy, Lond. (1935-43); Royal Portrait Society; Royal Society of British Artists; New English Art Club; Royal Scottish Academy; Royal Hibernian Academy, Ireland; Royal Inst. of Oil Painters; London Group; National Society; Royal Water Colour Society and Canadian Group of Painters. He is represented in the following public collections: National Gallery of Wales; Birmingham Art Gallery; Art Gallery of Ontario and the Edmonton Art Gallery.

References

Edmonton Journal, Alta., Apr. 14, 1933 "City Artist Wins Praise For Art Work"

Ibid, July 17, 1933 "L. Petley-Jones Carries Honors — Wins in Portraiture, Landscape and Still Life at Exhibition" by F.H. Norbury

Vancouver Sun, B.C., Nov. 4, 1933 "Artist 'Covers' Waterfront" by D.M.

Victoria Colonist, B.C., Aug. 31, 1934 "Private View of Pictures Given — Water-Colors Made by Edmonton Artist Visiting Coast Shown at Oak Bay"

Edmonton Journal, Alta., May 13, 1935 "Royal Academy Accepts Edmonton Man's Picture" (reported in other papers)

Ibid, May 18, 1937 "Edmonton Artist Receives Honors" (picture "Winter at Richmond" hung in R.A. show)

Ibid, Dec. 21, 1937 "Edmonton Artist Relates Paris Life"

Ibid, June 8, 1938 "Edmonton Artist Now in Paris Hangs Another Picture" ("Autumn on the Seine" shown at Soc. Nat. des Beaux-Arts — reproduction of painting with caption)

PETLEY-JONES, Llewellyn (Cont'd)

Ibid, Mar. 20, 1939 "Honor for Canadian Artist" (two pictures hung in Salon d'Automne, Paris)

Vancouver Province, July 14, 1939 "Fame For Canadian Artist" by A.C. Cummings

Ottawa Citizen, Ont., Aug. 1, 1942 "Canadian Artist's Success"

Toronto Star, Ont. Aug. 15, 1942 "Music and Art — Canadian Water-Colorist Rivals Camera and Corot" by Augustus Bridle

Edmonton Journal, Alta., May 8, 1950 "City Artist Displays Work of Past 15 Years" by F.H. Norbury

Vancouver Sun, B.C., Aug. 9, 1950 "Artist Here After Success In Europe" by Mildred Valley Thornton

Edmonton Journal, Alta., May 12, 1950 "Museum President Opens Display" (90 paintings of France, England and Canada shown at Museum of Arts)

Canadian Art, Vol. VII, No. 4, 1950 (reproduction of "Les trois françaises" by L. P-J)

Star-Phoenix, Saskatoon, Sask., Jan. 16, 1951 "Petley-Jones Painting at Art Centre"

The Albertan, Calg., Alta., Mar. 10, 1951 "Alberta Artist Shows Paintings"

Vancouver Sun, Mar. 31, 1951 (photo of portrait of W.H. Malkin by L. Pet-J)

Vancouver Province, B.C., Apr. 21, 1951 "In the realm of art — New, Lively Display At Fine Arts Show" by Palette (solo show at UBC Fine Arts Gallery)

Victoria Colonist, B.C., May 24, 1951 "Only Abstracts Missing From Art Centre Show" by John Kyle

Victoria Times, B.C., May 16, 1951 "Stunning Color Use In Jones' Paintings" by Audrey St. D. Johnson

Montreal Star, P.Q., Oct. 27, 1951 "In a High Key" (review of paintings)

Vancouver Province, B.C., Feb. 22, 1952 "from Banks to brushes" by Shirley Lynn (biographical article)

Ibid, Mar. 12, 1952 "Local Artist's Paintings Praised At Art Gallery"

Ibid, Mar. 27, 1952 "One-Man Show" (photo of Petley-Jones w/painting)

The Gazette, Mtl., Aug. 23, 1952 (photo of painting "Lodge Pole Pines" at Dominion Gallery)

newspaper, Victoria, B.C., April, 1954 "Canadian Artist Planning To Work In French Capital" (article and photo of Petley-Jones, wife, and children)

The Gazette, Mtl., Oct. 2, 1954 (photo of "Moulin Rouge, Paris" by P-J acquired by Max Stern)

The Times, Lond., Eng., Jan. 18, 1956 "Walker's Galleries" (review)

The Lady, Eng., March, 1956 (photo of Petley-Jones, wife and seven children)

Globe & Mail, Tor., Ont., Apr. 5, 1956 (CP Lond Apr. 3) "Canadian Artist To Paint Queen For Legislature"

Edmonton Journal, Alta., Sept. 11, 1956 "Royal Portraits Near Completion"

Calgary Albertan, Alta., Dec. 14, 1956 "Those Royal Portraits"

Vancouver Province, B.C., Dec. 15, 1956 "New Portrait Of Queen Elizabeth" (large photo of painting of Queen with P-J and two of his children viewing work)

Art News & Review, Dec. 8, 1956 "Portrait of The Artist" (reproduction and self portrait with biographical sketch)

Time, New York, Dec. 24, 1956 (controversy of Royal portraits)

Art Gallery of Ontario/the Canadian collection by Helen Pepall Bradfield, McGraw-Hill Co., Can. Ltd., Tor., 1970, P. 365

Calgary Herald, Alta., Jan. 28, 1957 "Cabinet Likes New Paintings"

Toronto Telegram, Ont., May 5, 1957 "A western province purchases a western artist's paintings of the Queen and Prince Philip"

Art News & Review, November, 1958 "Two Tone Exhibition" by Denis Bowen

Quebec Chronicle-Telegraph, P.Q., Nov. 19, 1959 "Artist To Rent His Paintings"

NGC Info. Forms May 24, 1950; Aug. 9, 1951; Jan. 16, 1959

PETRACHENKO, Leona (Mrs.)

She studied art nights and has been active with the Welland Brush and Palette Club and the Port Colborne arts clubs. A painter in various media her work has been accepted in juried shows. Her painting "Welland South Bridge" sponsored by the Rose City Art Festival Committee was chosen "Picture of the Month" and displayed at the Welland City Hall.

Reference

> *Welland-Port Colborne Tribune*, Welland, Ont., Mar. 14, 1973 "Welland South Bridge-Picture of The Month"

PETRALIA, George
b. 1936

Born in Catania, Sicily, he started woodcarving at the age of eight and by the age of eleven was considered a professional woodcarver. He did work for tourists and projects throughout Sicily and Italy in later years. At fourteen he enrolled in evening classes, studying painting and design under Professor Torrisi a noted Italian artist. He won first prize in a competition in Taormina, Sicily, for his carving of a miniature Sicilian cart (caretto). Working from a single piece of wood usually, he carves in mahogany, walnut, birch and after coming to Canada in 1953 has used maple. He settled in Oshawa and for thirteen years was employed in a furniture factory, then in 1966 assembled his own work and toured Winnipeg, Kenora, Port Arthur, Fort William, Sault Ste. Marie, Oshawa, Parry Sound and other centres. Petralia is also a painter. In all his work his subjects range from real to mythological. He admires the work of Raphael, Michelangelo and Leonardo da Vinci. Married, his wife Lisa is from Holland and they have a daughter. In 1967 Petralia was working in association with Del-Craft Metal Industries in Port Arthur.

References

> *News-Chronicle*, Port Arthur, Ont., Dec. 5, 1967 "Wood Carvings, Paintings by Local Artist on 'Show'" (photo of artist, work and article on him)
> Ibid, May 8, 1968 "Artist Shows Work" (photo of artist and his work)
> *Sudbury Star*, Ont., Aug. 15, 1968 "Promoting Art of Woodcarving His Dream for Young People" by Wray Roulston

PETREVAN, Charles Carl
b. 1919

Born in Aljmas, Yugoslavia, he received his first art training in Europe and arrived in Canada in 1940 and settled in Kirkland Lake where he attended high school and received further art training. In 1940 he moved to Toronto where he attended the Ontario College of Art and received instruction from Archibald Barnes, John Alfsen, George Pepper and Fred Finley. His studies were confined to evenings so that much of his progress was a result of his own study. He exhibited his work in the Hamilton annuals of 1957 and 1958. His paintings were used on different occasions to help raise money for the United Nations Relief Fund.

PETREVAN, Charles Carl (Cont'd)

Reference
NGC Info. Form July 7, 1959

PETRIK, John A.
1898-1965

Born in Hungary he lived and worked on his parents' farm until he was 18. He then attended the University at Budapest to study agriculture but soon discovered that it was art that really interested him and turned to fine art studies. He had talent and ambition, worked hard at his painting and finally became a university teacher. In 1938 he came to Canada with his wife Irene, and settled in Holbrook, Ontario, where he bought a farm and attempted to make a living from farming. He didn't have enough money or bank credit to buy the machinery necessary to work the land so he turned to painting as did his wife although they were reluctant to sell their work because they did not speak English very well. Finally John was able to buy material for making pottery, brooches, earrings, jewel boxes, table centrepieces and candleholders. He was soon able to build a studio on Dundas Street in Woodstock. People from coast to coast came to see his creations and one of his works "The Patchwork Quilt" was acquired for the collection of an Ottawa Museum. When he died in 1965 his wife had planned to carry on with his work. He was survived by a daughter, Mrs. Joseph Sztahura (Tor.); one sister Miss Maria Bozsejovzski (Hungary) and a grandson.

Reference
Woodstock-Ingersoll Sentinel Review, Woodstock, Ont., May 7, 1965 "Petrik The Potter — Famed Canadian Artist Buried at St. Mary's"

PETRISKA, Josef
b. 1930

Born in Arad, Romania, one of eight children of a steelworker, as a boy he watched the famous sculptor Constantin Brancusi at work and was inspired to create something himself. At the age of eleven he made his first piece of work, a mural in mosaics. He left Romania at the age of sixteen during the close of World War II. Since that time he has lived and studied art in many countries. From his travels he became fluent in nine languages. He arrived in most countries with little but the clothes on his back. He first learned the language and then worked at various jobs like mining, office services or any kind of job he could find to accumulate enough money to live on and save so he could take time off to do his sculpture. He arrived in Canada in 1952 after a sojourn in California. He settled in Oakville, Ontario in 1969 and set up a workshop and studio. In his work Petriska fashions metal with amazing skill using regular cutting and welding torches. His large frame of over six feet is a definite advantage in handling large pieces of metal or stone which he transforms into highly creative sculptures. At times he has had to resort to his trade as construction co-ordinator which has required the use of his diverse skills for

PETRISKA, Josef (Cont'd)

the different projects involved. In recent years however he has been receiving many commissions for shopping malls especially for Eaton's at the Sherway Mall; Scarborough Town Centre; the Eaton Centre where he did a mural of the Toronto skyline, refurbished the statue of Sir Timothy Eaton and made fifty entrance doors to the Centre with original plate and bar decorations. His chrome sculpture chandelier at Eaton's Scarborough Town Centre was described by *Globe & Mail's* Zena Cherry as a spectacular piece of work. He has also completed other major architectural commissions across Canada for a number of public buildings and outdoor centres. But Petriska also does table-sized sculptures which have proved popular with important collectors and he is a painter as well although sculpture has occupied much of his time in the past twenty years. His work has been exhibited at the Toronto Dominion Centre (1972); Oakville Centennial Gallery (1975); Art Gallery of Ontario and Place de Ville. He is represented in collections of the Firestone family (tire magnates), prominent movie script writer in Hollywood, Calif., insurance executives, developers and others. One of his works can be seen on the grounds of the Trafalgar Heights Apartments, Oakville, Ontario. Lives in Oakville.

References

Mississauga News, Ont., Nov. 12, 1969 "Unusual artistry" (photos)

Oakville Daily Journal Record, Ont., Jan. 3, 1970 "He writes his poetry with an acetylene torch" story by Bill Michelmore, photos by Murray Belford

Ibid, Nov. 11, 1970 "Oak sculptor stresses form where you see what you want" by Lillian Scott

Ibid, Mar. 6, 1971 "Globetrotter settles in Oakville" by Jane Wallace

Ibid, July 10, 1971 "They looked like they could hold back the bulldozers, but. . ." by Tina Breckenridge

Ibid, Feb. 12, 1972 "I have got a poor deal — sculptor" by Agnes McKenna (Petriska forced to move studio to make way for development on short notice)

Globe & Mail, Tor., Ont., Mar. 3, 1972 "Sculptor with Guardians" (large photo of Petriska with his sculpture)

Catalogue, The Oakville Centennial Gallery — Profile on sculpture by Josef Petriska, April 9 to May 4, 1975

Clipping (probably Oakville Daily J.R.), 1975 "Sculpture shows concern for society's problems"

Globe & Mail, Tor., Ont., Apr. 9, 1975 "After A Fashion — Following ancients" by Zena Cherry

Oakville Daily Journal Record, Ont., Jan. 10, 1977 "Sculptor creates mural for Eaton Centre" (photo by Bill Majesky)

PETROFF, Natan

b. 1916

Born in Poland, he came to Canada in 1929 and settled in Toronto. He studied art at the Art Gallery of Toronto under Arthur Lismer and Gordon Webber then enrolled at the Central Technical School, Toronto, where he studied under Peter Haworth, Charles Goldhamer, Carl Schaefer, and Elizabeth Wyn Wood. He twice won the Royal Winter Fair sculpture competition and was also winner of the competition to represent Canada at the Paris Exposition. He was awarded a scholarship in 1938 to attend the American Artists School in New York. His water colour "Modern Times" (a study of a young girl seated on a

PETROFF, Natan (Cont'd)

hassock with head resting on hands reading a newspaper spread out on floor) was acquired by the National Gallery of Canada in 1939.

References

Toronto Star, Ont., Sept. 13, 1938 "U.S. Scholarships Go To Toronto Artists — Central Technical Graduates Get Year's Tuition in New York"

Canadian Water Colour Painting by Paul Duval, Burns & MacEachern, Tor., Ont., 1954 (last page of text, also Plate 51)

NGC Catalogue, Vol. 3, Can. Sch. by R.H. Hubbard, P. 247

NGC Info. Form rec'd Dec. 20, 1937

PETRUCCI, Paul

A Montreal sculptor who has done among other things religious statues for churches including a statue of Jean de Brébeuf for the cité de Laviolette.

Reference

Le Nouvelliste, Trois-Rivières, P.Q., Nov. 2, 1964 "Une Statue" (photo with caption)

PETRY, Nancy (Mrs. Wargin)
b. 1931

Born in Montreal, P.Q., she studied art at McGill University under John Lyman and Gordon Webber graduating with her B.F.A. in 1948. She then studied in Paris at the Académie de la Grande Chaumière under Henri Goetz and at the Atelier 17 under William Hayter. She travelled extensively in Europe while living and painting in Paris. She held her first solo show at Galerie Voyelles in 1956 and exhibited in the Salon d'Automne (1957) and Salon des Jeunes Peintres (1958). She studied as well at the Slade School in London, England under Stanley Jones and established a studio there returning to both Paris and Montreal periodically. She married in 1958. A painter and print-maker she is highly regarded for her professionalism. She was described by *The Gazette* in 1971 as follows, "Nancy Petry is tiny and extremely feminine and you would never imagine her lugging huge canvases around, but she does, and she loves it. Nancy has been painting for 15 years and has managed to live on the income from her paintings for the past 10. Her canvases sing with color. She stains bright colors into the canvas with a brush so that they merge and blend harmoniously. Her canvases are a reflection of her personality; she is warm, cheerful and alive to life. . . .As a painter one works in the studio alone, but in order to produce prints it is necessary to participate in a group workshop. This contrast of working in a group with other artists and exchanging ideas is very necessary, Nancy feels. It fulfills the need to be with others, especially with persons who share the same interests. Nancy Petry has earned her professional status through hard work. She has had several shows of her own in Paris, London and this city. . . .Full of enthusiasm, she is working at present on a series of large canvases and more prints." Her solo shows include: Galerie Voyelles, Paris (1956); Galerie Agnès Lefort, Mtl. (1959, 1961, 1963); Western

PETRY, Nancy (Mrs. Wargin) (Cont'd)

Canada Art Circuit Travelling Exhibition of NGC (1963); Anthony Tooth Gallery, Lond., Eng. (1966); Commonwealth Inst., Lond., Eng. (1969); Galerie Malborough-Godard, Mtl. (1970); Nancy Poole's Studio, Tor. (1974); Ont. Assoc. of Architects, Tor. (1974) and many important group shows including: Young Contemporaries, Lond., Ont. (1961-2); Art Gallery of Ontario (1960, 1961, 1962); Mtl. Museum of Fine Arts (1960, 1961, 1962); Second Biennial of Abstract Art, Commonwealth Inst. Lond., Eng. (1965); Contemporary Canadians, Albright Knox Museum, Buffalo (1971); Association des Graveurs de Québec (1971, 1972); GRAFF (Atelier Libre, Mtl. — 1972, Paris; 1973, Simon Fraser Univ., Van.) and many others. She was awarded Canada Council Grants in 1969 and 1971 and is represented in the following collections: National Library of Canada, Ottawa; Musée d'Art Contemporain, Mtl.; Geigy, Mtl.; Canadian Industries Ltd., Mtl.; British Mortgage and Trust, Mtl.; Singer, Mtl.; Northern Life Assurance, Tor.; Toronto Dominion Bank, Tor.; Royal Bank of Canada, Tor.; Confederation Art Gallery, Charlottetown, P.E.I.; Scott James of Westminister, Lond., Eng.; Rothchilds Bank, Lond., Eng. and in many private collections in Canada, England, U.S.A., France and Italy. Member: Assoc. des Graveurs de Québec (on Exec.); S.A.P.Q.; C.A.R.; GRAFF (Atelier Libre, Mtl.). Lives in Montreal, P.Q.

References

Le Nouveau Journal, Oct. 21, 1961 "Nancy Petry Wargin: une femme de fond" par J.S.

The Gazette, Mtl., P.Q., Oct. 21, 1961 "At Galerie Agnès Lefort" by Dorothy Pfeiffer

La Presse, Mtl., P.Q., Oct. 21, 1959 "Galerie Agnès Lefort — Nancy Petry Wargin. . .ou l'abstraction reposante" par Jean Sarrazin

La Presse, Mtl., Oct. 23, 1961 "les beaux-arts — Nancy Wargin — Claude Girard" par Claude Jasmin

Leader-Post, Regina, Sask., May 24, 1963 "Two approaches to art show in city exhibit"

Montreal Star, Nov. 20, 1963 "Londoner Feels Vastness of Canada When in Europe" by Laureen Hicks

The Gazette, Nov. 30, 1963 "Nancy Petry Wargin" by D.Y.P.

La Presse, Mtl., P.Q., "Nancy Petry Wargin: modestie et sérénité"

Herald, Prince Albert, Sask., Apr. 20, 1963 "Art, Book Display At Public Library"

Montreal Star, Nov. 23, 1963 "A Quiet Art" by Robert Ayre

Peterborough Examiner, Ont., Oct. 23, 1969 "Canadian Painter Brings Sunny Colors To London"

Montreal Star, Feb. 12, 1970 "Galerie Godard Lefort — Smith sculptures and Petry acrylics" by Robert Ayre

The Gazette, Mtl., June 12, 1971 "Nancy Petry: Artist"

London Evening Free Press, Ont., Mar. 20, 1972 "Art exhibit combines color, message" by Lenore Crawford

L'Art au Québec depuis 1940 par Guy Robert, La Presse, Mtl., P.Q., 1973, P. 31, 319

Journal Pioneer, Summerside, P.E.I., Feb. 17, 1978 "Fire Destroys Exhibition" (some of Petry's paintings destroyed by fire)

PETTA, Angelo di

b. 1948

Born in Colle d'Anchise, Italy, settled in Canada and graduated from the Ontario College of Art majoring in ceramic design (1968-72). In 1973 attended

PETTA, Angelo di (Cont'd)

L'Instituto d'Art la Ceramica under an Italian Government Scholarship. Known for ceramic art, produces functional and non-functional works. Completed a ceramic mural for Marathon Realty, Peterborough (1975) and is represented in a number of private collections. First solo show at Merton Gallery Tor. (1975). Has participated in major exhibitions including: Tribute to O.C.A. at Pollock Gallery, Tor. (1974); Made to Order, 77, Tor.; One Hundred Years Evolution of the Ontario College of Art (1977). Represented in Canadian Crafts Collection and awards include C.C.C. Award (1975); Design Canada Scholarship (1975). Teaches part time at the Ontario College of Art and lives in Scarborough, Ont.

References

100 Years Evolution of the Ontario College of Art (catalogue, OCA/AGO, Tor. 1977, P. 66)

The Index of Ontario Artists, Visual Arts Ontario/Ont. Assoc. of Art Galleries, Tor., 1978, P. 66

NGC Lib. Info. on artist's file

PETTERSON, Andre
b.(c) 1951

A self taught sculptor and jazz musician living in Vancouver who has produced sculpture from found objects which include surrealistic musical instruments made from wood, fabric, brass, paint and recycled household furniture, also work called 'contraptional sculptures' which are built from a board base into various pieces decorated with old axe handles, plumb bobs, tiny chains and other objects. He has also produced oversized versions of real objects. Several solo shows of his work have been exhibited at the Bau-Xi Gallery in Vancouver.

References

Vancouver Sun, B.C., Sept. 5, 1975 "Wooden you know it" (photo and caption)

Ibid, Feb. 12, 1977 "Sculptor's manic work refreshingly original" by Wayne Edmonstone

PETTI, Mario Airomi
b. 1892

Born in Rome, Italy, he studied at the Academy of Art in Rome under Sartario and Gambilloti and in Austria for ten years where he also filled commissions. A painter of landscapes, portraits and still lifes he was best known for his religious paintings for churches throughout Italy, the Island of Malta, Austria and Australia. He painted portraits of the Queen of Italy, Pope Pius XI and XII and did portraits of Italian Cardinals. He came to Canada and settled in Prescott, Ontario, in 1949, with his wife and two children, Paulo and Rosetta. He held his first solo show in 1949 just after his arrival, at the Prescott High School where his oil paintings, charcoal and chalk sketches and water colours were shown. He conducted classes in painting for students in his Cornwall studio. Under the auspices of the Prescott Educational Recreation Commission he taught pupils charcoal sketching and oil painting. He was much impressed with the colours of Canada in the autumn and produced Canadian landscapes in all seasons.

PETTI, Mario Airomi (Cont'd)

References

Catalogue — Art Exhibition of Oil Paintings, Charcoal Sketches and Aquarels by Mario Airomi Petti, Prescott High School, Prescott, Ont., June 23rd-25th

The Ottawa Citizen, Ont., Oct. 14, 1949 "New Life In New Country For Artist Mario Petti" by Wilf Bell

Evening Telegram, Tor., Ont., Aug. 29, 1950 "Internationally Known Artist To Teach Prescott Aspirants"

NGC Info. Form rec'd Sept. 2, 1949

PETTIGREW, Hélène
b.(c) 1943

She started painting about the age of nine and is mostly self taught. A Frelighsburg, Quebec artist she travelled in Mexico and is known for her landscapes and abstracts which have been exhibited at Bedford, Quebec.

References

Le Canada Français, St-Jean, P.Q., June 23, 1966

newspaper clipping, June 27, 1966 "Vernissage de la collection Hélène Pettigrew, à Bedford" par Régent Lajoie

PEZZANI, Gino
b. 1927

Born in Glasgow, Scotland, studied at the Decorative Trades Institute and the Glasgow School of Art and came to Canada in 1957 and settled in Edmonton, Alberta. Became a member of the Alberta Society of Artists in 1963 and the "Focus" Gallery, Edmonton in 1960.

Reference

NGC Info. Form rec'd 1963

PFEIFER, Bodo
b. 1939

Born in Dusseldorf, Germany, he travelled widely in Europe, North Africa and North America over a six year period. Arriving in Vancouver, Canada in 1956 he was later hired as a logger in a lumber camp near Edmonton, Alberta and was a victim of an accident. He was confined indoors during his recovery and out of boredom made a mural on the four walls of his bedroom and suddenly realized how he enjoyed himself at this work. He became interested in painting and after his recovery moved east to Montreal where he attended the École des Beaux-Arts under Mario Merola. He won a German government grant and studied at the Academy of Fine Arts in Hamburg under Francis Bott, René Acht and Hunder Wasser noted colourist. He returned to western Canada and Vancouver where he studied at the Vancouver School of Art under

PFEIFER, Bodo (Cont'd)

Roy Kiyooka, Jack Shadbolt and Donald Jarvis. By 1967 Pfeifer had begun to attract the notice of several critics including Joan Lowndes who wrote, "Bodo Pfeifer's one-man show at the Douglas Gallery could stand up in any of the world's art capitals — Paris, London, New York, L.A. Along with the acclaim given to Arts of the Raven, it is one more proof of the great leap forward accomplished in Centennial Year by Vancouver's visual arts scene. . . .One of the most stimulating aspects of his show is its variety — of format, color and design. The ability to paint effective small canvases denoted an increase in control. . . .Pfeifer is experimenting further, no longer content to manipulate his great swathes of stripes upon fields of clear color, but making more of an over-all composition. Untitled No. 4, for example, eschews op effects altogether and should be read as a screen. Its forms are no longer geometrical but scalloped and graceful." Another reviewer, Eileen Johnson related how knowledgeable critics considered him B.C.'s most exciting colourist. Turning to avant-garde sculpture he erected an environmental piece on the site of the Burnaby Arts Centre complex near Deer Lake in 1970. The sculpture, consisting of nine concrete blocks set into the ground at an angle, was painted dandelion yellow with the top of each block covered with stainless steel. The grass around the blocks combined with the leaves from the trees, the blocks themselves, all bathed in sunlight cause an interaction of brilliant reflections. Pfeifer was awarded Canada Council Grants in 1966, 1967, 1968 for his work and received honourable mention in "Young B.C. Painters" show (1966) and was awarded a prize at the Canadian Group of Painters Exhibition at the Mtl. Mus. F.A. (1967) and at the Montreal Museum of Fine Arts show (1968). His solo shows include those at: Douglas Gallery, Van. B.C. (1967, 1968, 1969); Mazelow Gallery, Tor. (1968) and a two-man show at the Vancouver Art Gallery (1967). Did a mural for the Vancouver International Airport (1968). He is represented in the following collections: Vancouver Art Gallery; University of Victoria; Willistead Art Gallery, Windsor, Ont.; Agnes Etherington Art Gallery, Kingston, Ont.; National Gallery of Canada, Ottawa, Ont.; Canada Council, Ottawa; Montreal Museum of Fine Arts. He lives in Vancouver, B.C.

References

Vancouver Province, B.C. Sept. 22, 1967 "The Arrival of Bodo Pfeifer" by Joan Lowndes
Vancouver Sun, B.C. Sept. 20, 1967 "Pfeifer Does Well In Hard Edge Idiom" by Ann Rosenberg
Victoria Times, B.C. April 22, 1967 "Voice From The Gallery — This Way, That Way At 'Directions 67'" Tony Emery
Artscanada, November, 1967 "Reviews — Bodo Pfeifer, — The Douglas Gallery" reviewed by Richard Simmins
Vancouver Life, B.C., September, 1967 "Bodo The Bold" by Eileen Johnson
The Province, Van., B.C., June 13, 1968 "About Art. . ." by Ann Rosenberg
Globe & Mail, Tor., Ont., Oct. 28, 1968 "Other Galleries"
Vancouver Sun, B.C., Jan. 18, 1969 "Artists' Six New Works Show Air of Distinction"
Ibid, Mar. 12, 1969 "City Artist's Work on Display" by Charlotte Townsend
Vancouver Province, B.C., Mar. 14, 1969 "The new diagonal phase of Bodo Pfeifer"
Vancouver Sun, B.C., May 30, 1970 "'Bennett on a horse' taunt follows sculpture rejection" by Moira Farrow
Ibid, June 24, 1970 "Burnaby embraces rejected artist" by Moira Farrow
Star Weekly, Tor., Ont., Aug. 1, 1970 "What is that girl with the bronze flippers doing in Stanley Park?" by Moira Farrow

PFEIFER, Bodo (Cont'd)

New Westminster Columbian, B.C., Aug. 21, 1970 "Burnaby's Century Gardens" by Pat Cooper
Vancouver Sun, B.C., Aug. 6, 1970 "'It's an environmental piece'" by Leslie Plommer
Canadian Art Today, Ed. by Wm. Townsend, Studio Internat., Lond., Eng., 1970, P. 63, 112
NGC Info. Forms 1965, 1966, 1968

PFEIFFER, Gordon Edward
b. 1899

Born in Quebec City, the son of Adolphus Edward and Lillian (Wright) Pfeiffer, and brother of Harold and Walter (both artists). His mother was an accomplished painter in Ireland and in Cleveland, Ohio. Gordon began painting at the age of twelve under A. Bonham, a Quebec art teacher. He was educated at Quebec High School, Stanstead College, Rochester and Harvard Universities. In painting he was, however self-taught, although he was coached by friends including Horatio Walker (Ile d'Orléans), William Glackens (New York), André Biéler (Kingston), Robert Pilot (Montreal), René Richard (Baie St. Paul, P.Q.), Lieulf Claussen (Denmark), Dewey Albinson (Minneapolis) and others. He began painting seriously in 1925 while also working for his father. Gordon started work in the family business in 1923, then his father sent him to study for management (business administration, chemistry and history at Rochester and Harvard Universities). He became general manager of the firm in 1928 but following his father's death he sold the business. He remained associated with business through the years but spent more time painting. He lived in Paris where he visited museums and artists' ateliers and also visited other countries in Europe. Returning to Canada he painted rural Quebec in all its seasons which combined his interest in the outdoors and he painted in other regions of Canada and the United States. Viewing his 1966 show at the Arts Club of Montreal a *Gazette* writer noted, "Pfeiffer is a painter with an insatiable appetite for the Canadian landscape. In his present collection the interest centres on the most eastern Appalachians, the Long Range Mountains of Newfoundland. A romantic at heart, Pfeiffer relishes the dramatic settings of massive ridges against crystal-clear skies from which all moisture seems swept up by juicy clouds, sailing on brisk Atlantic breezes. Two large canvases,. . .of Long Range Mountain scenes, show some of Pfeiffer's finest brushwork. Above all, the painter appears to love his skies and his clouds." Some of his favourite painting spots included Old Quebec, the Lower St. Lawrence, Gaspé Peninsula, the Maritimes, and Newfoundland. He painted in England, Ireland and other countries. He married Dorothy Young in 1925 and they had three sons and one daughter. To date Pfeiffer has held over thirty-three solo shows, as follows (dates available are shown): Chateau Frontenac, Que. City (1931, 1932, 1936, 1938, 1948); Palais Montcalm, Que. City (1941 & 3 others); Galerie J.A. Morency, Que. City (1958 & 1 other); Galerie d'Art Lafayette-Saint-Jean, Que. City (1976); Galerie Kerhulu, Que. City; Stanstead College, Que. City; Galerie Le Seur, Que. City; W. Scott & Sons, Mtl. (1932); T. Eaton Co., Mtl. (1934, 1936, 1937); Canadian Hall of Fine Art, Mtl. (1944); The Arts Club of Montreal (1948, 1960, 1966, 1967); Montreal Museum of Fine Arts (1963 & 1 other); Galerie Colbert, Mtl. (1976); Silverman Gallery, Mtl.; Galerie Irla Kert, Mtl.; Recreation Centre of Aluminum Co. of

PFEIFFER, Gordon Edward (Cont'd)

Can., Arvida (1947); Artlenders, Westmount (1970); Gallery Ingenu, Tor. (1977); Alma College, St. Thomas, Ont.; The Art Centre, Cowansville, Que. (2 shows); Zwicker's Gallery, Halifax, N.S.; University of Ottawa, Ont. (1967); Robertson Galleries, Ott.; Fischer-Richer Gallery, Grand'mere, Que. (1968); The Lindsley Gallery, Boca Raton, Florida; Rockefeller Center, New York City. He has exhibited in many group shows including those of the R.C.A., O.S.A., N.G.C., Mtl. Spring shows and many others. He is represented in the following public and corporate collections: Cie d'Assurance Laurentien, Quebec City; J.B. Renaud Co., Que. City; Cercle Universitaire, Laval Univ., Que. City; Stanstead College, Que. City; Laurentide Acceptance Corp., Town of Mount Royal; Industrial Acceptance Corp., Town of Mount Royal; Mount Stephen Club, Mtl.; Thistle Curling Club, Mtl.; Mtl. Amateur Athletic Assoc.; The Arts Club of Montreal; McCord Museum, Mtl.; Redpath Library, McGill Univ., Mtl.; Divinity Hall, McGill Univ., Mtl.; Quebec Provincial Museum, Que. City; London Library & Art Assoc., Lond., Ont.; Alma College, St. Thomas, Ont.; Pickering College, Newmarket, Ont.; Dept. External Affairs, Ottawa; Southern Canada Power Company and in many private collections. Lives in Montreal and Rosemere, Quebec.

References

Le Soleil, Que. City, Dec. 7, 1931 "Une Exposition des oeuvres de M. G.-E. Pfeiffer"

Chronicle-Telegraph, Que. City, Dec. 7, 1931 "Painting Exhibition by Mr. G. Pfeiffer"

The Gazette, Mtl., Dec. 8, 1931 "Gordon Pfeiffer Shows Paintings"

Ibid, Sept. 27, 1932 "Autumn Art Shows Make Appearance"

Ibid, Dec. 7, 1932 "Art Exhibition Held in Quebec"

Le Soleil, Que. City, Dec. 4, 1933 (reproductions and caption)

The Gazette, Mtl., P.Q., Nov. 15, 1934 "Gordon E. Pfeiffer Shows Paintings"

Montreal Star, Nov. 15, 1934 "Pictures and Sketches By Gordon E. Pfeiffer"

La Presse, Mtl., P.Q., Nov. 21, 1934 "L'harmonie des neiges lourdes"

The Gazette, Mtl., P.Q., Feb. 6, 1936 "Gordon Pfeiffer Exhibiting Oils"

La Presse, Mtl., P.Q., Feb. 8, 1936 "Gordon E. Pfeiffer" (article & Photos)

Chronicle-Telegraph, Que. City, Nov. 14, 1938 "Stage Good Art Exhibition At Chateau Frontenac Here"

Le Soleil, Que. City, Nov. 15, 1938 "Natures Mortes A L'Exposition De Gordon Pfeiffer"

The Gazette, Mtl., Nov. 19, 1938 "Gordon E. Pfeiffer Showing Pictures"

Ibid, Apr. 22, 1939 "Gordon E. Pfeiffer Is Energetic Artist" (photo)

Ibid, Nov. 11, 1944 "Collection of Oils by Gordon Pfeiffer"

The Standard, Shawinigan Falls, P.Q., Oct. 28, 1947 "Gordon Pfeiffer Art Exhibition Popular"

Montreal Star, Jan. 12, 1948 "Gordon Pfeiffer Paints Quebec"

The Gazette, Mtl., P.Q., Jan. 12, 1948 "Arts Club Shows Work by Gordon E. Pfeiffer"

Chronicle-Telegraph, Que. City, Nov. 12, 1948 "Gordon Pfeiffer To Hold Showing Of Paintings At Chateau Frontenac"

Ibid, Nov. 19, 1948 "Traces of Kreighoff Influence Observed As Pfeiffer Art Exhibition Begins Here"

Le Soleil, Que. City, Apr. 14, 1958 "Pfeiffer expose une sélection de ses oeuvres"

The Gazette, Mtl., P.Q., May 21, 1960 "Gordon Pfeiffer" by René Chicoine

The Rosemere Journal, P.Q., Dec. 22, 1960 "Gordon Pfeiffer to Conduct Art Course"

Ibid, Nov. 21, 1963 "Gordon Pfeiffer's Art On Exhibit"

L'Evénement, Que. City, Nov. 26, 1963 "Exposition Pfeiffer-Braitstein au Musée des Beaux-Arts de Montréal"

The Gazette, Mtl., Nov. 30, 1963 "Gordon E. Pfeiffer" by Bill Bantey

Le Petit Journal, Mtl., Dec. 1, 1963 (photo and article)

PFEIFFER, Gordon Edward (Cont'd)

The Gazette, Mtl., Nov. 19, 1966 "Landscapes Unlimited: Pfeiffer at Arts"
Ottawa Journal, Ont., Nov. 18, 1967 (note on Harold & Gordon Pfeiffer)
L'Echo du St. Maurice, Shawinigan, P.Q., Oct. 2, 1968 "Le peintre Gordon Pfeiffer à la Galerie Margot Fisher-Richer"
Document from artist, 1970
NGC Info. Forms, 1943, 1931, 1928
Biographical Sketch (undated)
Canadian Art At Auction 1968-1975, Ed. Geoffrey Joyner, Sotheby & Co., Tor., 1975, P. 156
Kingdom of the Saguenay by C. Marius Barbeau, MacMillan, Tor., 1936
Who's Who in Canada, 1940-41, Ed. B.M. Greene, Internat. Press Ltd., Tor., P. 1153

PFEIFFER, Harold Samson
b. 1908

Born in Quebec City, the son of Adolphus Edward Pfeiffer and Lillian Braithwaite Wright (painter of horses and dogs and native of Ballyshannon, Ireland). His parents and older brothers, Gordon and Walter (Dr. W. Pfeiffer) all painted. Being the youngest of the family he was a little overwhelmed by all the painting talent in the household. During his summer holidays he turned to a different medium, clay. A little later he became interested in Eskimos as his mother was a follower of the activities of the Grenfell mission and he accompanied her to a lecture by Sir Wilfred Grenfell. His interest in Eskimos was to return in later years resulting in his remarkable series of portraits which have become valuable as a record for scholars today. At a young age he decided to study at the École des Beaux-Arts in Quebec where he attended night classes in modelling under Professor Jan Bailleul and later under Sylvia D'Aoust with intervals of study under Orson Wheeler of Montreal. While at the Beaux-Arts (1925-27) he met Marius Barbeau of the National Museums. It was Barbeau who persuaded him to research arts and crafts in remote parts of Quebec. During those early years he worked for various employers to pay for his studies. He next entered the Central Technical School in Toronto where he took pottery under Mrs. Peter Haworth. He received further studies at the New York School of Interior Decoration for design and handicrafts and making theatrical and decorative masks. In 1930 he spent six months in London, England, where he studied the antique sculptures in the British Museum, Victoria and Albert Museums, The Tate Galleries and he also lived a year in Paris where he visited and studied the treasures of the Louvre and the work of artists in galleries and workshops. He saw the original sculptures of Eric Gill, Jacob Epstein, Auguste Rodin and other famous sculptors. Returning to Canada he did experimental work with native clays for the Quebec Provincial Government. For twelve years he practiced interior decorating in Montreal and Toronto while he did sculptural portraits of prominent Canadians with excellent likenesses to his sitters. By 1939 he had done portraits of Capt. J.E. Bernier (Can. Arctic explorer); Thomas M. Forsythe (U.S. Consul, Lima, Peru); Col. Walter J. Ray; Lois Reynolds Kerr (Canadian playwright); Professor Luc Lacoursière; C. Anthony Law (Canadian painter); Miss Dalila Barbeau (daughter of Dr. Marius Barbeau), Arthur Leblanc (violinist); Ross Pratt (pianist) and others. It became evident that Pfeiffer had developed an unusual ability to make the eyes of his subjects very realistic. He himself feels much of the personality of

PFEIFFER, Harold Samson (Cont'd)

people is revealed through their eyes. He became highly esteemed as a portrait sculptor and in later years was given the singular honour of having his bronzes accepted and shown at the Royal Academy and the National Portrait Society in London, England. During World War II he became a war worker for General Engineering in the X-ray department of the Toronto plant. Despite the long hours at his job he was able to sculpt several subjects including the portrait of Mrs. Peggy MacKay, an employee of General Engineering who had been touched by the war with a son missing at sea, a sister killed in the blitz on London, three uncles and ten cousins lost on a trawler sunk three weeks after the outbreak of war, and a husband overseas in the army three years. Her portrait was entitled "War Worker". While in Toronto he lived and worked at his sculpture in "The Studio Building" on Severn Street. When first in the city Pfeiffer met the two well-known sculptors Frances Loring and Florence Wyle who encouraged him to do more sculpting. He became friendly with the great Swedish sculptor, Carl Milles, and Dr. Richmond Barthé of New York, who both gave him much encouragement. Because of his talent in many arts and crafts, Selective Service seconded him as a Crafts Specialist to organize Hobby Shops and teach at Army and Air Force camps. While a Flight Lieutenant at the R.C.A.F. Station in Moncton, in free time he organized many concerts, one of which was by the contralto, Portia White, whose portrait sculpture he did while she was in Moncton. After the war, he joined the staff of MacDonald College (McGill Univ.), 1945-49, where he taught Arts and Crafts and Interior Decoration. While there, he became acquainted with the world renowned violist, William Primrose, who was giving master classes in the viola and he did a portrait of Mr. Primrose at that time. In 1954 he was urged to join the Department of Indian and Northern Affairs by his artist friend James Houston and taught handicrafts in the occupational therapy section at Hôpital du Parc Savard, Quebec City, and later at Camsell Hospital, Edmonton, Alberta, where he had both Indian and Eskimo patients. He made three trips to the High Arctic as an assistant to a team of doctors making X-ray surveys and providing clinics for the Eskimos. In 1955 he did rehabilitation work with Eskimos for Northern Affairs Educational Department at Port Harrison and Povungituk and spent one year at Frobisher Bay, Baffin Island. For the first time he began to sculpt Eskimos in the Eastern Arctic. He was drawn to the pure-blooded Eskimos whose features were more defined, weather beaten, character revealing, and he realized their type would soon vanish forever. Students of anthropology and history will have his true-life portraits of native Canadians to study when all other tangible traces of these people are gone. He made many friends among them, some of whom he would visit again to sculpt for the Riveredge Foundation of Calgary and for the Government of the Northwest Territories. He joined the staff of the National Museum as chief cataloguer for the ethnology department then later became Custodian of the Canadiana Collection. In the course of his duties with the National Museum, with his knowledge of Antiques, the Director sent him on many trips through Newfoundland, the Maritimes and Quebec searching out and purchasing early Canadiana. Later, he was asked to prepare sketches of 12 rooms, covering historic periods from 1750-1900, using existing furniture, lighting fixtures, china, kitchen appliances, fire-place, wrought iron etc., all authentic to each period in history. He was awarded a grant from the Riveredge Foundation in 1968 to travel into the central and western Canadian Arctic to record some of the faces of the Eskimos and was given three months leave from the Museum to complete the commission. He worked up to sixteen hours a day to finish eleven heads and busts of Eskimos. During his treks he had to contend with climate and logistical problems and designed and made strong but light armatures, on which he built his portraits. As he was the first sculptor to have organized such a trip to the Arctic he had no precedent to guide him and had to improvise and invent ways to complete his task. He brought the necessary chemicals to manufacture styrofoam molds so that he would have light forms upon which to place his clay, saving the weight of the usual solid forms that had to be transported by air. He also used styrofoam molds into which he placed his finished work which eliminated heavy crates and packing materials. Details of his trip were published in *North* magazine issue of March-April, 1970. Over the years he has completed 44 bronzes of native peoples for the Glenbow-Alberta Institute in Calgary also 47 bronzes for the Government of the N.W.T. for the new Prince of Wales Heritage Centre in Yellowknife, N.W.T. By 1980 he had completed over 200 bronze busts including life-size portraits of: General George Vanier (former Governor General of Canada); Dr. Marius Barbeau (ethnologist, folklorist); Col. Patrick Baird (Arctic explorer); Yousuf Karsh (renowned Canadian photographer); Chief Dan George (noted Indian film star); Justice Thomas Berger (author, Berger Report on proposed Mackenzie Valley pipeline); Dr. L.Z. Rousseau (former deputy minister of forestry, Canada); Mrs. James Houston; Dr. Andrew Stewart (Chairman, Bd. of Broadcast Governors); H.W. Herridge (parliamentarian); Miss Portia White (Maritime contralto); Dr. Harold Geggie (Medical Doctor and humanitarian, founder of the Wakefield Hospital, P.Q.); Dr. Lotta Hitchmanova (Head, Unitarian Service Committee and humanitarian); Leo Ciceri (Shakespearian actor of Stratford National Theatre); Albert Faille (famous Nahanni River Hermit); Ross Pratt (pianist); Dr. Thomas O'Hagen (founder of Jasper, Alta. hospital); "Chief Jack Rabbit" H. Smith-Johanssen; Commissioner L.H. Nicholson (former head, R.C.M.P.); Normie Kwong (Athlete of the year, 1955); Mrs. Margaret "Ma" Murray (Editor and Publisher) and the following Commissioners of the Northwest Territories: Major-General Young; Gordon Robertson; Ben Siverts; Stuart Hodgson and John Parker; former Lieutenant Governor of Alberta the Hon. Ralph Steinhauer; Max Ward (Pres. Wardair); Hon. Justice Angelo Branca and many others. His sculpture is in many permanent collections including: Montreal Museum of Fine Arts; Glenbow-Alberta Inst., Calgary, Alta.; The J.B. Speed Museum, Louisville, Kentucky; Alberta House, London, England; Prince of Wales Heritage Centre, Yellowknife, N.W.T.; Eskimo Museum, Churchill, Manitoba and the R. Angus Co., Edmonton, Alta. He has sculpted over 125 portrait heads of Indians and Inuit as well as 7 Greenlandic Eskimos. This is a heritage of extraordinary importance. His solo shows include: Mtl. Mus. of Fine Arts (1953); Robertson Galleries, Ott., Ont. (1966); Univ. Ottawa, Ont. (1967); Calgary Galleries, Calg., Alta. (1972, 1978); Royal Ontario Museum, Tor., Ont. (1972); Brock Univ. Gallery, St. Catharines, Ont. (1973); Centennial Art Gallery, Halifax, N.S. (1975); Sherbrooke Village, N.S. (1975); Municipal Gallery, Ste. Foy, P.Q. (1976); First Canadian Place, Tor. (most major exhibition of native people, 1978) entitled "The Survivors"; Wells Gallery, Ott. (1979). He has exhibited with his brothers Gordon and Dr. Walter Pfeiffer several times as well. He has done many portrait sculptures in England, Greenland, Denmark, Switzerland, the U.S.A., Bermuda and Barbados. Lives in Ottawa.

PFEIFFER, Harold Samson (Cont'd)

References

Chronicle Telegraph, Que. City, Nov. 14, 1938 "Harold Pfeiffer"

The Gazette, Mtl., P.Q., Apr. 8, 1939 (photo of bust of C. Anthony Law by artist)

Saturday Night, Tor., Ont., Dec. 16, 1939 "A Quebec Sculptor"

GECO Fusilier, Scarboro, Ont., July 3, 1943 "War Worker" (article & 2 photos)

Toronto Telegram, Ont., Sept. 25, 1943 "Pictures, Pencils and Peas Displayed at Hobby show" (photo of artist with work & article about show)

Toronto Star, Ont., July 18, 1943 "Women's War Work — Canadian Woman Worker Symbolized in Sculpture" — Mrs. Peggy McKay Husband Overseas, Son Missing, Is Subject"

Transcript, Moncton, N.B., Oct. 5, 1945 "Canadian Sculptor Produces Fine Head of Noted Contralto" by W. Fraser Robb

The Gazette, Mtl. (Spring, 1951) photo and caption on portrait of Col. Patrick Baird

Chronicle Telegraph, Que. City, Dec. 2, 1953 "Quebec Sculptor"

Ibid, July 1, 1955 "Eskimos return home as 'C.D. Howe' leaves for North" (article and photo)

Edmonton Journal, Alta., Aug. 15, 1956 "Non Athlete stops Normie Kwong" (article and photo)

Ottawa Citizen, Ont., May 30, 1959 "Two Heads Are Better Than One" (photo of Dr. Marius Barbeau posing for artist)

The Gazette, Mtl., P.Q., Sept. 16, 1961 "The Brothers Pfeiffer"

Ottawa Citizen, Ont., Mar. 19, 1966 "This head-hunter brings trophies home in clay" by Carl Weiselberger (photos & article)

Ottawa Journal, Ont., Mar. 23, 1966 "Portrait Sculptor's Exhibition a Must" by W.Q. Ketchum

Ottawa Citizen, Ont., Nov. 18, 1967 "Brothers' Show" (two-man show of Gordon & Harold)

The Fulcrum, Ottawa Univ., Ont., Nov. 22, 1967 (review and photo)

Ottawa Journal, Ont., Nov. 23, 1967 "Bust of Vanier Exhibit Feature" by Jenny Bergen

Ibid, Nov. 23, 1967 "Brothers' works a Fine Art Display" by W.Q.K.

Ibid, Jan. 6, 1968 "Faces of Ottawa — Harold Pfeiffer" by W.Q.K.

Le Droit, Ottawa, Ont., Mar. 1, 1969 "Pour le sculpteur Harold Pfeiffer, une oeuvre doit représenter le réalité" par Rolland-E. Bouchard/photos par Champlain Marcil

Victoria Daily Times, B.C., Aug. 23, 1968 "Arctic Isolation Productive for Sculptor, Alan White" (article and photo)

Montreal Star, P.Q., Jan. 31, 1970 "Art — The White man who makes Eskimo heads with his hands" by Robert Ayre

North, Ottawa, Ont., Mar.-Apr., 1970 "Northern Heads Committed to Bronze" by Harold Pfeiffer

Peterborough Examiner, Ont., Nov. 6, 1970 "Sculptures Ciceri Bust"

Ottawa Journal, Ont., Apr. 3, 1971 "Ottawa Artist (25) — Remarkably Life-Like Sculptures" by Valerie Knowles

The Courier-Journal & Times, Louisville, Ky., Sept. 12, 1971 "Speaking of People — Sculptor takes role of historian" by Joan Kay

The Voice-Jeffersonian, Louisville, Ky., U.S.A., Dec. 2, 1971 "Artist Sculptor works in East End" (article & photo) by Charlotte Price

Toronto Daily Star, Ont., Nov. 26, 1971 "He portrays the Eskimos in Sculpture" by Helen Worthington

Globe & Mail, Tor., Ont., Dec. 3, 1971 "Art — Pursuing Arctic faces" by Kay Kritzwiser

St. Catharines Standard, Ont., Jan. 13, 1972 "Brock Exhibit of Sculptures Worth a Trip Up The Hill" by Joan Phillips

The Press, Brock Univ., Jan. 13, 1972 (article and seven photos)

Kainai News, Cardston, Alta., May 15, 1972 (double page story and 8 photos)

Edmonton Journal, Alta., July 14, 1972 "Bronze Eskimo Busts" (two photos and caption)

Mount Royal College Journal, Calgary, Alta., Nov. 17, 1972 (story, photos)

Cold Inferno, Yellowknife, N.W.T., Aug. 24, 1972 (article by T. Mailer)

The Reflector, Calgary, Alta., Nov. 29, 1972 "Sculpture, how it's done" by Steve Ramsey (article and photos)

PFEIFFER, Harold Samson (Cont'd)

Lethbridge Herald, Alta., Dec. 6, 1972 "Sculptor Displays His Work at U of L" (article and photo)

Canadian Golden West, Calg. Alta., Winter 1972-1973 "Harold Pfeiffer's Portraits in Bronze" by R. Gorman

Peterborough Examiner, Ont., (Calgary, CP), Jan. 6, 1973 "Preservation of Culture Kept By Ottawa Sculpture (Sculptor)"

Edmonton Journal, Alta., May 4, 1973 "Forms in ceramics, life in sculpture" by Jim Simpson

Bridge & River-Lillooet News, Lillooet, B.C., June 13, 1974 (photo of portrait of "Ma" Murray sculpted by Pfeiffer)

Ottawa Journal, Ont., Nov. 23, 1974 "Travel-Resorts — 'I loved every inch of it'" (artist's trip to Greenland) by C. Holland

Hamilton Spectator, Ont., Dec. 28, 1974 "Greenland great but coffee — $1?"

Vancouver Province, B.C., Jan. 28, 1975 "Eskimos old walnut faces fascinate Ottawa sculptor" by James Nelson

Ottawa Citizen, Ont., Feb. 22, 1975 "Eskimo faces softer now" by James Nelson

Canadian Golden West, Calg., Alta., Spring, 1975 "Faces of our Heritage" by Ruth Gorman (four photos)

Halifax Mail Star, N.S., May 3, 1975 (photo of opening night at Centennial Art Gallery Halifax)

Catalogue — exhibit at Centennial Art Gallery, Hal., N.S., May 1 to May 26, 1975

Sermitsiak, Godthaab, Greenland, June 13, 1975 (article & photo)

Northern News Report, Yellowknife, N.W.T., Vol. 5/19, 1976, "Northerners captured in bronze" by Don Wood

Ottawa Journal, Ont., May 21, 1977 "Around Town — Local sculptor will honor Berger in bronze" by Alixe Carter

Vancouver Sun, B.C., June 21, 1977 (photo of bust of Hon. Mr. Justice Thomas Berger and the artist)

News of the North Yellowknife, N.W.T., July 13, 1977 "Figures in Bronze" (caption & photo of Deput. Commissioner John Parker's portrait by artist)

The Interpreter, Yellowknife, N.W.T., August, 1977 "Sculpture project getting ahead"

The Sunday Sun, July 2, 1978 "The Art Scene" by Barney McKinley

The Royal Gazette, Bermuda, Dec. 5, 1978 "Carving a future for a forgotten people"

The Low down to Hull and back News, P.Q., June 23, 1978 (photo of memorial bust of Dr. H.J. G. Geggie, Wakefield Memorial Hospital, P.Q.)

Preview Magazine, Ottawa, Ont., July 1978 "The bronzes of Harold Pfeiffer" by Julie Maloney

The Low down to Hull and back News, July 27, 1978 "Mine is forever" (article and photo)

The Yukon News, Whitehorse, Yukon, Aug. 1978 "Sculptor looking for Yukon Indian works" (article & photo)

Toronto Star, Ont., Feb. 4, 1979 "Ottawa sculptor chipping away at art policies — Why is the art establishment ignoring Harold Pfeiffer?" by Sol Littman

Ottawa Citizen, Ont., Feb. 9, 1979 (article and photo) by K. Walker

Globe & Mail, Tor., Ont., Feb. 15, 1979 "Not too cold for Art" by Pauline King

Ottawa Review, Ont., Feb. 15, 1979 "Harold Pfeiffer at Wells Gallery" (article and photo)

The Index of Ontario Artists, Ed. Hennie Wolff, Vis. Arts Ont., 1978, P. 218

Who's Who In Canada, 1940-41, Ed. B.M. Greene, Internat. Press Ltd., Tor., Ont., P. 1151-2

NGC Info. Forms (undated; dated June 1, 1944)

Biographical notes on Harold Pfeiffer by Walford Reeves

Document from artist

Visit with artist

PFEIFFER, Dr. Walter M.
b. 1896

Born in Quebec City, the son of Adolphus Edward Pfeiffer and Lillian Braithwaite Wright Pfeiffer (of Ballyshannon, Ireland), he studied medicine and became a lung specialist. In his leisure time and especially around the age of thirty he did landscape painting during his motor trips to Baie St. Paul, Les Eboulements, Murray Bay and the Ile d'Orléans with André Biéler who showed him the rudiments of composition. His earlier influence was from his mother who painted horses and dogs and was known for her work on a professional level. While in England during the war he took the opportunity of studying traditional oil painting at the Farnham School of Art in Surrey (1941-43) under Professor McCannel and lessons in traditional water colour painting from L.M. Carter of the St. John School, London (1943-44). Later he studied contemporary painting at the Stanley Park Summer School of Art, Vancouver (1950) under Peter Aspel and Lionel Thomas. Chiefly a landscape painter who does the occasional portrait, he renders his realistic work in oils, water colours, pastel and oil pastels. His paintings have been hung in the National Gallery, London and Physicians' exhibitions in Edinburgh and elsewhere. He has won several prizes for traditional landscapes at the Physicians' Art Salon exhibitions in major cities in Canada. He has also exhibited with his artist brothers Harold and Gordon. Now retired from medicine he has devoted more of his time to painting.

References
    Document from artist
    Harold Pfeiffer by Walford Reeves

PFLIGER, Terry Lee
b. 1947

Born in St. Joseph, Michigan, he studied at the Lake Michigan College, Benton Harbor, Michigan (Assoc. of Arts, 1967); Western Michigan University, Kalamazoo, Michigan (B.Sc., 1969, M.A., 1970); studied under Dwayne Lowder (sculptor & painter). He is known for his dioramas (small box assemblages) and paintings. His avant-garde art won him a purchase award at the Ontario Society of Artists 100th Annual open exhibition in Toronto in 1972. A teacher in art he has been instructor at Loyalist Collegiate and Vocational Institute, Kingston, Ont. (1970-73); painting instructor for the Continuing Education Department, St. Lawrence College, Kingston, Ont. (1971-73); Co-ordinator and Painting Master, Visual/Creative Arts Department, St. Lawrence College, Kingston, Ont. (1973-   ). He held a solo show at Maud Preston Palenske Memorial Library, St. Joseph, Mich., U.S.A. (1969); group shows at the following: Kalamazoo Inst. of the Arts, Kalamazoo, Mich. (Spring Show, 1969) (Kalamazoo Artists, 1970) (two-man, 1971); Ball State Univ. Drawing Exhibition, Muncie, Indiana (1969); Art Park, Inc., Athens, Ohio (1969-70); Spring Show, South Bend Inst. of the Arts, South Bend, Indiana (1970); Agnes Etherington Art Centre, Kingston, Ont. (Spring Show, 1971) (Kingston Artists, 1975); (Small Objects Exhibition, Kingston, 1976); O.S.A. 100th Exhibition, Tor. (1972); St. Lawrence College Art Gallery, Kingston, Ont. (two-man show, 1973) (Faculty Exhibition, 1974); Rubber

PFLIGER, Terry Lee (Cont'd)

show, Plug-In Gallery, Winnipeg, Man. (1974); Monument to Miniature, Arts pace, Peterborough, Ont. (1975); On View, 76, T.D. Centre, Tor. (1976). He is represented in the collections of Western Michigan Univ., Kalamazoo, Mich.; I.B.M. Corp., Tor., Ont.; Agnes Etherington Art Centre, Kingston, Ont. and in private collections in Ontario, Manitoba, Michigan, Indiana and Illinois. He has written approximately thirty articles as art critic for the Western Michigan University publication *The Western Herald* from 1968 to 1970. Member of C.A.R.

References

NGC artist's file

Whig Standard, Kingston, Ont., May 9, 1972 "Kingston area artist wins award in Toronto"

Art Magazine, October, 1975 "Monument to Miniature" by Illi-Maria Tamplin

Canadian Artists in Exhibition, Roundstone Council for the Arts, Toronto, Ont., P. 129

The Index of Ontario Artists, Ed. H. Wolff, Visual Arts Ontario, Tor., 1978, P. 218

PFLUG, Christiane Sybille

b. 1936

Born in Berlin, Germany, by the time she was three, World War II was raging and she was left in the care of an elderly woman at Kitzbuyel, Austria, when her widowed mother enlisted as an army nurse. Her foster parent provided her with physical comforts and introduced her to books and paintings but Christiane did not have the same emotional security of a child with a natural parent and was alone in the world of adults. In her loneliness she visited local churches where she studied carved statues and stained glass windows and copied illustrations from prayer books and the Bible, spending hours on end drawing. Not long after the war at the age of twelve she was reunited with her mother in Frankfurt. She continued her interest in art and made sketches from their apartment window of the park which surrounded their dwelling. She attended school in Frankfurt until she was fifteen then went to live with her grandmother in Berlin. At seventeen she moved to Paris to study fashion design. She disliked the design course but loved the city. For the first time in her life she had a feeling of joy. She left designing and began to paint with the encouragement of three people, a medical student and artist, Michael Pflug whom she met on a train, Madame Marie Helene Vieira da Silva and Arpad Scenes both of whom had taught Michael. From 1954 to 1956 she painted many scenes in tempera, gouache and oils of the city especially of the Seine, also still lifes, buildings and landscapes of Normandy. She married Michael in Munich during the summer of 1956 then the couple departed for Tunisia where Michael began his internship. They rented a studio-apartment in a 600-year-old house in the centre of the Casbah, Tunis. Christiane painted a series of still lifes and interiors mostly in temperas described by Mary Allodi in *Artscanada* as ". . .among the most beautiful she ever produced." In Tunisia their two children, Esther and Ursula were born. Christiane and Michael held a joint showing of their work at the Alliance Française, Tunis in 1958. With the political violence growing in North Africa, Michael sent Christiane and the two children to Canada in the spring of 1959 and for a year she had to manage alone. Christiane's mother had remarried and gone to Canada too. Then

Michael arrived in 1960 and continued serving his internship and, in his free hours did some painting. Both Christiane and Michael underwent a difficult time trying to adjust to the new values of North America. Their apartment overlooked Yonge Street towards an abandoned railway yard which became her subject for a series of small canvases using a muted range of colours described by Mary Allodi as ". . .striking for their atmospheric quality which conveys an undefinable moodiness; the changing theme is that of the seasons and time of day. 'Railway Yard In Rain' is quite different from 'Early April Morning' or again from 'Railway Yard in Winter' and 'March Landscape,' but the changes are as subtle as the color of the air." Then in 1962 the family moved to Woodlawn Avenue in Toronto considered to be where she did her better-known paintings. It was a hard period for the Pflugs, four of them living on an intern's salary. But Christiane organized her life around her painting, rising at dawn and working until eight then preparing the children for school, then returning to her easel. When she painted night scenes she shifted her painting hours and slept during school time. She painted more detailed canvases at their Woodlawn Avenue home with its tree-filled garden and houses beyond. Her paintings became richer with the combination of interior and landscape in the same view looking out from the kitchen door past the balcony to the foliage of the backyard. She worked slowly on her paintings; for instance "Kitchen Door and Esther" took her seven months and "Kitchen Door with Ursula" nine months both considered among her masterpieces. Her series of still lifes were described by Gail Dexter in the *Toronto Daily Star* as follows, "When Christiane was not using her daughters Esther and Ursula as models, she used their dolls, because she says, 'They are so quiet, they just stand there.' The dolls — one black and one white, always rendered with the detail of a Flemish portrait — focus the emotional strain in these early paintings. They epitomize the silent, unfeeling world on which that kitchen door opens. No matter how beautiful the foliage, no matter with what exuberance it is painted, the little figures cannot sense it: they stare mechanically at the viewer or into the distance. Witnessing this scene from a child's perspective (remember the artist painted all this from a low stool) reinforces the contradiction between the sensuality of nature and the peculiar distortions of space and time within the paintings. Christiane insists that she thinks in neither symbolic nor formal terms. She just looks out the window and *wants* to paint what she sees. For her, realism is simply 'the tool I use to make my vision visible.' It is significant that she identifies her work with that of American pop artist James Rosenquist, who incorporates a variety of every-day images into vast paintings that have the 'realistic' look of billboard art. Christiane went to Ottawa last year to see the Rosenquist retrospective at the National Gallery and she was particularly impressed by his handling of detail." Virginia Nixon noted that in these paintings the detail is done with the utmost precision and never takes over from the scheme of the whole work. Two of her still life paintings with dolls are nicely reproduced in Paul Duval's *High Realism in Canada*, "On the Black Chair No. 2" (p.133) and "On the Balcony No. 2" (p.134). It was at Woodlawn Avenue that she painted the portrait of Avrom Isaacs (a frontal view) almost as if her subject had been transformed into a still life object. Isaacs came to know her paintings and drawings when she brought them to his gallery for framing. Seeing the high caliber of her work he arranged in 1962 an exhibition of her drawings and four of her paintings of the

PFLUG, Christiane Sybille (Cont'd)

railway yard. The show was a sell-out and Christiane turned to her painting with this very important new form of encouragement. Subsequent shows followed at the Isaacs Gallery. Between her work periods on large paintings she did pencil drawings. She also produced lithographs from her drawings. In 1966 the Winnipeg Art Gallery gave her her first retrospective show and continued to show an interest in her work ahead of any other public gallery in Canada. John Graham described her drawings as being so complete tonally and detailwise that they could almost be described as graphite paintings. The Winnipeg Art Gallery held an exhibition of her drawings between May 18 and July 15 of 1979 then circulated the show to galleries across Canada. In 1967 the Pflugs moved to the Birch Avenue apartment which looked across a park, over the roof of the Cottingham School towards an open view of the city. For the next five years until the end of her life Christiane Pflug did eight variations on this view described by John W. Graham as ". . .strongly constructed set of patterns organized from the urban minutiae of building shapes, people, cars, power poles, etc., set against the steep ground plane. As in her other series she contrasts the seasonal conditions, varies the cropping of her view, makes use of mirror surfaces, using both the school windows and water-covered roof, and reminds us of the subjective interpretation of her point of view by the color changes of the school flag." Christiane suffered from severe depression from time to time and near the end of her life spent more time at home. On April 4, 1972, she brought an end to her life "quietly" on the beach at Hanlan's Point, Toronto Island, which had been one of her favourite painting places. Some have attributed her unsettled and lonely childhood to be at least a factor in her distress, perhaps also the torment of a dedicated artist who was crushed by the pressures of daily living and stresses of an overwhelmingly materialistic world. Anne Halden of the *Winnipeg Tribune* explained, ". . .Christiane Pflug, living in Toronto in the 1960's, felt trapped by poverty, her foreignness and her personal insecurity." In her personal tragedy Canada lost a fine artist of outstanding talent. Solo shows of her work include: Isaacs Gallery (1962, 1964, 1966); Winnipeg Art Gallery (1966; 1974 retrospective circulated; 1977 40 drawings circulated); Hart House, U. of T. (1969); Peel County Museum, Brampton, Ont. (1969); Sarnia Art Gallery, Sarnia, Ont. (1971). She is represented in the following galleries: Winnipeg Art Gallery, Winn., Man.; McMaster Univ., Hamilton, Ont.; Hart House, Tor.; Agnes Etherington Art Centre, Queen's Univ., Kingston, Ont.; National Gallery of Canada, Ottawa, Ont. (drawings). Around 1969 she was paid $4,000 per large painting which would sell for considerably more today.

References

Tribune, Wpg., Man., Jan. 15, 1966 "Home-bound Toronto artist paints only according to mind's fancy"

Christiane Pflug, (catalogue), The Winnipeg Art Gallery, 1966, by Ferdinand Eckhardt, Director, WAG (36 works listed, 6 ill.)

Agnes Etherington Art Centre, Queen's Univ., Kingston, 1968, a catalogue by Frances K. Smith, No. 110

Daily Times & Conservator, Brampton, Ont., Feb. 1, 1969 "To Exhibit Here"

Toronto Daily Star, Sat., Jan. 11, 1969 "The strange reality of a housewife's kitchen paintings" by Gail Dexter

Hamilton Spectator, Ont., (CP) Feb. 4, 1969 "The Pflug bug bites"

The Hart House Collection of Canadian Paintings by Jeremy Adamson, Hart House Art Committee/Univ. Tor. Press, Tor., 1969, P. 115

PFLUG, Christiane Sybille (Cont'd)

Sarnia Observer, Ont., Sept. 16, 1971 "Opens Season" (Sarnia Art Gal.)

London Evening Free Press, Nov. 5, 1971 "Exhibitions in London; today and tomorrow"

Ibid, Nov. 8, 1971 "Larger-than-life art on display at gallery" by Lenore Crawford

Welland-Port Colborne Tribune, Ont., Mar. 9, 1972 "College Gets Art Exhibit" (CIL collection)

The Canadian Magazine, Tor. Star, Tor., May 11, 1974 "Christiane's World" by Paul Duval

Winnipeg Free Press, Man., May 25, 1974 "A Critique by John W. Graham — Pflug's Life Work"

Winnipeg Tribune, Man., June 15, 1974 "Pflug's work has magic atmosphere" by Jan Kamienski

The Gazette, Mtl., Nov. 16, 1974 "Window on the world of Pflug" by Virginia Nixon

The Albertan, Calgary, Alta., Dec. 14, 1974 "Christiane Pflug exhibition — Clarity 'not found' in life"

High Realism in Canada by Paul Duval, Clarke, Irwin & Co. Ltd., Tor., 1974, P. 132-141

Calgary Herald, Alta., Jan. 18, 1975 "Artist's private agonies evident in excellent work" by Carol Hogg

Leader Post, Regina, Sask., Apr. 12, 1975 "At the galleries — A look into the life of Christiane Pflug" by Lora Burke

Transcript, Moncton, N.B., Feb. 22, 1975 "Pflug Exhibit" (retrosp. at B.A.G.)

Telegraph Journal, Saint John, N.B., Feb. 18, 1975 "Exhibit At Capital"

Ibid, Feb. 25, 1975 "An Exhibition" (photo: "Cottingham Sch. After The Rain 1969")

Toronto Star, Ont., July 18, 1975 "Subway artists named" by Gary Michael Dault

Onion, Tor., Aug. 5-20, 1975 "At The Galleries" by Christiane Pflug

Winnipeg Tribune, Man., June 12, 1979 "Art gallery collection prelude to suicide?" by Laura Anne Halden

NGC Info. Form rec'd 1964

PFLUG, Michael

b. 1929

Born in Kassel, Germany, he studied medicine in Germany at Erlangen (1951-53) and also studied painting under Grimm at the Art School of Hamburg. Continuing his medical studies he moved to Paris where he entered the Sorbonne and graduated in 1956 to serve internship. While in Paris he took painting as well under Arpad Scenes and Vieira de Silva. There he met Christiane who had come to Paris to study fashion design but turned to painting. He encouraged Christiane in her painting and in the summer of 1956 they were married in Munich. Michael and Christiane departed for Tunisia where he became an intern. They lived in a 600-year-old house in the centre of the Casbah in Tunis. Michael served as well at two other places in Tunisia at Foum Tathouine and at Kasserine. He managed to do some painting during his free hours and held a joint show with his wife at the Alliance Française gallery in Tunis in 1958. When political violence broke out in Tunisia he sent Christiane and their two daughters, Esther and Ursula, both born in Tunisia, to Canada. He remained in Tunisia to complete his internship, then passed his final examinations for Doctor of Medicine in Paris. He emigrated to Canada in 1960 where he rejoined Christiane and the children and entered further internship in a Toronto hospital with the hope of eventually working in the field of medical research. In his painting he continued to be active when time permitted and participated in several shows including the Montreal Spring Shows (1962, 1963); Winnipeg Biennial (1962) and was represented by the Moos Gallery in

1657

PFLUG, Michael (Cont'd)

Toronto following a solo show there in 1963. Originally he painted landscapes for many years before turning to abstract painting in which some viewers still recognize traces of his earlier interest in figurative landscapes.

References

Toronto Telegram, Tor., Ont., Nov. 30, 1963 "from ultra modern. . .to representational" by Barrie Hale (article on Christiane and Michael Pflug)

Catalogue sheet, Moos Gallery, 1963 "Michael Pflug Paintings"

NGC Info. Form received 1960

PHENIX, Louis Serge

b. 1924

Born in Outremont, P.Q., he studied painting under Paul Emile Borduas and also at the École du Meuble where he also took furniture design. He became a member of the Contemporary Art Society in December of 1947 and in 1949 won a prize for painting in the Montreal Museum of Fine Arts Spring Exhibition. He held a solo show of his paintings at Galerie Agnès Lefort in Montreal when the reviewer of *The Montreal Star* noted that his landscapes were soft but he was more sure of himself in his small abstractions, and described them as follows, "He likes the hidden, the enclosed in cave or den, or the half disclosed, glimpsed through a thicket or a screen. His secrets are not too private to be shared, however, and there is pleasure in some of these little poems in smouldering color."

References

The Montreal Star, P.Q., Feb. 23, 1952 "Serge Phenix"

Invitation Card, Galerie Agnes Lefort, exhibition of paintings from February 18 to March 1, 1952

NGC Info. Form rec'd October, 1949

PHIFER, Michael

He created a sculptural set of large cedar blocks and carved cedar pillars for the Granville Centre in downtown Vancouver where passers-by can stop to contemplate the city.

Reference

Kelowna Courier, B.C., April 25, 1973 "People Forest" (CP photo and caption)

PHILIBERT, André

b. 1944

Born in Quebec City he moved to prominence for his effective paintings which have some elements of Claude Breeze and some of James Rosenquist although there is no actual similarity in his work to either artist other than the two worlds

PHILIBERT, André (Cont'd)

he himself straddles. He has explored the effects of LSD and other causes of human miseries. He has good design, draftsmanship and effective colouring in his portrayal of real subjects through distortion. He held his first solo show at Galerie MacKay in Montreal during the summer of 1968 where his work was very well received by the critics and then a fall showing of his work was held at the Cedarbrae Library in Scarborough, Ontario, indicating the impact of his first solo show. His work was exhibited at the Pavillon des peintres canadiens at Man and His World in 1970.

References

The Gazette, Mtl., P.Q., June 1, 1968 (Philibert at Galerie MacKay)

La Presse, Mtl., 1 juin, 1968 "Arts Plastiques — Le vide dans un univers rempli d'objects à voir"

Ste. Thérèse La Voix des Milles-Isles, Que., June 6, 1968 "Exposition Des Toiles D'André Philibert"

Globe & Mail, Tor., Ont., Sept. 21, 1968 "Other Galleries"

Biographical information on artist's file

L'Art au Québec depuis 1940 par Guy Robert, La Presse, 1973, P. 216

Quebec 74, Montreal Museum of Contemporary Art, Mtl., P. 113, 115

Sept-Jours, Mtl., P.Q., June 23, 1968 "Arts — André Philibert le graphisme en amour" par Claude Jasmin

PHILIPS, Bob

A former Vancouver businessman, he turned to making pottery and established a studio on Hornby Island, B.C., where he has experimented with unconventional decorations and glazes. When he builds up a stock of pottery pieces he fires his kiln usually once a month. Near his studio one finds a small room overlooking the sea where he relaxes and writes.

Reference

Vancouver Sun, B.C., Oct. 13, 1972 "Hornby Island blossoms in clay" by Alison Applebe

PHILLIMORE, Elizabeth (Mrs.)
b.(c) 1924

Born in Ontario, she graduated from the Ontario College of Art and then lived, painted, studied art history and restoration techniques in England for many years before returning to Canada to join the restoration department of the Royal Ontario Museum, Toronto. As chief conservator at the Museum she became responsible for restoring all sorts of objets d'art and paintings using as aids the latest scientific techniques and her own skills built up from years of study and practice. About 1969 after raising two daughters and experiencing a dissolved marriage she returned to her own painting and held her first solo show in 1974 at the Pollock Gallery when Sol Littman described her work as follows, "The long wait has not diminished her powers. As an art historian, she is familiar with the masterpieces of the ages; as an artist, she used them freely in

PHILLIMORE, Elizabeth (Mrs.) (Cont'd)

her own compositions." Referring to her painting "Spot Change" he went on, "A Renaissance style portrait of a young gentlewoman is suddenly transformed into a full bodied nude striding off into a series of stroboscopic variations. A monsterish face appears to interrupt the graceful flow of the design and then disappears again. The number of artistic games and puns that Mrs. Phillimore has managed to cram into one painting is amazing. There are suggestions of Veronese, Duchamp's Nude Descending a Staircase, Michael Snow's Walking Woman and Francis Bacon's phantasmagoric monsters. What is remarkable is not her virtuosity, but her ability to give her borrowed material a new, deeply personal meaning. . . .In other works, Mrs. Phillimore embraces Rosenquist's Pop Art, Op's optical games, the cold, rock strewn landscapes of the Group of Seven, Andy Warhol's silkscreens, Rousseau's naiveté and the richly patterned rugs on which realist Pearlstein poses his muscular nudes. Then in a tour de force, she organizes them all into a Mondrian grid. Curiously, what results is not a scholarly essay in art history, but an emotion-packed canvas that is both disturbing and satisfying. Dragons breathe fire and ravish young maidens; monkeys, in a state of shock, await their doom while enclosed in a plastic sack; Daddy, walled off in a glass cage, is both monumentalized and destroyed. . . . This is a complex, fascinating show, full of intense scholarship, bitter satire, hot resentment, revealing autobiography and brilliant technical achievement. Can one ask for more?" Also exhibited were her humorous drawings about Toronto landmarks. She lives in Toronto not far from her work in a house she decorated herself where she also has her studio.

References

Toronto Daily Star, Ont., July 29, 1970 "Artist reveals hidden beauty" by Lotta Dempsey
Ibid, May 14, 1974 "Historian's art full of Freudian symbolism" by Sol Littman
Exhibition notice/folder, Pollock Gallery Limited, Tor. May 14th-May 30th, 1974 w/reproduction of "Spot Change"

PHILLIPS, Doris Baillie (Mrs. George Phillips)

A native of Saint John, N.B., she has done woodcarving, made pottery, handicrafts and paintings. She has won several prizes for her plays and has had her poetry published in several periodicals. She lives in Halifax with her husband George Phillips.

Reference

Halifax Mail Star, N.S., July 5, 1969 "Playwright, Poetess and Artist Makes Mark in Ottawa Theatre" by Elizabeth Hiscott

PHILLIPS, Douglas
b.(c) 1941

Born in Willowdale, Ontario, a keen outdoorsman and naturalist he began carving birds as a hobby in 1956 making first duck decoys then song birds and others. Many of his birds are carved in lively form poised for flight. He

PHILLIPS, Douglas (Cont'd)

concentrates mainly on song birds. Describing his work a reviewer for the *Markham Economist and Sun* noted, "The workmanship and artistic design of each bird is very lifelife. There are blue jays, robins, cardinals, warblers and ducks, just to mention a few. He has also Canada geese in flight, a life-size pheasant, a herring gull and a couple of owls. By the way the wise old owl looks so natural that you expect its eyes to blink at any time." Phillips uses Balsa wood from Mexico which he buys in a rough state in three-foot by three-inch square lengths. From these rough pieces he is able to carve out about twenty specimens. His studio is located at the West end of Green River on Highway Seven north of Markham, Ontario. His work is known across Canada and the United States and his birds have been acquired by collectors in Australia, Africa and Europe.

References

Markham Economist & Sun, Ont., Feb. 16, 1967 "Green River Wood Carver Preparing for Big Spring Show"

Stouffville Tribune, Ont., Aug. 29, 1968 "Wood-carver at Markham Show"

PHILLIPS, Edward Openshaw
b. 1931

Born in Montreal, P.Q., the son of A. Lovell and Dorothy S. Phillips, he received his B.A. from McGill University, Mtl. (1953); L.LL., Université de Montréal (1956); A.M.T., for teaching English, Harvard University (1957); M.A., English Literature, Boston University (1962). He taught English for the Montreal Protestant School Board (1958-59, 1962-63); for Chauncy Hall School, Boston, Mass. (1960-62); Selwyn House School, Mtl. (1962-65). He studied at the Montreal Museum of Fine Arts School (1965-1968) under Arthur Lismer, Patrick Landsley, Gentile Tondino, Henry W. Jones, Hugh Leroy, François Déry and Roger Vilder and graduated with his diploma in 1968. He became known for his acrylic paintings (on unprimed canvas) and pen and pencil drawings. He held his first solo at Studio 23, Montreal in 1969 and subsequent solo shows at Studio 23 (1971, 1972); Dorval Cultural Centre (1971); Artlenders, Westmount, P.Q. (1973) and group shows at Studio 23 (1972); Society of Canadian Artists, Fifth Annual Open Juried Exhibition, Tor. (1972); Ontario Society of Artists 101st Annual Open Exhibition. His work has been described as modern hard edge, constructed with essentially traditional rules. His drawings of the human figure are very well done with an economy of line reminiscent of Matisse. Lives in Montreal.

References

La Presse, Mtl., P.Q., Nov. 22, 1969 "Peintures d'Edward Phillips, au Studio 23"

Ibid, Nov. 7, 1970 "Pas pareil et pareil"

The Gazette, Mtl., P.Q., Nov. 22, 1969 "Edward Phillips" (at Studio 23)

Canadian artists in exhibition, 1972/73, Roundstone, Tor., 1974, P. 170

PHILLIPS, Helen

An exhibition of her intaglio prints and sculptures was held at Gallery 1640, Montreal, in the fall of 1966.

Reference

Exhibition notice, Gallery 1640, Mtl., 1966 (Sept. 17 to Oct. 8th, 1966)

PHILLIPS, Jenny
b.(c) 1947

A Dutton, Ontario, artist, her paintings of horses and other animals have become popular in Southwestern Ontario. She also does cartoon work for the *Dutton Advance*. She does most of her paintings over the winter months using for reference, photographic material of horses and humans such as a Mennonite couple riding in their horse-drawn wagon or a Carlsberg Brewery wagon team or sometimes an oxen team. She has also done stage sets for the West Elgin Dramatic Society. Her husband David Phillips sometimes takes photographs of different activities involving horses or other subjects to add to her collection of reference material. She is a mother of four.

Reference

London Free Press, Ont., Nov. 26, 1976 "Boredom no problem — 'Resident artist' woman of many talents" by Steve Traichevich

PHILLIPS, John Kenneth (Ken Phillips)
b. 1909

Born in Toronto, Ontario, he studied at the Ontario College of Art under Arthur Lismer, C.W. Jefferys and for a short time at the Grand Central School of Art in New York City. He married a fellow student artist from the O.A.C., Marie Cecilia Guard, while in New York. They returned to Canada where John worked as a commercial artist in Toronto by day and spent his free hours painting scenes in sepia wash and conte of the older sections of Toronto also other places including cities and towns in England especially old churches and buildings of all sorts. Marie and John had two daughters and during this period Marie gave up her painting until Peri and Lisa were past their middle teens. Then she returned to her easel and they held joint showings of their work at the Port Credit Library and elsewhere and gave classes at the old Port Credit High School. Rae Corelli in reviewing John's paintings at the Toronto Central Library in 1964 noted, "He is at his superlative best when he reaches for mass and timelessness as in his studies of the Church of St. Martin-in-the-Fields at London, the Dunster Wool Market and St. Bartholomew's at Smithfield Market. . . .One gets the feeling that Phillips equates great age with dignity and the destruction of that which is old — merely because it is old — with indignity. And so he issues his protest. Nowhere does he do it better than in 'The Last of Elizabeth Street,' one of the few instances in which he has used full color." Marie and John Phillips were living at Cooksville, Ontario, in 1965.

PHILLIPS, John Kenneth (Ken Phillips) (Cont'd)

References

Toronto Daily Star, Tor., Ont., Sept. 18, 1964 review by R.F. Allen (photo of a painting of an old Toronto house by Phillips)

Ibid, Sept. 21, 1964 "His drawings are a protest" by Rae Corelli

article, undated c. 1963, probably Toronto Metro Area publication "Local Artists To Exhibit Paintings Next Week At Port Credit Library"

NGC Info. Form rec'd June 10, 1942

PHILLIPS, Myfanwy

b. 1945

Born in Dehra Dun, India, she was educated at the Royal School, Bath, England then followed her own self teaching plan for art. She worked for Crawfords Advertising Agency, London, England (1964-65) then emigrated to Canada in 1966. She was first represented by the Roberts Gallery, Toronto, in 1969 then in 1970 held her first solo show there when the *Globe and Mail* noted, ". . .Myfanwy Phillips' paintings are gay and spontaneous in a child's story-book way. Many of them, in fact, do tell a story, to be read with a child's slow-moving finger but understood with an adult's perceptive eye. . . .Miss Phillips first painted her bright patchwork dolls and animals on board and they are decorative and amusing. When she tried acrylics on canvas, the colors tended to sober up, like rich tapestries. Miss Phillips is at the stage where calico dogs and rag dolls spell cuteness. Whimsy is better for her, like 16 stoned green olives in Cornelius Chicken. That's done with a light hand and surely points the way to a whole marvellous cookbook." There is exceptionally fine drafting in her work and a unique blend of soft colours accented with bright colours. Her ideas are skilfully abstracted and arranged. She designed a four colour serigraph in a signed edition of 200 to raise money for the South James Town Defence Fund to help legal and other costs on behalf of tenants. The distinguished board of directors for the fund included Peter Akehurst, Jeremy Carver, June Callwood, Marilyn Cox, Jack Diamond, James Lorimer, Colin Vaughan and others. She is represented in the following collections: C.I.L., University of Waterloo, University of Western Ontario, Ontario Institute for Studies in Education, Etobicoke Board of Education, Elizabeth Fry Society, Levitt Safety Limited, Lincoln County Board of Education and J. Walter Thompson Limited, New York. She exhibited in the 100th annual exhibition of the O.S.A. and at the 23rd and 24th Annual Exhibition of Contemporary Canadian Art at the Art Gallery of Hamilton. She lives in Toronto.

References

Globe & Mail, Tor., Ont., May 9, 1970 (review)

Toronto Daily Star, Ont., Aug. 18, 1972 (review)

Biographical sheet, Wallack Galleries, Ottawa

PHILLIPS, Timothy
b. 1929

Born in Toronto, Ontario, the son of the late Col. W. Eric Phillips C.B.E., D.S.O., M.C., LL.D. and Doris Delano Gibson, he received his academic education at Upper Canada College and the University of Toronto where he entered pre-med courses to find human anatomy of particular interest to him. He obtained special permission to attend anatomy classes for two years and dropped all other subjects. He took private drawing lessons from several eminent Toronto artists and worked part-time at the osteopathic lab at the University of Toronto where he prepared anatomical drawings. In 1951 he travelled to England and where he enrolled in the Slade School (1951-52) then the Byam-Shaw School of Art in Kensington, London (1952-53) and attended classes (although un-enrolled) at the Royal College of Art (1958-59). He then studied at the Academy Simi Florence (1959-60) and during all the years of his European studies spent seven consecutive summers and autumns in Cadaquez, Spain, under the direction of Salvador Dali. While in Florence he studied with Pietro Annigoni mainly during the winters and springs when not at any school (1954-59). He experimented in the making of his own paints or mediums using his chemistry background from his pre-med studies and the help of his father, an industrialist, who had an interest in chemistry and successfully developed his own mixture of oils and synthetic resins which he has applied using his own technique. His main interest is in the human form. In a typical day he works from 9 a.m. to 6 p.m., six days a week, and tries to avoid missing his daily routine of drawing which he feels is the strength of his work. He returned to Canada in 1965. The next year McKenzie Porter in an article on the artist made these observations, "Timothy Phillips, who has studied under the late Augustus John, Salvador Dali, and Pietro Annigoni, reveals in his work the techniques of all three mentors. His sensual female nudes are imbued with the substance and anatomical verisimilitude of John figures. His backgrounds have the tremendous perspective depth and faintly dreamlike quality of Dali. And his taste for such fragile Grecian embellishments as garlands bring to mind Annigoni's immortal painting of Elizabeth II." Viewing his 1974 exhibit at the RM Gallery in Toronto William MacVicar noted, "An unusual collection of paintings and sketches hangs in the RM Gallery. There are canvases that bring Leonardo da Vinci to mind, and others that look like eighteenth-century sporting prints. Glimmers of light on polished brass suggest still lifes by Vermeer, and unfinished drawings are as unapologetic about traces left from false starts as those of Delacroix. So eclectic is the show, in fact, that it comes as a surprise to learn that they are all works by Timothy Phillips. . . .Some of Phillips' paintings are done in styles very possibly unknown to most of his contemporaries. He has worked in grisaille, a pearly monochrome where the paint, he says, is applied 'in a single, luminous layer of color.' In a moment Phillips is into a learned footnote about secret paint formulas in the seventeenth century. He speaks with knowledge and enthusiasm about all aspects of art, from the sublimities of Rembrandt to the chemistry of oils and temperas. As a matter of fact, he has just been doing research into the possibilities and effects of various kinds of paints. His goal is to obtain a 'translucency of tone' in which his darkest hues retain their light, and to combine chiaroscuro — light and shade — with brilliant color." Earlier Elizabeth Vaughan in the *Palm Beach Daily News* had mentioned his landscapes of northern Canadian lakes in early spring with a curious finish and then noted, ". . .a blend of oils and acrylics and he won't say what — that gives his paintings a brilliantly luminous

PHILLIPS, Timothy (Cont'd)

quality." His solo shows include: Upper Grosvenor Gallery, Lond. Eng. (1963); Galerie Ror-Valmar, Paris (1964); Collectors' Gallery, Lond. Eng. (1964); Mazelow Gallery, Tor. (1968); RM Gallery, Tor. (1972, 73, 74, 75, 76); James Hunt-Barker Gallery, Palm Beach (1973, 1977). He has participated in a number of group shows including: Daily Express Young Artists, Lond. Eng. (1954); Royal Academy, Lond. Eng. (1960, 1961); Kensington Artists, Lond., Eng. (1962); Kesketh Hubbard, Lond., Eng. (1962); Salon des Artistes Français, Paris (1963, 65, 66, 68); Nassau Artists, U.S.A. (1958, 59, 60); Palm Beach Gallery (1964, 65); Romanet Vercel, Palm Beach (1965); Ontario Inst. of Painters, Tor. (1966, 67, 68); RM Gallery, Tor. (1972, 73, 74, 75, 76). His awards include O'Keefe's Art Award (1950) and Paris Salon, Honourable Mention (1963). He is represented in the Lord Beaverbrook Museum of Fredericton, N.B. and in many private collections in Canada, England, the United States, Spain, France and South America. A member of the Ontario Institute of Painters (former Pres.). Lives in Toronto.

References

Sault Ste. Marie Star, Ont., (CP, London) June 12, 1963 "Too Busy To View Own Paint" (no time to attend show at Grand Palais, Paris, because preparing for London solo)

The Toronto Telegram, Ont., Feb. 2, 1966 "I See Abstract Art On The Way Out" by McKenzie Porter

Ibid, Oct. 25, 1968 "Watch that bare wall somebody will cover" by Bernadette Andrews

Ibid, Nov. 1, 1968 column by McKenzie Porter

Palm Beach Daily News, Wednesday, Mar. 25, 1970 "What meets the eye" by Elizabeth Vaughan

Globe & Mail, Tor., Ont., Apr. 5, 1971 "Canadian art" (letters to the Editor)

News-Chronicle, Thunder Bay, Ont., Apr. 3, 1974 "Salvation Army Exhibit Is Scheduled April 11"

Globe & Mail, Tor., Ont., Oct. 17, 1972 column by Zena Cherry

Palm Beach Daily News, Florida, Apr. 10, 1973 "Artist's Goal: Tone, Perspective" by Jamie Prillaman

Palm Beach Pictorial, Fla., Apr. 16, 1973 (events around Phillips' exhibit at Hunt-Baker Galleries)

Globe & Mail, Tor., Ont., June 8, 1974 "A painter looks back to the Old Masters" by William MacVicar

PHILLIPS, Tom V.

A Toronto artist who started painting about 1954 and attended the Doon School of Fine Arts in 1957 then returned to Toronto where he lived and studied with several teachers evenings and weekends while pursuing his regular occupation as an engineer. He became known for his water colour paintings of rural and city scenes and held a solo show of his work in 1961 at the Picture Loan Society, Toronto, when C.S. of the *Globe & Mail* noted, "Large, generous, attractive, were three adjectives which occurred to me when I looked at the first three of 19 watercolors by T.V. (Tom) Phillips. . . .Summer and winter street and rural scenes, with buildings of picturesque quality. . .are dominant features. All are on large watercolor paper, the color applied with controlled virtuosity in broad washes with a large brush. He is non-repetitive in design and in color scheme. In brief, these are among the best Canadian watercolors I have seen."

PHILLIPS, Tom V. (Cont'd)

References

Guelph Daily Mercury, Ont., Aug. 9, 1957 "An artist at work" (photo of Phillips painting at Elora, Ontario)

Exhibition notice, Picture Loan Society, Jan. 14 to Jan. 27, 1961 (with reproduction of a Phillips painting)

Globe & Mail, Tor., Ont., Jan. 21, 1961 "Phillips' Paintings" (exhibition review of solo at Picture Loan Society)

PHILLIPS, Walter John Herbert
b. 1912

Born in Salisbury Wiltshire, England, the eldest of six children of Walter Joseph and Gladys (Pitcher) Phillips, he arrived in Canada with his parents in 1913 barely eleven months old. He was educated in Winnipeg and studied at the Winnipeg School of Art under L.L. Fitzgerald and at home under his father the noted W.J. Phillips, R.C.A. He became a commercial artist and joined the firm of Brigden's of Winnipeg Limited in 1929 serving there for over nine years (probably much longer). Later he established his own studio where he employed twenty-five artists creating among other things animated characters for television commercials. During his off hours he enjoys sketching. He married Miss Edna Collins of Winnipeg in 1936 and was still living in Winnipeg in 1963. His only other brother Captain Ivan Phillips, the youngest in the family, was killed during World War II.

References

NGC Info. Form rec'd June 9, 1938

Calgary Herald, Alta., June 16, 1954 article on Walter J. Phillips (mentions his artist son)

Ibid, Nov. 23, 1960 article by Ken Liddell on occasion of Dr. Walter J. Phillips retiring to Victoria, B.C. (mentions his artist son making animations for T.V. commercials)

Victoria Times, B.C., July 6, 1963 "Well Known Artist Dies" (Dr. Walter J. Phillips, R.C.A.; mentions all members of the family)

PHILLIPS, Walter Joseph (W.J. Phillips)
1884-1963

Born at Barton-on-Humber, Lincolnshire, England, the son of Sophia (Blackett) and Reverend John Phillips, a Methodist minister. His encouragement to study art only came from his mother as his father did not approve of this uncertain and Bohemian vocation for his son. Following the Phillips' move to Barton-on-Trent, Walter attended evening classes at the local art school where the headmaster took a personal interest in developing his talent. Next he attended Bourne College (1899-1902), a boarding school near Birmingham, where he was active in sports and won a scholarship in mathematics which he promptly spent on fees to attend the Birmingham School of Art once a week under the instruction of Edward R. Taylor. Taylor did much to help him to further develop his art and he won first prize in drawing two years in a row at the examinations of the College of Preceptors. Then he became an usher at Yarmouth College where for a year he taught Latin and arithmetic at a salary of twenty pounds. He also had been awarded twenty pounds for general efficiency at Bourne College and with these two amounts he travelled to South Africa to try to earn enough money to study art in Paris. He chose South Africa because an uncle schoolmaster living there had suggested he try his luck in that country. There Phillips worked at many things to attempt to win his Paris study fees. He was a reporter for *The Diamond Fields' Advertiser*, a surveyor's assistant, a travelling salesman in South West Grinqualand, a lawyer's clerk and a diamond digger but he failed to make enough money to finance his art studies. He did some cartoons perhaps for his reporting job and continued to work at his painting when time permitted (John P. Crabb, Winnipeg, has a water colour "The South African Forest" 1905). Survival was probably the most valuable experience he was to learn during his stay in South Africa and he returned to England with little more money than he had at the outset. He next worked at commercial art for a year in Manchester (1908) then went to London where he tried his luck at free-lancing (probably a combination of writing and art) but was barely able to cover his expenses and after a short period abandoned this venture and became Art Master at Bishop Woodsworth School, Salisbury, England (1908-1911). There he met Ernest Carlos who had studied at the Royal Academy School and from Carlos learned techniques and acquired information he himself did not have. But this period also provided Phillips with the opportunity to do some landscape painting in water colours in the neighbouring countryside at Wiltshire and further afield off the coast of Land's End on the Scilly Islands and in Cornwall and Yorkshire accompanied by Ernest Carlos during their summer holidays (John P. Crabb has work from this period). On one of his outings at the village of Wylye he met Gladys Pitcher and they were married on Boxing Day, 26th December, 1910 in the Lady Chapel of Salisbury Cathedral. In November of 1911 he held his first solo show in Salisbury which proved a success both in sales and acceptance of his work. Then the following year a painting he had done in Newlyn, Cornwall was accepted for exhibit at the Royal Academy. By now he had become restless with the monotony of his artistic life and began thinking of seeking fresh horizons. Both he and his wife decided to emigrate to Winnipeg, Canada, simply because it was situated geographically in the centre of the country and they arrived there in June, 1913. He was appointed Art Master at St. John's Technical High School in Winnipeg by the superintendent of schools, Dr. Daniel McIntyre. His teaching job provided him with his family needs and by now the Phillips had two children. Weekend trips into the rural areas outside Winnipeg resulted in his water colours for which there was a good market. The sales of his paintings provided an additional income for his growing family. Shortly after his arrival in Winnipeg Phillips met Cyril Barraud who taught him how to etch. Barraud sold his tools and press to Phillips before leaving Winnipeg for service in France during World War I. Later Barraud became a war artist (1917) and remained in England after the war. From 1915 to 1918 Phillips did etchings which are quite rare since he only did a few copies of each. He mastered this medium in a remarkably short time. He was however more interested in producing his work in colour. After reading an article by Allen W. Seaby on printing from wood blocks he set to work to experiment in this medium (colour woodcut prints are produced by as many blocks as there are colours, one block for each colour). Phillips was also somewhat dissatisfied with the limited number of impressions that could be made from copper plate etching while the wood block method could produce more copies before showing signs of wearing out. His water colours, his main medium in painting, could be translated into colour woodcuts. His first successful colour woodcut "Winter" was produced in 1917 on unsized Japanese paper after he had experimented with other papers. So he turned to Japanese paper to produce his work. In 1919 six of his woodcut prints were reproduced in *The International Studio* with considerable praise for his work in an accompanying article. In his study of W.J. Phillips Michael Gribbon of the National Gallery of Canada illustrates how the artist was evidently influenced by Art Nouveau especially in the style of his monogram. Gribbon also noted that Phillips borrowed freely from many influences throughout his career and experimented with different types of wood to see what effects could be achieved from the grain of each wood. For instance he found that cherry-wood gave a tranquil effect to water while firwood left the impression of ripples on the water's surface. During the summers of 1917 and 1919 Phillips lectured at the University of Wisconsin and by now his work was being admired by viewers nationally, internationally and especially in his own city of Winnipeg. By 1923 he had published forty-two colour woodcuts, most of them in editions of fifty but a few in lots of one hundred. Much of his subject matter was found in the Lake of the Woods country from 1914 to 1924. He resigned from his teaching post in Winnipeg and took his family (by then five children) to Muskoka in Ontario where they stayed for three months and where he sketched and painted and gathered subject matter for his colour woodcuts. From Muskoka the Phillips went on to England for ten months where Walter met and studied colour techniques of print makers William Giles, Sydney Lee, Allen W. Seaby (whose book had influenced him earlier), Y. Urushibara and Martin Hardie. Phillips also contributed material to Giles' book *The Original Colour Print Magazine* as did Urushibara and Seaby. He learned from Urushibara the Japanese method of finishing or treating paper (sizing) to achieve the best effects for his colour woodcuts and wood engravings. He learned about the use of softer and lighter-coloured papers like Hosho and the use of powdered colours ground in water and applied with starch instead of using water colour pigment as it is prepared for water colour painting. He even altered Urushibara's recipe by adding more alum to achieve an egg shell surface. He wanted to remain in England but his children yearned for Canada and Winnipeg. For the children's sake they returned to Canada in June, 1925 stopping off again at Muskoka where he did a series of water colours which were later sent for showing to Herbert Furst's Galleries, The Little Art Rooms, The Adelphi, London. The family was back in Winnipeg in the fall and he entered a great period of productivity completing eleven woodcuts in 1926; fifteen in 1927 and thirteen in 1928. By now he had established the pattern for making his colour woodcuts: first the graphite sketch, next a finished water colour, then a further sketch to plan the woodcut and finally the woodcut itself. He also rearranged the actual scenes for the composition he desired. Like many other artists he drew his material from sketch books (see *Walter J. Phillips* by Michael J. Gribbon for details on stages for making a woodcut). During 1926 and 1927 he did a number of landscapes in egg-tempera which found their way into private collections and are rare items to be found today. His book *The Technique of the Colour Woodcut* was published in 1926 in New York. In July of 1926 Phillips' sixth child was born. He enjoyed teaching his children about the things he loved to paint himself, trees, flowers, birds and many other wonders a naturalist would seek out. He painted his own children into his pictures and paid them the going rate of ten cents a day to pose or help in some way, like row a boat. Many of his children's music lessons, medical bills and many of the household needs were paid for by the exchange of his work for the amount owing. He was one of the few artists able to make a living from his painting and woodcuts during the Great Depression. A former editor-in-chief of the Winnipeg *Tribune*, Carlyle Allison, described Phillips as follows, "Walter was six feet in height, weighed about 220 pounds at his peak, and, as C.B. Pyper of the *Toronto Telegram* put it, had 'a handshake like a navvy'. I remember him as a friendly man with a deep voice that had a smile or a laugh in it much of the time. When he worked he worked hard, 'from daybreak to dusk,' his son John says, and when he played he played hard, as in the weekend-long bridge sessions. He savoured life fully and accomplished a great deal, leaving behind him hundreds of watercolours and colour woodcuts, black and white engravings, hundreds of newspaper articles which still have interest today, and several illustrated books." Phillips by this time had made his first trip to the Rocky Mountains and during a solo show of this work a columnist, C.B.P. of the Winnipeg *Tribune* noted, "Mountain scenery is in the nature of new ground for Mr. Phillips, who has hitherto worked mostly on lakes and woods and rolling plains. He has made the ground his own on his first visit. His unerring eye for color has obviously revelled in the vivid greens and yellows, the mauves and purples and browns that lend their especial charm to lake and wood and stone in the Rockies; his sense of form is shown in his wonderfully successful treatment of rock formations and escarpments; his light and confident touch has enabled him to capture the delicate and varied tints of glacier and sky as seen in the color brillancy of the mountain air." The reviewer also noted some of Phillips' tempera paintings done on this trip. From 1925 to 1935 he had painted on the prairies mainly, but by 1936 was finding most of his material in the Rockies. From 1926 to 1942 his articles "Art and Artists" appeared in the Winnipeg *Tribune*. One of his busy years for book production was in 1931 when he illustrated three books: Robert Watson's *Women of the Red River* and *Dreams of Fort Garry*; *Highroads to Reading*. Other books he illustrated include: H.A.V. Green's *Death of Pierrot* (1923); H.G. Herklots' *The First Winter* (1935); Frederick Niven's *Colour in the Canadian Rockies* (1937); contributed ill. for Leacock's *Canada: the Foundations of its Future* (1941); F. Niven's *The Transplanted* (1944); R. Gard's *Johnny Chinook: Tall Tales and True from the Canadian West* (1945). Phillips made more trips to the west and became a member of the staff of the Banff Summer School of Fine Arts in 1940 and finally in 1941 moved to Calgary to take up his new position of instructor at the Institute of Technology and Art (he continued there until 1949). This gave him greater contact with people and much hapiness to share his skills and experience with his pupils and colleagues. He loved to play contract bridge and with his wife Gladys won the East-West Canadian Championship Contest sponsored by Ely Culbertson in 1939. In 1943 he moved to Banff where he painted and lived in an attractive home on Tunnell Mountain. His beautiful paintings of waterfalls, mountains and lakes were produced in this period when he also made more frequent visits to the West Coast. In 1945 his younger son Ivan, who had dropped a rank from Captain to Lieutenant so he could go to the front, was killed at Xanten, Holland, and left behind in Canada a widow and a baby son. By 1958 Walter Phillips' eyesight began failing and in 1960 he retired to

PHILLIPS, Walter Joseph (W.J. Phillips) (Cont'd)

Victoria. This same year the University of Alberta awarded him an honorary L.L.D. and Ken Liddell of the Calgary *Herald* wrote, "Fate has drawn a veil over the eyes of the man who earned an international reputation because of his ability to portray nature as he saw it and others enjoy it. His works, in oils, water colours, sketches and colored woodcuts, number in the thousands. He was an artist in the broad sense. His signature is his monument in public institutions around the world, in murals in railway cars, on jackets of books and on Christmas cards that would reach mountain heights if stacked. Now he is leaving the mountains where he has worked for so long and with such success. . .the accumulation of 76 years is being packed at the fine home in Banff that Dr. and Mrs. Phillips have shared and from which the family has scattered. One, a son, is making a reputation as creator of animated characters for television commercials. . . .After three major eye operations, talking was difficult for the man who had enjoyed 'the grandest life' and who now looked forward to taking recording machine microphone in hand to put it all down in words. 'We have the machine,' said Mrs. Phillips — she was one of his students in Salisbury — who had come back to the living room with board and dough she was kneading for home-made bread, in loving response to a quiet request: 'don't go away.'" In 1963 W.J. Phillips died in Victoria aged 78 and his ashes were scattered in the Alberta mountains where he loved to be and where he had painted for many years. At the time of his death he was survived by his wife Gladys; his son John (Winnipeg); four daughters: Mrs. Sherman Wright (Waterloo, Ont.); Mrs. Robert Adamson (Victoria, B.C.); Mrs. John Dufferin (Calgary, Alta.); Mrs. Barry Heimer (Winnipeg, Man.); 16 grandchildren; one brother, Arthur (England) and two sisters: Mrs. R. Sharp (Sechelt, B.C.) and Miss Irene Phillips (England). During his long career he held solo shows as follows: Bishop's School, Salisbury, Eng. (1911); Salisbury (1911); Church House, Salisbury (1912); Richardson Bros. Gallery, Winnipeg (1913); Art Gallery, Industrial Bureau, Winn. (1917); Winnipeg Gallery & School of Art, Winn. (1920); his home & studio, Bannerman Ave., Winn. (1923); Kendrick-Bellamy Co., Denver, Col. (1924); Eaton's, Tor. (1924); The Little Art Room, Duke St., Lond., Eng. (1925); Godspeed's Book Shop, Boston, Mass. (1926); Richardson Bros. Winn. (1926); W. Scott & Sons, Mtl. (1927); with F.H. Brigden, Richardson Bros. (1928); Convocation Hall, Univ. Sask. (1935); Coste House, Calg. (1944) (1945); Canadian Art Galleries (1947) (1951); Richardson Bros. (1953); Norfolk Gal., Vic., B.C. (1955); Coste House, Calg. (1957); Western Canada Art Circuit to various centres (1957); Winnipeg Art Gallery (retrospec., 1958); solos following his death include: Gainsborough Galleries, Lethbridge (1963); Winnipeg Art Gallery (1964); Glenbow Art Gallery, Alta. (1968); touring show by Hudson's Bay Co. to centres throughout Canada of 250 items from the John P. Crabb collection, Winnipeg (1970-72); subsequent shows by other sponsors. Phillips' work was shown in many group shows both nationally and internationally including the Royal Canadian Academy Annual Exhibitions; Canadian National Exhibitions; Canadian Society of Painters in Water Colour; Manitoba Society of Artists; Society of Canadian Painter-Etchers and Engravers; Ontario Society of Artists; British Empire Exhibition (Lond. Eng., 1925); Canadian Society of Graphic Art; New York World's Fair (NYC, 1939); 14th Internat. Art Exhibition of the City of Venice (1924); Internat. Exhibition of Lithography and Wood Engravings (several yrs.); Internat. Print Makers Exhibition (several yrs.); A Century of

PHILLIPS, Walter Joseph (W.J. Phillips) (Cont'd)

Canadian Art, Tate Gallery, Lond., Eng. (1938) and many others. He was awarded the following prizes: Storrow Prize for Colour Woodcut, California Printmakers Internat. Exhibition, Los Angeles (1924); Bronze Medal for colour woodcut, Graphic Arts, Tor. (1926); Gold Medal for colour woodcut, Society of Arts and Crafts, Boston, Mass. (1931); Honourable Mention, for wood engraving, Warsaw Woodcut Internat. (1933) (1936). He was a member of the following societies: Royal Canadian Academy (A.R.C.A. 1921, R.C.A. 1933); Canadian Society of Painters in Water Colour (Former Vice-Pres.); Manitoba Society of Artists; Alberta Society of Artists; Society of Canadian Painter-Etchers and Engravers; Printmakers Society of Calif.; Society of Print-Makers of Los Angeles; Society of Graver-Printers in Colour, Lond., England. His work can be seen in the following public institutions: Dartmouth College, N.S.; Art Assoc. of Mtl., P.Q.; Nat. Gal. of Can., Ott., Ont.; Public Archives of Canada, Ott.; Art Gal. of Ontario, Tor.; Hart House, Univ. Tor.; Metro Toronto Public Library; University of Winnipeg, Man.; The Winnipeg Art Gallery; St. John's High School, Winn.; Nutana Collegiate Inst., Sask.; Drake Hall, Regina, Sask.; Bessborough Hotel, Saskatoon, Sask.; Mendel Gallery, Saskatoon; The Glenbow Foundation, Calg., Alta.; The Univ. of Alberta, Edmonton; Calgary Public Library; Allied Art Centre, Calgary; Edmonton Museum of Arts; Banff School of Fine Arts; British Museum, Lond., Eng.; Victoria & Albert Museum, Lond., Eng.; Smithsonian Inst., Wash., D.C.; New York Public Library; Newark, N.J.; Art Institute of Chicago; Detroit Inst. of Arts; Los Angeles Museum, Calif.; San Diego Museum, Calif; Tokyo, Japan; Warsaw, Poland; Pietermaritzburg, Natal. Duncan Campbell Scott's *W.J. Phillips* (1947) was the first comprehensive book on the artist providing many biographical details, influences, list of articles written on the artist, list of works completed by artist to date of publication. John P. Crabb of Winnipeg assembled the largest single collection of the artist's work and other memorabilia including letters, school documents, medals, blocks and tools used by Phillips also sketches in water colour, pencil and ink; etchings; wood engravings, colour woodcuts, studio paintings and Christmas cards, in all about 500 items. With Crabb's assistance and help from the artist's widow and son John, Michael J. Gribbon, Curatorial Assistant of Prints and Drawings, NGC, wrote a superb book, *Walter J. Phillips, A Selection of His Works and Thoughts* (1978) a definitive study on the artist.

References

Books, periodicals, catalogues (listing is limited by space)

The Studio, Vol. 77, 1919, notes and colour woodcuts P. 35, 37, 38, 41 & 42

The Death of Pierrot by Harry A.V. Green, Winnipeg, 1923

The Original Colour Print Magazine, Ed. Allen W. Seaby, Eng. 1924 "The American Colour Print Movement" by W.J. Phillips, P. 14, 15

Ibid, 1925 frontispiece by W.J. Phillips; Notes on woodcuts and colour woodcuts by W.J. Phillips, P. 45, 47

The Technique of the Colour Woodcut by Walter J. Phillips, Brown-Robertson, New York, 1926

The Mountaineer, Aug. 15, 1926 article on Walter J. Phillips by Harry Green (ill. by W.J. Phillips)

Painting and Sculpture in Canada by M.O. Hammond, Ryerson Press, Tor., 1930

The Passing Show, April, 1931 (an English magazine) "The Wood Block"

Dreams of Fort Garry by Robert Watson, Stovel Co., Winnipeg, 1931 (ill. by Walter J. Phillips)

PHILLIPS, Walter Joseph (W.J. Phillips) (Cont'd)

The Canadian Graphic Year Book, 1931, P. 62, 63

Canadian Landscape Painters by A.H. Robson, Ryerson, Tor., 1932, P. 185, 202

Highroads to Reading, Book IV, Illustrated by Walter J. Phillips, Thomas Nelson & Sons, Tor., Ont., 1934; Book V, 1948; Book VI, 1948

The First Winter by H.G.G. Herklots, J.M. Dent & Sons, Tor. Van., 1935 (frontispiece & cover by W.J. P.)

The Beaver, Hudson's Bay Co., September, 1937 "Aboriginal Art" by W.J. Phillips (article with colour woodcuts, Pen and Inks and Wood Engravings)

Colour In The Canadian Rockies by Walter J. Phillips and Frederick Niven, Thomas Nelson & Sons, Tor., 1937

Canadian Mosaic by John Murray Gibbon, M & S, Tor., 1938 (8 drawings in coloured chalk by W.J. P.)

Canada: The Foundations of Its Future by Stephen Leacock, House of Seagram, Mtl., 1941 (ill. by W.J. P., P. 163, 187, 217, 242)

Canadian Art, Its Origin and Development by William Colgate, Ryerson, Tor., 1943, P. 210, 214-16, 222

Johnny Chinook by Robert Gard, Longmans Green, Tor., 1945 (ill. & cover by W.J. P.)

W.J. Phillips by Duncan Campbell Scott, Ryerson, Tor., 1947

The Canadian Forum, October, 1951 "Painting in the Rockies" by Walter J. Phillips

Canadian Water Colour Painting by Paul Duval, Burns & MacEach., Tor., 1954

Canadian Drawings and Prints by Paul Duval, Burns & MacEach., Tor., 1952

Canadian Paintings in Hart House by J. Russell Harper, Univ. Tor. Press, Tor., 1955, P. 11

University of Alberta Fall Convocation (Honorary Degree of Doctor of Laws conferred on Walter J. Phillips), October, 1960

National Gal. of Can. Catalogue of Paintings, V.3, Can. School by R.H. Hubbard, Queen's Printer, NGC, Ottawa, 1960, P. 247-8, 408

The Canadian Red Cross Junior, Vol. 12, April, 1962 by G. Joy Tranter

The Lyric, Spring, 1964 (poem dedicated to Death of an Artist by Virginia S. Hopper)

Graphics by Walter J. Phillips by John P. Crabb, Glenbow Alta. Inst., Calgary Alta., 1968 (catalogue for graphics show at Glenbow Art Gallery)

Painting in Canada/a history by J. Russell Harper, Univ. Tor. Press, Tor., 1966, (2nd Ed. paper, 1977), P. 314, 315, 381, 424

Information from John P. Crabb (biographical, bibliographical), Winnipeg, 1969

Winnipeg Sketch Club by Madeline Perry/research by Lily Hobbs, Winnipeg Sketch Club, 434 Assiniboine Ave., Winnipeg, 1970

Art Gallery of Ontario/the Canadian collection by Helen Pepall Bradfield, McGraw-Hill, Tor., P. 365-376

The Art of W.J. Phillips by Carlyle Allison, Hudson's Bay Company, Winnipeg, 1970 (an exhibit of 250 of Dr. Phillips' works assembled and loaned by John P. Crabb)

150 Years of Art in Manitoba by Ferdinand Eckhardt, Winn. Art Gal., Winn., 1970, P. 88, 89, 96

A Concise History of Canadian Painting by Dennis Reid, Oxford, Tor., 1973, P. 160, 181

Creative Canada, Volume One, McPherson Lib., Univ. Victoria/Univ. Tor. Press, Tor., 1971, P. 250-1

NGC Info. Forms: Aug., Oct., 1946; Jan. 1943, May 1920

Walter J. Phillips/A Selection of His Works and Thoughts by Michael J. Gribbon, NGC, Ottawa, 1978 (obtainable from any bookstore or from National Museums of Canada, Mail Order, Ottawa, K1A 0M8)

Newspapers (selection limited by space)

Tribune, Winnipeg, Man., June 12, 1920 "Winnipeg Artist in Wood Wins Praise" (International Exhibition of the Printmakers of Los Angeles, Calif.)

Free Press, Winnipeg, Nov. 27, 1920 "Winnipeg Artist Has Interesting Exhibit of Water Colors on View at Art School"

Tribune, Winn., Nov. 27, 1920 "Exhibition of Painting by Walter J. Phillips"

Free Press, Winn., Dec. 11, 1920 "Rare Canadian Art Exhibit" by Wm. A. Deacon (at Board of Trade Art Gallery)

PHILLIPS, Walter Joseph (W.J. Phillips) (Cont'd)

Ibid, Dec. 2, 1922 "Canadian Artist Paints Scenes in Noted Local Summer Resort" by Alec J. Musgrove (show in parish hall of St. Luke's Church)

Saturday Night, Tor., Mar. 15, 1924 "A Winnipeg Water-Colorist" (review of show at Eaton Art Galleries)

Tribune, Winn., Nov. 6, 1926 "Local Artist Records Beauty of Rocky Mts." by C.B.P. (quote from this review in text above)

The Globe, Tor., Sept. 20, 1930 "Leading Canadian Artists" by M.O. Hammond

Province, Van., B.C., May 4, 1935 "Artist Brings Honor to Empire" by Tom Matheson

Free Press, Winn., Feb. 8, 1937 "Phillips and Bergman Congratulated for Art Exhibit Honors" (success at Warsaw international exhibition)

Tribune, Winn., Man., Nov. 26, 1938 "Winnipeg Artist Displays Work" by R.H. (at Richardson Bros. Art Gal.)

Herald, Calgary, Sept. 12, 1941 "Noted Canadian Artist Joins Staff of 'Tech'"

Tribune, Winn., Sept. 17, 1941 "Winnipeg Artist Appointed to Calgary Post"

Herald, Calg., Mar. 9, 1944 "Phillips Exhibit Shows Mastery of Technique" by D. Geneva Lent (show at Coste House)

Ibid, Nov. 27, 1947 "Phillips' Art Display Features West Scenes" (show at Canadian Art Galleries)

Times Star, Geraldton, Ont., Jan. 12, 1950 (CP Winn.) "Forest Artist Animals Kibitz" (animals as onlookers as W.J. Phillips paints in mountains)

Herald, Calg., Mar. 16, 1951 "Art Display Features Outdoors" (at Can. Art Galleries)

Ibid, Feb. 16, 1953 "First Painting Sold Because of Car Crash" by Dushan Bresky (lady driver and her car land in local art dealer's show window — her husband buys Phillips' print on display)

Tribune, Winn., May 22, 1954 "Phillips Paints Mural For New Scenic Rail Car" (C.P.R. commission)

Herald, Calg., Sept. 14, 1957 (profile of Walter Phillips by Elizabeth Motherwell)

Ibid, Nov. 23, 1960 a column written by Ken Liddell (quotation from it appears in text above)

Albertan, Calg., Dec. 20, 1960 "Famed Artist Moves" (Phillips goes to Victoria)

Times, Vic., B.C., July 6, 1963 "Well Known Artist Dies"

Oak Bay Leader, B.C., July 24, 1963 "Artist Returns To Mountains" (ashes of W.J. Phillips are scattered in Alberta mountains)

Kitchener-Waterloo Record, Ont., Nov. 30, 1963 "Paintings Presented To Gallery" (W.J. Phillips' daughter, Mrs. Sherman Wright, presents six paintings to K.W. Art Gallery)

Tribune, Winn., June 23, 1967 "Phillips art show project" (John P. Crabb assembles 400 pieces of art of Walter J. Phillips)

PHILLIPSON, Gillian Saward (Gill Saward)
b. 1934

Born in Maidstone, Kent, England, she came to Canada in 1948 and studied at the Beal Technical School, London, Ontario, and at the Instituto Allende in Mexico. A painter in oil and tempera she began a style called "new realism" about 1967 and one of her paintings "Portrait for a Grandmother" done in casein, was awarded Third Prize at the 6th Annual Price Fine Arts Awards and reproduced in the catalogue for the travelling show of prize-winning paintings. She has exhibited her work at the Mazelow Galleries, Tor. (1973, 1975, 1976) and the Nancy Poole Gallery, Lond., Ontario and has exhibited in several group shows sponsored by the Ontario Society of Artists. She is represented in the London Art Gallery and was awarded grants from the Canada Council (1969) and the Ontario Arts Council (1975, 1977). Lives in Toronto.

PHILLIPSON, Gillian Saward (Gill Saward) (Cont'd)

References
> *The Index of Ontario Artists*, Ed. Hennie Wolff, Visual Arts Ontario/Ont. Assoc. of Art Gal., Tor., 1978
> *Price Fine Arts Awards*, 1970 (Catalogue by The Price Group of Companies)

PI, Lutzi

A Vancouver sculptor who erected a modern translucent plastic fountain outside the Daon Building on West Pender Street, Vancouver.

Reference
> *The Vancouver Sun*, B.C., Aug. 15, 1974 (large photo)

PICARD, Claude
b. 1932

Born in Edmundston, N.B., the son and 13th child of Vital and Brigitte (Toomay) Picard. He showed artistic ability at a very early age and at ten years received instruction from Dr. Paul Carmel Laporte who founded a private school where he gave free tuition. With Dr. Laporte's assistance Picard took a commercial art course from the International Correspondence School in 1947 which enabled him to earn a good part of his living from display advertisements for newspapers. Early in his career Picard became interested in portrait painting and in 1946 won 3rd Prize in a national contest to paint the portrait of Robin Hood. His first official commission came in 1950 from the Edmundston Rotary Club to paint the portraits of the late Archibald Fraser and William Matheson, founders of the Fraser Company (paintings displayed at the New Brunswick Museum, Saint John). Picard continued his studies at St. Louis College, Edmundston, with the help of Dr. Laporte, and after four years he graduated with his B.A. in 1954. While attending St. Louis he earned part of his tuition by painting thirty murals for the College, each six feet in width by eight or nine feet in height, mainly on subjects of religion, history and symbolism. He continued to do mural work for the College following his graduation. Because of his exceptional talent a fund-raising campaign was initiated by a local French-language weekly, *Le Madawaska* published by J.L. Boucher, to send Picard to Italy to study the Italian masters. The drive was successful and Picard was presented with a cheque by J.L. Boucher. With this money and savings of his own, Picard boarded the trans-Atlantic liner *Homeric* at Quebec City and finally reached Rome where he completed successfully a year's study in art. While there he received additional help from the Eudist Fathers and lived with various Italian families and learned to speak Italian fluently, a third language for him. He spent another two years in Europe studying in France and Spain then returned to Edmundston and a large basement apartment, owned by Dr. Laporte, which he uses as his studio. In 1960 Picard held his first solo show at the Edmundston Educational Centre where he exhibited religious paintings done in Rome (originals, and copies from ancient masters) also portraits, cityscapes and landscapes, commercial art and abstract paintings. His portraits

PICARD, Claude (Cont'd)

are exceptionally well done and include those of New Brunswick Premiers Hugh J. Flemming, Louis J. Robichaud and his wife; Hon. Senator A.H. McLean (Saint John, N.B.); Bishops Gagnon (Edmund., N.B.), Feeny (Portland, Maine); Archbishop Plourde (Ottawa, Ont.) and many others. His solo shows include those at the Educational Centre, Edmund., N.B. (1960-61-63); St. Joseph University, Edmund., N.B. (1961); Conference Room of L'Olympia, Sept-Isles, P.Q. (1964); Restigouche Regional Library, N.B. (1968); Campbellton Regional Library, N.B. (1968); La Tourbière, Rivière-du-Loup, P.Q. (1970); Shutter Art Gallery, Saint John, N.B. (1971). His other awards include: Best Decor at New Brunswick Drama Festival, Fred., N.B. (1965); Maritime Art Association painting award (1967). He is represented in the following collections: St. Louis College, Edmund., N.B.; Notre-Dame des Flots à Lamèque, N.B.; École de Métiers, Edmund., N.B. and the Hartland Memorial Room Museum and Art Gallery, Hartland, N.B.

References

Le Madawaska, Edmund., April 19, 1956 "Personnalité du peintre Claude Picard"

Telegraph-Journal, Saint John, N.B., Sept. 11, 1956 "Special Fund Sponsors Trip — Young Edmundston Artist On Way To Rome; Will Study Under 'Old World' Masters" by Ron Lebel

Le Madawaska, Edmund., Aug. 15, 1957 "Nouvelles de Claude Picard" par L.-J.L.

Ibid, Jan. 28, 1960 "Retour du peintre Claude Picard" Interview de Ls-J. Lachance

Ibid, June 23, 1960 "Peinture de Claude Picard pour l'église de Lamèque"

L'Evangeline, Moncton, N.B., Oct. 20, 1960 "Exposition des oeuvres de M. Claude Picard, peintre" par M. Guy Michaud

Le Madawaska, Edmund., N.B., Oct. 27, 1960 "A propos d'une exposition" par Marcel Sormany

Telegraph-Journal, Saint John, N.B., Oct. 29, 1960 "For Edmundston Painter — Ambition As A Youth Now Fully Realized" by Audrey Stevenson

Le Soleil, Quebec, Nov. 2, 1960 "Exposition de l'artiste-peintre Claude Picard à Edmundston"

Le Madawaska, N.B., Nov. 3, 1960 (photo of Picard with painting of his niece which she is holding)

Ibid, May 4, 1961 "Les Oeuvres de Claude Picard à l'U.S.L." par L.-J.L.

Telegraph-Journal, N.B., Oct. 26, 1961 "At Edmundston — U.S. Consul Visits Artist"

Ibid, Aug. 4, 1962 "Named Judge For Paintings At Maine Fair"

Le Madawaska, N.B., Dec. 5, 1963 "L'exposition de Claude Picard a attiré de nombreux visiteurs"

L'Evangeline, Moncton, N.B., Dec. 6, 1963 "Un artiste de chez-nous"

Le Madawaska, N.B., May 7, 1964 "Une autre oeuvre de Claude Picard"

Ibid, Oct. 29, 1964 "Claude Picard expose ses oeuvres à Sept-Iles"

Ibid, Mar. 24, 1966 "Murale confiée à M. Claude Picard"

Ibid, May 5, 1966 "Une murale de Claude Picard orne entrée de l'École de Métiers" (large photo of Picard and his mural)

Ibid, June 1, 1967 "A l'honneur"

Dalhousie News, N.B., Feb. 22, 1968 "Art Exhibits This Week Drawing Good Attendance"

Le Madawaska, N.B., Feb. 29, 1968 "Exposition à Campbellton" (photo of his work)

Ibid, June 24, 1970 "L'artiste-peintre — Claude Picard"

Evening Times Globe, Saint John, N.B., June 24, 1971 (photo of Picard during exhibition at Shutter Art Gallery)

Arts in New Brunswick, Ed. R.A. Tweedie, Fred Cogswell, W. Steward MacNutt, Brunswick Press (Univ. Press of N.B.) Fred., N.B., 1967, P. 160, 263

PICARD, Clément

b. 1926

After graduating from the École des Beaux-Arts, Montreal, in 1949 with his teaching diploma he taught at the Beaux-Arts from 1951 to 1969. He took further studies in Europe (1957-58) then started teaching three dimensional plastic arts at the Université du Québec in Montreal. With a grant in 1970 he did research into the different effects of polarizing light and the resulting work was his collaboration in "Pitrumac", the multi media production created by Trudeau (sculptor); Picard (painter); Maurice Macot (conceptual artist) and Claude Vivier (musician) with eight young artists and a choreographer, presented at the young musicians' camp at Mont Orford, August, 1970 and in a more elaborate version at the Musée d'art contemporain, Montreal. In 1975 he won first prize in an art contest of the International Telecommunications Satellite Organization for pieces to decorate the new Intelsat Headquarters in Washington, D.C. His submission was the polyester column "Totem 1" (6 ft. 2 in. high by 1 ft. sq.). He lives at Saint-Phillippe-De-Laprairie, Quebec.

References

Le Devoir, Mtl., P.Q., Jan. 13, 1956 "Evolution de Clément Picard" par Noël Lajoie

La Presse, Mtl., P.Q., May 13, 1961 "Galerie Libre" (photo and review of work)

Montréal-Matin, Que., May 25, 1974 "Quatre sculpteurs québécois à Paris"

La Presse, Mtl., P.Q., Feb. 28, 1975 "Le lauréat, un Québécois"

The Province, Van., B.C., Mar. 4, 1975 (large photo of Picard with winning sculpture "Pitumac")

Free Press, Winn., Man., Mar. 1, 1975 (photo of Picard with sculpture)

Le Nouvelliste, Trois-Rivières, P.Q. CNW, Mar. 3, 1975 "Premier prix de $5,000 au sculpteur Picard" (photo with article)

L'Art au Québec depuis 1940 par Guy Robert, La Presse, 1973, P. 418-19

PICARD, Françoise

b. 1923

Born in West Shefford, Quebec, she studied at the École des Beaux-Arts, Montreal, under René Chicoine; at the Montreal Art Association under Goodridge Roberts and Arthur Lismer and at Chouinard's Art Institute, Los Angeles, California under Dan Lutz, L. Burton and Mary Wirten, and in Paris with painters André Lhote and Fernand Léger. She participated in the 1947 exhibition sponsored by the National Council of Women of United States "Canadian Women's Exhibition" and at: the Montreal Spring Show at the Montreal Museum of Fine Arts; the Royal Canadian Academy of Arts; Canadian Society of Painters in Water Colour. She exhibited her water colours in Havana, Cuba and at Granby, Quebec.

References

La Voix de l'Est, Granby, P.Q., April 15, 1947 "Peinture de Mlle Françoise Picard exposée à N.-York"

The Montreal Star, P.Q., April 28, 1947 "Granby Woman Artist To Exhibit in New York"

La Voix de l'Est, Granby, Quebec, May 19, 1953 "Une exposition de peintures, oeuvres de Mlle Françoise Picard, aura lieu à l'hôtel de ville les 21, 22 et 23"

NGC Info. Form May 13, 1947

PICARD, Lucille Albert

She studied three and a half years under Mme. Cécile Rousseau and Anne-Marie Gagnon and exhibited her portraits, still lifes and landscapes in the Royal Bank at the Chateauguay Regional Shopping Centre, Quebec.

Reference
    St. Lawrence Sun, Valleyfield, Que., September 28, 1977 (photo of artist and her work)

PICARD, Maurice

Born in Montreal, P.Q., a graphic designer who created the 1968 Christmas Seal, he has been working in the field of photo engraving, art directing and designing and has won many awards for his work.

Reference
    Cochrane Northland Post, Ont., Nov. 21, 1968 "Christmas Seal Artist"

PICARD, Raymond
b. 1925

Born in Montreal, P.Q., he studied paintings of Great Masters in public libraries then took drawing classes at the École des Beaux-Arts, Montreal. He became ill during his art studies and while recovering at Ste. Agathe des Monts received instruction in oils and pastels from Stanley Tresider who was convalescing alongside him. Around 1960 he studied further at San Miguel Allende Saltillo and at Vera Cruz, Mexico. A figurative painter he held his first solo show at the Morency Gallery, Montreal in 1948, and subsequently a number of solo shows, including one held at the Ottawa Little Theatre in 1959 when Carl Weiselberger described his Laurentian landscapes as gentle, romantic, pleasantly handled with commendable skill in projecting atmosphere with mist and fog brewing over the hills and lakes. In 1959 Picard with car and trailer set out with his family on a North American painting and exhibition tour for eighteen months holding solo shows in Washington, D.C.; Richmond, Va.; Fort Lauderdale, Fla.; New Orleans, La.; Baton Rouge, La.; Dallas, Fort Worth and Houston, Texas; and in numerous locations in Mexico then returned north to Quebec in 1961. About 1966 he acquired an old house built in 1830 which is situated four miles from Sorel on the banks of the Richelieu River. He restored the house for a home and studio and gallery which he has named Atelier-Galerie, Arts et Artisans. There he displays his own work and the work of artisans. His own solo shows include: Galerie Antoine, Mtl. (1958); Galerie L'Art Français, Mtl. (1958); l'Hôtel Laurentien, Mtl. (1959); Ottawa Little Theatre, Ott. (1959, 1961, 1962, 1963); Sheraton Park Hotel, Wash., D.C. (c. 1960); Jefferson Hotel, Richmond, Va. (c. 1960); Pier 66, Ft. Lauderdale, Fla. (c. 1960); Roosevelt Hotel, New Orleans, La. (c. 1960); Canadian Counsul General, Baton Rouge, La. (c. 1960); Louisiana State Exhibition Museum, Shreveport, La. (c. 1960); Sheraton Dallas Hotel, Ft. Worth, Texas (c. 1960); Wedgewood Country Club, Ft. Worth, Texas (c. 1960);

PICARD, Raymond (Cont'd)

Warwich Hotel, Houston, Texas (c. 1960); Headliners Club, Austin, Texas (c. 1960); Heart of Palm Beach Hotel, Palm Beach, Fla. (c. 1960); Laurentian Hotel, Mtl. (1961); Beaurepaire, P.Q. (1961); Château des Gouverneurs, Sorel, P.Q. (1962, 1963) and a number of other centres in Quebec in 1964; Press Club, Tracy, P.Q. (1965); Caisse Populaire, Ste-Madeleine-Sophie, P.Q. (1967); Pillar & Post, Niagara-on-the-Lake, Ont. (1972); Centre Culturel, Drummond, P.Q. (1978).

References

Ottawa Citizen, Ont., Nov. 12, 1959 "His Landscapes Have A 19th Century Style" by Carl Weiselberger

La Patrie, Mtl., P.Q., Jan. 3, 1960 "États-Unis, Mexique et Canada en roulotte: tournée de deux ans du peintre Raymond Picard" par Pierre Saucier

Ottawa Citizen, Ont. (CP Washington) Feb. 29, 1960 "Few Rewards In Canada, Says Artist"

Ibid, Nov. 7, 1961 "Canvasses By Montreal Artist Show" by Carl Weiselberger

Le Sorelois, Sorel, P.Q., Mar. 22, 1962 "Exposition de tableaux sorelois"

Le Courrier, Sorel, P.Q., Mar. 22, 1962 "Expo au Château des Gouverneurs"

Le Sorelois, Sorel, P.Q., Apr. 5, 1962 "Un peintre nous revient. . ."

Ottawa Journal, Ont., May 8, 1962 "Paintings by Ray Picard Shown in Little Theatre" by W.Q.K.

Le Nouvelliste, Trois Rivières, May 31, 1963 "Les Maires De Sorel, Tracy et St-Joseph de Sorel — ont accepté de présider conjointement la cerémonie de vernissage de l'exposition. . ."

Le Courrier, St. Hyacinthe, P.Q., Mar. 12, 1964 "Raymond Picard exposera une trentaine de ses oeuvres à Saint-Hyacinthe"

La Voix de l'Est, Granby, P.Q., Mar. 16, 1964 "La 1ère d'une tournée provinciale de R.R. Picard"

Ibid, Mar. 21, 1964 "Sensibilité et subtilité dans les oeuvres de Raymond Picard"

Le Courrier, Sorel, P.Q., Sept. 29, 1965 "L'Artiste-Peintre Raymond Picard S'Etablit En Permanence A Tracy"

Montreal Star, P.Q., June 29, 1966 "Artist Takes Time Out To Decorate" by Helen Rochester

Le Courrier Riviera, P.Q., Dec. 14, 1966 "Raymond-R Picard Exposera Ses Oeuvres Au Club De Presse"

Progrès du Nord, Mtl., P.Q., Nov. 23, 1967 "Vernissage à la Caisse Populaire Ste-Madeleine-Sophie"

St. Catharines Standard, Ont., Aug. 3, 1972 "He Enjoys Best Of Two Worlds Raymond Picard — The Travelling Painter"

La Parole, Drummondville, P.Q., Jan. 11, 1978 (photo of Picard with work)

PICARD, Roger

b.(c) 1934

He studied at the École des Beaux-Arts, Montreal (1957-61) and worked in an architects' office for several years. He is known for his non-figurative sculpture (iron, bronze, metal, wood), paintings, drawings, graphics and the making of jewellery, all of which he has exhibited at Galerie Lulu, Granby, P.Q. (1964, 65, 66, —). He lived in Verdun with his parents before moving to Granby. Represented by a sculpture opposite the Verdun City Hall, P.Q.

References

La Voix de l'Est, Granby, Que., Feb. 12, 1965 "Exposition de peintures et sculptures de Roger Picard"

Ibid, Feb. 17, 1965 "Le Vernissage Picard Nous Révèle Un Artiste Honnête"

PICARD, Roger (Cont'd)

Dimanche-Matin, Mtl., P.Q., July 10, 1960 "Sans argent ni emploi, un oeil au beurre noir, il a trouvé sa voie: sculpter des vieux arbres"
La Voix de l'Est, Mar. 24, 1964 "Exposition de peinture sur le thème 'Recherche'"
Ibid, Oct. 22, 1966 "Le peintre Roger Picard, conférencier au Richelieu, lundi"
Ibid, Oct. 19, 1966 "Dessins, peintures et bijoux se complètent chez M. Roger Picard"

PICHÉ, Reynald
b. 1929

Born at Rock Island, Eastern Townships, Quebec, he studied at the École des Beaux-Arts, Montreal, where he specialized in printmaking and sculpture. He held his first solo show at Collège Bourget and subsequent shows at Collège St. Thomas, École Normale Monseigneur Emard, Théâtre des Apprentis Sorciers. He apprenticed himself in ceramics with Gaëtan Beaudin and studied as well, Arts of the Cinema, Psychology and art teaching methods, taught at the seminary at Valleyfield and was Director of the art courses for children at Valleyfield. He held his first solo show, outside the colleges, at Galerie Libre, Montreal, in 1966 and held a number of subsequent solo shows up to 1974 when he exhibited at Société des artistes professionnels du Québec, Montreal, and when Virginia Nixon of *The Gazette* noted, "He makes his 'aluchromes' by an anodyzing process which opens up the 'pores' of the metal, so that they can receive colors applied both by brush and in a way which permits them to spread out and grow in a semi-organic manner. Then the pores are closed, sealing up the surface so that the colors are actually enclosed within the metal. The result is a surface that can withstand even outdoor conditions without losing its color — an interesting possibility for architectural use. Piché's works, sized and shaped like paintings, are in abstract patterns which often look like undersea corals or still-growing crystal forms. The colors range from bright to delicate with considerable modulation, marble-type patterns, and plays of evanescent veining like the skeletons of fragile corals. . . .The combination of the gentle fluid patterns with the material strikes one as unusual, as one is accustomed to associating aluminum with a streamlined look. But Piché has brought it off in a very promising way." His other solo shows include: Galerie Libre, Mtl. (1968); Galerie La Relève (1974); Galerie l'Art Français, Mtl. (1976); Galerie du Parc, Trois Rivières (1977); Carmen Lamanna Gallery, Toronto. His group shows include Les moins de trente ans (1959); La jeune peinture (1960); Le Service des Parcs de Montréal (1964); Montreal Chamber of Commerce (Eatons, Mtl. 1964); L'exposition des Concours Artistiques de la Province de Québec (1965); Travelling Exhibition of the National Gallery of Canada (1965-66). He is represented in the collections of the National Gallery of Canada and the University of Montreal. Lives at Valleyfield, P.Q.

References

Le Progrès, Valleyfield, P.Q., Mar. 9, 1966 "L'exposition Reynald Piché"
Montreal Star, Mtl., P.Q., Mar. 10, 1966 "Reynald Piché" (at Galerie Libre)
Le Devoir, Mtl., P.Q., Mar. 28, 1974 "Les aluchromies de Piché: à voir" par Pierre Vallières
Le Journal de Montréal, P.Q., July 11, 1974 "Un Artiste Montréalais Expose À Paris"
The Gazette, Mtl., P.Q., Mar. 30, 1974 "Art" by Virginia Nixon

PICHÉ, Reynald (Cont'd)

Canadian artists in exhibition, 1972-73, Roundstone, Tor., 1974, P. 170

L'Art au Québec depuis 1940, par Guy Robert, La Presse, 1973, P. 157-8

PICHER, Claude
b. 1927

Born in Quebec City, the son of Edouard Boisseau and Clémence Mathieu Picher, he took art classes at an early age under Jean Paul Lemieux. He attended the Séminaire de Québec (1939-43) and in 1941 won first prize for design in the children's drawing section at the Quebec Provincial Exhibition. He next attended the Séminaire Joliette (1943-45) and in 1942 won first prize for design in the adult section of the Quebec Provincial Exhibition and in 1943 took first prize for painting and second prize for design. After his general education was completed, he entered the École des Beaux-Arts, Quebec, where he studied under Jean Paul Lemieux (1945-46) and he again won second prize this time for painting at the Q.P.E. in 1945. In 1946 he won first prize for painting (adult) at the Q.P.E. and for the next two years studied on his own (1946-47). At the age of nineteen four of his paintings were acquired by the Quebec Provincial Museum following his solo show at the Palais Montcalm in Quebec City in 1947. With the aid of a Quebec government bursary (1948-49, 1949-50) for study in Europe, and additional assistance from the French government (1948-49), he studied at the École Nationale Supérieure des Beaux-Arts, Paris, where he learned wood engraving under Demeter Galanis then returned to North America and studied painting under Julian Levi at the New School of Social Research in New York City (accompanied by his wife); studied further in Paris at L'École du Louvre in the latter part of 1948, and 1949 for General Art History under Coche de La Ferté; History of the Far East under Philippe Stern; History of Modern Art under Jean Cassou and study at Saint-Rémy de Province, France, with Albert Gleizes (1949-50). He returned to Canada in 1950 to begin various activities including a series of talks at the Quebec Provincial Museum in the fall of that year and he continued employment with the Museum in the presentation of exhibitions (1950-54) then as Director of Exhibitions (1951-58). He was active as well with painting and various research projects for the Province of Quebec including restoration work on historic sites and monuments. He won the Elizabeth T. Greenshields Memorial Foundation bursary for personal research in painting (1955-56). By 1957 he had enough paintings to present his fifth solo show at Galerie La Boutique in Quebec City where his work was well received and recognized as a significant break from the traditional Quebec painting as described by the *Chronicle-Telegraph* as follows, "A completely fresh approach to the problem of painting Quebec City may be currently seen in an art display at the Galerie de la Boutique. . . .Here, the traditional azure skies and blue tinted snow and bright red calèche and handsome horses are not to be seen. In their places are individual entities of art, which are not so concerned with these things as they are with a study of spatial division, a completely controlled sense of color, and, in general, interpretation and not photography. . . .Subjects vary from studies of roof tops to ducks to still lives to cubist abstractions. This is rather different from displays which have been seen in Quebec for some time now. An excellent variety of mood is revealed in these works. Picher can be gentle and Picher can be hard. One of the gentler pictures here is 'Le Séminaire,' which possesses an amost dreamlike quality. One of the more violent pictures is 'Les Toits dans la Nuit.' Dark areas are contrasted against very light ones." In 1957 and 1958 he studied in U.S.A. museums and in Mexico on a scholarship from the Catherwood Foundation awarded by Bryn Mawr University, Pa. He moved to national prominence as a painter in the 1960's as he held more solo shows in Toronto and was one of the artists included in *Canada Art's* survey of the work of young Canadian artists and also among those artists singled out by Guy Viau in his *Modern Painting in French Canada* in these words, "The landscapes of Claude Picher. . .are drained of colour: they show the city and its roofs, the river and its ice-floes, the forest and its glades, under snow or at night; and consequently they feature white, grey, and black almost exclusively. There is nothing drab or austere about them, however, because they are painted with passionate feeling. Picher makes one think of a great landowner who imposes on his domain, both man and beast, an inflexible authority, a severity which conceals real tenderness. The brutal and savage in him is exactly that part which is profoundly attuned to the elements — to the winds, the snow, space, and night. Yet it is surprising to see that this fierce enemy of abstract art has a strong tendency toward abstraction in many of his paintings, which is barely veiled by a title and by obscure allusions to nature." Picher had been influenced to a certain extent by the work of Van Gogh, Goya and from the musical works of Ludwig Van Beethoven, the power of which he attempted to transfer into his own works. Using as his media, oils and gouache, he made these forceful and original statements. From about 1964, as can be seen in his "Hiver canadien ensoleillé" reproduced in Irénée Lemieux's *Artistes du Québec* (1974), there was more colour in his work. Recognized as an important painter in Quebec his work was acquired by public galleries and by private collectors in significant numbers as can be found in the O.J. Firestone collection in Ottawa now part of the Ontario Heritage Foundation. While active as a painter he was equally active as an art critic and wrote for *Arts et pensée*, *Vie des arts*, *Revue des arts et lettres* and appeared on television programmes and wrote regular columns in *L'Evénement-Journal* and *Le Soleil*, also he was on the editorial staff of *Vie des arts* and was Quebec correspondent for *Canadian Art*. His activities did not end there as he appeared on C.B.C.'s *Arts et Pensée* and he was liaison officer for the Montreal Museum of Fine Arts, Hamilton Art Gallery (Ont.); London Public Library and Art Museum (Ont.); Willistead Library and Art Gallery (Ont.); Detroit Institute of Arts (Mich., U.S.A.); and the National Gallery of Canada serving as assistant curator there for a year (1963-64). His solo and two-man shows include: Palais Montcalm, Que. (1947); L'Atelier, Quebec (1952); Galerie Agnès Lefort, Mtl. (1955); Galerie La Boutique, Que. (1957, 1959 — two-man) Montreal Museum of Fine Arts (1958; 1964 — two-man); Here and Now Gallery, Tor. (1960); Galerie Zanettin, Que. (1960, 1964, 1967); Roberts Gallery, Tor. (1962, 1964); Agnes Etherington Art Gallery, Kingston, Ont. (1961 — two-man); Musée de Québec, Que. (1967); Galerie de la Grande Palace, Rimouski, P.Q. (1971); Galerie Michel de Kerdour, Que. (1974); Walter Klinkhoff Gallery, Mtl. (1977). He participated in many group exhibitions including those organized by the National Gallery of Canada: 2nd Biennial of Canadian Painting (1957); 2nd Paris International Biennial, Paris, France (1962); 5th Canadian Biennial of Painting, Commonwealth Inst., Lond., Eng.

PICHER, Claude (Cont'd)

(1963); 4th Biennial of Canadian Art (1961); 6th Biennial of Canadian Painting (1965). He is represented in the following public collections: National Gallery of Canada (Ottawa); Musée de Québec (Quebec City); Laval University Art Gallery (Quebec City); Art Gallery of Ontario (Tor.); Agnes Etherington Art Gallery (Kingston, Ont.); Canadian Embassies; American Embassy in Paris and in many private collections in Canada, United States, France and England. Lives in Quebec City.

References

L'Action, Quebec, Mar. 28, 1947 "Les Oeuvres du peintre Claude Picher au Musée De La Province" (photo of works)

Le Soleil, Quebec, Mar. 29, 1947 "Des tableaux de C. Picher au Musée"

Montreal Star, Mtl., Apr. 2, 1947 "Museum Procures Youth's Paintings"

The Gazette, Mtl., Apr. 5, 1947 "Claude Picher Works Acquired by Museum"

L'Evénement, Quebec, Oct. 24, 1952 "Exposition de peinture canadienne selon la conception de C. Picher" par P.-M.L.

The Gazette, Mtl., Apr. 6, 1956 "Quebec Painter Wins Oils Prize"

La Patrie, Mtl., Feb. 17, 1957 "Personnalité de Québec Le peintre Claude Picher"

Chronicle-Telegraph, Quebec, Apr. 5, 1957 "Fresh Approach In City Scenes"

L'Evénement, Quebec, Apr. 5, 1957 "Claude Picher Expose 'A La Boutique'" (photo and caption)

Le Soleil, Quebec, Apr. 5, 1957 "Exposition De Claude Picher A La Boutique" (photo and caption)

La Patrie, Mtl., Apr. 14, 1957 "Claude Picher" par Claire-P. Gagnon (two photos of work — one with artist)

La Presse, Mtl., Feb. 27, 1958 "Deux artistes de Québec exposeront au Musée dès demain"

Ibid, Mar. 1, 1958 (photos of two paintings and review of Musée des Beaux-Arts show)

Ibid, Mar. 28, 1958 "3 nominations à la Galerie Nationale: un nouveau service"

L'Evénement, Quebec, Jan. 21, 1959 "Les peintres Soucy et Picher exposent à La Boutique" par Guy Tremblay

Le Soleil, Québec, Jan. 23, 1959 "Deux Québécois exposent à la Boutique"

Chronicle-Telegraph, Que., Jan. 23, 1959 "Current Art Show Presents Pair of Opposite Styles" by S.S.

The Gazette, Mtl., Feb. 6, 1960 "Art — Vitality"

Globe & Mail, Tor., Feb. 13, 1960 "Art and Artists — Keep Eye on Quebec City Artists" by Pearl McCarthy

Le Soleil, Quebec, Dec. 3, 1960 "Les récentes toiles de Claude Picher: Vertige" par Paule France Dufaux

Chronicle-Telegraph, Quebec, Dec. 3, 1960 "Elemental Simplicity Keynote Of Picher Work" by R.T.

L'Evénement, Quebec, Dec. 3, 1960 "L'exposition de Cl. Picher: une transformation 'bouleversante'" par Paule France Dufaux

Le Soleil, Quebec, July 15, 1961 "Claude Picher: premier Québécois à participer à la Biennale de Paris" par Paule France Dufaux

Globe & Mail, Tor., Ont., Feb. 17, 1962 "Picher Art Canada's Gain" by Pearl McCarthy

Toronto Star, Tor., Ont., Feb. 24, 1962 "Picher" (a warm review)

Le Soleil, Quebec, Mar. 3, 1962 "Arts — Picher Peintre du paysage canadien" par Paule France Dufaux

Ibid, Mar. 6, 1962 "Bourse du Conseil des Arts au peintre Claude Picher"

L'Action Catholique, Quebec, Mar. 13, 1962 "Le peintre québécois Claude Picher"

L'Evénement, Quebec, Mar. 2, 1963 "Claude Picher nommé conservateur adjoint au Musée de la Province"

Chronicle-Telegraph, Quebec, Jan. 24, 1964 "Mural Shows Quebec in 1812" (mural in oils and gold leaf for Claridge apartments)

Ibid, Feb. 29, 1964 "Sombre and Powerful Art Compels Beholder To Look" by P.C.

PICHER, Claude (Cont'd)

Toronto Daily Star, Tor., Ont., Mar. 14, 1964 "Art and Artists" by Elizabeth Kilbourn

Globe & Mail, Tor., Ont., Mar. 14, 1964 "Some Pichers Garish; Most bold and Surging" by Robin Green

The Gazette, Mtl., P.Q., Apr. 11, 1964 "Gallery XII" (two-man show at Mtl. Mus. F.A.)

Books, Magazines, Catalogues

Second Biennial Exhibition of Canadian Art, 1957, NGC, Ottawa, 1957, No. 26

The Arts in Canada, Ed. Malcolm Ross, Macmillan Co. of Can. Ltd., 1958, P. 30

NGC Catalogue, Vol. 3, Can. School by R.H. Hubbard, NGC/Univ. Tor. Press, 1960, P. 249

Canadian Art, Vol. 18, No. 1, 1961 "A Survey of the work of 24 young Canadian artists" by Robert Fulford (photos by Philip Pocock) P. 38-9

Fifth Biennial Exhibition of Canadian Painting, 1963, NGC, Ottawa, 1963 P. 27

Modern Painting in French Canada by Guy Viau, Dept. Cultural Affairs, Quebec, 1967, P. 38-9

Permanent Collection, Agnes Etherington Art Centre by Frances K. Smith Queen's Univ., Kingston, Ont., 1968, P. 111

Art Gallery of Ontario, the Canadian collection by Helen Pepall Bradfield, McGraw-Hill Co. of Can. Ltd., Tor., 1970, P. 377

Creative Canada, Volume Two, McPherson Lib. Univ. of Victoria/Univ. Tor. Press, Tor., 1972, P. 220-1

L'Art au Québec depuis 1940 par Guy Robert, La Presse, Mtl., 1973, P. 39, 92, 104, 105, 132, 187, 189

Artistes du Québec par Irénée Lemieux, Editions Irénée Lemieux, Quebec, P.Q., 1974, 202-3

Canadian Art at Auction, 1968-1975 by Geoffrey Joyner, Sotheby & Co. (Can.) Ltd., Tor., 1975, P. 157

L'Information médicale et paramédicale, Mtl., 4 Jan., 1977 "Claude Picher, peintre de Québec et de la Gaspésie"

Firestone Art Collection by O.J. Firestone, McGraw-Hill Ryerson Ltd., Tor., 1978, P. 109, 110, 111

PICHER, Joseph

18..-1942

Born at St. Sophie, Quebec, he studied art at the École des Beaux-Arts, Quebec and also in Boston and New York. He became a close collaborator to Louis-Philippe Hébert, and together they designed the Monument of Monsignor Laval at Quebec; and in Montreal they worked together on the monument of Edward VII at Phillip's Square and the Chenier monument on Viger Square. He was in charge of construction operations at the time of the building of the Criminal Court edifice on Notre Dame Street East, Montreal. In 1942 he was killed by a runaway trailer while taking his daily walk. He was a prominent member of the Knights of Columbus, and served as an alderman for the City of Outremont from 1907 to 1919. He was survived by his wife the former Marie Louise duMaine; eight sons, duMaine, Lupien, George, Vincent, Louis, Philippe, Paul and François and three daughters, Rev. Sister Ste. Gertrude du Sauveur, Rev. Sister Marthe of Liberien, and Mrs. Edgar Tourangeau.

Reference

The Montreal Standard, Mar. 21, 1942 "Sculptor Joseph Picher Killed by Runaway Trailer"

PICHET, Pierre
b.(c) 1929

He attended St. Jerome College, Montreal; École Supérieur Chomedy de Maisonneuve; then studied five years at the École des Beaux-Arts, Montreal where he also received his diploma for teaching drawing. Following his graduation he joined the firm of H.J. Doran, Montreal, as draftsman and in the course of his employment drew up plans for Camp Gagetown for the Canadian government. He did his work so well that the government hired him to complete detailed drawings for the camp. He continued his art activity in his spare time and before leaving H.J. Doran, he completed with another employee J. Lauda, a large painting seventeen feet long (in two parts) for the foyer of the Doran office depicting six leading natural resources of Canada. Pichet works on his art in his free time.

Reference
The Montreal Star, P.Q. Aug. 29, 1955 "Montrealer's Painting Draws Art Plaudits"

PICHET, Roland
b. 1936

Born in Verdun, Quebec, he started working after school at the age of eleven to help make ends meet. He then left high school and before he was eighteen was working full time as a busboy, messenger and third chef while attending the École des Beaux-Arts, four nights a week for seven years. He studied painting, drawing and modelling and worked for a year and a half with painter Alfredo Monros. By 1960 his painting was for the most part influenced by the auto-matists who were followers of Paul Emile Borduas. At the Beaux-Arts he met Albert Dumouchel and became especially interested in printmaking and studied under Dumouchel for the next three years. His outstanding work in graphics was awarded two prizes in 1962; one from the Salon of Young Painters and the other from the Quebec Provincial exhibit. He became Dumouchel's assistant and the following year (1963) he was awarded a Canada Council grant for study in Paris for six months. During this period Pichet was gaining national and international recognition in graphics by his participation in important exhibitions like the 5th and 6th Biennials of Graphics in Ljubljana, Yugoslavia (1963, 1965) and 2nd Biennial of Graphics at Santiago, Chile (1965); 1st Biennial of Graphics, Cracow, Poland (1966) and others. He received a Canada Council grant to work in London, England (1966) covering the period 1967-68 when he studied at the Slade School of Art. Moving from the automatist influence in painting he worked in the hard edge style. During his visit to England he produced his zig-zag series (sharply defined colour bands forming a zig-zag pattern on the canvas surface) resulting in Optic Art. Returning to Canada in 1968 he first developed painting with rigid horizontal stripes in pinks, greys, pastel colours but not being satisfied with his results he destroyed many of his works. He also spent some time in New York City and there discovered that Kenneth Noland was doing on a twenty foot scale what he himself had planned to do on five by six foot canvases. Returning home he began doing work which he called "horizontals". In 1971 he had an especially busy year in his new studio of two thousand square feet located in a Montreal factory warehouse on St. Lawrence Boulevard. For twelve months he taught, painted, produced forty prints for a book *Miscible* by poet Marie F. Herbert; prepared an exhibition and also organized another show for teachers of the Université du Québec. He had developed such a frantic pace that when he made a chance discovery of a house hidden away in the forest on top of Mount Belvedere at Piedmont, he fell in love with the place, bought it and moved in with his wife. From this new rural environment he developed a whole new lifestyle. Instead of working through the night he found himself retiring early and working days. His isolation gave him more time and peace to concentrate on his work, and his work was now inspired by the mountain and its changes through the seasons. There he created his Laurentian Suite described by Terry Kirkman in *The Montreal Star* as follows, "Now, though the slightly inter-penetrating superbly harmonized tones are in a spectrum provided by nature, there are wide fields of 'sky', diverging lines that could be mountain ridges. They are still serene, yet more alive — reflections of the many moods of the country. As color fields that could also be considered windows to his new world they possibly reflect, too, his changed working hours." Pichet has been active as an illustrator for books including the following: *L'eau et la pierre* by Guy Robert (1964); *Apatride* by Michel Beaulieu (1966); *Mère* by Michel Beaulieu (1966); *Sous-Jacences* by Michel Beaulieu (1970); *Miscible* by Marie Hébert (1971); *Hommage à Dumouchel* (1972); *Elégie pour l'épouse En-Allée* by Alfred Desroches (1973); *Automne* by Alfred Desroches (1973). Following his return from Europe he was visited in his St. Sauveur studio by Claude Gadoury a local grocer who with his half-brother, J.M. Robillard, a partner in the grocery store, became Pichet's patrons. They had collected art for several years and upon their retirement from the grocery business they established *L'Apogée* gallery where Pichet's work has been featured on a regular basis. His solo shows include: Maison des étudiants canadiens, Paris (1966); Galerie St.-Laurent, Bruxelles, Belgium (1966); Galerie Libre, Mtl. (1966); Galerie 1640, Mtl. (1966); Carmen Lamanna Gallery, Tor. (1967); Richard Demarco Gallery, Edinburgh, Scot. (1968); Doris Pascal, Tor. (1970 — two-man); Galerie L'Apogée, St. Sauveur des Monts, P.Q. (1970, 71, 72, 73, 74, 75, 76); Galerie de l'Etable, Mtl. (1971); Galerie Bernard Desroches, Mtl. (1977). His recent work was a numbered portfolio of eleven silkscreens entitled *Blues pour un piquet de clôture* with texts by Beaulieu, Brossard, Carrier, Chamberland, Charlebois, Deschamps, Dor, Duguay, Royer and Vigneault, which was shown at L'Apogée in 1976. His work is also on view at Galerie Sussex, Ottawa, which opened in 1979. He is represented in the following public collections: Winnipeg Art Gallery, Man.; Art Gallery of Ontario, Tor.; University of Toronto; Metro Toronto Library; Queen's University, Kingston, Ont.; National Gallery of Canada, Ottawa; University of Ottawa, Ont.; Montreal Museum of Fine Arts, Mtl.; Musée d'art contemporain, Mtl.; Library, École des Beaux-Arts, Mtl.; Université de Montréal; Montreal Municipal Library; Redpath Library, McGill University, Mtl.; Concordia University, Mtl.; Université du Québec, Mtl.; Musée de la Province de Québec, Quebec; Bibliothèque nationale du Québec, Quebec; Museum of Modern Art, New York City, U.S.A.; Art Institute of Chicago, Ill., U.S.A.; British Museum, London, Eng.; Gloucestershire Collection, Eng.; Stedelijk Museum, Amsterdam, Holland; Kunsthaus, Zurich, Switzerland; Museum of Modern Art, Ljubljana, Yugoslavia; Museum of Contemporary Art, Skipje, Yugoslavia. He lives at Piedmont near Saint-Sauveur-des-Monts, Quebec, about ten miles outside Montreal.

PICHET, Roland (Cont'd)

References

Le Quartier Latin, Sept. 24, 1962 "Un Jeune Graveur" par Robert MacKay
École de Montréal par Guy Robert, Editions du Centre de Psychologie et Pédagogie, Mtl., 1964, P. 26, 69, 70
Le Devoir, Mtl., P.Q., Oct. 22, 1966 "Roland Pichet" (show at Galerie Libre)
Canadian Water Colours, Drawings and Prints, 1966, NGC, Ottawa, 1966, No. 101
Globe & Mail, Tor., Ont., Feb. 10, 1967 "Carmen Lamanna Gallery"
Ibid, May 30, 1970 "Gallery Pascal" (Pichet & Boyaner)
Montreal Star, Mtl., P.Q. Aug. 7, 1971 "Art — The arts and stripes of the Laurentians" by Terry Kirkman
The Gazette, Mtl., P.Q., Aug. 9, 1973 "'A bum' to his father, artist Pichet has 'arrived'" by Betty Shapiro
L'Art au Québec, depuis 1940 par Guy Robert, La Presse, Mtl., 1973, P. 32, *154*, 156, 313, 329, 330, *331*, 334
NGC Info. Forms, 1964, 1970
Books Illustrated by Pichet
L'eau et la pierre, poems by Guy Robert, Editions Robert, Mtl., 1964 (seven lithos)
Apatride, poems by Michel Beaulieu, Editions Esterel, Mtl., 1966 (ten intaglios)
Mère, poems by Michel Beaulieu, Editions Esterel, Mtl., 1966 (wood engravings)
Sous-Jacences, poems by Michel Beaulieu, Ed. Esterel, Mtl., 1970 (seriographs)
Miscible, poems by Marie Hébert, Editions du Songe, 1971
Hommage à Dumouchel, Editions P.U.Q., 1972
Elégie pour l'épouse En-Allée by Alfred Desroches, Editions M. Nantel, 1973
Automne by Alfred Desroches, Editions M. Nantel, 1973
Blues pour un piquet de clôture (portfolio) texts by ten authors, Editions du Songe, 1976

PICHÉ-WHISSEL, Aline-Marie Blanche Marguerite
b. 1919

Born in Trois-Rivières, Quebec, she attended the Collège Marie de l'Incarnation where she received her elementary and high school education (1927-37); and with Géraldine Bourbeau in Trois-Rivières (1943); evening courses at the École des Beaux-Arts, Montréal (1944-45) where she studied under Suzanne Duquet. In 1945 she was awarded an Honourable Mention at the Grand Prix de la Province de Québec and took part in the group show of winners at the University of Montreal. She was a teacher of ballet at Trois-Rivières (1946-47); exhibited with "Canadian Women Artists" which toured principal cities in Canada and at the Riverside Museum, New York (1947). She studied stained glass two years at the Beaux-Arts in Quebec under Marius Plamondon (1947-48) and won First Prize in the Stained Glass Section at the Grand Prix de la Province (1948). She studied ceramics at the Institut de technologie, Trois-Rivières (1959-61) also sculpture at the Art Centre at Trois-Rivières (1964). The following year she undertook a major project of stained glass for the chapel of the Grand Séminaire at Trois-Rivières (1965). She then taught plastic arts at Trois-Rivières (1965-69) and founded a workshop for creative education in 1969. She graduated in the field of plastic arts with her B.A. from the University of Quebec at Trois-Rivières (1971). Known for her work with stained glass, enamels, ceramics, enamel on leather and painting she held a solo show of her work in 1952 at Trois-Rivières and has participated in many group shows

PICHE-WHISSEL, Aline-Marie Blanche Marguerite (Cont'd)

including several in France, Haiti and cities in Quebec and Ontario. She married Percy Whissel, a forestry engineer in 1948.

References

Sélection du Reader's Digest, Juillet, 1949

Arts et Pensée, Juin, 1954 "Aline Piché-Wissell, Peintre et Verrier" par Yvon Thériault P. 153

Photo-Journal, 16 Aug. - 23 Feb., 1966 "Cinq peintres de la Mauricie" par Michelle Tisseyre

Le Nouvelliste, Trois-Rivières, Que., 2 Fev., 1966 "Artistes mauriciens à Montréal" par Thérèse Bernier

The Gazette, Mtl., 12 Fev., 1966 "Cinq Artistes de la Mauricie" by Rea Montbizon

Le Nouvelliste (undated) "Aline Piché révèle dans ses oeuvres une personnalité forte — Au Vernissage" par Y. Thériault

Ottawa Journal, Ont., June 8, 1976 "Imaginative Graffiti; Hungarian graphics" by W.Q. Ketchum

Le Nouvelliste, Nov. 24, 1976 "Aline Piché-Whissel expose à Paris" par Michelle Guerin

L'Art au Québec depuis 1940 par Guy Robert, La Presse, 1973, P. 351

NGC Info. Form rec'd Nov. 8, 1948

PICK, Kathy

A resident of Sandspit, Queen Charlotte Islands, B.C., and originally from Australia, she arrived in Canada in 1968. A nurse who studied painting with Ruth Harvey and Muriel Patterson and held a solo show of her acrylic paintings of seascapes, scenes along the Copper River, wildlife, lake scenes and other subjects at the Art Gallery, Museum Building, Prince Rupert, B.C.

Reference

Prince Rupert News, B.C., Nov. 29, 1973 (photo and text)

PICKEL, Patricia
b. 1931

Born in New Jersey, U.S.A. she studied fine arts at Skidmore College. Coming to Montreal in 1952 she entered McGill University where she studied with John Lyman and Gordon Webber receiving her B.F.A. in 1953. She studied painting with John Fox for many years then established her own studio. During her exhibit at Wallack Galleries, Ottawa, an *Ottawa Citizen* reviewer noted, "Despite the calculated emotional splashes of color, Pickel's art is soothing and liveable. The transparent colors are pleasantly cohesive — blues, greys, blacks and tans with just a touch of salmon pink for contrast. . . .The artist also has a flair for composition, balancing large solid expanses with dribbled, splashed, calligraphy-like areas. Highlights are the bold paintings, Vierge and Vaton, both quite a departure from the soft, pastel works that comprise the majority of her display." She has also shown at Galerie Gilles Corbeil, Montreal.

PICKEL, Patricia (Cont'd)

References

Ottawa Journal, Ont., Mar. 25, 1976 "Airy quality to abstracts" by W.Q. Ketchum
Ottawa Citizen, Ont., Apr. 3, 1976 "Wallack Galleries"

PICKERING, Bernard
b. 1903

Born in Toronto, Ontario, he studied art at Central Technical School, Toronto and at the Ontario College of Art under Emanuel Hahn and Arthur Lismer and while at the College won a scholarship and poster competition. He has exhibited with the Royal Canadian Academy and the Ontario Society of Artists.

Reference

NGC Info. Form rec'd Sept. 4, 1956

PICKERING, David

A Kingston, Ontario, artist who exhibited his sculpture at the Agnes Etherington Art Centre Spring Exhibition of 1974.

Reference

Kingston Whig-Standard, Ont., Mar. 26, 1974

PICKERING, Jack
b. 1928

A Saskatchewan artist, his great grandfather was a British romanticist painter and his grandfather, a cartoonist and woodcarver, taught him to sketch, carve on apple box ends and to paint in oils. Jack farmed for ten years while continuing his interest in art. He became a storekeeper in Milestone then finally decided to study commercial art through the Famous Artists correspondence course. Following his completion of the course he was hired by a Regina printing firm as a commercial artist. After five years with the printing firm he free-lanced for a year then joined the staff of the Museum of Natural History in Regina. A wildlife painter he enjoys spending a period of each summer camping in some part of Saskatchewan with his wife and five children. His subjects include coyotes, rabbits, porcupines and landscapes. He uses mainly acrylics with a water colour technique that gives his landscapes a softness. One of his projects was to record the changing face of Saskatchewan through the seasons by doing a painting each day of the year. He has exhibited his work at the Saskatchewan Museum of Natural History and the Saskatoon Public Library gallery.

PICKERING, Jack (Cont'd)

References

Star Phoenix, Saskatoon, Sask., Oct. 29, 1976 "Accent on art with Nancy Russell — More than a grain elevator"

Leader-Post, Regina, Sask., Nov. 30, 1971 "Display of museum artists' works shows love of wildlife" by Harvey Linnen

PICKERSGILL, Peter (Pic)
b. 1945

Born in Ottawa, Ontario, the son of John Whitney Pickersgill (former Federal Cabinet Minister) and Margaret Beattie, he received his early education in Ottawa where he attended Lisgar Collegiate. He then studied architecture at the University of British Columbia graduating in 1972. No doubt he was stimulated politically by his father's involvement in politics which combined with his interest in drawing led to his activity in caricature. He did work for the *Montreal Star* and the *Vancouver Sun* and when he moved to Ottawa in 1972 he became back up cartoonist to Rusins of the editorial page of the *Ottawa Citizen*. A free-lance cartoonist his work also appeared in the *Ottawa Journal, Guardian* of London, *Saturday Night, Time,* and *Financial Post.* He experimented with animation and for a time contributed to the production of daily political animated cartoons for Global Television and later twice weekly on local evening news shows coast to coast on CBC. In 1974 a solo show of his political and social cartoons was held at Gallery 93 in Ottawa when Kathleen Walker of the *Ottawa Citizen* noted, "Once upon a time, PIC was interested in architecture and even went so far as to become a qualified architect. But somewhere along the line (probably because he is the son of Jack Pickersgill and therefore had a steady diet of politics at the dinner table), he decided to give cartooning a try. And I'm rather glad he did. PIC is a good draftsman. He also dreams up some good 'punch lines'. . .is at his best when he follows in the tradition of Aislin and the marvellously subtle caricaturist from the New York Review of Books, David Levine." With Gordon Henderson he produced in 1979 the book *Sandy Mackenzie, Why Look So Glum?,* a colourful and entertaining book about Canadian prime ministers with verses by Henderson and illustrations by himself. He is working free-lance in architectural design specializing in solar-heated domestic architecture. He married Lisa Young in 1968 and they live in the greater Ottawa area at Pointe Gatineau, Quebec. They spend summers at Salvage, Newfoundland.

References

Ottawa Citizen, Ont., Nov. 30, 1974 "Around the galleries" by Kathleen Walker

The Hecklers, A History of Canadian Political Cartooning and a Cartoonists' History of Canada by Peter Desbarats and Terry Mosher, M. & S., Tor., 1979, P. 159, 247

Sandy MacKenzie, Why Look So Glum?, Rhymes and Pictures about our Prime Ministers, Verses by Gordon Henderson and Illustrations by PIC, Deneau & Greenberg Publishers Ltd., Ottawa, 1979

PICKETT, Frederick Albert
1868-1904

Born at Oak Point, N.B., where his father, the Rev. David Wetmore Pickett, was an Anglican church minister. The ninth child in a family of ten he showed an early interest in drawing, colour and form. He made his own colours from powder scraped from coloured pebbles and stones along Oak Point beach, then he mixed them with water to make his primitive paints. Later in life he became a partner in the engraving firm of F.C. Wesley and Company in Saint John while he also gave lessons and produced illustrations for magazines. Around 1900 he went to the United States where he worked for a newspaper in New York City and painted miniature portraits in water colour on ivory working as well in Providence and Newport (R.I.). One of his favourite subjects was children. He rose to considerable prominence as a portrait painter and was praised by the noted portraitist John Singer Sargent. Throughout his life he suffered from repeated attacks of sciatica and rheumatism and further success was curtailed by his illness. His work was executed so delicately that it is difficult to detect the brush strokes in the paintings. In the winter of 1903-4 he contracted pneumonia and shortly afterwards died at Newport, R.I., and was buried in the church yard beside St. Paul's Church, Oak Point at his birthplace. In 1963 an exhibition of his work was organized by his relatives and held in the Main Hall of the New Brunswick Museum. Biographical details were provided by his niece Miss Beatrice Welling of London, Ontario. A number of his works are owned by Ed. and Lorraine Pickett of Salisbury, New Brunswick, part of their greater collection of antiques housed in a special addition to their home. They have more than 100 pieces of Frederick Pickett's works including water colours, charcoals, pen drawings and engravings. Frederick Pickett is represented as well in the New Brunswick Museum, Saint John, and also a museum in Hampton (probably Kings County Museum), N.B., and elswehere.

References

St. John Evening Times-Globe, N.B., Sept. 7, 1963 "Museum To Exhibit Famous Miniatures"
Moncton Transcript, N.B., Oct. 1, 1977 "Salisbury couple working on unique home-museum" by George Taylor

PICKETTS, Marcia
b. 1928

Born in Asquith, Saskatchewan, she studied painting techniques with Glyde and Taubes at the Banff School of Fine Arts. In 1967 she completed an historical mural (two paintings back to back each 4' × 8') of scenes entitled "Riverboat Northcote" and the "Dirty Thirties" both on permanent display at Elbow Park near the Saskatchewan River Dam. When she retired from operating a dress shop in North Battleford she became more actively involved in the visual arts. She taught weaving and painting and spent three years as assistant at the North Battleford Arts Centre. She began her weaving around 1972 first on a small Salish loom then in 1975 on a larger loom which can produce weavings up to 3 × 7 feet. Viewing her weaving in 1977 Lora Burke of the *Leader-Post* in Regina noted, "Ms. Picketts combines traditional techniques, both European and Salish, with a contemporary flair for imaginative experimentation. The result is an interesting and colorful show with works ranging from pictorial pieces to the abstract. Some hangings verge on the three-

PICKETTS, Marcia (Cont'd)

dimensional with tufts and tassels of yarn or with off-loom weaving super-imposed on the basic design. . . .Ms. Picketts incorporates all sorts of materials into her work. . . .A hanging called Wheels combines 26 different yarns in Rya knots with the colors radiating out from the centre. The brightly-colored Fighting Cocks uses phentex and polypropolene." Her solo shows include those at the Richmond Art Centre, Richmond, B.C. (1972); the SPC, Gallery on the Roof, Regina (1977) and she has exhibited her paintings in juried shows in Saskatchewan. A Charter member of the North Battleford Art Club (former Pres.), she lives in North Battleford, Sask.

References

Star-Phoenix, Saskatoon, Sask., Apr. 27, 1949 (photo of her painting "Blue Monday")

News-Optimist, North Battleford, Sask., Aug. 1, 1967 "Art Notes — Marcia Picketts Commissioned To Paint Mural For Elbow Park"

Leader Post, Regina, Sask., Nov. 18, 1977 "Weaving exhibit colorful" by Lora Burke

Catalogue sheet — "Marcia Picketts — Weaving" at the Saskatchewan Power Corporation, Gallery on the Roof, Regina

PICOTTE, Michel
b. 1947

Born in Montreal, he studied at the École des Beaux-Arts and at the University of Quebec where he obtained his D.E.C. in Plastic Arts in 1971. He is known especially for his calm, almost meditative linear painting and has experimented with the action of non-complementary colours and the impact of the 3rd dimension of the eye of the viewer. He mounted pictures with false frames to bring painting and sculpture together in a happy synthesis. These paintings were abstractions composed of horizontal lines bathed in restrained colours. He also does realistic allusions flooded with bright metallic colour. He won the first provincial prize for painting in 1974. He has exhibited in solo shows including one at Galerie Claude Luce, Montreal, in 1977.

References

Le Devoir, Mtl., Que., Oct. 15, 1977 "Un entretien avec Michel Picotte — L'art est-il devenu une science?" par Jean-Claude Leblond

Le Journal de Montréal, Quebec, P.Q., Feb. 18, 1977

Galerie D'Art Claude Luce — biographical information included in communiqué

PIDDINGTON, Helen Vivian
b. 1931

Born in Victoria, B.C., the daughter of Mr. and Mrs. A.G. Piddington, she attended the University of British Columbia where she graduated with her B.A. in anthropology in 1952. Subsequently she attended the Slade School of Fine Arts, London, England, where she studied wood carving and drawing with F.W. McWilliam (1952-53); Central School of Arts and Crafts, London, for wood-cuts with Gertrude Hermes (1953-54); lived in Ottawa and worked for the Arctic Division of Northern Affairs of Canada when she conducted research

PIDDINGTON, Helen Vivian (Cont'd)

for ten months at Fort Chimo on the history of women's crafts in the Arctic and studied life drawing at the Ottawa Municipal Art Centre with Gerald Trottier (1955-58); in Vancouver she followed a self study course in painting receiving criticism and encouragement from B.C. Binning (1958-60); then back to France to the École Nationale Supérieure de Beaux-Arts, Paris for lithography with P.E. Clairin (1960-62); Atelier 17 Paris, for etching with S.W. Hayter (1963-65). Sometimes in order to make ends meet she taught English and worked for Air France. She was aided in her studies by awards, prizes and scholarships as follows: Canada Council Arts Scholarship to study etching (1962-63); Leon & Thea Koerner Foundation grant (1963-64, 1964-65); Canada Council Arts Award for research in coloured etching (1967). Viewing her work in 1972 Joan Lowndes of the *Vancouver Sun* noted, "A two-month sailing trip last September to the Queen Charlotte Islands has wrought a radical change in the prints of Helen Piddington. Seduced by the coast scenery, she has relinquished the abstract idiom for lyrical seascapes. This should not be interpreted as a definitive conversion to representationalism. Some abstractions remain, and an artist should be free to move from one zone to another, or to rest midway in abstracted but recognizable forms if he so chooses. What is important is that Helen Piddington brings to her more realistic subject matter all her mastery of craft, plus a fabulous new delicacy of color. . . .Her present show at the Priestlay Gallery has several reminders of her former imagery. These are boldly outlined shapes pressed right to the foreground, all their intricate textural effects perceived as in close-up. They suggest great rocks, almost menacing in their massive confrontation. . . .A lively group of some 20 small drawings provides source material for the prints. In impulsive line they record the wind-driven clouds and the rip of the tide. But in the prints the movement is stilled and the images distilled by memory. Whereas Piddington's work hitherto has been distinguished by wit, decorative opulence and dramatic impact, it now is permeated with an unsuspected tenderness. This feeling is conveyed chiefly by means of the color. The single plate monocolor etching, in which diverse inks are applied to a plate, has rarely yielded such evanescent results. . . .Despite the tendency of some prints to be too literal. . .this exhibition is a reminder of the high standard that Piddington maintains." Her solo shows include: George Loranger, Ottawa (1957); La Maison du Canada, Paris (1965); Montreal Museum of Fine Arts (1965); Dorothy Cameron Gallery, Tor. (1965); New Design Gallery, Van. (1965); Curwen Gallery, Lond., Eng. (1965); Greater Victoria Art Gallery, Vic., B.C. (1965); A.L. Lowe Gallery, New Orleans, USA (1966); Institute of Contemporary Art, Lond., Eng. (1967); Fleet Gallery, Wpg. (1967); Griffiths Gallery, Van. (1967); Gallery Pascal, Tor. (1967); Gallery 1640, Mtl. (1967); Print Gallery, Vict. (1968); Picture Framing Shop & Gal., Van. (1969); Gallery 1640, Mtl. (1970); Print Gallery, Vict. (1970); Wells Gallery, Ottawa (1970); Priestlay Gallery, Van. (1972); Gallery Pascal, Tor. (1972) and in many group shows including: 3rd and 4th Biennales de Paris (1963, 1965); 20th Salon Réalités Nouvelles at the Musée Municipal d'Art Moderne, Paris (1965); Canadian Printmaking Today, Dorothy Cameron Gallery, Tor. (1965); Salon D'Art Sacré 1965 at Musée Municipal d'Art Moderne, Paris (1965); Segunda Bienal Americana, Chile (1965); 1st Biennale de la Gravure, Cracov, Poland (1966); 4th International Triennale of coloured graphics, Grenchen, Switzerland (1967) and others since that time. She is represented in the following public collections: Grosvernor-

PIDDINGTON, Helen Vivian (Cont'd)

Laing, Van., B.C.; The Art Gallery of Greater Victoria, B.C.; University of Victoria, B.C.; Regina Public Library, Sask.; Norman Mackenzie Art Gallery, Regina, Sask.; Richardson Building, Wpg.; Winnipeg Art Gallery; Sarnia Public Art Gallery & Museum; Lambton College, Sarnia; London Public Library & Art Museum; Art Gallery of Ontario, Tor.; York University, Tor.; Erindale College, Mississauga; Scarborough University, Ont.; Imperial Life, Tor.; Toronto-Dominion Bank; Montreal Museum of Fine Arts, Mtl.; T. Eaton Co.; Canadian National Railway; Mount Allison University, Halifax, N.S.; Memorial University, St. John's, Nfld.; and elsewhere. She is represented in many private collections in many countries of the Western World. Lives in Victoria, B.C.

References

> *Montreal Star*, Mtl., Que., Oct. 6, 1974 "Canadian Artist's View — 'Paris Is for Hermitesses'" by Lisa Balfour
>
> *Toronto Daily Star*, Ont., June 10, 1965 "Printmaker calls her art 'stately, intoxicating dance'" by Gail Dexter
>
> *Victoria Times*, B.C., Oct. 18, 1965 "City Artist Wins First Prize In Paris Show"
>
> *Vancouver Sun*, B.C., Dec. 1, 1967 "City Printmaker Displays Quality" by Ann Rosenberg
>
> *Vancouver Province*, B.C., Dec. 4, 1967 "The enriching of Helen Piddington — brings glowing colour to the scene" by Joan Lowndes
>
> *Victoria Times*, B.C., Nov. 30, 1968 "From Little Boxes Spiritual Safaris" by Ted Lindberg
>
> *Winnipeg Free Press*, Man., Apr. 28, 1969 "A Review by John W. Graham — Fare Better"
>
> *Vancouver Province*, B.C., Dec. 3, 1969 "Prints and Etchings — Piddington's new prints suggest massed energy" by Joan Lowndes
>
> *Ottawa Journal*, Ont., Oct. 2, 1970 "Graphics, Sculpture Show Opens"
>
> *Montreal Star*, Que., Feb. 17, 1970 "Art scene — Color etchings fascinating" by Robert Ayre
>
> *Vancouver Sun*, B.C., Jan. 5, 1972 "Coast scenery seduces artist" by Joan Lowndes
>
> *Winnipeg Free Press*, Man., May 16, 1972 "A Critique by John W. Graham — Coastline Etchings"
>
> NGC Info. Form dated Aug. 12, 1965, May 1, 1967; data June, 1970
>
> *Art Gallery of Ontario, the Canadian collection* by Helen Pepall Bradfield McGraw-Hill, Tor., 1970, P. 377

PIEKENBROCK, Henry

An Oshawa, Ontario, artist he has drawn a number of portraits and has been interested in designs for coins. The Lions Club of Oshawa has one of his works which is on display in the lobby of the Hotel Genosha of that city.

Reference

> *Oshawa Times*, Ont., Thursday, May 6, 1965 "City Artist Reproduces Columbus From Old Coin"

PIER, Roland

b. 1936

Born in France he came to Canada in 1965 and travelled throughout the country working in a variety of jobs including those at construction and gold

PIER, Roland (Cont'd)

mining sites as far north as Fort Nelson and Dawson City. Occasionally during this period he did cartoons of his fellow employees. Finally he settled in Montreal where he free-lanced for several publications. Then he joined the staff of *Le Journal de Montréal* as political cartoonist. This publication has now grown to be the largest French-language newspaper in North America. His work also appears in *Le Journal de Québec*. He is known for his incisive line style work.

References

> *Le Journal de Montréal*, Que., July 15, 1972 "Exposition à voir"
> *The Hecklers* by Peter Desbarats and Terry Mosher, M. & S., Tor., Ont., 1979, P. 188, 248

PIERCE, Gordon
1883-1975

The son of John Pierce and Harriet Lucinda Singleton, he married Ellen Bracken in 1915 and for many years farmed the old Pierce homestead in the Rideau Lake area. In 1950 after he had retired from farming to Newboro, Ontario, he started carving as a hobby and displayed his work at Brockville at the Carvers' Fair in 1973. His carvings were of teams of farm horses pulling wagons (the works being two feet in length) or horses pulling sleighs; police dogs; squirrels; paddlers in canoes; and a variety of other subjects including a Hindu priest in prayer. His favourite subject was horses because of the many years he had worked with the animals. He took orders for his carvings from tourists during the summers and always had the commissions ready for the following summer. He did many other remarkable things like building his own grandfather clock in which he crafted wooden gears, balance wheels and he even made the metal springs. It took him three winters to build the clock simply by taking a clock apart to see how it was made and using these parts as a design for his own hand-made parts which were reproduced exactly three times larger than the original. At the age of 92 he died in Kingston, Ontario and was survived at that time by his widow; a sister, Mrs. Charles Bass of Portland, Ontario and a brother Harold of Kingston, Ontario.

References

> *Athens Report*, Ont., March 13, 1969 "Craftsman from Newboro prefers carving horses" (article with photos)
> *Brockville Recorder and Times*, Ont., Feb. 18, 1975 "Gordon Pierce, Newboro carver, died in 92nd year" (photo and article)

PIERE-LÉON

A Montreal painter who held his first solo show of landscapes at Galerie Anette, Montreal.

Reference

> *Le Petit Journal*, Mtl., Que., "A la Galerie Anette" (photo with caption)

PIERRE, Isabelle

She studied drawing and painting at the École des Beaux-Arts, Montreal before devoting most of her time to singing. She did not however completely abandon the visual arts and from time to time accepted commissions for graphic art work and continued to draw for her own pleasure. She completed a number of charcoal sketches which she was to exhibit in the spring of 1970. Among her subjects are landscapes of the country around St. Jovite.

Reference
> *Nouvelles Illustrées*, Mtl., P.Q., Feb. 28, 1970 an article by Richard Constantineau

PIERRE, Marcel

Born in France he studied psychology of art at Collège de France under René Huyghe. He studied Baroque art in several European countries then he won a scholarship in the France-Quebec cultural exchange and in 1966 received a teacher's diploma and a specialized certificate from the École des Beaux-Arts in Quebec City. He taught plastic arts in Tilly-Sainte-Foy, Quebec. He was planning a study trip to Poland on a French government grant in 1967. He exhibited his work at Petit Champlain de Québec theatre in Quebec City with sculptor-ceramist Claude Desconteaux.

Reference
> *Le Soleil*, Québec, 10 June, 1967 "Les artistes québécois recherchent une forme d'art plutôt futuriste" par Louis Duvernois

PIESINA, Raymond
b. 1945

Born in Germany of Lithuanian parents, he came to Canada at an early age. He studied at the École des Beaux-Arts, Montreal (1963-67) while free-lancing as a graphic designer. In 1966 he was awarded first prize at an art exhibition sponsored by the City of Lachine, Quebec. He later exhibited at arts shows in Montreal, Toronto and the United States. In 1972 he held a solo show of his paintings at the Ottawa Little Theatre when he was interviewed on CBC's "Four For The Road." He has been art director for the Canadian Radio-Television Commission in Ottawa.

Reference
> Biographical information in artist's file at NGC Library

PIETRANGELO

A creative jeweller from Montreal who has exhibited his work there at La Galerie Kaleidoscope.

PIETRANGELO (Cont'd)

References
Notice of his exhibitions held at Galerie Kaleidoscope 1967, 1968
L'Art au Québec depuis 1940 by Guy Robert, La Presse, Mtl., 1973, P. 372

PIFKO, Ted L.
b. 1935

Born in Budapest, Hungary, he studied at the Müvészeti Gimnazium (art school) and the Szinhaz és Film Müvészeti (Academy of Theatre and Film) in Budapest. As a student in the visual arts he was particularly interested in the works of French Impressionists Pierre Bonnard and Edouard Vuillard and the sculptures of Michelangelo. He spent some time in Italy and Austria where he studied works of the Great Masters. He settled in Montreal, Canada, in 1957 then moved to Toronto where he became a creative consultant. A visual artist he has a particular interest in drawing and painting but he has done sculpture as well. An admirer of the work of the Group of Seven and Tom Thompson.

Reference
Information from artist

PIGOTT, Marjorie
b. 1904

Born in Yokohama, Japan, of an English father who had commercial interests in Japan, and a Japanese mother of noble birth. She and her sisters were of British nationality according to Japanese law which determines the nationality of the family through the father. She and her four sisters received an education from English governesses until they were old enough to attend English boarding schools in Britain and Japan. But Marjorie was too delicate to travel abroad. Her mother had a thorough knowledge of Japanese art and their home was filled with priceless treasures of ancient Japan. Marjorie's aptitude for art was recognized by her mother (her father died while she was very young) and she was sent to the Nanga School where she studied under master artists for twelve years. This school of painting is almost abstract in method and stresses the importance of the skilful use of brush in applying black ink in various ways of light and shade to express how the artist feels about the subject. She received her Seal Diploma and a Master Diploma (Teacher's Certificate) designating her a Nanga Master. Part of her teacher's name Shutei is on the Seal Diploma as an honour for her achievement in certain atmospheric misty effects in her paintings. The great earthquake of 1923 destroyed 90 percent of the ancient treasures in the Pigott home. A second trauma was caused by the imminence of World War Two. With her family's British nationality she and her sister Edith were advised to leave Japan. In 1940 aged 36 she arrived in Canada settling first in Vancouver. The climate was hazardous to her health so she and her sister moved east and settled in Toronto. For the first few years she kept active doing floral studies (many in lacquer) for a commercial firm. Then she taught the

PIGOTT, Marjorie (Cont'd)

Nanga technique to Japanese in Canada for the next ten years (1955-65). Afterwards she began a series of water colours of landscapes around Muskoka. She never paints on the spot but absorbs nature around her then paints from memory when she returns to her studio using photos to accurately portray the size and shape of various weeds and flowers in her paintings. From the disciplined brush-strokes of the Nanga School she developed a technique of semi-abstract wet-into-wet water colour. In 1950 she first employed the Nanga School brush strokes in depicting Canadian scenes incorporating the ancient technique in her work and gradually developing her present style of semi-abstract landscape and floral paintings. Viewing her work in 1975 Kathleen Walker of *The Citizen* noted, "The majority of the paintings are what might be termed 'interior' landscapes — close-ups of grasses and wild flowers imbued with a feeling of late summer's lazy heat. This is especially evident in Droning Bees and Last Rose of Summer, both reminding one of the full-bloomed works in Keats' ode to Autumn. But the artist is occasionally crisp, using a spatter technique and that 'trade secret' to heighten the chill in Frozen Landscape. One of her latest works, Dancing Grasses effectively combines a peachy soft, mottled background with the more harsh sumi-e brush strokes. These close views expressing as they do, a quiet love for natural beauty, are the highlights of Marjorie Pigott's collection." Her solo shows include: Roberts Gallery, Tor. (1962, 64, 66, 68, 70, 72, 74, —); Wallack Gallery, Ottawa (1971, 73, 75); Kensington Fine Art Gallery, Calgary (1969, 72); Gallerie Fore, Winnipeg (1972) and she has participated in many important group shows including: 4th Biennial Exhibition of Canadian Art, Ottawa (1961); Canadian Society of Painters in Water Colour; C.N.E. Art Gallery, Tor.; London Art Gallery "Six Ways with Water Colour" (1961); Annuals of Art Gallery of Hamilton (1962, 1963); Ontario Society of Artists; Spring Exhibition of Montreal Museum of Fine Arts (1964, —); St. Catharines Arts Council (1964). She is represented in the following collections: Sony of Canada Ltd., Winnipeg, Man. (1973); London Art Gallery, Ont.; Art Gallery of Sarnia, Ont.; University of Western Ontario, London, Ont.; Dominion Foundries & Steel Ltd., Hamilton, Ont.; Hamilton Club, Hamilton, Ont.; University College, Tor.; Steel Company of Canada; I.B.M., Tor.; York Club, Tor.; The Ladies Club, Tor.; Canadian Imperial Bank of Commerce, Tor.; McLaughlin Public Library, Oshawa, Ont.; Atlantic Inst. of Education, Halifax and elsewhere. Member: Royal Canadian Academy (ARCA 1971; RCA 1973); CSPWC (1964); O.S.A. (1963). Lives in Toronto.

References

Globe & Mail, Tor., Ont., July 18, 1959 "In Oriental Manner"

Ibid, May 11, 1961 (photo of artist at work)

Ibid, May 27, 1961 "Oriental Mysticism Flavors Local Scene" by Colin Sabiston

Ibid, Oct. 22, 1966 review by Kay Kritzwiser

Ibid, Mar. 4, 1970 "Some paintings for sale — Art gives flower show new scope" by Kay Kritzwiser

The Silhouette, Hamilton, Ont., Nov. 27, 1970 "Who is Marjorie Pigott? Just a very fine artist" by Stephen Rand

Ottawa Journal, Ont., Oct. 14, 1971 "Landscapes, floral scenes soft, poetic" by W.Q.K.

Ottawa Citizen, Ont., Oct. 15, 1971 "Exhibition fascinating combinations of styles" by Jenny Bergin

Globe & Mail, Tor., Nov. 25, 1972 "Marjorie Pigott"

PIGOTT, Marjorie (Cont'd)

Winnipeg Tribune, Man., Nov. 4, 1972 "Pigott paintings on view"
Winnipeg Free Press, Man., Nov. 25, 1972 "A Critique By John W. Graham — Saying Much With Little"
Ottawa Journal, Ont., Oct. 3, 1973 "Marj Pigott's canvases have Oriental touch" by W.Q.K.
Ottawa Citizen, Ont., Oct. 5, 1973 "Flower paintings capture delicacy" by Jenny Bergin
Journal Pioneer, Summerside, P.E.I., Oct. 11, 1973 "Centre Presented Paintings"
London Evening Free Press, Ont., Dec. 2, 1961 "Color on Canvas — Marjorie Pigott Water Color Added to London Collection" by Lenore Crawford
Ottawa Citizen, Ont., Oct. 25, 1975 "Art — Canadian landscape in a Japanese style" by Kathleen Walker
NGC Information Forms 1964; 1973, 1975
Who's Who in American Art
Dictionary of International Biography, England
The World's Who's Who of Women (1977)
Sotheby Canadian Art at Auction (1968-1975)
The Index of Ontario Artists by H. Wolff, Visual Arts Ontario/Ontario Assoc. of Art Galleries

---

PIHAY, Georgette

Originally from Belgium she first studied water colours then graphic arts and finally sculpture. A painter of landscapes in figurative style she exhibited her work in the foyer of the Palais Montcalm, Quebec City in 1972 in a joint show with painter Sylvie Papillon.

Reference
Le Soleil, Quebec, Mar. 15, 1972 "Le retour de la porcelaine — Arts plastiques"

PII, Ole

He studied art and architecture at the Academy of Arts in Copenhagen, Denmark, and came to Canada in 1955. A versatile artist he does pen and ink sketches, oils, water colours, woodcarving and ceramic sculpture. His wood carvings have been displayed at the Vancouver Art Gallery. Was living at 100 Mile House, B.C. in 1977.

Reference
Williams Lake Tribune, B.C., Sept. 20, 1977 "Three artists show at PG Gallery"

PIKE, Alfred Leonard (Leonard Pike)
1890-1977

Born in London, England, he studied art, especially in the field of ecclesiastical and domestique stained glass at the Central School of Arts and Crafts in London and became a protégé of Sir Christopher Whall. During the First World War he put aside his art and volunteered for service in the army with the

1698

PIKE, Alfred Leonard (Leonard Pike) (Cont'd)

Royal Fusiliers in France until he was wounded and returned to England where he received a discharge due to the seriousness of his wounds. When he was well enough to work again he continued his art career and for some years operated a studio on the estate of the Earl of Plymouth at Hewell Grange, Worcester, England. He continued work in the studio until the climate caused difficulties with his wound and he was advised by his doctor to find a drier climate. In 1929 he accepted a post as designer in Toronto, Canada, where he worked until 1939 when he joined the federal civil service in Ottawa. There he carried out work in the Department of Mechanical Maintenance designing badges, buttons, victory loan posters until the end of the war. He then opened up his own studio, Colonial Art Glass Studios, in Ottawa, specializing in stained glass windows and related work. Over the years he completed commissions for many churches in Ottawa including: Wesley United; St. Matthew's Anglican; St. Matthias Anglican; Bell United and windows for the Grey Nuns Convent, Orleans, Ontario (demolished by jet fighter crash). His work for which he won many awards can be seen in churches across Canada from coast to coast. His wife Gladys Pike is the Canadian water colourist and former proprietor of Ye Olde Booke Shoppe, well known to Ottawa book lovers for almost half a century. Mrs. Pike still resides in Ottawa with her son Miklejohn. Alfred Leonard Pike's name is recorded in the Book of Remembrance at the Regimental Chapel of the Royal Regiment of Fusiliers in the Church of the Holy Sepulchre, London, England.

References

The Ottawa Citizen, Dec. 16, 1955 "Historical Society Hears Talk On Stained Glass Art"

The Ottawa Journal, Mar. 4, 1959 "Stained Glass Art Described By Leonard Pike"

The Ottawa Citizen, May 13, 1958 "Wesley Window Unveiled"

The Ottawa Journal, Jan. 21, 1961 "The Healing Window" (stained glass window created by Leonard Pike is dedicated at St. Matthew's Church, Ottawa)

Ibid, May 13, 1961 "Memorial Window Dedicated" (stained glass window created by Leonard Pike dedicated at St. Matthias Church, Ottawa)

Letter, December, 1975 to Mrs. L. Pike from C.E. Manser, Chief Clerk, The Royal Regiment of Fusiliers, London, England

The Ottawa Citizen, 1977 (undated) "Stained-glass artist, area craftsman dies"

Biographical details provided by Gladys Pike as requested for this entry, 1980

PIKE, Gladys

Born in England she lived in London and came to Canada in the late 1920's to join a sister who had suffered a bereavement. Shortly afterwards she met Leonard Pike, noted stained glass artist who had settled in Ottawa and it was through him that she was encouraged in her drawing. They married and she continued with her art with classes opened by Phyllis Flood, wife of the then British High Commissioner. She studied under Wilfred Flood noted artist and became an accomplished water colourist exhibiting her work with the Ontario Water Colour Society. In later years she studied abstract painting for two years under Duncan de Kergommeaux and another internationally known artist Gerald Trottier. She exhibited in local exhibitions where she was presented with numerous awards. She is known for her fine floral subjects and is represented in

PIKE, Gladys (Cont'd)

many private collections in England, New Zealand and Canada. She is a member of the Ottawa Society of Painters in Water Colour. Her husband died in 1977. She lives in Ottawa with her son Miklejohn who is an avid tennis player and active in other sports. For almost half-a-century she owned and operated Ye Olde Booke Shoppe specializing in rare and second-hand books as well as a tracing service for hard to find titles.

References

Interview with artist in September, 1980

The Ottawa Journal, Ont., Mar. 27, 1973, P. 25 "Ye Olde Booke Shoppe — Gladys Pike: For 43 years Ye Olde Lady has been buying and selling books to people of all ages" Photostory by Eric Minton

PILBY, Kyra

A Palgrave, Ontario, artist who attended the Doon School of Fine Arts, the Huckley Art School and took additional night classes and sketching courses. She is known for her quick sketch portraits which she calls pastel shadow drawings. Her sitters include the Hon. Darcy McKeough, Harold Danforth, Garnet Newkirk (mayor of Chatham) Wallace Young and others. She has appeared as guest artist at the annual Chatham Sportsman's Show; Canadian National Exhibition, Toronto, and at the Western Fair, London, Ontario. The wife of Eric Pilby they live in Palgrave with two of their five children.

References

Free Press, London, Ont., Sept. 14, 1967 "Quick sketch artist at Fair turns hobby into paying job" by Vicki Martin

Chatham News, Ont., Feb. 2, 1968 "Portrait Artist Show Feature"

PILBY, Lind

She studied portraiture at the Central Technical School, Toronto, under Robert Ross then studied and worked in New York City. She returned to Canada at Montreal where she did commissions first by knocking on doors and then by selling her work through a photographer Richard Holden. Before leaving Montreal she was receiving $300 a portrait. She also worked in Vancouver. She went back to Toronto where she established a studio in the Toronto Dominion Centre working full time on pastel and sepia portraits in traditional style. She takes photos of her subjects before the actual sittings which are an average of 90 minutes. Her work bears a good likeness to her subjects.

Reference

Globe & Mail, Tor., Ont., June 15, 1968 "Lind Pilby's artist's loft is 48 stories in the clouds" by Paul King

PILCHER, Steve

A Hamilton, Ontario area artist working in pencil, acrylics and water colours who portrays people, animals and other subjects in their environments in super-realistic style. A solo show of his work was held at the Art Gallery of Hamilton.

Reference
>   Biographical note with sample of his work in NGC Library artist's file

PILGRIM, John

Born in England where he was educated, he later came to Canada and served in the Princess Patricia's Light Infantry and rose to the rank of major. A painter of portraits and other subjects he is especially interested in marine paintings and has done a painting of the famous sailing ship the Bluenose. He painted the portrait of Patricia Brabourne, Colonel-in-Chief of the PPCLI and daughter of Lord Louis Mountbatten. This portrait was then given to the 2nd Batallion, PPCLI's officers' mess. He has travelled and painted in England and Europe.

Reference
>   *Winnipeg Tribune*, Man., May 20, 1975 "Ex-major in Princess Patricia's to paint Lord's daughter" by Nick Hunter

PILL, Miriam
b. 1927

Born in New Zealand she came to Ottawa, Canada in 1956 and has been active as a weaver and member of the Ottawa Valley Weavers Guild (Pres. 1966, 1968, —). She exhibited her work at the London Weavers show of 1962 where she received honourable mention. She exhibited as well in the Canadian Fine Crafts prepared and circulated by the National Gallery of Canada (1966-67).

References
>   NGC Info. Form rec'd July 17, 1967
>   NGC Catalogue (sheets) for the Canadian Fine Crafts exhibit (1966-67)

PILLAI, Mohandas
b. 1936

Born in Penang, Malaysia, of East Indian parentage he grew up in Kerala in the southern part of India. He studied at the College of Art in Delhi for five years during which period he travelled extensively throughout India visiting the architectural monuments. His talent was spotted by art critic Miss Marie Seaton who gave him full support. He held his first major exhibition in 1961 at the All India Fine Arts and Craft Society in Delhi and received a very favourable review from the late Dr. Charles Fabri, English art critic and authority on Indian art and architecture. He spent 1964 travelling across Asia

1701

PILLAI, Mohandas (Cont'd)

to Europe visiting Pakistan, Iran, Turkey, Bulgaria, Yugoslavia, Austria, Germany, Holland and Belgium and arrived in Canada in 1965. He held a solo show of his works inspired by Indian mythology, at the Llewellyn & Picard Gallery in Montreal.

Reference

Biographical information supplied by Llewellyn & Picard Gallery, Mtl.

PILON, Paul
b. 1909

Born in Hull, Quebec, he studied art in a commercial art studio in Detroit (c. 1926) at the age of 17 but also studied informally by visiting museums and galleries in Chicago and Montreal. In 1931 he started painting portraits and supported himself this way until he went to work for Famous Players in 1934 designing posters and stage settings. Later he worked as a toy designer. During World War II he joined the services and was posted to Toronto where he painted regimental badges, out-of-bounds signs and other routine service art work. In 1963 he went into semi retirement spending half his time in Florida and the other half in Caledon, Ontario. His winters are spent in Palm Beach where there are more galleries for the size of the community than anywhere else. He does portraits solely in pencil and also works for the *Palm Beach Daily News* as an artist. In Palm Beach his subjects include mainly society people and some of these portraits appear twice weekly in the local newspaper.

Reference

The Daily Times & Conservator, Brampton, Ont., May 28, 1968 "Paints In Palm Beach And In Caledon Hills" by Randy Glover (photo of artist at work in his studio with article)

PILOT, Robert Wakeham
1898-1967

Born in St. John's Newfoundland, the son of Edward Frederick and Barbara (Merchant) Pilot. His mother, a widow, remarried, Canadian artist Maurice Cullen, in 1910 and they returned to Cullen's home in Montreal. For the first few months Pilot lived in his stepfather's large skylighted attic studio which was decorated with mementos gathered by years of travel abroad. In the studio he watched Cullen work on many important paintings and experienced the excitement of visits by artists, architects and collectors. In 1910 Pilot enrolled in the Montreal High School where he was a student until 1914. Many evenings after school he would hurry back to the studio to sketch or carve frames or help his stepfather with studio chores. This gave him the opportunity of learning his craft from the bottom up in the tradition of the apprentice painters of old. Other evenings he attended night classes of the Monument National where he learned drawing first by studying cubes, prisms, spheres and plaster casts. The human form was next with parts of the face — noses, ears, the complete head and finally the whole figure. Later he attended night classes at the Royal Canadian Academy where he continued to study the human form working from the live model under the direction of William Brymner. At other times he painted landscapes when he accompanied his stepfather on week-end sketching expeditions to the country and summers with his stepfather who was allowed the use of the camps by friends and patrons. His R.C.A. School instructor, William Brymner offered him classes at the Art Association of Montreal and knowing that the boy had no money, told him he could pay the Association later, ". . .in ten years' time, or whenever you have the money." So Pilot started classes and continued there until March, 1916, when he enlisted for active service in the army during World War I. He served overseas as a gunner on trench mortars in the Canadian Expeditionary Force, Fifth Division Artillery, until the end of the war. In the spring of 1919 he returned to Brymner's classes and there won the Wood Scholarship. He was considered exceptional for his time and was even invited to participate in the first Group of Seven show which was held in May of 1920. He felt somewhat overshadowed by his stepfather in painting so he decided to develop his skills in etching as his stepfather did not work in this medium. He made eight or ten etchings nearly all of Quebec City and its suburbs which were considered by art dealer William Watson, ". . .the best etchings ever made in Canada." Apparently there were a limited number of prints and his etchings are collectors' items today. In 1929 he wrote an appreciation of etchings by Clarence Gagnon and was probably influenced by Gagnon in this medium. In 1920 while attending a farewell dinner for Edwin Holgate on the occasion of Holgate's departure for Paris, one of the guests, Walter Hislop, offered Pilot enough money to study in Paris for two years on the condition that he pay him back when he could. The next week he was on the boat to France. There he studied at the Académie Julian in Paris under Pierre Laurens (1920-22). He exhibited in the Paris Salon in 1922 and was elected member of the Salon Nationale des Beaux-Arts. He painted at Concarneau where he met American painter Charles Formuth who had known Cullen and was very helpful in finding Pilot a studio in Paris. Pilot painted with Canadian painter Edwin Holgate at Concarneau as well in 1922. Holgate stayed at Pilot's studio for several months. Pilot returned to Canada this same year and opened a studio in Montreal. In 1925 he was elected an Associate of the Royal Canadian Academy and his "Quebec From Levis" was exhibited at the R.C.A. show and acquired by the National Gallery of Canada this same year. In this painting one can see the blend of softer French Impressionism with the new treatment developed by Cullen in portraying the clarity of the Canadian atmosphere especially in winter. He was also a great admirer of J.W. Morrice whose influence can be found in his work as well. Pilot emerged however very much his own man and developed a gentle but colourful approach to painting Canadian landscapes. A second painting of his "Houses, St. John's Newfoundland" was acquired by the National Gallery of Canada in 1926. In 1927 he held his first solo show at the Watson Art Galleries and it was very successful. This same year he also travelled and painted abroad in France, Spain and Northern Africa, stopping at the famous cities of Toledo, Madrid, Tangiers, Teutuan and elsewhere. He returned to Canada with many colourful canvases. In 1930 he executed the first of two mural commissions for Montreal High School and the second in 1931. He continued with his smaller work and in 1931 A.H. Robson in his book *Canadian Landscape Painters* used the words "masterly manner" to describe Pilot's pastel paintings. By 1934 he had won his second Jessie Dow Prize (the first awarded in 1927) and during his solo show at the Watson Art Galleries in 1935 *The Gazette* noted, "The pictures are new not merely in time but also in ideas and manner and they make the best showing of Mr. Pilot's work that he has given. There are winter and summer landscapes, the winter ones mostly in the Laurentians, near Piedmont and St. Sauveur, the summer ones at Metis and other places down the river. . . .Mr. Pilot has always painted snow very sympathetically and there are some good snow pictures here. In some of them the snow helps to show up the gay colours of French Canadian houses, and the same colours without snow are in several cheerful pictures painted at Beauport and on the isle of Orleans." He completed as well this same year a mural for The Chalet, Montreal. In 1938 he became professor of Engraving at the École des Beaux-Arts and continued in this capacity until 1940. In 1941 he went back into the Canadian Army serving with The Black Watch as camouflage staff officer with the First Canadian Corps and Headquarters attached to the 8th Army in England and Italy. While in Italy he was mentioned in dispatches and was made a Member of the Order of the British Empire (1944). After the war he returned to his chosen profession. He held his first Toronto solo show in 1948 at the Laing Gallery when Pearl McCarthy commented, "Broad, joyous use of pigments marks his pictures. . .little figures are put in with a deftness which recalls Morrice's sketches; The Cabstand, Quebec, has poetic unity; and, if one wants romance, there is the wistful painting of the Saguenay's solemn promontories contrasted with flaming foliage. It holds the essence of Autumn feeling." She made a general reference to a good collection of his work to reward the gallery visitor. T.R. MacDonald a close personal friend described his full palette and attitude to his work as follows, ". . .blue, ultramarine blue, viridian, mars brown, light red, yellow ochre, zinc yellow, cadmium orange, rose madder, vermilion was frequently simplified to cobalt blue, mars brown, yellow ochre and rose madder. He exercised great care in the selection and preparation of panels and canvases. Painting was his life and he gave himself to it without reserve. His love and respect for his profession made it impossible for him to work with less than complete sincerity." In 1952 Pilot was elected President of the Royal Canadian Academy and held that office until 1953 when he was awarded the Coronation Medal; was elected member of the National Academy of Design, U.S.A. (1953); Doctor of Civil Laws (Honoris Causa), Bishop's University (1953); presentation of his paintings to Sir Winston Churchill on his 80th Birthday (1955), to Queen Elizabeth and Prince Philip by Prime Minister Diefenbaker to commemorate their visit to Canada (1957), to Earl Alexander of Tunis. Pilot died in 1967 aged 69 and was survived at that time by his wife the former Patricia Dawes and a son Wakeham. Writing in 1969 on the occasion of the retrospective exhibition of the work of Robert W. Pilot organized by the Montreal Museum of Fine Arts and shown at the National Gallery of Canada and the Art Gallery of Hamilton as well, Paul Duval noted, "Although he earned wide public recognition throughout his career, he never received the acclaim of a major one-man show during his lifetime. . . .Throughout a career of half-a-century, Pilot quietly explored the impressionist vein of art. Although aware and appreciative of the works of other, more volatile artists, he was never tempted to stray from the artistic tradition which best suited his temperament and purpose. Pilot was particularly attracted to those quiet hours of dusk in winter when the last wash of sun is still in the sky and the first lights of evening are being lit. He found a visual magic in that short period when night and day over-

PILOT, Robert Wakeham (Cont'd)

lap and shapes dissolve into one another. As a pictorial poet of twilight, Pilot understood and portrayed the atmosphere of a scene as have few Canadian artists. . . .Geographically, Pilot's painting ground included Europe and North Africa as well as Canada, but it was to Quebec Province that he gave his deepest allegiance. There, he found the source material for some of the most poetic landscapes ever achieved by a Canadian." His solo shows included: Watson Art Galleries from 1927 to 1958; The Arts Club of Montreal (1946, 1951, 1952); Laing Gallery, Tor. (1948); Victoria College, Tor. (1951); Continental Galleries, Mtl. (1961); Kitchener-Waterloo Art Gallery, Ont. (1967) and the retrospective initiated by the Montreal Museum of Fine arts with the cooperation of the NGC and HAG shown at the three galleries (1969). He is represented in the following public collections: Art Gallery of London, Ont.; Art Gallery of Hamilton, Ont.; Art Gallery of Ontario, Tor.; National Gallery of Canada, Ottawa; Montreal Museum of Fine Arts, Mtl.; McGill University, Mtl.; Museum of the Province of Quebec; Confederation Art Gallery & Museum, Charlottetown, P.E.I.; and at the following city clubs: Club Saint-Denis, Mtl.; The Engineers' Club, Mtl.; The Mount Royal Club, Mtl.; The Mount Stephen Club, Mtl.; St. James Club, Mtl.; University Club, Mtl.; The Hamilton Club, Ham., Ont.; Corporate collections: Dominion Bridge Co. Ltd., Lachine, Que.; Power Corp. of Canada, Mtl.; The Royal Bank of Canada, Mtl.; I.B.M., NYC. As a member of the Royal Canadian Academy the following are important dates in his membership: A.R.C.A. (1925); R.C.A. (1935); P.R.C.A. (1952-54); also was a member of the Pen and Pencil Club of Montreal.

Selected References

Newspapers, periodicals, solo show catalogues

The Gazette, Mtl., Quebec, Oct. 29, 1920 "To Study In Paris — Mr. Robert Pilot Sails for France Today"

Le Revue Populaire, Avril, 1927 "A l'Atelier De Robert Pilot" par Jean Chauvin

Periodical (unidentified) April, 1929 "The Etchings of Clarence Gagnon"

The Gazette, Mtl., May 11, 1934 "Painters Awarded Jessie Dow Prizes"

The Montreal Star, Que., Nov. 24, 1935 "Robert Pilot's Exhibition At Watson's"

The Gazette, Mtl., Jan. 15, 1938 "Works By R.W. Pilot, R.C.A., Reveal Variety at Watson Art Galleries" by St. G.B.

Ibid, Feb. 18, 1939 "Landscapes by R.W. Pilot, R.C.A. On View At Watson Art Galleries — Montreal Painter Shows Works Done Below Quebec and in Nearby Laurentian County — Trend Is Towards More Brilliant Color" by St. George Burgoyne

Ibid, Feb. 25, 1939 "Art News and Reviews — Paintings by R.W. Pilot Brilliant in Color" by Robert Ayre

The Montreal Star, Sept. 4, 1941 "Captains Take Lower Ranks To Join Group" (notice of overseas postings)

The Gazette, Mtl., Feb. 1, 1946 "Robt. W. Pilot, R.C.A., Exhibits Small Oils — Laurentian Scenes and Subjects on Lower St. Lawrence At Arts Club"

Globe & Mail, Tor., Apr. 10, 1948 "Art and Artists — Robert Pilot Has Exhibit Of Quality" by Pearl McCarthy

The Gazette, Mtl., Jan. 29, 1949 "Paintings Are Varied In R.W. Pilot Exhibit — Quebec and Laurentian Subjects Feature Collection at Watson Art Galleries"

The Montreal Star, Feb. 3, 1949 "New Pictures by R.W. Pilot" by H.P.B.

Le Devoir, Mtl., Nov. 5, 1949 "Exposition aux Beaux-Arts"

La Patrie, Mtl., Jan. 23, 1951 "La peinture — Robert Pilot garde son équilibre dans un monde des plus instable"

Montreal Standard, Mtl., Jan. 27, 1951 "Speaking of Art — Robert Pilot Exhibition. . . ." by Michael Forster

La Presse, Mtl., Jan. 27, 1951 "L'exposition de Robert W. Pilot" par Jean Dénéchaud

PILOT, Robert Wakeham (Cont'd)

The Montreal Star, Feb. 3, 1951 "Taylor, Pilot Have Common Ground Here" by Robert Ayre

Globe & Mail, Feb. 17, 1951 "Art and Artists — Pilot, Donges Represented in One-Man Exhibitions" by Pearl McCarthy

St. John Telegram, Nfld., Aug. 25, 1951 "Artist Painting At Corner Brook"

Western Star, Curling, Nfld., Sept. 7, 1951 "Famous Canadian Artist Says Nfld. 'A Marvellous Country To Paint'"

Times-Globe, St. John, N.B., Oct. 7, 1951 "To Represent N.B. — Montreal Artist In City To Do Saint John Scene For N.Y. Canadian Club"

The Gazette, Mtl., Dec. 1, 1951 "Paintings by Pilot Shown at Arts Club"

The Hamilton Spectator, Ont., Dec. 15, 1951 "Purchase Prize" (photo of the painting "The Governor's Garden, Quebec" and caption)

The Gazette, Mtl., Nov. 1, 1952 "Landscapes by Pilot Shown at Arts Club"

Ibid, Nov. 17, 1952 "Royal Canadian Arts Academy Elects Robert Pilot President"

The Montreal Star, Nov. 18, 1952 "New President Installed by Arts Academy"

Ibid, Nov. 28, 1952 "Noted Artist and Wife Do Paintings for St. Andrew's Ball"

La Presse, Mtl., May 20, 1959 "Galerie d'art mobile conçue, puis réalisée"

The Ottawa Journal, Ont., May 21, 1954 "Two Former Ottawa Men To Paint Murals for CPR Cars" (photo of Pilot finishing mural of Revelstoke Park, B.C. for sleeper lounge car)

Globe & Mail, Tor., Ont., Nov. 20, 1954 "80th birthday gift" (photo of Pilot's painting of the St. Lawrence River from the ancient Citadel of Quebec presented to Sir Winston Churchill)

Ibid, Jan. 25, 1955 "Sir Winston Lauds Painting; Canada Secure in Memory"

Portneuf-Presse, St. Basile, Que., Oct. 25, 1956 (photo of mural for lounge sleeper CPR car)

Ottawa Citizen, Ont., Oct. 16, 1957 "Queen And Prince Philip Attend Black Tie Dinner At 24 Sussex" (Prime Minister Diefenbaker presents their Majesties with painting of Parliament Buildings by Pilot) by Phyllis Wilson

Ottawa Journal, Ont., Oct. 16, 1957 "Oil Painting Canada's Gift To the Queen"

La Presse, Mtl., Oct. 16, 1957 "Peinture remise à la reine"

Le Droit, Ottawa, Jan. 22, 1958 "Un peintre canadien a peint pour la reine" par Robert Rice (painting of Quebec City for their Majesties)

Sun Life Review, Vol. 15, No. 2, April 1958 "Recollections of an art Student" by Robert W. Pilot

Robert Pilot (exhibition notice by Continental Galleries of Fine Art, Mtl.) Nov. 1st to 15th, 1961

The Montreal Star, Dec. 19, 1967 "Canadian painter Robert Pilot dies"

Robert Pilot (catalogue) The Kitchener-Waterloo Art Gallery by Bert Henderson, 1967

Recollections of An Ex-Patriate, February, 1967, by Robert W. Pilot (a talk by Robert Pilot — copy deposited in NGC artist's file)

The Gazette, Mtl., Dec. 19, 1967 "Painter Robert Wakeham Pilot Dies at 69"

Western-Star, Corner Brook, Nfld., June 8, 1968 "Painting presented to province's people" (Charles R. Bronfman presents Pilot's painting of Churchill Falls to the people of Newfoundland)

Robert W. Pilot Retrospective (catalogue) by David G. Carter/Harold Beament/T.R. MacDonald — liberally illustrated) MMFA, Mtl., 1968 (55 pages)

La Presse, Mtl., Nov. 9, 1968 "Le peintre de la neige sale" par Normand Thériault

Hamilton Spectator, Ont., Jan. 25, 1969 "Art Gallery of Hamilton — Pilot showing is home grown" by Paul Duval

Ibid, Jan. 29, 1969 "Full range of artist's work on display"

Books and general catalogues

Canadian Landscape Painters by A.H. Robson, Ryerson, Tor., 1932, P. 169, 170, 171

Painting in Canada, A Selective Historical Survey, Albany Inst. of History and Art, Albany, New York, 1946, P. 35

Canadian Drawings and Prints by Paul Duval, Burns & MacEachern, Tor., 1952, Plate 9

Canadian Art, Its Origin and Development by William Colgate, Ryerson, Tor., 1943 (Ryerson Paperback, 1967), P. 141, 142, 222, 237, 239

NGC Catalogue, Vol. 3, Can. School by R.H. Hubbard, Univ. Tor. Press/NGC, Ottawa, 1960, P. 249, 250

PILOT, Robert Wakeham (Cont'd)

Check List of The War Collections by R.F. Wodehouse, NGC, Ottawa, 1968, P. 187

The Group of Seven by Peter Mellen, M. & S., Tor., 1970, P. 99

Art Gallery of Ontario, The Canadian collection by Helen Pepall Bradfield, McGraw-Hill, Co. of Can. Ltd., Tor., 1970, P. 378

Creative Canada, Volume One, Ref. Div., McPherson Lib. Univ. Victoria/Univ. Tor. Press, Tor., 1971, P. 252

Canadian Art at Auction 1968-1975 by Geoffrey Joyner, Sotheby & Co. (Can.) Ltd., Tor., 1975, P. 158, 159

Retrospective Recollections of a Montreal Art Dealer by William R. Watson, Univ. Tor. Press, 1974, P. 47, 48

Painting in Canada, a history by J. Russell Harper, 2nd Edition (paperback), Univ. Tor. Press, Tor., 231, 234

PILOTE, Clode

He exhibited his very creative sculptural pieces at Galerie Signal, Montreal, in November of 1976.

Reference

Exhibition notice from Galerie Signal with photos of Pilote's work

---

PINCHBECK, Irene (Mrs. Cyril Pinchbeck)

A Kamloops, B.C., artist she was commissioned in 1969 to do eight large-sized caricatures to decorate the hall where presentations for the Seagram Stone Senior National Curling Championships were made. Her work caused great amusement amongst the 350 guests attending the banquet as her art was poking fun at the House of Seagram and greatly amusing the House of Seagram representatives who were attending the banquet.

Reference

News Advertiser, Kamloops, B.C., Feb. 27, 1970 "Local Artist Commissioned for Seagram Stone portraits"

PINCKNEY, Joyce

A Saskatoon, Saskatchewan artist and member of the Fifth Street Studio in that city, she exhibited her batiks in a group show at the Saskatoon Public Library Gallery. The pieces she exhibited included one of a figure of a dancer made by the process of Procion dye on raw silk and another work of an apple and pear design by Procion dye on cotton. The reviewer of the show found her work impressive considering the patience necessary to produce the detail Ms. Pinckney had achieved in her work.

PINCKNEY, Joyce (Cont'd)

Reference

Star Phoenix, Saskatoon, Oct. 14, 1977 "Where it's art" article, with photos by Tammy Tompalski

PINE, John Michael

b. 1928

Born in Wolverhampton, England, a painter-sculptor he graduated in architecture qualifying as an A.R.I.B.A. and worked in London for some years. In sculpture he started out as a constructivist in plaster and then turned to wood-carving, working in St. Ives, Cornwall with Barbara Hepworth and exhibiting at the Penwith Gallery. Using wood as his medium, he chose techniques that permitted his ideas to take physical shape as quickly as possible. In London he joined with James Stirling and Richard Matthews to form the "Group of 8" and participated in their show "This is Tomorrow" at the Whitechapel Gallery, London (1956). He also showed work at Gimpel Fils and was included in the collection of new sculptors and painter sculptors at the Institute of Contemporary Arts. He came to Canada in 1957 and settled in Ottawa where he held his first exhibition in Canada. Subsequently he exhibited at the Dorothy Cameron Gallery and elsewhere in Toronto and his work was included in the Ottawa Mall, Canadian Exhibition in Poznan, Tokyo and Cleveland and the Canadian Home of the Year (1965); Expo '67, Montreal; Sculpture 67, Toronto and other shows. After arriving in Canada he took up welding and became known for his pendulum series of welded steel sculptures. He has been experimenting with moving space involving light, sound and synthetic materials especially elements that create problems of assembly into coherent spaces. He is a consultant with the Central Morgage and Housing Corporation in Ottawa. Lives in Ottawa.

References

NGC Info. Form rec'd September, 1958

Exhibition notice for the Massot-Loranger Gallery, Ottawa

Blue Barn Gallery, Bell's Corners, Ottawa, Sept. 16, 1964 exhibition notice with biographical notes

Sculpture '67 by Dorothy Cameron, NGC shown at Toronto City Hall, Summer, 1967, P. 60-61

Canadian Sculpture, Expo 67, Graph, Mtl., 1967, Plate 31

PINGWATUK, Makituk

b. 1931

An Eskimo artist of Cape Dorset, West Baffin Island, she took up ceramics because of the good quality clay that had been found in her area. She attended school in Nelson, B.C., to learn ceramics and while there won one of the top prizes in an international ceramics competition in Italy. The local clay near her home is sand coloured and is strengthened by adding chips and dust from the soapstone carvings. In 1968 she was invited to place an exhibition of her

PINGWATUK, Makituk (Cont'd)

work in the Women's Pavilion of the "Hemisphere 1968" Exposition at San Antonio, Texas. She was one of the representative women of North America to be featured in this pavilion.

References

The Ottawa Citizen, Ont., Sept. 23, 1967 "Top prize for Eskimo"
Nelson Daily News, B.C., Mar. 14, 1968 "Art School Student Asked To Exhibit At U.S. Exposition"

PINHEY, John Charles
1860-1912

Born in Ottawa, Ontario, the son of John Hamnet Pinhey he studied at the Central School of Art, Toronto and in Paris for five years at the Académie Julian, under Boulanger, Lefebvre and at the École des Beaux-Arts under Gérôme. Returning to Canada he established a studio in Ottawa, married, then later moved to Hudson Heights on the lower Ottawa River near Montreal. A painter of figures, portraits, landscapes and other subjects he was described by E.F.B. Johnston as a painter of allegoric pictures with broad colour effects that delight the viewer. He is represented in the National Gallery of Canada R.C.A. Diploma Collection by a painting of a woman in a dreamy pose with a lyre by her side. J. Russell Harper notes that he was principally a portrait painter who also did landscapes and genre subjects. Member: Royal Canadian Academy: A.R.C.A. 1885; R.C.A. 1897; O.S.A. 1886; Pen and Pencil Club of Montreal, 1890.

References

Canada and Its Provinces, Vol. 12, Tor., 1914 "Painting" by E.F.B. Johnston, P. 625
The Fine Arts in Canada by Newton MacTavish, MacMillan, Tor., 1925, P. 176
Nat. Gal. Can. Catalogue, Vol. III, Can. School by R.H. Hubbard, NGC/Univ. Tor. Press, Tor., 1960, P. 408
Early Painters and Engravers in Canada by J. Russell Harper, Univ. Tor. Press, Tor., 1970, P. 251
NGC Info. Form undated; biographical notes in artist's NGC Lib. file

PINKERTON, Kathleen Louise Campbell Ward (née Campbell; K. Ward, 1926-45; K. Pinkerton, 1945-) b.1902

Born in Toronto, Ontario, the daughter of Mary Walker Kieghley and William M. Campbell she attended Bishop Strachan School where she first studied art under Mary Wrinch Reid then attended art classes at the Central Technical School with Frederick Challener and others (1920); Ontario College of Art, summer schools at Meadowvale (1920) with William Beatty and Frederick Varley, OCA at Port Hope (1924) with William Beatty and George Reid; full time at the Ontario College of Art where she graduated in 1925 after studies with Reid, Beatty, Manly, Holmes, Lismer, Casson, Varley and A.Y. Jackson; OCA Summer School, Port Hope (1930) with William Beatty and later in her career at OCA (1957) and with Jock Macdonald in his studio (1958). She feels

PINKERTON, Kathleen Louise Campbell Ward (née Campbell; K. Ward, 1926-45; K. Pinkerton, 1945-) (Cont'd)

that much of her training in painting was assimilated on the many sketching trips with J.W. Beatty and Alice Innes and the mid-winter sessions at Burks Falls, Ontario, when twelve to sixteen painters gathered together including Beatty, Innes, Hortense Gordon, George Paginton, Sir Frederick Banting, Norm Marshall, Tom Stone, Dr. Campbell and others. The groups would stay at the Birks Falls Hotel and would go out in the snow to make two sketches each day. The evenings were spent in discussion with their day's output around them. Kathleen Pinkerton believes she is the first artist to have prints by the silk screen process accepted for juried shows in fine art galleries. She was employed for four and a half years in war work which required crash courses to equal two years' engineering study. Afterwards she was employed for ten years in statistical research which took her away from her art for that period but she returned to painting and printmaking and was still active in 1978 working in acrylic, water colours, oils and silkscreen in representational style. She has exhibited extensively including shows at the Canadian National Exhibition, Women's Building; Women's Art Association in Ontario; and shows at the Art Gallery of Ontario; Art Gallery of Windsor and elsewhere. She married Horace H. Ward in 1926 and they had one son John (1927); married George McGill Pinkerton in 1946 and they had one daughter Shan (1946). Member: Fakirs Art Club, Windsor, Ont. (1930); Canadian Society of Graphic Art (1936) held all offices except Presidency; Heliconian Club (1972); Print and Drawing Council of Canada. Lives in Thornhill, Ontario.

References

NGC Info. Form rec'd Dec. 19, 1955; May 2, 1973; letter May 5, 1973 in NGC Lib. file from K. Pinkerton

The Index of Ontario Artists by Hennie Wolff, Visual Arts Ontario/Ont. Assoc. Art Galleries, Tor., 1978, P. 219

PINKHAM, Jack

A Vancouver, B.C., sculptor originally from New York City who works in traditional style with bronze, stone, ceramics and wood. He has explored the plastic field to reproduce facsimiles of his original work which take on the appearance of actual materials of slate, wood, ivory, bronze and volcanic rock. The plastic techniques he uses are applicable to both bas-relief and full-round sculpture. Lightness and durability make his plastic pieces adaptable to both interior and exterior use. He has travelled in the Orient, Mexico and through-out British Columbia and has been influenced in his art by his travel. In creating his facsimiles the kind of sculpture chosen decides which plastic technique he must use from his stock of Drape Styrene, polyester, epoxy and other materials. First he creates his original sculpture in clay then makes a copy in his chosen synthetic material. From Drape Styrene for instance it is possible to turn out relief wall paper for large areas. One of his mediums is a modern version of papier-mâché which he calls Celastic. His work has been recognized by top architects and interior designers. Pinkham is also a painter.

PINKHAM, Jack (Cont'd)

Reference

Vancouver Sun, B.C., Aug. 28, 1959 "Plastics Bring Murals Into Home — Sculptured Beauty Available To People of Modest Incomes" by Cecilia Smith (photo by John Askew)

PINNEO, Georgiana Paige (Paige Pinneo)
b. 1896

Born in Waterville, Nova Scotia, the daughter of Wylie D. Pinneo and Maud Clark. Her father was descended from Peter Pineo, a planter and French Hueguenot settler who came to Nova Scotia in 1761. Her mother's paternal ancestors who came to Nova Scotia from the United States in 1780 originated with John Clark, mate and pilot of the Mayflower. She studied at Acadia University where she graduated with her B.A. in 1916. She then studied at the Victoria School of Art and Design (now Novia Scotia College of Art) with Elizabeth S. Nutt; attended the Nova Scotia Provincial Teachers' College and became a teacher in the Nova Scotia public and high school system (1920-1930). For ten years after that, she followed domestic pursuits during which time she also studied. She gave up painting almost entirely until 1936. She went into the business world at Windsor, Ontario and then settled in Montreal where she became a teacher for the Protestant School Board (1939-1960). At the time of her retirement she was head of the art department for the Verdun High School. She also taught art with Arthur Lismer at the Montreal Museum of Fine Arts (1940-44) and evenings at Sir George Williams College (1940-54). She was a frequent speaker on art teaching during her years in the Montreal Schools to home and school groups, local art associations and other groups (1940-60). She was a contributor to *Canadian Art* magazine during the 1940's and 50's and wrote book reviews on art education for the *Educational Record* (1940-60) and articles on art teaching for professional magazines. At the same time she studied art with Aleksandre Bercovitch in Montreal (1940-42) with Lester Stevens and Stanley Woodward at Rockport, Massachusetts (five summers). She held her first solo show in Montreal at the Henry Morgan & Company gallery in January of 1942 when the Montreal *Gazette* reviewer noted, "The exhibition. . .contains much interesting material and reveals the painter as a watercolorist of direct, bold methods who sees and handles her subjects in a big way. Her arrangements are uniformly effective, her values true and her treatment is free, washy and clean. Unnecessary detail has no place in her work which is marked by force and individuality." During her early retirement (1960-1970) she lived in Nova Scotia and travelled and painted in Indonesia, Bali, Spain, Italy, England, France, Sicily, Thailand, Philippines and elsewhere in the Far East (for periods, 1960-1970) also on the Island of Mallorca and elsewhere in the Balearic Islands off the coast of Spain. Her solo shows include: Henry Morgan, Mtl. (1942); Royal Victoria College, Common Room, Mtl. (1943); Willistead Art Gallery, Windsor, Ont. (1944); Art Association of Mtl. (1945) Cowansville Art Centre (1974) and other solo shows. She appeared regularly in Montreal Spring Shows, R.C.A. shows and occasional travelling shows of the National Gallery of Canada. Up to 1977 she had sold between 400 and 450 paintings. She is represented in the Quebec Provincial Museum; Cowansville Art Centre; St. Mary's College, Halifax, N.S. She lives in Cowansville, Quebec.

PINNEO, Georgiana Paige (Paige Pinneo) (Cont'd)

References

The Gazette, Mtl., May 6, 1940 "Loan Exhibitions Help Teach Art" (photo of Miss Paige Pinneo and her art class and loan exhibition on surrounding walls)
Ibid, Jan. 24, 1942 "Miss G. Paige Pinneo Holds 'One Man' Show"
Ibid, Nov. 13, 1943 "Watercolors Shown By G. Paige Pinneo — Montreal Artist Exhibits Group In Common Room of Royal Victoria College"
Ibid, Nov. 27, 1943 "Watercolor Exhibition Is Ending This Evening"
Ibid, Mar. 20, 1944 "Montrealer to Show Paintings in Windsor"
Ibid, June 10, 1944 "Works by Montrealer Exhibited in Windsor — Watercolors by G. Paige Pinneo at Willistead Art Gallery Win Approval"
The Windsor Daily Star, Ont., June 3, 1944 "Vigorous Art in watercolor" by Valerie Conde
The Gazette, Mtl., Jan. 20, 1945 "Fine Arts, Crafts and Decoration — G. Paige Pinneo Shows Group of Watercolors"
La Voix de l'Est, Granby, Que., Jan. 18, 1974 "Un peintre figuratif expose à Cowansville"
NGC Info. Forms of Oct. 1, 1941 and Mar. 9, 1977

PINSKY, Alfred

b. 1921

Born in Montreal, Quebec, he received early encouragement in the arts from his public school teacher, Miss Fraser, then studied art with Anne Savage at the Baron Byng High School; with Goodridge Roberts, Arthur Lismer and Eldon Grier at the Montreal Museum of Fine Arts where he won a scholarship for the period 1938-39; studied in New York City at the Art Students' League, also at the Contemporary Arts School under John Senhauser and at St. Mark's Art Centre with Viviano and B. Kerr. His training was interrupted by the Second World War when he volunteered and served five years in the Royal Canadian Air Force. He returned to art studies at the Montreal Museum of Fine Arts School after the war. He opened a school in cooperation with Ghitta Caiserman, Harold and Barbara Goodwin (from U.S.A.) and Karl Rix. They named their school "Montreal Artists' School" which was based on the system of the Art Students' League of New York of offering students freedom, a place to work and close association with the teacher of their choice. Many students were 'carried' at the school as they didn't have the money to pay the fees. In 1950 the school closed because there were too few paying students. Pinsky turned to his first love of children's classes and instigated the Child Art Council to stimulate teachers to improve child art education in both French and English schools on the Island of Montreal. The Council made international ties. Its ideas centered around the goals of bringing children up in a happy creative process and developing their whole personality. He taught art at Teachers' College, Saskatoon (1959) and summer sessions at the University of New Brunswick art centre. In his own art he joined with his associates to produce a series of prints and also had an interest in producing murals. By the 1970's he was creating work dealing with certain aspects of Conceptual art and joined with Joan Rankin in producing the show "Conceptual Art and Other Things" when Irene Heywood described the idea around the exhibition in her words and theirs, "'We are more and more aware that what is visual (in art) depends on non-visual data for understanding. . .what you see is influenced by what you already know.' They both felt that an exhibition of records of people looking at

PINSKY, Alfred (Cont'd)

a landscape rather than painting it, of listening to sounds of traffic rather than hearing the sounds, of time shown passing on the face of a clock, should allow the viewer the chance to complete the cycle between sight or sound and emotion. . . .It's the involvement of every man and woman and child that Alfred Pinsky wants. He hasn't changed at all from his original philosophy that through the senses comes true maturity." For many years Pinsky has been active in art education and is a member of the Canadian Society for Education Through Art (Pres. 1963-65); former Chairman, Department of Fine Arts, Sir George Williams University before its amalgamation with Loyola College to form Concordia University; Professor of Fine Arts at Concordia University. He has been art reviewer for CBM-CBC. Lives in Montreal. Member: Canadian Society of Graphic Art; College Art Association of America; American Federation of The Arts.

References

Canadian Art, Vol. 7, No. 4

Windsor Daily Star, Ont., Mar. 8, 1952 "Graphic Art at Gallery" by David Mawr

Ibid, Mar. 15, 1952 (photo of lithograph 'Still Life' by Alfred Pinsky)

Photo Journal, Mtl., Que., July 9, 1953 "Artistes de Montréal — Alfred Pinsky"

Fredericton Gleaner, Aug. 10, 1954 "Art Exhibit Opens" (photo of Pinsky's Students' work with Pinsky and Colin B. MacKay, U.N.B. Pres., in attendance)

Evening Times-Globe, Saint John, N.B., May 22, 1957 "Says Local Artists Have Own Culture"

Regina Leader-Post, Sask., May 22, 1959 "Artist criticizes collegiate art"

Ibid, May 19, 1959 "School art show opens Thursday"

La Presse, Mtl., Oct. 27, 1962 "Pinsky et Roussel"

Arts in New Brunswick, Eds. Tweedie, Cogswell, MacNutt, "Painting in New Brunswick After 1880" by Alfred Pinsky, Brunswick Press, Fredericton, N.B., 1967, P. 149-161

Montreal Star, Mtl., Que., Mar. 18, 1972 article by Irene Heywood (joint show by Pinsky and Joan Rankin)

Ibid, Feb. 10, 1972, "Around the Galleries" (joint show by Pinsky and Rankin)

Who's Who In American Art, 1976, P. 442

Document from artist, 1962

NGC Info. Forms rec'd: Sept. 25, 1941; Aug. 12, 1965

PIOTROW, Roger

b. 1945

Born in Nottingham, England, he came to Canada and Toronto where he studied at the Ontario College of Art and graduated with his diploma. He participated in group shows at the Aggregation Gallery (Gallery Artists, 1969-72) and Hart House (1969) Toronto; at the Agnes Etherington Gallery, Kingston (1969); at the Glenhyrst Arts Council, at the Art Gallery of Brantford (1969); holding his first solo show at the Aggregation Gallery (1972) when Kay Kritzwiser noted, "Piotrow's drawings make remarkable rapport with the gallery space. . . .Piotrow's graphite and turpentine black works on corrugated cardboard in the rear gallery at Aggregation. . .Pewter-like frames and non-glare glass, . . .are important physical complements to his drawings. . .sensitivity is acute in all these drawings, but particularly in the color he finds (eggshell, white) by simply arranging the grain of paper, and in the subtle differences he discovers between his pencil mark and scissor cut." He has won a number of

PIOTROW, Roger (Cont'd)

awards in Canada and the United States. He is represented in the collection of the Ontario Institute for Studies in Education and many private collections.

References

Collingwood Enterprise-Bulletin, Ont., Apr. 3, 1969 "Roger Piotrow Won Art Award"
Globe & Mail, Ont., Feb. 5, 1972 review by Kay Kritzwiser
Aggregation Gallery biographical information on Roger Piotrow

PIOTROWSKI, Adolph
b. 1931

Born in Toronto, Ontario, he attended public school and Parkdale Collegiate there and graduated as top student in 1949. He entered the University of Toronto medical school graduating in 1956 and then becoming a partner in a medical practice as general practitioner associated with the Queensway General Hospital in Mississauga. His father had come from Poland in 1929 and had stressed the great importance of education to his son. Adolph studied violin, art and achieved academic excellence at school. Later he gave up the violin as he realized it would be difficult to master three areas of endeavour but continued art with the encouragement of his father and continued high academic achievement. Both his parents wanted him to take all of the opportunities available for an education they themselves never had. He studied with Gordon Payne, Carl Schaefer, the University of Toronto Anatomy School, the Ontario College of Art and Three Schools. Working in oils, acrylics and soapstone his subjects include landscape, figure and abstraction. He has travelled extensively in his search for subject material in Mexico, The West Indies, Europe, North Africa and elsewhere. Viewing his carving in 1971 the *Globe & Mail* writer noted, ". . .Piotrowski paints and sculpts the female torso with unusual versatility, most successfully using Canadian soapstone as one medium. On one grey surface he etches a face or a portion of the female form. The stone turns to reveal another version of the same figure. This combination of etching and carving adds an agreeable dimension." The Polish Alliance of Canada presented one of his sculptured torsos to Prime Minister Trudeau on the occasion of the Prime Minister's visit to Place Polonaise at Grimsby, Ontario. Viewing his paintings at the Wayne Art Gallery in 1976 Tony Wanless noted, "Pitrowski paints the constant, repetitive cycles of the universe that provide it with stability and, paradoxically, an easy motion. . . .His last two shows explored serenity and horizons, each giving the same well-being to the viewer. . . .' There's an order to everything in the universe,' he explains, 'Everything flows and ebbs. To really achieve peace with yourself, you have to tune into this rhythm.' Piotrowski's collection at the Wayne Gallery shows he has tuned into this rhythm. Dreamy, foggy and showing a distorted perspective that borders on the abstract, his series of landscapes has a symphonic quality. One feels he should see the series in paintings in a quick series as a slide show set to some grand classical piece of music. By diffusing his light sources Piotrowski leaves his paintings with vague definitions. There is just enough there to let you know what you are looking at, but not enough to force you to concentrate on the details, enabling you to explore yourself." One of his other series of paintings and stone images was on the theme "The Flight of Icarus"

PIOTROWSKI, Adolph (Cont'd)

(yearning of man to fly). The stone was collected from some of the oldest boulders on earth and considered a found object in its original shape with fissures, gouges and holes produced by time and weather onto which Piotrowski adds only pigment and gold leaf to bring out the spirit within the object. His solo shows include: Port Credit Library (1966); Kar Gallery, Toronto (1971, 1973, 1975, 1977); Wayne Art Gallery, Windsor (1976) and others. His large mural of sailboats can be seen in the entrance foyer of the Queensway General Hospital in Mississauga. Married with three children, Dr. Piotrowski makes sure that he takes time out to unwind with squash or tennis and he remains conscious of the need for the family visits to the theatre by planning to 'waste a day' lest he should one day suddenly realize the joys of doing things together with his wife and children were missed. Lives in Mississauga, Ontario.

References

Mississauga News, Ont., Sept. 4, 1968 "The New Mississaugans — This physician wears two hats" by Arthur Lowe

Globe & Mail, Tor., Ont., Dec. 4, 1971 review of solo show at Kar Gallery, Toronto

Hamilton Spectator, Ont., May 13, 1972 "PM gets sculpture of a nude woman"

Toronto Star, Ont., Dec. 17, 1975 "Success as artist led him to reveal his role as doctor" by Bob Pennington

Windsor Star, Ont., Nov. 11, 1976 "This physician heals himself by painting" by Tony Wanless

Catalogue sheet from Kar Gallery of Fine Art, Toronto, Nov. 19, 1977

PIPER, Audrey

Originally from England, she settled in Saskatoon, Saskatchewan, where she has become known as a very successful artist working in the unique process of batik on paper using acrylic paints. Her subjects include those based on views from the windows of her own home situated in the city's oldest streets, memories of scenes in England or from her own imagination. She works from sketches and/or photographs and produces paintings usually on sheets 14½ × 22 inches. She starts her process by painting the lightest colour on first which she then waxes over then proceeds with the next slightly darker colour until she finishes with the darkest. By using acrylics she has a vast range of colours. She achieves special effects when the wax does not totally obliterate each colour making the process quite different from ordinary painting. The wax is eventually ironed off to reveal what are often exciting results. Each batik takes approximately two weeks to complete. She held a solo show of her landscapes at the Shoestring Gallery, Saskatoon in 1978.

Reference

Star Phoenix, Saskatoon, Sask., April 15, 1978 "Accent on art — Paintings sold in first hours of show"

PIQTOUKUN, Dave

Born in Paulatuk, N.W.T., he hunted polar bear, caribou and white fox all of his life until he decided to leave his parents, eighteen brothers and sisters for a new life in Alberta and British Columbia. He served an apprenticeship in Vancouver to learn how to carve jade. Before then he had been carving in soapstone. Using jade from north central British Columbia he roughs the carving mechanically then does the finishing by polishing and sanding. He has concentrated on carving Canadian wildlife out of jade although he has also done figures, faces and masks. He enjoys carving miniatures out of soapstone and gets his soapstone from Hope, B.C. One of his miniature pieces for example includes eight tiny eider ducks on a cliff complete with nests and eggs. Many of his larger carvings have been described as having excellent motion. He has exhibited at various places including Arctic Arts on 104th Street in Edmonton, Alberta.

Reference

Edmonton Journal, Alta., Oct. 30, 1974 "Counter Points — Jade presents Eskimo with new fascination" by Nancy Clegg Buck

PIROCHE, Setsuko
b. 1933

Born in Tokyo, Japan, she studied painting there and for a number of years was apprenticed to the well-known Japanese artist, Setsu Asakura. In 1959 she studied Islamic art in India. She produced sculptural weaving, paintings, pottery and illustrated five Japanese children's books. She came to Canada in 1968 settling in Vancouver and first attracted public notice in 1972 when she received "Best-in-the-show" award in the British Columbia Craft exhibition held at the Simon Fraser University Gallery. Her winning work was a woven sculpture "Horse and Woman". In her weaving she shapes figures and animals by double-weaving on a loom, then inserts wire hoops and paper padding to achieve the desired form. Viewing her show in 1977 at the Artists' Gallery in Vancouver Wayne Edmonstone of the Vancouver Sun noted, "Piroche's people, made from cobwebby-looking woven colored fabric and tiny strands of wire, hang from the gallery's ceiling with the lightness of a breeze, executing stately little half-turns as they dangle to the best of their own quiet melody. About 20 pieces make up the show, with half being a series of large multi-colored stuffed dolls which lounge and preen and pose within a single room, like contestants in a Raggedy Ann beauty contest. Another character, who rides a bumbershoot off into the air with all the panache of a Mary Poppins, obviously loves the rain (coming down the day of the reviewer's visit) with all the ardor of a young desert flower; an Unidentified Flying Object with curling Saul Steinberg wheels trails little smoky bits of fabric as if it were seeding crops, and a handlebar moustachioed figure stands encased in what looks like a cocoon made from spun cotton candy." Her solo shows include: North Vancouver Picture Loan Show, N.V. Senior Sec. Sch. (1972); Burnaby Art Gallery, B.C. (1973); Arts Centre Gallery, Penticton, B.C. (1973); Vancouver Art Gallery, Van., B.C. (1974); Artists' Gallery, Van., B.C. (1977); Surrey Art Gallery, New Westminster, B.C. (1978).

PIROCHE, Setsuko (Cont'd)

References

Vancouver Sun, B.C., Apr. 11, 1972 "Horse-and-woman sculpture awarded first crafts prize" by Joan Lowndes

N. Vancouver Citizen, B.C., Apr. 25, 1972 "Award Winner Will Display Art Works"

W. Vancouver Lions Gate Times, B.C., Apr. 27, 1972 "Winner Guest Artist At N.V. Picture Loan"

New Westminster Columbian, B.C., Jan. 20, 1973 (photo of work at Burnaby Art Gallery)

Penticton Herald, B.C., Mar. 6, 1973 "Sculptural Weaving Show Contains Unusual Pieces"

Vancouver Sun, B.C., Aug. 12, 1974 "Piroche's fantastic soft sculpture" by Joan Lowndes

Ibid, B.C., June 10, 1977 "Ethereal art with a funnybone"

Vancouver Province, B.C., June 18, 1977 "Entertainment — Sculptor probes the human condition" by Art Perry

Columbian, New Westminster, B.C., Apr. 20, 1978 "Surrey presents Piroche works"

PIROT, Jean-Marie

b. 1926

Born in France he graduated from the École Nationale Supérieure des Beaux-Arts of Paris and taught at the École des Beaux-Arts of Grenoble in 1950. From about 1950 on he produced paintings, sculptures, leaded glass mosaics, frescos, jewellery, book illustrations and set designs. He completed many commissions for the French government, public bodies and private collectors. He held solo shows at Grenoble (1959-69), at Lyon (1963) and participated in group shows in Paris, Ostende, Berlin, Munich and Panama. Coming to Canada in 1969 he held his first solo show at the Visual Arts Centre of the University of Ottawa. In 1971 viewing his second solo show at Galerie Spectrum Capricorn, Ottawa, W.Q. Ketchum of the *Ottawa Journal* noted, ". . .There is a splendid engraving 'The Kiss' and some highly individualistic works which are a metal with oils and acrylics superimposed. He contends that though the surface extends outward they are not sculptures and still have a flat plane. He says his paintings reflect everyday life in a poetic state. When he uses biblical themes for his inspiration his reactions are symbolical and poetic. Mr. Pirot veers from the figurative to the nonfigurative, but whatever he turns his hand to results in something imaginative and technically sound." He taught for the Department of Fine Arts of the University of Ottawa in 1969. He is represented in the Fine Arts Museum of Grenoble and in private collections in Bordeaux, Metz, Nancy, Nantes, Paris, Strasbourg, Chambery, Berlin, Munich, Madrid, Bruxelles, Ottawa, Waterloo (Ont.), New York City and Cuernavaca (Mexico).

References

Ottawa Journal, Ont., Apr. 17, 1970 "Pirot Art On View" by W.Q. Ketchum

Le Droit, Ottawa, Apr. 17, 1970 "Très bonne exposition de Jean-Marie Pirot"

Ibid, Apr. 18, 1970 "Arts Plastiques"

Ottawa Journal, Ont., Feb. 26, 1971 "One-Man Show At Capricorn Imaginative" by W.Q. Ketchum

PISKO, Michael
b. 1913

Born in Lethbridge, Alberta, he became interested in art during his early years at school but being a member of a large family he had few toys, pencils, crayons and paper to fulfil his need to explore the creative world of a child. During the Depression he was unable to attend art school and he embarked on a self-teaching plan and spent much of his time in the 1930's sketching and painting. Later he studied under H.G. Glyde at summer courses sponsored by the Lethbridge Sketch Club (1935-50) and attended the Banff School of Fine Arts in 1941. Influenced in his work by Glyde and A.Y. Jackson he became a landscape painter in impressionistic and realistic styles working in oils. Viewing his work at the Bowman Arts Centre, Lethbridge in 1967 the *Herald* noted, "Mr. Pisko paints his boldly conceived works in large sweeping brushstrokes. He has been greatly influenced by Tom Thomson of the Group of Seven. . . .There is also some influence by other members of this Canadian group. Mr. Pisko takes brush and palette to sketch outdoors. These trips have produced Glimpses of Sunny Alberta, a collection of 97 paintings." He earns his living as a commercial artist and is a member of the Alberta Society of Artists and the Lethbridge Sketch Club. He has supervised art classes under the sponsorship of the Lethbridge Sketch Club. Lives in Lethbridge.

Reference

Lethbridge Herald, Alta., Oct. 16, 1967 "Michael Pisko Opens One-Man Art Showing"

PISKUNOWICZ, Paul
b.(c) 1914

Born in Poland he was keenly interested in art and was able to draw animals before he could write his name. He came to Canada about the age of 16 and settled on a homestead outside Tomahawk, Alberta. During the years that he farmed he continued painting. After his retirement he turned to art full time. He held his first solo show in 1977 at the Stony Plain Multicultural Centre when Bob Remington of the *Edmonton Journal* noted, "On canvas he has captured scenes witnessed daily as a farmer — a calf crying for food, a deer slipping silently through winter woods. An idyllic painting of a snow-covered log cabin that was his homestead near the hamlet of Tomahawk near Dryton Valley is one of his works. All are currently on display. . .some selling for $300. Unfortunately, some of his best paintings are not for sale. They contain too many fond memories, mainly from his boyhood in Poland. One of his schoolteacher; another of a rabbi. Two are striking portraits of old peasants he sketched in his homeland. As a hunter, he says his specialty is wildlife. But it is his portraits that most easily attract interest." In earlier years Piskunowicz entered his work in the Edmonton Exhibition where he won prizes.

Reference

Edmonton Journal, Alta., Mar. 15, 1977 "He has worked, painted the land" by Bob Remington

PISSUYUI, Martine
b. 1933

Born at McConnell River 35 miles south of Eskimo Point, N.W.T., where she later settled. A widow she started to carve in 1966 when Gabriel Gély was arts and crafts adviser to the Department of Northern Affairs. Many of her pieces are human figures with her inspiration mainly coming from family life as Diana Trafford a writer for the Canadian Government noted, ". . .she seems to take her inspiration from family life, as in her sculpture of a boy crying, holding his hands over his eyes. She has a highly individual style, and depicts human emotions effectively."

References

"Pissuyui, Soapstone Carver, Eskimo Point" Dept. Indian Affairs & Northern Develop., Ottawa, 1968 (biographical sheet with photo)

Sculpture/Inuit (catalogue), Univ. Tor. Press, Tor. 1971, P. 283

Sculpture of The Eskimo by George Swinton, M & S, Tor., 1972, P. 207

PITALOOSIE
b. 1942

Born in the Arctic she spent several years at the sanitarium in Hamilton, Ontario, first arriving at the hospital when she was ten years old. During her convalescence she learned English. After her recovery she returned to Cape Dorset. In 1967 she accompanied the noted Inuit sculptor, Pauta, to Toronto on the occasion of the installation of one of his large sculptures in High Park. They returned to Cape Dorset where they were later married. Following her marriage, Pitaloosie began her drawing between her duties as mother of four children. The local Co-operative took an interest in her work and began reproducing her drawings by tracing them onto soapstone slabs so that a skilled carver could carve out the design on the surface of the stone from which the prints are then made. One of her favourite subjects is the mother and child theme to which she relates in a very personal way. Because she is at ease in her use of English she often translates at gatherings of Eskimo women. Her name had been mistakenly printed as Pitalouisa but she herself made the correction to establish the right pronunciation.

References

Eskimo Graphic Art, 1969, West-Baffin Eskimo Co-op., Cape Dorset, NWT, 1969, P. 40, and photo on last page of catalogue

Kitchener-Waterloo Record, Ont., Feb. 4, 1974 "Eskimo artists realize small profit" by Susan MacKenzie

The Spectator, Hamilton, Ont., Feb. 5, 1974 "A woman whose views look best in print" by Marjorie Wild

Dorset 76, Cape Dorset Annual Graphics Collection, M.F. Feheley Publishers Ltd., Tor., 1976, P. 71

PITMAN, Lewis

A potter from Kenora, Ontario, he has produced pottery using the traditional potter's wheel. Taking his clay from Dryden, Ontario (which is red in colour),

PITMAN, Lewis (Cont'd)

he specially prepares it before forming it on the potter's wheel. His pottery is then fired in a kiln for approximately twelve hours, sprayed by hand with a glaze or "frit" (powdered glass suspended in water) then fired for another twelve hours. Applying his colour on the pieces before their first baking he achieves very successful results. Reviewing his work at the Public Library at Kenora, the *Daily Miner and News* noted, ". . .articles of excellent craftsmanship, samples of which may be seen at the Public Library. They show beauty of form and design, and they range in interest from utilitarian to the decorative. There are ornamental vases, candle holders, salt and peppers, mugs, bowls, flower pot, ash trays and ear-rings. The colours include soft blues and greens, navy and tones of brown." Steps in making his pottery were also displayed by photos showing him at work. Actual samples of the clay at various steps towards becoming a finished product were also shown adding an educational dimension to his display. Formerly on the staff of King George School, Kenora, Pitman moved from Kenora to eastern Ontario in 1958.

Reference

Daily Miner & News, Kenora, Ont., May 8, 1958 "L. Pitman Creates Works of Art With His Potter's Wheel"

PITRE, James A.
1918-1969

Born in Bathurst, New Brunswick, where he was educated, the son of Doran and Henrietta (Glazier) Pitre, he served in the Canadian Army for seventeen years through the 2nd World War and the Korean conflict. After his discharge in 1952 he returned home to Bathurst where he settled. While serving in Germany he began painting through the encouragement of a roommate. Pitre visited every art gallery he could in Europe, Korea and the United States and other countries as part of his art education. Following his return home he painted a wide variety of subjects including landscapes, historical sites in and around Bathurst and at Papineau Falls, Connolly Falls, Tetagouche Falls and Cherry Brook, forest scenes, wild flowers and even sites of local industries like Bathurst Paper Limited and the Belledune Smelter. He painted as well a series of portraits (probably from photographs or other visual records) of Sir John A. Macdonald, Queen Elizabeth II, Queen Victoria, Laura Secord, Winston Churchill and John McCrae (author of the poem "In Flanders Fields"). For a Canada Centennial project he produced a variety of paintings and sought out antique picture frames from all over New Brunswick then mounted fifty of the paintings and put them on public view at the City Motel in Bathurst. After settling in Bathurst he worked as a gatekeeper for Consolidated-Bathurst and Red Pine Knoll park and spent most of his off hours painting. He died suddenly at Red Pine Knoll and was survived by his mother and three sisters, Edna (Bathurst), Mrs. Ernest Lapointe (South Bathurst) and Mrs. Donald Jones (Montebello, California); two brothers Edward (Port Hawkesbury, N.S.) and William (Bathurst).

References

Moncton Times, N.B., Mar. 14, 1967 "Bathurst Artist To Open Showing Today" by Mrs. J.C. MacLaggan

PITRE, James A. (Cont'd)

Telegraph-Journal, Saint John, N.B., June 13, 1969 "Gloucester Artist Dies In 52nd Year"
Bathurst Northern Light, N.B., June 18, 1969 "Talented City Artist Mourned"

PITSEOLAK

b.(c) 1900

Born on the island of Tugjak (Nottingham Island), Hudson Strait, N.W.T. Her family later moved to Baffin Island where she spent most of her life. They lived mainly in the area of Foxe Peninsula. From her father she learned about Eskimo legends, the spirit world and the shamans. After her father died she married her childhood friend, Ashoona and they had seventeen children; five survived. During a family hunting trip her husband died of an illness. To survive she became an excellent seamstress and she decorated the clothing she made with embroidery designs. She began print making in the 1950's when James Houston introduced the idea to the Eskimos during his term as civil administrator for the Government of Canada. Encouraged by Houston to produce drawings about "the old ways" of the Inuit she became known for her colourful prints. She has also done textile designs and the occasional sculpture. Her subjects are based on her life past and present and ancient ways and legends of her people. The West Baffin Eskimo Co-operative has produced over 144 of her prints. Her work has been included each year in the Co-operative's editions of graphics since 1960. Before becoming an artist she made parkas and duffel socks and decorated them with designs of animals and all kinds of living things and sold them for about twelve dollars each. Now she is making a good living from her art and is supplied by the Co-operative with coloured pencils, felt pens and paper to produce her work. She lives in a comfortable hut of one of her sons and is able to buy clothes, tea, food for all the family. She still misses life in the camps and the freedom associated with camp lifestyle. Four of Pitseolak's sons are among the finest carvers at Cape Dorset (Kimwartok, Kiawak, Kaka and Ottochie). Her daughter Napachee is a noted printmaker. The Pitseolak family held a large exhibition of their prints and carvings at the Robertson Galleries, Ottawa in 1967. Then in 1971 Dorothy Eber, a Montreal writer, produced the book, *Pitseolak: Pictures out of my life* in English and Eskimo from tape recorded talks with Pitseolak aided by young Eskimo interpreters. Ninety of Pitseolak's engravings, stone cuts, and drawings in colour and black and white illustrate the book with animals, birds, monsters, spirits and early experiences. Following the publication of her book she visited various cities as part of the promotional programme of the publishers and her work was featured in a retrospective exhibition which toured galleries throughout Canada. Her work has been acquired for important collections including the National Gallery of Canada. In 1977 she was awarded the Order of Canada and a 14 cent postal stamp was issued in 1978 with her woman on foot reproduced on its face. The National Film Board of Canada in 1973 made a 13 minute coloured film "Pictures out of my life" which is about her work.

References

Eskimo Graphic Art, 1966, West-Baffin Eskimo Co-op., Cape Dorset, N.W.T., 1966, P. 39, 40
Cape Dorset, A decade of Eskimo prints and recent sculptures, NGC, Ottawa, 1967, Nos. 29-33

PITSEOLAK (Cont'd)

Eskimo Prints by James A. Houston, Barre Publishers, Barre, Mass., U.S.A., 1967, P. 56-65

Eskimo Graphic Art, 1969, West Baffin Eskimo Co-op., Cape Dorset, N.W.T., 1969, P. 1-11

Pitseolak: Pictures out of my life, Edited by Dorothy Eber, Design Collaborative Books, Mtl./ Oxford Univ. Press, Tor., Ont., 1971

Sculpture Of The Eskimo by George Swinton, M & S, Tor., 1972, P. 131, 136

Inunnit, The Art of the Canadian Eskimo by W.T. Larmour, Info. Canada, 1974 (reprint from 1968) P. 78, 82, 86, 87

Canadian Art Auctions, Sales and Prices, 1976-1978, Ed. by Harry Campbell, General Publishing Co. Ltd., Don Mills, Ont., 1980, P. 195

Newspaper and periodical articles (selected)

The Ottawa Journal, Ont., April 18, 1967 "Pitseolak Show Fresh, Vigorous" by W.Q. Ketchum

The Ottawa Citizen, Ont., April 29, 1967 "Saga of an Eskimo family"

Ibid, Oct. 2, 1971 "Old Eskimo lady recalls past times and illustrates her story"

The Toronto Telegram, Ont., Oct. 8, 1971 "Great Eskimo artist here to publicize her first book" by Elizabeth Dingman

The Ottawa Citizen, Ont., Oct. 5, 1971 "Life in words, pictures — Vigor yet unspent" by Anne Carey

Globe Magazine, Tor., Ont., Oct. 23, 1971 "Crisp visual memories of hard but simple lives"

Montreal Star, Quebec, Oct. 8, 1971 "Eskimo artist Pitseolak exhibiting — and in print" by Terry Kirkman and Judy Heviz

Montreal Gazette, Quebec, Oct. 2, 1971 "Eskimo artist visits big city" by Michael White

Toronto Daily Star, Ont., Oct. 7, 1971 "Eskimo artist sees city for first time"

Quill & Quire, Tor., Ont., September, 1972 "Pitseolak to be published in U.S."

Winnipeg Free Press, Manitoba, Nov. 20, 1971 "A Critique By John W. Graham — Native Theme Clicks"

Business Quarterly, Autumn, 1972 "Art and the Businessman — Eskimo Art in the White Man's Market" by Ross Woodman

New Westminster Columbian, B.C., Mar. 4, 1972 "Pitseolak decorated her own book"

The Ottawa Citizen, Ont., May 10, 1975

Pitseolak — Fifteen Years of Drawings — photo and biographical information sheet for exhibit, Simon Fraser Gallery, Burnaby, B.C., 1976

Vancouver Sun, July 9, 1976 "She will draw, if she can, beyond death" by Mary Fox

Ottawa Citizen, Ont., Oct. 27, 1977 "Indian woman 'proud' to win Order of Canada medal" by Louise Crosby

---

PITSEOLAK, Peter

1904-1973

A Cape Dorset Eskimo who was regarded as a fine hunter and leader among his own people. He was introduced to photography by a white man who was terrified of polar bears but wanted a photograph of a bear close up. He asked Pitseolak to take the photo. After handling the camera Pitseolak became interested in photography and was the first known Eskimo photographer to record the era of igloos, dog teams before the move of his people to settlements. He recorded many portraits of friends, relatives, some spectacular shots of icebergs, seal hunts and Husky dog teams. He used five different cameras and purchased his first camera from the Baffin Trading Company in 1942. He used his igloo as a darkroom. He documented the old ways as well, in drawings, paintings and historical writings and his book *People from our Side* was published by Hurtig in 1975. The National Museums Council purchased his family album which consists of 1,200 photos and negatives, and placed them

PITSEOLAK, Peter (Cont'd)

on permanent loan at the Notman Photographic Archives in Montreal. His drawings were exhibited at the Innuit Gallery of Eskimo Art in Toronto and lithographs of his work were shown at the Waddington Galleries in Montreal.

References

> The Gazette, Mtl., Feb. 21, 1976 "'Family album' preserves old Eskimo ways" by Marguerite Senecal
>
> Drawings by Peter Pitseolak of Cape Dorset, March 13-27, 1976, The Innuit Gallery of Eskimo Art, 30 Avenue Road, Toronto (exhibition notice with brief biographical notes)
>
> Peter Pitseolak (sample folder with colour reproductions of lithographs), Waddington Galleries, Montreal

PITSIULAK, Lypa (Lipa)

The son of an Eskimo whaler, Marcusie Pitsiulak, he lives at Pangnirtung, N.W.T., where he is a print maker. He draws upon ancient tales and Inuit life for his subject matter. His work has been included in the book of *Prints Pangnirtung* and exhibited at Arctic Arts, Edmonton, Alberta and elsewhere.

References

> Prints/estampes, 1973 Pangnirtung, Govt. N.W.T., see Items 16, 17 and photo of him at front of catalogue
>
> Edmonton Journal, Alta., Sept. 10, 1977 "Prints reflect Inuit traditions"

PITTS, Arthur D.J.

After studies at the Westminster School of Art, London, England, he became well known as a cartoonist. Later he settled in Canada where he continued with his art and produced a good number of fine water colours. In 1933 he exhibited his water colour portraits and views of Vancouver at the Richmond Arts, Hornby Street, Vancouver, when a reviewer for *The Province* noted, ". . .Mr. Pitts has a facile touch, and his portraits are remarkably alive. One particularly, of an old soldier, is an almost speaking likeness, while another of a gentleman in formal dress, is well done. There is almost that touch of caricature, in the artist's brush, that catches the fleeting characteristic of the subject, but in a flattering way. In addition there are half a dozen sketches of familiar spots around Vancouver that will interest many." In the mid 30's Pitts travelled 4,000 miles along the coast of British Columbia and Alaska, a journey taking two years. He visited Indian villages on Vancouver Island and elsewhere he painted portraits and recorded his experiences. Some of his travel accounts appeared in articles for *Canada's Weekly* published in London, England, where he exhibited 70 water colours of Indians and Indian life at Whiteley's, Queen's Road. He painted in London either before or after he came to Canada, as his water colours of buildings and streets as they appeared prior to World War II, were exhibited at the Art Gallery of Greater Victoria in November of 1961. Another show of his work took place at Shady Creek United Church, Victoria,

PITTS, Arthur D.J. (Cont'd)

B.C. in 1969. The British Columbia Government and the Glenbow Foundation, Calgary, both have water colour portraits of Northwest Indians by him.

References

> *Vancouver Province*, B.C., July 15, 1933 "In The Domain of Art"
> *Canada's Weekly*, London, England, Jan. 10, 1936 "An Artist Among the Indians — I" by Arthur D.J. Pitts
> Ibid, Jan. 17, 1936 "An Artist Among the Indians — II" by Arthur D.J. Pitts
> *Bulletin of Art Gallery of Greater Victoria*, November to December, 1961 "London Scenes by Arthur Pitts"
> *Victoria Times*, B.C., Nov. 8, 1969 "Art Show at Bazaar"

PLAMONDON, Antoine-Sébastien
1804-1895

Born at Ancienne-Lorette, Quebec, the son of Pierre and Marie (Hamel) Plamondon. His father, described as a farmer, innkeeper and grocer, may have been all three at overlapping periods. Apparently his father was working as an innkeeper at Faubourg Saint-Roch, a suburb of Quebec City, when Antoine, then fifteen years old, was apprenticed to Joseph Légaré. Légaré was busy restoring paintings which had been gathered by Abbé Desjardins and his associates in France and sent to Quebec to be safe from wanton destruction during the French revolution. Much of Plamondon's learning period was spent on the restoration of these works. By the time he was twenty-one he had become a trained artist. He opened a temporary studio at Côte du Palais where his first known work "Jeune fille en rose" (Girl in Pink) was done. He had also begun filling commissions for churches at Beaumont, Bécancour and Cap Sainté. In 1826 he met the Vicar-General of Quebec, Descheneaux, who recognized his talent and secured funds for him to go to France to study. There he took instruction from Paulin Guérin (1783-1855), portrait painter to Charles X, and follower of neo-classic painter Jacques-Louis David. While in Paris Plamondon became involved in supporting Charles X against anti-aristocratic followers of Louis Philippe. When Charles X abdicated Plamondon left Paris in disgust and travelled to Venice, Florence and Rome where he copied works of early Italian painters, then returned to Quebec. A few of his Paris paintings returned with him which include "A Young Man" (1827), "Abbé Philippe Desjardins" and "Portrait de Femme" (A Lady, c. 1826), this last portrait revealing a strong influence of neo-classicism in marked contrast to his "Jeune fille en rose" done two years earlier. His neo-classical trend in portraits did not continue in a straight line as he moved through his career but varied with his subjects. Sometimes he painted austere canvases and at other times he included more detail around his subjects. It is estimated that he painted over fifty portraits of the upper bourgeoisie of Quebec City which included bishops, clerics, parish priests, seigneurs, politicians, doctors, notaries, merchants, businessmen and their families. It is acknowledged by several scholars that Plamondon's most productive years and his best work was done between the 1830's and the mid 1840's. Among his very fine portraits are a series of nuns of Hôpital général; "Soeur Saint-Alphonse", one of these, is owned by the National Gallery of Canada. John R. Porter, Assistant Curator of Early Canadian Art at the Gallery, did an excellent study in which he provided background and an

PLAMONDON, Antoine-Sébastien (Cont'd)

analysis of the paintings of these nuns in the publication *Antoine Plamondon, Soeur Saint-Alphonse* (NGC, 1975). One of Plamondon's other remarkable portraits is of Monseigneur Joseph Signay, Archbishop of Quebec (coll. Archevêché de Québec). While he always regarded himself as a student of the French School of painting, he moved to a freer style at times as in 1866 when he painted "The Flute Player" in which one sees a surprisingly lyrical, almost impressionistic rendering of a boy, high above the St. Lawrence on a cliff with the St. Lawrence and a ship at anchor below all bathed in a glowing sunset. Plamondon intended the painting to be a romantic serenade to the first French warship to arrive at Quebec since the fall of the Citadel to the British. One can detect the joy of the artist at seeing this exciting link with his ancestral home. He used his nephew, Siméon Alary (Alarie) as his model. Three versions of this canvas were painted by him. Then in 1871 he began to paint portraits from photographs. His last known portraits for clients were of Joseph Doré, Abbé J-H. Desruisseaux and Abbé Ulric Rousseau. He did a remarkable but austere self-portrait in 1882 which is in the collection of the Musée du Séminaire de Québec, Quebec City. He also did many religious works for churches most of which were copies. One such commission, done between 1837 and 1839, consisted of fourteen pictures for Stations of the Cross for Notre-Dame Church, Montreal, each measuring approximately eight by five feet, however when acceptance time came the paintings were rejected on the grounds that they were too radical. Rather than suffering great despair, Plamondon exhibited them in the anteroom of the Quebec Parliament Buildings and charged admission for the viewing public. Following the show the paintings were returned to his studio at Hôtel-Dieu where they were stored. Some years later the church official who had commissioned them finally accepted them and they were hung in the Seminary of Notre-Dame. They were moved from Notre-Dame and years later they were discovered in the attic of St. Patrick's Church, Montreal and were then kept by L'institut des Sourds-Muets, Montreal, until 1961. Six of them are known to have survived and were acquired for the Montreal Museum of Fine Arts. Two were rescued from a trash pile. All six were reproduced in R.H. Hubbard's catalogue *Antoine Plamondon/Théophile Hamel, Two Painters of Quebec* (NGC, Ottawa, 1970, Pages 20-21, 132-133). J. Russell Harper gives a partial list of churches in Quebec for which Plamondon executed commissions (see *Early Painters and Engravers in Canada*). During his career Plamondon lived and worked at the following places: Sainte-Hélène Street, Que. City (1825); Côte du Palais, Que. City (1825-26); France (1826-1830); Rue Sainte-Famille, Que. City (1830); Chambers of House of Assembly, Que. City (c. 1830-38); Storeroom, Hôtel Dieu, Que. City (1838); Rue Desjardins, Que. City (1842-45 where fire destroyed much of his work); Château St. Louis (Governor's residence) Château Haldimand, Que. City (1845-1850); Neuville, Quebec (1851-1895). Those who studied under him include Francis Matte (portrait, 1834-38); Zacharie Vincent (guidance in portraiture, 1838); Théophile Hamel (apprenticeship, 1838-40); Siméon Alary (Alarie, nephew, painting & decoration, c. 1854). Plamondon was also drawing master both at the Quebec Seminary (1830-41) and at Hôpital-Général (c. 1841). He lectured on art periodically as well. He felt Quebec City was his domain and when other painters made attempts to establish themselves and he didn't think their work was as good as his own, or he just didn't like what they did, he made bitter attacks upon them as on the following dates on: James Bowman (1833); Henry

PLAMONDON, Antoine-Sébastien (Cont'd)

D. Thielke (1838); Victor Ernette (1842); Andrew Morris (1844) and E. Martino (1874). His honours include a medal (1838) by the Société Littéraire et Historique de Québec for his portrait entitled "Le dernier indien" (The Last Indian); the subject of this canvas was Zacharie Vincent, last pureblooded Indian of Lorette. The portrait was purchased by Lord Durham as a tribute to Canadian artistic achievement. In 1880 he became a founding vice-president of the Royal Canadian Academy. He decorated the church at Neuville with 18 paintings between the years 1881-82. He never married and near the end of his career he lived with his mother, a brother and a sister and enjoyed the life of a gentleman farmer. He was musical and played the piano and violin and was accompanied on occasions by his nephew, Siméon Alary. He became the mayor of Neuville. When he died he had outlived all of his family and left his estate to Eugène Soulard, one of the younger members of the family of the farmer who worked his farm. A large exhibition, organized by the National Gallery of Canada and researched and catalogued by Dr. R.H. Hubbard was exhibited at the Musée du Québec (1970), Art Gallery of Ontario (1970-71) and the National Gallery of Canada (1971). Ninety-one works by Antoine Plamondon and Théophile Hamel were shown and the catalogue contained a wealth of information and excellent reproductions. Plamondon is represented in the following collections: Hôpital-Général, Que. City; Hôtel Dieu, Que. City; Jesuit Chapel, Que. City; Laval University, Que. City; Library of Parliament, Que. City; Musée du Québec, Que. City; Mtl. Mus. Fine Arts, Mtl.; McGill University, Mtl.; Nat. Gal. Canada, Ottawa; Willistead Art Gallery, Windsor, Ont.; Art Gallery of Ontario, Tor. and in many private collections.

References

The French Canadian Tradition in Painting by R.H. Hubbard, Univ. of Wisconsin, 1940 (Master of Arts Thesis) excerpt "Antoine-Sebastien Plamondon"

Canadian Art, Its Origin and Development by William Colgate, Ryerson, Tor., 1943 (paperback 1967), P. 109-111

Painting in Canada, A Selective Historical Survey, Albany Inst. of History & Art, 1946, P. 26, No. 20

National Gallery of Canada Catalogue, Vol. 3, by R.H. Hubbard, NGC, Ott., 1960 P. 250-51

The Development of Canadian Art by R.H. Hubbard, NGC, Ott., 1963, P. 57-58

Peinture traditionnelle du Québec, par Jean Trudel, Musée du Québec, 1967, P. 82-91

Three Hundred Years of Canadian Art by R.H. Hubbard and J.R. Ostiguy, NGC, Ott., 1967, P. 90-91

Art Gallery of Ontario, the Canadian collection by Helen Pepall Bradfield McGraw-Hill, Tor., 1970, P. 378-379

Early Painters and Engravers in Canada by J. Russell Harper, Univ. Tor. Press, 1970, P. 252, 253 (see bibliography)

Antoine Plamondon/Théophile Hamel, Two Painters of Quebec by R.H. Hubbard NGC/Info. Can., 1970 (see excellent notes under title and provenance section, P. 65-88 also text)

The National Gallery of Canada by Jean Sutherland Boggs, Oxford Univ. Press, Tor. 1971, P. 108-109 (excellent reproduction)

The Canadian Art Auction Record Vol. 5 by H.C. Campbell, Tor. Pub. Lib., Amtmann, Mtl., 1974, P. 56

Trésors Des Communautés Religieuses De La Ville De Québec, Musée du Québec, Que. City, 1973, P. 91

A Concise History of Canadian Painting by Dennis Reid, Oxford Univ. Press, Tor., 1973, P. 49-52

Canadian Art At Auction 1968-1975, Edited by Geoffrey Joyner, Sotheby & Co., Tor., Ont., 1975, P. 160

PLAMONDON, Antoine-Sébastien (Cont'd)

Antoine Plamondon, Soeur Saint-Alphonse by/par John R. Porter, Assist. Curator, Early Can. Art, NGC, Ottawa, 1975 (excellent source of infor.)

The Ontario Community Collects, a survey of Canadian painting from 1766 to the present by William C. Forsey, Art Gallery of Ontario, Tor., 1976, P. 152-155

Enjoying Canadian Painting by Patricia Godsell, Gen. Pub. Co. Ltd., Don Mills, Ont., 1976, P. 44, 48-50

Painting in Canada a history, 2nd Edition by J. Russell Harper, Univ. Tor. Press, Tor., 1977, P. 73-76

Canadian Art Auctions 1976-1978 compiled & edited by Harry Campbell, Gen. Publishing, Don Mills, Ont., P. 196

newspaper articles

Toronto Telegram, Ont., May 23, 1942 "At The Galleries — Painting by Plamondon Art Gallery Acquisition ("La Chasse aux Tourtes")

Windsor Star, Ont., April 22, 1966 "19th century still life — Plamondon for Windsor"

La Renaissance, Mtl., 24 Août, 1935 "Arts et Lettres — Deux Chefs-D'oeuvre De Plamondon" par Gérard Morisset

The Ottawa Citizen, Ont., June 26, 1948 "Canadian Art 100 Years Ago" by Josephine Hambleton

The Gazette, Mtl., Sept., 1960 "All our Yesterdays" by Edgar Andrew Collard

Ibid, June 3, 1965 "At The Museum — Plamondon Works 'Salvaged'"

Le Droit, Ottawa, Ont., Oct. 29, 1970 "Exposition de deux peintres québécois du siècle dernier"

Québec l'Action, Que. City, Nov. 2, 1970 "Deux peintres canadiens au Musée du Québec"

PLAMONDON, Irénée

A landscape painter who does summer and winter scenes in representational style. He is director of graphics for Bleau, Duperry, Giguères and Associates, advertising consultants.

Reference

Le Journal de Québec, Que. City, Feb. 24, 1977 "Irénée Plamondon, Peintre" (photo of paintings and caption)

PLAMONDON, Marius Gérald
1919-1976

Born in Quebec City, a descendant of the same family of noted Quebec painter Antoine Sébastien Plamondon, he studied sculpture and stained glass at the École des Beaux-Arts, Quebec, and stained glass on a Quebec provincial scholarship in France with Henri Charlier, also took further study in Italy. He returned to Quebec City, set up a studio and filled commissions for sculpture in wood, metals, stone and stained glass (windows) for churches and buildings. A master glass worker he soon became best known for his stained glass work. By 1944 he was completing, part time, thirteen windows for the Novitiate of Les Clercs de Saint-Viateur, at Joliette, Quebec, with the assistance of Ernest Rose, cutter, and Fred Barbeau, lead-glazier. The project, begun in 1940 and completed in the autumn of 1944 was made up of 6,000 pieces of glass weighing 1,500 pounds assembled. Plamondon first made his design, cut patterns from

1727

PLAMONDON, Marius Gérald (Cont'd)

the design, cut glass from the patterns, then waxed the glass pieces into an assembled whole on plate-glass. In this stage the line work was drawn on with a stipple then disassembled and the pieces placed in the firing kiln for a permanent finish. Retouching was done and the pieces assembled into sections again, leaded and soldered; cemented with putty to stiffen, weatherproofed, then (after cement dried) installed. Producing figurative and non-figurative designs, Plamondon's simplified charm was once described as, ". . .bringing imagination, humor and a vigorous human style to the art of stained glass." In 1956 he was awarded a Royal Society fellowship to take further research in stained glass in France. On his return to Canada, Plamondon was commissioned to create a sixty foot artifically lighted stained glass window as a mural for Les Voyageurs cocktail lounge in the Queen Elizabeth Hotel. The mural depicting the port of Montreal during the period when the fur trade was flourishing, consisted of half a ton of lead and glass imported from France and England and assembled by a four-man team of Benoit East, Olivier Ferland, Aristide Gagnon and Plamondon himself. The work was mainly done at Plamondon's studio at Sillery, a suburb of old Quebec where Plamondon was born. Using a variety of colours, additional tonal effects were brought out by the use of grisaille-copper or iron oxides mixed with turpentine and vinegar. The glass was then baked in a potter's kiln at a temperature of 1200 degrees for about eight hours. Plamondon also did decorations for the grill room, Beaver Club, adjoining the cocktail lounge at the Queen Elizabeth (the original Beaver Club being open only to traders who had wintered in the Northwest) where he recreated in glass, one of the mock canoe trips held after a banquet by the members of the original club, founded in 1775, when they sang the songs of the voyageurs. Another of Plamondon's commissions can be found at the Basilique de l'Oratoire Saint-Joseph du Mont Royal (1959) where 164 square feet of glass depict Sister Catherine of Saint Augustin's vision of St. Joseph in paradise at the head of the elect. Plamondon travelled to Europe to choose his supply of glass. An exhibition of his stained glass work was featured at the Art Gallery of Toronto (Ontario) in 1958. Plamondon spent considerable time teaching his art and was head of the stained glass and sculpture departments at the École des Beaux-Arts, Quebec and, also taught at Laval University and the Beaux-Arts in Montreal between 1943 and 1949. Was a member: Sculptors' Society of Canada (former Pres.); Royal Canadian Academy (A.R.C.A.); Stained Glass Association of America; International Association of Plastic Arts, UNESCO (Vice-Pres.).

References

Montreal Standard, Quebec, Sept. 23, 1944 "Stained Glass — Ancient Craft Modernized in Quebec Monastery Windows"

La Presse, Mtl., Dec. 4, 1957 "Vaste verrière de Plamondon sur le 'vieux Montréal'"

Chronicle-Telegraph, Que. City, Dec. 4, 1957 "Stained-glass Murals Set For New Montreal Hotel"

Montreal Star, Quebec, Feb. 8, 1958 "Hotel Window to Reflect History" by Boyce Richardson

Ottawa Citizen, Ont., Feb. 22, 1958 "Glass Window Recalls Montreal Of Long Ago"

Globe & Mail, Tor., Ont., Sept. 20, 1958 "Stained Glass Display Opens at Art Gallery"

Le Droit, Ottawa, Ont., Feb. 2, 1959 (article on Lake Bouchette church)

Ibid, Dec. 28, 1959 "Quatre Verrières Installées En 1959" (photo & caption)

La Presse, Mtl., Dec. 29, 1959 "Durant l'année écoulée — Importants travaux réalisés à l'Oratoire"

PLAMONDON, Marius Gérald (Cont'd)

Le Nouvelliste, Trois Rivières, Que., Jan. 6, 1960 "Des travaux importants effectués à l'Oratoire"

L'Art au Québec depuis 1940 par Guy Robert, La Presse, Mtl., 1973, P. 376

Le Devoir, 9 Oct., 1976 "La mort d'un grand artiste — Marius Plamondon, assembleur de lumières" par Jean-Charles Falardeau

Who's Who in American Art 1976, Ed. by Jaques Cattell Press, R.R. Bowker Co., NYC, 1976, P. 443

NGC Info. Form Feb. 13, 1957

Document from artist, 1962

PLANGG, Warner

A Calgary artist who was honoured by becoming a member of the Society of Animal Artists (only 65 members in the world in '69) following his exhibition of paintings at Cody, Wyoming, U.S.A. in 1969.

Reference

Calgary Albertan, Alta., Dec. 4, 1969 "Calgary artist honored" (photo and caption)

PLANIDIN, John I.

A Burnaby, B.C., artist who does portraits and landscapes in oils, water colours, wash and pen and ink and has shown with the Western Art Circle; Federation of Canadian Artists; Art, Historical and Scientific Association of which he was or is a member. He has also exhibited his work at the Orpheum and the New Museum in Vancouver.

Reference

Burnaby Courier, B.C., Sept. 9, 1959 "Portraiture and Landscapes" (photo of artist at work/caption)

PLANT, Stafford Donald

b. 1914

Born in Georgetown, Ontario, he studied at the Western Technical School and at the Grange, Toronto under Fred Brigden, Archibald Barnes and L.A.C. Panton. Was living at Qualicum Beach, B.C., in 1958.

Reference

NGC Info. Form rec'd June 25, 1958

PLANTA, Ethel Ann Carson (née Copeland)
b. 1896

Born in Newcastle, N.B., the daughter of Mr. & Mrs. James Copeland she moved to British Columbia with her family in her early teens and received formal education in Vancouver where she attained distinction as a talented concert violinist and followed her musical career until 1941 when she moved to Ottawa. She commenced study in painting seriously in 1943 first under the direction of British water colourist Emily M.B. Warren, R.A., and later with Dutch artist Peter Van Den Braken of Nijmegen and Amsterdam who maintained studios in Ottawa and Montreal from 1947 to 1954. Ethel Planta became known for her landscapes and seascapes, flower studies and still lifes. She worked in the media of oil, water colour, tempera, pen and ink and pen and crayon. She painted in Newfoundland, Ontario, Quebec, British Columbia, Rocky Mountains and in the Caribbean. She held exhibitions of her work in St. John's, Ottawa, Montreal, Quebec City, Victoria, and Vancouver. A collection of 32 of her paintings toured centres across Canada. She also exhibited at the following galleries: Bowrings, St. John's, Nfld. (1952); Robertson Galleries, Ottawa (1957, 1963); Odeon Theatre, St. John's (1959); Palais Montcalm, Que. City; Montreal Museum of Fine Arts, Mtl. (c. 1955). She exhibited at the Montreal Spring Exhibition twice (1952, 1956). She is represented in the collection of Memorial University, Nfld. Wife of Clive Planta, one time Deputy Minister of Fisheries for Newfoundland.

References

The St. John's Evening Telegram, Nfld., May 23, 1952 "Ethel Planta's Painting Selected for Montreal Museum of Fine Arts Display"

Ottawa Citizen, Ont., Apr. 11, 1957 "Exhibition By Ethel Planta At Galleries"

St. John's Evening Telegram, Apr. 10, 1957 "Mrs. Planta's Paintings Praised"

Fredericton Daily Gleaner, N.B., Apr. 22, 1957 "Newcastle Woman Stirs Art Circles With Paintings"

Clipping — "Une Hulloise expose aux Beaux-arts de Montréal" par Gaston Lapointe

St. John's Daily News, Nfld., Jan. 15, 1959 "Planta Picture Is Given To University"

St. John's Evening Telegram, Nfld., Jan. 15, 1959 "Oil Painting Is Donated To University Collection"

Le Droit, Ottawa, June 15, 1963 "La Vie Artistique — Le rideau se lève. . ." par Edgar Demers

NGC Info. Form rec'd Aug. 31, 1956

PLANTE, Carole

She studied art at Trois-Rivières and exhibited her ink drawings, some engravings and gouache paintings at Cambuz'art in Trois-Rivières. René Lord described her work as creative and imaginative. She illustrated poems for Jean Ferrat.

Reference

Le Nouvelliste, Trois-Rivières, P.Q., May 26, 1977 "détente — Exposition Carole Plante" par René Lord

---

PLANTE, Léopold

He exhibited sixty of his paintings on a variety of subjects in the basement of Saint-Pie-X in Trois-Rivières (1969) also showed his work at la galerie d'art du Centre commercial Les Rivières (1977).

References

> Le Nouvelliste, Trois-Rivières, Que., May 8, 1969 "Exposition de toiles au souper de l'Age d'Or"
> Ibid, July 14, 1969 "Le Productif Peintre Léopold Plante" (photo and caption)
> Ibid, Feb. 16, 1977 "La galerie d'art du Centre. . ."

PLANTENGA, Stansje
b. 1947

Born in the Netherlands, she studied at the École des Beaux-Arts, Montreal, and is known for her drawings, paintings and printmaking in the media of oil, etching, silkscreen and linocut. She has exhibited her work at the following places: "Les Moins de 35"; dual show at Galerie 90/40, Mtl. (1972); "L'Exposition des Femmes" Vehicule Art, Mtl. (1972); dual show at Power-house, Mtl. (1974). Viewing her show at the Galerie 90/40 Michael White of The Gazette noted, "Gaiety and naïveté are not often the main qualities of the work of young Montreal artists but they are in the paintings, drawings and prints of Stansje Plantenga. . . .paintings and pastels express an involvement with her immediate environment — her friends, her husband (musician Andrew Cowan) and their home, stand out. There is more heat and movement in her fantasies of jungles or of the city jungle. This young Dutch-born artist works in harmonious colours and simple forms of the German 'Blue Rider' Expressionists of the 1900's, but her subjects are more personal, less tense than the erotic blue horses and vibrant color contrasts of the pre-First World War Germans."

References

> The Gazette, Mtl., Aug. 17, 1972 "Tranquility, violence at 90/40" by Michael White
> Canadian artists in exhibition, 1972-73, Roundstone, Tor., 1974, P. 171
> exhibition notice — at Powerhouse, 1210 Green, Mtl., 1974 (Jane Adams and Stansje Plantenga)

PLASKETT, Aileen Anne
b. 1905

Born in London, England, she came to Toronto, Canada in 1911 then moved to Ottawa. She studied drawing at the Ottawa Technical School under A.F. Newlands and also painting under Franklin Brownell; life painting with Ernest Fosbery and, in London, England at the South Kensington Museum then returned to Canada. She became active with the Ottawa Art Association (1926). Following her marriage in 1938 she painted under her married name. See DUFFY, Aileen Plaskett, V.1.

PLASKETT, Aileen Anne (Cont'd)

References

NGC Info. Form, June 25, 1930
A Dic. Can. Artists V.1

PLASKETT, Joseph Francis
b. 1918

Born in New Westminster, B.C., the son of Frank and Mary (Draper) Plaskett, his mother was born in England and his father in Ontario. Joe Plaskett lived in the Anglican Rectory in New Westminster (his father was Canon Frank Plaskett). His home was located near the Fraser River and surrounded by fields, bush and large Victorian mansions. The setting was described by Alvin Balkind in these words, "Cows used to graze nearby; and close at hand were ruins, abandoned gardens, a Shinto temple, and cemeteries. His childhood saw the last of an idyllic setting, a combining of country living with town life. Then, life was quiet, parochial, old-fashioned, English in tone. For Plaskett, it was, perhaps, the Golden or Silver Age which he still seeks." He attended Sir Richard McBride primary school at Sapperton, then the Duke of Connaught Secondary School at New Westminster where he began to copy paintings, and work from nature or his imagination. He pursued academic studies and after finishing high school he entered the University of British Columbia where he took an Honours B.A. in History, graduating with first class honours in 1939. He then attended teachers' college at U.B.C. and after finishing this course taught in B.C. schools for five years (North Shore College, N. Van., 1940-45; Coquitlam High School, B.C., 1945-46). During this period he began formal instruction in art, evenings. He received encouragement to paint from G.G. Sedgewick, Lawren Harris and Jock MacDonald when he attended the Vancouver School of Art between 1940 and 1942 where he studied with P.V. Ustinov, Charles Scott, F.A. Amess, Jack Shadbolt and B.C. Binning. He spent his summers painting and studied at the Banff Summer School in 1944 with A.Y. Jackson. The following year he became a member of the B.C. Society of Artists (won a bronze medal for work in pastel from this society in 1944). In 1946 he was awarded an Emily Carr Scholarship and was the first recipient of this award which enabled him to study art at the California School of Fine Art, San Francisco under William Gaw, David Park, Clay Spohn and Clyfford Still (at San. Fran., Sept. '46 to Feb. '47). By this time he was painting landscapes chiefly of the southern Okanagan Valley and the Cariboo District of British Columbia while also doing imaginative figure paintings and abstractions. He now had a fine background of academic studies, five years of teaching experience, thirteen years as a practising artist exploring drawing and painting with a grasp of varied points of view, styles, theories and was ready to assume the principalship of the Winnipeg School of Art. At the school he gave guidance and inspiration to his students from 1947 to 1949. His summers were spent in further study in New York City and Provincetown under the noted abstractionist Hans Hofmann. In 1949 he began to long for more time to paint and finally resigned from the school, passed the summer as instructor at the Banff School of Fine Arts before sailing from New York to Paris where he studied with Fernand Léger, Jean Lombard and Marzelle. He found a place to live, a salon on the Boulevard St. Germain. His apartment was filled with precious objects which were to attract him to use them as subjects in a series of fine interiors and drawings, and gradually draw him away from the world of abstraction. That summer (1950) he set out on a walking and hitch-hiking tour of France, Spain, Portugal, Morocco, Tunisia, Italy and other points. In his travels he used mainly pastels which were suitable for mobility. He then returned to Paris for another season of study. He had learned in American schools the theory and technique of art but it was in Paris and in Europe that he became aware of the reverence for the created object. The following summer he toured the British Isles, Holland, Belgium and Germany and returned to Venice and back to Paris. In 1951 he moved to London, England, to study at the Slade School with a bursary awarded by the British Arts Council. By the end of 1951 he had returned to New Westminster where he prepared his drawings, pastel paintings and oils done over the past two years for showing at the Vancouver Art Gallery and at the University of British Columbia Art Gallery. Viewing his work at V.A.G. Palette of the *Province* described his work as follows, "The new pastels are delightful, being particularly exciting in their freedom of expression and use of color, employed sensitively but in a rich, forceful manner. Many of the subjects are in Paris and other places in France visited by the artist during recent years abroad. Joe Plaskett gives a distinctly original twist to his interpretations, which are primarily based on powerful aesthetic impulse and his own method of expression. His poetic rather than realistic or descriptive viewpoint provides rich entertainment for those who appreciate strong creative tendencies in contemporary art." His work was also exhibited in Winnipeg, and Toronto. He taught nights at the Vancouver School of Art (1952-53). In 1953 he returned to Paris with the assistance of a Canadian Government Overseas Scholarship to study etching and engraving with Stanley Hayter. On his return to Canada in 1955 he took a teaching post with the Extension Department of the University of British Columbia and continued to travel and paint in his native province, especially in the Kootenay and Cariboo Districts. He was accompanied by fellow painter and former pupil Takao Tanabe. In 1956 he also taught at the Vancouver School of Art and at Emma Lake in Saskatchewan. He returned to Paris in 1957 to become a full-time painter free from any teaching duties. By now he had left the world of abstraction, no longer satisfied with its results and had turned to figurative painting. Abstraction had developed his taste, sensitivity and knowledge of controlling space. There were greater possibilities in abstraction but he found limitations by its exclusion of the actual visual world with the endless ways to interpret that world. In 1960 with his friend, he purchased two floors of a small 15th Century, four-storey building not lived in for over twenty years, located near the western boundary of the Marias (or March) district of Paris close to the Right Bank of the Seine River. They set to work and installed electricity, proper plumbing and in his section of the apartment, Joe proceeded to decorate with Louis 16th styled furniture and assorted bric-a-brac selected from local flea markets. The district, with historical roots going back some 800 years, is bordered by the old market of Les Halles on one side and the Place de la Bastille on the other. It had fallen into disrepair until being rediscovered following World War II by a new history-conscious generation. Now it has become inhabited by scholars, intellectuals, artists, writers, and "reconstituted semi-aristocrats" who live in its restored apartments. Here Plaskett over the

PLASKETT, Joseph Francis (Cont'd)

years has created countless studies of his apartment's interior, still lifes and portraits of his friends and neighbours. In 1967 he was awarded a Canada Council fellowship to travel and paint "out of the way" places across Canada from Labrador to British Columbia. He renewed his ties with Canada visiting small communities and making hundreds of sketches and paintings which were subsequently exhibited at various centres across Canada. Then he returned to Paris and in 1971 an exhibition was organized, entitled "Joe Plaskett And His Paris — In Search Of Time Past", by the Fine Arts Gallery of the University of British Columbia and shown at that gallery then circulated across Canada through the auspices of the extension services of the National Gallery of Canada. A catalogue written by Alvin Balkind, organizer of the show, provided excellent background material on Plaskett, his home and studio, and some insight into his daily routine with brief notes on the artist's many friends and neighbours, whose portraits he has painted. Photos of his studio and some of his work were also included. In the prologue to the catalogue Balkind states, ". . .Joe Plaskett's life and his art could not be considered apart from one another; for his life feeds his art, and his art, in turn, feeds his life; and the cycle continues. Indeed, it would be difficult not to see these two aspects of Plaskett as having become completely and totally inseparable, with both revolving like electrons around the nucleus of his house at 2 rue Pecquay, Paris." Paris however, was soon not to be his only working location overseas. He purchased some years back a cottage in Suffold, England, where he has been developing new paintings, in contrast to his Paris interiors, filled with sunlit English country fields rendered in his own personal interpretation. He continues to return to Canada to paint and exhibit. His solo shows include: Vancouver Art Gallery, B.C. (1940, 43, 45, 52, 56); University of B.C. Fine Arts Gallery, Van. (1952, 60, 71 & circ. across Canada); Holy Trinity Memorial Hall, New Westmstr. (1956); New Design Gallery, Van. (1960, 63, 65); Little Gallery, New Westmstr. (1965); Griffith Galleries, Van. (1968); Burnaby Art Gallery, B.C. (1976); Pub. Lib., New Westmstr. (1961); Bau-X1 Gallery, Van. (1974, 75, 77); Kelowna Art Gal., B.C. (1976); Topham Brown Gal., Vernon, B.C. (1977); Coste House, Calg., Alta. (1953); Lefebvre Gal., Edmon., Alta. (1977); Winnipeg Art Gal., Wpg. (1952, 69); Fleet Gal., Wpg. (1970); Brandon Univ., Man. (1969); Brandon Art Centre, Man. (1960); Picture Loan Soc., Tor. (1953, 58, 60, 70); Jerrold Morris Gal., Tor. (1970); Robertson Galleries, Ott. (1963, 67, 70, 73); Wallacks Gallery, Ott. (1977); Waddington Gal., Mtl. (1960); Walter Klinkhoff, Mtl. (1973); Univ. N.B. Arts Centre, Fred. (1968, 69 & touring 5 other Atlantic galleries); Canadian Cultural Centre, Paris (1978). He is represented in collections of New Westminster Pub. Lib. B.C.; Vancouver Art Gallery, B.C.; Edmonton Art Gal., Edm. Alta.; Winnipeg Art Gallery, Wpg., Man.; London Public Library & Art Museum, Ont.; Art Gallery of Ontario, Tor.; Nat. Gal. Canada, Ott.; Firestone Coll., Ott.; Concordia Univ. (Sir Geo. Wms. Univ.), Mtl.; Beaverbrook Gallery, Fred., N.B. and many important private collections in North America and Europe.

References

Books and catalogues

The Arts in Canada, Ed. Malcolm Ross, Macmillan, Tor., 1958, P. 29, 30

NGC Catalogue, Vol. 3, by R.H. Hubbard, NGC/Univ. Tor. Pr., 1960, P. 251-2

The Development of Canadian Art by R.H. Hubbard, NGC, Ottawa, P. 130

PLASKETT, Joseph Francis (Cont'd)

Sir George Williams University (Concordia) Collection of Art by Edwy Cooke

150 Years of Art in Manitoba, Winnipeg Art Gal., Man., 1970, P. 62

Art Gallery of Ontario, the Canadian Collection by Helen Pepall Bradfield, P. 380

Joe Plaskett and His Paris — In Search of Time Past by Alvin Balkind, Fine Arts Gallery, UBC, Van., 1971/NGC, Ottawa

Creative Canada, Volume Two, Ref. Div. McPherson Lib. Univ. Victoria/Univ. Tor. Pr., 1972, P. 222

Four Decades, The Can. Group of Painters by Paul Duval, Clarke Irwin, Tor., 1972, P. 167

Canadian Art Auction Record, Vol. 5, 1973 Compiled by H.C. Campbell, Bernard Amtmann Inc., Mtl., 1974, P. 56

Canadian Art at Auction 1968-1975, Ed. Geoffrey Joyner, Sotheby & Co. Tor., 1975, P. 160

The Ontario Community Collects by William C. Forsey, Art Gal. Ontario Tor., 1976, P. 156

Canadian Art Auctions Compiled by H.C. Campbell, Gen. Pub. Ltd., Don Mills, Ont., 1980, P. 196

Firestone Art Collection, Ont., Heritage Foundation, McGraw-Hill Ryerson Ltd., Tor., 1978, P. 112

Newspapers, books & catalogues (selected)

Vancouver Province, Van., B.C., Sept. 13, 1945 "Plaskett Pictures Featured — City Gallery Display Discloses Creative Spirit" by Palette

Vancouver Sun, Van., B.C., July 27, 1946 "Plaskett Awarded Carr Scholarship"

Winnipeg Tribune, Nov. 21, 1947 "Art School Head Talks on Sculpture"

Ibid, May 28, 1948 "Opportunity in Art Lies In Hard Work, Grads Told" (Plaskett speaks to students at Wpg. Sch. Art)

Ibid, Feb. 21, 1949 "Art Principal Opens Informal Show — Keep Mentally Alive, Artists Told"

Vancouver Province, Nov. 8, 1952 "Plaskett Art Exhibit Proves To Be Popular" by Palette

The Free Press, Wpg., Man., Nov. 26, 1952 "Plaskett Paintings" by K.M.H. (show at Wpg. Art Gal.)

Globe & Mail, Tor., Ont., Dec. 12, 1953 "Plaskett's Work Illustrates Role of Picture Loan Bodies" by Pearl McCarthy

British Columbian, New Westmstr., B.C., Jan. 3, 1951 "Scholarship Awarded to City Artist"

Vancouver Province, Oct. 3, 1952 (informative article by J. Delisle Parker)

British Columbian, New Westmstr., — 28, 1955 "National Gallery Buys Plaskett Art"

Ibid, Apr. 7, 1956 "Plaskett, Hardman Show Paintings, Sculpture"

Vancouver Province, Sept. 10, 1956 "Plaskett oils depict a more graceful age" by Palette

Daily Sun, Man., July 5, 1960 "Canadian Artist From Paris Arranges Display" by Daye Rowe

The Gazette, Mtl., Nov. 5, 1960 "Art — Joe Plaskett Exhibition" by Dorothy Pfeiffer (show at Waddington, Mtl.)

Montreal Star, Nov. 5, 1960 "Quebec Painters Well Represented. . . ." by Robert Ayre (show at Waddington, Mtl.)

Globe & Mail, Tor., Nov. 12, 1960 "Concrete in Abstract Joseph Plaskett's Art"

British Columbian, New Westmstr., Oct. 22, 1962 "Joe Plaskett and Royal City Show their mutual admiration" by Priscilla Jackson

Ottawa Journal, Ont. (CP), Dec. 20, 1963 "Artist Scores In Paris" by Alan Harvey (finds 15th Century dwelling not lived in for 23 years)

Columbian, New Westmstr., B.C., July 26, 1965 "Canadian artist returns home" by Mildred Jerre

Vancouver Sun, Oct. 15, 1965 "Artist Will Melt Hardest Heart" by David Watmough

La Frontière, Rouyn-Noranda, Québec, Juillet 5, 1967 "Un peintre canadien-anglais à Paris, Joe Plaskett" par Jean-Pierre Bonneville (photos: Robert Martino)

Ottawa Citizen, Ont., Oct. 11, 1967 review by Jenny Bergin (show at Robertson, Ott.)

Brandon Sun, Man., Nov. 22, 1967 "Artist Joseph Plaskett Paints Out-Of-Way Places" by Kaye Rowe (cross Canada painting trip assisted by C.C.)

Vancouver Province, B.C., Feb. 28, 1968 "Plaskett loses mystique and magic to technical skill" by Maija Bismanis

Brandon Sun, May 20, 1969 "Plaskett the Painter show shared day of convocation"

PLASKETT, Joseph Francis (Cont'd)

Winnipeg Free Press, Man., May 24, 1969 "A Review By John W. Graham — Brandon U Displays Plaskett Collection"

Montreal Star, Que., April 18, 1970 "Joe Plaskett in Paris" by Francean Campbell

Globe & Mail, Tor., Apr. 25, 1970 "Wings, glitter, gaiety" by Kay Kritzwiser

Columbian, New Westmstr., July 25, 1970 "enjoys 'busman's holiday'" by Winnifred Thorpe

Winnipeg Free Press, Man., Dec. 15, 1970 "Critique By John W. Graham — Plaskett Display In Fleet Gallery"

Vancouver Sun, B.C., Nov. 21, 1971 "Joe knows people are awful, but he won't admit it" by Joan Lowndes

London Evening Free Press, Ont., Mar. 4, 1972 "Plaskett inspires ageless quality" by Lenore Crawford

Calgary Herald, Alta., Dec. 1, 1972 "Paintings by Joe Plaskett; an art highlight of the year"

Ottawa Citizen, Ont., Nov. 17, 1973 "Long route to art" by Ann Walker

Vancouver Sun, B.C., Sept. 25, 1974 "The contradictions in Plaskett's garden do grow" by Joan Lowndes

Columbian, B.C., New Westmstr., B.C., June 4, 1976 "Library receives Plaskett paintings" by Maggie Leech (photo by Peter Battistoni)

The Canadian Review, October, 1976 "Joe Plaskett, A Canadian in Paris" by Susan Hallett

Vancouver Sun, B.C., Oct. 4, 1976 "Joe Plaskett's record of a vanished B.C." by Mary Fox

Kelowna Courier, B.C., Dec. 6, 1976 "Joe Plaskett Pastels On Display At Gallery"

Vernon Daily News, B.C., Jan. 14, 1977 "Topham Brown Gallery — Pastel exhibition well worth visit" by Jack Nittel

Ottawa Journal, Aug. 27, 1977 "Joe Plaskett — a Canadian in Paris" by Marianne Ackerman

Edmonton Journal, Alta., Jan. 29, 1977 "Art review — A show to delight lovers of Impressionism" by Jean Richards

Vancouver Sun, Aug. 5, 1977 "The self-exile of 28 years as a painter in Paris"

Le Droit, Ont., Jan. 10, 1978 "Exposition à Paris — Le peintre Joe Plaskett veut s'attaquer au marché européen" par Jacques Bouchard

NGC Info. forms: July 2, 1947, 1959, 1966

Document from artist, 1960

Copy of letter from J. Plaskett to J. Hardman, Aug. 23, 1976 (NGC artist's file)

PLASSE, Gill

A Charlesbourg, Quebec, artist who works in both abstract and figurative styles of painting which includes portraits, still lifes, town and country scenes and geometric based abstractions. His work can be seen at La Galerie des Artisans in Charlesbourg.

Reference

Brochure by La Galerie des Artisans, Charlesbourg, Quebec

PLATKAIS (Mrs. Anna Mierzynski)

A graduate of the Ontario College of Art, Toronto, she moved to Sault Ste. Marie, Ontario, where she taught painting at the local Y.M.C.A. and exhibited her own paintings there including oils and mixed media. Viewing her work in 1961, Gwen Keatley noted, "Paintings such as Grevant Hill, Poppies, Whirling

PLATKAIS (Mrs. Anna Mierzynski) (Cont'd)

Wind, The Field, Late Afternoon, Storm Birds, Twilight and Harvest are so intimate in their conception that they glitter like jewels despite the vibrant colors and bold design of the rest of the show. . . .Along with her oils Platkais has exhibited a number of small works of mixed medium. In these she has again excelled in color or achieving the raw brilliance of medieval stained glass."

Reference

Daily Star, Sault Ste. Marie, Ont., July 6, 1961 "Platkais' Palette Knife Breaks Vibrant Prisms" by Gwen Keatley

PLATNER, Rae Katz

b. 1905

Born in Poland, she came to Canada with her family around 1910 and they settled in Toronto. She studied art at the Central Technical School in Toronto under Elizabeth Wyn Wood; evenings at the Ontario College of Art under Emanuel Hahn; and under Frances Loring and Florence Wyle at their Toronto Glenrose Avenue studio. Known for her portraits she has also done figures and compositional pieces. In 1940 she won first prize for a sculptural portrait at the Canadian National Exhibition. She held solo shows of her work at the Towne Cinema, Tor. (1954, 58) and Hart House (1954) and participated in the Toronto Art Exhibition held at Nathan Phillips Square (1973) where her larger than life heads of former Prime Ministers, John Diefenbaker and Lester B. Pearson were shown (two in her series of portraits of noted world personages, done in bold and vigorously textured style). The wife of writer Israel Platner, she has exhibited her work with the Sculptors' Society of Canada, the Ontario Society of Artists, at the Art Gallery of Ontario and elsewhere.

References

Canadian Jewish News, Tor., Ont., Sept. 20, 1968 "Diefenbaker Sculpture Praised" (photo and caption)

Toronto Sun, Ont., June 19, 1973 "The largest outdoor art display in Canada, the Toronto Art Exhibition" (photo of two sculptures by Rae Platner and caption)

NGC Info. Form rec'd Feb. 11, 1959

PLATZ, Gayle

A Winnipeg, Manitoba, textile artist who has exhibited wall hangings and banners at the Winnipeg Art Gallery.

Reference

Winnipeg Free Press, Man., Dec. 21, 1973 (large photo, showing Platz and Marilyn Foubert, another textile artist, surrounded by work during an exhibition at the Winnipeg Art Gallery)

PLAYFAIR, Charles Paul Gregory
b. 1917

Born in Hagersville, Ontario, he studied art in Hamilton with John and Hortense Gordon; at the Art Students' League, New York under George Bridgman, Jon Corbino (1937-41). He joined the army and served in the Intelligence Corps in England, France and the Low Countries and after his demobilization in 1946 returned to Hamilton, Ontario. By 1949 he was exhibiting his paintings at the Hamilton Art Gallery annual winter exhibitions and attracted considerable attention with his work. During his solo show in 1959 at the Upstairs Gallery, Toronto, Colin Sabiston of the *Globe & Mail* noted, "Mr. Playfair's drawings in ink and pencil are in the tradition of fine line delineation. They reveal highly developed capacity for selecting the most significant features of subject matter, and for using them with discrimination and taste. . . .The oil paintings have a higher proportion of abstract and non-objective subjects than the drawings, and show the same thoughtful approach. Relying on the world of visible realities, Mr. Playfair seems to move from representationalism to abstraction only a certain distance before realizing the emotive impulses begin to weaken. He then returns to basic subject matter from nature, falling back upon his accomplished draughtsmanship. While the exhibition has high pictorial appeal as it hangs, there is an equal, or even greater interest in its promise of Mr. Playfair's future development into the ranks of Canada's major artists." He exhibited for the first time in the national show of the Third Biennial Exhibition of Canadian Art held at the National Gallery in 1959 and again in 1963 (Fifth Biennial. . .Painting). By 1966 he showed his support for the Canadian Peace Research Institute and donated the proceeds of the sales of his exhibition held at the Port Credit Library, to the Institute. He taught art in Hamilton; was a designer for television production settings at the C.B.C., Toronto, exhibiting his personal work at the Pollock Gallery. Over the years he also held solo shows at Hart House, Tor.; George Loranger, Ottawa; in Regina, Sask. and probably other locations.

References

> *The Hamilton Spectator*, Ont., Dec. 3, 1949 "Distinguished Paintings on View" (photo of Playfair's "Portrait of an Old Man"
>
> *London Free Press*, Ont., Jan. 18, 1950 "Painting Series Listed Tonight"
>
> Ibid, Apr. 28, 1951 (photo of Playfair's "Christ Washing Peter's Feet")
>
> *Regina Leader Post*, Sask., Nov. 8, 1954 "Drawings by Playfair" (solo show)
>
> *Globe & Mail*, Tor., Ont., Mar. 13, 1959 "A Pair of Art Firsts" by Colin Sabiston
>
> *Daily Journal-Record*, Oakville, Ont., Nov. 26, 1966 "Playfair Oil Painting Show Set Proceeds To Aid Peace Research"
>
> *Third Biennial Exhibition of Canadian Art*, 1959, NGC, Ottawa, 1959, No. 45
>
> *Fifth Biennial Exhibition of Canadian Painting*, 1963, NGC, Ottawa, 1963, No. 57
>
> NGC Info. Form rec'd May 1, 1947; NGC Info. Form undated, but later

PLESKOW, Lisa

She exhibited a series of oil and fabric constructions of portraits in a show entitled "Damsels in Relief" at the 567 Gallery, Toronto.

PLESKOW, Lisa (Cont'd)

Reference

Notice from 567 Gallery with reproduction of her work.

PLISIK, Vera

Born in Waddesdon, Buckinghamshire, England, she had an early interest in art and received her first real colour box at the age of five and her first oil paints at twelve. She won an art scholarship when she was sixteen and attended the West of England College of Art. She came to Canada, married Paul Plisik and they have one son Michael. Mrs. Plisik returned to her art and has become known for her portraits in pastel. She also does flower and scenery paintings as well and makes brooches on which she paints tiny scenes on an oval surface which have been described as beautiful. Lives in Galt, Ontario.

Reference

Galt Evening Reporter, Ont., June 6, 1969 "Pastel Portraits The Specialty Of Local Artist Vera Plisik" by Pat Keachie

---

PLITZ, Gus

A carver from Pickering Township, he began his craft when he was in the Armed Services. His father, founder of G. Plitz Co. Ltd., (dealers, shippers of genuine Canadian hand-made souvenirs) saw his son's work as a marketable product and the carvings soon became known further afield. Gus spends some of his time buying up drift wood and pine roots for his raw materials and from them he produces life-like wild life figures which include fish of all shapes and sizes, ducks, birds of many kinds mounted on plaques and painted with exquisite detail, also other items. He built his home, a thirty-five foot sailboat as well, and has enjoyed flying as a hobby. Lives on Sandy Beach Road, Pickering Township, Ontario.

Reference

The Bay News, Pickering, Ont., Mar. 7, 1973 "An Old Time Art" by Dilys Sutton

---

PLOMTEUX, Léon

b. 1905

Born in Belgium, he became a notary and was also interested in painting. He met Raymonde, an artist in her own right, and they married and continued their artistic interests; emigrated to Canada in 1951 and settled on a farm just outside Dunham, Quebec. From there they attended classes at the Cowansville Art Centre. Léon and Raymonde studied art as well at the Instituto Allende at San Miguel Allende, Mexico. After their children had grown up, one of their sons

PLOMTEUX, Léon (Cont'd)

built them a chalet just across the road from their farm and there they established "Studio Clarement" where they have their studios, exhibit their own work and conduct classes for local residents. In his painting Léon has become known for his portraits, figure studies and local scenes around Stanbridge East, Dunham, Cowansville, and elsewhere in the Eastern Townships also his colourful scenes done during his visits to Mexico and Italy.

References

Granby La Voix de l'Est, Que., Feb. 19, 1960 "La Peinture Moderne — Un peintre dit sa valeur artistique et culturelle"

Leader-Mail, Granby, P.Q., Nov. 16, 1960 "Three artists hold exhibit in art centre"

Le Yamaska, Cowansville, P.Q., Nov. 23, 1960 "Three Artists Hold Exhibit in Cowansville Art Centre"

Sherbrooke Record, Que., Nov. 4, 1963 "Last '63 art exhibition opens" by Fred Pattemore

Ibid, June 9, 1965 "Dunham couple has own art gallery — way of life centered on life long hobby" by Dan Karon

Le Yamaska, June 30, 1965 "Une Nouvelle Galerie D'Art Ouvre Ses Portes A Dunham"

Granby La Voix de l'Est, Que., Aug. 30, 1968 "La technique de la peinture doit être personnelle, dit M. Plomteux"

Sherbrooke La Tribune, Que., Nov. 20, 1968 "Raymonde et Léon Plomteux Exposent à Lac-Mégantic"

PLOMTEUX, Raymonde
b. 1905

Born in Liège, Belgium, she studied art in Belgium, France, Italy and Mexico and came to Canada with her notary and artist husband in 1951. They settled on a farm just outside Dunham, Quebec, and from there attended painting classes at the Cowansville Art Centre with A. Zodorozy. They established a studio across from their farm named "Studio Clarement" where they have done their painting, exhibited their work and conducted classes for local residents. Her landscapes of Mexico have particularly been cited for their colourfulness especially effective by her application of paint almost in its pure form with fairly heavy impasto brush strokes. Also cited are her still lifes and flower arrangements.

References

Granby La Voix de l'Est, Que., Aug. 30, 1968 "La technique de la peinture doit être personnelle, dit M. Plomteux"

See also references under PLOMTEUX, Léon

PLOMTEUX, Tiziana Tabbia
b. 1938

Born in Turin, Italy, from a family of artists, she studied at the Albertine Academy of Fine Arts specializing in drawing and art history. She then graduated from the University of Turin; travelled in Europe and Latin America, returning with notebooks filled with her felt pen drawings. She taught arts and literature for five years and was assistant to the curator of the Turin Gallery of

PLOMTEUX, Tiziana Tabbia (Cont'd)

Early Art. She married a Canadian and moved to Quebec. Known for her water colours, drawings, pastels and oils she held her first solo show at the Cowansville Cultural Centre, Quebec, in 1971 and subsequent shows at: Rothman's House, Sherbrooke (1976); Cowansville Cultural Centre (1977 — two-woman); St. Lambert Cultural Centre (1978) and in a number of group shows including the Craftsman's Show at Jay Peak in 1976 when she won 2nd Prize for her water colours.

References

La Voix de l'Est, Granby, Que., Sept. 27, 1976 "Peintre de chez nous à l'honneur" (photo and caption)
Sherbrooke La Tribune, Que., Dec. 9, 1976 "Tiziana Tabbia Plomteux expose"
La Voix de l'Est, Granby, Que., Oct. 12, 1977 "Au Centre culturel. . ." par Ginette Laurin
Sherbrooke Record, Que., Mar. 17, 1978 "E.T. artist exhibits"

PLOSKER, Oscar
b. 1953

Born in Regina, Saskatchewan, he studied visual arts at the University of Saskatchewan, Regina Campus, and at the Emma Lake Artists' Workshop and graduated with his B.F.A. in 1976. In 1974 he was awarded a Saskatchewan Arts Board grant and travelled in Canada and Europe. During his solo show at the Norman Mackenzie Art Gallery in 1976 a reviewer for the *Leader Post* noted "Mr. Plosker, who was given a one-man show in the Mackenzie's "Other Space" series last August, is a non-objective painter. His paintings are color statements, curling, swirling masses of brilliant shades. It's very much a continuation of the work shown last summer except that the current compositions seem a little more compacted, the masses more deliberately shaped. . .It's a great show for this time of year. . .like stepping out of the cold into a warm conservatory full of exotic blooms."

References

Leader Post, Regina, Sask., Aug. 29, 1975 "Artist's work displayed"
Ibid, Jan. 17, 1976 "Plosker exhibition"

PLOTEK, Leopold

He participated in Quebec 75, with seventeen other artists and during the same year held a solo show at Concordia University when Georges Bogardi reviewing his work noted, "Leopold Plotek's paintings. . .Painted on raw, unstretched, shaped canvas, are built of architectonic elements of vivid color. In Swiss Movement, a compelling work, the semi-circular surface is set in motion by overlapping segments of color. The space created is ambiguous; as in the works of the French Support surface school, the segments of bare canvas act as breathing space. They separate the colored areas and prevent them from creating space. In Plotek's other paintings, color is totally absolved of this traditional responsibility; the elements are assembled into dynamic structures."

PLOTEK, Leopold (Cont'd)

References

Montreal Star, Mtl., P..Q., Mar. 8, 1975 "Toward definitions" by Georges Bogardi
Ibid, Oct. 30, 1976 "Beyond history" by Georges Bogardi

PLOURDE, Raymond M.

From Valleyfield, he began painting in hospital using charcoal. After leaving hospital he organized a group of amateur painters under a teacher from Montreal. In the spring of 1959 the group "Club des Arts" held a show with great success. Plourde has worked with serigraph and has been interested in making reproductions of coins. He held a solo show of his paintings at Sept-Iles Municipal Library when he received praise for his high quality of work.

Reference

L'Avenir de Sept-Iles Journal, Sept-Iles, Que., Mar. 6, 1969 "Exposition de Tableaux Du Peintre Plourde"

PLOURDE-SIMARD, Ginette

Known for her work in pen, pencil and water colours of landscapes, and science fiction subjects, she has exhibited her work in Jonquière at the community Café and at the Gosselin restaurant.

References

Sagueney Le Quotidien, Chicoutimi, Que., Mar. 6, 1976 "Ginette Plourde-Simard nous déçoit" par Yvon Paré
Ibid, (date unknown) "Ca mijote chez Ginette Plourde-Simard" par Yvon Paré

PLUHATOR, Mike

After finishing high school at Wadena, Saskatchewan, he attended the University of Saskatchewan and graduated with his Bachelor of Arts (1959); took post graduate studies at the University and majored in art and drama. During this period he studied under noted Canadian, American and Dutch artists. He exhibited his paintings at the home of Mr. & Mrs. O.E. Fraleigh in Wadena, in 1965. Was active with the Wadena Theatre.

Reference

Wadena News, Wadena, Sask., May 20, 1965 "Paintings of local artist to be displayed at tea"

PLUNGUIAN, Mrs. Mark (née Rosner)

(c) 1905-1962

Born in Germany, she came to Montreal, Canada in 1935 where she studied sculpture at the École des Beaux-Arts. She met Dr. Mark Plunguian in Montreal and following their marriage they moved to Chilicothe, Ohio, then settled in Princeton, N.J. where she did the portrait of Albert Einstein which is now in the collection of the Tel Aviv Museum. Was a member of the Artists' Equity; Delaware Council of Artists; National Association of Women Artists; Knickerbocker Artists; College Art Association of America and the National League of American Pen Women. She died in Newark, N.J. in her fifty-seventh year and was survived at that time by her husband; two daughters, Mrs. Edith Frank (Buffalo, N.Y.) and Miss Clair (Newark, N.J.), her mother Mrs. Jetty Rosner and a sister, Mrs. Friga Markovits (Mtl.) and two brothers Carl (Mtl.) and Vid (Los Angeles, Calif.).

Reference

Montreal Star, Quebec, Nov. 14, 1962 "Mrs. M. Plunguian"

PLUSCH, Alice

She exhibited her paintings of geometric figurative interiors at Gallery O, Markham Street, Toronto in 1977.

Reference

Notice — New Paintings by Alice Plusch, Sept. 29 to Oct. 18, 1977, Gallery O, 589 Markham Street, Tor.

POCOCK, John

b. 1912

Born in Toronto, Ontario, he was a junior officer in the English army and was wounded in the invasion of France and sent home in 1944. A designer and jeweller, he established his studio in Yorkville Village, Toronto, where he created jewellery which is known in many parts of the world. He has won many prizes at the C.N.E., Toronto, and handicrafts shows in Montreal, Toronto, Brussels, Paris, Ottawa and elsewhere. He exhibited his work at the Art Gallery of Ontario (Tor.), National Gallery of Canada (Ott.), and at World's Fairs at Brussels, Paris, and New York. Amongst his important commissions is a large gold cross and necklace set with a ruby for Mrs. Scott Symon and he has done many wedding and engagement presentation pieces. He taught fine crafts at Northern Vocational School (nights); Madsen Folk School, Markham, Ontario; Muskoka Works, and at the Central Technical School, Toronto and elsewhere. Married Nancy Meek in 1942 and they have one daughter Judy.

Reference

NGC Info. Form rec'd in 1967

PODESVA, Yehuda
b. 1926

Born in Poland, he came to Canada in 1948 and settled in Toronto. A still life and figure painter in impressionistic style, he produces his work in pen and ink, water colours, oils, acrylics and etching media. He held his first important solo show in Toronto at the Pollock Gallery in 1965. Viewing his work at Gallerie Fore, Winnipeg, in 1970 Jan Kamienski *Winnipeg Tribune* critic noted, "He is. . .a brilliant colorist. There is no hesitation in his use of strong color, but there is restraint in its application. A red is redder when set against a brown, and a white will show many paces away when it's surrounded by a neutral background. Yet, with all this, Podesva uses color deliberately and discreetly. . . drawings are light in touch and immensely skillful. Perhaps the best proof of this is his small, delicate drawing entitled Homework, done with no more than a couple of dozen lines sufficient to give a clear and concise image." His solo shows include: Pollock Gallery, Tor. (1965, 67, 68); Gallery Fore Wpg. (1970, 75); Estee Gallery, Tor. (1974, 1977).

References

>Globe & Mail, Tor., Ont., Oct. 30, 1965 (solo at Pollock)

>*Winnipeg Jewish Post*, Winn., Man., Oct. 15, 1970 "Galerie Fore Shows Podesva"

>*Winnipeg Free Press*, Man., Oct. 24, 1970 "Podesva Exhibition" (at Gal. Fore)

>*Winnipeg Tribune*, Man., Oct. 31, 1970 "Podesva sets old values against mad, modern world" by Jan Kamienski

>*Globe & Mail*, Tor., Ont., Nov. 30, 1975 "Y. Podesva" (at Estee Gal.)

>*The Index of Ontario Artists*, Ed. H. Wolff, Vis. Arts Ont./Ont. Assoc. of Art Galleries, Tor., 1978, P. 219

PODGRABINSKI, Miet (Mieczyslaw Podgrabinski)
b. 1901

Born in Lublin, Poland, he showed an early interest in art. At twelve he was asked to teach drawing to other students. At eighteen he entered the Warsaw Technical College where he studied Mechanical Engineering (1919-1923) then the Warsaw Academy of Art where he concentrated on Monumental Sculpture (1924-28) and after two years there, was appointed teacher at the Warsaw College of Art (1927-1939). He executed several busts of national heroes and was active with the Polish Professional Artists' Association until 1939. He travelled to Paris, Berlin and Florence in 1937 for further study. He won awards in Warsaw and Paris both for his medals and posters. When Poland was attacked by the Nazis, Podgrabinski went to the defence of his country and eventually served with the free Polish army stationed in Edinburgh, Scotland. In his spare hours he managed to produce portrait heads including "Head of Pilot" and "Head of Woman." He remained in Scotland after the war and continued with his chosen field producing a number of memorial plaques including one to Frédéric Chopin which he completed in 1948. His work was exhibited in the Royal Academy of Art, Edinburgh, and the two portrait heads mentioned above, completed during the war, were selected to tour North America. In 1956 he emigrated to Canada and for the next ten years worked as a graphic artist. He returned to his sculpture and to producing portrait busts, medals (sports and memorial) and monumental sculpture working between figurative and abstract styles in the media of clay, wood, metals and plastics.

PODGRABINSKI, Miet (Mieczyslaw Podgrabinski) (Cont'd)

He was elected to the Sculptors Society of Canada and was active with this society. His work has appeared in: Endobannah, 77, St. Clements Church, Tor. (Boy Scouts of Canada); Ethnic Artists, 76, Tor. (Ont. Science Centre); Group 74, Tor. (C.N.E.); Group 75, Robt. McLaughlin Gallery, Oshawa and periodically with the Sculptors Society of Canada annuals. Lives in Toronto. Represented in the Polish Museum in Great Britain and in many private collections.

References
Info. Form rec'd from artist in 1972 with biographical notes
The Index of Ontario Artists, H. Wolff, Ed., Vis. Arts Ont. & Ont. Assoc. Art Gal., 1978, P. 220

POELZER, Allan

A Canadian Indian carver from Victoria, B.C., who, with his wife Gloria, markets his work at locations within the City of Victoria.

Reference
Victoria Times, B.C., June 20, 1974

POESIAT, Dorothy

Born in Amsterdam, Holland, she has been interested in art since she was a small child and held her first show at the age of thirteen in Java. She then studied at the Academy of Fine Arts in South Holland until her late teens. At nineteen she attended contemporary art classes at Cambridge, England. She then travelled for several years and in 1958 came to Canada and resumed her art career, teaching at the West Vancouver Academy of Fine Arts and then working with Canadian artist Robert Wood. She established her own studio in New Westminster and has also been conducting painting classes at the New Westminster Community Centre.

Reference
New Westminster Columbian, B.C., Nov. 24, 1972 "Art work readied for 'open house'"

POGGI, Vincent

A Montreal artist, he is known for his stained glass windows and his commissions include those for the Cardinal Léger Institute and the Crémazie Boulevard Church in Montreal.

POGGI, Vincent (Cont'd)

References
La Presse, Mtl., Jan. 11, 1958 "A l'Institut Cardinal-Léger" (large photo of window)
Clipping, Mtl., May 30, 1959 "Symphonie de lumière et couleur" (large photo and article)

POHLMANN, Gordon W.H.
b.(c) 1925

Originally from British Columbia, for many years he did landscape painting, cartooning, murals, heraldry and other forms of fine art. A member of the Canadian Armed Forces he served with the 1st Batallion, Canadian Scottish Regiment, joining them at Caen, France in 1943 and other sectors until the end of the war. In peace time he was a member of the militia and rose to the rank of sergeant. He returned to active duty with the Lord Strathcona Horse in 1952 and served in Korea and in Indo-China with the truce advisory commission in 1959. After suffering injuries during exercises at Wainwright he was unable to join his regiment for service in Germany and was posted to Camp Borden attached to the Royal Canadian Armoured Corps School (Trials and Evaluation Establishment). For years he produced cartoons for the *Borden Citizen* and painted crests on mahogany shields, two of which were presented to Generals Tedlie and Stovel on their departure for new duties at Canadian Forces Headquarters. Married with four children, Pohlmann was living on base at Camp Borden in 1968.

Reference
Borden Citizen, Ont., Dec. 18, 1968 "Master artist at work"

POIRIER, Denys

From Jonquière, Quebec, the son of Mr. & Mrs. Donat Poirier, he began painting at an early age and took courses from Jean-Jacques Jolois. He exhibited his work in a joint show in the basement of Convent Ste-Marie where thirty of his landscapes of Gaspé and Jonquière regions were shown.

Reference
Le Réveil, Jonquière, Quebec, Feb. 5, 1964 "Exposition Des Oeuvres De Deux Jeunes Artistes"

POIRIER, Elizabeth
b. 1945

Born in Trois-Rivières, Quebec, she studied two years at the École des Beaux-Arts de Québec, and two years at the École des Beaux-Arts de Montréal. An engraver and painter she travelled in France and Morocco. She shows powerful lines with hot fiery colours rendered with a play on form and colour.

POIRIER, Elizabeth (Cont'd)

There is a strength in her work reminiscent of Rita Letendre. She also creates abstract wooden forms in three different colours which can be put together in several different ways. Some of her work is done in the tradition of Jean Noël, Yvon Cozic or Serge Tousignant. Her solo shows include: Galerie Jolliet, Quebec (1968); Palais Montcalm, Quebec City (1969); Concours artistiques du Québec (1969); Maison des Arts, La Sauvegarde, Mtl. (1970).

References

Québec Le Soleil, Que., Apr. 20, 1968 "Deux expositions à la Galerie Jolliet"
Le Devoir, Mtl., May 5, 1970
Info. Form in artist's file at NGC Library Doc. Centre

POIRIER, J. Gérard
b. 1912

Born at Ste. Elizabeth, Berthier, Quebec, he began his interest in art by making drawings on paper with coloured pencils. He attended the Académie St. Vinteur, Joliette, until 1929 and continued his studies at Mount Assomption Institute at Plattsburg, N.Y., U.S.A. from 1929 to 1932. He did linoleum cuts while serving in the army in Newfoundland in 1943. Serious art activity started with him in 1964 and he took courses from Père Maximilien Boucher, a painter-sculptor from the Séminaire de Joliette and evening courses in advanced oil painting from Gaetan Therrien at the Joliette C.E.G.E.P. (1972). Known for his landscapes and still lifes he works with spatula and brush to apply his colours. He held his first important solo show at the Galerie Plexi, Joliette, Que. (1970) and has participated in the following group shows: C.E.G.E.P. Joliette (1965, 66, 67, 68); École Ste. Anne, Rawdon, Que. (1970, 71, 72, 73, 74); Galerie "Coup D'oeil", Joliette (1970). His other interests include photography, stamp and coin collecting and he is writing the history of his regiment. Lives at Joliette, Quebec.

Reference

Biographical form dated September, 1974 in artist's file at NGC Lib. Document. Centre, Ottawa

POIRIER, Luc
b. 1950

Born at Rawdon, Quebec, he studied art two years at C.E.G.E.P., Joliette and two years at the University of Montreal (Trois-Rivières campus). A sculptor he works in wood, metal, cement, plastic, glass and other materials. He has exhibited his sculpture at the following locations: C.E.G.E.P., Joliette (1970); Rawdon (1971); Joliette (1973) and one of his works is on permanent display at the Rawdon school commission.

References

Horizon, juillet, août, 1973
Joliette Journal, novembre, 1973

POIRIER, Luc (Cont'd)

Ibid, janvier, février, 1974
Biographical form in artist's file at NGC Library Document. Centre, Ott.

POIRIER, Marcel

A former school teacher, he became interested in art as a young man. His fiancée, a graduate of the École des Beaux-Arts, gave him further lessons and after their marriage he became a goldsmith and fine craftsman specializing in religious art. Working in the tradition of the master-craftsmen of yesteryear his workshop became a family enterprise with his wife working alongside him while raising their seven children. They made sacred vases, ciboria, chalices, patens, and other religious objects either in solid gold or silver covered with gold, sometimes enriched with stones or sculptured ivory, engraved or chased after having been modelled according to the original drawing. Poirier always arranges to work with the architect to fit his creations into the style of each church. They also do pectoral crosses and chains, rings, altar candlesticks, crucifixes and other items. He has done commissions for bishops, large religious communities in Canada, United States and elsewhere. He has done commissions for Cardinal Paul-Emile Léger whom he knew as a child in the village of St. Polycarpe, Quebec. The Poiriers show their work each year to make their art known in seminaries across Quebec. Their work can also be seen at St. Boniface, Winnipeg, Edmonton, Vancouver and as far east as Halifax, Nova Scotia.

References

La Patrie Du Dimanche, 19 Mars, 1961 "Marcel Poirier, Instituteur qui, pour l'amour de Dieu se fit orfèvre d'art" par Manuel Maitre, photos par Jacques Senecal
Le guide des artisans créateurs du Québec par Jean-Pierre Payette La Presse, Mtl., 1974, P. 18

POIRIER, Marcel
b(c) 1948

A landscape painter, he wanted to study art after finishing high school by enrolling in the École des Beaux-Arts but was discouraged from doing so by his family. He joined the Dollard des Ormeaux police force in 1967. While on duty he was injured and during his recovery period his wife bought him some art supplies. He proceeded to do copies of old masters and other famous works of painters like El Greco and Rembrandt. It was in this way that he taught himself how to paint. Then he began working on his own, turning to Quebec rural realism for which he soon became known. He received encouragement from his friends, then from the Policemen's Brotherhood who bought several of his works. By 1973 he had held four solo shows and had been mentioned in artistic publications such as *Les Moins de 35, Artistes Canadiens — Expositions 1972-73* and noted in *Vie des Arts*. He was invited to work at Leo Ayotte's studio and was advised by Narcisse Poirier who had worked with Picasso and leading French painters, on technique and colour. On occasion he has worked with Luigi Galante, a neighbour, on paintings to which they placed the name Magi.

POIRIER, Marcel (Cont'd)

Poirier still looks for the opportunity to study abroad. One of his working principles is not to reproduce a painting even if he knows it will sell, although the pressure to go commercial is very great. By 1976 he had been invited to hold an exhibition of his work in a New York gallery. He has exhibited his work at Residence Les Cascades and La Galerie Du Gobelet, Montreal.

References

La Presse, Mtl., Que., Dec. 8, 1973 "Le Québec découvre son peintre-policier" par Lily Tasso
Vie des Arts, Mtl., Printemps 1974 "art-actualite — Montréal — La Galerie Du Gobelet" par Jean-Claude Leblond, P. 71
Montreal Star, Quebec, March 16, 1976 "Policeman in Dollard — Struggling artist wears a gun at work" by Rosemary McCracken

POIRIER, Narcisse
b. 1883

Born in St. Félix de Valois, a small town in the Province of Quebec, he began his artistic career at the age of five, sketching likenesses of friends of the family and visitors to the Poirier household. His father was a miller and with this rural setting the young man would seem destined to earn his living by farming. But Narcisse had a slight build, was not inclined toward farm work and had a keen interest in art. So at sixteen he left St. Félix for studies in Montreal. He enrolled in night classes at the Monument National and there studied drawing, painting and modelling from 1905 to 1912. During this period he received instruction from a number of prominent teachers including Edmond Dyonnet, Maurice Cullen, William Brymner, Georges Delfosse, Joseph Saint-Charles and sculptor, Alfred Laliberté. At the Monument National he won a number of prizes for his work both in drawing and modelling. He worked with Suzor-Côté in the painting of religious pictures and later worked alone on the same type of decoration in his home town. In 1914 he became a founding member of a group of painters known as "Peintres de la Montée Saint-Michel", originated mostly by artist Ernest Aubin, which included Joseph Jutras, J.O. Legault, O.E. Leger, Elisée Martel, Paul Pépin, and J.O. Proulx. These painters had studied together at the Monument National, and had in common their interest in painting the wooded part of old Montreal within the area of Saint Sulpice. They met at the workshop of Ernest Aubin in an old warehouse of Desmarais & Robitaille, also on Sundays at 22 Notre Dame, an old mansard-roofed house formerly known under the name of L'Archite (The Ark). In 1920 Poirier studied in France at Académie Julian, Paris, with Jean-Pierre Laurens and Paul Chrétien then travelled in Italy returning to Montreal in 1921. In 1922 his painting "La Vieille Maison d'Henri IV" was purchased by the Quebec Provincial Government. Poirier participated in numerous group shows including those of the R.C.A., Montreal Spring Exhibitions and at least once at the C.N.E., Toronto (1927). He held at least twelve solo shows. He was described by art critic Frank Getlein in 1970 during an exhibit of his work, from the collection of his daughter, at the Canadian Embassy in Washington, D.C., as follows, "He was never committed to any one art gallery, preferring to sell his paintings on the spur of the moment to people to whom he took a liking. A compassionate man, he could not conceive that a life could be complete unless it was shared: twice widowed, he married a third time at 79. At 87, he is still active, rising early to put in a good day's work at the easel. A happy and unassuming man, his paintings reflect a zest for living and a complete lack of pretension. Only the rather austere self-portrait is not true to life, no one can ever remember seeing him taking himself quite so seriously. . . .He carries on, as a professional, a double tradition — the landscape and the still life — long after both are popularly supposed to be outmoded in the changing stream of art styles of our time. The views of Montmartre, painted half a century ago, recall the environs of Paris in a quieter time. They also show an infallible sense of place. We know exactly what city we are in, even though none of the universally familiar monuments are given. The same sense informs his Canadian landscapes, the feeling of a tough, proud land much loved by its painter. As a still life painter, Poirier is in the center of an appealing tradition of understatement and modesty. He relates to Zurbaran's patient scrutiny of a handful of earthenware vessels on a shelf rather than to the elaborate, elegant and often allegorical Dutch arrangements of exotic blossoms and clinging insects. He relates also, at his best, to the austere geometry whereby Chardin and Cézanne approached Euclid. Consider the small picture of a basket of raspberries in the present exhibition. It seems utterly casual, an ordinary fruit basket tipped on its side so the berries roll out. But look at the line of the berries against the box. . . .The parts are locked into place exactly as they are in Chardin and Cézanne. If the picture were repainted in grays and browns, the box and the berries left out in favour of abstract forms, it would be a Cubist minor masterpieces of, say, 1920. But Poirier does not leave out the berries. All their cheerful juiciness is there, almost asking to be crushed between the tongue and the palate. Moreover, his subjects, the fruits and vegetables, glasses and kettles, are as unmistakably those of his native Quebec province as Zurbaran's ceramics are from the earth of Seville and no place else. There is the remembrance of a cold climate, a short growing season, a hard earth in these berries and apples. They could never be mistaken for the overblown produce of California and Florida. They are tart and tasty, the more precious for growing in a latitude less than lush. We always know, in the presence of Poirier's paintings, that these flowers and fruits have grown and will decline and die. That intimation of mortality, set in the eternal truth of pure form, is the ultimate value of still life painting and is the heart of the work of Narcisse Poirier." His daughter Mrs. Louis Dupret of Washington, D.C., made the paintings available from her collection of her father's work. Recorded solo shows of Poirier include: Galerie des Arts, Mtl. (1925); Bibliothèque Saint-Sulpice, Mtl. (1925) (1926) (1927) (1928); Galerie Morency, Mtl. (1942); Galerie d'Art Français, Mtl. (1942); 4490 Sherbrooke St. W., Mtl. (1946); Canadian Embassy, Wash., D.C. (1970); Bank, Chicoutimi, Que. (1973).

References

(only a few of the *La Presse* articles have been included)

La Presse, 1925 (day and month unknown) "L'Art Et Les Artistes — Remarquable Exposition Par Le Peintre N. Poirier — Des natures mortes d'un riche coloris et fort décoratives et de pittoresques paysages." par Albert Laberge

Ibid, 1926, "L'Art Et Les Artistes — Exposition De Tableaux Par M. Narcisse Poirier — Intéressante collection de natures mortes, de scènes d'hiver et de paysages d'été à la bibliothèque Saint-Suplice"

Ibid, 1928 "L'Art Et Les Artistes — Exposition de tableaux par le peintre Narcisse Poirier —

POIRIER, Narcisse (Cont'd)

Paysages représentant les coins le plus pittoresques de la vieille province de Québec et toute une serie de natures mortes"

Mon Magazine, Novembre 1931 "Les Artistes de chez nous — M. Narcisse Poirier" par M. Emmanuel Desrosiers

Peintres de la Montée St-Michel (catalogue) Aux Galeries Morency, 458 Est. Rue Sainte-Catherine, Montreal, Du 15 au 30 Avril, 1941

Le Petit Journal, Mtl., Que., Sunday, Aug. 15, 1965 "Un Maître de la nature morte — Narcisse Poirier" par Emile Falardeau de la Société historique de Montréal

L'Information, Sudbury, Ont., Mar. 3, 1966 "Narcisse Poirier, peintre canadien"

Narcisse Poirier (catalogue with biographical info. and critical notations) by Frank Getlein, Art Critic, *The Washington Star*, 1970

Letter from J. Jutras to Jean René Ostiguy (NGC) dated Dec. 10, 1971

Québec Le Soleil, Que., May 19, 1973 "Narcisse Poirier, 90 ans, expose"

Curriculum vitae de Narcisse Poirier par Laurent Hardy, 12 juillet, 1965

Canadian Art Auctions/Sales and Prices, 1976-1978, by Harry Campbell, General Publishing Co. Ltd., Don Mills, Ont., 1980, P. 196, 197

Royal Canadian Academy of Arts, Exhibitions and Members, 1880-1979 by Evelyn de R. McMann, Univ. Tor. Press, Tor., 1981, P. 331

POIRIER, Normand ("Fracas")

A Montreal artist, he paints under the pseudonym of "Fracas" and tries to show his vision of man evolving with nature. He is known for his figurative drawings in pen and india ink. He has worked at a variety of occupations including: salesman, buyer, social worker and rehabilitation assistant. He has travelled extensively across Canada. He held his first solo show at the boutique Diogène in the village of Carré Saint-Louis, Quebec.

Reference

Dimanche-Matin, Mtl., Que., Sept. 10, 1967 "Un jeune peintre aux idées fracassantes: Normand Poirier"

POIRIER, Pierrette

Known for her work as co-director of a free workshop since 1963, her own painting is characterized by its delicacy and sensitivity. She has taken part in numerous shows in Quebec and abroad. She lives at Shawinigan, Quebec.

Reference

Le Nouvelliste, Trois-Rivières, Que., Feb. 25, 1978 "Exposition de groupe"

POIRIER, Roland

An artist who exhibited his serigraphs at Studio 23 in Montreal in 1971.

Reference
   La Presse, Mtl., Quebec, April 10, 1971 (review)

POIRIER-MCCONNELL, Edmonde

Exhibited tapestries at Galerie de l'anse-aux-barques, Quebec City, in 1977.

Reference
   Notice from Ministère des Affaires culturelles, Musée du Québec, 1977

POISSON, Christiane

Born in France, she was a creative designer in Paris for a major textile design studio. She came to Toronto, Canada in 1965 with her Dutch photographer-husband, Robert Van der Hilst. They set up a studio on Church Street and in 1969 she held a solo show of her paintings at La Cimaise gallery when Kay Kritzwiser of the *Globe & Mail*, noted, "The colors swim about the walls and drop in silk cascades of banners. . . .Her designs demand long, fiddly preparation and then frantic haste, in the case of her big works. When the colors are flowing, she must leap about with the flexibility of a gymnast. Miss Poisson works on Chinese paper or on white silk and sometimes on wool, instead of canvas. She establishes her theme or design with wax and glue, then applies her colors with lightning brush strokes because the inks or dyes move very fast on the material at this stage. The paintings and the color-fast washable banners are a lyrical interpretation of what she thinks, what she reads, what she remembers."

Reference
   Globe & Mail, Tor., Ont., Nov. 25, 1969 "The swimming colors of Poisson" by Kay Kritzwiser

---

POISSON, Gaston

A painter and sculptor who has taught at the Polyvalente de Louiseville, Quebec. He is known for his sculpture in wood, plaster and metallic thread and his painting in conventional media. He held solo shows of his work in Louiseville at the Town Hall (1967) and at the Caisse Populaire (1971).

References
   Le Nouvelliste, Trois-Rivières, Que. (photo of Poisson's paintings with caption)
   Ibid, May 1, 1971 "Un sculpteur qui a beaucoup d'avenir" (photo of Poisson's sculpture with caption)

POISSON, Jacques

Born in east end Montreal, he is a sculptor who studied three years with Paul Barbeau at the École des Arts Appliqués de Montréal. He exhibited his work at the Rockland commercial centre; The Press Club, Sorel; and at the Salon Antoine, Montreal. One of his pieces was awarded a prize in the Quebec Provincial Competition.

Reference

Montreal E. End News, Quebec, Jan. 11, 1968 "Exposition de sculptures réalisées par un artiste originaire de l'Est" (photo of artist with some of his work)

POKLEN, Jeffrey Ervin
b. 1934

Born in Carmel, California, he served in the United States Air Force in Korea and in New Mexico (1953-57). Following his service he studied art at: New Mexico State University; Monterey Institute of Foreign Studies; sculpture with Robert Thomas, painting with Howard Warshaw at the University of California (graduated 1961, B.A.); sculpture with V.E. Colby and Jack Squier, and painting with John Hartell at Cornell University, Ithaca, N.Y. (graduated 1963, M.F.A.). A figurative and non-figurative painter, sculptor and graphic artist he came to Canada in 1963. Taught painting and sculpture: Univ. Saskatchewan, Regina (1963-64); Fine Arts, Mount Allison Univ., Sack., N.B. (1964-   ); University of Guelph, Guelph, Ont. (1972-   ). From 1964 on he participated in a number of important Canadian shows including: 81st Annual, Mtl. Museum of Fine Arts (1964); 9th Wpg. Show (1964); 6th Biennial Canadian Painting, NGC (1965); Ten Young Artists, Beaverbrook Art Gallery, Fred., N.B. (1965); 7th Biennial of Canadian Painting (1968); McLaughlin Library, Univ. Guelph (1973); two-man shows at: Art Centre, Univ. N.B. (1965); Confederation Art Gallery, Charlottetown, P.E.I. (1965); "Innovation '66" Mtl. Mus. F.A. (1966). His solo shows include those at Cornell Univ., Ithaca, N.Y. (1963); Owens Art Gallery, Mount Allison Univ., Sackville, N.B. (1964); Art Gallery, Memorial University of Newfoundland, St. John's, Nfld. (1965); Owens Art Gallery, Mount Allison Univ. (1965); Art Gallery, Dalhousie Univ., Halifax (1965); Galerie Libre, Mtl. (1966) Carmen Lamanna Gal., Tor. (1966) and others since then. Has been producing ink drawings and creative photographic images in recent years.

References

Halifax Mail-Star, N.S., Nov. 26, 1965 "Opens Wednesday At Dalhousie Art"

Ibid, Dec. 6, 1965 "Works Cannot Be Termed Paintings" by Martin Kemp (sculptural effects added)

Sixth Biennial Exhibition of Canadian Painting, 1965, NGC, Ott., P. 36

Seventh Biennial of Canadian Painting, 1968, NGC, Ott., P. 53

Canadian Art Today, Ed. by Wm. Townsend, Studio International, Lond., Eng., 1970, P. 112

Canadian artists in exhibition, 1972-73, Roundstone, Tor., 1974, P. 171

NGC Info. Form rec'd 1964

POKRANT, Luther
b. 1947

Born in Rosenfeld, Manitoba, he attended the University of Manitoba School of Art (1965-69) and in 1969 was awarded a Canada Council grant to develop his painting through graduate studies at the New Mexico University where he received his master of arts degree (1970). In 1976 he received the highest award at the Mid-Western Exhibition of Art for his "Time and Time Again". He was associated for a time with the visual arts department of the University of Regina before moving to Ninga, Manitoba. Viewing his drawings, prints, mixed media works and three-dimensional pieces at the Assiniboia Gallery, Regina, Saskatchewan, Lora Burke of *The Leader-Post* noted, "The mixed media work. . .watercolor, pen, sometimes a bit of collage. . .is marvellously intricate and complex. These paintings are a maelstrom of minute images: figures, flowers, trees, numbers, letters, all sorts of bric-a-brac. The over-all intent seems to be social commentary. . .drops of the sociological pond water viewed through Pokrant's highly personalized lens. . . .The drawing is meticulously observant, the handling of watercolor perfectly beautiful. A collage in one of the paintings is so complicated in cut and shaping that it looks like one of those strange animal-vegetable creatures that grow at the bottom of the sea. I very much liked two pencil drawings and a work called Keep It Up: a clean drawing in sepia ink with a touch of color. And I liked best Creation Of Adam. This is actually six separate works hung in the shape of a cross. Pokrant's interpretation manages to combine genesis according to the Bible with contemporary theories of evolution; witty bits of visual commentary are scattered along the way. There's something awfully familiar about Eve in the final scene. . .she has the plump bounciness of a good-natured showgirl. And Adam isn't entirely naked; he's wearing a fancy tattoo on his left arm." Pokrant's other solo shows include: Fleet Gallery, Wpg., Man. (1969); Gallery 21, Wpg. (1970); Norman MacKenzie Gallery (-). In 1977 he participated in a group show at the University of Manitoba at the University Centre Building. Lives and works at Ninga, Manitoba.

References

Winnipeg Free Press, Man., Dec. 19, 1969 "Don't Miss The Exhibition"
Ibid, Oct. 17, 1970 "A Review by John W. Graham — Incisive Social Comment"
Winnipeg Tribune, Oct. 24, 1970 (review on solo at Gallery 21, Wpg.)
Ibid, June 3, 1976 "Regina man takes top art award" (wins Mid-Western award)
Leader Post, Regina, Sask., Jan. 24, 1978 "Works are intricate, complex" by Lora Burke

POK-YUN, Kim

Born in Korea, a painter and potter, he began his study of Oriental painting when he was still in high school. He earned his master of arts degree from a Korean university. He also studied under prominent Korean artists Lee Sang-Won and Kim Chong-Hi. He travelled to the United States and was visiting professor of Oriental painting at Luther College, Decorah, Iowa and Waldord College Forest City, Iowa. In producing his work Pok-Yun paints on thin, delicate rice paper, spreading it on the floor and putting in the black portion of the work first, before adding the others. The white portions are left unpainted,

POK-YUN, Kim (Cont'd)

utilizing the white of the paper itself. He uses only one brush for all his works, making the finest hairline to the broadest brush stroke simply by manipulating the brush. When the work is done, he submerges it in water and then mounts it on silk, or other backing using a special mixture of water, flour and salt. His colours will not fade or wash out even when his work is submerged in water. The work is believed to remain clear and in its original state for thousands of years. He has held solo shows of his work at the University of Minnesota, Minneapolis; Upstairs Gallery, Wpg.; Gallery 115, Wpg.; Manitoba Museum of Man and Nature, Wpg. (1974). He was planning to study and teach at the University of Manitoba in 1974.

Reference

Winnipeg Free Press, Man., May 30, 1974 "Artist Says His Paintings Could Last Thousand Years" (photo of artist with one of his paintings)

POL, Ebel

Born in Holland, he came to New Westminster, B.C., in 1953 and worked for two years in a plywood mill. He then began sign painting, establishing his own business which he named "Success Signpainting." When his sign work became successful he began to look for other challenges and ventures and started making totem poles for tourists made of rubber and then fibreglass (11 feet tall). In the process he turned to picture painting by experimenting with resins and adaptable colors, putting them down on sheets of hardboard and fibreglass. In order to apply one colour over another he found a chemical to add to the mixture to make it dry faster. He never uses a brush, but runs the mixtures over the hardboard or uses a piece of cardboard on his fingers to create the pattern he wants. David Watmough viewing his works at The Canvas Shack in 1966 and finding them not too challenging in an artistic sense did note them as ". . .full of friendly color and the world evoked is invariably a smiling one." But this is exactly the goal Pol had in mind as he wishes to please people with his art in a direct and uncomplicated way.

References

The Columbian, New Westminster, B.C., July 22, 1965 "Around the Shops" by Pat Preston
Burnaby Courier, Burnaby, B.C., Oct. 7, 1965 "Ebel's Art One Big Drip"
Vancouver Sun, B.C., Aug. 25, 1966 "Pol Art 'Friendly' But Too Obvious" by David Watmough

POLDAAS, Jaan Aare

b. 1949

Born in Kristjanstad, Sweden, he came to Canada in 1949 and studied architecture at the University of Toronto and began painting in 1971. He quickly moved into experimental or conceptual art using a variety of techniques to explore colour effects through the use of tools like the Xerox 6500 Color Copier from which he creates colour images as described by Joyce Zemans. In

POLDAAS, Jaan Aare (Cont'd)

her review of his work at the Colour Xerography show at the Art Gallery of Ontario she noted, ". . .his use of the Xerox technology departs dramatically from the pattern established by the other artists. Having selected the format for his art — a painterly color-field — Poldaas casts dice to randomly select the color settings. No image is present, only the patterns of light generated by the machine. Poldaas uses the 6500 Color Copier not to copy but to create elegant color images, and in many ways he, of all the artists represented, has used the machine in the most unique fashion. Two colored papers created in this manner form the two panels of a diptych which, because of its limited size, is mounted with other diptychs to create an overall composition of subtly varied color-fields, juxtaposed to highlight similarities and contrasts. This uncomplicated approach is both intellectually and visually captivating." His solo shows include: A Space Gallery, Tor. (1974); Artists Cooperative, Tor. (1977) and group shows as follows: "Four Painters", Art Gal. Ont. (1975); "Colour Xerography", Art Gal. Ont. (1976). He was awarded grants from the Ontario Arts Council in 1975, 1977 and from the Canada Council in 1977. He is represented in the Art Gallery of Ontario. Lives in Toronto.

References

Impetus, December, 1975, P. 16

Artscanada, March/April, 1977, Issue No. 212/213 "Reviews — Colour Xerography Art Gallery of Ontario" by Joyce Zemans, P. 63

The Index of Ontario Artists, Edited by Hennie Wolff, Visual Arts Ontario, Tor., 1977, P. 220

POLE, Howard

An artist who exhibited his still lifes, landscapes and a figure in interior at the Towne Cinema, Toronto, where they were well received by reviewer Colin Sabiston who noted, ". . .characterized by. . .placid quietude in subtly muted tones that, in the hands of a thoughtful painter like Pole, achieve variety without straining for effects, a feeling of newness without indulging in novelty for its own sake."

Reference

Globe & Mail, Tor., Ont., May 9, 1959 "Pole Is Between Poles" by Colin Sabiston

POLGAR, Vladimir
b. 1941

Born in Zagreb, Croatia, Yugoslavia, he studied electronics, music and art and graduated with an electronics engineering degree from the University of Zagreb in 1968. This same year he moved to Canada where he joined Northern Electric's Research and Development labs in Ottawa. He started oil painting in 1969 and also became interested in the study of mosaics and in the process came upon mention of nail murals by David Partridge. About two years later he began working with nails, wood, and hammer which appealed to him as they could be carried in the back of his car and be available for him to work at

POLGAR, Vladimir (Cont'd)

during his free moments of leisure. He took these materials with him on holidays when he travelled south to Florida. They were also materials he could obtain in most places. During these trips he was inspired by what he saw, as in the case of his visit to the Bahamas when he got the idea for his Coral Reef mural which was later installed on a wall of the main branch of the Ottawa Public Library. Polgar has added his own innovations in his nail murals and sculptures which include painted wood backgrounds, gold-headed tacks, gold and silver painted nails resulting in his stunning and highly creative designs. His solo shows include those at Juanita Stephens Gallery, Hamilton (1974); Royal Trust Building, Ottawa (1977) and his work has also been exhibited in galleries at Pensacola, Florida; Chicago, Ill.; Montreal and elsewhere. His mosaics and sculptures are in the following collections: Art Gallery of Hamilton; Lakeshore General Hospital, Pointe Claire, Quebec; Mr. & Mrs. Pero Baljevic, New Haven, Connecticut, U.S.A.; Mr. Frank Cacciotti, Ottawa, Ont.; Dr. Donald Chisholm, Ottawa (Pres. Bell Northern Research); Dr. Marijan Jurcevic, Rijeka, Yugoslavia; Mr. & Mrs. Martin Kasumovich, Tor., Ont.; Mr. Byron Kavadias, Mtl. (Pres. C.A.E. Electronics Ltd.); Dr. Sylvester Krzaniak, Ottawa; Robert McQuarrie, M.P.P., East Ottawa; Mr. & Mrs. Zygmunt Nowak, Ottawa; Mr. Radoslav Planic, Zagreb, Yugoslavia; Mr. James Powers, Cincinnati, Ohio, U.S.A.; Mr. & Mrs. Dick Parlow, Ottawa; Mrs. Philece Rosada, New Rochelle, New York, U.S.A.; Mrs. Justina Saunders, Mtl.; Mr. Emilio Schulder, Dorval, Quebec; Mr. & Mrs. Senecal, Baie D'Urfe, Quebec; Victor Temporaries, Ottawa, and many others. Was a computer systems analyst with the Department of Regional Economic Expansion in Ottawa in 1976.

References

Ottawa Journal, Ont., Oct. 2, 1976 "This artform hits a nail on the head" by Kit Irving

Saguenay Le Quotidien, Chicoutimi, Quebec, Aug. 25, 1977 "Sculpture Cloutée" (photo of work)

Catalogue sheet — Royal Trust Art Show, June 20-July 4, 1977 (33 works)

Biographical sheet with exhibition notice, The Juanita Stephens Gallery, Hamilton, Ont., August 31, 1974

POLIDORI, Mario

A graduate of the Institute of Art, Florence, Italy, specializing in drawing and painting; studied set designing at the Academy of Fine Arts, Italy (two years); moved to the United States in 1960 and studied at the Art Students' League, New York City; with Hans Hofmann at Provincetown, Mass.; at the Instituto Allende, San Miguel, Mexico. He came to Canada and studied at the Ontario College of Art (A.O.C.A.); became director of the Glenhyrst Arts Council, Brantford, Ontario. Moved to Brantford, Ontario, with his wife and children in 1966.

Reference

Brantford Expositor, Ont., Aug. 29, 1966 "New Glenhyrst Art Director Hopes to Broaden its Scope"

POLIQUIN, Jean-Noël

b. 1927

Born in Trois-Rivières, Quebec, he studied at the Institut des Arts Graphiques, Montreal, with Albert Dumouchel. He travelled to Europe, where he studied different methods of artistic education, especially children's art education under the direction of Arno Stern. He worked at the Académie de Jeudi, France, then returned to Canada. Once back in Montreal he opened a painting workshop for children and then went ahead with the opening of five more similar workshops in other localities in Quebec. In his own work he held his first solo show of sculptures and drawings at Galerie Libre in 1962. In the years that followed, his abstract work was noted for its purity, some of which was compared to the sculpture of Arp, and his architectural collaborations proved to be dynamic and rugged. His solo shows include: Galerie Libre, Mtl. (1962, 1963) and group shows: Salon de la Jeune Sculpture, Musée Rodin, Paris, France (1965); Stratford Festival, Ont. (1966); Troisième exposition internationale au Musée Rodin, Paris (1966); Confrontation 66-67, Quebec. His commissions include: Mural for Ville Jacques-Cartier (1967); retaining wall for the Université de Montréal (1968) and others. He was nominated president of the Quebec Association of Sculptors in 1966. Lives in Montreal.

References

Le Devoir, Mtl., Jan. 25, 1962 "Ceramiques du Québec. . .Sculptures et dessins de Jean-Noël Poliquin à la Galerie Libre" par Laurent Lamy

La Presse, Mtl., Jan. 27, 1962 "Jean-Noël Poliquin"

Le Nouveau Journal Mtl., Jan. 27, 1962 "Jean-Noël Poliquin des notes de Bach"

The Gazette, Mtl., May 11, 1963 "Sculpture by Poliquin" by D.Y.P.

École de Montréal par Guy Robert, Editions du Centre de Psychologie et de Pédagogie, Mtl., 1964, P. 108, 128

L'Art Au Québec Depuis 1940 par Guy Robert, La Presse, 1973, P. 235, 256, 298, 299

Biographical Info. from documentation centre of NGC Library, Ottawa

POLISOIS, Antoine

He studied architecture in Italy but had to leave school in 1934. Later he became a highly skilled construction manager and supervised the building of such colossal stage sets as those for the movies "Cleopatra" and "The Ten Commandments." He came to Montreal, Canada from Egypt in 1970 to be with his children. He met Dr. David Giles Carter of the Montreal Museum of Fine Arts and told him of his idea to build plaster models of famous religious architectural landmarks representative of several major civilizations. Dr. Carter was excited by the idea and arranged facilities for Polisois to work at the Museum and the project went ahead. Using the scale of 1 to 100 Polisois created twelve architectural models over the next six years and they were placed on exhibit at the Museum under the title "Aspects of Religious Architecture." Accompanying each model were photos of plans and, where possible, photos of the original buildings with details about their architects. Cut away sections in the models allowed viewers to examine the inner wooden supports in the buildings. Viewing this show in 1977 Henry Lehmann of The Montreal Star noted, ". . .aside from their instructional value, Polisois' constructions demand to be contemplated as powerful presences in their own right — each one is a tour de

1758

POLISOIS, Antoine (Cont'd)

force put together using a unique technique. Indeed, the meticulous and loving way in which Polisois has built each work from precisely moulded pieces of plaster can be seen as extension of the kind of craftsmanship of the past that Polisois admires so much." Polisois has received many awards and commendations for his work.

References

> *Montreal Star*, Quebec, July 16, 1975 "Antoine Polisois recreates great architectural feats" by Henry Lehmann
>
> Ibid, Dec. 15, 1977 "Expressions of major civilizations — Polisois creates stunning architecture" by Henry Lehmann
>
> *Le Devoir*, Mtl., Dec. 15, 1977 "Exposition de maquettes de Polisois"

POLKINGHORNE, Ted

He exhibited a showing of paintings under the title of "Occular Events" at the 1.2.3.4.Five.Six.Seven Gallery in Toronto in 1975. His work in this show was from his random and chance study of arrangement and accidental composition related to work by Marcel Duchamp.

Reference

> Exhibition sheet of 1.2.3.4.Five.Six.Seven Gallery, Tor., "Ted Polkinghorne — 'Occular Events'" May 10 to 30, 1975

POLL, Frank
b. 1932

Born in Austria he served his apprenticeship in stone carving and wood carving with his uncle; studied sculpture at the Academy of Art Innsbruck with Professor Pontiller; travelled and worked for several years; studied sculpture and ceramics at the Academy in Vienna with Professor Heinz Leinfellner. He came to Canada in 1963 and settled in Vernon, B.C., where he established a studio. There he produces his sculptures, drawings, pots, glass and concrete designs. He has conducted classes in modelling at the Kamloops Museum and on occasion has opened his studio to visiting visual arts groups.

References

> *News Advertiser*, Kamloops, B.C., Feb. 11, 1970 (photo of Poll with a student at Kamloops Museum)
>
> *Vernon News*, B.C., Oct. 13, 1970 (Poll opens his studio to VSSS Photography Club and Fine Arts Club)
>
> NGC Info. Form rec'd September, 1967

POLLACK, Harry

A Montreal, Quebec sculptor of exceptional talent whose portrait bust of Dr. Alexander Brott, founder and conductor of the McGill Chamber Orchestra, is on display at Place des Arts.

Reference
>   *The Canadian Composer*, Tor., Ont. March, 1975 (photo of Pollack's portrait bust of Dr. Brott who stands beside the work)

POLLAK, Ludo

Born in Romania, he lived in Paris before coming to Montreal. His humorous painting of Montreal appeared on the cover of *Montreal Scene* of June 26, 1976. He is known for his paintings and illustrations of children's books.

Reference
>   *Montreal Scene*, Mtl., Quebec, June 26, 1976 (note on cover design)

POLLARD, Irene

A graduate of Northern Vocational School and the Ontario College of Art, Toronto, she is a free-lance commercial artist and illustrator who has done murals and paintings for restaurants, hotels and motels. In her personal painting she is known for her portraits; one of her son, representing a Canadian child as part of a UNICEF collection of children's portraits from different countries, travelled around the world. A landscape artist as well, working in pastels, water colours and oils, she has done scenes in many countries including England, France, Germany, Switzerland, Bermuda, United States and has held solo shows at the Lakeshore East Pemberton Gallery, Oakville; Decker Gallery, London, Ont., also in Toronto, Vancouver, Detroit, Chicago and California. The mother of two children (Gary and Christine) she lives in Oakville, Ontario.

Reference
>   *Oakville Daily Journal Record*, Ontario, June 25, 1970 "Featuring Women — Art commissions keep her busy" by Luella Broughton (article and photo of artist at work)

POLLARD, Tootsie

A North Bay, Ontario artist known for her pottery, battik, spinning, weaving, and other crafts, she exhibited her woven fabrics on frames at the upper level of the North Bay Art Association in December of 1976. She had also exhibited her

POLLARD, Tootsie (Cont'd)

woven fabrics earlier that year at Kirkland Lake. Her unique idea has been well received.

Reference

North Bay Nugget, Ont., Dec. 3, 1976 "Tootsie's dream of 'woven fabrics' comes true" by Elaine Oshell

POLLOCK, Dr. Allan D.

An Owen Sound, Ontario artist known for his fine landscapes in oils, acrylics and water colours, he received first prize for his oil painting "The Green Door" at the Canadian Physicians Art Salon. Many of Dr. Pollock's scenes are of the Georgian Bay area such as Kemble, Fraser Bay, Presquile and New Dundee. Viewing his work in 1974 Liane Heller of the *Owen Sound Sun Times* noted, "Dr. Pollock's love for the outdoors — flowers, trees, quiet retreats of water and silent boats — is reflected in tender and visually fluid works such as More Memories, Autumn Fantasy and Reflections. . . .The rich reds, yellows and purples of the fall foliage provide an ideal foil for the royal blue sky that melts into the water. . . .Dr. Pollock retains the perennial dictum to paint what he sees. 'There are so many beautiful things in the world. I paint what makes me happy.'" His solo shows include those held at Owen Sound at the Tom Thomson Memorial Gallery (1965, 1974); Gallery of Foto-Art Studio (1967); Gallery 10 (1978). Dr. Pollock is an Owen Sound surgeon.

References

Sun Times, Owen Sound, Ont., Oct. 6, 1965 "City Doctor and Niece Combine In Art Exhibit"
Ibid, March 13, 1967 "Local Artist, Dr. A. Pollock Holds Show"
Ibid, Nov. 9, 1974 "Glowing colors of nature attract Dr. Allan Pollock" by Liane Heller
Ibid, Feb. 18, 1978 "Third week of Artsfest — You can see or buy city artist's work"

POLLOCK, Allan L.
b. 1918

Born in China, he moved to Canada where he became an outstanding artist and designer especially in the field of Canadian stamps. He was chosen by the United Nations committee with two other artists to design stamps for the World Meteorological Organization, the International Monetary Fund, the Atomic Energy Commission, the Security Council and for the International Geophysical year.

References

Ottawa Citizen, Ont., Dec. 15, 1951 "Buy Postage Stamp Designs"
Medicine Hat News, Nov. 30, 1956 (first time for Canadian to be chosen to design stamps)
Ottawa Citizen, Dec. 1, 1956 "Canadian Artist Busy On U.N. Pictorials"
Ottawa Journal, Jan. 24, 1958 "New Stamp Will Mark IGY Year"
La Presse, Mtl., Sept. 6, 1958 "Le Canada émettra le 10 septembre un nouveau timbre-poste"

POLLOCK, David Raymond
b. 1926

Born in Toronto, Ontario, the son of Mr. & Mrs. George Pollock, he won prizes in public school for his painting and later studied art in Toronto at the Northern Vocational School under L.A.C. Panton and Leonard Brooks and at the Ontario College of Art with Rowley Murphy, Charles Comfort and J.S. Hallam; in Montreal at the Montreal School of Art and Design. At sixteen Pollock had a painting accepted for showing at the Ontario Society of Artists exhibition and at eighteen was also accepted by the Royal Canadian Academy of Arts jury for showing at the Academy's exhibition held at the Art Gallery of Toronto in 1944. He served in the Canadian army in New Brunswick and elsewhere and was in Montreal in 1948.

References

The Toronto Star, Ont., Sat., Nov. 18, 1944 "Portrait of 18-year-old Private Hung By Canada Royal Academy" (photo of David Pollock in army uniform with his painting that was accepted by RCA)

NGC Info. Form rec'd Mar. 3, 1945

POLLOCK, Florrie (LARK)

An Ottawa, Ontario artist who works in collaboration with Rosalyn Anisman of Montreal to produce creations to which they sign the pseudonym "Lark." Viewing their work at the Pollock Gallery in Toronto in 1972 the Globe & Mail writer noted, "The exhibition is polished, inventive and very professional. The theme is Reflections, actual and imaginary. It's an exploration of the illusionary possibilities of their materials. What aids the theme enormously is their use of plexiglass and polyester resin. Sometimes they give the plexiglass metallic qualities, as in a pair of spheres in green and silver, suspended from the ceiling. Or they make surfaces reflect like a mirror, as in Microscopes, which makes for multi-eye trickery." Florrie Pollock was trained as a painter while her associate Anisman is a sculptor. They have exhibited their work at Galerie Libre, Montreal.

Reference

Globe & Mail, May 27, 1972 "Lark"

POLLOCK, Jack Henry
b. 1930

Born in Toronto, Ontario, he was one of six children of an Irish Protestant father and mother of Canadian Indian origin. He attended the Perth Avenue Public School, Bloor Collegiate, then paid his way through the Ontario College of Art by working in the fancy packaging department of Neilson Chocolates. At the College he studied with Jock MacDonald and following his graduation from a four-year course in 1954 he worked as an interior decorator at Gliddon Paints. When he had saved enough money he went to London, England, for art studies at the Slade School and supported himself with odd jobs and by performing as a folk singer. When his sister was killed in a car crash Pollock decided to return home. He had no money so he hitchhiked from London to Liverpool and stowed away on a Norwegian iron ore ship. He was left off at Wabana, Newfoundland, and several days later arrived in Toronto. He found a place to live at Ossington and Queen, had little money and found life very difficult. He spent some time in hospital and after recovering he settled in a dwelling on Elizabeth Street in the heart of the old Gerrard Street Village. He had a few of his own paintings which he hung on his walls and decided to sell them along with paintings of his college friends and others who lived in the neighbourhood and thus established the first Pollock gallery in his flat. Popular in the community, and considered by its residents as mayor of the village, he tried to save it from demolition by collecting 1,000 signatures and with the backing of the rest of the village residents approached City Hall. This action was believed to be the first instance of citizen participation in Toronto which focused public awareness of alternatives to allowing the wrecker's hammer to deprive the city of artistic or heritage oriented community areas. But the day was lost, the village was turned into a parking lot and Pollock was left without a place to live. By then he had become known for his gallery and was invited by Ed Mirvish to open a new gallery at Bathurst and Bloor where Mirvish was encouraging development of an artistic community. So in 1961 at a low rent Pollock moved into a house owned and renovated by Mirvish where he was to operate his gallery for the next nine years. In other activities he became director of the Toronto Outdoor Art Exhibitions and served in this office for the next five years (1960-65); taught summer classes in painting at Queen's University (1964-65) and in his own work became especially interested in printmaking. In the summer of 1965 for instance, he spent six weeks at Queen's University making over 300 monoprints and in an exhibition at his own gallery, later that year, he exhibited a selection of these prints under the title "Remembered Images" (in memory of his former teacher Jock MacDonald). Viewing his work a *Globe & Mail* writer noted, "Basically he uses a sheet of glass, masking tape and oil paints. . . .He begins with non-objective arrangements of resists — torn scraps of newspapers, for example — and with brush and roller, he achieves the beautiful floating forms on paper. Sometimes, the Kingston summer scene where he taught emerges in abstract; a traffic network works through in another. In contrast, he tries a subtle color idea in 'Integration.' He puts softness into the hard-edge approach and makes it work. Pollock's colors are particularly successful." While Pollock was exhibiting his prints at his own gallery, ten of his oil paintings (on the same theme) were shown at the Towne Cinema, Toronto. His life soon became a frenzy of activity from his lecturing on art, proprietorship of his gallery, conducting six art classes a week, judging art shows, acting as auctioneer at charity fund raising art sales, and continuing his exploration of printmaking. A visit to his Markham studio by Kay Kritzwiser provides us with further details, "His prints are stamped with professionalism: nothing slipshod, and every line is firm, the color and design forming that blissful union possible only from painstaking discipline. 'Monoprints are the most accidental of the print media,' Pollock said, as he pushed a roller over a squirt of purple oil and a sheet of ordinary window glass. 'But what I've done has nothing to do with accident,' he said, as he made rapid placement of geometric paper forms on the oiled surface. More pressure, more color, more swift placing of the big sheets of expensive paper, high in rag content, luxuriously smooth, over the glass, and then the final decision: does the print work? He pointed out the unexpected flaws which can curse a printmaker. A fleck of dried-out pigment or a dab of dust can ruin the work that's gone before. . . .The average monoprint takes 15 minutes. Some of Pollock's prints on display took 4½ hours for the final pull, and were built up from as many as 12 colors." In his Markham gallery Pollock built up an impressive inventory of internationally known graphic artists which included Ben Nicholson, Victor Vasarley, Claes Oldenburg; in these three artists alone was a span of three generations and three countries. After nine years Pollock yearned to own his own gallery space. His search for suitable quarters ended in his purchase of two old but sturdy houses on Dundas Street opposite the Art Gallery of Ontario. He financed their acquisition by a bank loan using part of his inventory as collateral and the balance of costs including renovations from cash sales through a special offer of graphics to his regular customers. They would pay $1,000 cash for $1,500 worth of graphics and in two separate offers he brought in $139,000 to cover the renovations to the houses to make them into an exceptionally fine gallery. With renovations finally completed under the direction of architect Peter Hamilton, the new Pollock Gallery opened in the fall of 1972 with a showing of abstract work by Joseph Albers. This ideal location opposite the entrance of the Art Gallery of Ontario should have provided a rewarding situation but the temporary closing of the Art Gallery of Ontario, his expansion to a second gallery in the Toronto Dominion Centre and a recession in the art market proved too much of a financial drain and he was forced to sell out most of his inventory at drastically reduced prices, close out the second gallery which was running at a loss despite the fact that its premises were rent free, and sell his renovated Dundas Street gallery. In the process he suffered an emotional setback. He recovered, rebuilt his confidence and established his current gallery in Yorkville on Scollard Street where he handles a selected number of Canadian artists and a collection of master drawings. One of his recent ventures was the collaboration with Lister Sinclair in the writing of the book on the Canadian Indian artist, Norval Morriseau, whom Pollock discovered and promoted since 1960. John Bentley Mays wrote in the *Globe & Mail*, ". . .Pollock has lost none of the impulsiveness and gambling instinct that originally propelled his gallery to the top of the Canadian art world. . .(he) appears to have kept most of the innocence and optimism he brought to his gallery on opening day 20 years ago." Describing Pollock's drawings (done in his south of France home) at the Soho Gallery, Mays continued, ". . .brief notations about what the artist saw around the house on certain days: a window-box overflowing with flowers, a lone candlestick on a bare table, pears and a jug of milk set out for a simple lunch. His pen touches only the edges of leaves, furniture, pots and window frames — then moves on, rarely pausing to fill in the details. The open, incomplete diagrams reach out to the viewer, invite him to visit and bring into the room his notions of color and detail — to supply, in other words, the other half of the picture." His drawings and prints done in France were reproduced in his book *We All Are All* (1980). His solo shows include: Art & Graphics Centre, Cornwall, Ont. (1963); Queen's University, Kingston, Ont. (1966); Library, Barrie, Ont. (1969); Pollock Down-

POLLOCK, Jack Henry (Cont'd)

town Gallery, Tor. (1975); Soho Gallery, Tor. (1980) and he is represented in the collections of: Queen's University, Kingston, Ont.; National Gallery of Canada, Ottawa; Dept. External Affairs, Ottawa; Cleveland Museum of Art, Ohio, U.S.A. and elsewhere. Lives in Toronto.

References

Canadian Champion, Milton, Ont., Jan. 24, 1963 "Toronto Artist Shows His Style"

Toronto Star, Ont., June 8, 1963 "The Star Talks To Jack Pollock"

Cornwall Standard-Freeholder, Ont., Oct. 16, 1963 "Exhibition Of Paintings Is On Display In City"

Barrie Examiner, Barry, Ont., May 14, 1965 "Toronto Artist Guest At Dinner"

Globe & Mail, Tor., Ont., Aug. 21, 1965 "Mr. Pollock Goes Back To His Palette"

Ibid, clipping, October, 1965 (how Pollock makes prints)

Whig-Standard, Kingston, Ont., Feb. 2, 1966 "Art Show On Today At Queen's"

Canadian Water Colours, Drawings and Prints, NGC, Ott., 1966, No. 103

Prints and Drawings, Canadian Government Pavilion, Expo '67, No. 18

Woodstock-Ingersoll Sentinel Review, Woodstock, Ont., Feb. 27, 1967 "Mono-Printing Artist Shows Method To Club"

Times, Oshawa, Ont., Nov. 4, 1967 "Art, Living Similarities Pointed Out By Pollock"

Globe & Mail, Tor., Ont., Jan. 20, 1969 "Art — Printmaker Pollock painfully pulls 400 to show 30" by Kay Kritzwiser

Orangeville Banner, Ont., May 15, 1969 "Art Demonstration By Toronto Art Lecturer"

Barrie Examiner, Ont., Nov. 4, 1969 "Jack Pollock Show" (photo of work being hung for show)

Lindsay Daily Post, Ont., Mar. 4, 1970 "Outstanding artist coming" (photo of Pollock and article)

Peterborough Examiner, Ont., Mar. 13, 1970 "Toronto Artist Has Positive Views, He's Critical of Van Gogh, 'Grandma'"

Toronto Telegram, Ont., Nov. 13, 1970 "No chauvinism in art, urges Toronto dealer" by Bernadette Andrews

Barrie Examiner, Ont., Aug. 3, 1972 "Pollock To Open Art Festival 200 Artists, Craftsmen Ready"

Globe & Mail, Tor., Ont., Sept. 28, 1972 "Art — A new Homage to Painting" by Kay Kritzwiser (photo of model of gallery held by architect and Pollock)

Toronto Star, Ont., Sept. 29, 1972 "What's happening — Friends help Pollock pay for new gallery" by Nora McCabe

Toronto Sun, Ont., Oct. 6, 1972 "Around Town" (photo of Mae Pollock, Jack's mother, in his new Dundas Street gallery)

Financial Post, Tor., Ont., May 12, 1973 "Arnold Edinborough — Jack Pollock turned 87¢ into a $350,000 gallery — that's art!" by Arnold Edinborough

Toronto Sun, Ont., Sept. 12, 1974 "Lifestyle — Elegance from the eclectic" by Gloria McDade

Globe & Mail, Tor., Ont., Jan. 11, 1975 "At The Galleries — Idle, disturbing hands from Eskimos" by Kay Kritzwiser"

Ibid, Mar. 3, 1976 "Art — Pollock Gallery starts from scratch once again" by James Purdie

The Citizen, Ottawa, Ont., Apr. 15, 1978 "Jack Pollock keeps wild eye on art" by Kathleen Walker, P. 45

Toronto Sun, Ont., Nov. 23, 1979 "Lifestyle — Pollock: Man of Motion and emotion" by Sandra Naiman

Sunday Star, Tor., Ont., Feb. 3, 1980 "Sutton's Place — Jack Pollock celebrates his amazing survival" by Joan Sutton

Globe & Mail, Tor., Ont., Dec. 12, 1980 "Art dealer puts himself on view" by John Bentley Mays

NGC Info. Forms rec'd Aug. 23, 1965; undated

POLLOCK, R.G.
b. 1915

Born in Martintown, Ontario, he grew up in Winnipeg and in the 1960's began painting seriously from his sketches, photographs and remembered scenes from his travels made while performing his daily duties as a business maintenance technician. His acrylic on masonite paintings have been exhibited at the Manitoba Society of Artists Show (1970); Great River Road Show, Man. (1971); Manisphere (1971); Manitoba Provincial Exhibition (1971). His awards include: Purchase Award, City of St. James, Man. (1969); Grand Award and First Prize at Manitoba Provincial Exhibition (1971). He is represented in the collections of: Hon. J.W. McKeag, Lieut. Governor, Manitoba; Hon. D. Rowland, M.P.; Dr. E. Sirluck, Pres. Univ. Manitoba; T. Hayashi, Consulate of Japan; I.B.M. Wpg.; Wawanesa Mutual Ins. Co., Wpg.; Peat Marwick & Mitchell Co., Wpg.; Reliance Mfg., Wpg.; Tri Graphic, Van., B.C.; City of St. James, Man.; Sampson Shaen and Company and elsewhere.

Reference
Biographical sheet in artist's file, NGC Lib., Ottawa

POLLOCK, Wayne

A potter who teaches for the extension department (pottery studio) of the University of Regina. He exhibited his functional pottery at the Dunlop Gallery in the Regina Central Library in 1977 including tea pots, bowls, plates, lidded casseroles, pitchers and jugs. Lora Burke, reviewer for *The Leader-Post* found the basic shapes of his pottery appealing.

Reference
Leader Post, Regina, Jan. 19, 1977 "Pottery display" by Lora Burke

POLUSHIN, Valentina

Born in Shanghai, China, of Russian parents she arrived in Canada when very young and grew up in the cities of Victoria and Vancouver, B.C. Ever since childhood she had been drawing and later she won a scholarship to enter the Vancouver School of Art where she studied with Jack Shadbolt and Fred Amess. She married and for a time left her art but returned to painting in 1961 and later took further studies at the University of Victoria. Her first canvases were of religious paintings in the tradition of the old Russian ikons. Then she turned to other subjects including a series of nudes which were exhibited in a joint show at the Utley's Gallery, Victoria. Viewing this work Eileen Learoyd for the *Victorian* noted, ". . .it is a comparative newcomer, Polushin, whose bold and bizarre nudes shout, 'stop!' They stare with long Slavic eyes and purple hair. They seem to have emerged from some damp primeval jungle where the light is uncompromisingly blue, red, green or yellow. They sit, crawl and stand in a way that is so awkward that it becomes touchingly human. The violent color grabs you first, and then shock at the primitive composition, but

POLUSHIN, Valentina (Cont'd)

before you know it, something fresh and magnetic claims more lasting attention. A certain indefiniteness, a naïveté keeps the figures alive. They never become static, but more and more demanding like creatures who want your attention and sympathy. . . .The surprise of the Polushin nudes is partly that her use of strong color is foreign to the usual West Coast scene where viewers see so much forest green, sea blue and muted light. She obviously does not see the ordinary colors all around her, but paints from some burning palette in her inner eye. . . .All her work contains excitement. . . ." She has been influenced by Oriental masters from Hokusai to Munakata, but also by German expressionists. She received honourable mention for her work in 1971 and also received appreciation from Canadian art figures like Colin Graham, Pat Martin Bates, Karl Spreitz, Don Harvey, Herbert Siebner and others. Married to John Polushin of Russian ancestry as well, they live in Victoria.

References

Victoria Colonist, B.C., June 14, 1969 "Artist's Firm Belief: Creator, Creativity Linked" by Don Gain

Victorian, Vict., B.C., May 20, 1977 "Wild and wonderful" by Eileen Learoyd

POLUTNIK, Jose

b.(c) 1938

Born in Yogoslavia, after coming to Canada he studied at the Vancouver School of Art and graduated in 1962. He worked for a period as a landscaper while spending his evenings at his sculpture. A painter-sculptor he has visited Hawaii regularly and has been inspired in his art from these visits. He held an exhibition of his paintings and sculptures in 1976 at the Open Space Gallery in which he displayed his work in three parts: paintings entitled "universal chasm", "Hawaii" and a third section made up of three stone sculptures. He held solo shows as well in Victoria at the Open Space Gallery (1973) and the NCIA gallery (1974).

References

Victoria Times, Vict., B.C., May 6, 1972 (short article on Polutnik demonstrating his sculpture at seven schools)

Ibid, July 3, 1976 "One-man Show"

POMANTI, Maria (née Phillips)

A landscape and still life painter, the daughter of Mr. and Mrs. V. Phillips of Port Arthur, Ontario, she moved to Toronto where she held a solo show of her work at the St. Lawrence Galleries in 1966.

Reference

News-Chronicle, Port Arthur, Ont., May 31, 1966 "Former PA Woman Holds Toronto Show"

POMMINVILLE, Louise

b. 1941

Born in Montreal, she had an early interest in art and at the age of ten was producing drawings of flowers, trees, animals and children in a very creative way. She studied at the École des arts appliqués de Montréal four years; École des Beaux-Arts, Paris, one year. She worked in the animation department of the National Film Board for four years and also served as a graphic artist with Radio-Québec. Especially interested in enamels she took extensive studies in the field both in Canada and France and is known for her plates, medallions, compacts, engravings and paintings on enamel. She is known as well for cushions, hassocks and has illustrated three children's books. She has given evening courses in enamelling and has taken part in a group art concept of enamellers under the auspices of the Government of Canada. She has an endearing lyrical fairy tale touch to her work.

References

Le guide des artisans créateurs du Québec par Jean-Pierre Payette, La Presse, Mtl., 1974, P. 114, 115

Châtelaine, Mtl., Que., March, 1975 "C'Est Charmant Frais Et Naïf" par Thérèse Alier, P. 32

POND, Francis (née Snider)

A graduate of the Toronto Central Technical School in art she is the daughter of Mr. & Mrs. Alex Snider of Kirkland Lake, Ontario. Known for her portraits and landscapes in oils, water colours, wood blocks and monoprints. She has exhibited her work at the Allied Arts Centre Gallery, Kirkland Lake (1962, 1966). Taught art at Sault Ste. Marie, Ontario, where she was living in 1966.

Reference

Northern Daily News, Kirkland Lake, Ont., June 11, 1966 "30 Paintings by Tech Artist In Exhibition"

POND, Wilfred

A Simcoe, Ontario, artist and school teacher known for his landscapes. He gave four of his paintings, each four feet by nine feet, to the Simcoe Lions Club to be auctioned off by the Club to raise money for its various community projects. His subjects include historical landmarks and scenes in the Simcoe area.

Reference

Simcoe Reformer, Ont., May 23, 1969 "Local Artist Donates Paintings To Lions"

PONTONI, Dr. Andrea
b.(c) 1914

Born in Italy he received his elementary schooling and instruction in painting and restoration at the world famous Monte Casino monastery. He finished his studies there at the age of eighteen and then took his higher education at the State University in Rome where he received his Ph.D.s in Psychology and Medieval Literature. He also received his teacher's certificate from the Department of Education of Rome. He studied art with Mingorance (from Academy of Malaga, Spain). He travelled to 128 countries earning his way by teaching, lecturing and doing other jobs. He didn't paint for a number of years but in the early 1950's in the process of touching up old works began doing original compositions again. While a professor on the staff of a Mexican University he travelled in the summer of 1956 to Houston, Texas, where he was having a showing of his paintings. There he met a Vancouver school teacher, a Canadian, fell in love with her and courted her in French, the only language they had in common. Three days later they married. They lived in Mexico for several months then they moved to Vancouver, Canada, where they settled. Dr. Pontoni learned to speak English and became a Canadian citizen. While learning English he managed a Vancouver Italian theatrical café in which his paintings were shown. He soon qualified for a teaching certificate. He taught Spanish, Latin and French in Burnaby and gave art instruction in Surrey and Burnaby Adult Education Programmes. His unusually fine memory has enabled him to learn languages and assimilate information easily. He is the author of books on the following subjects: barbarians in Europe, a geography of Guatemala, a history of San Salvador, a profile of Pope Pius XII for the Catholic Youth in Rome, and a book on the theory of knowledge leading to the reform in education, entitled, *The Labrynth*. He works quickly in his painting and usually finishes a canvas in one day. He has painted in classical, surrealist and expressionist styles but favours painting in impressionistic manner. His solo shows since coming to Canada include: Edmonton, Alta. (1961); Mady's Coffee Shop, Windsor, Ont. (1963); Arlington Hotel, Port Alberni, B.C. (1967) and others. Lives in Vancouver.

References

Edmonton Journal, Alta., July 7, 1961 "Will Explain Them, Too — Artist Displays Paintings Here"

Windsor Daily Star, Ont., July 13, 1963 "Artist in Rush — One-Man Whirlwind" by Mike Vickers

Twin Cities Times, Port Alberni, B.C., Sept. 20, 1967 "Artist, Author, Traveller Dr. Pontoni Teaches Here"

POOLE, Dr. Franklin Dayton
1904-1972

Born in Keewatin, Ontario, he went to St. Thomas, Ontario, in his early youth. He studied medicine at the University of Western Ontario and spent some years in research at Yale University and the Ford Hospital, Detroit. It was in Detroit during the 1930's that he became interested in painting and studied in that city at the George Rich Studio. He returned to St. Thomas and began the practice of medicine while continuing with his painting during his free hours. He studied with Lila Knowles of St. Thomas and later at the Beal Technical

POOLE, Dr. Franklin Dayton (Cont'd)

School, London, Ontario and with the London Gallery Painting Group. During World War II he served in the Canadian Army and at the end of the war went back to his practice. He retired from medicine in 1955 and turned to full time professional painting. He made trips outside Ontario which included the East Coast and the State of Maine as well as recording local landmarks in Elgin County. He painted in oils, acrylics, and water colours and depicted historic landmarks. Following his death a retrospective show of some of his work was held at the Art Gallery of St. Thomas and Elgin in 1973. The paintings were assembled by his family and a number of local collectors, and viewed by the St. Thomas *Times-Journal* as follows, "Frank Poole's years in painting were almost like a voyage of discovery as he moves easily through the various mediums of sketching, oils and acrylics. Once into watercolors, he progressed quickly and surely in this sensitive and difficult medium. . . .In his abstract oils with their 'cells under microscope' emphasis, he seemed subconsciously to reflect his medical training." His solo shows included: Anderson's Ltd., St. Thomas, Ont. (1967); Collingwood Collegiate Auditorium, Ont. (1969); Art Gallery of St. Thomas, Ont. (1973) also at the St. Thomas Public Library; Western Art League Shows; Rothman's Gallery, Stratford; Glenhyrst Gallery, Brantford; Rodman Hall, St. Catharines, and he is represented in the permanent collection of the Art Gallery of St. Thomas and Elgin; Parkside Collegiate Institute, St. Thomas and elsewhere.

References

Times-Journal, St. Thomas, Ont., Jan. 21, 1967 "F.D. Poole Paintings Have Different Style"

Elmvale Lance, Ont., Oct. 23, 1969 "Franklin Poole to be guest artist at 'Simcoe Art '69'"

Orillia Packet & Times, Ont., Oct. 22, 1969 "Simcoe Art '69 Features Artist Franklin Poole"

Times-Journal, St. Thomas, Ont., Nov. 12, 1973 "Paintings of Dr. Frank Poole will be shown at art gallery"

Ibid, Nov. 14, 1973 "Opening Night" (photo of Mrs. Poole, Dr. Clare Bice & Jiri Hanzalek Dir. Art Gal. St. Thomas)

London Evening Free Press, Ont., Nov. 14, 1973 "Show pays tribute to late artist" by Lenore Crawford

Franklin Dayton Poole (retrospective exhibition sheet with biographical information, photo of Dr. F. Poole and some of his work) 1973

POOLE, Jaqueline Lynda

b. 1944

She is known for collage, figure drawings in acrylics, water colours, oils, inks and charcoal but has been doing perhaps more non-representational work in her recent painting. She has exhibited her work in solo shows at the Creative Arts Centre, Ingersoll, Ontario (1977) and a dual showing with John Palchinski at the Woodstock Public Library and Art Gallery (1977) and group shows at the Woodstock Public Library and Art Gallery (1976); Betty McArthur Gallery, Woodstock (1975, 1976); Ingsersoll Creative Arts Centre (1975, 1976). She lives in Woodstock, Ontario.

References

Notice of show — Woodstock Public Lib. & Art Gal., Nov., 1977 Jaqueline Poole & John Palchinski

POOLE, Jaqueline Lynda (Cont'd)

London Free Press, Ont., Feb. 3, 1977 "Exhibition of paintings planned for Woodstock"
The Index of Ontario Artists, Ed. H. Wolff, Vis. Arts Ont. & Assoc. of Art Galleries, 1978, P. 220

POOLE, Judith
1943-1973

Born in Tunbridge, England, she studied at St. Martin's School of Art and in 1966 came to Saskatchewan, Canada, where she became a vital part of the local art scene. She worked as a medical illustrator, art instructor with the Extension Division of the University of Saskatchewan, a taxi driver and graphic artist. In 1967-68 she was awarded a Canada Council grant and exhibited nationally. Did colourful optical art often involving flowers. Married Don Buckle in the spring of 1972 and was studying for her Master's in Fine Arts in drawing and sculpture at the University of Saskatchewan when her death occurred. A retrospective show of her paintings was shown in January of 1974 at the Mendel Art Gallery, Saskatoon.

References

Exhibition folder with biographical notes, Mendel Art Gallery, January, 1974, *Judith Poole 1943-1973*
Saskatchewan: Art and Artists, Norman Mackenzie Art Gallery/Regina Public Library Art Gallery, April 2-July 31, 1971, P. 42

POOLE, Leslie
b. 1942

Born in Halifax, Nova Scotia, the son of Mr. & Mrs. Milton O. Poole, he spent most of his early life at Roseneath, P.E.I., where his family made their home. He attended the local county school and then Montague High School and went on to the Prince of Wales College in Charlottetown. He studied next at the University of Alberta and graduated with his B.F.A. in 1967. For a year he taught art in a Langley high school before being accepted (he was first Canadian to be so) on a scholarship in the fine arts course at Yale University where he graduated in 1970 with his M.F.A. His first solo show was held in Toronto at the Nightengale Gallery in 1970. He painted and lectured at the University of Alberta for the period 1971-72 and in 1973 put twelve of his large canvases on tour as his own celebration of Prince Edward Island's Centennial. These works were described by Norman Yates as follows, ". . .it seems to me that three major elements interlock as expressive structure. One is a hard edge geometric grid which delineates and controls the relationships of rhythmic movement of colour and space. The second element is the delicately rendered human figure, a light dark richly fleshed phantom in, out, and on the surface, whose presence even when left out of a painting pervades. . . .The third element of this trilogy is the paradox of the illusion of the depicted actual confronting the formal illusion of the non-objective color and space." These paintings measuring up to five feet high and 20 feet long were shown in the Maritimes in 1973 at Confederation Centre Art Gallery, Charlottetown; Memorial University

POOLE, Leslie (Cont'd)

Art Gallery, St. John's; Mount St. Vincent University, Halifax and then across Canada to the Musée d'art contemporain, Mtl.; Wells Gallery, Ottawa; The Winnipeg Art Gallery, Wpg.; Mendel Art Gallery, Saskatoon; The Edmonton Art Gallery, Edm., The Art Gallery of Greater Victoria, Vic., B.C. In 1975 he completed a new series of paintings "Cloud Series" derived from his fascination in observing the Vancouver sky from a fifth-floor rooftop. In 1977 his "Studio Paintings" made from observations in his studio of light and shadow on the corners, doorways and angles of empty rooms. Viewing this work at the Bau-Xi Gallery in 1977, Art Perry in the *Vancouver Province* noted, "Poole's studio has a large rambling wooden floor that stretches over 100 feet across a Gastown loft. In such a place, light and shadows can push and pull itself to exaggerated lengths, and Poole used this effect in his recent paintings. His approach to paintings is a hybrid of figurative and formalist ideals. Using the corners and the linear planking of his studio, Poole tilts and colors reality into an explosion of bright stripes and geometric shapes. The cracks between the floor boards become Poole's most effective formal device. These lines divide his color-panels, and create the flat, spaceless two-dimensionality captured in many of his works. If he excels in one area, it is in relating color to space perception. . . . In his studio paintings, Poole is extremely regular in his choice of canvas size. All are formulated around a four foot square. This is quite a change from his earlier Cloud Series, 1975, which consisted of large canvases showing clouds pierced by bands of colors. . . .Poole obviously holds a particular sensitivity to color, and to color's ability to toy with our perceptual reality. His studio paintings are enjoyable explorations into our perception of space." In 1978 he did a series of paintings and drawings on sailboats in his continued voyage of discovery. His solo shows include the following: Nightengale Gallery, Tor. (1970); Confederation Centre Art Gallery (1972 on tour across Canada as mentioned); Edmonton Art Gallery, Edmonton, Alta. (1974); Art Gallery of Greater Victoria, B.C. (1974); Bau-Xi Gallery, Van., B.C. (1975); Penticton Art Gallery, Pent., B.C. (1975); Bau-Xi Gallery, Van., B.C. (1977). Bau-Xi Gal., Tor. (1978). He has been the recipient of several Canada Council grants (1973, 1974,   ). He is represented in the following collections: Confederation Centre, Charlottetown, P.E.I.; Montague Regional High School, P.E.I.; Lord Beaverbrook Gallery, Fred., N.B.; Mt. Allison Univ., N.B.; Univ. of New Brunswick Art Centre; Canadian Broadcasting Corp., Mtl.; Art Bank, Ottawa; Globe Theatre, Tor.; Alberta Art Foundation; Shell Oil Collection, Calg., Alta.; Government Art Access, B.C.; Crown Zellerback, Van., B.C. Lives in Vancouver, B.C.

References

Charlottetown Guardian, P.E.I., Sept. 4, 1969 "Does Painting For High School"

Pictou Advocate, N.S., Jan. 29, 1970 "Life Before Death — and Life After Death. . ." (painting in Montague Reg. H.S.)

Charlottetown Guardian, P.E.I., Sept. 2, 1970 "Roseneath Artist To Have Toronto Showing This Fall"

Ibid, Feb. 7, 1973 "Island Show Opens"

Fredericton Gleaner, N.B., June 28, 1973 "Beaverbrook Gallery Re-Opens Sunday" (travelling show of Poole paintings)

Ibid, July 19, 1973 "Canadian Artist" (photo of one of the 12 paintings on exhibition)

St. John's Evening Telegram, Nfld., May 17, 1973 "Artist's works on display"

Le Droit, Ottawa, Ont. (PC) Edmonton, Jan. 14, 1974 "Une difficile vie d'artiste" par Marvin Zivitz

POOLE, Leslie (Cont'd)

Montreal Star, Que., Jan. 3, 1974 (CP) Edmonton "Poole finds artist's life 'hell so far'" by Marvin Zivitz

Vancouver Sun, B.C., Jan. 8, 1975 "Head in the cloud's" (photo of Poole's painting "Second Coming No. 2")

Ibid, Jan. 10, 1975 "A young artist given a chance to dare" by Joan Lowndes (Cloud Series shown at Bau-Xi)

Vancouver Sun, B.C., July 8, 1977 (review by Wayne Edmonstone — Studio paintings at Bau-XI)

Vancouver Province, B.C., July 4, 1977 "Poole explores colors of space" by Art Perry

Ibid, Feb. 13, 1978 "Poole's boats too romantic for his style" by Jarvis Whitney

Biographical Information sheet from Bau-Xi Gallery, Dundas St. W., Tor.

Canadian artists in exhibition, 1972-73, Roundstone, Tor., 1974, P. 160, 171

POOLMAN, AL

b.(c) 1913

A Peterborough, Ontario artist, he began painting in 1934 and became known for his landscapes which he did by the hundreds. He also did portraits, especially of Indians from the Curve Lake Indian Reserve. The remarkable fact about Poolman is that he successfully painted all these pictures knowing he was colour blind to browns, greens and blues. He overcame his handicap by working by the 'shade' method. It is for this reason that he favoured using pastels that are already mixed, labelled and kept in strict order of colour arrangement. He feels that his partial colour blindness has worked to his advantage in that it gave him better colour values and balance. His portraits are done in his home studio from photographs. His work was exhibited at the Eskimo House gallery in the Royal York Hotel, Toronto, in the mid 1960's and he is represented in collections throughout Canada and the United States. In 1964 he was set designer for CHEX Television Station in Peterborough.

Reference

Peterborough Examiner, Ont., Aug. 21, 1964 "Color-Blindness No Problem For Artist Working By The 'Shade' Method Found Helpful" by Earl McRae

---

POOTOOGOOK

Originally a hunter and leader among the Kingnaimuit he died in 1959. He was skillful and first rendered fine drawings which inspired others of his community to contribute their drawings and prints to help build a new industry of Eskimo art. A fine example of his strongly-designed prints is reproduced in James Houston's book, *Eskimo Prints* entitled "Joyfully I See Ten Caribou." It depicts a hunter holding up his arms with open hands displaying ten fingers. The red of the hunger's parka and black outline of the hunter's head, the white of the paper for his face, teeth and hands and background makes a striking and effective design. Many of his prints were made by stone cuts. He died in 1959.

POOTOOGOOK (Cont'd)

References

Eskimo Graphic Art, West-Baffin Eskimo Co-op., Cape Dorset, N.W.T., 1966, No. 61, 62
Eskimo Prints by James A. Houston, Barre Publishers, Barre, Mass., U.S.A., 1967, P. 32, 33
The Citizen, Ottawa, Ont., Feb. 25, 1978 "Art — 20 years after — Inuit prints still exciting" by Norman Hay, P. 37

POPE, E.H.

A Victoria, B.C. sculptor. On his land near Elk Lake he found trees he selected for his carving, particularly those with shapes suggestive of a subject. One such work "The Lady of the Rainforest" he produced from red cedar with the use of good tools, careful workmanship and applications of wood hardener which allowed him to produce fine features in the carving. Leaving a block of cedar below the statue's knees gave him a sense of the point of origin. A photo and article about this work appeared in the Victoria Colonist.

Reference

Victoria Colonist, Vict., B.C., May 23, 1965 "Anchored in Serene Repose — Lady Emerges from Cedar In 'Impossible' Sculpture" (photo by Patrick O'Neill)

POPE, Robert
b.(c) 1957

Born in Windsor, N.S., he graduated from Acadia University with a major in math (1977). Interested in art for most of his life he has produced a variety of artwork including a cover for record album; outdoor signs; book jacket illustrations; newspaper ads; silkscreen designs for T-shirts; pen and ink drawings for private collections and illustrations for Heather MacKinnon's book of poetry. While establishing himself in the world of illustrative and commercial art he plans future studies at the Nova Scotia College of Art.

Reference

Halifax Chronicle-Herald, N.S., Jan. 13, 1978 "Two young artists combine efforts" by Beth Page

POPE, William
1811-1902

Born in Maidstone, Kent, England, an amateur naturalist, he was educated there and at Sevenoaks, Kent. He visited Canada in 1934 travelling by steamer to New York then proceeding to Toronto. On his way to Toronto on the steamboat Queenston he made notes in his diary on the ducks and other water birds he saw on Lake Ontario and continued to make notes during his continued travels in southwestern Ontario. He hunted birds and also painted them. By 1847 he completed nearly 100 paintings then returned to England but was back

POPE, William (Cont'd)

in Canada in 1859 and settled permanently for nearly 40 years on a farm on the shores of Lake Erie at Port Ryerse, Norfolk County, Ontario. He did many water colour paintings combined with pen and ink, of birds and wildlife using the pen for detail for bird plumage or hairs of animals. He also did the occasional landscape. When he died in 1902 his son William E. Pope, succeeded to his farm. In 1917 John Ross Robertson, publisher of the *Telegram* purchased 226 framed water colours by Pope which he presented to the Toronto Public Library. Subsequently the library acquired another 52 water colours of birds attributed to Pope. His work compares favourably with the work of John James Audubon. In 1977 Harry Barrett's book *The 19th Century Journals and Paintings of William Pope* was published by M.F. Feheley with introduction by noted Canadian wildlife artist, J. Fenwick Landsdowne.

References

Canadian Antiques Collector, Tor., Ont., January, 1969 "William Pope Paintings" by H.C. Campbell, Chief Librarian, Tor. Pub. Lib.

Early Painters and Engravers in Canada by J. Russell Harper, Univ. Tor. Press, Tor., 1970, P. 254

London Free Press, Ont., Oct. 16, 1976 "Canada's 'Audubon' Western Ontario bird painter left treasure" (book review by John K. Elliott)

St. Catharines Standard, Ont., Jan. 29, 1977 "Niagara Outdoors — Talented artist recognized" by Gerry Wolfram (book review)

POPESCU, Cara (POPESCO)

Born in Munich, Bavaria, she studied at the Academy of Fine Arts, Florence, Italy, and in Germany at the Academy of Fine Arts, Stuttgart with Otto Baum and Willi Baumeister. She came to Canada in 1951 and in 1956 became a Canadian citizen. Working in water colours, oils, engravings and sculpture she exhibited her work first in Quebec at Galerie Agnès Lefort (Mtl.), Galerie Martin (Mtl.), Verdun Cultural Centre (1968) then in Ontario at Gallery Danielli, Toronto (1976) when reviewer for the *Globe & Mail* noted, "If your taste in sculpture responds more readily to the beauty of form and finish usually associated with carving in the classical mainstream, Cara Popescu, a German-born sculptor now resident in Toronto, has some lyrical works waiting for you. . . .The abstract and semi-abstract forms can't be faulted and the finishes are flawless. Popescu is showing marbles, bronzes, some aluminum reliefs and drawings. 'For me,' she says, 'Composition of form in space and space in form, the play of light on surfaces, the play of shadows in the negative forms, the unity of these elements. . .have become essential to my existence.'. . . .If you are drawn to the poetic, contemplative vision, these works won't let you down."

References

Verdun Messenger, Que., Jan. 3, 1968 "Le Passé, le Présent et l'Avenir"

Lasalle Messenger, Que., Oct. 2, 1968 (photo of Cara Popescu with her work)

Globe & Mail, Tor., Ont., Nov. 13, 1976 "Cara Popescu" (review of her show at Gallery Danielli)

POPESKI, Mrs. Jessie (née Jessie Liss)
b. 1926

Born in Kowal, Poland, she came to Canada with her family in 1930 and began to show her interest in art in elementary school. Later she started serious study while still attending school, with the Hollywood School of Art (1937); night classes at the Winnipeg School of Art (1936-49) with J. Lemoine Fitzgerald and Joseph Plaskett; Banff School of Fine Arts with H.G. Glyde where she received a scholarship and purchase prize for her work (1942-44). Later she studied with Fernand Léger, André Lhote and Jean Lombard in Paris and elsewhere. In her painting she was first influenced by the work of Burcafield, Glyde, Russell Flint and later André Lhote, Henri Matisse and Georges Rouault. Working in water colours, tempera, oils, most of her painting is impressionistic and some abstract. She also works in mosaics. A commercial artist she worked for Western Engraving, Rapid Grip and Batten, McConnell Eastman Advertising and some other firms for shorter periods, creating folders, magazine advertisements and other types of commercial designs. Lives in Brandon, Manitoba.

Reference
Document from artist

POPLONSKI, Alexander Jan
b. 1933

Born in Warsaw, Poland, he studied at the University of Warsaw (grad. 1959) and the Academy of Fine Arts in Gdansk (Danzig). There he took both sculpture and painting including the study of the nude for six years. He received a scholarship from the State Art College in Poland and during this period worked on reconstruction of sculptures of an 18th Century Building (1956-59) for the Ministry of Culture and Art. In 1965 he travelled to Vienna on a three day excursion where he discovered the remarkable work of Velasquez. He was so taken with the light in the master's work that it changed his whole future. He decided to strive for that magical glow found in Velasquez's work and in so doing was to become one of the few contemporary painters to employ the technique of the Old Masters. He found a job gilding frames for three months in Vienna where he could be near the museums that housed important paintings. Next he went to Dusseldorf where he was employed designing furniture, bathroom units including a two-way faucet that resembled a sculpture. He did well as a designer but found only weekends to work on his paintings. He gave thought to changing his entire routine and decided to go to Canada where he would turn to full-time painting. He had had the encouragement of an earlier solo show in Warsaw (1965) which had been a complete sell-out to buyers from Canada and the United States. In 1968 he arrived in Montreal where he made arrangements to have a showing of his work the next year at Gallery Moos. Then he went on to Toronto. He showed a sample of his work to Gerd Untermann, owner of the Collector's Cabinet and a solo show of his work was arranged and held in the spring of 1969 when the reviewer for the *Globe and Mail* noted, "Alexander Poplonski. . .who came to Canada last October shows the kind of painting one seldom sees today. He works very much in the technique of the Old Masters. His subjects, similarly have a Medieval

POPLONSKI, Alexander Jan (Cont'd)

connotation. The glow of light in paintings like Pieta-Procession and The Non-Existent Knight is in the tradition of Rembrandt and his contemporaries. There is a richness of color in his canvases which seems to seep up slowly. With as many as 20 glazes built up on his canvases, this is no trick of the imagination. It will be interesting to watch the Canadian development of this newcomer." It was during this period that he met G.S. Vickers, Chairman, Fine Arts Department, University of Toronto, who introduced him to John Hall, associate professor with the University's School of Architecture. Poplonski was given the use of the studio for resident artists for the summer where he was able to produce more of his unique work. Subsequently, he taught fine arts at the department's summer school course. In the fall of that year a successful show of his work was held at Galerie Moos with an exceptionally fine review by Catherine Bates of the *Montreal Star*. In 1974 reviewing his show at the Canadian Fine Arts Gallery, Kay Kritzwiser noted, "Poplonski's technique is never subordinate to subject. In his few new paintings, he continues with a simple female form, classical as a Greek marble, and in its carved outline just as sculptural. His female form seems to be at the point of emerging from marble or bronze and though there are no anatomical distractions, no skin qualities, the figure is there, mysterious, provocative. But the forms are like armatures for Poplonski's technique. His slowly built up glazes, his capturing of light and his hairline brushwork for the delicate traceries of lace and jewels on the shoulders and heads of his forms certainly qualify him as an extraordinary painter. Strength and delicacy, balance of dark and light are sometimes combined with painting as kinetic as an original oil by Vasarley. . .but what he puts into his paintings is a heritage of emotion and skill we seldom see." His solo shows include: Collector's Cabinet, Tor. (1969); Galerie Moos, Mtl. (1969); Canadian Fine Arts Gallery, Tor. (1974); Scarborough College, The Gallery, Tor. (1977); Goethe Inst., Tor. (1977) and a group show at Ellen Burka Gallery, Tor. (1976). He is represented in the Gdansk City Hall, Poland, and many private collections. A member of the Print and Drawing Council of Canada and the Sculptors' Society of Canada. Lives in Toronto.

References

    Globe & Mail, Tor., Ont., Apr. 19, 1969 (review of show at Collector's Cabinet)

    Ibid, May 8, 1969 "Art — Poplonski's hunt for Velasquez' light" by Kay Kritzwiser

    Montreal Star, Mtl., P.Q., Oct. 3, 1969 "Inviting repeated meditation" by Catherine Bates

    Globe & Mail, Tor., Ont., Dec. 23, 1972 "Alexander Poplonski (one painting a year for gallery)

    Ibid, Nov. 2, 1974 "At The Galleries — Ships of war with vivid personalities" by Kay Kritzwiser

    The Index of Ontario Artists, Hennie Wolff, Ed., Visual Arts Ontario & Ontario Association of Art Galleries, Tor., 1978, P. 221

POPOV, Vasil

b.(c) 1932

Trained in applied arts at the Sophia Academy of Fine Arts, Bulgaria, he left that country with his wife Mellie in 1970 ostensibly on a trip to Hungary but they went on to Yugoslavia then crossed the Italian border at Trieste and on to southern Italy. They lived in Italy for eight months during which time Popov

POPOV, Vasil (Cont'd)

held two solo shows of his work in Rome. Looking for a better life they decided to come to Canada. After their arrival they took a Canadian Manpower English language course in Elliot Lake, Ontario, before settling in Vancouver in 1971. After a period Popov established himself in a studio-home in Gastown. Earning his living by commercial art he continued with his fine art at every opportunity. In 1973 he had assembled 88 pieces for a solo show at the H.R. MacMillan Planetarium when Scott MacRae of the *Vancouver Sun* noted, "More than half the exhibit is devoted to abstract pencil sketches portraying a whole range of emotions — entitled Tranquility, Sympathy, Love and the like. But the natural focus of interest would seem to be his copper, wood, plastic resin and cement sculpture. . . .He uses combinations of copper and wood to produce generally warm bas-relief panels. . . .Two standing sculptures, Gracefulness, a metal representation of a peacock, and Temple, a three-pronged free-form, are all ready to go as fountains — the plumbing is installed and all they need is an exterior location. Other panel configurations use acid-etched and blowtorched copper colorations with wood pieces and cement. A slick finish is then applied with a glossy plastic resin."

Reference

Vancouver Sun, B.C., July 21, 1973 "The other Vanity in men's eyes" by Scott MacRae

---

POPOVIC, John

b. 1938

Born in Yugoslavia, he has painted since the age of twelve and at the age of twenty had completed fine arts studies in England, France, Italy and Germany. He came to Montreal, Canada in 1960. He later spent some time out of the country in New York also in the Bahamas where he learned to swim under-water and found a beautiful new world he had not seen before. This experience was later to influence his painting. At first he did the usual traditional figurative work on a variety of subjects including portraits. While painting a portrait one day he suddenly realized how restricted he was when a patron complained about having to sit too long. Popovic turned to new ideas in painting which were to prove highly successful. During a showing of his work at the Queen Elizabeth Hotel, Montreal, in 1968, Michael Ballantyne described his work in *The Montreal Star* as follows, "Most of the more than forty canvases are concerned with experiences and objects on the loftiest of scales — whales, mammoths, volcanic eruptions, the creation of the earth, the music of the singing spheres, all in all a rather Blake-like vision of the universe although carried out with great style and sophistication and a superbly subtle palette — if palette is the word since Mr. Popovic's particular technique and combination of materials is, in his own words, a jealously guarded secret. Popovic depicts (although that is too simple a word to describe his sorcery) nature at its most violent and majestic. His fiery images convey the old-fashioned and, I suppose, unfashionable notion of the painter possessed, his eyeball in a fine frenzy rolling. There are glorious sunbursts of infinitely varied color like the coronas which leap in immense arcs from the solar rim, and moons as cool and translu-cent as nacre. These are paintings not to be appreciated in a single viewing but studied, absorbed quietly, lost in — and if this sounds unabashedly romantic,

POPOVIC, John (Cont'd)

so be it. Mr. Popovic is a creator of strange, exotic blooms —. . .and he is doing his own thing,. . .and doing it beautifully. Let there be light!" Popovic mixes his special paints himself and once refused a large sum of money from American businessmen to divulge his secret. His work has a lacquered brilliance and he doesn't seem to use brushes to paint. He calls his work Celestial Art. Terry Kirkman also described his work in 1971 as follows, "His Celestial paintings. . . are dynamic explosions of fused, bright color that fill his canvases in a tumultuous flood. They show a sensible artistic temperament that has adopted the conquests of abstract expressionism to translate a particular vision of the universe." He is represented in the collections of Pierre E. Trudeau, the Van Beurens, David Rockefeller of New York as well as in other prominent art collections. No news filed on this artist since 1971.

References

La Presse, Mtl., Que., Sept. 14, 1968 "Popovic, peintre concret d'expression abstraite"

Montréal-Matin, Que., Nov. 11, 1968 "Apprécié de Trudeau Et Rockefeller" (at Galerie Moos, Mtl.)

Montreal Star, Que., Nov. 16, 1968 (at Galerie Moos)

Globe & Mail, Tor., Ont., Dec. 8, 1969 (show at Galerie Ustel, Tor.)

Montreal Star, Aug. 10, 1968 "Exhibitions around town — Early Canadian, late celestrial" by Michael Ballantyne (appearing in Mtl. Star of Aug. 21, 1968 see below)

Ibid, Aug. 21, 1968 "An Event of Extraordinary Interest To Every Collector in Montreal"

Le Droit, Ottawa, Ont., Oct. 11, 1969 "Arts Plastiques — Célestialisme"

Montreal Star, Que., Feb. 17, 1971 "Entertainments — Popovic's art doesn't need the hoopla" by Terry Kirkman (show at Galerie St. Paul, Mtl.)

PORTAL, Marcel

A painter of the Chicoutimi area who has done a wide variety of subjects. His folklore paintings, usually in bright colours, reflect the customs of the people who live in his subject country, as in his paintings of Portugal, Maine (U.S.A.) and the Gaspé region of Quebec. He has also produced a series of small paintings, almost miniatures, which reflect his interest in legends, landscapes, people, and even works containing stained glass, mosaics and puzzles. In these he tries for simplicity. His legends reveal his lyricism which he depicts in a primitive style by disregarding the usual concern for perspective. In his paintings of people his work is strong and impressive. He has painted women without mouths to symbolize women of old who suffered in silence. Other of his figurative subjects include houses, chateaux, still lifes of flowers and birds. His solo shows include: Royal Bank, Chicoutimi (1973); Maison des Arts, Chicoutimi; Société des Arts, Chicoutimi (1978).

References

Le Soleil, Que., Jan. 20, 1973 "Exposition Marcel Portal" (at Royal Bank)

Newsclipping unknown, "Spectacles" par Andrée Barrette

Saguenay Le Quotidien, Chicoutimi, Que., April 1, 1978 "Une exposition sous le signe de la lumière" par Yvon Paré

PORTELANCE, Joseph Eugene Donald
b. 1938

Born in Vancouver, B.C., he studied art at the University of British Columbia with J.A.S. MacDonald, Gordon Smith and Sam Black and graduated in 1964. He also attended the Vancouver School of Art (extra-sessional) where he studied with Ian MacIntosh and Peter Aspell; took graduate studies in art at the Western Washington State College where he received his Master of Education in Art (1968). A printmaker, painter, and teacher, he held his first solo show at the Little Gallery in New Westminster in 1966 of his "Landscape Impressions" when Neil Godin in a two-column review in *The Columbian* noted, "Over-all impression on stepping into the gallery is one of immediate, strong color, diversification in approach and technique. . . ." The review was favourable and Godin expressed the belief that Portelance was an artist who was moving toward prominence. David Watmough of the *Vancouver Sun* gave a favourable review as well in very much the same way. During his second year at U.B.C. Portelance started his teaching career at Austin Heights Elementary School in Coquitlam and continues today at Coquitlam's Centennial High School. In the *B.C. Art Teachers' Journal* Portelance's paintings were described as follows, "Don's paintings show his love for colour and strong tone. There are many flat areas balanced carefully with complex, intricately detailed areas. He enjoys using reflected images and shapes with symbolism hinting religious overtones. Almost all his paintings have ambiguous interpretations on both the visual and literal levels." By 1960 he was exhibiting in group shows. In 1967 he participated in "Northwest Artists" a show at the Crossroads Gallery in Seattle, Washington; in 1974 he showed at the "14th Annual Calgary International Drawing Exhibition at the Alberta College of Art Gallery and many other shows. The above Journal mentioned how drawing every day is an integral part of his work as follows, "Apart from working in a flexible environment at school, which is conducive to melding the teaching of art with working in art, he also works with very portable equipment — a pencil, eraser and paper. 'I draw during staff meetings and other snatches of minutes throughout the day. I sit in front of the TV and listen to the hockey game while I'm drawing. '. . . .Don always carries a sketch book, which contains not only objects of interest, but also philosophical notes and many lesson plans. Portelance explains, '. . . .Sometimes I work on a drawing that I began at noon hour. The next noon hour, I may have started the drawing again. By redoing an idea three or four times, the students witness an integral part of the end product. Apart from showing the effort involved in the process, it also makes discipline easier if the students respect your ability and involvement as an artist. It works both ways. Students bring inspiring objects, ideas and enthusiasm.'" During a solo show at the Burnaby Art Gallery in 1976 Portelance explained that he had longed to work with the human figure as he had done in the past but time and money and his working methods rendered the use of live models prohibitive. Photographic sources were unsatisfactory for him as well, so he began to use toys as a temporary means and they proved so accessible he soon found that they had a life of their own as he further explained, "Old discarded dolls, in particular, seemed to possess wistful auras which echo the mystery, adventure and hope in the human experience in surrogate fashion. The works. . .record my attempts to grasp the spirit of those objects and the poetry of their circumstance." In 1978 his paintings of doll images were shown at the Penticton Art Gallery in conjunction with an exhibition of actual dolls on loan from private collections. Each exhibit enhanced the other. Judith Foster in

PORTELANCE, Joseph Eugene Donald (Cont'd)

reviewing the show noted, ". . .the dolls (real dolls). . .seem to express an air of contentment and happiness in one another's company, while the dolls in the Portelance paintings appear lost and helpless in various cold and forbidding environments. In their discarded and broken state, these doll images evoke the fragile and vain hopes of human beings as they try to grasp the ungraspable, or form a viable and harmonious relationship with their environments. Most of the time, unfortunately, they are alienated from their surroundings, and in this respect are representative of many contemporary life situations. If this overall theme of hopeless endeavor and pathetic isolation is disturbing to the viewer, he or she can find more than adequate compensation in the very skillful brushwork and design formats which display an abundance of rich detail and patterns." Solo shows of Portelance include: "Landscape Impressions", The Little Gallery, New Westminster, B.C. (1966); "Play Things and Other Things", Avelles Gallery, Van. (1972); New Westminster Public Gallery (1973); Place Des Arts Municipal Gallery, Coquitlam, B.C. (1975); Bau-Xi Gallery, Vic., B.C. (1975). His paintings are in private collections in British Columbia, Ontario, Quebec, Washington and California.

References

The Columbian, New Westminster, B.C., Mar. 29, 1966 "Little Gallery Exhibit — Local painter shows promise" by Neil Godin

The Vancouver Sun, B.C., Mar. (clipping, no date), 1966 "Portelance Exhibit Solidly Endowed" by David Watmough

The Columbian, Tues., Jan. 12, 1971 "Arts & Clubs" (photo of artist's optic painting "Spectrum No. 1" at Burnaby Art Gallery)

Port Coquitlam Herald, B.C., May 2, 1972 "Coquitlam Artist In One-man Show"

The Columbian, Apr. 29, 1972 "Portelance has fantasy show"

BCATA Journal for Art Teachers, Volume 14, No. 4, April, 1973 "Meet Don Portelance"

The Columbian, Jan. 12, 1974 "Portelance on view"

Canadian Artists in Exhibition, Roundstone Council for the Arts, Tor., Ont., 1974, P. 209, 285

Don Portelance (catalogue) Burnaby Art Gallery, 1976

Penticton Herald, B.C., Jan. 19, 1978 "Dolls, doll paintings on display at gallery" by Judith Foster

Ibid, Jan. 27, 1978 "Gallery Focus" (review of show at Penticton Art Gallery)

NGC Info. Form rec'd Mar. 22, 1966 & biographical sheet 1976

PORTEOUS, Frances Esther Dudley
1896-1946

Born at Ste. Petronille (Beaulieu), Ile d'Orléans, Québec, the daughter of Mrs. C.E.L. Porteous of Les Groisardières, Ile d'Orléans, she studied at the Art Association of Montreal with William Brymner and Randolf Hewton; in London, England at the London County Council School of Design; in Paris, France then returned to the Ile d'Orléans. A landscape, still life, town and city scene painter she exhibited her work at the Stevens Art Gallery, Montreal, in 1940 when a reviewer from The Gazette noted, "Miss Porteous. . .has in the neighborhood of her home on the Island of Orleans much lovely country to paint, and of this area is 'Autumn Morning,' with its distant blue hills, figures in a field, and, in the foreground, a house typical of rural Quebec. An old fence, too, plays its decorative part. 'Autumn Hills,' which introduced a glimpse

PORTEOUS, Frances Esther Dudley (Cont'd)

of river and shows old barns, is 'washy' and free in handling, the cloudy sky being brushed in with confidence. 'From Nine Mile Road' is another effective work which shows a wide stretch of fenced meadowland that loses itself at the base of distant hills. 'The Last Load' introduces a haycart near a barn, with a glimpse of water in the background." She painted in Bermuda and Montreal. She exhibited with the Canadian Group of Painters at the Art Association of Montreal (1939); with the Royal Canadian Academy (1929, 1940). Taught art classes at King's Hall, Compton, Quebec (1934-35); attended classes for teachers at the Art Association of Montreal under the direction of Arthur Lismer (1940). Was member of the Federation of Canadian Artists. She died in Montreal aged fifty. She was niece of Mrs. H.A.K. Drury and Mrs. George Younger of Ottawa.

References

The Gazette, Mtl., Quebec, Apr. 13, 1940 "Watercolors Shown By Frances Porteous"

News clipping (paper unknown) Sept., 1946 "Miss Frances Porteous" (obituary)

NGC Info. Forms: June 14, 1930; Aug. 12, 1943

Royal Canadian Academy of Arts, Exhibitions and Members, 1880-1979 by Evelyn de Rostaing McMann, Univ. Tor. Press, Tor., 1981, P. 332

PORTEOUS, Piercy Evelyn Frances (Mrs. George Robert Younger)
b. 1907

Born in Montreal, Quebec, an aunt of artist Frances E.D. Porteous, she lived in Montreal, then in Ottawa probably after her marriage. A landscape artist she exhibited her scenes of Ile d'Orléans at the Royal Canadian Academy 1927 (etchings) and 1947 (oil painting); the latter date she signed her married name, Younger. Was living in Ottawa in 1946 according to her niece's obituary notice.

References

Royal Canadian Academy of Arts, Exhibitions and Members, 1880-1979 by Evelyn de R. McMann, P. 332

Obituary (news clipping unknown) September, 1946 "Miss Frances Porteous"

PORTER, Ann Pearson (Mrs.) (née Ann P. McCurdy)
b. 1929

Born in Halifax, N.S., she studied painting at the Nova Scotia College of Art with Donald MacKay and an instructor by the name of Hunter; at Mount Allison Summer School, Sackville, N.B., with E.B. Pulford. She won the Elizabeth S. Nutt Memorial Prize at the N.S. College of Art in 1951 for Best Woman Painter. Was living in Halifax in 1956 also registered as living in Dorval, Quebec (date unknown).

Reference

NGC Info. Forms: Feb. 22, 1956; undated

PORTER, Brian
b. 1948

Born in Yarmouth, N.S., he graduated from the Nova Scotia College of Art in 1970. He held a solo show of his paintings at the College's Anna Leonowens Gallery in 1972 when nine of his backdrops painted on canvas for the musical melodrama "Threepenny Opera" were shown under the title "Images of the Three Penny Opera." Gretchen Pierce of the *Halifax Mail Star* viewing this exhibit noted, "The nine black and white backdrops painted on canvas have a strength as paintings on their own. Although Porter's original works were primarily the result of his collaboration in the staging of the play, they make an interesting group of studies. Without even knowing the story of the Opera one may appreciate his sense of humor, far-reaching imagination and tightly-controlled draughtsmanship. The massive canvases bear Porter's recognizable style. It has a cartoonish-quality somewhat whimsical with unsparing attention to detail. . . .Porter's surrealistic approach worked well in his backdrops which range in size from close to seven feet high to 10, 12 and 14 feet wide. . . .The paintings are charged with symbolism which may or may not have any reference to the play. . . .Porter's interpretations provided a vivid backdrop for the stage production, and as an exhibition they are provocative and thought-provoking." In 1977 the National Film Board produced a film "Porter's Magic Dreams" about the real world of the artist and the world he paints. Porter once explained "All my ideas come from dreams. . . .I don't go any further than that. Who am I to question a dream?" The NFB film was directed and edited by James Rottboll. In 1978 the Art Gallery of Nova Scotia exhibited a series of his oil paintings dealing with dream imagery of the artist. Porter was awarded a Canada Council bursary in 1971. He lives in Chebogue near Yarmouth.

References
> *Halifax Mail Star*, N.S., Mar. 24, 1972 "Porter's works on exhibition"
>
> Ibid, July 8, 1974 "Porter's surrealist backdrops charged with symbolism" by Gretchen Pierce
>
> *Halifax Chronicle-Herald*, N.S., Aug. 8, 1977 "NFB produces two films on artists" by Liz Stevens
>
> *Lethbridge Herald*, Alta., Jan. 6, 1978 "Southern Alberta Art Gallery — Watercolors, pottery and poems" by Allan MacKay
>
> Film — NFB "The Magic of Porter" (Porter's Magic Dreams) 15 minutes Directed and Edited by James Rottboll

PORTER, C.G.
(c) 1872-1957

Born in Kent, England, he came to Canada and settled in Saskatoon, Saskatchewan. He worked for the Saskatchewan Government as Deputy Registrar in the Lands Titles Office, Saskatoon. A painter in oils it is believed that one or two of his paintings were in the collection of William Lyon Mackenzie King. Porter died in Victoria, B.C., where his daughter Mrs. E.A. Eckdahl lives.

Reference
> *Letter from Mrs. Eckdahl to NGC dated January 4, 1978 giving brief biographical facts (see artist's file in NGC Library Documentation Centre)*

PORTER, Edward Clark

b. 1935

Born in New York, N.Y., he studied at the Wesleyan University, Middletown, Conn., U.S.A. and graduated with his B.A. in 1957; at Yale School of Art and Architecture, New Haven, Conn., where he received his M.F.A. in 1961. A printmaker he has exhibited in numerous national print shows including: Brooklyn Museum Biennial; Virginia Museum Annual; National Academy of Design, N.Y.; Society of American Graphic Artists, N.Y.; American Color Print Society; The Canadian Society of Graphic Art; Canadian Printmaker's Showcase; The Society of Canadian Painter-Etchers & Engravers and others. Has taught printmaking at the following schools: Old Dominion College, Norfolk, Va. (1961-65); Philadelphia College of Art (1965-71); Nova Scotia College of Art & Design, Halifax, N.S. (1971-   ). His solo shows include: Norfolk Museum, Norfolk, Va. (1961); Wesleyan Univ., Middleton, Conn. (1962); Twentieth Century Gallery, Williamsburg, Va. (1963); Petersburg Art League, Petersburg, Va. (1964); Bangor Public Library, Bangor, Me. (1966); Print Club, Philadelphia, Pa. (1967); Gallery 252, Philadelphia, Pa. (1967, 1969); Prints for People, Bala Cynwyd, Pa. (1968); Friends Neighborhood Guild, Philadelphia, Pa.; Neptune Theatre, Halifax, N.S.; Gallery Moos, Tor., etchings (1978). Represented in the following collections: Wesleyan Univ.; Lessing J. Rosenwald Collection, Jenkintown, Pa., Free Library of Philadelphia; Philadelphia Museum of Art. Proprietor of Saturday Press and private publisher of books and other material. He married Elaine Snow in 1963; they have two children and live in Lunenburg, N.S.

Reference
NGC Info. Forms: November, 1972; August, 1973

PORTER, John

Originally from England, he began potting with friends of the family in England and then took serious study at the Central School of Arts and Crafts in London graduating with his arts and crafts diploma with distinction. He worked for the Kenneth Clark Pottery firm until he made a visit to Canada in 1960. He became employed with a Calgary ceramics firm on a temporary basis until 1963. He moved to Medicine Hat where he worked in a pottery for the next three years then returned to Calgary in 1966 to become manager of the firm he had been employed by for three years. This firm is engaged in making articles ranging from coffee mugs to lamp bases, urns, decorated bowls, stemware and other objects which are supplied to selected stores from Victoria to Toronto. The firm also fills commissions for businesses, architects, interior designers, collectors and others. His own work has been exhibited annually at the CNE, Toronto. Most of his work is made from clay that originates in Alberta with glazes formulated and made up within the company. He received a CNE award and design of merit listing with the National Design Branch in Ottawa for a jar set made of hard fired stoneware (fired in a reduction atmosphere to about 2300 F). Exhibited his work with his associates in the Arcade Building, Medicine Hat in 1970. Hopes to undertake training of Eskimos in the far north in the ceramics field.

PORTER, John (Cont'd)

Reference
>   *The Medicine Hat News*, Alta., Jan. 12, 1970 "Potter is ex-Hatter"

PORTER, John E.

A Nova Scotia artist who exhibited his landscapes, seascapes, flower studies, abstracts, over a hundred water colours in all at the Izaak Walton Killam Memorial Library in Yarmouth, N.S., in 1963, where his work was well received.

Reference
>   *Yarmouth Light-Herald*, Yarmouth, N.S., Oct. 24, 1963 "Many Enjoy Local Artist's Exhibit"

PORTER, Kathleen (Mrs.)
b. 1911

Born in Johannesburg, South Africa, she came to Canada in 1920 and settled in British Columbia. A member of the Victoria Hand Weavers Guild Standards Committee she has won various prizes at the C.N.E. and P.N.E. shows for her weaving, leathercraft and other work. Lives on the Trans-Canada Highway near Victoria, B.C.

References
>   NGC Info. Form dated Aug. 3, 1967
>   NGC *Canadian Fine Crafts 1966-67* Cat. No. 135

PORTER, Robert

Born in Saskatoon, Saskatchewan, his interest in art was kindled by visits with Canadian artist Ernest Lindner. He kept his interest alive during his student days at the University of Saskatchewan, and even serving overseas with the Regina Rifles. Returning home he studied library science at the University of Toronto on a veterans' (D.V.A.) course. He became librarian at Port Arthur, Ontario, and began carving after meeting Ken Campbell, wood sculptor. As Chief Librarian of the Peterborough Public Library he has continued his art in both carving and sculpture. To produce his work he usually sketches a form on paper then realizes his sketch in wood by using chisels to form the rough work, wood rasps for the smoothing out process, then various grades of sandpaper to the finest to create a smooth surface. He applies a coat of linseed oil to bring out the grain. Finally he applies wax to the finished form. His work was described by a *Peterborough Examiner* writer as follows, "He is essentially an innovator, so far only slightly influenced by the many international sculptors he so admires, who has moved from realistic carvings in both wood and stone, to pleasing abstractions with great beauty and grace of line. He makes masterful use of grain and surface texture to enhance his carvings and produces splendid

PORTER, Robert (Cont'd)

work in a short space of time." Porter works with mahogany, cherry, cedar, red and white birch and oak. He also carves in stone. He has exhibited his work over the years in group or solo shows in Ottawa, and at the Peterborough Public Library. He lives in Peterborough with his wife. They have two sons.

References

Globe & Mail, Tor., Ont., Aug. 15, 1957 "Peterborough Librarian Does Wood Sculptures"

Peterborough Examiner, Ont., Dec. 31, 1958 "A Study In Birch" (large photo of one of Porter's sculptures with caption and critical comment)

Ibid, Mar. 1, 1958 "Portrait of A Librarian For Whom Carving Is A Hobby" (photos of his work and article about him)

Ibid, Apr. 22, 1974 "Exhibition Opens At Library" (Peterborough Group of Painters hold exhibition with Robert Porter as guest artist)

PORTER, Royce

Born in Annapolis Valley, Nova Scotia, he studied under Milen Cezak of Montreal and Professor Ian James, Department of Fine Arts, Acadia University, Wolfville, N.S. A painter in both figurative and abstract styles he has exhibited his work in group shows at the Atlantic Winter Fair; Harbourfront Gallery, Tor.; Maritime Art Assoc.; two-man show at the Centennial Art Gallery, Citadel Hill, Hal., N.S. (1978); solo shows at the Heritage Museum Gallery, Dartmouth, N.S.; Acadia University, Wolfville, N.S.; Kipawo Little Theatre, Wolfville, N.S. (1977) and others. Lives at Kentville, N.S.

References

Halifax Chronicle Herald, N.S., Sept. 10, 1977 "Porter has exhibit at art gallery"

Halifax Mail Star, N.S., May 3, 1978 "Kentville art works shown"

PORTER, Yolande
b. 1917

Born in Jamaica, she began her art education there when only eight and continued studies under a number of teachers. Her art was very much influenced by the vivid colouring of the Jamaican landscape and by the luscious gardens of the family plantation. She became a textile designer in Jamaica creating decorative patterns for garments. She left home and spent a year living and studying at Pebble Beach, California with artist Abel G. Warshawsky. She came to Canada in 1955, settled in Montreal where she married and continued with her art, studying painting with Michel Lacombe. Her husband, a businessman, suffered severe losses which turned him to alcohol and eventually alcoholism. Her marriage was devastated and she found herself retreating to her painting as her only way to get through each day. A further tragedy came about when their Westmount home burned to the ground; Yolande suffered burns to her hands and arms but the family miraculously escaped. Two months later her husband died and for the next two years she went into a vacuum and did not paint. Searching in her apartment locker one day for Christmas decorations she came upon a partially burned typewriter and boxes of ruined

PORTER, Yolande (Cont'd)

books she had packed after the fire. The memory of her nightmare returned, which in turn triggered her sudden urge to express her feelings about her experience through her art. For the next ten months she set to work on a series of canvases, collages and sculptures entitled "Journey Through Hell" a visual account of life with one whose spouse has been afflicted by alcoholism. The paintings were exhibited at the Ontario Institute for Studies in Education and at the Addiction Research Foundation of Ontario and she felt that her work would be useful in bringing home to alcoholics the impact of the pain they inflict on others. During the period 1960 to 1968 she had painted some 300 canvases and participated in several group shows in Montreal before moving to Toronto. She is known for her fine nude studies, landscapes, collages and portraits. She has experimented with sculpture for a number of years and has been described as an excellent carpenter. She has one daughter Anne who is married. Her shows include: The Arts Club of Montreal (1968, 1969); Mullins Crescent Street Gallery, Mtl. (1969); Place Bonaventure Art Committee, Mtl. (1970); Addiction Research Foundation (1976) and others.

References

Press release, biographical data by Sklov, Mtl., Mar. 18, 1968 "Yolande Porter Exhibits At Arts Club"

Westmount Examiner, Que., Mar. 21, 1968 "Westmount Painter — Yolande Porter at Arts Club"

Toronto Star, Ont., July 21, 1977 "Tragedy finds release in painting" by Lotta Dempsey

Globe & Mail, Tor., Ont. (CP) Aug. 29, 1977 "Nightmarish life with alcoholic chronicled in series of paintings"

The Index of Ontario Artists Ed. by Hennie Wolff, Vis. Arts Ont., Tor., 1978, P. 221

PORTNALL, Francis Henry

b. 1886

Born in Caterham Valley, Surrey, England, he took architectural studies with William A. Pitre, F.R.I.B.A. in London. Self taught in art he began sketching in charcoal, pastel, water colours and oils. He came to Regina, Saskatchewan in the spring of 1906 and took up residence in that city. When the First World War was declared he enlisted in 1915 and arrived in England the same year. He served in France from August 1916 to May 1919. He arrived back in Regina in June of 1919. He returned to architecture and to his interest in painting and became a member of the Regina Sketch Club (1925-36). He exhibited a water colour at the Royal Canadian Academy show of 1935 entitled "My hunting partner." Member: Saskatchewan Association of Architects (1928-29); Fellow, Royal Architectural Institute of Canada (1930).

References

NGC Info. Form dated June 15, 1936

Royal Canadian Academy of Arts, Exhibitions and Members, 1880-1979 by Evelyn de R. McMann, Univ. Tor. Press, 1981, P. 332

PORTUGAIS, Louis

A Montreal artist who did a large action painting in a go-cart in Dominion Square using spray cans which he held in his hands while the go-cart carried him over a huge piece of paper taped to the pavement. The exercise was part of a colour film being produced by the National Film Board as a feature on modern painting. The film was temporarily interrupted when an elderly woman, who was a regular of the park, felt her civil rights were being encroached upon. It was explained to her that the film crew had permission from City authorities to be there, but to no avail. Finally a policeman from a nearby station offered to take down particulars of her complaint if she would first giver her name. Finally the lady retired to a bench as she was reluctant to give out that information, and the production continued.

Reference

    The Gazette, Mtl., Aug. 8, 1968 "'Art-in-action' display stalled by lady in red" by Paul Thurston

PORUBSZKY, Istvan J.
b. 1927

Born at Kispest, near Budapest, Hungary, his father was a prominent sculptor and his mother a textile engineer; he studied art there and became a master painter. He married Anna Maria (Aniko) Prandocku, a childhood friend, and they have two children, Anna and Peter. He was a freedom fighter during the Hungarian revolution in 1957 and was wounded critically. Two of his friends carried him forty miles to the Austrian frontier and across the border. He suffered a broken back and a deep bullet wound. He spent time in hospitals overseas. He arrived in Canada about 1958 and for the first few months was hospitalized in a Montreal hospital for his wounds. He became a naturalized Canadian citizen. After his recovery he turned to his painting to support his family. He sold his first canvas which took him two days to paint, for only four dollars. By 1966 his paintings were selling for between $175 and $500, but one he sold in 1962 brought him $1,700. In his painting he combines the use of brush and palette-knife which enables him to portray great depth in his work. He is particularly interested in landscapes but has also done many other subjects. His group shows include: St. Mary's University, Halifax, N.S. (1966); St. Mary's Church Hall, St. John's, Nfld. (1966); McGill University, Mtl., Que. (1967); Shopping Mall, Place LaSalle, LaSalle, Quebec (1967) and solo shows at the Shopping Mall, Place LaSalle, LaSalle, Que. (1967); St. Laurent Shopping Centre, Ottawa (1976) and he has also exhibited in Boston, New York, Hollywood, Toronto, Quebec City and elsewhere.

References

    La Presse, Mtl., Sept. 14, 1963 "Istvan Porubszky"

    Mail-Star, Halifax, N.S., July 2, 1966 "Artist Paid For Freedom"

    Ibid, July 2, 1966 "Admires Nova Scotia Scenery" (exhibit at Saint Mary's Univ., Halifax)

    Messenger, LaSalle, Que., Nov. 29, 1967 "Well-Known Artist Holds Exhibition in Place LaSalle"

    Ibid, Dec. 20, 1967 "Well-Known Artist Holds Painting Exhibition Locally"

POSA, Andrew

b. 1938

Born in Budapest, Hungary, he had to flee his country during the student-led uprising in 1956 when he was 18. He arrived in Canada a few months later (1957) where he had friends. For a time he worked at a variety of jobs including tobacco picking, dishwashing, building computers and as an employee of a jewelery store he became interested in sculpture. He designed some pieces of jewelery and in the process became interested in metal sculpture. What formal training he had was a three-month session at the Artists' Workshop in Toronto. He worked on aircraft guidance systems at Malton (1963-64) to make a living while he continued the development of his sculpture in his spare time. He held four solo shows during that period then he turned to his art full time. In 1967 he moved into an old farmhouse north of Oakville on the Trafalgar Road and built a studio and workshop at the back of the house which he has continued to improve. His wife in the meantime reduced living costs by baking her own bread, making her own clothes, and maintaining a large garden. This in turn helped give Andrew more time with his family rather than working extra long hours to make more money. He received his first commission in 1964 and was exhibiting with the Pollock Gallery by 1966. From 1969 to 1971 he was busy building a foundry to accommodate his large sculpture commissions, while he was also filling numerous commissions for apartments and office buildings in Toronto, London and Ottawa. Some of his larger commissions could now be done. George Mann, President of Mann and Martel (brokers) commissioned Posa to do a large sculpture for the newly built Toronto Real Estate Board. Posa set to work in his own backyard under a plastic shelter during the coldest months of the year with his wife's help to create his "Flying Form", a thousand-pound bronze sculpture which looks very much like a large orchid. Posa's smaller sculptures are never done in more than seven copies. Some collectors prefer copies. His favourite form of expression is light, graceful, flying figures for his more modest sized pieces. His larger commissions in marble or bronze require a more massive design. He is represented in the following collections: Dundas Secondary School, Dundas, Ont.; Hamilton Senior Citizen project; Mr. & Mrs. Joseph Berman ("Soaring" 12 ft. bronze); Mr. & Mrs. Martin Goldfarb; Mr. & Mrs. Mark Levy; Controller Paisley, North York; Meridian Properties; Temple Sinai; Dental College, U. of T.; Highland Secondary School, Dundas, Ont.; and in numerous collections in Canada and the United States. His smaller work can be seen at the Beckett Gallery, Hamilton, Ont., where he held a solo show in 1971. His awards include: First Prize, Aviva Exhibition, Tor. (1969 for the entire show); First Prize Aviva Exhibition, Tor. (1970 for sculpture). He has taught life sculpture to Oakville Art Society classes. The Posas have three children.

References

Globe & Mail, Tor., Ont., April 30, 1970 "A gnarled root in bronze" by Kay Kritzwiser

Forest Hill Journal, Ont., May 1, 1970 "Half Ton Bronze Sculpture Dedicated at TREB Building"

Globe & Mail, Tor., Ont., Feb. 18, 1972 "A bronze weathering the winter"

Oakville Daily Journal, Ont., Jan. 15, 1974 "Sculptor puts life before art" by Agnes McKenna

Toronto Star, Ont., Mar. 31, 1978 "Art auction features abstract candelabra" by Warren Potter

POSLIFF, Kathi

She exhibited her painting "Miss Gaudy's House Lives In My Cupboard", an imaginative and colourful folding panel or triptych painting of a woman, cat, trees, lawn and house, in the 33rd Annual Western Ontario Exhibition at the London Public Library and Art Museum, London, Ontario. Forty-five works were selected from 335 entries. Her work was illustrated in the catalogue.

Reference

Catalogue, 33rd Annual Western Ontario Exhibition, London Public Library and Art Museum, Lond., Ont., May 4-June 4, 1973

POSSELT, Irmgard

A weaver trained in design at art schools in Germany she came to Canada with her family around 1970 and settled in country beyond Burns Lake, in the northern part of British Columbia. She totally controls the quality of her yarns by raising her own sheep and by carding, dyeing and spinning her own wool. She has won many awards for her intense "hot" colours. More recently she turned to adopting in her work, Eskimo weaving techniques which have resulted in her experimentation with subtler earth tones. She exhibited her tapestries under the title "Weaving the Wilderness" at The Maples Gallery in Victoria, B.C., in November of 1976.

Reference

Victoria Times, B.C., Nov. 20, 1976 "At The Galleries"

POST, Estelle

A Toronto, Ontario batik craftsman who in 1966 discovered the availability of "Procion" dyes which were developed in the dyestuffs laboratories of Imperial Chemical Industries Limited in England in 1956 and marketed in Canada by Canadian Industries Limited. These particular dyes are vivid in colouring (as the dyes of old) with the modern advantages of light fastness and wash fastness. They are reactive dyes which combine with the fabric through a chemical process whereas regular dyes merely adhere physically to the surface of the fibres. The dyes are safe for pure silk, pure linen, pure cotton, cotton or silk velvet and wool. Post has been largely responsible for stimulating the batik revival on the Prairies and in eastern Canada. She has a boutique on Balmuto Street, Toronto.

Reference

Sherbrooke Record, Que., July 8, 1970 "Batiking is a new fashion" (article repeated in several papers in Canada during 1970)

POST, Rose Salloum

She was a newspaper artist, a commercial artist and had her own studio in Vancouver, B.C., where she also taught painting in water colours and oils. She moved to Kelowna, B.C. in 1973, where she has continued with her art and has held over four solo shows including one of her water colours at The Trove, Mission Park, Kelowna, in 1977.

Reference

Kelowna Capital News, B.C., May 11, 1977 "Paintings exhibited"

POTEMPKA, Joe

b.(c) 1926

Originally from Germany where he studied art, he came to Canada in 1959 and settled in Winnipeg where he has become known for his painting of scenery of the City and of Manitoba. He is a realistic painter who takes care for exact details. Working in water colours he wets his paper before painting on it to achieve a gentle subdued tone of soft colours. He likes very much to paint historical places of the province which include: Old Fort Garry (copied from old pictures he found in the library); St. Andrew's Church; Ross House, deserted barns and scenery along the Red River. In his work he uses only brushes (some have only three or four bristles for fine details). He prefers painting in the spring, fall and winter when the colours are more real. Many of his paintings of the old section of Winnipeg and historical sites of Manitoba will become important records (because of his eye for detail) when some of these places have vanished due to the march of progress. Potempka also teaches art classes at the German Society of Winnipeg. He exhibited his water colours at Smith's House of Art, Winnipeg in 1970.

Reference

Winnipeg Free Press, Man., Jan. 2, 1970 "Old Manitoba Put On Canvas" by Carmen-Litta Magnus

POTOENIK, Frank

A sculptor in wood, he spent his childhood in Yugoslavia. The school he was attending in Austria (when he was fifteen) was demolished by a bomb and he had to move to a displaced persons camp. Later he arrived in Montreal, where a French-Canadian co-worker helped him through a difficult period. He finally made his home in Port Arthur and became a papermaker with the Abitibi company. He first began carving in 1959 using his childhood memories to select subjects of significance to him. Later he began creating a variety of subjects from religion and literature including: "Last of the Mohicans", "Praying Madonna", a pair of outstretched hands, and wildlife (moose, bears, buffalos, etc.). An exhibition of his work was held at the Thunder Bay Museum in 1975. Potoenik has been President of the Lakehead Area Craft Association of which he is a founding member. He is active in the Northwestern Association

POTOENIK, Frank (Cont'd)

for Community Crafts. He has given his time and talents to students interested in learning the fine points of wood sculpture.

Reference

The Chronicle Journal, Thunder Bay, Ont., Sept. 30, 1975 "Local Woodcarver Opens Show Today" (photo of artist and one of his sculptures)

POTTER, Debby

A graduate of the University of Regina Fine Arts Department she held her first solo show at the Department of Visual Arts Gallery, Norman Mackenzie Art Gallery at the University of Regina. She exhibited pottery, drawings, prints and dozens of small clay sculptures described by Lora Burke as follows, "Ms. Potter tweaks her clay into pendulous bosoms and massive haunches, but the figures are seldom entirely human. Bird beaks and lizard heads, prehensile tails and heavy claws sprout from the human torso. The viewer may interpret this as a depiction of the evolvement from animal to man. . .or, more likely, as Ms. Potter's notation that the beast exists in all of us below the civilized veneer. . . . The drawings range from figures similar in concept to the sculptures through portraiture. There is a collection of pottery. . .thin bowls and plates decorated with landscape themes. . .There are also three rather pleasant representational landscape paintings with figures. Ms. Potter is, apparently, a dedicated and prolific artist."

Reference

Leader Post, Regina, Sask., Sept. 9, 1976 "Figures seldom entirely human" by Lora Burke

POTTER, Geoffrey Gilbert
b. 1944

Born in Saskatoon, Saskatchewan, the son of Earl and Hilda (Hilton) Potter, he studied art at Saskatchewan Teachers' College (1963-64) with Wynona Mulcaster; University of Saskatchewan art education course as well as pottery, drawing and painting (1967-73); Univ. of Saskatchewan painting course with Eli Borenstein (1968-69); Univ. of Saskatchewan etching course with Warren Peterson and pottery (clay work) with James Thornsbury (1971-72). He is represented in the Mendel Art Gallery, Saskatoon by a clay piece entitled "The American Dream — Apple Pie and Motherhood" and in the collection of Gary Essar of Kindersley, Saskatchewan, by several oil paintings. Potter has taught art in several communities in Saskatchewan and in 1973 was employed by the Murray Memorial Library at the University of Saskatchewan. He lives in Saskatoon.

Reference

NGC Info. Form dated Feb. 24, 1973

POTTER, Joseph
1884-1945

An Ottawa artist, the son of the late Henry Potter and Dora (O'Brien) Potter, he was a resident of Sandy Hill. In 1912 he married Olive Wells who predeceased him. He was survived by four sons, Gordon, Ollie and Earl of Ottawa, Lorne of Carleton Place and a daughter Mrs. Henry Lavergne of Ottawa; one brother Harry Potter of Ottawa.

Reference

Ottawa Journal, Ont., Nov. 3, 1945 "Well-known Painter Joseph Potter Dies"

POTTHAST, Heribert
b. 1935

Born in Bensberg, Germany, he came to Canada in 1955 and lived in Kingston, Ontario, before moving to Niagara Falls where he works with Joseph Grosso, a tailor. Potthast began painting in 1964 and is self taught. He has done surrealistic paintings which portray his interest in philosophy and religion. In 1967 he exhibited his work in Victoria, B.C., through the sponsorship of Joseph Grosso.

References

Oak Bay Leader, Victoria, B.C., May 31, 1967 "Paintings Meant To Talk"
NGC Info. Form dated 22nd January, 1968
Letter of January 26, 1981 with information and slides of paintings from artist

POTTRUFF, Richard Phillip
b. 1945

Born in Hamilton, Ontario, his encouragement in art came from his secondary school teacher, Robert Agnew. He attended McMaster University in Hamilton and graduated with B.A. in Fine Art, majoring in Art History (1964-68). At McMaster he studied painting with Tony Urquhart and George Wallace. He then taught art at a school in Waterford for two years and in Brantford at the Pauline Johnson Collegiate and Vocational School for two years. In 1972 he entered the University of Toronto where he studied for his Bachelor of Education and graduated in 1973 (B.Ed.). In September of 1973 he attended the Oxford University Ruskin School, Oxford, England. He then returned to Brantford. Earlier during the Art Gallery of Brant's 3rd Invitational show in 1972 his paintings were noted by Maureen Peterson as follows, "Rick Pottruff. . .is represented mainly by large and masterfully colored oils. . . Pottruff is a painter, with all the mystical Parisian nuance implicit in the word. . . .In his work there is something of 'the great French art' of the second quarter of this century. . .It is perhaps in Pottruff that one can sense the greatest potential." Viewing his work in 1977 in a group show at the Arts Place, Brantford, David Moore noted, "Tending towards a more representational and figurative kind of art is Rick Pottruff's work. . . .His prints and drawings are strong, dense, robust works that amass people and forms and environments in a slightly distorted, disorienting manner. His figures have qualities reminiscent of

POTTRUFF, Richard Phillip (Cont'd)

expressionist interpretations of psychological states, and comic-book and editorial cartoons, and are both affectionately humorous and misanthropically biting at the same time. They are very successful works." Most of his important work has been done in oils, acrylic, ink, pencil and woodcuts. His awards include: Honourable Mentions at the Brantford Jury Shows (1964, 1969); Sanderson Award (1965); Glenhyrst Arts Council Award (1966, 1967) and he has had two shows at McMaster University in 1966 and 1967. He has exhibited at the Brant Gallery Invitational Show for several years. A member of the Society of Canadian Painter-Etchers & Engravers he is represented in a number of private collections including those of: B.L. Baig, Waterford, Ont.; D.G. MacDonald, Brantford, Ont.; D.M. Sherman, Tor., Ont.; J. Darville, London, Eng.; B.T. Roberts, Tor., Ont. and others. Pottruff was a member of the provincial rugger team in 1971. He married Jennifer in 1968 and they have a son Christopher.

References

Brantford Expositor, Ont., Apr. 20, 1966 (large photo of collage in oils by Pottruff which won Glenhyrst Arts Council award)

Simcoe Reformer, Ont., Aug. 3, 1972 "Third Annual Brant Gallery Holds Invitational Show"

Brantford Expositor, Ont., August (date missing), 1972 review by Maureen Peterson

Ibid, Oct. 22, 1977 "The Roving Eye — A varied display of. . ."

NGC Info. Form dated July 15, 1973

POTVIN, Dominique

b. 1959

He has been painting since the age of six and has been described as an artist with an astonishing technique. He has a fine sense of colour, equilibrium and light. He is known for his portraits, landscapes and enjoys drawing in his leisure time. An archeology student at Alma College he comes from a family that enjoys drawing. An exhibition of his work took place at the Alma Plaza in Alma, Quebec in 1977.

Reference

Saguenay Le Quotidien, Chicoutimi, Que., Mar. 9, 1977 "Du barbouillage qui se termine en peinture"

POTVIN, Gabrielle

A Quebec painter who has exhibited her work in many centres in Canada including Montreal (1976), Ottawa (1977) and abroad in Japan at Gallery Mikimoto (1977) the show was sponsored by the Quebec Government and opened by the former Japanese ambassador to Canada, Shin-ichi Kondoh.

References

Brochure, Gallery Mikimoto, 1977

POTVIN, Gabrielle (Cont'd)

Exhibition notice, Gabrielle Potvin at Holiday Inn, Ottawa, 1977
Exhibition notice, Gabrielle Potvin, Hotel Meridien, Montreal, 1976

POU, Polly

A painter, she taught flower arranging and painting in Hong Kong, from about 1952 to 1976. She came to Ottawa in 1977 when she held a solo show of her work at the Ottawa City Hall art gallery. There she exhibited sixty ink drawings of misty landscapes of mountainous southern Chinese highlands, flower and pine bough still lifes and figure studies in historic dress. She also exhibited her tools for making her art which included groups of brushes each for achieving different effects; ones used to make bamboo trees, others used for making the sky and water; and still others for painting figures. She also gave an explanation of how to mount rice paper onto the silk panels which frame each work and was present at the exhibition to discuss her work.

Reference

The Ottawa Citizen, Ont., July 26, 1977 "Art — Chinese artist paints with love" by Robert Smythe

---

POULIN, A.

Born in the province of Quebec, he worked in logging camps until an injury to his legs prevented him from walking for two years. During that period he took up a pastime of carving with pen knife, scenes of his native province at different times of the year. Each scene represented one month of the year and the activities carried on during that month. They included logging activities, harvesting with old fashioned scythe and threshing by flailing the wheat and a Christmas scene. Poulin exhibited his work at Bowmanville, Ontario. The public was asked for a small donation when seeing the exhibit which he presented with special lighting and accompanied viewers around the exhibit to discuss each scene. He was still having difficulty walking and could not return to the heavy work he had done before. Poulin was described by the *Statesman* as a clever and skilful artist.

Reference

Statesman, Bowmanville, Ont., Oct. 27, 1938 "Cripple Carves Quebec Miniatures Depicting Seasonal Scenes in Wood"

POULIN, Bernard Aimé
b. 1945
Born in Windsor, Ontario, the eldest of nine children of Jose Aimé Poulin (Prof. at Collège Technique d'Amos) and Marie-Jeanne (Lauzière) Poulin. He

POULIN, Bernard Aimé (Cont'd)

attended elementary school at Windsor, and at fifteen years of age decided to be on his own. He moved to Ottawa where he found work in a store. He was persuaded to attend school in Ottawa and became a pupil at Collège du Sacré Coeur. Continuing his education he returned to Windsor to Corpus Christi High School where he completed his secondary school education. Being away from home at the age of fifteen made him keenly aware of the needs of the very young and would later cause him to devote a good part of his life to working with youths with special problems. As a fully bilingual student, he attended the University of Ottawa Teachers' College while he earned income to make ends meet as a tutor and secretary to the Brazilian Ambassador's son in Ottawa (1963-64). In his art he had become interested in drawing and painting at the age of eight which was encouraged at home and was part of the activity at his early family environment. He attended art classes briefly at the Willistead Art Gallery, Windsor, but continued his interest and learning on his own. His attendance at the Ontario Ministry of Education Course at the Ontario College of Art to qualify for his Elementary Art Teacher's Certificate in 1964 fortified his studies. As a painter his main interest became realisitc subject matter and his early influences were derived from the work of Caravaggio, Paul Peel, Winslow Homer and from the association of his best friend Normand Fortin, a jewellery artist and sculptor. Poulin produced drawings, paintings of nature, of heritage buildings and of children. Working in oils, water colours, pencil and in terra cotta in sculpture, he was developing his art towards the day of his first one-man show. In his daily duties he assumed the job as Head of Child Care at Mount St-Joseph Treatment Centre, Ottawa, which was an in-residence responsibility (1965-68) while he was also a teacher for the Ottawa Separate School Board (French) in the Student Services Department where he participated in the organization and planning of in-patient children "Home-school" concept; organization and planning of the first services to non-resident emotionally disturbed children; organization of second and third special education classes; and teacher for the severely disturbed pre-teens and many other activities in education culminating in his appointment as Professor at the University of Ottawa in the Faculty of Education, Teacher Training in Special Education Course (1965-73). From 1973 to 1977 he was teacher and consultant for individual and group programming for the M.F. McHugh School, Ottawa, where resident and non-resident children of Ottawa hospitals and detention centres receive their education. Working at his painting throughout those years he was ready to hold his first solo show which took place at the Sandy Hill Art Gallery, Ottawa (1967) and the same year he worked with his friend Normand Fortin in Windsor on a huge outside mural for a Centennial Project (the mural measured 50 ft. by 20 ft.). He held subsequent solo shows in Ottawa at Gallery 5 (1972-74); Crossroads Gallery (1975); Galerie Rodrigue Lemay (1976); York Gallery (1977, 79); Galerie De LaSalle (1978). He worked with Eleanor Kish in the creation of the first pictorial stamp diorama for the Canadian Postal Museum, Ottawa (1974). He took time out in 1975 to follow personal studies in Florence, Italy. Then in 1977 he became a full time professional artist and moved to Sudbury, Ontario, with his wife Marie-Paul, a CBC executive, and their two children. There he established a home and studio and, in 1979, held a solo show under the title "People, Places and Things" at the Bell Museum, Laurentian University, Sudbury, when Carolyn Fouriezos for *Northern Life* noted, "In Bernard Aimé Poulin's world, the 'things' are vibrant,

POULIN, Bernard Aimé (Cont'd)

the 'places' are vivid and the 'people' memorable. The people are mostly children — children sleeping, stretching, removing slivers, posturing, pondering or playing. Their faces mirror the mischief, defiance, resignation and, at times, the bewilderment of the young in an adult world. . . .The colours in Poulin's paintings range from the dark, earth tones reminiscent of the Flemish school to the brighter lighter shades of nature reflected in strong sunlight. . .the work is imaginative, perceptive and on each viewing, different levels of meaning emerge. For a trip into Bernie Poulin's world, I'd advise you to see the exhibition. . . ." Poulin has now published limited editions of reproductions of some of his work obtainable from various galleries, and distributorship in Canada and Bermuda. These issues have been described by Carolyn Fouriezos as being, "beautifully reproduced." As a full-time artist he also does a wide range of commercial work including posters, billboards, cover designs, book illustrations and other items. He is also a professional photographer and in 1969 produced a poster for the United Appeal. His photo work includes portraits and artistic renditions. His paintings have been exhibited in many group shows including: Contemporary Tendencies in Figurative Painting, Univ. Ott. (1976); Franco-Ontarian Painters, Univ. Ott. (1977); Big Brothers Art Auction and Exhibition, Ott. (1970-77); Norart Juried Exhibition, Laurentian Univ., Sudbury (1979); Bermuda Society of Arts Exhibition, Hamilton, Bermuda (1980) and many others. He was a CBC (Radio Canada) French researcher-interviewer from July to Nov. 1976. He is represented in the following collections: Le Droit Newspaper, Ottawa; M.F. McHugh School for Emotionally Disturbed Children, Ottawa; Royal Ottawa Hospital, Draper Memorial Fund, Ottawa; Chorale International Satya, Amos, Que.; Hi-Roy Guest Home, Bermuda; Palazzo Antinori Estate, Florence, Italy; Pensione Quissisana e Ponte Vecchio, Florence, Italy; Bass Lake Lodge, Lombardy, Ontario and in over one hundred private collections in Canada, Bermuda, England, France, Switzerland, Italy and Australia. He is a member of the Canadian Artists Representation (CARO); International Society of Artists (ISA); Bermuda Society of Artists (BSA), also United Commercial Travellers of America; Big Brothers Assoc. of Ottawa; Association des Enseignants Franco-Ontariens; Ontario Public School Men Teachers' Federation; Highway Radio Patrol International; SOS Children's Village of Canada; Club Richelieu, Ottawa; Cursillo. He has been guest speaker and lecturer to many educational programmes and Children's Aid Societies and the Ontario Association of Foster Parents. Elected Citizen of the Week, Ottawa (1967); Hon. Life Member of Distinguished Citizens Club of Ottawa (1968).

References

Ottawa Journal, Ont., Jan. 26, 1967 "Fine Showing At Sandy Hill Art Gallery" by W.Q. Ketchum

Ibid, April 3, 1972 "Poulin works at Gallery 5 splendid" by W.Q. Ketchum

Ibid, Mar. 12, 1973 "Gallery 5 exhibit includes miniature oils and drawings" by W.Q. Ketchum

Le Droit, Ottawa, Mar. 17, 1973 "Arts Plastiques — Bernard Poulin l'espace en miniature" par Michel Dupuy

Ottawa Journal, Ont., Sat. Oct. 6, 1973 "Faces of Ottawa — Bernie Poulin" by W.Q. Ketchum

Ottawa Citizen, Ont., Mar. 29, 1974 "Artist evokes nostalgia" by Kathleen Walker

Le Droit, Ottawa, Mar. 30, 1974 "Arts Plastiques — Bernard Poulin: redécouverte" par Michel Dupuy

Ottawa Citizen, Ont., Nov. 25, 1977 "Art" (review) by Robert Smythe

POULIN, Bernard Aimé (Cont'd)

Northern Life, L.S., Sudbury, Wed., July 18, 1979 "The Entertainers — Bernie Poulin: full-time artist" by Carolyn Fouriezos

Ibid, Wed., Nov. 21, 1979 "The Entertainers — Bernie Poulin's world of enigma and allegory" by Carolyn Fouriezos

Film, CBC *Hope Is A Good Word* (a film of 30 minutes running time about Poulin's work with children) produced 1966

Io e Firenze by Bernard A. Poulin, limited edition, 1975 (on the art legacy, the people of and the modern way of life in Florence) with 40 original drawings

Of Fools And Laughable Things, N.Y.P. (poetry and children's observations, re: adults)

POULIN, Carol
b.(c) 1947

A painter from Beauce County, Quebec, who started painting about 1964 and studied applied arts at the École des Beaux-Arts, Quebec. He held his first solo show at Chantauteuil, Quebec City, which was well received. His work shown then was surrealistic in nature and revealed Poulin's ability to place his subject beyond its habitual space by drawing on his imagination. He worked as a designer at Parc de l'Artillerie where one of his projects was to decorate the top of the well at the park with birds. He sees the possibilities of his subjects in terms of images.

Reference

Le Soleil, Québec, Qué., Dec. 7, 1974 "Arts Visuels — Carol Poulin: parler en images" par Jean Royer

---

POULIN, Robert
b.(c) 1949

Born in Quebec, he studied architecture. Two years before finishing he turned to sculpture and spent four months in Copenhagen working in collaboration with the Royal Academy of Fine Arts there and exhibited his work at the Max Staal Gallery (1972); lived six months in Poland, mostly in Warsaw then held a solo show in Elblag at Galerie El Laboriatoriumsztuki (1973); in Tokyo, Japan at Mr. K. Ando's Factory in Meguro (1973-74); in Tokyo again at Mr. Ando's factory and afterwards he exhibited his work at Gallery 5610, Tokyo (1975); returned to Quebec where he continued his iron rod sculpture receiving the backing of several companies which enabled him to complete a series of works which he exhibited at the Musée de Joliette (1978). During that show his work was described by Jean-Claude Leblond as having exquisite spacial calligraphy in deep accord with its environment. Earlier in 1975 his work had been described by Masakazu Horiuchi in Japan as follows, "He does his work in one corner of a small welding shop, using an electric welding machine. His main material is iron rods, but he seldom leaves them straight. He generally bends them into circular arcs or curves that are almost parabolas. He claims that this is his revolution against the great number of rectilinear shapes found in most modern sculpture today. Among his works, there is one that is almost two meters high that has strong curves which are like tightly strung bows, curves which jut out

POULIN, Robert (Cont'd)

in various directions and loop back on each other, giving the general feeling of giant waves reverberating off each other with a loud roar of energy. When I asked him if he had done this particular work with the movement of waves in mind, he answered that he had. Besides this work that expresses the movement of waves, he has sculptures that give the feeling of the vigorous growth of plants and those that express the great broad space of a dome. In this way, his works take on a fantastic variety of shapes and forms, but in each and every one, there is a feeling of a strong, majestic heart, indicative of his own personality and character. . . .It was a solemn and magnificent sight. There were works ranging from one to two meters in height, but Robert explained that these were only maquettes for architectural scale structures. He had been wanting to put them on display for some time, but since they are all built upon architectural structural principles, he felt that it would be necessary to display them outside and was being held back due to the lack of an appropriate outdoor gallery." Poulin is certainly one of the more interesting and talented of sculptors not only in Quebec but in all of Canada.

References

Booklet, text, photos from Gallery 5610, Tokyo "Robert Poulin à Tokyo Sculptures en fer et maquettes pour structures architecturales" May 30 to June 8, 1975 (text in French, English, Japanese)

Booklet, text, photos from Musée de Joliette, "Robert Poulin" work made possible by the support of the following: Jean-Marc Carrier of Tube Bend Ltée. (Mtl.); Charles A. Decelles of Bend-All Ltée. (Mtl.); Russellsteel Ltée. (Mtl.); Georges Dupuis of Wolf Power Tools Ltée. (Mtl.); l'atelier de soudure, Léo-Paul Pelletier (St. Ours, Que.)

Le Devoir, Mtl., 10 Mai, 1978 "Arts et Spectacles — Expositions/Les folles sculptures de Robert Poulin" par Jean-Claude Leblond

POULIN, Roland
b. 1940

Born in St. Thomas, Ontario, he studied art at the École des Beaux-Arts, Montreal. He became interested in effects with beams of light and exhibited the first effective use of the laser in an art work in Montreal. With the assistance of McGill Physicist Dr. A. Gunjian, he prepared the work 'Immaterial Structure' which made use of two compact helium-neon gas lasers and small mirrors that direct fine red beams into a smoke-filled environment (25 by 40 ft.). He had plans to produce forms of light for other immaterial structures including one with the form of Toronto's modern City Hall, another within a wooded landscape and still another in theatre performances. Whether he produced any of these is not here known but he did go on to a new form of art expression which involved wood or concrete beams placed in various shapes to induce the viewer to contemplate the relationships of the outer and inner spaces created by the arrangements of the beams and any differences to one another in the beams themselves within each arrangement. His beam arrangements were chosen for the 1980 exhibition "Pluralities 1980" at the National Gallery of Canada. An accompanying text to his various sculptures was included in the catalogue. Nineteen artists participated in the show selected by a committee of four (Philip Fry, Willard Holmes, Allan MacKay and Chantal Pontbriand). His laser work stands as his more exciting creations to date but no doubt he will

POULIN, Roland (Cont'd)

continue to experiment with various elements to create new art forms. He has participated in over thirty-three shows national and international. Lives and works in Montreal.

References

Structure Immatérielle by Roland Poulin, Musée d'Art Contemporain, Mtl., 1971 (Rayons Lasers et Faisceaux — catalogue with sketches and photos about laser beams as decoration)

The Gazette, Mtl., October 30, 1971 "Roland Poulin is showing his laser art at the Museum of Contemporary Art" (review and photo of artist viewing his laser beams)

Le Soleil, Que., 5 Mai, 1973 "Jeux de lumière et d'espace" (article and photo of artist with his light beams)

Vie des Arts, Mtl., Vol. 18, No. 73, Winter, 1973 "Roland Poulin: Structures immatérielles et utopies" par L. Vermette

L'Art au Québec depuis 1940 par Guy Robert, La Presse, Mtl., 1973, P. 440, 441

Canadian artists in exhibition 1972-73, Roundstone, Tor., 1974, P. 171

Artscanada, July/August, 1976 206/207 "Quebec 75/Arts: 1" by David Burnett, P. 16, 17

Ibid, Vol. 34, No. 20, November, 1977 "Site Work: Some Sculpture at Artpark 1977" by E. Thalenberg

Parachute, No. 1, Autumn, 1975 "Notes 1974-1975" by Roland Poulin

Ibid, No. 5, Winter, 1976 "Roland Poulin à la Galerie B" par France Morin

Ibid, No. 8, Autumn, 1977 "Artpark 1977" by France Morin

Ibid, No. 19, Summer, 1980 "Roland Poulin" by Jean Papineau

Vie des Arts, Vol. 24, No. 96 Autumn 1979 "Mongrain et Poulin" par Jean Tourangeau

Pluralities 1980 (catalogue) an exhibition coordinated by Jessica Bradley, NGC, Ottawa, 1980 P. 91-96 (photos, text, list of exhibitions, selected bibliography)

POULIN, Suzanne

She exhibited her sculptural hangings eight to ten feet high which produced rhythms and colour zones from their contrasts. The exhibition took place at the Maison des Arts, La Sauvegarde, Montreal in 1975.

Reference

Notice — La Maison des Arts, La Sauvegarde "Suzanne Poulin: sculptures"

POULIOT, Aline

She studied painting for five years with Lionel Fielding Downes, André Garant and Francesco Iacurto. About 1969 she began to market her work with Club artistique de Ste. Foy at Maison Routhier under the sponsorship of the Centre de Loisirs of Ste. Foy and in different art boutiques in Quebec. She won honourable mention at a symposium at Place de l'Hotel de Ville de Québec during the Festival of Quebec. Her work shows some cubistic and some impressionistic influence and she is mainly in the figurative domain. Her subjects include old buildings of Quebec City, landscapes and portraits. She held her first solo show at the Solidarité, Quebec, in 1971 and subsequently exhibited at the Palais Montcalm (1974). Her work has been well received. A mother of four she lives in Quebec City.

POULIOT, Aline (Cont'd)

References

Québec l'Action, Que. City, Sept. 25, 1969 "Pour une jeune femme habile — Un passe-temps devient un art" par Thérèse Dallaire

Quebec Chronicle-Telegraph, May 5, 1971 "Girl's Portrait" (large photo of her painting of a girl's portrait)

Le Journal de Québec, Que. City, Mar. 11, 1974 (notice of her show at Palais Montcalm)

POULIOT, André
1919-1953

Born in Quebec City he attended the Jesuit College there and after graduation went on to the University of Ottawa. He attended the School of the Montreal Museum of Fine Arts where he studied painting with Goodridge Roberts then later attended the Pratt Institute of Art in New York City. He studied both painting and sculpture. He served with the R.C.A.F. during World War Two and painted murals at St. John's depot and at Rockcliffe Station hospital. He was employed by *La Presse, Canadian Press* and did independent newspaper work. He died in Montreal and was at that time survived by his wife Muguette Jobin; a son, Francis; his mother Mrs. Rachel Pouliot; two sisters: Miss Camille and Mrs. Thérèse Chadwick; two brothers: René of Montreal and Jean of Toronto.

Reference

The Gazette, Mtl., Oct. 17, 1953 "Funeral Set For Sculptor André Pouliot"

POULIOT, Andrée

An Ottawa painter who exhibited her landscapes and portraits at the Sussex Annex Works in Ottawa in 1974. At that time she had painted scenes of Old Chelsea, Quebec and scenes of the Rideau Canal. She was a member of the Canal Painters, a group made up of six artists.

Reference

Ottawa Journal, Ont., Feb. 6, 1974 "Group of Six exhibits" by W.Q. Ketchum

POULIOT, Mario
b.(c) 1949

From Sherbrooke, Quebec, he studied engraving at the Université de Québec, Montréal, and is known for his incorporation of various objects like wood and metal in his forms for his prints which he produces in soft colours with evocative titles. He was the only Canadian whose work was selected by the International Triennial of Engraving on Wood in Fribourg, Switzerland (only 224 engravings were selected out of 1,399). The two works selected were entitled

POULIOT, Mario (Cont'd)

"Hiver au soleil" and "Nids d'hiver" and there were only nine prints pulled from each original. One of these prints was reproduced in the catalogue XYLON 7. As well as engraving on wood he does serigraphs and some etchings. He held a solo show of his work at Galerie Mena'Sen, Sherbrooke (1974).

References

La Tribune, Sherbrooke, Nov. 22, 1974 "Une exposition de Mario Pouliot: ses gravures ont une grande douceur"
Ibid, March 27, 1976 "Des Variétés — Oeuvres d'un graveur sherbrookois sélectionnées par hasard"

POULIOT, Paul R.
b. 1909

Born in Joliette, Quebec, he wanted to draw from an early age but had poor eyesight. In 1964 he had an eye operation with unexpectedly good results and shortly afterwards joined painting classes at C.E.G.E.P. at Joliette (1966-74) studying with R.P. Max Boucher (painter and sculptor), Gaston Thérrien and Paul Turgeon. Working in oils and acrylics he has preferred doing portraits over other of his painting subjects. He is represented in collections in London, Ontario; Montreal, Quebec and the region of Lanaudière. He has exhibited at the Seminaire de Joliette (1966, 1974) and at Rawdon, Quebec (1967-1974). Has won a number of prizes in shows both at Joliette and Rawdon. Member of Cercle des Artistes de Rawdon. Lives in Joliette.

References

NGC artist's file with biographical information and letter
Dictionnaire Biographique des Créateurs de la Région de Joliette par Réjean Olivier, Le Centre de Documentation, Musée Du Québec, 1975

POULTON, Michael
b. 1948

Born in Winnipeg, Manitoba, he studied at the Epsom & Ewell School of Art, England (1967-68) and the Camberwell School of Art, London, Eng., and graduated with a Diploma in Art and Design, B.A. (1968-72). He returned to Canada and settled in Toronto and became known for his prints, creative illustrations and book jacket designs. Mainly a figurative artist he has exhibited in the following shows: "500 Years of Printmaking", O.I.S.E., Tor. (1974); Soc. of Can. Artists, St. Mary's Univ., Halifax (1975) and Gallery Danielli, Tor. (1976); "On View, 76", Tor. Dom. Centre, Tor. and touring Ont. (1976); travelling show of Vis. Arts Ont. (1976); Graphex 4, Art Gallery of Brant, Brantford, Ont. and touring Canada (1976); "Soft Touch", Art Gal. Brant (1976). He is represented in the Art Gallery of Brant, the Carlsberg Foundation, and his work is available at the Art Rental Gallery, Art Gal. Ontario, Tor.; Art Rental Gallery, Art Gal. Windsor, Ont.; Art Rental Gallery, Art Gal. of Hamilton, Ont. His awards include: Carlsberg Foundation, Lond., Ont. (1971); Central & Northern Gas Award, "On View" (1976); Purchase

POULTON, Michael (Cont'd)

Award, Art Gal. of Brant "Graphex 4" (1976); Ont. Arts Council, Editions Award "Graphex 4" (1976); Aviva Chapter, 2nd prize in graphics (1978). Member: Soc. of Can. Artists and Print and Drawing Council of Canada.

References

Wallack art editions, 204 Bank St., Ott. (biographical sheet on artist)
Andre Tom Macgregor, a novel by Betty Wilson, Macmillan (Can.), Tor. (jacket ill.)
The Index of Ontario Artists, Ed. Hennie Wolff, Vis. Arts Ont./Ont. Assoc. Art Gal., Tor., Ont., 1978, P. 221 & cover design

POUPLOT, Jacques

Originally from France, he served in the French military service in Africa where he became inspired by masks and sculptural heads. He arrived in Quebec in 1967 from France and at first worked as a clerk in a bookstore while developing his craft at nights. A sculptor, he is known for his fine works in wire which include: sunbursts, heads, birds, masks and other interesting pieces. One of his pieces for instance "Le Heron" is six feet high and is suitable for an interior decoration. In designing his work he makes his pieces mathematically regular. On occasion he has produced work in cooperation with Michel Gibout as in the creation of the work "La Vie", a sunburst with metal rods representing rays of the sun with two human figures, a man and woman, walking towards the centre of the work. A member of the Société des Artisans du meuble québecois, he has exhibited his work with other members of the Society at the Maison des artisans in Old Montreal (1969, 1970).

References

La Presse, Mtl., Que., Feb. 22, 1969 "Quand un héron se regarde dans un miroir. . ." par Madeleine Berthault
Ibid, Apr. 21, 1970 "Un vernissage"

POW, Robert
b. 1942

Born in Montreal, Quebec, he studied art at Western Technical School, Toronto, and established his home in Toronto. He began concentrating on wildlife art in 1975 especially Canadian mammals. He creates his subjects with careful attention to detail and feeling. Working in pencil, water colours and scraperboard he reflects his profound respect for the animal world with beauty and vitality. His goal is to eventually draw all North American wildlife. A few of his subjects include: Bears, Beaver, Bobcat, Bighorn Sheep, Buffalo, Caribou, Cougar, Deer, Foxes, Lynx, Mice, Moose, Otter, Owls, Polar Bear, Raccoon, Squirrels, Sparrow Hawk, Weasel, Wolves, Wolverine and many others. He produces limited edition prints of his wildlife subjects from fifty of some animals and birds to a maximum of 500 for others per edition. Many of his original paintings and drawings, as well as over four thousand limited edition prints, have been purchased for private collections in Canada, the

POW, Robert (Cont'd)

United States and Europe. His work has appeared in the following shows: First Canadian Place, Tor. (group show); Federation of Ontario Naturalists at Guelph University, Ont.; The Art Loft, Peterborough, Ont. (group show, 1978); The Dawn Gallery, Tor. (group show, 1979); Etobicoke Civic Centre (group show, 1980); The Davidson Gallery, Tor. (1980); The Dawn Gallery, Unionville, Ont. (1980) and annual exhibits at the C.N.E. (Arts Bldg.), Tor.; Wildlife shows in: Kingston, Ont. (Aug.); Clayton, N.Y. (July); Buckhorn, Ont. (Aug.); Ottawa (Nov.). His Wolverine was featured in the 1979 Spring issue of the *Ontario Naturalist* magazine.

References

Sunday Sun, Tor., Ont., May 14, 1978 "The art scene" by Barney McKinley (photo of artist and one of his bear drawings)

Robert Pow Wildlife Art Catalogue, 1980 (31 illustrations), Robert Pow Wildlife Art, 250 Scarlett Rd., Tor., Ont.

Robert Pow, Wildlife Artist (folder with biographical information and list of limited edition prints)

POWE, Larry

Born in Montreal, Quebec, he studied art at the Monument National and with Edwin Holgate. A muralist and illustrator he served with the R.C.A.F. during the 2nd World War and produced a number of murals for the service. He exhibited his work at the Art Association of Montreal, the Arts Club of Montreal and at the Price Fine Arts Award shows and elsewhere in Montreal and in Quebec. He taught illustration at Sir George William University in Montreal and mural techniques at the Art Centre, Le Vieux Moulin in Saint-Pie de Bagot, Quebec.

Reference

Granby La Voix de l'Est, Quebec, July 29, 1968 "M. Larry Powe enseigne la peinture murale à St-Pie"

POWELL, E.J.

An artist who moved to B.C. about 1973, who is known for his work with pastels. He uses pigment of a special French sanded pastel ground. Has exhibited his pastel paintings throughout Canada and in the States of Washington, Oregon and California. He held a solo show of his work at the New Westminster Public Library Gallery in May of 1973. He fills commissions and gives lessons in pastel painting. Member of the Federation of Canadian Artists.

Reference

New Westminster Columbian, B.C., May 14, 1973 "New Art Exhibit At Public Library"

POWELL, Fred
b. 1924

Born in Toronto, Ontario, he was educated there at Upper Canada College. Following graduation he served with the Canadian army in Europe (1942-46) and returned home at the end of the war. He picked up with his two interests of music and sculpture, exhibiting his carvings in leading galleries in Canada (1949-51). As he became more serious with his carving he realized the likelihood of not becoming a full-time musician. He felt however the limitations financially of being a sculptor in Canada full-time would not adequately provide for him and his wife and son. Finally he decided to move to California with his family settling at Malibu Beach where new opportunities for development awaited him. He established a home and workshop with the considerable advantage of a warmer climate. After settling at the Beach he was much inspired by his surroundings. The sea gave him a new sense of form as did the wonders everywhere along the coastline. In 1952 his work was exhibited in a group show at the Landau Gallery, Los Angeles, and also he held his first American solo show at the Santa Barbara Museum of Art. His sculptural wooden pieces of shells, birds and figures revealed his early mastery of the medium. He stayed in California until 1958. Then he moved on to New York City to study and work with leading sculptors learning how to handle steel, plastics, fabrics and other materials (1958-63). He returned to California until 1969. He decided next to live in Mexico and settled in a small town where the simplicity of life and the freedom to move about nurtured considerable inspiration. He concentrated fully on his sculpture and at times was even able to see the finished work in his mind before it was begun. Mexico was a wonderful creative period for him but he longed for a new challenge and to renew his old ties. Finally he loaded all his work on an old truck and returned to Toronto in 1975. He held his first showing of some work at Galerie Dresdnere that same year when James Purdie, *Globe & Mail* reviewer noted, "Fred Powell is a Canadian sculptor who recently returned to Toronto after many years in the United States and other countries. He works with wood, for the most part, but produces some interesting mixed-media pieces as well. Among these is his sombre and symbolic Los Angeles Freeway. Another, which illustrates Powell's understanding of wood, is his piece called Temptation. It shows a single apple growing from a sinister tree. . . .He is an important new presence on the Toronto art scene and is at work now on pieces for a one-man show to be held at the same gallery next year." In 1976 his solo show at Galerie Dresdnere was again reviewed by James Purdie who noted, "When Fred Powell came home to Toronto last year. . .he drove up from San Miguel de Allende in an old truck piled high with the best of his Mexican sculptures. . .Powell adjusted as the coldest, windiest, stormiest winter in memory laid layer after layer of snow and ice over Toronto, but the truck couldn't. It fought the new climate like some stubborn Mexican burro,. . .The sculptor pushed and kicked and drained batteries all winter long, but he's turned the experience to good use. He got back at the truck by using it as a model for a new sculpture he calls Gear Strip. It's a carved wood piece, black as the mechanical heart of the model, and it's unlike anything else Powell had done to date. . . .It's a depiction of the truck, barely visible under a rolling pall of thick, oily smoke. . . .The truck and the other two Toronto works, Overcoat and Split, are carved from wood blocks laminated by the artist. . . .Overcoat is exactly what Powell says it is: a dark symbol of the winter environment. It stands on its own tails, less than two-feet high, half-open but empty and in Powell's hands it has become much more than protection for the body. Its interior cradles all the mysteries of caves, shrines and shells in the dark recesses of both of the ocean floor and the mind. . . .Among the Mexican pieces in the exhibition are two monumental constructions, Buddha in the West and Gateway to Meditation. Powell says he built them from 100-year-old, worm-eaten timbers acquired from a wrecker. 'Buddha in the West means many things.' Powell says 'If you look to the right, you'll see the decay of our western cities. Poised above them, curving up from the pillar of time and the wheel of evolution, is the Chinese horse, final judgement, whatever you want to make of it. And in the centre, eternal, unchanging, the Buddha remains. 'Similar forces are at work in Gateway to Meditation, but it also has an interior, a private place to be shared only with the person who looks within.' Powell says Toronto has already influenced his works, urbanizing it, toning down the colors of Mexico to that truck-engine black that leaves his simplified forms to speak for themselves." In 1978 for his show at the Moos Gallery Theodore Heinrich in an introduction for the catalogue perhaps best describes Powell's work, ". . .satirically penetrating and good-humoured, we find in his comments a double-edged bite. The familiar essences that he discovers make us laugh. The hollowness he has created in his startling new sculptural invention gives us a sociological shudder. Together they fuse mysteriously into presences that we cannot forget. Powell is now working with laminated pine. This permits him as carver a wonderfully fluent line and as sculptural engineer structures independent of armature. He has had to invent new tools to carve out the vivid emptinesses that command the expressive outer forms. Each of the sixteen pieces in the show that represent a furiously concentrated working period of only a year and a half is lovingly finished in polished black or white lacquers rubbed to the sheen of prized old Mexican leather saddlebags. His universal city is not necessarily all of just now nor are its denizens even of their own precise time. The marvellous 'Jesse' is a Jesse James translated into one of the Sheiks of 20's street-corners. Absolutely everything is said by the coat, the slouch hat and the aggressive pose. The fact that there is literally nothing inside the costume is the stinger. This sculpture is not an illustration, it is a remarkably perceptive comment." Powell's solo shows include: Santa Barbara Museum of Art, Calif. (1952); Park Gallery, Tor. (1960); Rex Evans Gallery, Los Angeles (1963); Charles Fiengarten Gallery, Los Angeles (1964, 1967, 1969); Santa Barbara Museum of Art, Calif. (1967); Belles Artes, Mexico City (1971); Roberts Gallery, Tor. (1973); Galerie Dresdnere, Tor. (1976); Gallery Moos Ltd., Tor. (1978) and in many group shows in the United States at California, New York, Texas, Illinois, Indiana and in Ontario, Canada. He is represented in the following collections: Phoenix Art Museum, Arizona; Museum of Modern Art, Mexico City; Canadian Embassy in Mexico City; Art Bank, Ottawa and in private collections in the U.S.A. and Mexico.

References

Globe & Mail, Tor., May 14, 1960 "Powell Sculpture On View"
Exhibition sheet — Santa Barbara Museum of Art, 1967 (biographical notes and photos)
Catalogue sheet — Roberts Gallery, Tor., Nov. 7-17, 1973 "Fred Powell Sculptures"
Globe & Mail, Tor., Nov. 16, 1973 "Art — Sombre looks carved from solid wood" by Kay Kritzwiser
Ibid, Dec. 27, 1975 "At The Galleries — Fred Powell" by James Purdie
Ibid, Mar. 29, 1976 "Powell: dark symbols and peeping tongues" by James Purdie

POWELL, Fred (Cont'd)

Ibid, Jan. 13, 1978 "Canadian culture booms in Mexico" by Scott Symons

Catalogue — Gallery Moos, Tor., 1978 "Fred Powell" (forward by Theodore A. Heinrich & photos of artist's work)

Sunday Star, Tor., Ont., Feb. 19, 1978 "The Arts — Vaguely nasty, despite the whimsy" by Sol Littman

POWELL, W. (William Benjamin Powell)
b. 1938

Born in Hamilton, Ontario he has been cited for his colourful canvases described as dynamic and at times explosive. He works in acrylic, water colour and mixed media applied in a wash-like technique. He has a wide range of subject matter including landscapes, boats, figures and colourfield (abstract image painting). He is interested in the inner feeling of the movement and its evolution within each subject. A painting from his Boat series was described by Tully Kikauka as follows, ". . .one displayed shows simultaneously the successive images of masts swaying as result of the wave action. This type of superimposed images again adds that active ingredient which is part of Powell's exuberance, and love for motion." Powell opened his Hamilton, Ontario, Canvas Gallery in 1973 where the public has been encouraged to come in, ask questions about art, meet artists and learn to judge a piece of art. Funds for his gallery were obtained from the sale of his paintings. The main part of the gallery consisted of two rooms in the front part of the building. He and his wife were living in the apartment above the gallery with their two children Kim and Bill. He participated in a two-man show at his gallery with artist Robert Green in December of 1973 when his work was favourably reviewed. Subsequent shows have been: Alan Gallery, Hamilton (solo, 1973); Canvas Gal. (two-man, 1973, 1974); Gairloch Gardens Gallery, Oakville, Ont. (*Three from Hamilton*, 1976); McMaster Univ. Medical Centre Art Gal. (solo, 1977). He completed a mural for the Opera House (jazz club), Guadalajara, Mexico (1976). He is represented in the collection of CKOC Radio, Hamilton.

References

Hamilton Spectator, Ont., May 8, 1972 "Bill's canvassing support for art" (photo of artist in his gallery, with article about gallery opening)

Ibid, Dec. 1, 1973 "Artviews — Two-man show continues until Dec. 14" by Tully Kikauka

The Index of Ontario Artists, Ed. by Hennie Wolfe, Vis. Arts Ont./Ont. Assoc. of Gal., Tor., 1978, P. 221

POWNING, Peter

He studied fine arts at the University of Connecticut and pottery with Minnie Negoro. He came to Canada in 1970 and established the Markhamville Pottery on a farm near Sussex. There with his wife Beth they earn their living, she by her free-lance writing and he by his skills as a potter. They grow most of their own vegetables and have a meatless diet, keep goats for milk and raise chickens and ducks. He operates his own kiln which has a firing temperature of

POWNING, Peter (Cont'd)

2,380 degrees Fahrenheit. He works for a full month handthrowing clay, making lamp bases, tea pots, cups and saucers, mugs, planters, vases, bowls and ornaments, then lets them air-dry and fires them all at once to make it an economical venture. He uses about ten different glazes none of which have lead in them. The characteristic look of his work is a pale green tint glaze which he applies, leaves to dry, before firing the pieces for eighteen hours. One load can total about 400 articles. His work is sold in a pottery store named Jabberwock which he jointly runs with Lee Danisch, another potter from the same locality. Powning was the largest wholesale exporter of pottery in New Brunswick supplying pottery stores in Toronto, Montreal and Vancouver, prior to establishing his own retail pottery store in Sussex.

References

Evening Times Globe, Saint John, N.B., Mar. 29, 1978 "Pottery Exhibit Set For Handicraft Centre"

Moncton Transcript, N.B., July 19, 1975 "Leisure/Living — The Land, The Wheel, The Artist" by Anne Leslie

PRAGER, Eva Sophie
b. 1912

Born in Berlin, Germany, the daughter of Fanny and Joseph Oppenheimer, her father, a prominent portrait painter, came from Würzburg and her mother from Munich. Following a visit to a zoo at the age of four Eva drew and modelled animals by cutting out images and painting in water colours. Later she watched her father work and even sketched children as they sat for him. After reaching school age she modelled in clay, plasticine and wax and showed outstanding ability in art. Following completion of regular schooling she attended the Academie der Feinen Künste, Berlin, in 1929. Once she accompanied her father when he was working on the portrait of Albert Einstein who lived in the country. While walking through the woods one day between sitting sessions with this great scientist, they heard the most beautiful chamber music coming from a house. It was the two Prager brothers playing together. Eva and her father knocked on the door and were invited in by the family. That night they attended a party at the Prager's home which began the romance between Eva and Richard that led to their marriage in 1934. Her father had lived in England from 1898 to 1908 and had made frequent trips there until 1933 when he decided to make London a permanent home. Eva and her mother were soon able to join him. In London she studied at the Royal College of Art, and also in Paris at the École Paul Colin. As she developed her painting she was influenced by artists of many ages including the European Masters, Impressionists, Chagall, Japanese and Chinese Masters and by her own father who gave her guidance throughout her student years. She became known for her paintings in London and completed many portrait commissions. During the war years she was involved in creating stage decor. Within fifteen years she had become well established in her work. In 1944 in London her son Vincent was born. Her husband, now a businessman, had been making trips abroad and in 1949 they visited Montreal and shortly afterwards settled there. Eva continued with her art and it was not long before she had established herself in Canada.

PRAGER, Eva Sophie (Cont'd)

With a wide range of subject matter she produced still lifes, interiors, seascapes, city scenes, and many illustrations for magazines, papers, and portraits, especially of children. She received commissions in the United States and painted portraits of children of Hollywood personalities Elizabeth Taylor (daughter Liza); Debbie Reynolds (son Todd, daughter Carrie Fisher); Jayne Mansfield (son Mickey, son Zoltan, daughter Jayne Marie); Alan Ladd (son David) and in Canada, children of the Eatons, Molsons, Mr. & Mrs. Colin Gibson; grandchildren of Alan Bronfman; and in England she had already painted portraits of members of Lord and Lady Sainsbury's family. In 1959 she donated her time to create a mural for the X-Ray Room of the Montreal Children's Hospital which delighted the children themselves and she also gave of her time for the production of paintings for Unitarian Service Committee of Canada Christmas Cards to finance aid to the World's hungry children as well as for paintings to raise money for The Canadian Save The Children Fund. Explaining Eva's feelings about painting children's portraits, Janet Kask wrote "She says she finds a 'tremendous change from those of 10 years ago' and it's for the better. 'They're extremely well-mannered and interested. The whole world exists for them.' She prefers painting them when they are 'expressing their personalities — lying on a couch playing, or sitting on the stairs doing their home-work.' And she says they make better subjects in their 'everyday' clothes. One engaging boy was wearing football togs in his portrait. One of her most rewarding jobs was sketching children who attend the UN International School in New York. One reason is that she has strong feelings about the importance of children of all backgrounds growing up and learning together. 'Children must know each other on the playgrounds before they can partake of each other's culture.'" Virginia Nixon in an article on portrait painters of Montreal noted, "The best known is probably Eva Prager. Prager is particularly popular for her children's portraits — light in touch and color and tending towards an impressionistic style — and she does have an ability to capture childish sweetness and at the same time bring out character, but in fact she does as many adults as children. Prager has an unfailing ability to find something of personal worth in everybody she paints — perhaps one of the reasons she's never had the experience of dealing with a dissatisfied sitter." Her portraits of leading figures include: Linus Pauling (Nobel Prize Winner, scientist); Yehudi Menuhin (violinist); Rudolph Nureyev (ballet dancer); Sol Hurok (American theatre impresario); Pierre Elliott Trudeau (Prime Minister); John Turner (former Federal Cabinet Minister); Mr. & Mrs. Colin Gibson; Gerald Fauteux (former Chief Justice, Supreme Court of Canada); Jean V. Allard (General); Jacques Dextraze (General); S.C. Waters (General); Dr. Douglas Cameron, (Physician-in-Chief, Mtl. Gen. Hospital); Dr. Harold Griffith and Dr. James Griffith for the Queen Elizabeth Hospital, Mtl.; Dean Vincent MacDonald (Dalhousie Univ., Halifax); Heads of the Law and Dentistry Departments of McGill University; Headmaster of Trinity College; 'Jack Rabbit' Johannsen (on his 100th birthday); Pierre Berton (author, broadcaster, T.V. personality); Adrienne Clarkson (writer, broadcaster, T.V. personality); Commodore Aram Oganov (Head of the Russian Merchant Marine); His Eminence, The Metropolitan Saliba, Archbishop of the Antiochian Orthodox Christian Church, Archdiocese of New York and all of North America; and many others. Wini Rider writing in *The Gazette* in 1972 noted, "Eva Prager paints a dustbin in the snow as if it were a Japanese landscape, sees a rotating apartment ventilator

PRAGER, Eva Sophie (Cont'd)

as a Russian crown, and views today's youth as the most beautiful of all sights. Two areas of North America delight her and her emotions are tugged between them — the Laurentians which she sees as bright, warm and full of flowers — oranges, reds, pinks, yellows. . .The other is Cape Cod, — water, weathered wharves, and old sail boats — blues, greys, taupe, mauve. One location indeed represents her joie de vivre, the other her serenity. She does not seem to show any despondency in her moods or paintings — they are either bright, exciting, warm or they are serene." She is represented in the McCord Museum, Mtl.; Palais de Justice, Mtl.; Trinity College, Tor.; Dalhousie University, Halifax; Supreme Court of Canada, Ottawa; Maritime Museum, Leningrad, U.S.S.R. and elsewhere. Her work has been exhibited at the Beckett Gallery, Hamilton, Ont.; Hamilton Gallery, Lond. Eng.; Kastel Gallery, Mtl.; Galerie Martal, Mtl.; Dominion Gallery, Mtl.; Women's Club, New York; Salon d'Automne, Paris; Montreal Museum of Fine Arts. Member: Media Club of Canada; Montreal Museum of Fine Arts; Committee of Canadian Save the Children Fund; Women's Press Club; Conseil de la peinture du Québec; Canadian Club. Has been subject of CBC film for "Focus" (1967); French Canadian T.V. network (1971) and has appeared on other CBC programmes with her paintings. She lives in Westmount, Quebec, with her husband Richard and her mother Fanny (now over ninety) who is still active. Her son Vincent is a Montreal lawyer.

References

The Gazette, Mtl., Apr. 30, 1959 (photo of Children's Hospital mural)

La Presse, Mtl., Apr. 30, 1959 "Première murale de Mme Prager" (article and photo)

Toronto Daily Star, Ont., June 11, 1960 "One Type Emerging? — Artist Starts Search For Canadian 'Look'" (article on artist while visiting Toronto to paint portrait commissions)

Weekend Magazine, Vol. 11, No. 37, 1961 "'I Like Hollywood Children" by Eva Prager as told to Frank Lowe (photos of her portraits of Hollywood children and article about them)

Ibid, Vol. 12, No. 34, 1962 "Fairs Are Fun All Over" (fairs in France, England, and Canada illustrated by E. Prager)

Chatelaine, April, 1962 "Eva Prager — The way to be beautiful is to be happy and confident"

The Ottawa Citizen, Ont., Sat., Nov. 30, 1963 "All children appeal to Montreal artist" by Janet Kask (photo of Eva and article)

L'Evangeline, Moncton, N.B., Nov. 30, 1963 "Une artiste de renom Mme Prager"

The Gazette, Mtl., P.Q., Mar. 16, 1964 "Painting Theatre's Sol Hurok — 'Giant Among Men'" by Joan Forsey

Ibid, Nov. 17, 1966 (photo of artist in her studio with her painting of UNICEF child)

Ibid, Jan. 20, 1968 "Facts & Fancies" with Harriet Hill (a film about her sketching at Expo '67)

Ibid, Sept. 12, 1968 "Facts & Fancies" with Harriet Hill "Go With An Artist" (Eva finds everything interesting at Expo '67 as she sketches on the grounds)

Ibid, Oct. 15, 1968 "Man and His World: The people made the exhibition" (full page of sketches by Eva Prager)

The Canadian, May 10, 1969 (Her portrait of Trudeau commissioned by *The Canadian* for article "Trudeau's first year: How is he doing?"

Toronto Daily Star, Ont., Nov. 28, 1969 "PM is ultimate human being, artist says" by Lotta Dempsey (article and photo of artist at work)

The Tribune, Winnipeg, Man., May 1, 1970 "Life is painting to Eva Prager" by Mary Bletcher (large photo of artist at work and article about her)

La Presse, Mtl., Feb. 17, 1971 "Elle était comme chez elle à la Cour Suprême du Canada"

Toronto Daily Star, Ont., May 20, 1971 "Artist's studio was a courtroom" by Lotta Dempsey (artist completes portrait of Chief Justice Gerald Fauteux)

PRAGER, Eva Sophie (Cont'd)

Montreal Star, Aug. 7, 1971 "Ontario Place — as seen by Montreal artist Eva Prager" (full page of illustrations by artist)

The Gazette, Mtl., Jan. 17, 1972 "The Good Life — Eva Prager — sensitive artist who sees only beauty" by Wini Rider (large colour photo of artist at work on a canvas of young people, also photos of her home — artist standing with her husband before fireplace in front of a portrait of her done by her father, Joseph Oppenheimer) P. 21, 22

The Chronicle Review, Tor., Ont., Jan.-Feb. 1975 (photo of artist with her lithograph to be sold to raise funds for Israel Family Counselling Assoc.)

The Gazette, Mtl., Sept. 29, 1975 "Home now alive with children's noises" (Eva Prager makes sketches of children for exhibit to support Project 80 — a project to help children develop in impoverished areas)

Ibid, Feb. 19, 1976 "Artist's eye sees beauty everywhere" by E.J. Gordon (photo of artist at work and an article about her)

Ibid, Mar. 4, 1978 "Art Notes — Want your portrait? Prices start at $200"

The World Who's Who of Women

Correspondence with artist 1970 to 1980

Visit with artist in Ottawa

Document from artist

PRAGNELL, Bartley Robillard
1908-1966

Born in Moose Jaw, Saskatchewan, he studied at the Winnipeg School of Art with Keith Gebhart and L.L. Fitzgerald (won Mundell Prize Scholarship); Banff School of Fine Arts with B. Middleton and H.G. Glyde (won high honours); Department of Education in Victoria, B.C. with W.P. Weston, and J.W.G. MacDonald; at the Montreal Art Association where he attended lectures by Arthur Lismer (1947); Hans Hofmann in New York (c. 1952). He was Head of the first Art Department at Moose Jaw Technical High School then became general art supervisor for all public and technical schools and colleges in Moose Jaw (1932-39). Served as public relations artist with the R.C.A.F. at No. 4 Training Command Headquarters. In 1944 he won third prize for his "Jimmy's Corner", a water colour submitted in the R.C.A.F. service-wide art competition for which there were 700 entries. He was an exceptionally fine water colourist, basically figurative, and at times tended towards impressionism. He was experienced in the field of commercial art. Following his release from the Air Force he took a post graduate course in Montreal with Arthur Lismer then was appointed principal of the Winnipeg School of Art in 1949 and in 1950 turned to full-time painting at Lethbridge, Alberta, before becoming Director of the Lethbridge Art Centre. In 1963 he joined the faculty of the University of Alberta, and was presumably teaching there until his death in 1966. He died in Calgary, Alberta. He was a member of the Art Association of Saskatoon (1937); Moose Jaw Sketch Club (1939); Winnipeg Sketch Club (1928-29); Saskatchewan Provincial Art Association (1938). He exhibited with the art societies to which he belonged also the R.C.A. in 1939.

References

Times Herald, Moose Jaw, Sask., June 13, 1941 "Bart Pragnall Gets Fellowship Canadian Artists"

Calgary Herald, Apr. 29, 1944 "Calgary Street Scene Wins Award For Artist"

PRAGNELL, Bartley Robillard (Cont'd)

The Standard, Mtl., May, 1947 "Veteran Show — Six Montreal Students Exhibit Work on Their Own" story by Mavis Gallant
Winnipeg Tribune, Man., Sept. 12, 1949 "Former Pupil Named To Head School of Art"
Ibid, Apr. 19, 1950 "Little Folk May Express Emotions in Their Drawings"
Brandon Sun, Man., May 8, 1950 "Brandon Art Club Met Saturday at Prince Edward — Bart Pragnell of Winnipeg School of Art Guest Speaker"
Lethbridge Herald, Alta., Feb. 21, 1951 "Artist Comes Here To Do His Painting"
Winnipeg Sketch Club, Wpg., Man., by Madeline Perry and Lily Hobbs, WSC, 1970
Saskatchewan: Art and Artists, Norman Mackenzie Art Gallery, 1971 P. 42, 56, 74
Royal Canadian Academy of Arts/Exhibitions and Members, 1880-1979, by Evelyn de R. McMann, U of T Press, Tor., 1981, P. 333
NGC Info. Form rec'd June 27, 1940

PRAGOFF, Ettie Richler

She exhibited her etchings at the fifth annual arts exhibition held at the Laval Jewish community centre near Montreal, in May of 1978.

Reference
The Gazette, Mtl., May 15, 1979 "Laval's art show had a difference" by Jane Tetley

PRANKE, Walter W.

b. 1925

Born in Czechoslovakian Sudetenland, the son of an artist and art professor. Receiving encouragement from his father he studied at the Dresden Art Academy and during the war travelled all over Europe including Russia continually sketching and collecting impressions of different people and regional scenes. In 1945 he emigrated to the United States where he studied with Professor Scott of Utah. He filled several commissions for large murals in various government buildings in Texas and Oregon. He returned to Europe in 1947 and studied further painting techniques in Hanover and Dusseldorf. Worked in various styles but decided to continue with figurative painting favouring a degree of impressionism. In 1955 he came to Canada with his family and established a studio in Montreal where he worked and lived for twenty-five years. At first he worked as a transport driver then as a stockbroker while continuing his painting in his free time. It was while he was working as a stockbroker that an enthusiastic patron suggested he should paint full time. Pranke took his advice and has never regretted making that decision. Since then he has held over eight solo shows and has been interviewed on television and radio programmes. Now a resident of Ottawa he has travelled extensively over eastern North America in search of interesting subjects especially historical sites, village, town and city scenes. He is partial to autumn colours but also paints his subjects in other seasons. His work has been reproduced on many Christmas cards and he has donated his talents for the decoration of Christmas cards sold to raise funds for the Multiple Sclerosis Society of Canada. Pranke is known for his masterful handling of his palette knife. His work has been

PRANKE, Walter W. (Cont'd)

available through the Koyman's Galleries Limited in three locations in Ottawa and galleries elsewhere. In 1967 he produced three portfolios of reproductions of his pen-and-ink drawings of Old Montreal and Quebec City as his Centennial project.

References

Visit with artist in Montreal
Conversation with artist after his arrival in Ottawa, 1981
Walter W. Pranke, folders with biographical information
The Intelligencer, Belleville, Ont., Nov. 2, 1974 "Adopted Country Inspires Artist" by Jim Smelle

PRAT, Annie
1860-1960

Born in Paradise, Newfoundland, the daughter of Mr. & Mrs. Samuel (Morse) Prat, one of five children. She showed artistic talent when very young. She went to live in Halifax with her grandfather and attended the Morse Street school. She went on to the Art Institute of Chicago and following graduation lived in New York where she first established her reputation for painting miniatures on ivory. She had a studio in New York with her sister Mrs. Starr who worked at leather book-binding. Annie taught painting in various parts of New York State. She returned to Windsor, N.S., where she did her paintings of Nova Scotia wildflowers and fungi which were presented by her to the Nova Scotia Archives. Five of her portraits were acquired from her estate by the same archives. She wrote poetry for recreation and won a prize from the Nova Scotia Poetry Society for her "The Bells of St. Paul's" and was made a life member of the Society. Also a member of I.O.D.E.; King's College Alexandria Society; and the Canadian Author's Society. She died aged 99 in Nova Scotia.

References

Halifax Mail-Star, N.S., Feb. 7, 1959 "Display Art Of Windsor Woman"
Halifax Chronicle-Herald, N.S., Sept. 29, 1961 "Archives acquire paintings — Gift of N.S. artist's sister"

PRATT, Christopher (John Christopher Pratt)
b. 1935

Born in St. John's, Newfoundland, the son of John Kerr and Christine Emily (Dawe) Pratt, he had close ties with his grandfather James C. Pratt who started painting as a hobby shortly after his 60th birthday in 1940. Christopher attended Holloway Primary School in St. John's (1939-46); Prince of Wales College Secondary School, St. John's (1946-52); Engineering, Memorial University, St. John's and started painting as a hobby (1952). He changed courses and enrolled in pre-med at Mount Allison University in Sackville, N.B., in 1953 but again changed courses to general arts at that University this same year. He was interested about this time in poetry. He did not take alcoholic beverages nor tag along with a group of students. In his English class he became friends with

PRATT, Christopher (John Christopher Pratt) (Cont'd)

Mary West, a fine arts student. Mary took up water colours to work along with Christopher and share something in common. It was Mary who eventually persuaded him to switch to fine arts because of his unusually fine talent in painting. He entered fine arts and studied for two-and-a-half years before becoming restless and anxious to try painting full time in his home city of St. John's. As early as 1953 attention was drawn to his coastal scenes and recorded in the *Daily News* whose columnist felt there was "excellent painting for the days ahead" for him. Pratt worked mainly in water colours at that time selecting local architectural themes and averaged selling a painting a week. Finally he felt he was ready for further study. Mary and Christopher realized how compatible they were and married in 1957. After seeking advice from their former professors on what and where to study they decided Christopher should attend the Glasgow School of Art. They sailed on the freighter-passenger vessel *Nova Scotia*. In Glasgow Christopher followed a rigorous course in drawing, sculpture, design, lettering, crafts and graphics. He received important direction from Miss Alex Dick. After almost two-and-a-half years (1957-59) Mary and Christopher felt lonesome for Canada. They returned home and continued courses in fine arts at Mount Allison, graduating together with their B.F.A. (1959-61). Afterwards they moved to St. John's where Christopher took a job of running the gallery at Memorial University and teaching extension classes at the University at night. His classes were made up of somewhat indifferent non serious students which was disappointing for him and his programme left him little time to himself. He was waiting for the break to paint full time. In 1958 while they were in Scotland the Pratt's first child John was born. Their box-like CMHC house was located in a transient neighborhood which had the frequent traffic of moving vans. He continued at the University until 1963 when his family had grown to three children; Anne was born in 1960 and Barbara in 1963. In the spring of 1963 he quit his job to fulfil his plans of painting full time. He took his family to St. Catherine's, St. Mary's Bay, where they set up home in an old summer house owned by his father. After visiting them sometime later, Harry Bruce described the location in *Maclean's* as follows, "The place is on the banks of the Salomonier River, where the river joins St. Mary's Bay, and the Pratts live there under Canada geese, eagles, bitterns, gulls, ospreys, black ducks, golden ducks, mergansers, 'practically every bird in Newfoundland.' Seals cruise and otters romp in their river pond. Their four kids boat there, swim there, skate there. Mary can call them home for supper from the kitchen door; and supper, on any summer day that anyone feels like fishing, will be trout caught just off their lawn. Moose sometimes amble in among the flowers, the pretty hardwoods, the blackberries, gooseberries, the vegetable garden, and loose toys and sports gear that surround the house. A stone-lined creek splits the sloping grass, and rattles down to the river." Their fourth child, Edwyn, was born in 1965. After settling there Christopher's first works were water colours and drawings of old shops, closed places of business and other architectural themes. During his studies he had found certain artists past and present of great interest including Giotto, The Van Eycks, Bruegels, Rembrandt, Eakins, Hopper, Balthus, Pollock, Henry Moore, Cézanne and others. "At Mount Allison," he once explained, "although I was registered in courses of which he (Colville) was the head, I never was in a classroom in which he taught. Most of us worked at home and then brought our painting in for criticism. While it is logical to make a comparison, I think if our works were seen side by side, the

PRATT, Christopher (John Christopher Pratt) (Cont'd)

differences would be rather more striking than the similarities. Lawren Harris Jr. was already working in a very precise hard-edge style and actually I think an analysis might suggest that I got more from him." Nevertheless Pratt's figure paintings do suggest some Colville influence (see Paul Duval's *High Realism in Canada* for good quality reproductions also Patricia Godsell's *Enjoying Canadian Painting* for a straightforward analysis of his painting *The Bed*). Describing Pratt's work in 1977 Michael Greenwood in *Artscanada* wrote, "Pratt is absorbed by the task of giving visual shape to dimensions of consciousness that are essentially metaphysical without recourse to a purely non-objective sign language. He chooses to clothe the abstraction of his ideas in recognizable forms not from any particular interest in naturalism as such but to add a psychological component of symbolic reference and tension to the underlying proposition. But when Pratt has applied his visual razor to the familiar motifs of windows, doors, walls, architraves and newel posts the latter have been pared down to the barest bones and retain only a nominal connection with their real functions in the context of human existence. What finally remains is an elemental system of dynamic relationships based on the square, the circle and the triangle, quite as abstract in its way as anything in the work of Mondrian, Newman or Rothko, artists who also were concerned with the pursuit of universal truths." Pratt's taking of real objects and eliminating their flaws, eg. broken shingles or window panes, warped or broken timbers which a realist might meticulously include, and further refining his selected elements by eliminating nature's normal clutter, makes a statement of such clarity and stillness that the viewer tends to be drawn into meditation by the sheer quiet or calm of the work and its apparent timelessness. His figure studies are also rendered with equal perfection. He rarely does a painting which represents a specific place or person, but rather one that represents an idea expressed through his modified real objects. He did his first figure painting in oils "Woman at a Dresser" in 1964 which was completely worked out before he called in a live model. When in doubt he sticks to his original working drawing if his model's proportions tend to change it too much. For the above painting he created his own furniture design and selected the wall paper from an Eaton's mail order catalogue. Michael Greenwood goes on to explain that Pratt's work in printmaking is even more demanding of him as follows, "In his graphic works the intensity and strenuous concentration of Pratt's vision surpasses even the formidable level achieved in the paintings. To ensure the absolute precision of his images in the medium of the serigraph demands an almost inhuman accuracy of registration with the various color separations and screens involved." He usually makes editions between thirty and sixty prints. He was commissioned in 1978 by the Canada Council Art Bank to make a print suitable for government offices. Although he has done considerable work in serigraph he hopes to spend more of his future time as a painter. He works so carefully at his paintings that he produces only about three a year. Their market value has risen from $8,000 in 1973 to $30,000 in 1980. One work consisting of five panels, entitled "Me And Bride" sold for something between $65,000 and $70,000. His silk screens have also risen in price from $200 in 1973 to well over $850 in 1980. He produced one silk screen for each of the three parts of the book *Christopher Pratt*, a limited edition of 279 copies. The overall production in addition to the silk screen prints, contains 60 colour and 16 black-and-white plates along with numerous studies and documentary photographs. Each book is bound by hand using high

PRATT, Christopher (John Christopher Pratt) (Cont'd)

quality materials. The text for the book was written by David Silcox, a personal friend of the artist, and Meriké Weiler. The book was designed by Ken Rodmell. The publishing house, Quintus Press of Toronto, is a partnership of Mira Godard, Anna Porter, Ernie Herzig, Roderick Brinckman and Michael de Pencier. At home in St. Catherines, Mary and Christopher have separate studios but share their breaks together. Mary, a realist painter, has become increasingly popular over the years (see PRATT, Mary). Christopher's other interests include: Design for a Newfoundland flag; stamp collecting and stamp designing; politics (supportive of PC's); writing poetry (He has given readings in various centres in Canada. E.J. Pratt a noted poet, was his grand-uncle.); and sailing. He acquired his first boat in 1961 and moved to larger and larger craft until he owned *Dry Fly*, a Cuthbertson and Cassian 43 foot sloop worth an estimated $100,000. He sold *Dry Fly* in 1980 to purchase a smaller craft. He has sailed his own yacht from Newfoundland to Ontario and back, twice (1974 and 1977) to attend his solo shows at Mira Godard Gallery in Toronto. His activity in sailing is reflected in his work, as in his serigraph *New Boat* (1975) described by Michael Greenwood as follows, ". . .New Boat. . .not only reaches an extraordinary standard of technical perfection but as an image lacks none of the formal subtleties and inner meanings that distinguish his finest paintings. The graceful but stringently functional and dynamic lines of the ship's hull suspended in space like a vision of hope (a Noah's Ark) against the cosmic infinities of time and space seem to epitomize the historic adaptability of human life to the forces of the universe." For his achievements Pratt has received the following honours: A.R.C.A. (1965); Hon. D. Litt., Mount Allison Univ., N.B. (1972); Hon. D. Litt., Memorial Univ., Nfld. (1972); Order of Canada (1973). He has participated in many group shows including Canadian Biennials in 1961, 1963, 1965, 1968; Winnipeg Biennial, 1966; Magic Realism, London (1971); Canadian Society of Graphic Arts (annual shows); Atlantic Artists of Canada (1971); Canada Trajectoire at Musée d'Art Moderne, Paris, France (1974); and other shows since then. His solo shows include: Memorial Univ., St. John's Nfld. (1966); Memorial Univ./Gal. Godard-Lefort, Mtl., travelling retrospective (1970); Memorial Univ., St. John's, Nfld. (1972); Malborough Godard Gal., Mtl. (1973); Memorial Univ. for Atlantic Provinces Art Circuit (1973); Malborough Godard Gal., in Mtl., Tor., NYC. (1976); Malborough Godard Gal. & Van. Art Gal. a two-man travelling show Gaucher/Pratt (1977); Mira Godard Gal. Tor., Mtl. (1978); Mira Godard Gal., Tor. (1980); Memorial Univ., St. John's, Nfld. (1980) and others. He has appeared as guest speaker on numerous occasions in centres across Canada. He is represented in the following collections: London Public Library & Art Museum, Ont.; York University, Tor.; Art. Gal. Ontario, Tor.; Dept. External Affairs, Ottawa and elsewhere; Canada Council, Ott.; National Gallery of Canada, Ott.; C.I.L., Mtl.; P.F. Bronfmann, Mtl.; Mount Allison Univ., Sackville, N.B.; Univ., of Moncton, N.B.; Dalhousie Univ., Halifax, N.S.; New Brunswick Museum, Saint John, N.B.; Beaverbrook Art Gallery, Fred., N.B.; Memorial Univ., St. John's, Nfld.; Confederation Art Gallery, Charlottetown, P.E.I.; Northern & Central Gas and others. Pratt is also represented in private collections in Canada and abroad.

References (newspapers, magazines and catalogues)
  The Daily News, St. John's, Nfld., Feb. 28, 1953 "I knock on a door — And These Are The People I Meet" (early comments on Pratt's work)

Evening Telegram, St. John's, Nfld., Nov. 25, 1965 "Artist here honored" (Pratt receives A.R.C.A.)

Ibid, Feb. 7, 1966 "Pratt has first one-man show" by Rae Perlin

Time, Aug. 5, 1966 "The Arts — Life Without Evasion"

Fourth Biennial Exhibition of Canadian Art, 1961, No. 71

Fifth Biennial Exhibition of Canadian Art, 1963, No. 58

Sixth Biennial Exhibition of Canadian Art, 1965, No. 86

Seventh Biennial Exhibition of Canadian Art, 1968, No. 114

Evening Telegram, St. John's, Nfld., Dec. 20, 1968 "Christopher Pratt: Passionate realist" by Michael Cook

Vancouver Sun, B.C., Oct. 30, 1970 "Christopher Pratt" by Joan Lowndes

Ibid, Nov. 6, 1970 "Art of intense concentration" by Joan Lowndes

Artscanada, October/November, 1970 No. 148/149 "Christopher Pratt — Photographic essay and words" by John Reeves, Tor., P. 63 to 67

St. John's Evening Telegram, Nfld., May 26, 1972 "Honorary degree conferred on artist Christopher Pratt" by Michael Benedict (from Memorial Univ.)

St. John's News, Nfld., May 26, 1972 "Christopher Pratt awarded degree" (from Memorial Univ.)

Corner Brook Western-Star, Nfld., Oct. 11, 1972 "Artist to receive degree" (from Mount Allison Univ.)

St. John's Evening Telegram, Nfld., Dec. 22, 1973 "Two Newfoundlanders named to Order of Canada"

Evening Times Globe, Saint John, N.B., Apr. 2, 1973 "Art Exhibitions Open At Museum Wednesday" (working drawings & preliminary sketches for major serigraphs of period)

Maclean's, Tor., Ont., Dec., 1973 "Christopher Pratt: Magic as reality" by Harry Bruce

Toronto Star, Ont., Jan. 18, 1974 "Artist's passion is tidiness" by Sol Littman

St. John's Evening Telegram, Nfld., June 15, 1974 "The Pratt exhibition" by Peter Bell (Christ., his grandfather and Mary's works shown together)

Globe & Mail, Tor., Ont., Oct. 20, 1976 "Art — Pratt wants to leave the realist pack" by James Purdie

Toronto Star, Ont., Oct. 25, 1976 "Maritimes artist more than a realist" by Gary Michael Dault

Ottawa Citizen, Ont., Dec. 13, 1976 "Entertainment — Canadian artists — The tough go of making it in New York" by Norman Hay

The Canadian Magazine, Tor., Ont., Nov. 26, 1977 "A Rarer Reality — Christopher Pratt invests everyday objects with mystery" by Harry Bruce

Halifax Chronicle Herald, N.S., Dec. 6, 1977 "Special exhibit of graphic art"

Artscanada, December, 1976/January, 1977 No. 210/211 "Christopher Pratt" by Michael Greenwood, P. 30-33

St. John's Evening Telegram, Nfld., Jan. 28, 1978 "Unusual exhibition contrasts artists" by Peter Bell

St. John's News, Nfld., May 2, 1978 "Pratt commissioned by Canada Council"

Globe & Mail, Tor., Ont., May 19, 1978 "Art — Pratt practices his art of smaller, excellent parts" by James Purdie

Brantford Expositor, Ont., June 10, 1978 "Focus on Art — Pratt-Gaucher link is strong"

Globe & Mail, Ont., July 25, 1978 "Survey of prints superlative show" by James Purdie

London Evening Free Press, Ont., Apr. 27, 1979 "Newfoundland artist 'enriches reality'" by Dennis Kucherawy

Ibid, Apr. 30, 1979 "Concert probes inter-relationship of arts" (Pratt's poetry set to music and dance) by Dennis Kucherawy

Globe & Mail, Tor., Ont., Dec. 13, 1980 "Pratt's precise offerings reward the patient viewer" by John Bentley Mays

Toronto Star, Ont., 1980 (Dec. day unkn.) "Art — Pratt paintings rare and expensive" by Lisa Balfour Bowen

The Gazette, Mtl., July 26, 1980 "Art — Artist's book will sell for $2,100" by Virginia Nixon

Kingston Whig Standard, Ont., Aug. 29, 1980 "In the tradition of E.J. Pratt: Making

PRATT, Christopher (John Christopher Pratt) (Cont'd)

something from nothing" by Ed Walters (Pratt's sloop to be sold)

Medicine Hat News, Alta., Apr. 12, 1980 "Artist uses land to portray a theme" by Sarah Jones

Moncton Transcript, N.B., Feb. 25, 1981 "Pratt never paints from photographs"

References — (books)

Canadian Art Today, Ed. Wm. Townsend, Studio International, Lond., Eng., 1970, P. 94

Creative Canada, Volume One, McPherson Lib. of Univ. Victoria, B.C./Univ. Tor. Press, Tor., 1971, P. 252-253

Four Decades, The Canadian Group of Painters and their contemporaries, 1930-1970 by Paul Duval, P. 183, 184

High Realism in Canada by Paul Duval, Clarke Irwin & Co. Ltd., Tor., 1974, P. 142-151

Enjoying Canadian Painting by Patricia Godsell, General Publishing Co. Ltd., Don Mills, Ont., 1976, P. 252-253

Canadian Art Auctions, Sales and Prices 1976-1978, Gen. Publishing Co. Ltd., Don Mills, Ont., P. 197

Christopher Pratt by David Silcox and Merike Weiler, Quintus Press, Tor., Ont., 1980 (limited edition of 279 copies, each book in three parts with an original silk screen for each part made by artist in the same process and equipment as his other prints)

PRATT, Elva (Mrs. O.F. Pratt)

A potter and ceramist from Abottsford, B.C., she has been active since 1965 when she entered classes of Mrs. Herm Baker. She has produced a wide variety of items including plates, planters, figures, vases, dinner sets and other items. Her prizes include: 2nd Prize, Central Fraser Valley Agricultural Association Fair (1966); three 1st Prizes at the Aldergrove Fall Fair (1966); four 1st Prizes, two 2nd Prizes, and one 3rd Prize in the Abbotsford Fair (1967). Her main market is in Squamish, B.C. She is represented in private collections in British Columbia and also in Ontario, Manitoba and the United States.

Reference

Abbotsford, Sumas & Matsqui News, Abbotsford, B.C., Feb. 1, 1967 "Talented potter hand models clay pieces" (article and large photo of Mrs. Pratt)

PRATT, George Forbes

b. 1939

Born in Minden, Ontario, the son of Robert and Edna Pratt, he studied sculpture with E.B. Cox in Toronto (1970-75) then lived and studied tundra life at Fort Churchill, Manitoba (1957-59). He married Marjorie in 1958 and they have three children. He settled in Vancouver and established a gallery in his home where collectors from all over have purchased more than 500 stone carvings of various sizes. Pratt has a lovely smooth round look to his sculpture which shows the influence of his teacher E.B. Cox but has very much his own style as well. A number of interior designers have purchased his sculptures for their clients. His stone (glacierite) carvings of animals and birds are obtainable from: Images For A Canadian Heritage, in Vancouver and Gold Design Gallery in Calgary, Alberta. He is represented in the following collections: Crown-Zellerbach, Van., B.C.; B.C. Telephone, Van., B.C.; McDonald's

PRATT, George Forbes (Cont'd)

(restaurant chain), Van., B.C.; Luscar Ltd., Edmonton, Alta.; Czar Resources, Calg., Alta.; Topaz Petroleum, Calg., Alta. and others. He has been teaching B.C. Indian carvers to carve in stone (members of the B.C. Indian Arts and Crafts Society) under the sponsorship of the Department of Indian and Northern Affairs. His home and gallery is located on West 27th Avenue in Vancouver.

References

Ontario Craft Foundation Publication, Summer, 1974

Canadian Interiors, Tor., Ont., May, 1975

Vancouver Sun, B.C., Feb. 7, 1980 "Sculpture that's a chip off the old block" by Andrew Scott

La Presse, Mtl., Que., May 26, 1981 "Sculpture de Terry Fox" (photo of artist beginning work on a sculpture of Terry Fox from a large piece of granite)

Info. Form NGC Feb. 12, 1980

PRATT, James C.

1880-1956

Born in St. John's, Newfoundland, the son of the Reverend John and Fannie (Knight) Pratt and brother of E.J. Pratt, noted scholar and poet, he started painting as a hobby shortly after his 60th birthday and continued to paint scenes of Newfoundland for the next twelve years. Although he had no formal training he read a great deal about art and periodically received valuable assistance from Reginald Sheppard, R.C.A. (elect). He exhibited at local art exhibitions on several occasions. In 1974 his work was again shown with that of his grandson Christopher and his grandson's wife, Mary Pratt. This show was put on in aid of the Canadian National Institute for the Blind at the Art Gallery of Memorial University of Newfoundland in 1974. Much of his work is in the private collection of Mr. J.K. Pratt (his son) and Mrs. Pratt.

Reference

A Personal View of James Pratt, Mary Pratt, Christopher Pratt from The Private Collection of Mr. & Mrs. J.K. Pratt, Memorial University of Newfoundland, Art Gallery, St. John's, Nfld., June 10 to July 2, 1974

PRATT, Mary (Mary Frances West Pratt)

b. 1935

Born in Fredericton, N.B., the daughter of Katherine E. (MacMurray) and Hon. W.J. West, Q.C. Both her parents were amateur painters and her father used to illustrate her bedtime stories with drawings. Mary received considerable encouragement from her parents who put her pictures up on the walls and kept them in scrapbooks. This encouragement built up a wonderful confidence in the young child. When she was eleven one of her paintings was selected for an international exhibition in Luxembourg. From that point on Mary was dedicated to the idea of becoming a professional painter. She attended Charlotte Street School and Fredericton High School. During her high school years she studied art with Lucy Jarvis, John Todd, Fritz Brandtner and Alfred Pinsky. After finishing her schooling in Fredericton she consulted with Mount

PRATT, Mary (Mary Frances West Pratt) (Cont'd)

Allison University's registry office in Sackville about studying fine arts and was confronted with suggestions about choosing something more practical like teaching or nursing. She turned to her father for advice and received a sympathetic reply that she should go ahead with her main ambition lest she would regret it later in life. That's all Mary needed to fortify her own convictions and she enrolled in the Fine Arts Department course at Mount Allison. There from 1953 to 1956 she studied with Ted Pulford and Alex Colville. In her first year English her seatmate was Christopher Pratt who was then a pre-med student still searching for something he wanted to spend the rest of his life doing. In his spare time he did water colours and Mary, anxious to find something further in common took up water colours herself. She was also intrigued by his interest in poetry and that he was a grandnephew of the famous E.J. Pratt, English scholar and poet. Mary saw Christopher's great potential as a painter and urged him to consider changing his course to fine arts. This he did in 1953 and continued to study for over two years. By the end of 1956 Mary had a good background to become a professional painter. Christopher in the meantime had decided to paint full time in St. John's, Newfoundland, and managed to sell a painting a week. Then Mary and Christopher decided to get married and go to Scotland where he would study at the Glasgow School of Fine Arts. After almost two-and-a-half years they felt lonesome for Canada and returned to study at Mount Allison where Mary continued her course in Fine Arts with Lawren Harris. In 1961 both Mary and Christopher graduated together with their degrees of B.F.A. Their first child had been born in 1958 and now Mary turned all her attentions to being a mother. They moved to St. John's, Newfoundland, where her husband took a teaching job with the extension services of Memorial University during the evenings while he ran the art gallery of the University in the daytime. Their family had grown to three children with Anne born in 1960 and Barbara in 1963. But Christopher was biding his time to paint full time and finally made the break in the spring of 1963. They moved to St. Catherines on the edge of the wilderness where they set up home in a summer house of the Pratt family. It was the place Christopher had dreamed of since he was a boy but Mary, more accustomed to urban life, found it rough going. Harry Bruce related her struggle as follows, "Nobody had ever used the place year-round. It was a sort of ranch-style semi-wreck and, the first winter, viciously cold. Again and again, as the short days died, electricity failures forced them to use coal-oil lanterns. Shortly before Christmas the stove blew up and hurled a blanked of inky soot over everything in sight including, to the older children's horror, Mary's freshly baked gingerbread men. 'It was so isolated down here,' she remembers, 'and there was no running water. We used to crack a hole in the brook, and drag all the water up, for everything. The kids got lice, the whole bit. It was very hard.'" From the time her first child was born, Mary did not paint a thing for nearly five years. She devoted all her time to looking after her children in the way she believed children must be looked after. Their fourth child, Edwin was born in 1964. The isolation and the free moments between her housewife duties began to play on her nerves. Just at the right time she was given a commission to illustrate an ornithologist's book on the snipe. The job was originally offered to Christopher but he was too busy on his own projects. The work was exacting and absorbing but after completion of the project her perception was sharpened and she began to make quick studies of friends and objects around her in the kitchen which were affected by the light from the windows. When the children were still young she would snatch 30 minutes of work in oils of a fruit bowl or other item as they slept or had not yet arrived home from school. She began to accumulate a number of these small paintings and they were seen by Peter Bell, Curator of Art, Memorial University, who offered her a solo show. In a modest note in the exhibition catalogue Mary wrote, "When one has four small children to look after, it is not easy to paint. This is not an excuse — it is a simple statement of fact. If one allows one's ambitions as a painter to soar beyond the reality of one's responsibilities as a mother, one must be frustrated with the resulting work. If, on the other hand, one surrenders to the housework and the household, there is an emptiness, a frustration which is no less real. As in all things — what is needed is a balance — an equilibrium. For me, this consists of accepting the fact that the time I have for painting is limited, and allowing the size and scope of my work to reflect the small packages of time into which it must fit. It means accepting the simple things around me as they are and taking from them the maximum pleasure they will provide. That is what I have tried to do in these paintings." Her show of sixty works done over several years, some going back to her student days, was well received. As her children became older Mary had more time to herself and was able to do more ambitious paintings. But often certain effects that she wanted to capture would disappear before she had put them down on canvas. Christopher made the suggestion that she use a camera to catch the right moment, instead of waiting each day at the same time for the sunlight to be in the exact position to finish her work. This proved to be a successful solution for achieving as much as possible a working reference for the perfection she sought. But Mary continued to draw upon subject matter in her immediate surroundings. Christopher was very insistent that she not give up her painting for her housework and she also received support from his parents who, on their visits to St. Catherines would ask Mary to show them her recent work. Her subjects continued to be such items as dirty dishes, grocery bags, raw chicken, fish, onions, cabbage, potatoes, apples, nasturtiums, a wedding dress, kittens and other items she encountered daily. By 1973 Mary's paintings were being shown in Toronto at Erindale College, University of Toronto and the same year a retrospective show of her work was held at Memorial Hall in St. John's which was reviewed by Alan Annand as follows, "These oil paintings by Mary Pratt at once impress upon the viewer the artist's strong use of light and colour. There is a warmth and beauty that is immediately recognizable in the most familiar of objects. . .Initially a housewife painter concerned with the intimacies of her particular role in the home, Mrs. Pratt left behind this 'age of innocence' and began to move outside into a larger, more transient world. Her canvases immediately became larger and although the intimacy of her former works evaporated, she was still able to convey her sense of joy and wonder in the contemplation of her subjects. Often working from photographic slides, Mrs. Pratt combines technical expertise with love to produce paintings that are at once lively, evocative and ordered." In 1975 a show of seven Canadian women artists was held at the National Gallery of Canada, a result of visits to studios of nearly 200 women artists by Mayo Graham, assistant curator of contemporary Canadian art at the National Gallery. Mary was initially notified by telephone that her work had been chosen for this important show. Twelve of her works were included in the exhibition and made an impact on reviewers and public alike. Included with her fine work

PRATT, Mary (Mary Frances West Pratt) (Cont'd)

was the superb painting "Fredericton" which she painted in 1972. It is a view of a residential street bathed in early morning sunlight which falls across the roadway creating long shadows from the tall trees, and bars of light that stretch across the sidewalks and lawns and come to rest on the fronts of stately homes. This work brings to mind the sunbathed buildings found in the paintings of 18th Century artist Giovanni Antonio Canal. During her exhibition, *Mary Pratt, a 12-year survey* (1981-82) at the London Ontario Regional Art Gallery, David Livingstone in *Maclean's* concluded his review of the show as follows, "While the food Pratt depicts is quite traditional, her interest in modern materials such as aluminum foil and stretch-and-seal plastic prevents such sights as currant jelly and steamed pudding from seeming nostalgic. And rather than pitting the man-made against the natural, she seems quite capable of delighting in both history and progress. At first glance, it might seem from Pratt's closeups of fillets and broken eggshells that she is occupied by parts and pieces. In fact, more characteristic of her talent is an ability to celebrate the whole of a world in which pleasure and wisdom are borne on shafts of light." In this show there were several masterful figure studies of young girls which were rendered with great sensitivity in the treatment of light and shadow especially apparent in "Girl in My Dressing Gown" painted in 1981. In Toronto her work can be seen at the Aggregation Gallery. Her solo shows include: Memorial University, St. John's, Nfld. (1967); Morrison Art Gallery, Saint John, N.B. (1969, 1971); Erindale College, Mississauga, Ont. (1973); *Mary Pratt: A Partial Retrospective*, by Art Gal. Memorial Univ. (1973) *touring* the Maritimes; — Cassel Galleries, Fred., N.B. (1973); *Mary Pratt: Paintings & Drawings* by Art Gal. Memorial Univ. (1975) *touring* Dalhousie Univ. Art Gal., Halifax; Univ. N.B. Art Centre, Fred.; Simon Fraser U. Art Gal., Van., B.C.; Moose Jaw Art Mus., Sask.; Open Space Gal., Vic., B.C.; Burnaby Art Gal., B.C.; Peter White Gal., Banff Centre, Banff, Alta.; — The Gallery, St. John's, Nfld. (1975); — *Mary Pratt: A Seven-Year Survey*, Aggregation Gal., Tor. (1976); — *Mary Pratt: Paintings and Drawings*, Aggregation Gal., Tor. (1978); — *Mary Pratt: Recent Paintings & Works on Paper*, Aggregation Gal., Tor. (1981); — *Twelve Year Survey* (1981-82) *touring* Lond. Reg. Art Gal., Lond., Ont.; Saskatoon Gal. & Conserv. Corp.; Mendel Art Gal., Saskatoon; Glenbow Museum, Calg., Alta.; Art Gal., Windsor, Ont.; Art Gal., Hamilton, Ont.; Rbt. McLaughlin Gal., Oshawa, Ont.; The Gallery, Stratford, Ont.; New Brunswick Mus., Fred., N.B.; Beaverbrook Art Gal., Fred., N.B.; Memorial Univ., Art Gal., St. John's, Nlfd.; Aggregation Gal., Tor., Ont. Her group shows include: *Newfoundland Painters*, Picture Loan Gal., Tor., Ont. (1971); *9 out of 10: A Survey of Contemporary Canadian Art* (1974) *touring* The Gallery, Stratford, Ont.; Art Gal., Hamilton, Ont.; Kitchener-Waterloo Art Gal., Ont.; — *The Acute Image in Canadian Art*, Owens Art Gal., Mount Allison Univ., Sackville, N.B. (1974); — *Some Canadian Women Artists*, NGC, Ott., Ont. (1975); — *Aspects of Realism* (1976-78) *touring* across Canada; — *50 Canadian Drawings*, Beaverbrook Art Gal., Fred., N.B. (1977); — *Selecting & Collecting*, Harbourfront Art Gal., Tor., Ont. (1977); — *Realism in Canada*, Norman McKenzie Art Gal., Regina, Sask. (circulating exhibition, 1977-78); — *Strictly People* (1978-79) *touring* Canadian Embassy, Wash., D.C.; Canadian Consulates General, Chicago, Ill.; Boston, Mass., Atlanta, Georgia. She is represented in the following collections: C.B.C., Calgary; London Art Gallery, Lond., Ont.; University of Guelph, Ont.; Dofasco Art Coll., Hamilton, Ont.; Norcen Energy

PRATT, Mary (Mary Frances West Pratt) (Cont'd)

Resources, Tor., Ont.; U. of T., Erindale College, Ont.; Canada Council Art Bank, Ott., Ont.; National Gallery of Canada, Ott., Ont.; Beaverbrook Art Gal., Fred., N.B.; Univ. N.B., Fred., N.B.; N.B. Museum, N.B.; Confederation Art Gal., Charlottetown, P.E.I.; The Art Gal., Memorial Univ., St. John's, Nfld.; Canada House, London, Eng. and elsewhere. In the private collections of Mr. & Mrs. Arthur Irving, Saint John, N.B.; Hon. W.J. West & Mrs. West, Fred., N.B.; Hon. Frank Moores & Mrs. Moores, St. John's, Nfld.; John De Visser, Tor., Ont.; Mr. & Mrs. H.G. MacNeill, Mississauga, Ont. and others. Member: Royal Canadian Academy, R.C.A. (Elect); Member: Newfoundland Government Task Force on Education (1973); Federal Cultural Policy Review Committee (1981).

References

Periodicals, Newspapers, Catalogues

St. John's Evening Telegram, Nfld., Mar. 25, 1967 "Mary Pratt: 'Delicate and sensitive'" by Rae Perlin

Evening Times Globe, Saint John, N.B., Nov. 13, 1969 "Paintings And Pottery Scheduled For Showing"

Toronto Daily Star, Ont., Feb. 13, 1971 "Fifteen artists have captured the flavor of Newfoundland" by Peter Wilson (Newfoundland painters at Picture Loan Gallery)

Erindalian, Mississauga, Ont., Apr. 10, 1973 "Mary Pratt Paintings" by Tanya Abolins

U. of T. Bulletin, Mar. 23, 1973 "Flying from Newfoundland for reception at Erindale"

Globe & Mail, Tor., Ont., Apr. 21, 1973 "At The Galleries" by Kay Kritzwizer

Mary Pratt: A Partial Retrospective by Peter Bell (catalogue) June 26, 1973

The Brunswickan, Nov. 9, 1973 "A Partial Retrospective, Mary Pratt" by Alan Annand

Mary Pratt: Paintings and Drawings, Cassel Galleries, Fred., N.B., Oct. 29 to Nov. 17, 1973

Charlottetown Patriot, P.E.I., Feb. 1, 1974 "Exhibit opened in Art Gallery"

A Personal View of James Pratt, Mary Pratt, Christopher Pratt from the Private Collection of Mr. & Mrs. J.K. Pratt, June 10 to July 2, 1974, Memorial Univ. Art Gal.

Mary Pratt: Paintings and Drawings, Memorial Univ. of Nfld., June, July, 1975

Ottawa Citizen, Ont., Nov. 22, 1975 "Seven, but not a Group" by Kathleen Walker

The Chronicle-Herald, Halifax, N.S., Dec. 12, 1975 "Painting a 'celebration' for realist Mary Pratt" by Gretchen Pierce

Some Canadian Women Artists by Mayo Graham, NGC, Ottawa, Ont., 1975, P. 54-66

Mary Pratt: Paintings — A Seven Year Survey, Aggregation Gallery, Tor., Ont., 1976

Globe & Mail, Tor., Ont., Feb. 28, 1976 "Mary Pratt"

The Canadian Review, May, 1976 "Art — Mary Pratt, The Redeeming Realist" by Susan Hallett

Globe & Mail, Tor., Ont., Apr. 6, 1978 "At The Galleries — Realist takes a step toward the surreal" by James Purdie

Toronto Star, Ont., May 6, 1978 "Artist Mary Pratt — 'I like paint better than realism'" by Gary Michael Dault

The Canadian Magazine, Tor., Ont., Nov. 29, 1975 "The Fine Art of Familiarity" by Harry Bruce

Atlantic Insight, September 1979 "Cover Story — Mary Pratt, artist" by Stephen Kimber, P. 24-26

London Evening Free Press, Ont., May 18, 1979 "Mary Pratt top artist despite busy role as wife, mother" by Dennis Kucherawy

St. John's Evening Telegram, Nfld., Mar. 14, 1981 "Newfoundlander named to cultural committee"

Maclean's, July 6, 1981 "Art — The wrought irony of the real world" by David Livingstone

Mary Pratt, Recent Paintings & Works on Paper, Aggregation Gallery, Tor., Ont., May 23 to June 10, 1981 (biographical notes)

Books

High Realism in Canada by Paul Duval, Clarke Irwin, Tor., Ont., 1974, P. 145

PRATT, Mary (Mary Frances West Pratt) (Cont'd)

Enjoying Canadian Painting by Patricia Godsell, General Publishing, Don Mills, Ont., 1976, P. 236-237

100 Years of Canadian Drawings by Jerrold Morris, Methuen, Tor., Ont., 1980, P. 169

Royal Canadian Academy of Arts, Exhibitions and Members, 1880-1979 by Evelyn de R. McMann, Univ. Tor. Press, Tor., Ont., 1981, P. 333

Visual media

"Telescope Show" CBC TV "The Pratts of Newfoundland"

"Take 30" CBC TV (interview) 1970

Audio

Interview on CBC, Fredericton, N.B., 1973

PRATT, Mildred Claire
b. 1921

Born in Toronto, Ontario, the daughter of Viola L. (Whitney) and E.J. Pratt, author, lecturer and poet, she studied art with Gordon Payne at the Payne School of Fine Art and at the Boston Museum of Fine Arts School with Richard Bartlett, Ture Bengtz and Tuleschewsky. Known for her woodcuts described as lyrical she has given talks to groups on her work. A member of the Society of Canadian Painter-Etchers and Engravers, she served as its secretary (c. 1963). Was living in Toronto in 1960.

References

Lindsay Watchman Warder, Oct. 2, 1963 "Artist Claire Pratt Addresses Art Guild"

Owen Sound Sun Times, Ont., May 16, 1964 "Current Show At Gallery By Two Experts"

NGC Info. Form, 1960

PRATT, Thomas
b.(c) 1953

A Toronto, Ontario artist, he has been drawing for most of his life and is known for his prints and jewelry. He started making beaded jewelry in 1970 along with his sister Joanne Pratt. They sold their work at the farmer's market in Kingston. By 1973 however Thomas began full-time work on sterling silver jewelry. From 1974 to 1976 he studied jewelry-making with Kingston metal artist Neil Aird at St. Lawrence College where he learned many techniques and did considerable experimentation. In 1976 he won an award and three honorable mentions in the De Beers' Diamonds Tomorrow competition. His work was also included in "Hand to Hand" a juried show held in Kingston during the Olympics. His 1978 solo show "Homage To The Disco Beat" held at the Shetani Gallery in Toronto, was the result of his inspiration from science fiction, architectural forms, geometric shapes and art books. On display were 22 pieces of jewelry and 21 framed black and white drawings. Pratt works full time on his jewelry and drawings in his George Street studio in Toronto.

Reference

Toronto Star, Ont., Oct. 14, 1978 "Intricate works span the ages" by Susan Himel and Elaine Lambert

---

PRATTE, Fernande

Born in Montreal, she attended the École des Beaux-Arts there (1958-60, 1962-63) and is known for her large colourful abstract-expressionist paintings which she has exhibited in group and solo shows including the following: Gemst Gallery (1963); Centre d'Art de Ville Saint-Michel, Que. (1964); Galerie Art Den (1966); La Maison des Arts La Sauvegarde, Mtl., Que. (1967); Centre des Jeunesses Musicales, Mont Orford, Que. (1970); Kensington Fine Art Gallery, Calgary, Alta. (1972); Galerie d'Art Benedek-Grenier, Que. (1973); Galerie L'Apogée, Saint-Sauveur-des-Monts, Que. (1968, 1970, 1972, 1976). She lives at Pointe aux Trembles on the edge of Montreal East.

References

    L'Echo du Nord, St. Jérôme, Québec, Oct. 9, 1968 "A la Galerie des arts l'Apogée de Saint-Sauveur — Les Oeuvres récentes de Fernande Pratte" par Gariepy

    The Gazette, Que., June 20, 1970 "Fernande Pratte 'show of color'"

    L'Echo du Nord, St. Jérôme, Québec, May 26, 1972 "Fernande Pratte, un très grand peintre canadien" par Marie-Odile Vézina

    Canadian artists in exhibition 1972-73, Roundstone, Tor., 1974, P. 172, 173

    Québec 74 (catalogue), Mtl. Mus. of Contemporary Art, Mtl., Qué., 1974, P. 26, 27

    L'Art au Québec depuis 1940 par Guy Robert, La Presse, Mtl., Qué., 1973, P. 150, 151

    La peinture au Québec depuis ses origines par Guy Robert, Iconia, Sainte-Adèle, Qué., (1978) 2nd Ed. 1980, P. 148, 149

PRENT, Mark
b. 1947

Born in Montreal, Quebec, the son of a hardware salesman who came from Poland as a survivor of the Nazi invasion and Russian labour camps, Mark attended Outremont High School and then studied art at Sir George Williams University under painter and printmaker Yves Gaucher and sculptor John Ivor Smith. In reviewing Prent's work in 1971 Michael White suggested that he developed a sense for formal aesthetic relationships from Gaucher and respect for form and shape as the key meaning of sculpture from Smith. But there Prent's relationship to his mentors' work ends. Moving into the world of nightmares and of horror, using the language of realism in his carefully defined human forms, he peels off the various layers of security of the romantic, the heroic, the hopeful, the sentimental that many viewers seek. Michael White, art reviewer for *The Gazette* described his technical approach in 1971 as follows, "Mark Prent's own particular quality is for the things that create realism. It appears in drawings of horses done in high school. At first glance they seem the usual adolescent's work, semi-romantic, semi-realistic — 'nice.' But in each, one or more details give these little sketches an uncanny vivacity, the bulge of an eye, hairs about the horse's mouth, that draw your eyes back again and again. In his present work Prent has complete control over his resin glazes and dyes. From his imagination he is able to recreate the painfully real copies of flesh, bone and organs that are the details of his harsh vocabulary on the hardness and blindness of modern man. Prent, like most young people, is looking for a world without war, a world without hatred and a world without cruelty. So far, in his own experience and through the machines of high school and university he has not found them or has not seen fit to express them. His

1825

poetry, and however horrifying the language be, is a form of poetry. It is competent and powerful and is real and poignant today. Prent himself admits that it seems to lack love or even hope. 'The closest I can come to hope is in humor.' And there is no doubt that the large gallon jar of 'Pickles' from Mark Prent's newest assemblage sculpture called 'Delicatessen' is humor for our age, a little macabre, definitely phallic and very real." Prent chooses horror as his form of protest against our acceptance of the "dog eat dog" business world, the paranoia of nations scrambling for possession of more efficient weapons to kill greater numbers of each other's populations. He creates a butcher shop of human parts in trays and bottles offered at the counter, or a cold storage room stocked with human carcasses, a table set in all its splendor of a special dinner with the featured roast of a human torso. He shows man's inhumanity to man by his renderings of twisted human torsos in painful confinements of tied hands or feet, and reflects on our ruthless disregard for the aged and handicapped by his assemblage of withered and rotting creatures in wheelchairs. Nor has capital punishment escaped his wrath, shown by his life-sized model of a man in overalls, devoid of his identity ready for execution in the electric chair. During Prent's first solo show at the Isaacs Gallery in 1972 charges were laid against the gallery owner for exhibiting "a disgusting object" (parts of the human anatomy) as a result of a complaint of a private citizen, in sympathy with the Western Guard, a group formerly known as the Edmund Burke Society who protested in the streets of Toronto against the show. The charge was laid by activating a law on the books since 1892 seldom if ever evoked. Eventually the charge was withdrawn. His work had been exhibited without incident in Toronto at the Art Gallery of Ontario, in New York at the Warren Benedek Gallery, in Paris at the Museum of Modern Art and in Montreal at Sir George Williams University. Another show at the Isaacs in 1974 again brought charges and they were also later withdrawn. Both proceedings attracted wide attention, stimulated articles in *The Toronto Star*, *The Globe & Mail*, *The Gazette*, *The Montreal Star*, *Time*, *Art Magazine*, *The Canadian Forum*, *Maclean's Magazine* and other publications. Both exhibitions broke all previous records of attendance as the public flocked to see what the fuss was about and in many cases returned with their friends. In the overall scrutiny by the critics, Prent fared well for his craftsmanship and skill in presenting his work. He received Canada Council grants for five successive years (1971-72, 72-73, 73-74, 75-76, 77-78). These grants were needed as his work is not saleable for the average collector although a few individuals and institutions have acquired some of his pieces. The Canada Council Art Bank acquired his "Death in the Chair." In 1975 he was awarded the German Kunstlerprogramme DAAD Fellowship for artists of international merit. Through that fellowship he lived and worked in West Berlin for one year. Only one other Canadian has received that honour. The award pays a large proportion of studio space and allows the artist to participate in events of the West German cultural scene and the Kunstlerprogramme directors help line up shows and produce fine quality catalogues. Around 1975 a film which documents Mark Prent's methods and works of the early 1970's was produced by Peter Bors and Tom Burstyn in Montreal and given the title of one of Prent's environmental pieces "If Brains Were Dynamite, You Wouldn't Have Enough to Blow Your Nose." In 1977 Prent was awarded the much sought after Guggenheim Foundation Award. In 1978 he was given a solo show at the Stedelijk Museum in Amsterdam, considered to

PRENT, Mark (Cont'd)

be one of the most prestigious contemporary museums in Europe. The last Canadian artist invited to exhibit there was Paul Emile Borduas in the early 1950's. Prent's solo shows include: Sir George Williams University, Mtl. (1971); The Isaacs Gallery, Tor. (1972, 74, 78); Warren Benedek Gallery, NYC (1972); York University Art Gallery, Tor. (1974); Akademie der Junste, Berlin (1976); Kunsthalle, Neurenberg (1976); Concordia University, Mtl. (1978); Stedelijk Museum, Amsterdam, Holland (1978); Musée d'art contemporain, Mtl. (1979); SAW Gallery, Ottawa (1979). After his return from Germany he resumed working on his sculpture in a large studio space in one of Concordia University's art annexes. He works days in his studio and spends evenings at home with his partner, Susie. He spends the occasional Sunday dinner at his parents' house.

References

The Gazette, Mtl., Que., Apr. 3, 1971 "Art — Mark Prent — power through horror" by Michael White

Ibid, Oct. 2, 1971 "The reality as horror" by Michael White

The Montreal Star, Mtl., Que., Oct. 9, 1971 "A macabre wit that cuts both ways" by Adrian J. Gatrill

Toronto Daily Star, Ont., Feb. 22, 1972 "It may not look pleasant but art show is a must" by Merike Weiler

Globe & Mail, Tor., Ont., Feb. 28, 1972 "Art — Artist's work a true horror show" by Kay Kritzwiser

The Gazette, Mtl., Que., Mar. 14, 1972 "For 'disgusting' show — Defence fund formed"

Calgary Herald, Alta., Mar. 20, 1972 "The National Gallery wants to tour it — Is it art or a freak-out horror show?" by Roy Shields

Time, March, 1972

Toronto Star, Mar. 11, 1972 "Stinging exhibit revitalizes stale art world" by Robert Fulford

The Gazette, Mtl., Que., Mar. 18, 1972 "Case dismissed"

L'Express, Drummondville, Qué., 17-23 Septembre, 1973 "L'art de la grande bouffe"

Toronto Star, Ont., Jan. 11, 1974 "Artist probes the esthetics of horror" by Sol Littman

Toronto Sun, Ont., Jan. 22, 1974 "Show goes on"

The Montreal Star, Que., Jan. 22, 1974 "Entertainments — Life-size electric chair is a hot item" by Dusty Vineberg

Toronto Sun, Ont., Jan. 29, 1974 "True Davidson — Monsters"

Toronto Star, Ont., Jan. 31, 1974 "'Disgusting object' is true sculpture artists protest"

Time, February 4, 1974, P. 12

Toronto Star, Feb. 5, 1974 "Police focussed attention on artist, he says"

Toronto Sun, Ont., Feb. 25, 1974 "Realistic or disgusting — but sculptor goes ahead with show at U of T"

York University, "A Chilly Diet for the Gods" by Michael Greenwood, Curator of Art, York Univ., Tor., Ont., 1974

Globe & Mail, Tor., Ont., July 13, 1974 "Art — Prent given award to work in Berlin" by Kay Kritzwiser

Art Magazine, Summer, 1974 "Mark Prent Perceived — A Discourse on Art and Reality" by Joyce Zemans

Canadian Forum, Tor., Ont., August, 1974 "Interviews with Canadian Artists: Joyce Zemans interviews Mark Prent"

The Gazette, Mtl., Jan. 17, 1976 "Mark Prent: Out of scandal, only shock" by Eric Johnson

Montreal Star, Dec. 11, 1976 "Mark Prent" by Henry Lehmann

Globe & Mail, Ont., Mar. 19, 1977 "Another prophet without honor. . .Prent's excursions into darkness find a haven in Germany" by Peter White

Toronto Star, Ont., June 2, 1978 "Obscene sculpture? Never, says Prent" by Gary Michael Dault

PRENT, Mark (Cont'd)

Maclean's Magazine, Tor., Ont., Sept. 25, 1978 "Art — Those not-so-obscure objects of disgust" by Christopher Hume

Globe & Mail, Tor., Ont., Sept. 30, 1978 "Sculpture bound hand and foot" by James Purdie

The Gazette, Mtl., Oct. 27, 1978 "Art Notes — Sculpture lets you pull the switch on an electric chair" by Virginia Nixon

Le Devoir, Mtl., Qué., Dec. 5, 1978 "Mark Prent — Le visage de l'horreur?" par René Viau

The Gazette, Mtl., Qué.,Dec. 22, 1978 "Art Notes — Prent's sculpture: Is it a sick joke or a work of art?" by Virginia Nixon

Catalogue sheet, Stedelijk Museum, Amsterdam, 17.2-2.4.1978 — Mark Prent

Le Devoir, Mtl., Qué., Jan. 30, 1979 "Les expositions cette semaine — Grand guignol et déjà-vu" par René Viau

Kitchener-Waterloo Record, Ont., Feb. 6, 1979 "Monstrous Images Shock Viewers — Artist doesn't care how people react" by Trish Wilson

The Gazette, Mtl., Que., Feb. 9, 1979 "Art Notes — Prent, Gadbois highlight Musée exhibits" by Virginia Nixon

Halifax Mail Star, Feb. 10, 1979 "Controversial realist to present Halifax lecture"

Montreal Star, Que., Feb. 17, 1979 "Hostile but not aggressive" by Henry Lehmann

Ottawa Citizen, Ont., Nov. 14, 1979 "Controversial artist — Police say sculptures okay" by Kathleen Walker

Ottawa Revue, November 22-28, 1979 "Art — A modern master of the Dance of Death, Mark Prent at SAW Gallery" by Jennifer Dickson

Alberta Report, Edmonton, Alta., Dec. 21, 1979 "Arts — Drawing the line - Prent's tortured torsos are out, decides SAIT"

Royal Canadian Academy of Arts, Exhibitions and Members 1880-1979, by Evelyn de R. McMann, Univ. Tor. Press, Tor., Ont., 1980, P. 333

PRESCOTT, Ken

Born in Ontario, now living in Vancouver, he has travelled widely in his search for wildlife subjects. During his recent exhibition Kerry McPhedran writing in the *Vancouver Magazine* noted, "In this related series, Prescott uses several mediums to explore and define the relationship between man and his fellow creatures, moving from absolute realism to abstract impressionism to exaggeration in an attempt to force us beyond our built-in perceptions and myths. Even at its most realistic and detailed, though, Prescott's work is never merely romantic, and the animals never cute. The dignity and spirit of wild creatures underlies all his studies." Jean Richards in reviewing his work in the *Edmonton Journal* described his marine paintings as follows, "Ken Prescott's Marine Life series comprises sensuously-colored acrylic abstracts. Here his love of design is given full play. The large works are warm and rhythmic, showing us, through a number of 'openings' (some like portholes, face-masks or binoculars) the wonderful and fascinating world under the sea. By eliminating detail, and using flat surfaces of pure and mixed color free from tonal gradations, he abstracts his creatures and breaks them into individual forms. They retain some reality, though, enough to be recognizable in most cases." His recent exhibits include those at the Lefebvre Galleries Ltd., Edmonton, Alta. (1978) and the Federation Gallery, Vancouver (1979).

References

Edmonton Journal, Jan. 21, 1978 "Feathers, fur and fins" by Jean Richards

Vancouver Magazine, July, 1979 "Up Front" by Kerry McPhedran

PRESCOTT, Robert

A graphic artist, he produced a series of sketches of Ottawa Streets during the late 1950's which appeared in *The Ottawa Journal*. At that time Prescott was serving with the R.C.A.F. as graphic artist.

References
> *The Ottawa Journal*, Aug. 9, 1958 (sketch of Elgin and Wellington Sts. looking down toward the Chateau Laurier, entitled "Old World Ottawa")
> Ibid, Aug. 16, 1958 (sketch from corner of Sparks and O'Connor Sts. entitled "Centre Town in Summer")
> Ibid, Aug. 22, 1958 (sketch of By Ward Market entitled "The Market Place")

PRESCOTT, Terrance Ormand

A Vancouver, B.C. artist, he spent five years in Europe and then returned to his home city where he exhibited close to one hundred works all in black and coloured inks with the odd touch of pencil or charcoal. Viewing his work at the Bau-Xi Gallery David Watmough in the *Vancouver Sun* noted, "In his severe paring away of the clutter of detail as well as in his basically romantic response to landscape and topographical detail, Prescott brings Toni Onley's name to mind. But here again I think coincidence is a determining factor — the coincidence of inhabiting the same northwest region and of inheriting a tradition of watercolor temperateness and a reluctance to shout when a gentler voice is thoroughly audible. . . .For Terrance Prescott, as I think this show indubitably suggests, is above all a natural artist who, whether in abstraction or semi-figuration, works out of compulsion stirred profoundly by romantic, free-flowing impulse. The species seems to be becoming rarer, and apart from the distinctiveness of his art, this alone makes a visit to his show an experience not to be missed."

References
> *Vancouver Province*, B.C., Aug. 26, 1966 (review of show at Bau-Xi Gal.)
> *Vancouver Sun*, B.C., Aug. 26, 1966 "Prescott Displays Manifold Merit" by David Watmough

PRESCOTT, Yves
b. 1957

Born in Drummondville, Quebec, he studied at Concordia University, Montreal where he graduated with distinction with his Bachelor of Fine Arts. He was in the N.F.B. film "La fougère et la Rouille" (a documentary on Quebec painters). He was awarded a bursary from the Quebec Government in 1977 to study Visual Arts at York University with Claude Breeze and Bruce Parsons. He worked on a field painting by Bill Vazan for the Oscar Wilde Festival, Toronto. He participated in the following shows: NoHo Gallery, NYC (1980); Montreal Harbour Anniversary Show (1980); V.A.V. Gallery and the Undergraduate show in the Weisman Gallery both at Concordia University (1980); Centre d'art du Mont-Royal (1980). In 1980 he also held a solo show at Radio-Canada, Montreal and the same year received the Walter Steinhouse Bursary. In 1981 he

PRESCOTT, Yves (Cont'd)

participated in a number of group shows including the Third Biennale of drawing and prints at the University of Sherbrooke which toured centres across Canada. He is represented in both of the Sales and Rentals Galleries of the Art Gallery of Ontario and The Montreal Museum of Fine Arts. Represented in collection of Musée d'art contemporain. Lives in Verdun, Quebec.

Reference
Biographical material filed with NGC, Ottawa, Documentation Centre

PRESHAW, Bente

A ceramic artist known for her organic landscape-influenced porcelain inlaid with oxides. She studied ceramics at: Humber College; Banff Centre; University of Calgary (1975) and numerous workshops and courses relating to ceramics across Canada. Her work was selected "best in show" by popular vote during the group juried show "Mud 77" at the University of Calgary. She was invited to exhibit her work at the Commonwealth Games in Edmonton (1978). She held a solo show of her porcelain at the University of Calgary Art Gallery (1978) and the "Canadian Folk Artists" group show at the Thomas Gallery, Wpg. (1980). She is represented in The Alberta Potters Association Collection and numerous private collections.

Reference
Calgary Albertan, Alta., Oct. 22, 1978 "Four showings at the university"

PRESSON, Phyllis

A Sault Ste. Marie, Ontario artist she exhibits with the Northern Ontario Art Association and has been mentioned for her fine paintings of nature. Works in water colour and other media.

Reference
Sault Ste. Marie Star, Ont., Oct. 10, 1972 "Jurors select work of five Sault artists"

PRETTY, Lloyd

Born in Chapel Arm, a small fishing village in Newfoundland, the son of Mr. and Mrs. Clarence Pretty and one of ten children, he became interested in art at an early age. He left school in 1961 to work with his father cutting pulpwood in a lumber camp. Spending so much of his time in the forest made him more aware of the beauty in nature. In 1965 he moved to Montreal where he took a job as a seaman on an oil tanker. During his travels as a seaman he visited galleries and museums in major art centres throughout Canada, the United

PRETTY, Lloyd (Cont'd)

States and Europe. Then he decided to settle in Montreal where he found a job days at an oil refinery while he attended art workshops evenings (1969-1974). In 1975 he returned to the Maritimes and took up residence in Sydney, N.S. where he settled with his wife Daphne and son David. By 1976 he had assembled enough work to hold a solo show at the Sydney Credit Union. As an employee at the Glace Bay heavy water plant he was looking forward to working at his art full time. In 1978 he held a solo show at the Lord Nelson Hotel in Halifax where all his paintings sold on opening day. Known for his depiction of rural scenes and seascapes of Atlantic Canada, by 1979, Pretty's work was being shown in major galleries in Nova Scotia, Newfoundland, Toronto and Montreal. By 1981 he was living at Stephenville, Newfoundland with his family and was a feature artist of the Atlantic Art Gallery in Halifax. His dealers in Ontario, St. John's and Cornerbrook were experiencing quick sales of his work. Memorial University Art Gallery selected his paintings with the work of five other artists to go on a six-month tour of Newfoundland and mainland Canada. Pretty was selected in 1980 to teach at Silver Glen, a 250 acre retreat for art lovers in Antigonish, N.S. He is represented in the collections of Rt. Hon. Pierre Elliott Trudeau, Premier Brian Peckford, Madame Vanier and the late Bing Crosby.

References

Cape Breton Post, Sydney, N.S., June 10, 1976 "Lloyd Pretty recalls childhood — Maritimes Inspiration For Painter" by Julie Zatzman

Ibid, June 10, 1976 "Art Work on Display" (photo of artist with his work)

St. John's News, Nfld., Nov. 6, 1978 "Artist pursuing full-time career"

Cornerbrook Western Star, Nfld., Nov. 9, 1978 "Newfoundland artist to hold one-man show"

Halifax Chronicle Herald, N.S., Nov. 16, 1979 "Artist fulfilling a lifelong dream"

Halifax Mail Star, N.S., Nov. 16, 1979 (same article as above)

Cornerbrook Western Star, Nfld., Jan. 17, 1980 "Painting For Premier" (large photo of Brian Peckford accepting a painting by L. Pretty from Stephenville Chamber of Commerce and the Harmon Corporation)

Ibid, Mar. 15, 1980 "S'ville artist to display work at Halifax show"

Halifax Chronicle Herald, N.S., Mar. 25, 1980 "Realist Pretty's paintings"

Ibid, Apr. 3, 1981 "Artist depicts local scenery" (show at Atlantic Art Gallery, Halifax)

Halifax Mail Star, N.S., Apr. 8, 1981 (large photo of Pretty, his work and Judy Yorke, owner of Atlantic Art Gallery)

PRÉVAL, Guerdy

Born in Haiti, he became established in Montreal in 1972. He has held at least thirteen solo shows. Some of his pictures show voodoo séances, highly coloured, where luminously contoured shapes of people dance on cabalistic figures traced on the earth. He feels there are some positive aspects of voodoo as an everyday religion and a political force which enabled his ancestors to liberate themselves from slavery and to survive many difficulties. Préval also paints subjects with Québecois themes and is influenced by Pelland and Borduas. He exhibited his work at the Place Royale, Quebec in 1979 under the patronage of the Confederation of Linguistic and Cultural Associations of Quebec.

PRÉVAL, Guerdy (Cont'd)

Reference
> *Québec Le Soleil*, Qué., Oct. 10, 1979 "Précédent à place Royale avec l'exposition d'un peintre haïtien" par Regis Tremblay

---

PRÉVOST, Antoine
b. 1930

Born in Quebec City, he attended the Collège des Jésuites where he received his education and strict training which still holds its influence on him today. Raised in a family keenly aware of the history of Quebec and of the arts, he was encouraged to express himself through writing and painting from childhood. Antoine wanted to be a painter but growing up during a period when parents looked for practical careers for their children, he was discouraged from being an artist full time. To compromise the wishes of his parents and his own needs he went into business for himself as an antique dealer where he could be practical while still being close to art, history and books. Later he became involved with historical reconstructions which led to his creation of the Chambly Historical Village which in turn led to his appointment as Executive Director of the Corporation of Urbanists of Quebec. He then moved to a similar post with the Town Planning Institute of Canada in Toronto. He had during this period done some 'Sunday painting' and wanted to try it full time. In 1971 he returned to Quebec to paint with his wife and children to the village of Cacouna on the south shore of the St. Lawrence River not far from the town of Rivière-du-Loup. By 1977 Prévost had emerged as an important artist. Jacques Breton writing in the *Montreal Star* noted him as follows, "Antoine Prévost. . .after four successful one-man exhibitions and five years since first appearing on the art scene, is now attracting the kind of critical and popular attention needed to transform an artist's solitary statements into meaningful communications. Solitude is an important theme to Quebec writers and poets and Prévost is no exception. His paintings express this in a gripping manner. The lonely figures aimlessly wandering through infinite snow deserts, the bishops and their clergy solemnly progressing toward unreachable churches, the flowing brides lost in winter roads, all of these cry out their loneliness, their solitude. If they become so effectively, so convincingly present despite the dream-world in which the painter presents them, it is because of the way in which they are painted. Prévost has chosen watercolor as his medium, what is so unusual about his painting is his approach to watercolor. His pictures, every single anonymous figure in them, are painted with an infinity of minute strokes which the artist uses to depict in an almost 'realistic' manner, texture, volume, color and shading. The effect thus achieved is one of almost 'magic realism,' the illusion that the figures can be touched. In contrast to the vast expanses of snow-white landscapes animated by the merest suggestions of time and place, in which they evolve, the figures become 'surreal' in their reality. Thus understood Prévost's message comes across loud and clear; the folk-like world he depicts, the historical past to which he constantly refers, the 'Québécois' memories in which he and most of those of his generation were steeped, all of this, Prévost tells us, was a dream, a reality distorted into a dream. That dream could be very tender, very touching, or alarming, a nightmare, serene, peaceful or devastating, but a dream from which 'real' reality not 'magic' reality must be

PRÉVOST, Antoine (Cont'd)

distilled so that the trance may be broken. In that lies Prévost's originality his meaningfulness as a painter of today." By 1980 Prévost had moved to Quebec City and into a house that had been closely connected in the 1800's with members of his own family. He discovered portraits of the original owners of the house which heightened his sensitivity to the historical past of his own kin. Cyrice Têtu and Julie Caroline Dionne the original occupants were the subject of a series of Prévost's paintings based on events of their lives described in an exhibition folder of Galerie Dresdnere as follows: "So let us follow him through the corridors of time to meet first Cyrice Têtu and Julie Caroline Dionne, the couple whose lives provide the theme for this cycle of works. Beginning with their humble origins in the early 19th Century, theirs is a saga which contains all the elements of a morality play: the rise to power with the unpleasant by-products engendered by it, and finally — the hand of retribution precipitating the Fall. Cyrice Têtu was born on the rugged north shore of the St. Lawrence. During his days of power he never forgot that he was a self-made man and sensing perhaps the ephemeral nature of success, he built his baronial abode like a signet for posterity. He died an exile at La Prairie du Cheval Blanc in Manitoba about 1870. During his lifetime he witnessed the 1837 uprisings, the waves of Irish immigrations, Confederation and the Riel rebellion. He travelled extensively on the Continent, married his children into aristocracy — and died a pauper leaving his widow destitute!" Prévost's solo shows include: Galerie Morency, Mtl. (1972, 73); Walter Klinkhoff Gallery, Mtl. (1974, 76, 78); Galerie Dresdnere (1980). He has published a number of serigraphs including the illustrations for Claude Jutra's *Mon Oncle Antoine*.

References

The Gazette, Mtl., Nov. 11, 1972 "Art — At the galleries: A 'Sunday painter' tackles trouble" by Virginia Nixon

Montreal Star, Que., 19 Nov., 1977 "Art — Active dreamer creates a magic realism" by Jacques Breton

The Gazette, Nov. 17, 1978 "Art Notes" by Virginia Nixon

"Antoine Prevost — La Maison Têtu — A cycle of recent works", Galerie Dresdnere, Tor., 1980 (exhibition folder)

PREYSS, Witold Ludwik
b. 1919

Born in Danzig, Poland, he studied art at the Liverpool School of Art in England under William Penn and Martin Bell. He came to Toronto, Canada in 1948 where he worked as a free-lance artist. He executed several mural decorations in collaboration with Architects in Toronto before joining the staff of Hillfield School, Hamilton where he taught art and woodworking. During his free hours he painted landscapes and figure studies and also designed and executed murals for a number of new schools in the Hamilton area including decoration of glass windows for the chapel of Hillfield School. Preyss is represented in the National Gallery of Canada collection by a casein on board painting "Gore Park, Hamilton" acquired by the gallery in 1955. This painting is skillfully designed with trees in the foreground whose bare branches divide the background of buildings into sections giving a stained glass effect. Preyss

PREYSS, Witold Ludwick (Cont'd)

moved to the United States sometime in the late 1950's. He was a member of the Contemporary Artists of Hamilton.

References
> *Hamilton Spectator*, Ont., Nov. 24, 1955 "National Gallery Grabs City Artist's Painting"
> Ibid, Jan. 7, 1956 "Art Notes" (article on Preyss and photo of his "Ballet Dancers")
> NGC Info. Form rec'd Dec. 5, 1945
> *NGC Catalogue of Paintings and Sculpture, Vol. 3, Can. School* by R.H. Hubbard, Ottawa, 1960, P. 252, 253

PRÉZAMENT, Joseph
b. 1923

Born in Winnipeg, Manitoba, he studied at the Winnipeg School of Art under Wm. LeMoine Fitzgerald; at the Montreal Art Association with Arthur Lismer and Goodridge Roberts and at the Montreal Artists School with Ghitta Caiserman and Alfred Pinsky. Known for his paintings and drawings exhibited over the years at the Vancouver Art Gallery, The Montreal Art Association and the Art Gallery of Toronto (Ontario), he held a solo show of his drawings at the Artlenders in Westmount, Quebec in 1968. Was living in Winnipeg in 1950.

References
> *Le Devoir*, Mtl., Apr. 23, 1960 "Joseph Prézament"
> Artlenders exhibition notice, 1968
> NGC Info. Form rec'd July 12, 1950

PRICE, Art (Arthur Donald Price)
b. 1918

Born in Edmonton, Alberta, the third of four children of Malen Lemuel and Mary Emily (Courtenage) Price. His parents were of Welsh and Pennsylvania Dutch extraction. Art's father was a builder and contractor. In 1921 the family moved east to Ontario and eventually to Waterford, then to a farm five miles away. Art rode his bike to high school in Waterford, from the beginning of the school year right through the winter. Coming in from the snow or rain he spent long hours drying himself out but was resolved to attend and seldom missed a day. At home on the farm his chores included milking cows, grooming horses and feeding the livestock which gave him an early sense of responsibility. He helped his father in his workshop, first handing him the tools he needed then working with wood under his father's direction. His father felt a farm was an ideal place for children as it gave them lots of room. Art liked everything about his father's carpenter's shop, the smell of the wood, the sound of the saw ripping through the boards and the crunch of shavings under his feet as he walked about. There was one thing however that gave him even greater pleasure and that was doing art work at high school which eventually led to his decision to become an artist. He attended Western Technical School were he received a bursary to study at the Ontario College of Art, evenings, under various teachers including Franklin Carmichael, Eric Aldwinckle, George Pepper, Fred Haines and others. Days he worked at various jobs from being a butler and chauffeur for a private family to, later on, free-lance commercial art. He studied dancing with Boris Volkoff. He designed and built sets for the Volkoff Ballet Company and appeared in productions. But finally, like most young men, he got the urge to travel and hitchhiked to New York, Chicago, California and along the border of Mexico then up to Vancouver where he joined the Merchant Navy as a cook's helper shipping between California and Alaska. During his travels he became acquainted with the art of the North West Coast Indians. He returned east to Toronto in 1938 where he continued designing for the stage then the same year went to New York for a short course in fashion design at McDowell College where he also took pattern-making and industrial design. In 1939 he returned to Canada where he completed preliminary army training but with his previous experience at sea he chose service in the Merchant Navy this time in the Atlantic where he served as a steward. Between sailings he had a chance to see the Maritimes and Newfoundland. After a convoy shakeup he had the opportunity to return to Toronto where he joined the army and was soon designing sets for the Canadian Army Shows. He crossed Canada with the first show and designed sets for travelling shows overseas to all the war theatres. This period was a great source of happiness to him as there was plenty of hard work, activity and warm associations. Many of his sets were used by the famous comedy team Wayne and Shuster. In 1943 he went on loan from the army to the National Film Board as a set designer and part-time animator working with Norman McLaren. The N.F.B. was engaged in making war related films. It was while working at the N.F.B. that he met and married Dalila Barbeau, daughter of noted ethnologist and folklorist Dr. Marius Barbeau. Dalila and Art were to have five children: Hélène (1945), Caroline (1948), René (1949), Nina (1953) and Tania (1957). In 1946 they moved to Hollywood, California where Art intended to continue set designing for films but they arrived at the outbreak of the big studio strikes and the kind of work he sought was simply not to be had. He switched to cabinet making and fared very well. But he returned to Vancouver in 1947 to work for the National Museum of Canada under the direction of Dr. Barbeau. He visited Indian villages on the east and west coasts of Vancouver Island and up the coast to Prince Rupert and vicinity also the Queen Charlotte Islands, taking notes and photographs and making drawings of Indian art. He arranged the purchase and removal of totem poles, house posts, a community house and other pieces which established the Indian village at the University of British Columbia. Many of the natural forms sketched during this period he later transformed into bronze sculpture and other of his sketches went into the western phase of his "Native Arts of Canada" series used by the Canadian Pulp and Paper Association. In 1948 he moved to Ottawa where he resumed set designing for the N.F.B. on a free-lance basis. During the summers of 1948 and 1949 he lectured to teachers in Toronto on Indian art. He finally decided to make Ottawa his permanent home and with his father's help he built a house at Cyrville just outside Ottawa. His house doubled as living space and studio but as his family grew the room was too limited so he decided to build a studio and shop on the property where he was able to continue wood-carving and in 1950 metal work in wrought iron, copper and later sterling silver. He had replica tools made of the original tools used by B.C. Indians. This work was done by his friend Leo Mainville, a local blacksmith at Blackburn Corners. From his new shop Price turned out an impressive number

PRICE, Art (Arthur Donald Price) (Cont'd)

of commissions for wood carvings from private collectors, associations, public institutions, hotels, corporations, churches and museums. In the summer of 1951 he took time out for a sketching assignment for the Hudson's Bay Company magazine *The Beaver*, when he travelled along the Mackenzie River in the Northwest Territories making drawings of the settlements and the countryside reproduced in the article "A Mackenzie River Sketch Book." Some of the paintings based on his sketches were acquired by the Hudson's Bay Company and the Ford Motor Company. With his considerable experience in set designing he was appointed Technical Director for the Canadian National Exhibition grandstand show in Toronto for 1952. In 1953 he was commissioned to carve two large totem poles (Grizzly Bear and Raven Totems) and three other large carvings (Thunderbird & Whale, Coat-of-Arms of Canada, and Thunderbird with Branch) for Jasper Park Lodge in Alberta. He installed all five works on location. In 1954 he began casting in aluminum, iron and bronze which led directly to much of his major work. In 1955 he completed "The Blackboard" for Blackburn Public School using bronze, aluminum and copper images mounted on a large slab of purple slate, itself carved with recessed abstract shapes of a fish and a hand. During a two-man show of sculpture at the Montreal Museum of Fine Arts in which Price was a participant, Robert Ayre noted, "Art Price, whose widespread circulation on Canada's five-cent postage stamp and who is exhibiting some of his sculpture in the Montreal Museum of Fine Arts this month, is a man of many skills. He is still under forty but he has had many careers and there is an astonishing variety in the contributions he has made to Canadian life. . . .His sculpture includes everything from silver bracelets and carved wooden boxes and trays to trophies, weather-vanes, crucifixes, pulpit panels, standing figures and three-dimensional murals. Much of it is original in concept, most of it owes its inspiration to West Coast Indian art. As a designer, and as a craftsman who loves materials and tools and has a powerful way with them, Price has a deep respect for native traditions, and his knowledge owes not a little to the privilege of working with his father-in-law, the distinguished Canadian ethnologist, Dr. Marius Barbeau. When a museum wants a totem pole and the great originals are not to be had, or the Canadian Government needs one for an exhibition abroad, they can depend on Price to carve a replica marvellously accurate in style and spirit. Along with all this, he has painted landscapes, published travel sketches, illustrated books of legends, and designed sets for motion picture and television productions." In 1958 Price carved some of his fine totems, plaques and panels for the Royal York Hotel's British Columbia Room. In this year too, he completed the casting and installing of the Coat-of-Arms of the City of Ottawa for its new city hall. A note on this work was carried in Foseco Foundry Practice as follows, "Artist, Craftsman, Foundryman — We feel sure that all our readers will join in our congratulations to Art Price of Ottawa, Canada — particularly when it is realized that the cores were carved from dried sand blocks. Here are some extracts in his own words from his description of the making of the casting. 'When I started casting I felt I wanted to try carving directly in the material in which the metal was to be poured. This being the purest, simplest and most direct method, similar to carving wood or working stone. The large shield in Aluminum was cast from a pattern which I made, as were the parts of the ribbon or banner. The small elements in the shield, crown, mapleleaf, etc., and the letters on the ribbon were cast in manganese bronze from patterns I made. All the other parts of the Coat-of-Arms were carved by myself in green sand, with cores where needed carved from large chunks of baked sand." He thought of the possibilities of carving directly into the material in which the metal was to be poured while watching foundry operations. He found a sympathetic foundryman in William Bond, owner of Bond Brass Limited, and working together they carried out a series of experiments in casting metals with the assistance of Canada Council funding. After five years he finally achieved the degree of proficiency necessary to undertake monumentally sized sculpture. Since then he has produced a remarkable number of works. A few of them are: the magnificent "Family Group" for the lobby of the Prudential Assurance Company of England's head office building in Montreal (1960). This work contains 5,950 pounds of bronze. Five statues comprise the "Family Group," with over-all dimensions of 8 ft., 7 in. tall; 9 ft., 6 in. long; and 5 ft. wide. The artist explained his procedure for this work in *Foundry*, January, 1961. His original 19" model for "Family Group" was produced in 1959 with an edition of four. In 1961 he completed "Girl with Cat" for display at the Canadian Conference for the Arts in Toronto. He explained to G. Joy Tranter, writer, how this work was conceived as follows, "Suddenly I hit on the idea of doing Nina, our fourth child, sitting in the large rocking-chair which Dr. Barbeau of the National Museum had given us some time ago. Then, to relax my model, I felt she should hold her dearest little friend the cat, who is called Sammy. I had always felt I would like to do Nina. Her straight hair with the bang, her almost sad face and compact little figure had always intrigued me. We all love the cat, so he was easy to include. After weeks of strenous work and very long hours. . .I finally completed the piece, crated it, and Nina, Sammy and the first French Canadian rocking chair in bronze were on their way to the big city." The process for producing this work was carried in the February, 1963 issue of *Foundry*. In 1962 Price completed a bronze bust of Queen Elizabeth II which was presented by the *Victoria Daily Times* to the City of Victoria on the occasion of the City's centennial. The original bust, done by Peggy Walton Packard of Victoria, had been damaged by vandals in 1963. "Man above Matter" a 25-foot sculpture was produced for the entrance of the Coliseum Building in the Canadian National Exhibition Grounds in Toronto. It consisted of 300 separate mold pieces which had to be made for casting by Price. He produced them in his studio, and then moved them to the foundry where the bronze casting was poured. Sixteen realistic objects appear in the sculpture to illustrate the events held in the Coliseum. The shape of the work is basically three poles in a triangular arrangement with banners attached to each of them. On the banners are the realistic objects representing the activities held within the Coliseum. At the top of the sculpture, on a spar joining two of the poles is a human figure with arms stretched upwards. *Canadian Coppermetals*, Spring, 1964 and *Foundry*, June, 1964 describe details of how the work was carried out. In 1964 Price was awarded the grand prize in Montreal's National Monument and Fountain Competition for his "Not even a sparrow falleth." He chose the fountain to be dedicated to the memory of Jeanne Le Ber, recluse and humanitarian of New France. The 22-foot-high bronze sculpture was to consist of 20 airborne angels, cohorts with the leading angel holding a small bird outstretched in her hands. Price's design was cited for its very moving allegorical expression (see *Canadian Coppermetals*, Spring 1966). "Your Daily Citizen" was his 1965 three-dimensional mural collage for the lobby of The Citizen Building which included elements that go into the daily production of news. In this work he combined mats, stereo plates, linotype and news rolls. Carl Weiselberger described it as "a highly attractive, logically developed three-dimensional mural in the shape of a circle." Price's 12½-foot-diameter stainless steel sphere "The Universe is You" was commissioned by the Department of Public Works' fine arts programme and was designed and supervised by himself. He was awarded in 1971 the coveted "Citation for Excellence in Fine Art in Steel" for the sphere. One thousand entries in fourteen categories were entered in the competition. The work was constructed by welding nickel stainless steel sheets together into two sphere halves then joining them together. The surface of the sphere was brought up to the highest finish possible (No. 7 finish) making joints undetectable to the naked eye. The sphere was installed on the outside front grounds of the Administration Building of the National Research Council of Canada located on the Montreal Road near Ottawa. The installation was completed in 1966. In 1967 Price's "Unity in Diversity", a fountain of nickel stainless steel forms was completed and installed in the Ottawa Sparks Street Mall. Almost rectangular in shape each stainless steel piece looks like a replica of a modern building but placed in an angular position to each other they present a fine artistic backdrop for streams of water that fall from the front of each of the forms. In 1968 he designed the huge 30 foot high sculptural shell motif which decorates the 22 story Shell Head Office Building on University Avenue in Toronto. Working for architects Marani, Rounthwaite & Dick, the work was produced by C.J. Rush Architectural Metals Limited of Toronto. Price had to design the sculpture so that it could be manufactured and be strong enough to hold together. It was decided to make the sculpture in two parts; a lower section approximately 8 ft. by 10 ft. and an upper section about 16 ft. by 20 ft. Projected wind and ice loads involved aerodynamic considerations. Other problems had to be solved including the best way of attaching the sculpture to the already completed building and lighting up the work in the most effective but practical way. Finally the work was assembled and hoisted into place by using a 100 ton crane with a 280 ft. long boom. The weight of the giant shell symbol is 15,000 pounds. In 1969 Price was made adviser to Indian Affairs for setting up the show at Man and His World. The display was to show artifacts from the collection of the anthropology museum of the University of British Columbia. The museum curator, Audrey Hawthorn was able to organize 5,000 artifacts of West Coast Indian culture together in one space for the first time after their storage in the basement of the museum for many years. Price designed "Communigraph '70" for Ottawa's new Postal Terminal. Government spending cutbacks of the day reduced his budget by 30 percent. This meant he had to use less metal and make radical alterations in the design. Originally he had intended to make rough-textured cylindrical forms but the casting would have been too expensive for the budget reductions. Instead he changed the forms to flat fins which were cast in a clay and sand mixture and welded together, giving the illusion of enclosing an actual volume, but in fact using much less aluminum. The work was carried out at Alloy Foundry in Merrickville. The concept of a three dimensional graph symbolized the lows and highs of human physical and mental communication potential (see *La Fonderie Belge* 8-9-10, 1971, Bruxelles). In 1973 he completed "Sails Aflame" sculpted of cast aluminum 18 by 10 by 6 ft. for the pool at the entrance of the Harbour Castle Hotel, Toronto (see *The Ottawa Journal*, Sept. 27, 1975). In 1973 he was also

PRICE, Art (Arthur Donald Price) (Cont'd)

commissioned to create an interior hanging sculpture in glass and stainless steel for the new main branch of the Ottawa Public Library in downtown Ottawa. For the National Capital Commission he restored an 80-year-old facade "Tin House." The galvanized iron pieces remaining from the original structure had deteriorated over the years. He made new pieces and rusted them to match the old and sculpted other missing parts for the assembly. Completed, it now hangs on a brick wall facing a courtyard off Sussex Drive. In 1974 he was appointed to the advisory committee on design of the National Capital Commission. Over the years he has created sculpture to listen to by first producing a small flute carved from grey slate made after the fashion of west coast Indians. The flute was commissioned by the Canada Foundation for a musical trophy and won by Anne Eggleston in 1953. Anne didn't believe the trophy would play but couldn't resist trying to make sounds with the sculpture. Surprised to find it worked she described the experience of hearing an ocean wind and tasting its salt. Price conceived the idea of producing sculpture to make sounds from this experience. In the following years he produced a maquette or model of a 10-note "Music Machine" cast in bronze and stainless steel. The model was fitted with various sizes of bronze bars and steel plates to make an carillon sound by pressing different pedals and levers. Next he made a bronze music trophy in the shape of a large tuning fork with musical diversity close to that of a Xylophone. Five successive bars cross over the fork to give it the entire musical scale in harmony depending on the mood of the player and what material is used to strike the fork. His "Unity in Diversity" on the Ottawa Sparks Street Mall has a subtle and pleasing sound which refreshes many visitors who pause awhile. When planning the fountain he designed five nickel stainless steel pillars of varying heights set at different angles in the fountain pool to bounce the sound from surface to surface. His "Sound Pods" for the exterior of Bell Canada in St. Lambert, Quebec give a wail in several tonal keys when teased by the wind. "Rhythm in Rods" consists of 36 cast aluminum bars joined to a horizontal part 48 inches long. The bars vary in lengths and diameters to create a multitude of sounds when tapped with a solid material. "Musical Interlude" was an 8-foot-tall by 5-foot-across sculpture of welded steel, cast aluminum, bronze and wood. It made music when cranked and drew attention of crowds at the Royal Canadian Academy show at the National Gallery of Canada in 1970. For details on his sound sculptures see *The Ottawa Journal*, Saturday, Feb. 9, 1974. In 1975 he completed a bronze plaque with Canada's old Supreme Court Building on it for the Canadian Bar Association who presented it to the Wellington Street Supreme Court building on the occasion of the Court's 100th anniversary. He designed in 1976 a sundial for the National Capital Commission who had received savings of Max Florence of Toronto to help beautify the capital city as his token of appreciation for living in Canada. The sundial, a four-foot cube time-piece carved from Beebe, Quebec granite is located near the official residence of the Prime Minister of Canada and is dedicated to Max Florence. In 1977 Price restored heraldic figures for the foyer of the Opera House in the National Arts Centre. The figures had been stored in government warehouses for twenty-five years. The originals stood guard over the entranceway to Westminster Abbey during Queen Elizabeth's coronation. Price has been recently working at his studio and home on Innes Road at Blackburn Hamlet where he has established a gallery. Visiting there in 1981 Nancy Baele in Art Reviews for *The Citizen* noted, "Widely known as a

PRICE, Art (Arthur Donald Price) (Cont'd)

sculptor, his attention has shifted over the last three years to the graphic arts. His studio reflects this change of focus with more than half its floor space now used for painting on different types of tracing and acid free papers. He also uses the pattern-making fabric of the fashion industry and there is lots of evidence that he hasn't abandoned oil and canvas. He pulled out rolls of paintings from one of the bins and shelves which line the walls of his studio to show his recent buoyant works of roller skates and bacchanalian revels done with acrylic dyes on large sheets of tracing paper. When wet, the paper wrinkles, collecting heavy colors in its creased pockets and creating an unusual textured shading on its translucent surface. Price routinely works in his studio from 8 a.m. until 6 p.m. with many evenings spent there as well, experimenting with an idea or technique that excites him." He is represented in hundreds of private and corporate collections in Canada and elsewhere, also many museums. A member of the Sculptors Society of Canada (1958), Royal Canadian Academy (ARCA 1960, RCA 1973); The Arts Club, Mtl. (1958); American Craftsmen's Council (1960).

References

NGC Info. Forms and biographical data, artist's file, NGC Library

Vancouver Daily Province, July, 1947 "*Alaska Beckons* by Marius Barbeau" reviewed by Torchy Anderson (Arthur Price, brilliant young artist)

The Beaver, Hudson's Bay Co., Wpg., Mar., 1952 "A Mackenzie River Sketch Book" by Art Price

Road & Wheel, August-September, 1954 "CGRA To Make Good Roads Education Award" (A.P. creates trophy for best publicity for better roads and streets)

Ottawa Journal, Ont., Jan. 16, 1954 "Razor-edged Adze Carves Career For Ottawa Artist" by Stephen Franklin

Ibid, Sept. 29, 1954 "Canada Furnishes Decorates Room in Rome FAO" (Price carves map, coat-of-arms and crests for Food & Agriculture Organization of U.N. in Rome)

Ottawa Citizen, Oct. 1, 1954 "Many-sided Arthur Price Turns To Postage Stamps" by Fred Inglis

Timber of Canada, Vol. 15, No. 6, February, 1955 "Gillies' White Pine Office" (A.P. carves front panel for desk)

Lincoln-Mercury Times, Dearborn, Mich., U.S.A., July-August, 1955 "The River Nobody Knows" by Richard L. Neuberger/paintings by Arthur Price

Globe & Mail, Tor., Ont., Apr. 25, 1956 (photo of Tanya Moiseiwitsch, scenic and costumes designer for film "Oedipus Rex", Marie Day, maker of masks for cast and Art Price, art director of film)

Canadian Art, Winter, 1957 "An Appreciation of the Native Art of Canada" by Robert Ayre (Art Price's work)

Alcan Ingot, Mtl., March, 1957 Vol. XVI, No. 3 "An Artist and Aluminum"

Montrealer, January, 1957 "Art Price. . .Man of Skills" by Robert Ayre

Ottawa Citizen, Oct. 22, 1958 "Cyrville Studio Producing Bits of 'Canadiana'"

The Arts in Canada, Ed. M. Ross, Macmillan, Tor., 1958 "Sculpture" by William S.A. Dale, P. 40-41

Canadian Hotel Review and Restaurant, Feb. 15, 1959 "History, traditions, folklore, scenery, products and geography give artists, architects chance to show. . .how they build decor around Canadian themes" P. 40-41

Foseco Foundry Practice, No. 134, April, 1959 "Artist, Craftsman, Foundryman" (City of Ottawa crest cast from mould carved in greensand)

Canadian Art, August, 1959 Vol. XVI, No. 3 "Coast to Coast in Art" (The Welcoming Birds installed for opening of new air terminal at Gander, Newfoundland), P. 203

Canadian Metalworking, September, 1959 "Foundryman's craft creates works of art"

Imperial Oil Review, December, 1959 "The Man with the Wooden Wife" by Marius Barbeau (illustrations by Art Price)

The Canadian Red Cross Junior, March, 1960 "Art Price", Part One by G. Joy Tranter

PRICE, Art (Arthur Donald Price) (Cont'd)

Ibid, April, 1960 "Art Price", Part Two by G. Joy Tranter

Ottawa Journal, Sept. 24, 1960 "Versatile Art Price Ranks High Among Today's Top North American Artists" (Creative Canadians — First of a Series on Ottawa Artists) by Scott North

Canadian Art (Special issue on architecture and allied arts), November, 1960 "Art Price" by Alan Jarvis, P. 364-365 (photos of "Sound Symbols" Bell Canada, St. Lambert, Que.; "Collecting Cosmic Rays" Bell Canada, Chicoutimi, Que.; "Coat-of-Arms", Ottawa; "Family Group", Prudential Ins., Mtl.)

Foundry, Cleveland, Ohio, U.S.A., January, 1961 "Sculptor Carves in Sand in Statuary Molding Process" by Art Price

Canadian Metalworking, Don Mills, Ont., April, 1961 "How would you do the casting?" by V.H. Furlong (research by Art Price and Bond Brass)

Canadian Copper & Brass, Tor., Summer, 1961 "Artistic Metalwork"

Ibid, Fall, 1961 "Castings — A Few Examples of the Work of An Outstanding Canadian Sculptor"

Halifax Mail-Star, N.S., Oct. 30, 1961 (Dalhousie Univ. acquires small version of "Family Group")

La Fonderie Belge, Brussels, Belgium, November, 1961 "Fonderie et art moderne" par A. Pirson, P. 299-303, 329

The Canadian Red Cross Junior, February, 1962 "Arthur Price's Girl With a Cat" by G. Joy Tranter

Canadian Catholic Institutions, March-April, 1962 "Working with copper. . .To Produce Liturgical Art" by R. Wardell

Copper, Lond., Eng., Spring, 1962 "Sculptor — Foundryman" (translated excerpts from *La Fonderie Belge* above)

Victoria Daily Times, B.C., May 23, 1962 "At Work on Times Centennial Gift" (casting of bronze bust of Queen Elizabeth by A.P.; original made by Peggy W. Packard damaged by vandals)

Ibid, July 30, 1962 "New Bronze Bust of Queen Unveiled Sunday at 3 p.m."

Foundry, Cleveland, Ohio, U.S.A., February, 1963 "Girl With a Cat" by Art Price, P. 152

Design Engineering, Tor., June 1963 "'New frontier' for foundrymen — Metal sculptor uses polystyrene patterns" by A.A. Knapp

Globe & Mail, Tor., Ont., Mar. 28, 1964 "Man over Matter" (sculpture for Coliseum, CNE)

Canadian Coppermetals, Tor., Spring, 1964 "Man Above Matter" (25 ft. sculpture for Coliseum Bldg., CNE cast in bronze)

La Fonderie Belge, 3 Mar., 1964 "Art et technique" par Alex Pirson

Foundry, June, 1964 "Man Above Matter" by Art Price

The Montreal Star, Oct. 28, 1964 "Sculptor From Ontario Wins Fountain Prize"

Journal of Royal Architectural Inst. of Can., Tor., Ont., September, 1965 "Montreal. . . Achievement and Faith" by A. Aarons

Canadian Coppermetals, Fall, 1965 "'Pop' Art — A study of sun and shadow striking contrasts and surface texture. . ."

Ottawa Citizen, Ont., Sept. 16, 1965 "Art tribute to a daily wonder of production" by Carl Weiselberger

Canadian Coppermetals, Spring, 1966 "Creative Casting" by Art Price (treatment of molds)

Time (Canada), Apr. 22, 1966 "The Arts" P. 11

Allied Arts Catalogue, Vol. 1 (RAIC), October, 1966, P. 31

Agnes Etherington Art Centre Permanent Collection, 1968, No. 112

Shell News, June 6, 1968 "Super Shell!"

The Ottawa Journal, Sat., Dec. 14, 1968 "Scallop Shell Motif"

A Cross-section of Work by Art Price, 2797 Innes Rd., Ottawa, 1968

Engineering & Construction, January, 1969 "Problem sculpture poses many challenges" (Emblem for 22 storey Shell Bldg., Tor.)

Time (Canada), Aug. 8, 1969 "The Arts — The People of the Potlatch" (Price advised Indian Affairs for exhibit)

Ottawa Journal, Sat., Aug. 16, 1969 "Faces of Ottawa — Arthur Donald Price" by W.Q. Ketchum

PRICE, Art (Arthur Donald Price) (Cont'd)

Ibid, Oct. 10, 1970 "Ottawa Artists (1) — 'Ours is not simply to fill an empty space'" by Valerie Knowles

Ottawa Citizen, Sat., Dec. 5, 1970 "Three years' hard labor — City's shining new sculpture survives the 'squeeze'" (budget cutbacks on 'Communigraph '70) by Jenny Bergin

Globe & Mail, Tor., Ont., Feb. 4, 1971 "A tribute to Communication" by Kay Kritzwiser

The Despatch, DPW, Ottawa, Fall, 1971 "Fine Arts Sculpture Wins Award"

La Fonderie Belge, October 9, 1971 "Communigraph 70" P. 179-181

The Citizen, Ottawa, Sat., Sept. 8, 1973 "Saga of Tin House — A wonderfully-accurate restoration" (restoration by A.P.) by Barbara Lambert

Happiness is where you find it by Art Price, 2797 Innes Rd., Ottawa, 1973 (photos of his work)

Globe & Mail, Tor., Ont., Dec. 29, 1973 "Sculpting the past to fit the present" by Kay Kritzwiser

Ottawa Journal, Wed., Feb. 6, 1974 "City artist named to advisory team"

The Citizen, Ottawa, Ont., Jan. 19, 1974 "Library: More than reading place" by Valerie Knowles

Ottawa Journal, Sat., Feb. 9, 1974 "Leisure — Sculpture to listen to. . ." by Kit Irving

The Citizen, Ottawa, Ont., Sat., Mar. 20, 1974 "5-year plan — Drawing takes control" by Kathleen Walker (A.P. moves to graphic arts)

Ottawa Journal, June 24, 1975 "Chief Justice Laskin and the plaque — Some relief from the 'bar'"

Le Droit, Ottawa, Ont., June 24, 1975 "La Court suprême a 100 ans"

Ottawa Journal, Sat., Sept. 27, 1975 "The Arts — Anatomy of a sculpture" by Kit Irving

The Citizen, Ottawa, Ont., Dec. 9, 1976 "Max Florence's niche in history carved as selfless Canadian" by Doug Small (granite sundial — designed by Art Price)

Ottawa Today, Ont., Oct. 18, 1977 "Queen's Beasts" (photo of carved heraldic figures restored by Art Price)

The Citizen, Ottawa, Ont., Sept. 5, 1981 "Art Reviews — Subversion a gentle art in Price's varied works" by Nancy Baele

Some illustrations, covers and book designs by Art Price for publications

Alouette! Nouveau recueil de chansons populaires avec mélodies. . ., Nat. Mus. Canada, Les Editions Lumen, Mtl., 1946

Alaska Beckons by Marius Barbeau, Macmillan (Can.), Tor., 1947 (ill. by A.P.)

L'arbre des rêves by Marius Barbeau, Les Editions Lumen, Univ. Mtl., 1947 (ill. by A.P.)

Les contes du Grand-Père Sept-Heures by Marius Barbeau (12 booklets), Chantecler, Mtl., 1950-53

Totem Poles, Bulletin No. 119 (2 vols) by Marius Barbeau, Nat. Mus. Canada, Ottawa, 1950-51 (research on north Pacific coast also photographic & museum work, preparation of illustrations by A.P.)

Haida myths illustrated in argillite carvings by Marius Barbeau, Nat. Mus. Canada/Queen's Printer, Ottawa, 1953 (cover, map & end papers by A.P.)

The Tree of Dreams by Marius Barbeau, Oxford, Tor., 1953 (ill. by A.P.)

Haida Carvers in Argillite by Marius Barbeau, Nat. Mus. Canada/Queen's Printer, Ottawa, 1957 (cover & book design by A.P.)

I have seen Quebec by Marius Barbeau, Macmillan, Tor., (English version of *J'ai vu Québec*) cover & ill. by A.P., 1957

Trésor des anciens Jésuites by Marius Barbeau, Bulletin No. 153, Nat. Mus. Canada, Ottawa, 1957 (cover design, mounting & retouching of Ill. by A.P.)

J'ai vu Québec, Lib. Garneau, Quebec City, 1957

National Ballet of Canada, souvenir programme, 1957-58 (cover design by A.P.)

The Golden Phoenix by Marius Barbeau, retold for children by Michael Hornyansky, Oxford, Tor., 1958 (ill. by A.P.)

Pathfinders in the North Pacific by Marius Barbeau, Caxton, Idaho, 1958 (cover design & end papers by A.P.)

Medicine-men on the north Pacific coast by Marius Barbeau, Nat. Mus. Canada, Bulletin No. 152, Ottawa, 1958 (covers, end papers, map and photo retouching by A.P.)

Indian days on the western prairies, Bulletin No. 163 by Marius Barbeau, Nat. Mus. Canada,

PRICE, Art (Arthur Donald Price) (Cont'd)

Ottawa, 1960 (book design, map, end papers and covers by A.P.)

Tsimsyan myths illustrated by Marius Barbeau, Bulletin No. 174, Nat. Mus. Canada, Ottawa, 1961 (cover, frontispiece and illustration by A.P.)

Le rossignol y chante, Première partie du Répertoire de la chanson folklorique Française au Canada, Bulletin No. 175, Nat. Mus. Canada, Ottawa, 1962 (cover, end papers & retouch of ill.) by A.P.

Jongleur songs of Old Quebec by Marius Barbeau, Ryerson, Tor., 1962 (decorations by A.P.)

The Magic Tree and other tales by Marius Barbeau, retold for children by Michael Hornyansky (ill. by A.P.) originally titled *The Golden Phoenix*, Scholastic Book Services, NYC (4th printing) 1969

PRICE, Caroline

b. 1948

Born in Ottawa, Ontario, the second of five children of Dalila and Art Price. She grew up in a rich cultural background provided by her grandfather, noted ethnologist and folklorist Dr. Marius Barbeau and her versatile artist father and mother. She benefited from both French and English cultures coming together. Her home was always filled with activity where she witnessed many of her father's projects being assembled. She took classical studies at school followed by a four year course in plastic arts. She worked as a graphic artist for the Federal Ministry of Lands and Forests then was graphic artist and producer at the National Film Board in the multi media department where she produced five films, three on legends for children. A free-lance artist she lives at Saint-Jean de Matha where she has immersed herself in Old Quebec culture which has changed so much and yet so little — the houses grouped around the church, the maple sugar shacks, the farms, and barns in the fields. She enjoys winter and spring and reflects this interest in her paintings which she exhibited in 1974 at Galerie Sauvegarde in Montreal when Henry Lehmann for *The Montreal Star* noted, "Price's washes seem to glide off her brush and spontaneously to assume the shapes of the stones, boards, leaves, cows that populate her world of smalltown life and pasture land. She does not paint, she pours it in a way recalling the marriage of gesture and precision that has made King Dongman's illustrations famous. In pieces like Deux Granges, Gate and Maison Bleu thin washes of paint are amazingly metamorphosed into solid, three dimensional volumes that at the same time have weight and are transparent. . . .Price focuses on details, the most poignant relics and wrecks of man's unending effort to make his mark, to preserve his footprints in the sand. It is in the psychological area which separates the hard, precise little shadows that momentarily project the sun's position onto an awning, and the passionate fluidity of our subjective experiencing of life, that we enter a vague nether world commonly known as nostalgia."

References

Communiqué de Presse, La Maison des Arts, La Sauvegarde, Mtl., "Caroline Price: Aquarelles"

The Montreal Star, Quebec, July 20, 1974 "Entertainments — Galerie Sauvegarde — Caroline Price" by Henry Lehmann

---

PRICE, Daniel
b.(c) 1947

Born at Keswick, New Brunswick, just a few miles from Fredericton, he grew up near his grandfather's farm. He moved about New Brunswick as logging jobs took his father from camp to camp with occasional seasons at the fish-packing plants in the harbours. Keswick Ridge, on the St. John River has remained home to him and a place to come back to. His father as well as being a woodsman liked to draw and paint in water colours. Danny began his interest in art by imitating his father. He exhibited first at the Keswick Fair where his Grade Three drawing won first prize. He did water colours at that time as well. In his twenties he bought a set of cheap oil paints and a book on how to paint. He attended Fredericton High School where he completed an industrial arts course. After graduation he apprenticed as a meat-cutter at various stores and at one of them met and married Theresa Scholton, a cashier in her family's small grocery-store chain. He injured his back at meat-cutting and was advised by his doctor to change his work. So with the encouragement of Theresa he looked for something closer to his serious interest of painting. He worked for Unipress, a Fredericton commercial printing plant where his high school drafting came in handy and he also took a correspondence course in commercial art. However fine art was his primary interest so after a year he turned to full-time painting, learning from art books as he went along. From the outset his subjects have been abandoned farms, trees, deserted trucks, bridges, country stores and other scenes that evoke the life of rural New Brunswick. When Theresa and Danny had their first child, he finished an apartment in his parents' basement and they moved in until he had sufficient funds to have a home of their own. He took some of his paintings to Capital Art Gallery where Julius Fazekas hung them on the walls and when they sold, Price took more in and Fazekas became his agent. In 1976 the Royal Trust Company bought one of his paintings for their 1977 desk calendar issue. His "Covered Bridge, Welsford, N.B." was the painting chosen and now hangs in the company's Montreal head-office board room along with other artists' paintings selected over the years. More than 600,000 copies of the calendar were printed. Price is particularly interested in painting the area surrounding Fredericton in a twenty-mile radius. Since the Royal Trust purchase and five or more solo shows behind him, Price's paintings have been in great demand. His exhibitions have over several occasions been early sellouts. By 1978 he had established his own studio and gallery in a separate level of his home in Fredericton where he lives with his wife and three children.

References

Fredericton Gleaner, N.B., Oct. 8, 1974 "First Exhibition" (photo & caption)

Ibid, May 22, 1975 "Artist's Theme Is New Brunswick" by Marion Owen-Fekete

Halifax Mail Star, N.S., Jan. 27, 1977 "Price paintings on view"

Halifax Chronicle Herald, N.S., Jan. 28, 1977 (photo of artist and one of his large rural paintings)

The Atlantic Advocate, April, 1977 "Danny Price" by Jo Anne Claus

Fredericton Gleaner, N.B., June 15, 1978 "Artist Blooms In Our Midst — Paints What He Sees" by A.E. Leutchford

PRICE, Howard

A graduate from the University of Washington (B.A. in painting) and from Syracuse University, N.Y. (M.F.A. in sculpture) his work covers a variety of media from woodwork to plastics, tooling, pattern-making and drawing in ink and other mixed media. He has exhibited his paintings in many group shows and several solo shows in the United States and Canada. In 1977 he held a solo show of drawings at the University of Calgary art gallery and subsequently a show of his constructions at the Canadian Art Galleries in Calgary. Was academic supervisor and former chairman of the drawing division of the Alberta College of Art at that time.

References
University of Calgary news release, 17 January, 1977
Calgary Albertan, Jan. 22, 1977 "One-man show"

PRICE, Peter

A metal sculptor and ceramics artist who exhibited his fine work at the Bow River Folk Arts Fair at Lacombe Centre in Calgary. He has been working at his art since 1972.

Reference
Calgary Albertan, Alta., July 24, 1976 "Family Living" Edited by Linda Curtis (large photo of Price at work on his pottery)

PRICE, Winchell (Addison Winchell Price)
b. 1907

Born in Toronto, Ontario, the son of Dr. and Mrs. Walter Price, the family moved to a large tract of land near Port Credit overlooking the Credit River. He attended Riverside and Forest Avenue Public School in Port Credit and graduated from Parkdale Collegiate in Toronto. At thirteen he received some help from a water colourist Mrs. Andrew Harris who summered near his family's cottage. Price asked her to teach him how to use brush and palette and later she took him on a visit to the Art Gallery of Toronto. At high school he received encouragement from Elizabeth Ferguson, a geography teacher. He sold a large number of his early paintings to teachers at high school. Following his graduation from collegiate he attended the Ontario College of Art in Toronto where he studied under Fred S. Haines, Robert Holmes, Yvonne McKague Housser, J.W. Beatty and G.A. Reid. During the summers he attended the Port Hope School of Art under J.W. Beatty (1927-31). At the age of twenty-three he attracted the attention of *Revue du Vrai et du Beau*, a leading art magazine in Paris who invited him to submit two or three photos of his paintings and biographical data. His first painting was accepted for hanging by the O.S.A. when he was only nineteen. He established a studio at Forest Hill Village on the outskirts of Toronto. He exhibited at the Eaton Galleries on College Street, Toronto for a number of years. He was elected member of the Ontario Society of Artists in 1941. In 1943 he held a solo show at Laing

PRICE, Winchell (Addison Winchell Price) (Cont'd)

Galleries when R.S. Lambert for *Saturday Night* noted, "He has always been interested in the effects of light, particularly in association with trees. But during the past year he has turned away from the woodland, and come out into the open to depict the changing moods of sky and cloud, in sunlight and storm. Like Emily Carr, Price is an artist with a spiritual outlook; he strives to reveal the hidden beauty that lies behind the outward form. A collection of some dozen of his skyscapes — the fruit of the past year's patient workmanship — is now on view. . . .Price takes an open landscape, with meadowland or prairie dotted with birch or poplar copses and single trees, and uses it as foreground for expansive treatment of sky, and cloud under varying weather conditions. In this collection you can find almost every kind of lighting and form of cloud. Here are bars of sunlight streaming earthward from behind a raincloud; a curving double rainbow silhouetted against the dull grey of a departing rain-cloud; a flash of forked lightning glimpsed in a distant thunderstorm; and summer lightning at night illuminating with an eerie glow the thick foliage of nearby trees." He exhibited with the Royal Canadian Academy periodically and was elected A.R.C.A. in November of 1947. For ten years or more he retired from full-time painting and chose instead to travel extensively. In 1965 he returned to the art scene and assembled 100 paintings for exhibit at the Texaco Room of the Port Credit Library in the spring of 1965. The exhibition was opened by Dr. Clare Bice and the *Port Credit Weekly* described Price's paintings as follows, "Mostly the presentation is landscape, of which Mr. Price is such a master. Some are impressionistic and play with light to such an extent that it seems to jump out at the observer. A few approach non-objectivism and in these one may conjure up one's own images. This is to the good, since they make Mr. Price a painter, not only of beautiful objective pieces but of modern art as well. . . .Of the paintings themselves, most are in oils with perhaps a dozen in water colours. . .'Embers of the Year', . . .is a masterpiece of the water colorist's art and would stand proudly beside any water color painted anywhere in the world. Priced at $1,000, the painting has evoked gasps of incredulity when it was realized it was a water color and not an oil. . .to play with light as Mr. Price has done in this painting, seems impossible until it is realized he has become such a master with this elusive quality, a quality found in so many of his paintings, oils included. . . .Of the oils, so many different subjects are presented that it seems impossible they should come from brushes and knives wielded by the same hand. Many have Mr. Price's well-known trade-mark on them — brilliant and deftly-executed sky and cloud formations." At his summer home at Doreas Bay near Tobermory, Price moves out to paint the surrounding countryside. He is particularly known for his paintings of spring in Canada but enjoys doing subjects in other seasons as well. His solo shows include: Eaton Galleries, Tor. (1936, 37, 38, 70); Laing Galleries, Tor. (1943); Port Credit Library, Ont. (1965, 66, 67, 68, 69, —); Bruce Peninsula & Dist. High School, Lions Head, Ont. (1967); Tom Thomson Memorial Gallery and Museum of Fine Art, Owen Sound, Ont. (1969,   ). Price lives in Port Credit.

References

Saturday Night, Tor., Ont., Oct. 17, 1931 "Winchell Price" by J.M. Elson
Ibid, Jan. 18, 1936 "World of Art" by G. Campbell McInnes
Ibid, Feb. 6, 1937 (review)
Ibid, Feb. 5, 1938 (review of show at Eaton Galleries) by G.C. McInnes

PRICE, Winchell (Addison Winchell Price) (Cont'd)

Globe & Mail, Tor., Ont., Mar. 13, 1943 (review of show at Laing Galleries)

Saturday Night, Tor., Ont., Mar. 27, 1943 "Art and Artists — Winchell Price's Show" by R.S. Lambert

Port Credit Weekly, Port Credit, Ont., Apr. 1, 1965 "Local Artist To Hold Exhibit of Paintings" (Port Credit Library)

Ibid, Apr. 22, 1965 "Winchell Addison Price Paintings Attract Many To 1965 Exhibition"

Ibid, May 6, 1965 "Artists and Curator"

Ibid, Apr. 20, 1966 "Winchell Addison Price Exhibition Opens May 3"

Ibid, Apr. 27, 1966 "Personality Profile Of The Week"

Ibid, May 4, 1966 "Outstanding Works Shown At 1966 Exhibition Here"

Mississauga News, Clarkson, Ont., Mar. 29, 1967 "Art Foundation Is Solid Says Port Credit Artist"

Owen Sound Sun Times, Ont., July 19, 1967 "50 Painting Exhibit Lion's Head Aug. 4"

Wiarton Echo, Ont., Aug. 10, 1967 "Open Art Show"

Mississauga News, Clarkson, Ont., Apr. 17, 1968 "Studies of spring by Price at Port Credit"

Ibid, Apr. 24, 1968 "Spring exhibit by W.A. Price"

The South Peel Weekly, Port Credit, Ont., May 1, 1968 "Price Still Has Skies He Wants To Paint" by Muriel Moore

Ibid, Apr. 23, 1969 "Well Known Artist To Hold Exhibition"

Owen Sound Sun Times, Ont., July 9, 1969 "Winchell Price to exhibit work from July 12-27"

Ibid, July 15, 1969 "Reception Sunday opens Winchell Price art exhibit"

Mississauga Times, Port Credit, Ont., Apr. 22, 1970 "Port Credit artist Winchell Price received honorary appointment"

NGC Info. Forms dated 1930, 1943, 1953

PRIDDAT, Fritz

Born in Germany, he learned the painting trade and then took a two-year course at the art school in Hannover. Subsequently he took more courses in handicrafts at a special school in Lemo. He married in 1946 and for a time operated a small farm while continuing his studies in art which included history and church art. He operated a paint business before leaving Germany. Arriving in Winnipeg with his wife and two children in 1961 he worked for a construction firm, then established a paint business and after making a success of it left the business in the hands of his employees while he supervised. Turning to easel painting he filled many commercial orders. In his own painting he chose landscapes and became fairly prolific. In 1965 he held a solo show of his paintings at the Rose Room of the Marlborough Hotel, Winnipeg. Most of his work deals with Manitoba scenery. He is represented in the guest house of the atomic plant at Pinawa. He is also represented in collections in Chicago, Minneapolis, Winnipeg and elsewhere.

References

Der Nordwesten, Wpg., 21, Sept. 1965 (German language paper) translated heading "Love of Nature Leads the Brush" by Vera Oberholz

Winnipeg Free Press, Man., Sept. 29, 1965 "Priddat To Exhibit 100 Oil Paintings"

PRIESTNER, Maureen

A Cambridge, Ontario artist of Irish stock she grew up in England where she attended school and was encouraged by her teachers to develop her artistic talents. She won a number of contests for her art and one of her paintings was presented to the Queen Mother. When she was 14 she moved to Canada with her parents who settled in Hamilton. Later she married Dr. Vincent Priestner and they moved to Cambridge where her husband set up a general practice. She took art lessons from Margaret Massey of Bridgeport, Ontario. Back at her painting after many years she paints a wide range of subject matter including boats, seascapes, birds, gypsies, town, country and city scenes in soft blues and mauves. In 1977 her work was shown at the Pinnochio Shop in Galt. Maureen and Vincent have four children.

Reference
Kitchener Waterloo Record, Ont., Sept. 8, 1977 "Area artist specializes in children's paintings" by Lynda Coates (photo of artist with her work)

PRIMEAU, Claude

A self taught sculptor and son of Alex Primeau (painter and one-time Automatiste), Claude has produced sculpture of polish and colouring overflowing with exotic sensuality. He also produced chair-sculptures of both artistic and functional qualities. He has worked in Montreal, Europe and in California with Bernard Zakeim and Paco Sandow. With his father he opened a gallery in San Francisco in 1967.

Reference
La Patrie, Mtl., 23 July, 1967 "La sculpture québécoise à San Francisco" par C.D.

PRINCE, James Hubert
b. 1935

Born in Toronto, Ontario he attended Western Technical School and then attended the Ontario College of Art evenings. He won Honourable Mention from the I.O.D.E. art competition (1953) and also won a prize at Western Tech which was offered by the Sketch Club.

Reference
NGC Info. Form rec'd Apr. 14, 1954

PRINCE, Jean-Guy

An artist working in many mediums including those used in sculpture, he exhibited his experimental work in Montreal at galerie Media Gravures et Multiples in 1974 and also the same year at La Société des artistes professionnels du Québec.

PRINCE, Jean-Guy (Cont'd)

References
   La Presse, Mtl., P.Q., Feb. 2, 1974 "Les fétiches de J.-G. Prince"
   Montréal-Matin, Mtl., P.Q., May 1, 1974 "Jean-Guy Prince à la S.A.P.Q."

PRINCE, Richard
b. 1949

Born in Comox, B.C., he attended the University of British Columbia and graduated with B.A. (Arts) 1971; University of British Columbia Post Graduate Work (1972-73); Emma Lake Workshop, University of Saskatchewan (1970). Noting his background, Avis Lang Rosenberg in *Artscanada* explained in 1973, "The fact that his father is a high school shop teacher and that Prince has held jobs as diverse as making polyurethane foam topographical models and working on card catalogues in the library have helped nourish and direct his art. The library job perhaps engendered in him an awareness of the kinds of human tendencies and attitudes that give birth to museums and libraries, attitudes involved with categorization, evaluation, compartmentalization. . . . Richard Prince is unequivocally an object-maker. His works are usually quite small, intimate, and playful, and always well-crafted. To many people they seem precious. They have a child's curiosity and delight in the world, captured and held by an adult's understanding of things like electricity, use of materials, the power of three-dimensionality, and Marcel Duchamp. They have titles such as *Landscape for Lawyer's Office* and *Navigation Aid for Howe Sound Island*. . . . Most of Prince's pieces can in one way or another be classed iconographically as landscape, but this is an urban creature's landscape, experienced not slowly, constantly, subtly, uninterruptedly, but rather by occasionally looking out the window, down the street, across the skyline, or by walks in the park. A bit of still life creeps into the landscape via the miniaturization, finiteness, and tangibility. A sense of symbolic shorthand rather than direct naturalistic representation informs the component parts: two trees, three trees, a hill, a pond. For nearly all of Prince's works you must commit yourself to an active physical and mental involvement, a participation. There are boxes to open, drawers to pull, shelves to slide, handles to turn, and stereoscopic slides and viewer to deal with. You must consciously move in close enough to see, for these are not large powerful structures that overwhelm, that emphasize the viewer's passivity or the involuntary aspects of perception. And yet the ubiquitous boxes do in fact command and direct your vision." By 1977 Prince was producing larger works like "Windcatcher's Trap Table For Field Use Only" described by Art Perry in *Artmagazine* as follows, ". . .is similar to *Large Windcatcher*, only a fan still simulates the wind and the twig wire embedded into the table top in order to trap the wind is again a model from nature. Yet the table is full-scale and it has a roughness of presence that is new to Prince's usual perfected craftsmanship. All in all it can be seen as a definite part of Price's new growing sensibility towards open sculptural space." From these larger pieces he moved to an entirely different sculptural concept as described by Andrew Scott in *The Vancouver Sun* in 1979 as follows, "Now his interests, like those of so many other artists, have turned to the human figure. Using plaster-casting orthopaedic bandages, Prince took moulds from the sides of a number of female volunteers, and then cast thin translucent fibreglass

1849

outlines which he has arranged in all sorts of architectural poses. There's a mother and daughter arch, twin figures forming a Palladian window, a flying buttress made from arm and torso, two columns, a ring of identical pixie-like models suspended gently from the ceiling, and more. The results are futuristic fantasies, very light and airy, almost like spirit-creatures — or supernatural beings who have fled a problem planet, leaving behind them these strange discarded husks. . . .Prince's concern with the human figure is echoed by many North American sculptors — Duane Hanson, George Segal, Edward Kienholz and John De Andrea in the U.S.; Colette Whiten, Mark Prent, Liz Magor and Joe Fafard in Canada. And these are just to name a few. . . .Prince, while never a formalist, helps reveal how far from exhaustion is the human figure as a source for artmaking." His solo shows include: "Woodlore and Other Romances", Anna Leonowens Gallery, Nova Scotia College of Art & Design, Halifax (1974); Isaacs Gallery, Tor., Ont. (1976, 1978); Equinox Gallery, Van., B.C. (1977); "Figure Structures", Burnaby Art Gal., B.C. (1979) and numerous group shows including "Pacific Vibrations", Art Gallery of Greater Victoria (1973); "Nine Out of Ten, a Survey of Contemporary Canadian Art", Art Gallery of Hamilton & Kitchener Waterloo Art Gallery (1974); "Young Contemporaries", London Art Gallery, Ont. (1975); "Pacific Coast Consciousness", Robert McLaughlin Gal., Oshawa, Ont. (1975) travelling show; "Eleven Artists from the West Coast", Wpg. Art Gal., Wpg., Man. (1976); "Young Contemporaries '77", Art Gal. London, Ont. (1976), travelling show; Professional Art Dealers Assoc. of Can. Exhibition, Harbour Front Art Gal./Ontario Arts Council, Tor., Ont. (1977); "Performance", Harbour Front Art Gallery, Tor., Ont. (1978); "Obsessions, Rituals, Controls", Norman Mackenzie Art Gal., Regina, Sask. (1978); "Four From Vancouver", Alberta College of Art Gallery, Calg., Alta. (1980). He is Assistant Professor in the Department of Fine Arts at the University of British Columbia. Represented in the following collections: Vancouver Art Gallery; Burnaby Art Gallery; B.C. Central Credit Union; Government of Province of B.C. Art Bank; City of Vancouver Art Collection; Canada Council Art Bank, Ottawa; National Gallery of Canada, Ottawa; Gulf Oil Company; Thorne Riddell & Co.; Canadian Parapelegic Association. Juror, City of Vancouver Art Purchase Award Programme (Dec. 1976). Member: Royal Canadian Academy (R.C.A. 1979); Board of Directors, Vancouver Art Gallery (1978-80); Pres., Board of Directors for Green Thumb Theatre for Young People (1979); Juror, Canada Council Art Bank Purchase Programme (1980). Taught sculpture at the following educational institutions: Instructor, Vancouver School of Art, Night School (1973-74); Instructor, Vancouver Community College, Langara (1974-75); Artist in Residence for Nat. Mus. of Canada, Queen Charlotte Islands (1975); Instructor, University of British Columbia (1975-76, 1976-77); Visiting Lecturer, University of British Columbia (1977-78) then became Assistant Professor of Sculpture in 1978. His awards include: Canada Council Arts Bursary (1972-73); Purchase Award, Art Vancouver for 1974 (1973-74); Canada Council Arts Grant (1974-75) (1977-78). Lives in Vancouver, B.C.

References

Artscanada, Tor., February-March, 1973 "Richard Prince" by Avis Lang Rosenberg, P. 39-40

Art in Boxes by Alex Mogelon & Norman Laliberte, Van Nostrant Reinhold, N.Y., 1974

Vancouver Province, B.C., Aug. 16, 1975 "Miniature boxes, rooftop marvels" Art Perry

Capilano Review, Capilano College, N. Van., Spring 1975 "Interviews & Images"

PRINCE, Richard (Cont'd)

Toronto Star, Ont., Apr. 30, 1976 "Sculptor turns wind into tangible poetry" by Gary Michael Dault

Vancouver Province, B.C., Apr. 29, 1977 "Art with poetic intelligence" by Art Perry

Western Living Magazine, Van., B.C., April, 1976 "Tales of the Pale and Silvery Moon" by Mary Fox

Vie des Arts, Hiver, 1976-77 "La Hantise du Vent" par Art Perry

Vancouver Sun, B.C. (clipping) "Little Boxes, little boxes, full of wonder"

Art Magazine, Tor., May-June, 1977 "Vancouver: Richard Prince & Alan Wood — Pacific Coast Constructions" by Art Perry, P. 57-60

Artscanada, Tor., October-November, 1978 "Richard Prince: bringing the outdoors in" by Joan Lowndes, P. 43-47

Richard Prince, Burnaby Art Gallery, 1979 "Figure Structures" September 19 to October 21, 1979

Vancouver Province, B.C., Sept. 20, 1979 "Prince grows away from puns" by Art Perry

Vancouver Sun, Sept. 21, 1979 "It's a fantastic show and a joy to the eye" by Andrew Scott

Royal Canadian Academy of Arts, Exhibitions & Members 1880-1979 by Evelyn de R. McMann, U. of T. Press, Tor., 1981, P. 334

PRINGLE, Alex

He was a newspaperman for forty years and a one time night editor for the *Mail & Empire*. He studied art at the Ontario College of Art and the Art Students' League of New York. For many years he was a member of the Ontario Art Club of Toronto where he studied amongst other things life drawing and painting. He held a solo show of his oil paintings in Acton, Ontario, in March of 1958 and also had plans of holding solo shows in Kitchener and in Hamilton, Ontario.

Reference

Free Press, Acton, Ont., Mar. 13, 1958 "A. Pringle Was Newspaperman Now Artist, Displays Paintings"

PRINGLE, Annie White

1867-1945

Born in Leith, Scotland, the daughter of P. White Greive and Jean A. (Boyd) Greive. She received her primary education in public school in Leith where she was awarded a first prize for free hand drawing. Subsequently she attended evening classes at Edinburgh School of Art under Miss Wone. She came to Canada in 1889 and continued her studies at day classes at the Monument National (1909) and for fifteen years with Jobson Paradis also life classes in painting with Edmund Dyonnet; John Johnston; sculpture at the Monument National with Alfred Laliberté. As a student in Montreal she won prizes for drawing and painting. She studied at the Montreal Art Association with William Brymner; at the Women's Art Studio with Adam Sherriff Scott, Lilias T. Newton and Randolph Hewton. She received constructive criticism from G. Horne Russell. She exhibited the following at the Art Association of Montreal: a landscape "Turn in the Road" (1923), "Grandma" (1926), "Portrait Study"

1851

PRINGLE, Annie White (Cont'd)

(1935), "Autumn Tints" (1936); Royal Canadian Academy "Eleanor" (1931). She also exhibited at the Women's Art Society exhibition, Eaton's, Morgans, Ogilvy's, Johnson's Art Gallery. Member: Women's Art Society. Married James B. Pringle in 1889. Died in Smith's Falls, Ontario aged 78 while staying with her daughter, Willa B. Milne (Mrs. George Milne).

References

Letter, 2nd June, 1946 from Willa B. Milne to H.O. McCurry (Dir. NGC)

Biographical entry (possibly from *National Reference Book on Canadian Men & Women* by Canadian Newspaper Serv., Registered, undated)

NGC Info. Form stamped NGC June 4, 1946 sent by W.B. Milne

Early Painters and Engravers in Canada by J. Russell Harper, Univ. Tor. Press, Tor., 1970, P. 256

Royal Canadian Academy of Arts, Exhibitions and Members, 1880-1979 by Evelyn de R. McMann, Univ. Tor. Press, Tor., 1981, P. 334

PRINS, Nick

An Alberta artist, he exhibited his water colours at The Lock Art Gallery in Winnipeg when John W. Graham noted, "Mr. Prins is an excellent water colorist who has selected the western rural landscape for his subject matter. He handles it with affectionate perception, describing the derelict remnants of abandoned homesteads in a nostalgic but never sentimental manner. His technique combines the wet fluidity of the traditional water colorist with a surface toning application of dry brush texturing. He directs a great deal of his attention to describing the tactile qualities of weathered boards, rusted iron, battered tin, flaking whitewash, disintegrating plaster and peeling paint which, in contrast with the wet insubstantiality of overcast skies, the obliterating mantle of snow or tracery of unmowed grass, reinforces the illusion of reality, a reality in which time has stopped. . .in every case he proves himself to be more than an illustrator. He is a commentator, too."

Reference

Winnipeg Free Press, Man., Apr. 5, 1973 "Critique By John W. Graham — 'Affectionate Perception'"

PRIOR, Frances

A Richmond, B.C. artist who is known for her landscapes including interior scenes of B.C., she has exhibited her work with the Delta Sketch Club & Richmond Artists Guild at the Richmond Square Mall (1968) and held a solo show in the cafeteria of the B.C. Hydro and Power Authority in Richmond (1968). She also paints still life canvases.

PRIOR, Frances (Cont'd)

References
> *Richmond Review*, B.C., Mar. 27, 1968 "Artist in Action" (photo of artist at work on landscape)
> Ibid, Nov. 13, 1968 "Cariboo Holiday Canvases Show At B.C. Hydro"

PRITCHARD, Chris

Living in Brantford, Ontario, he became known for his batiks which he creates with his wife Wendy Pritchard. They were described as, "experts in their medium, bringing visual variety and vigour to a craft that is demanding in technique." Created a Japanese mythological mural for the Brantford General Hospital measuring 12 x 10 feet. Participated in a group show at the Art Gallery of Brant with three other artists in 1972.

References
> *Simcoe Reformer*, Ont., Aug. 3, 1972 "Third Annual — Brant Gallery Holds Invitational Show"
> *Brantford Expositor*, Ont., Mar. 5, 1973 "Japanese Mural" (photo of artist standing by mural)

PRITCHARD, Deborah

She exhibited her oil pastels under the title "Fences" at the Scarborough Public Library in the spring of 1978.

Reference
> Scarborough Public Library exhibition notice "Fences" April 10-May 13, 1978 an exhibition of oil pastels by Deborah Pritchard

---

PRITCHARD, Wendy

Living in Brantford, Ontario, part of the team of Wendy and Chris Pritchard, creators of batiks. Their work has been described as being vigorous and adding visual variety to the craft in the area. She participated in the five person show with her husband and three other artists at the Art Gallery of Brant in 1972.

Reference
> *Simcoe Reformer*, Ont., Aug. 3, 1972 "Third Annual — Brant Gallery Holds Invitational Show"

PRITTIE, Mary Elizabeth
b. 1908

Born in St. Catharines, Ontario, she became head nurse at the Children's Hospital in Buffalo, N.Y. After she married and had children, she took up painting. She received lessons from Mrs. A. Porter in Welland (two years); from Mr. A. Sisti of Buffalo, N.Y. and later studied with Gordon Ferrier, John Martin, Tony Urquhart, David Partridge and others. She attended the Doon School of Fine Arts, Queen's University and New York State University classes. Known for her oils, water colours, acrylics, graphic art and batiks. Her subjects include historic buildings, town and country scenes, still life and others. Her solo shows include: Ye Olde Fire Hall Gallery, Niagara-on-the-Lake, Ont. (1967); Gordon Hill Advertising, C.I.L. Bldg., Tor. (1977); Grimsby Art Gallery, Grimsby, Ont. (c. 1979); Niagara College of Applied Art & Tech., Hennepin Art Gallery, Welland, Ont. (1980) and others, also Three-woman show, Oak Hall, Niagara Falls, Ont. (1974); Jury Show, Rodman Hall, St. Catharines, Ont. (1979); major juried shows including: Ontario Society of Artists, Royal Canadian Academy (1950, 1964); Hamilton Art Gallery, London Public Library and Art Museum, Society of Canadian Artists (1967) and others. She is represented in the collections of: Port Colborne Hospital, Public Library and City Hall; Hamilton City Hall; Royal Trust, Mtl.; and Governor-General Schreyer and his wife. Member: Port Colborne Art Association (founding member); Port Colborne Art Club (Pres. 1950); Niagara District Art Association. Lives at Port Colborne, Ontario.

References

Welland-Port Colborne Tribune, Ont., Dec. 9, 1963 "Local Artist's Work Accepted For RCAA Show"

Niagara-on-the-Lake Advance, Aug. 3, 1967 "'One Woman's art exhibit at Niagara'"

Welland-Port Colborne Tribune, Ont., Oct. 17, 1967 "Local Artist Has Painting In SCA Show"

Ibid, May 6, 1972 "Over 300 From Municipal, Sports World Honor Peart" (photo of painting by Mary Prittie presented to Peart)

Ibid, July 31, 1974 "Three Port Lady Artists Exhibited At Oak Hall"

Ibid, Nov. 20, 1974 "Cellar Studio Exhibits At Plaza" (photo of Mary Prittie with her batiks)

Evening Tribune, Welland, Ont., Dec. 17, 1977 "Local artist shows paintings in Toronto"

Ibid, Feb. 13, 1979 "Prittie collection at library oils, water colors, and inks"

Ibid, Jan. 14, 1980 "Paintings show 'guts and rhythm'" by Gloria Katch

St. Catharines Standard, Ont., Jan. 19, 1980 "Art with Linda Crabtree — Mary Prittie — College gallery features Port Colborne artist"

NGC Info. Forms 1950, 1964

PRITZ, Alexandra Lecia (née Lecia Polujan)
b. 1945

Born in Austria, the daughter of Anna (Loban) and Simon Polujan. Her family moved to England and then to Canada in 1951 and settled in Edmonton, Alberta. Lecia attended Eastglen Composite High School where she studied art for three years. In her senior year she painted a 28 foot mural in the school rotunda. She also took private lessons from Professor J. Bucmaniuk (1961-62). She entered the Fine Arts course at the University of Alberta (Edmonton) where she studied with H.G. Glyde, Norman Yates, R. Sinclair, Jonathan Knowlton, Stephen Andrews, Jeremy Moore, Ron Davies and graduated in

PRITZ, Alexandra Lecia (née Lecia Polujan)

1968 with a B.F.A. (in studio art). She was awarded a Province of Alberta Scholarship in 1967 during her final year at university. She was also awarded a National Gallery of Canada Museum Training Scholarship in 1968 and took the Gallery's Museology Course in Ottawa (1968-69). She joined the staff of the National Gallery of Canada as documentalist in 1969 and with other duties also prepared the first edition of *Artists in Canada* and worked on its revision up until her resignation in the summer of 1977 when her husband's job took them to the West Coast. She taught art for exceptional children in Highland Park High School, Ottawa (1969-70); received a teaching fellowship to attend the University of Ottawa (1970-71); graduated with her M.A. from the University (1977). She also gave lectures on "The Impressionists" at the NGC (1969); "Taras Shevchenko — artist" at Carleton University, Ottawa (1970). In her own art she has done sculpture, drawings, print-making and painting, working with perspex, wood, etching and lithography media, graphite for drawings, oil and acrylics for painting. She has been cited for her flawless draughtsmanship and great sensitivity in drawing. Her group and juried shows include: Ukrainian Artists Centennial Exhibition, Jubilee Auditorium, Edmonton (1967); Ukrainian Canadian Women's Art Exhibit, Harbourfront Art Gallery, Tor., 1975; "Ukrainian Painting", Ottawa City Hall (1976); "Art Experience '77", Focus Gallery, Tor. (1977). She is represented in the University of Alberta Collection and in industrial and private collections across Canada. Active in recreational folk dancing she was artistic director and choreographer for a Ukrainian Dance Company. She was free-lancing in commercial art and portraiture in British Columbia in 1981.

References

Ottawa Journal, Ont., Jan. 31, 1976 "Ukrainian art exhibition opens Monday at City Hall" by W.Q. Ketchum

Ibid, Feb. 2, 1976 "Ukrainian art show at city hall"

Art Experience '77 (exhibition sheet by Christina Senkiw, show organized by Maria Ochrymowych

Ukrainian-Canadian Women's Art Exhibition catalogue sheet, paintings selected by Kay Kritswiser (former art critic, Globe & Mail) Maria Ochrymovych (Fine Arts Dept., Cedarbrae Library) and David Samila (Dept. Fine Arts, York Univ.), Harbourfront Art Gallery, Nov. 9-30, 1975

NGC Info. Form, 1972; Document from artist, 1977

Artists in Canada, NGC, Ottawa, 1975 compiled by Alexandra Pritz

Ibid, 1977

PRIVETT, Molly

b. 1905

Born in Streatham, England, she came to Canada in 1927 to Limerick, Saskatchewan then later settled in British Columbia. She studied four years with Herbert Siebner in Victoria (1954-55, 1958) and became a member of the B.C. Society of Artists (Assoc. Member, 1964; Member, 1966); was active with The Point Group (1960-62). She held solo shows at the Grant Gallery, Wpg., Art Gallery of Greater Victoria, and the Point Gallery, Victoria. Was guest artist at the Annual Saanich Peninsula Art Show, Sidney (1966) and has

PRIVETT, Molly (Cont'd)

participated in group shows at Bau-Xi Gallery, Van.; with B.C. Society of Artists at Point Gallery and at Pandora's Box Gallery, Victoria (1966). She received honourable mention at the juried show of the Art Centre of Greater Victoria (1965). Lives in Sidney, B.C.

Reference
    NGC Info. Forms (c) 1955, 1966

PROCH, Don
b. 1944

Born in Inglis, Manitoba, he lived in a coal-warmed log cabin on his grandparent's farm at Grandview, Manitoba, where they grew wheat and raised eight cows. His Ukrainian grandfather drove him to school by horse and buggy. During those early years while his father helped his grandfather, Don's chores included filling the cracks between the logs of the cabin with a mixture of clay, straw and dung. They had no electricity and their existence was a frugal one. Finally Don's father, after trying farming on his own for a year with little or no profit, left the land to work in the automobile factories of southern Ontario. Saving his hard earned money Don's father made a down payment on a rural hotel (Inglis Hotel) at Inglis, Manitoba. The hotel was a corrugated-tin covered structure with a beverage room. Hydro gangs, road workers, and travelling salesmen stopped overnight as an interval in their daily routines. With the exception of electricity the town of Inglis had little traces of urbanism. Don was eight years old when his family moved into the hotel. He used to bicycle down the highway to the deserted settlement of Asessippi, a village which was later to provide him with so much of his material in his art. Asessippi had been by-passed by progress when the railroad was built further to the south. Eventually farms became deserted and farm machinery lay dormant in the sheds and fields, material which he was to use in his art later. He drew a lot as a boy and even entered the Robin Hood Contest to draw the archer. He assembled boats, aeroplanes and other items with various materials with great concentration and perfectionism. At sixteen he enrolled in engineering at the University of Manitoba but was not happy with university life and returned home to find a job. His father persuaded him to return to university but this time in fine arts studies. He enrolled in the University of Manitoba School of Art where he proved to be an active student with an independent mind. The school was then under the direction of George Swinton and Ivan Eyre and although influenced by them Proch emerged very much an artist with his own style. He painted for a year but was not satisfied with his results. He put aside his brushes and taught high school art from 1967 to 1970. During this period he pondered what direction his own art would take. He became interested in the concept of drawing on three-dimensional surfaces, subjects derived from his rural experiences, his sense of history (Ukrainian heritage and the prairie pioneers), urban pressures on rural life, the interaction between nature, man and the land. In 1970 he submitted his first three-dimensional drawing to the Winnipeg Biennial entitled "Asessippi Tread." This work is about a boy on a bicycle in action along the Asessippi road. The theme is the return of the human presence to the deserted village of Asessippi. The spikes on the bicycle are symbolic of the human presence on the land once more making the land bleed as once the farmers did with their ploughs and the villagers with their traffic. In an article on Proch, Philip Fry noted, ". . .*Asessippi Tread*, a multi-media assemblage representing a boy crouched low on a bicycle. The formal impact of the piece is due mainly to a play between the flat, upper surface upon which the image is drawn, and various three-dimensional elements that form the legs of the rider and lower half of the bicycle. The image is completed by a sheet of chromed metal cut to echo the outline of the upper surface. Serving as a base, the metal reflects a fuzzy image of the rider and, in clear focus, the bicycle tread. The opposition between the two and three-dimensional aspects of *Asessippi Tread* is resolved by Proch's careful calculation of angles of vision, slight modifications of parts of the assemblage, and his overall treatment of the surface. . .the piece is best seen, not on a flat horizontal surface, but on a slightly inclined plane. . . . All the elements are either chromed or finished with gesso and very fine silver-point drawings. The pattern of the drawing, sometimes rather loose and open, reminiscent of the design of frost on a window, but often tight and dense, is always made up of small, sharply pointed lines. The tire treads are drawn in silver-point, but they bristle with very real, sharpened chrome spikes." Proch formed a tongue-in-cheek group of friends and relatives under the name Ophthalmia Company of Inglis. The original group included his father Dymetro (shop foreman), Bill Lobchuk (printer and boss of The Grand Western Canadian Screen Shop), Thomas Melnick (sander/finisher), Steve Chachula (welder), Bertie Duncan (bird sculptor). Others joined including Doug Proch, Kelly Clark, Glen Tinley, Ernest Mayer, Gord Bonnell and Patrice. The sculpture "Asessippi Tread" was acquired by the Winnipeg Art Gallery through the Purchase Award of the Winnipeg Biennial Show. In 1972 his solo show "The Legend of Asessippi" was held at the Winnipeg Art Gallery when John W. Graham in his review of the show noted, "Though Mr. Proch and company have chosen to try to capture and express the inner spirit of a particular place which still bears the marks of a former intrusion, this is not an exercise in maudlin nostalgia. Like most contemporary exhibitions which deal with systems, forces and elements, it is an investigation into the nature of an environment and the interaction of the agencies which operate within it. By examining the particular, they have attempted, by translation into expressive images in new contexts, to give more universality of meaning to what they have recorded. The environmental nature of the show begins with the Shell River valley and its relics, and concludes with the physical relationship of the gallery space and two and three-dimensional elements created and positioned within it. . . .The administration of the gallery is to be congratulated for presenting Asessippi and Mr. Proch and the Ophthalmia Company have used the opportunity to create one of the most important exhibitions to be assembled anywhere. Don't miss it, but don't expect to take it all in just one visit." Proch next participated in several group shows, then in the winter of 1975 held another show at the Winnipeg Art Gallery exhibiting his prints, sculptures and masks. The show was Proch's continuation of expressing themes based on the rural dwellers' struggle to adapt to the complexities of urban life and the necessity of making compromises between two essentially different lifestyles. In 1976 his work was chosen for showing at Place Bonaventure in Montreal for the all-Canadian Olympic show. In 1977 he completed a mural for the Winnipeg Convention Centre measuring 8 ft. by 12 ft. of a prairie scene, half of which was fashioned in chromed steel. His work went on a travelling show organized by the Winnipeg Art Gallery. Reviewer Brooks Joyner viewing the show at the Southern Alberta Art Gallery in Lethbridge, noted, "One of the most splendid shows of my experience. . .The sculpture and drawings of Manitoba artist Don Proch. . .is a masterful exhibition that does real justice to the magnificent craftsmanship and remarkable imagination of this young Canadian sculptor. . . .His subjects, both landscape metaphor and people, derive from his immediate extended family in Asessippi. . . .His sculptures are laced with rhythmic lines of graphite that form contour maplike landscapes. The more magical-shamanistic heads or busts are anonymous humanoids, whose faces and features reveal cloud patterns and prairie terrain. They are beautiful sculptures, superbly finished and tremendously compelling." Proch's silkscreen prints are printed at the Western Canadian Screen Shop and are made by the use of roller-bearing graphite mixed with bronzing varnish. The graphite technique was described by Robert Enright as making the prints ". . .almost indistinguishable from drawings, a confusion increased because the prints were produced in such small editions. Many were printed in both grey and color editions and there are as few as six copies of the color variation of Prairie Nude and Asessippi Elevator. Summer Fall, a seductive mouth composed of Proch's favorite trinity of elements — earth, horizon and sky — was produced in a color edition of three copies, which makes it hardly an edition at all!. . . .Any artist who makes print-making an off-shoot of drawing is a collector's delight." Enright was viewing Proch's prints at the Brian Meinychenko Gallery, Winnipeg, in the spring of 1981. Kenneth Hughes writing in the *Canadian Dimension* described Proch as follows, "His heritage he neither can nor will forget, and it therefore becomes a constitutive element in his art. So while in his person and in his art Don Proch is most obviously a prairie Canadian, his Canadianness has been mediated through the Ukrainian experience of settlement in Manitoba. A great distance in space and time separates the traditional Ukrainian decorated egg and Proch's space-age masks, but with his space-age masks Proch transforms the rigid old tradition of the decorated egg belonging to a simple world of the ancestral past and transports it into the brave new world of modern complexity. So sure is his vision that when he transforms the traditions of the people from whence he came, at the same time he transcends those traditions and speaks in more universal terms to a larger audience of non-Ukrainian-Canadians and others. . . .The concept of the Ophthalmia Company has two main sources, one old the other new. On the one hand the idea of the company has its origins in the mutual help situation of prairie rural peasant and populist society. On the other hand, there is the obvious connection between a name such as Ophthalmia Company and similar names associated with rock groups in the so-called counter-culture in the sixties. This counter-culture side is important, for it gives us a clue as to the implications of eye irritation. For as we shall see, what Proch commonly does is to take familiar scenes, things, concepts, and distort them in order to (a) break the patterns of habituation that prevent us from seeing those things, scenes or events clearly, or (b) to cause us to see things anew so that justice is done to the past even as the (rural) past is brought under control of the (rural and urban) present. In fact, the Ophthalmia Company seeks to inflame the eye of the viewer only to shift his mechanisms of perception, to change the way in which the viewer actually sees." Proch lives in Winnipeg.

PROCH, Don (Cont'd)

References

Artscanada, Early Autumn, 1972 (Nos. 169/170/171) "Prairie space drawings" by Philip Fry, P. 40-56

Winnipeg Free Press, Man., Sept. 11, 1972 "A Critique By John W. Graham — 'Asessippi' Lauded"

Winnipeg Tribune, Man., May 19, 1973 "A Paris showing for two Winnipeg artists" by Rosalie Woloski

Canadian Artists In Exhibition, 1972-73, Roundstone, Tor., 1974, P. 172

Ibid, 1974, (Part 2), P. 147, 285

Winnipeg Free Press, Man., Jan. 11, 1975 "The Gallery — Urban and rural relationship explored" by William Kirby

Catalogue — "Don Proch's Asessippi Clouds" — The Winnipeg Art Gallery, notes by William Kirby, Curator of Contemporary Art

Ottawa Citizen, Ont.,Jan. 25, 1975 "Lifestyle of Asessippi in prints and sculpture"

Winnipeg Free Press, Jan. 23, 1976 "Art gallery plan meets problems"

Winnipeg Tribune, May 13, 1976 "Art goes to the Olympics" (photo of work by Proch bound for Olympics)

Saturday Night, Tor., January/February 1977 "The magic masks of Asessippi — Don Proch is the shaman of prairie art" by Adele Freedman

Winnipeg Free Press, Mar. 5, 1977 "Sculptor spends four months before getting the right man" (Proch selects Cliff McPherson to work on his mural)

Windsor Star, Ont., Aug. 27, 1977 "Prairie farm boy sees art in machines" by Tony Wanless

Winnipeg Free Press, Sept. 26, 1977 "Woodsmoke, seagulls, flowers — an artist's world in prints" (photo of Proch's print "Woodsmoke II, 1977")

The Albertan, Calg., Alta., Oct. 15, 1977 "Visual Arts — The Proch wizardry" by Brooks Joyner

Canadian Dimension, Wpg., Man., Aug.-Sept., 1978 "The Art of Don Proch" by Kenneth Hughes

Winnipeg Free Press, Apr. 4, 1981 "Proch's 'visual pun' reflects strengths of art gallery show" by Robert Enright

Ibid, Apr. 18, 1981 "Proch exhibition offers calm portrayal of prairies" by Robert Enright

---

PROCTOR, Alexander Phimister
1862-1950

Born in Bozanquit Township, Lambton County, Ontario, the son of Alexander and Tirza (Smith) Proctor, he moved with his family to Michigan and then by wagon to Des Moines, Iowa and from there to Denver, Colorado. He took an early interest in drawing. He became fond of hunting and spent summers in the Rocky Mountains with sketch book and rifle. At sixteen he killed a grizzly bear and bull elk in the same day. He spent months alone on trips in the mountains of Colorado subsisting on game almost entirely. He sketched wild animals and also hunters and Indians with whom he spent many months. Later he tried prospecting to raise money to study in New York but was not successful in this venture. He sold a ranch at Grand Lake and went to New York about 1882. He spent a few summers sketching domestic animals on his uncle's farm in Ontario. In New York he studied at the National Academy of Design School and at the Art Students' League. After each year of study in New York he headed west for the open spaces of Colorado. It was not until the Chicago World's Fair in 1893 that the attention he deserved, came to him. He was engaged to create wild animals for various locations on the grounds of the Fair including: moose, elk, mountain lions, polar bears, lions for the Art Building

PROCTOR, Alexander Phimister (Cont'd)

and two equestrian pieces "Indian Scout" and "Mounted Cowboy". From these commissions he was awarded a Rhinehart Paris Scholarship. In the meantime he met Daisy Gerow and they married then sailed for Paris where Proctor studied under Inglebert and Puech, winning a Gold medal for his work shown at the Paris Exposition of 1900. He was called back to New York to make the first models of horses for statues of noted sculptor, Augustus St. Gauden and benefited greatly from a year's work with him. He returned to Paris for three more years before settling in the United States. In the years that followed Alex and Daisy had four sons and four daughters. Proctor continued to win honours for his work including: Gold Medal, St. Louis (1904); Gold Medal, San Francisco (1915); Medal of Honor, Architectural League, New York (1911). His works can be seen at the following places: Robert E. Lee Memorial, Dallas, Texas; Pioneer Mother group, Kansas City; Pioneer Scout and Indian, grounds of Wichita High School East, Wichita, Kansas; colossal Lions for McKinley Monument, Buffalo, N.Y.; Lions in front of Public Library, 5th Avenue, N.Y.C.; Tigers on approach to Princeton University, N.J.; Indian, for park, Lake George, N.Y.; Pioneer Circuit Rider, Salem, Oregon; "Bronco Buster" and "On The Trail", two heroic figures (cowboy and Indian) for the grounds of Denver Civic Centre, Colo.; equestrian statue of Col. Theodore Roosevelt as Rough Rider, Portland, Ore. and others. He is also represented in a number of museums including the National Gallery of Canada by three bronze works "Indian Warrior", "Standing Puma", "Prowling Panther" all acquired by the Gallery in 1909; Metropolitan Museum of Art, N.Y.C.; Corcoran Gallery of Art, Washington, D.C. and elsewhere. Was a member of: Canadian Art Club; National Academy of Design; Architectural League of New York; American Watercolor Society, National Sculpture Society; New York Art Commission. He lived in New York City. Died at Palo Alto, California in 1950 at the age of 88.

References

Canadian Men and Women of the Time, Morgan, Wm. Briggs, Tor., 1912, P. 920

Who's Who 1928, A. & C. Black Ltd., Lond., Eng., 1928, P. 2453

New York Times, N.Y., Feb. 2, 1936 (large photo of Rbt. E. Lee Memorial for City of Dallas)

The Wichita Beacon, Wichita, Kansas, Sunday, Oct. 25, 1931 "Phimister Proctor Is Product of Pioneer Days, Prouder of Marksmanship Than of His Widely-Known Statues" by Guy G. Gentry

clipping, Jan. 29, 1938 "Phimister Proctor, N.A." by Agnes Joynes

Canadian Art, Its Origin and Development by William Colgate, Ryerson, Tor., 1943, P. 75

National Gallery of Canada, Volume 3, Canadian School by R.H. Hubbard, NGC, Ottawa, 1960, P. 356

NGC Info. Forms

PROCTOR, Carol

She studied at the Art Institute of Chicago and settled in Vancouver. An illustrator, her work has appeared in magazines, newspapers and books including children's books. An exhibition of her work took place at the Art Gallery in Woodstock, Ontario in the fall of 1968.

PROCTOR, Carol (Cont'd)

Reference
>Woodstock-Ingersoll Sentinel-Review, Woodstock, Ont., Nov. 6, 1968 "Exhibition of Water Colors Planned"

PROCTOR, Edward D'Arcy
b. 1919

Born in Toronto, Ontario, the son of Albert and Florence (Kemp) Proctor, a self-taught artist he started serious painting in 1969. He is known for his realistic acrylic paintings of town and country scenes, historical places and other subjects which have been exhibited at the juried annual shows of the East Central Ontario Art Association, First Prize (1972) and the Durham Agricultural Fair, First Prize (1973). His solo shows include: Magpie, Port Hope, Ont. (1974); Nancy Poole's Studio, Tor. (1979). His work has become popular with private collectors and one large canvas, "The Liftlock", Peterborough, Ont., commissioned by Ethicon Sutures Limited (subsidiary of Johnson & Johnson) now hangs in the Head Office of Johnson & Johnson in New Jersey, U.S.A. He married Lorna C. Dewar in 1940 and they have two children, Brian (1943) and Sheila (1946). Proctor's recreations include trout fishing, golf, photography, golf course design and maintenance. Lives at Pontypool, Ontario, north of Port Hope. Member of the East Central Ontario Art Association.

References
>Evening Guide, Port Hope, Ont., April, 1974 (photo of Proctor with one of his paintings)
>NGC Info. Form dated Apr. 12, 1974

PROCTOR, Florence Evelyn
1886-

Born in Montreal, Quebec, the daughter of Sir Edward and Lady Kemp, she studied painting in school when she also did outdoor sketching. In 1933 when she was forty-seven, she started doing still lifes with the encouragement of Ronald McRae in Toronto where she had settled. By 1936 she was exhibiting in New York City at the Studio Guild where after viewing her work Thomas Simonton wrote in the *American*, "She finds her models in flowers, sculpture and bric-a-brac. Her paintings flash with color. They have glossy surfaces. They are decorative and presumably intended to be decorative." Carlyle Burrows of the *Herald Tribune* noted, "She has original ideas about composition and has a vast repertory of unusual objects which she combines with inventive taste in her work." She exhibited with the National Association of Women Painters and Sculptors in 1938 and one of her paintings was reproduced in the Toronto *Saturday Night* of the same year.

References
>Art digest, April 1, 1936 "A Canadian Woman Exhibits"
>New York Herald Tribune, N.Y., April 4, 1937 "Notes and Comment on Events in Art" by Carlyle Burrows

PROCTOR, Florence Evelyn (Cont'd)

Saturday Night, Tor., Ont., Mar. 19, 1938 (photo of Proctor's still life "Africa")
NGC Info. Form rec'd May 5, 1934; April 6, 1936

PROKOP, George
b. 1925

Born in Czechoslovakia, his father died in a concentration camp during the Second World War. His guardian, a painter, started giving him lessons when he was fourteen years old. Later he entered the Academy of Fine Arts in Prague where he studied three semesters under Professor Jakub Obrovsky. He won a scholarship in 1946 to study at the École Nationale Supérieure des Beaux-Arts in Paris where he completed three semesters under François Narbonne and François Desnoyer. He returned to Prague in 1948 when his mother took ill. In the meantime all passports were cancelled by the new government who took over in a coup d'etat. He could not return to Paris so he enrolled in the Industrial Art School in Prague where he studied with Professor Joseph Filla, a specialist in the cubist style of art. The political climate cut short his study and he worked at painting backdrops in a theatre and later made cartoons for a film production company but finally had to flee his country through West Germany and was allowed to come to Canada in 1949 where he first worked as a farm labourer. He lived in Chatham until moving to Blenheim in 1968. He married in 1953 and became an employee working nights at International Harvester in Chatham. In the afternoons he did his painting in his Blenheim home studio. His work has been exhibited in Prague, Brno and Pardubice in Czechoslovakia; in Paris, France; at Stuttgart, West Germany and in Cleveland, Detroit and Bridgeton in United States. He has also exhibited his paintings at the Thames Theatre Art Gallery in Chatham where his work was well received. He donated a monumental mural to St. Mary's Roman Catholic Church in Blenheim entitled "Flight into Egypt" in gratitude to God and Canada for his good life here. The mural is triangular in shape (18 ft. long at the base and 7 ft. 9 in. high). He is also represented in the Chatham City hall by a painting entitled "Prayer For Peace" done during the Vietnam War. The Prokops have three sons and one daughter.

References
> *Windsor Star*, Ont., April 26, 1969 "Artist's donated mural gesture for freedom" by Blair McKinnon
> *London Free Press*, Ont., Nov. 4, 1972 "Fighting words in 1948 — Chatham man combines art, factory job" by Win Miller
> *Chatham News*, Ont., Nov. 3, 1972 "One-man Show Readied" (photo of Prokop beside his mural "Flight into Egypt")
> Ibid, Nov. 18, 1972 "Chatham Buys Oil Painting"
> Ibid, Nov. 28, 1972 "Artist's Gift To Chatham" (photo of Prokop and his donated painting "Prayer For Peace" with city officials)

PROSPERO, Marie
b.(c) 1939

An Etobicoke, Ontario, painter who does landscapes and portraits which she exhibits with the Etobicoke Art Group of which she is a member. She has been painting since 1954. She demonstrated her painting skills at the C.N.E. in 1979.

Reference
> *Toronto Star*, Ont., Aug. 23, 1979 "Mother of 7 takes break with easel and palette" by Frances Kelley

---

PROSSER, Harvey Thomas
b.(c) 1930

Born in Ottawa, he attended Children's Classes at the National Gallery of Canada and subsequently studied art three years at the Ottawa High School of Commerce with Robert Darby; advanced drawing and painting at Ottawa Technical High School with Robert Walker; Studio Commercial Art at Fisher Park High School with Robert Walker; Portraiture and Colour Harmony with Ernest Fosbery, R.C.A.; Drawing and Painting with Robert Hyndman; Studio Design Apprenticeship with the Canadian Bank Note Company Limited under the direction of Master Designer Herman H. Schwartz (5 years); Advanced Art Communication, University of Ottawa with Gerald Trottier; Advanced Figure Drawing with Robert Hyndman. As Staff Designer for the Canadian Bank Note Company Limited he designed close to forty stamps for Canada Post.

Reference
> Document from artist, May 25, 1978

PROULX, Anne
b. 1923

Born in Timmins, Ontario she began painting in 1947 and attended part-time classes under Jean-Paul Lemieux at the École des Beaux-Arts in Quebec City (1947-49) and from 1955-57 exhibited with the Noranda Arts & Crafts group and the Northern Ontario Artists Association and won top awards for her work in shows at Timmins, Kirkland Lake, North Bay, Rouyn, Sudbury and Sault Ste. Marie. She has moved a number of times to follow her husband in his work and has been active in community art groups. Her first solo show was held at Le Café des Artistes, Montreal in 1960 and subsequent solo shows as follows: Le Café des Artistes (2nd show, 1960); Holiday Inn, Côte de Liesse, Mtl. (1961); Holiday Inn, Port Credit (1965) and elsewhere. Living in Port Credit, Ontario in 1967.

References
> *Globe & Mail*, Tor., Ont., Oct. 19, 1964 (article on Anne Proulx)
> *Port Credit Weekly*, Ont., July 15, 1965 "Local Artists Display Work At Lindsay"
> Ibid, Dec. 9, 1965 "Local Artist Has One Man Show"
> *Globe & Mail*, Ont., Oct. 3, 1967 "Arranges exhibits — Artist tries to sell Canadians to Buffalo" by Kay Kritzwiser

PROULX, Anne (Cont'd)

Port Credit Weekly, Ont., Oct. 11, 1967 "Mrs. Anne Proulx" (becomes coordinator for Sisti Galleries)

NGC Info. Form rec'd 1961

PROULX, Carol

b.(c) 1946

Originally from Jonquière, Quebec, he began his study of fine arts at the C.E.G.E.P. there. His meeting with Armand Vaillancourt and Charles Daudelin in Montreal began his serious interest in sculpture. He studied and worked in Montreal for six years. He was involved with animation. His chance to work in sculpture came when he was restoring murals by Jordi Bonet for the Arvida City Hall. He then did the 50th Anniversary monument and his sculptures followed. He has worked in wood, granite, aluminum and cement. Of special interest is his fine work in wood from which he creates mythical personages which escape all traditions, often mysterious female beings. He is a sculptor who suggests outlines. The material which he chooses has much to do with his conception of the subject. He has done a series of statuettes of the female body, the human form and of couples, which were well received during their showing. His shows include: two-man, Crafts Boutique, La Chaouinière, Chicoutimi (1974); solo, Arche de Jonquière, Jonquière (1977); solo, Arvida City Hall (1980); Chicoutimi Symposium of Environmental Sculpture (1980).

References

Progrès Dimanche, Chicoutimi, Qué., Sept. 24, 1977 "Carol Proulx — Une approche essentiellement sensitive" par Yvon Paré

Ibid, Sept. 8, 1974 "Arts — Quand deux sculpteurs 'pigrassent'!" par Claude Genest

Le Quotidien, Chicoutimi, Que., Jan. 12, 1980 "'Un artiste doit vivre" Texte: Yvon Paré/Photos: Paulo Rousseau

Ibid, Apr. 3, 1980 "Sculpture-synthèse pour le oui" (photo of Proulx clowning beside one of his wood sculptures)

Ibid, July 22, 1980 "Arts et spectacles — Un tracteur a le dernier mot sur Carol Proulx" par Yvon Paré

Ibid, Mar. 15, 1980 "Un dialogue matière/artiste" par Yvon Paré

PROULX, Elyse

An artist from Quebec City, she is known for her serigraphed landscapes which have been described as soft, luminous, agile, delicate with thin dancing lines. She has exhibited her work at Atelier de Réalisations Graphiques, St. Jean, Quebec (1976); Galerie Rodrigue LeMay, Ottawa (1976) and elsewhere.

References

notice — Atelier de Réalisations Graphiques, St. Jean, Qué., 1976

Le Droit, Ottawa, Ont., Sept. 11, 1976 "Les imprimés — Une jeune histoire d'amour" par Pierre Pelletier

---

PROULX, Laure

A Sherbrooke, Quebec artist she has been studying art seriously for a number of years and has spent much of her free time painting. Mother of seven children she is very active in parish associations and the St. Jean Baptiste Society.

Reference
> *La Tribune*, Sherbrooke, Qué., 11 Mars, 1964 "Mme L. Proulx attend beaucoup de la S.S.J.B. pour la femme. . ."

PROULX, Martial

Originally from Baieville, Quebec, he is known for his enamels on copper. His subjects include flowers, landscapes, sunsets which he depicts in hot colours often enhanced by black. He prefers bare expressive lines stripped of structured geometric forms. He has been teaching plastic arts for the St. François Regional School Commission. He also conducts workshops in ceramics in Drummondville at the Centre Garceau, St. Jean Baptiste Recreation Centre and at his home. He exhibited in a two-man show in 1977 at the Caisse populaire St. Pierre, Drummondville. Lives in Drummondville.

Reference
> *La Tribune*, Sherbrooke, Que., Feb. 14, 1977 "Drummondville — Une exposition dans une caisse"

PROULX, Mike

He exhibited his interesting and colourful work at several places including the SAW Gallery, Ottawa, during July of 1974 when W.Q. Ketchum noted, "The display is introduced as 'Eyes and Mind' and consists of three-dimensional paintings. The artist uses both oils and acrylics. Intricate patterns are followed. In one of his works he uses bottle tops imbedded in paint on a plywood base obtaining an unusual effect. In his creations he uses string in some cases and in others metal. . ." Subsequently he exhibited his electric photographs at the David Mirvish Gallery, Toronto (Upstairs) during November of 1976.

References
> *Ottawa Journal*, Ont., July 26, 1974 "3-dimensional paintings" by W.Q. Ketchum
> Exhibition notice, DM Upstairs Gallery, Tor., Nov. 30, 1976 — Michel Proulx — ". . .an exhibition of electric photographs"

PROULX, Rachel

She is known for her figurative paintings in pastel tones including nudes and flowers which have been exhibited at Alexis Nihon Plaza, Montreal (1972)

PROULX, Rachel (Cont'd)

and in a solo show at the Stable Gallery of the Montreal Museum of Fine Arts (1972).

References

The Gazette, Mtl., July 20, 1972 "Students at Alexis Nihon Plaza — Art moves into the light where the people are" by Sharon McLeod

Montreal Star, Que., Feb. 17, 1973 "Stable Gallery — Rachel Proulx"

La Presse, Mtl., Feb. 17, 1973 "Ambiguïté du modèle"

PROULX, Rolland E.

Born in Ottawa, Ontario he studied and painted in Ottawa, Montreal, Vancouver and Toronto. He held his first solo show at the Elmdale Theatre Gallery, Ottawa in 1966 when his work was described by Carl Weiselberger as follows, "The artist experiments a good deal with simplifying forms such as circles, cog-and-wheel-like shapes. . .his color schemes are bright, and applied in such a manner that they give the impression of transparency — almost as if painted on glass. His favorite colors are luminous blues, greens and reds, justifying somehow such fanciful titles as 'Carmina Burana' (a tribute to composer Carl Orff), 'Firmanent', a bold conglomerate of balloon-like shapes in gay blues and greens." In 1967 he received a Canada Council grant to travel and study in Europe and in 1969 was awarded a Quebec government grant. One of his later shows in Toronto was a series of acrylic paintings entitled "Other Worlds". Proulx became director of a new gallery in the lobby of La Cantinette Restaurant in Toronto which featured such artists as John Palchinski, Avemarie, David Kaye, Olive Blewchamp, Mimi Shulman, Della Burford and Dale Bertrand and others. He was involved in various projects to do with the Recreation and Parks Service of Montreal. In his painting his solo shows include: Carleton University, Science Bldg., Ottawa (1970); Le Gobelet, Mtl. (1973); Le Centre Culturel de Verdun, Mtl. (1975); New Academic Bldg., Victoria University, Tor. (1976).

References

Ottawa Journal, Ont., Jan. 8, 1966 "Contemporary Art Show at Theatre"

Ottawa Citizen, Ont., Jan. 13, 1966 "Ottawa painter displays oil abstracts on nature" by Carl Weiselberger

Le Droit, Ottawa, Ont., Jan. 15, 1966 "Fantaisie et recherche chez Rolland-E. Proulx" par Denise Côté

Ottawa Journal, Ont., Jan. 29, 1970 "Proulx Art Show Opened"

La Presse, Mtl., Qué., Dec. 23, 1972 "La 'Féerie sous la Neige' — loisirs et récréation" par Dollard Morin

Montréal-Matin, Que., Nov. 27, 1973 (exhibit at "Le Gobelet")

La Presse, Mtl., Mar. 5, 1975 "Expositions"

Globe & Mail, Tor., Ont., Dec. 3, 1975 (Rolland Proulx director of new art gallery)

Exhibition notice — Rolland E. Proulx "Acrylic Paintings", New Academic Building, Victoria College, 73 Queen's Park Crescent East, Tor., Oct. 18-Nov. 5th, 1976

PROUSE, G.J.

Born in England, he received his art education in London and exhibited there in the National Portrait Gallery. He came to Canada in 1946 and was active in the Toronto area. He exhibited his Northern Ontario landscapes, seascapes of Maine (U.S.A.) and scenes done by him in England at the North York Public Library in the winter of 1961. He also exhibited his work with the Ontario Society of Artists and the Canadian National Exhibition.

Reference

Willowdale-Lansing Enterprise, Ont., Feb. 9, 1961 "New Exhibit of Paintings At The Public Library"

PROUSE, Rod

b. 1945

Born in England the son of William Prouse, who did war art while serving in the R.A.F. In 1947 the Prouses moved to Toronto, Canada where Rod grew up and attended high school then the Ontario College of Art where he studied drawing, painting and print-making under Carl Schaefer, John Alfsen, Eric Freifeld, William Roberts, Gustav Weisman, Frederick Hagan, graduating in 1968. He worked for a brief period as a book illustrator then commercial artist but disliked the rigid routine which tied him to the city. He broke free and worked at his art by supplementing his income truck driving, selling, teaching and carpentry while travelling in North America from coast to coast and from the Arctic to the tropics. In 1975 he moved to a farmhouse 40 miles from Halifax. His father had also moved there to Hubbards and the two of them exhibited their Maritime scenery at the Manuge Galleries in Halifax. That same year Rod returned to Toronto and felt his art needed a change of direction. He abandoned using brushes and turned to working directly on paper with pencil, pastel and conte. Pleased with his results he accumulated enough of this new work for a solo show at the Canadian Fine Arts Gallery, Toronto, in 1977 when James Purdie noted, "Prouse didn't stop to analyse this new shorthand that seemed to be emerging from unknown regions of his mind. He just worked and kept on working until he was sure he really had found the personal expression that the active search of 10 years failed to release. 'My work was rapid and continuous,' he says, 'It was direct, an immediate transfer of the moment contained in the scene. Now I find that the faster I work the more valid the piece becomes' . . .Prouse has a hit show on his hands, and it's his first solo performance in Toronto: 34 landscapes in pencil, pastel and conte. . .fragments of Ontario streams, rocks and hills — but original and astonishingly harmonious in execution." Viewing his work a year later at the same gallery Purdy made these favourable comments, "Rod Prouse, whose pastel drawings with water-color are among the most accomplished and inventive of their kind to be produced in Canada since the death of David Milne, appears to be moving effortlessly from strength to strength. . . .Among the works is a series of 20 made by Prouse at this year's Canadian National Exhibition. They are so orchestrated, so full of controlled exuberance and dancing energies of line and color, that most viewers, myself included, find the pictures a more rewarding experience by far than the Ex itself has ever been. This come to think of it, is

PROUSE, Rod (Cont'd)

one of the things art is supposed to do, isolate the essences of joy and movement from the clutter of experience and give them a permanent existence on their own terms. Prouse achieves this with line and color applied with such rapidity and apparent ease that the great explosion of crowd energy, Toronto's annual farewell party for summer, seems to echo yet from wall to wall in the gallery. The Ex series should go a long way toward establishing Prouse on the Toronto scene as something more than a passing phenomenon. It shows, among other things, that drawing alone is not his only major skill. He can also make color dance to a new set of tunes." Subsequently Prouse's impressions of the Canadian National Exhibition (100th Year Anniversary) were hung at the McMichael Gallery at Kleinburg, Ontario, where they were very well received. He is represented in the collection of the Metropolitan Toronto Library (Canadian History Section) and in many private collections both in Canada and the United States. His shows include: Two-man (with father), Manuge Galleries, Halifax (1976, solo 1979); Solo, Canadian Fine Arts Gallery, Tor. (Jan. 1977, Oct. 1977); Father and Son Gallery, Chester, N.S.

References

Halifax Mail Star, N.S., Sept. 2, 1976 "Paintings by the Prouses, father and son"

Globe & Mail, Tor., Ont., Jan. 25, 1977 "Art — An artist liberated by discarding brushes" by James Purdie

Ibid, Oct. 1, 1977 "At The Galleries — Colors dancing to a new set of tunes" by James Purdie

Halifax Mail Star, N.S., Sept. 15, 1979 "Prouse exhibition opens next week"

Halifax Chronicle Herald, Sept. 20, 1979 "Watercolours and Pastels" (photo of Prouse's painting "Harbour, Halifax" being viewed during his show at Manuge Galleries)

Biographical material from The Canadian Fine Arts Gallery Ltd., Tor.

PROUSE, William
b.(c) 1914

Born in England, he studied art in London at Southampton Row and Bolt Art Schools and under prominent water colourists. He served with the R.A.F. during the Second World War and part of that time was commissioned to paint various war activities. In 1946 he came to Toronto, Canada and over the years visited Nova Scotia on painting trips. In 1972 he moved to Hubbards, Nova Scotia, where he now spends most of the year painting. He has exhibited with his son Rod Prouse at the Manuge Galleries in Halifax. He has participated in many group shows in England and Canada and also at the Father and Son Gallery, Chester, N.S.

Reference

Halifax Chronicle Herald, Nova Scotia, Sept. 2, 1976 "Paintings by the Prouses, father and son"

PROVENCHER, Paul
b.(c) 1901

A painter, photographer and forestry explorer for 35 years with the Ontario Paper Company and the Quebec North Shore Paper Company, he carried

PROVENCHER, Paul (Cont'd)

portable painting materials which included sketch book and water colours. He learned many secrets of survival in the bush from the Indians and in 1953 was requested by the Canadian Army to give a course in forest survival to commandos. In the forest he carried his 16 mm camera on the butt of his rifle and he entered his photos in different competititons. His films were to be presented in 1966 at the Camping Salon, Centre d'Art de Manicouagan, about sixty miles north of Baie Comeau. His paintings and photos evoke scenes and memories of the great Canadian North. He married a Quebec girl and brought up his family in the forest.

References
>*Photo-Journal*, Mtl., April 13 to 20, 1966 "Il mangeait de la panse surie de caribou! — Paul Provencher, notre Tarzan canadien" par Pol Chantraine
>*La Côte Nord Journal*, Baie Comeau, Qué., June 15, 1966 "Avis Aux Amateurs D'Art" (photo of Provencher with one of his paintings)

PROVOST, Aurette

Born in Montreal, she studied drawing with Simone Dénéchaud and Cécile Gravel Raymond. She showed artistic tendencies and interests in music, poetry and drawing at an early age. She later turned her attentions to poetry and then painting. Mainly self-taught in painting, her subjects have been realistic, done in fanciful, symbolic, poetic and surrealistic styles and also non-figurative with all its variations. She is known for her portraits and still lifes which she presents in modern and traditional methods. She has been cited for her concept of space, clarity, vigorous drawing and cleanness of statement in her work. She held her first solo show at the Ritz Carlton, Montreal in 1949 and again in 1955, then held subsequent solo shows at the following: Salon de La Maison Modèle, Mtl. (1957); at the home of Mr. & Mrs. Robert Allard, Bois-des-Filions, Que. (1957); Salon of the Statler Hilton Hotel, Hartford, Conn. (1959); a series of 14 pictures entitled "Vacances Interplanétaires" in Quebec City warmly received by the Quebec Cultural Ministry and the French Consular Corps at Quebec (1962); "Matinées Bonne Entente", Sainte-Foy, Quebec (1964); "L'oiseau d'Or", Musée du Québec (1966). Her series "Vancances Interplanétaires" which she created between 1947 and 1960 foresaw the advances of science of our era. Some of her group shows include: Salon d'Automne des Amis de l'Art, Mtl. (1950); Salon du Printemps, Mtl. (1951); Salon de l'Exposition Provinciale, Que. (1953, 54, 56); "La Matière chante", Galerie Antoine, Mtl. (1954); Salon des Jeunesses Musicales du Canada, St-Hyacinthe, Que. (1958); Salon d'Été des Jardins du Carré Dominion, Mtl. (1959); Festival de Peintures du Carnaval de Québec, Que. (1960); VII Salon International de Vichy, Vichy, France (1960) when she was awarded the "Diplôme d'Honneur", Prix Hors Concours, which was presented by C.S. Daupin, Chevalier de la Légion d'Honneur; IX Salon International de Vichy (1962). Her other honours include: "Femme Peintre de l'Année", L'Univers de la Femme, Mtl. (1963); Prix Hors Concours lors de l'Expo "L'oiseau d'Or" for two compositions inspired by mineralogical specimens (1966); Guest Exhibitor, Cercle Culturel de Château-Richer, Quebec (1968). Member: Société des Artistes Professionnels du Québec.

PROVOST, Aurette (Cont'd)

References

Unidentified clipping, 1960 "La Femme — au Foyer et dans le Monde — Aurette Provost artiste-peintre" par Cécile Brosseau

La Presse, Mtl., July 28, 1961 "Avec Aurette Provost — vous vivrez de beauté à travers la peinture" par Nicole Mongeau

Quebec Chronicle-Telegraph, Nov. 13, 1962 "Artist Deplores Lack Of Galleries In Canada"

Ibid, Sept. 21, 1963 "Chosen Painter Of The Year"

Le Banlieusard, Ste. Foy, Que., Oct. 9, 1963 (photo of artist and caption announcing that she will write an article on the arts for *Le Banlieusard*)

Aurette Provost — biographical information

PROVOST, Jean

b.(c) 1926

Born in Montreal, he began painting as a youth of ten and later studied art at the École des Beaux-Arts. He held his first solo show in Sherbrooke in 1948. He is a figurative and figurative-abstract painter of a wide variety of subjects including landscapes and wildlife. Other solo shows of his work in Quebec include those at Mont-Joli (1958), at Matane (1964), at Knowlton (1966) and at Salle des Chevaliers de Colomb, Boulevard Rosemont, Mtl. (1967). Provost is well known in the Eastern Townships especially on the French radio networks. He was an announcer on CHEF and CHLT-TV in Sherbrooke, CKBL in Matane and CHLC in Hauterive. In 1965 he became an instructor at the Cowansville Institute where he was responsible for the entire educational programme for the inmates including art instruction. In this capacity he has become much respected by those in his charge. Living in Knowlton, Quebec in 1966.

References

Leader-Mail, Grandby, Que., June 22, 1966 "Jean Provost holds art exhibit at Knowlton's La Galerie"

Progrès de Rosemont, Mtl., Qué., Nov. 8, 1967 "Exposition de peinture"

Nouvelles de l'Est, Mtl., Qué., Nov. 9, 1967 "Exposition de peintures"

PRUDENTE, Steve

A Winnipeg sculptor, he exhibited his work in a two-man show with sculptor Ted Luba at the Plug-In Gallery, Winnipeg, when John W. Graham noted, "Both artists have an excellent sense of the power of the profile silhouette and its ability to unify and give their work a real sense of presence. Because of this, their exhibition had a surprising sense of unity which overcame any sense of duality which the dimensional contrast of the full scale constructions of Luba and the miniature images of Prudente might easily have produced. . . .Expressive symbolists, both artists make great use of their materials and techniques. Steve Prudente achieves his sense of monumentality by the miniaturized detail and encrusting of agglomerate forms upon otherwise simple masses or clearly discernible structural models. In many of his pieces there is a deliberate sense of

PRUDENTE, Steve (Cont'd)

time lapse or suspension. The Three Bricks presents a sequence of increasing detail from insects to embryonic extrusions to fungal growths, the whole endowed with a green patina. Gotterdammerung is a great symbolic and monumental pyloned gateway, while Parade Through a Teeming City is like a kind of frozen hysteria or pandemonium. Many of the formal shapes found in his sculptural fantastics were also to be seen in a series of paintings in which the spatter color overlays, with their submarine images, served as a visual link between the implied monumentality of his sculptures to the actual monumentality of Ted Luba's constructions."

References

Winnipeg Free Press, Man., May 7, 1975 "A Critique By John W. Graham — Stress Implied In Sculptures"

Exhibition notice — Ted Luba and Steve Prudente at Plug-In, Wpg., March 14-April 2, 1975

PRUD'HOMME, André

Born in Montreal, a self-taught sculptor he works mainly in stone but also wood. He creates as well, ceramics, enamel and gold plate jewellery and engravings. In his stone sculpture he carves his shapes with a chisel and his work shows some influences derived from Eskimo sculpture although he takes a different path to arrive at comparable results. His work shows simplicity, monumentality, generosity of form with a discreet and restrained human presence. He travelled in Europe for two short periods. His solo shows include those at Galerie Libre, Mtl. (1965, 1967) and he has participated in group shows which include: Université de Montréal, Mtl. (1957); "Confrontation '65" and "Confrontation '66", Mtl.; "Sculpteurs du Québec" at Musée d'Art Contemporain, Mtl. (1968). He was one of seven artists participating in the production of Jacques Godbout's book *Salut, Galarneau!* issued in a limited edition of 150 copies at $525 a copy.

References

Le Devoir, Mtl., Qué., April 17, 1965 "Les Beaux-arts" par Laurent Lamy (solo show at Galerie Libre)

La Presse, Mtl., Qué., April 17, 1965 "André Prud'homme" (solo show at Galerie Libre)

Ibid, February 19, 1977 "Salut Galarneau! de Jacques Godbout — Sept artistes, un livre d'art" par Nicole Charest

Biographical sheet, NGC Library's file on artist

PRYDE, Ian

b.(c) 1949

Born in Toronto he attended commercial and fine art courses at Sheridan College of Applied Arts and Technology in Oakville and after graduation he moved to St. Catharines, Ontario. A sculptor, graphic artist and painter he is known for his murals which he has painted for the public Libraries in St. Catharines and other places in the city. One of Pryde's ambitions was to

1871

PRYDE, Ian (Cont'd)

decorate the exteriors of old buildings in bright cheerful designs. Describing the artist when viewing one of his murals, Joan Phillips noted, "Ian does 'everything and anything' when it comes to art around the library. . .love of primary colors is evident in the mural with his use of yellow mainly and in the posters and pamphlets and other graphics on the walls of the library."

Reference
St. Catharines Standard, Ont., July 20, 1972 "World of Art by Joan Phillips — Painting Colorful Murals Is His Thing — Our Library Benefits From Artist's Work"

PRYNE, Rolf E.
1914-1979

Born in Toronto, Ontario, of Anglo-Saxon and Pennsylvania Dutch descent, he completed his Senior Matriculation and in 1934 commenced employment as a commercial artist with Legge Brothers, a Toronto engraving house. He then moved over to Rapid Grip and Batten Limited as illustrator-designer for the next eleven years (1934-45). In 1945 with two partners he founded the firm of Art Associates Limited specializing in advertising, art design and commercial photography working with ad agencies and advertisers. He became President and senior partner of Pryne Scott, a subsidiary of Art Associates Limited, specializing in all phases of corporate design. In 1968 he retired from active participation and ultimately relinquished all duties and responsibilities in 1970 when he turned to full-time painting. He began working in water colours in rural southern Ontario and on the East Coast. He held his first solo show at Nancy Poole's Studio in 1973 both in London and Toronto, Ontario, and subsequent solo shows there in 1974, 1975, 1976, 1977; also at Galerie de L'Esprit, Mtl. (1975); Saskatoon Art Gallery (1976 circulating); Brampton Public Library and Art Gallery (1977); Downstairs Gallery, Edmonton (1977) when Paul Duval in the introduction to the exhibition folder wrote, "Rolf Pryne has emerged during the past few years as one of Canada's most able figurative painters. He first came to prominence as a water colourist of superb technical ability, with a sure and free calligraphy and an outstanding tonal sense. His earlier career as a commercial illustrator has supplied him with an unusually sure control of technique, a control that he has now extended to the demanding medium of egg tempera. Pryne's themes have ranged from Mennonite elders to nudes, but whatever he portrays, his compositions are marked by a notable affection and conviction." Pryne was preparing for his sixth solo show at Nancy Poole's Studio at the time of his death. A memorial exhibition of his work was held at Nancy Poole's Studio in February of 1980. He participated in the following group shows: "Through the Looking Glass", Realism, Art Gallery of Ontario, Tor. (1975); T-D Centre "On View", Visual Arts Ontario travelling show (1976); "Spectrum Canada" Montreal/Kingston, R.C.A. travelling (1976); C.S.P.W.C. 51st Annual Exhibition, circulating (1976); O.S.A., First Canadian Place, Tor., juried (1976); "Ontario Now", Art Gallery of Hamilton and Kitchener-Waterloo Art Gallery (1977); O.S.A. juried travelling exhibition, throughout Ontario (1977); "Realism in Canada", Norman Mackenzie Art Gallery, circulating, extension (1977). Pryne was a member of the C.S.P.W.C. and O.S.A. He is represented in the collection of Rothman's of Pall Mall Canada Limited and many private collections.

PRYNE, Rolfe E. (Cont'd)

References
London Free Press, Ont., Nov. 5, 1973 (article by L. Crawford)
Globe & Mail, Tor., Dec. 7, 1974 (article by K. Kritzwiser)
Ibid, Apr. 5, 1975 (article by J. Purdie)
Montreal Star, Que., Dec. 3, 1975 (article by H. Lehmann)
Prince Albert Herald, Sask., May 1, 1976 "Artist's Works On Display" (photo of water colours on display)
Leader-Post, Regina, Sask., June 7, 1976 "Photography and painting well mixed in exhibition" by James Roe
Globe & Mail, Tor., 1976 "Other Galleries" (notes on Pryne's nudes)
The Index of Ontario Artists, Ed. by H. Wolfe, Vis. Arts Ont./Ont. Assoc. of Art Gal., 1978, P. 223
Royal Canadian Academy of Arts, Exhibitions and Members, 1880-1979 by Evelyn de R. McMann, Univ. Tor. Press, Tor., 1981, P. 334

PSUTKA, Frank
b.(c) 1955

A Kitchener, Ontario artist, the son of Carl and Sophie Psutka, he studied art at Cameron Heights Collegiate in Kitchener and following graduation turned to full-time painting. He is especially interested in portrait work and in 1978 completed a 60″ by 38″ portrait in oils of Frank Groff (known as the General) who for a number of years worked as an unofficial school crossing guard in Kitchener until his death in 1978. Frank also does portraits in pencil and scrape-a-board.

Reference
Kitchener-Waterloo Record, Ont., May 2, 1978 "The Bridgeport General is captured on canvas" by Trish Wilson

PUCHTA, Siegfried Rudolf (Siggy Puchta)
b. 1933

Born in Greiz, Germany, he studied woodcarving there from 1948 to 1951. He settled in Canada in 1953 and became a Canadian Citizen in 1958. Once in Canada he taught himself stone carving mainly working in granite. He also studied modelling and sculpture evenings at Northern Vocational School, Toronto with Dora de Pedery-Hunt. Puchta's work includes monument making (often religious figures) and bronze portraits and figures. His work is mainly realistic. He held his first solo show at the Craft Gallery of the Canadian Handicraft Guild (1976) and subsequent solo shows at: Shaw-Rimmington Gallery, Tor. (1968); The Guild Inn, Scarborough, Ont. where he worked and exhibited at the Old Sculpture Studio (1969); Eaton's Fine Art Gallery, Tor. (1976); Madison Gallery, N.Y.C. (1977); Eaton's Art Gallery, Toronto Eaton Centre (two-man, 1980) and in the following group shows: International Exhibition of Contemporary Medals, Cracow, Poland (1975); Olympic Coin Tour, National Sports Centre (1976, travelling show); "Foreign Friends of Acapulco", Annual Exhibition, Acapulco Hilton Hotel, Mexico (1971, other

PUCHTA, Siegfried Rudolf (Siggy Puchta) (Cont'd)

years including 1976 when he won 1st, 2nd & 3rd prizes) and in shows of the O.S.A. His commissions include: The Sovereign Award for the Jockey Club of Canada (1976); portrait, Hilroy Envelopes & Stationery Ltd., Tor. (1977). Member of the Sculptors' Society of Canada. Lives in Toronto.

References
    NGC Info. Form, 1961
    Document from artist, 1971
    The Index of Ontario Artists, Ed. H. Wolfe, Vis. Arts Ont./Ont. Assoc. of Art Gal., 1978, P. 223

PUGEN, Diane (Diane Fern Pugen Burton)
b. 1943

Born in Toronto, Ontario, she studied at the Art Institute of Chicago and the Art Students' League, New York and returned to Toronto where she settled and held her first solo show at the Pollock Gallery in 1966. She established herself as a printmaker known for her lithographs, etchings and for her charcoal and graphite drawings and paintings. Viewing her work at Studio 3 in Hamilton in 1979 Grace Inglis in the *Hamilton Spectator* noted, "Diane Pugen enjoys working in several different areas. Her draughtsmanship is strong. . . The show has large spacious Ontario wilderness drawings in charcoal — spare, open, strong on composition and understood landscape conventions. She does these on location. . .here is a fine space captured. There are also detailed drawings in a semi-surrealist vein combining figures, landscape, abstract design. . .these are strong, resolute works, fun to look at, with spirit and wit. The best of them combine the energy in the gouache abstracts with the structure of the drawings." Pugen teaches at the Toronto School of Art, the University of Toronto life drawing classes and Arts Sake Incorporated which she founded with her husband in 1977. Pugen and Burton met in 1965 on their way to classes at the New School of Art; she was a part-time model working to help support her print-making and he a teacher. Burton mentioned he was looking for an etching press and Pugen said she happened to own one. When viewing her press, Burton discovered she was a serious and proficient artist. They married in 1970 and Maihyet, their daughter was born in 1971 (see Frank Rasky's article in the *Sunday Star*, Sept. 24, 1978). Diane has participated in many shows since 1966 including these later ones: Hart House Art Gallery, Tor. (solo, 1976); Upper Level Gallery, North Bay, Ont. (solo, 1978); Margot Samuel Gallery, Oshawa, Ont. ("By Women", group show c. 1978) ("From Life", group show, May, 1979) (four A.C.T. artists, June, 1979); A.C.T. Gallery, Tor. (Pugen/Van Damme, 1979); Studio 3, Hamilton, Ont. ("Hamilton The City", four artists, June, 1979) (Pugen/Van Damme, September, 1979) (seven artists, November, 1979); The Isaacs Gallery, Tor. ("Ceramics" 12 artists, 1979). Her "Elephantasy" a graphite and collage work was reproduced in Jerrold Morris' *100 Years of Canadian Drawings*. She shares studio space in Toronto with her husband.

References
    Globe & Mail, Tor., Ont., Mar. 5, 1966 (note on her solo show at Pollock Gallery)
    The North Bay Nugget, Feb. 4, 1978 "The Intaglio never stops" by Bobbi Eberle (Pugen shares

PUGEN, Diane (Diane Fern Pugen Burton) (Cont'd)

expertise with 14 artists — photo-story)

Sunday Star, Tor., Ont., Sept. 24, 1978 "Garterbeltmania got her — The Other Half" by Frank Rasky

Oshawa Times, Ont., May 24, 1979 "From Life at Samuel gallery"

Ibid, May 31, 1979 "The ACT opens at Samuel gallery"

Ibid, June 8, 1979 "Four Toronto artists at Samuel gallery"

Hamilton Spectator, Ont., June 23, 1979 ". . .Hamilton as art subject"

Ibid, Sept. 15, 1979 "Artviews — Two artists with contrasting styles" by Grace Inglis

100 Years of Canadian Drawings by Jerrold Morris, Methuen, Tor., 1980, P. 151

The Index of Ontario Artists, Ed. H. Wolfe, Vis. Arts Ont./Ont. Assoc. of Art Gal., 1978, P. 38

PUGH, Dene

She spends most of each year at her small tourist camp "Tonomo" on the Marten River in the Temagami area and there paints landscapes in the changing seasons. Her home is in North Bay where she has been active with the North Bay Art Association and was the first member of the group to have a solo show at the Upper Level Gallery (1976). She also exhibited at the Manamek Gallery, Northgate Shopping Centre and Railton Studio & Camera Shop, North Bay. Originally from Burlington, Ontario she became active in the promotion and establishment of nursery schools and day care centres for pre-schoolers. The mother of five (four daughters and a son) she creates her pictures with palette knife using oils.

Reference

North Bay Nugget, Ont., Nov. 19, 1976 "Meet the artist and her landscapes tonight" by Rosalie Little

---

PULEY, Geraldine Mae (Mrs.) (Gery Puley)
b. 1925

Born in Summerland, B.C., she is from a family of artists and musicians. She played violin and piano and studied voice. Later she became more interested in the visual arts. She attended the Calgary Collegiate Institute and the Alberta Institute of Art and Technology. She travelled east in 1946 and studied at the Ontario College of Art with Fred Hagan, Rowley Murphy and others. She also studied at the Doon School of Fine Arts with Carl Schaefer, Henry Masson and John Martin; Art Students' League of New York and the Dundas Valley School of Arts. Painting a wide variety of subjects in water colour, acrylic and oils she is especially known for her portraits of people, old houses, historic buildings, barns and orchards. Viewing her work in 1975 Jenny Sheppard in the *Hamilton Spectator* noted, ". . .she. . .works primarily in watercolor. It is a medium which she handles with very great sensitivity and delicacy. Pastel tones, diffuse and sometimes barely there characterize the paintings as a group and yet occasionally perhaps, along the edge of a flower petal, they are focussed into rich, vibrant colors. . . .Mrs. Puley is drawn towards natural subjects, flowers, landscapes and trees, and she is also fascinated by old houses which

PULEY, Geraldine Mae (Mrs.) (Gery Puley) (Cont'd)

have suffered the ravages of time. They are all subjects which admirably lend themselves to the creation of the kind of mood pictures which modern photographers love to make. Mrs. Puley's approach is in fact to some extent photographic. She uses the selective focus technique which blurs and mutates color and forms in background and sometimes foreground in order to subtly emphasize a detail of especial beauty. In spite of the illusion of profuse detail, it is really the understatement of line, form and color to just the right degree which characterizes Mrs. Puley's work. It is an attractive show, particularly appealing, I should think, to those of contemplative disposition with perhaps just a hint of the romantic." Her solo shows include: Beckett Gallery, Hamilton, Ont. (1967); Damkjar-Burton Gallery, Hamilton, Ont. (1972); Burlington Central Library (1972); Alice Peck Gallery, Burlington, Ont. (1973, 1979); Peel Museum & Art Gallery, Brampton, Ont. (1974); Art Gallery of Hamilton, Ont. (1975); Oakville Centennial Gallery, Ont. (1978); Cultural Centre, Burlington, Ont. (1979); Shaw-Rimmington Gallery, Tor. (1979). Her awards include: Central Ontario Art Association, Best Drawing (1965), Best In Show (1972); Tom Thomson Memorial Gallery, Gen. Marine Hospital Award (1972); Burlington Kaleidoscope, Judges Choice (1972/73); C.S.P.W.C. Hamilton Spectator Award (1973). A member of the C.S.P.W.C. she has exhibited in many shows with this Society also with the Central Ontario Arts Association (Director, 1969). Her other activities include: Adviser, Burlington Fine Arts Assoc.; Instructor: Oakville Art Society, Ontario Department of Education, and Sheridan College. She is represented in the following collections: Central Ontario Art Association; National Gallery of Canada; Canada Council Art Bank; City of Hamilton; Clarkson Gordon Co. Ltd.; National Steel Car Company; Dofasco. Lives in Burlington, Ontario.

References

Hamilton Spectator, Ont., Nov. 10, 1967 "Finishing Touches" (photo of Gery Puley making finishing touches to portrait of her daughter Lorraine)

Oakville Beaver, Ont., Jan. 23, 1969 "Teaching art — Gery's paintings hang everywhere"

Oakville Daily Journal, Ont., Oct. 19, 1972 "Watercolor exhibit extended"

Hamilton Spectator, Ont., Dec. 27, 1972 "Woman paints old buildings, but on canvas"

Oakville Daily Journal, Ont., Nov. 28, 1973 "Artist will lead tour of England"

Brampton Daily Times, Ont., Mar. 25, 1974 "Artist Gery Puley's Work Coming To Art Gallery"

Hamilton Spectator, Ont., Feb. 17, 1975 "Artviews — Old houses fascinate artist" by Jenny Sheppard

Ibid, Feb. 18, 1975 "Around & About — Happiness is a gallery show" by Stan McNeill

Ibid, Oct. 18, 1975 "Artviews — Paintings reflect 3-D image" by Jenny Sheppard

Film — *Reflections In A White Space* by James Aquila & Al Thomson, Colour 23 min., Canada, 1975 (A personal documentary film about Gery Puley that conveys her philosophy of life through her paintings. The film outlines the artist's various stages of expression, from the urgency of capturing the fine old architecture before it disappears, to the apparent calmness of flowers and still life.)

Fifty Years, The Canadian Society of Painters in Water Colour, 1925-1975 by Katharine Jordan, AGO, Tor., 1975, P. 13

The Index of Ontario Artists, Ed. by H. Wolfe, Vis. Arts Ont. & Ont. Assoc. Art Galleries, Tor., Ont., 1978, P. 224

Hamilton Spectator, Ont., May 26, 1979 "Artviews" by Grace Inglis

PULFORD, Edward (Ted) Berwyn
b. 1914

Born in Saskatoon, Saskatchewan, his interest in drawing and painting began at an early age. In the thirties he attended night-school where he began serious study in classes conducted by Ernest Lindner at the Saskatoon Technical Collegiate. He helped support himself during the Depression by delivering packages six days a week on a bike for $4 a week (even in winter). The outbreak of W.W. II interrupted his studies and in 1940 Pulford joined the R.C.A.F. and trained as a wireless-air gunner and served in Europe, Africa and Asia. Following the war he returned to Fine Art studies in 1945 under the Department of Veterans' Affairs' Educational Allowance. He chose Mount Allison University which was the only degree-granting Fine Arts course in Canada at that time. There he studied under Lawren P. Harris and Alex Colville and graduated with his B.F.A. in 1949. He was an outstanding student and after completion of his course found a place on the teaching staff of Mount Allison alongside Harris and Colville. There for over thirty years he taught basic courses in drawing, painting and design. He contributed considerably to the reputation of the school as an excellent art training centre. Keilor Bentley, Director of the Owens Art Gallery noted that Pulford ". . .played an inspiring role in the development of some of Canada's foremost artists, and. . .added to the lustre and laurels of an outstanding art school." A list of his students includes such artists as D.P. Brown, Tom Forrestall, Christopher Pratt and Mary West Pratt. In his own painting he moved out from Sackville, where he lived for many years, to points in the Maritimes which included the Marshes of Tantramar and the Bay of Fundy coast in Westmorland County in New Brunswick. A love of water colours was instilled in him through his association with Lindner and it became his main medium. Pulford over the years travelled widely in search of his subjects including the Dew Line but his main concern and enthusiasm today is for the landscape of the Maritimes, particularly the shores of the Bay of Fundy. He completes most of his paintings on location catching the varying moods of the seasons. Now devoting his full time to painting he has travelled as far as Ireland. Louis Rombout reviewing his water colours in 1966 noted, "Almost all of the watercolors on exhibit deal with the local and surrounding areas from which the artist has perceptively selected and extracted segments of land and seascapes of rare, and to the untrained eye often unnoticed, beauty. Coupled with this affection for his environment he displays admirable control over a medium which needs considerable skill if it is to be applied effectively. His treatment of skies, water and fog in many of his works attests to this competence and he is unquestionably one of few Canadian artists who display this measure of technical command." One of the highest prices paid at the Maritime Art Exhibition in 1959 was for Pulford's "Fundy Shoreline, Port Grenville, N.S." which received First Prize. His work was also selected by Canadian Oil Companies Limited for ads in nationally circulated magazines like *Maclean's*. He is represented in the collections of former Governor General and Mrs. D. Roland Mitchener; Prime Minister Pierre Elliott Trudeau; former Premier of New Brunswick, Louis J. Robichaud; Minister of National Resources of New Brunswick, J. Wallace Bird; Canadian Embassies overseas; Canada Art Bank; New Brunswick Art Bank; New Brunswick Museum; University of New Brunswick and Mount Allison University. A major exhibition of his water colours, officially opened by Alex Colville, was organized by the Owens Art Gallery, Sackville in 1980 and circulated through the Atlantic Provinces Art Circuit.

PULFORD, Edward (Ted) Berwyn (Cont'd)

References
> *Saint John Telegram-Journal*, N.B., Nov. 28, 1959 "More Than $2,000 Paid For Paintings"
> *Mount Allison University Collection of Canadian Art*, Sackville, N.B., 1965
> *St. John's News*, Nfld., Jan. 25, 1966 "New Brunswick Exhibit Will Visit MUN Gallery"
> *The Tribune-Post*, Sackville, N.B., Jan. 6, 1966 "Watercolor Paintings By E.B. Pulford On Exhibition At Gallery" by Louis Rombout
> *Toronto Telegram*, Ont., Feb. 23, 1970 "Depression kids didn't freak out"
> *High Realism in Canada* by Paul Duval, Clarke, Irwin & Co. Ltd., Tor., 1974, Pgs. 44, 88, 117, 145
> *Halifax Mail Star*, N.S., May 30, 1980 "Artist Ted Pulford" (photo of artist with one of his portraits and caption)
> NGC Info. Form May 25, 1951
> Document from artist 1978

PULLEN, Dorothy (Mrs.)

Born in England she attended the Chelsea School of Art, London and studied fashion drawing in Bournemouth where she lived with her musician husband Ed who was the lead guitarist in the Billy Cotton band and later Billy Bissett's Band at the Savoy Hotel in London. The Pullens came to Brampton, Ontario with their children in 1948. Dorothy worked at her art for a living and soon became known for her portraits of famous persons, landscapes and figure paintings. She has also been conducting art classes in Brampton for a number of years for school teachers, art teachers and other pupils. Her paintings can be found in hotels, factories and private collections. Her subjects have included such notables as Winston Churchill, John F. Kennedy, Robert F. Kennedy, Floyd Patterson and a host of others. Both Dorothy and Ed have been interested in collecting, cutting and mounting gems which they found during their travels in Wyoming, Arizona, Montana and North Carolina including jade, turquoise, sapphire, ruby and garnet stones also many others. Dorothy made pottery for a period but has discontinued this area of the arts. Ed conducts classes in guitar in Brampton.

References
> *Georgetown Herald*, Georgetown, Ont., June 10, 1965 "Sends Churchill Portrait to Prime Minister Pearson"
> *Woodbridge News*, Ont., Aug. 24, 1967 "Constellation Gallery"
> *Brampton Guardian*, Ont., June 19, 1968 "See portraits of Kennedys"
> *Times & Conservator*, Brampton, Ont., May 8, 1967 "Strolling Around Town — Voice Betrays Enthusiasm" by Diane Grell
> Ibid, July 5, 1968 "Guitar, Easel and Now Gems — The Artistic Pullens Are Turning To Stone"
> Ibid, June 3, 1970 "Painting And Panning For Gems Play A Major Part In Her Life" by Colleen Knights

PULVER, William A.
b. 1922
Born in Hamilton, Ontario he studied at the Ontario College of Art in Toronto under L.A.C. Panton then at the Art Students' League, New York and worked as a commercial designer in New York and Toronto. He began teaching art in 1961 for the Toronto Board of Education. He was active with the Canadian Society of Painters in Water Colour (was on the executive, 1963-65). Was living in Scarborough, Ontario in 1961.

Reference
NGC Info. Form rec'd 1961

PUNDLEIDER, Heinz V.
b. 1925
Born in Salzburg, Austria, he started painting as a boy. His father was an employee of the post and telegraph department of the Austrian government and in his spare time made fine wood carvings. During W.W. II Heinz served as a lieutenant in the 34th Ski Battalion of the 18th (Austrian) Infantry Division where as a ski instructor he trained mountain troops (1943-45). He attended the Engineering School at Salzburg and graduated as an electrical engineer. He also studied at the Academy of Fine Arts in Salzburg. He came to Canada with his family in 1951 and worked with the American Can Company at Niagara Falls. In his free time he studied oil painting techniques and colour coordination. He moved to Ottawa in 1960 where he established his own electronics repair shop then joined the firm Computing Devices of Canada Limited where he became director of the Engineering Services Division. During his leisure hours he carried his sketch pad with him to make sketches of scenes that interested him. Known for his landscapes and floral paintings he held his first solo show at the art gallery in the St. Laurent Shopping Centre, Ottawa in 1969. Viewing his work in 1974 Max Palmer writing in *The Clarion* noted, "I have never seen so many, or so good painting scenes from around the Ottawa valley, local scenes and scenes from the east coast of Canada. Scenes that have been captured on canvas that will never be able to be seen in reality again, a picture of the old Beaver Creek before its beauty was ruined by the building of Arlington Woods or of the old farm houses and barns now gone to make room for the new and modern buildings of Craig Henry Farms. Heinz has captured these and many more of the local landscapes in his painting, the old mill at Manotick makes you feel that you are standing on the bridge and looking up river at this old landscape. Someday this too will be gone, but not in the painting that Heinz has painted." Pundleider uses both brush and palette knife when creating his scenes. His other solo shows include: Koyman Gallery, Lincoln Fields Shopping Centre, Ottawa, Ont. (May 1973, May 1974, Nov. 1974); Koyman Gallery, Bayshore Shopping Centre, Ottawa, Ont. (Apr. 1975, Nov. 1975, Apr. 1976); Julianne Galleries, Tor., Ont. (1976); The Palette Art Gallery, Oshawa, Ont. (1976); Group Show, Janrielle Gallery Niagara Falls, Ont. (1980). He has a large farm between North Gower and Smith's Falls and has had a keen interest in horses. He is represented in collections in Europe, the U.S.A., South America and in Canada by Governor-General and Mrs. Edward Schreyer and many others. He was awarded a prize at the CKOC Arts

PUNDLEIDER, Heinz V. (Cont'd)

Competition in Hamilton and his winning picture "A Ray of Sunshine" was purchased for the Station's permanent collection. He married Herma Danes and they have one daughter Karin (Mrs. Joseph Streit). Pundleider has a working knowledge of French, Italian and Russian besides German and English. Member: Can. Soc. of Mechanical Engineers; Inst. of Electronic Engineers and The Engineering Inst. of Canada.

References

The Ottawa Journal, Ont., May 25, 1973 "Austrian artist's work on view at Lincoln Fields" by W.Q. Ketchum

Ibid, May 23, 1974 "Engineer exhibits"

Ibid, Aug. 10, 1974 "Faces of Ottawa — Heinz Pundleider" by W.Q. Ketchum

The Nepean Clarion, Ottawa, Ont., Nov. 13, 1974 "Manordale/Woodvale — Manordale — Woodvale men" by Max Palmer

The Ottawa Journal, Ont., Nov. 14, 1974 "Devoted painter shows 45 works" by W.Q. Ketchum

Ibid, Apr. 17, 1975 "Vivid landscapes of Ottawa Valley" by W.Q. Ketchum

Ibid, Apr. 28, 1976 "Colorful mirages"

Ibid, Mar. 22, 1977 "Living — The accent is Austrian" by Helen Turcotte (photos by Armand Legault)

Ibid, Dec. 29, 1977 "and preview of art" (Pundleider received award from CKOC)

Ottawa Citizen, Ont., May 17, 1978 "Mill of Kintail painting might be yours" (Pundleider's "Mill of Kintail" becomes grand prize for Melodie Fair sponsored by Women's Committee of Ottawa Choral Society)

St. Catharines Standard, Ont., April 12, 1980 "Art — Two landscape shows in area" by Linda Crabtree (Pundleider exhibits at Janrielle Gallery, Hamilton)

The Index of Ontario Artists, Ed. by Hennie Wolff, Vis. Arts Ont./Ont. Assoc. of Art Galleries, Tor., 1978, P. 224

Document from artist

Conversation with artist

PUPLETT, Terence
b.(c) 1940

Born in England he became a free-lance commercial artist. He arrived in Canada in 1968 and soon became known for his fine realist paintings in acrylic on masonite. He held his first solo show at the Merton Gallery, Toronto when Kay Kritzwiser noted the artist and his work as follows, "The quality of light — sunlight, lamplight — challenges Pulplett in the way candlelight obsessed the seventeenth century painter Georges de la Tour. But in his big painting, Mrs. Boles, which dominates his small collection at the Merton Street gallery, the lamps are a symbol, frankly spiritual. They are also a kind of unexpected personal icon, for this engaging young Londoner who came to Canada as a freelance commercial artist in 1968. . .In the painting, the exquisitely painted lamps hang with such certitude against the light, the figure of Mrs. Boles becomes secondary, even blending with the green of the wall. One blue lamp seems to hold light within itself. 'That blue lamp represents Mr. Boles to me,' said Puplett. 'I painted it in his memory.' This blend of emotion and a respect for painting techniques characterizes each work in Puplett's collection. The painting Michael captures a joyous, spontaneous moment of childhood, with trees, sand, lake only a means of projecting light around the small boy. The

PUPLETT, Terence (Cont'd)

frustration and concentration of a violinist are balanced against the violin, painted as a lyrical extension of the player. His painting of three derelicts recognizes the marks of tough times on their faces, but with compassion. For Puplett is a realist. 'But without any fancy tags.' he insisted. 'Art comes in so many forms, so many categories and I think one form enhances the other. I'm interested in light. I like the way the light bounces back and forth in this room.'"

Reference
> *Globe & Mail*, Tor., Ont., Nov. 13, 1973 "Puplett's lamps pay homage to the spirit" by Kay Kritzwiser

PURA, William

b. 1948

Born in Winnipeg, Manitoba, he studied at the School of Art, University of Manitoba where he graduated with his B.F.A. (Honors), 1970; attended the Indiana University, Bloomington, Indiana and graduated with M.F.A., 1973. In notes on Pura's exhibition in 1976 Daniel Mato wrote, "Bill Pura states that the shapes and forms found in his prints come from nature and reflect a visual reality. He also shares a deep empathy with music as he has studied composition and written musical scores. The abstraction of the prints are impressed with the structure of music as themes, and thematic variations appear in the ordering of the compositions." Pura's exhibitions include: United States Information Service, Prints for American Embassies (1973); Gallery Oseredok, Wpg. (1973); Canadian Printmakers Showcase, Carleton University, Ottawa (1974); Winnipeg Artists Invitational, The Winnipeg Art Gallery (1975); Thomas Gallery, Wpg. (solo); Gallery One One One, School of Art, University of Manitoba, Wpg. (1976); Arthur Street Gallery, Wpg. (1977). Member of the faculty of the School of Art, University of Manitoba (1973-   ).

References
> *Winnipeg Free Press*, Wpg., Man., Sept. 21, 1973 "Pura Exhibit To Open Soon"
> Gallery One One One, School of Art, Univ. Manitoba — Lithographs by K.J. (Jack) Butler and William Pura (biographical data), 1976

PURCELL, Joseph Douglas

b. 1927

Born in Halifax, N.S., the son of Mr. & Mrs. John Purcell, he showed an early interest in drawing and painting and at fourteen began serious work in painting. A year later he was exhibiting his work in important shows. He entered the Nova Scotia College of Art where he studied for three years on scholarships and then began a series of paintings interpreting Nova Scotia towns, farmlands, fishing villages and activity of the East Coast and Atlantic fishing industry. By 1947 he had established himself as a professional painter. Viewing his work at the Granville Galleries that year the writer for the *Halifax Mail* noted, "The show is made up of 12 scenes of Lunenburg, where Mr. Purcell is working. The

PURCELL, Joseph Douglas (Cont'd)

most outstanding of these works are those of the Lunenburg waterfront, with the fishing schooners in their berths. All the paintings show a maturity and knowledge unusual in so young an artist. The use of color is excellent and the choice of subject matter in all the paintings is typically Nova Scotian, showing the atmosphere of the sea and the nautical air of the home of the fishing fleet." He also completed a series of murals in the private dining salons in the Nova Scotian Hotel, Halifax, and the Victoria General Hospital. In 1953 he moved with his artist wife to Lunenburg. There they found much of their subject matter for their paintings over the years. In 1967 Marion Moore noted Joe Purcell's work as follows, ". . .most of his scenes are sketched in rambles about Lunenburg County with his wife (also an artist) and their young family. Because of the beautiful coastal scenery in that area, most of his paintings have the sea as its theme, but also there are comfortable farm-houses, country lanes and similar subjects. . . .The artist seems to prefer working with watercolors — which he handles particularly well — and for most of the work in this show he has chosen this medium, with some oils, and a few interesting experiments with mixed media. Perhaps the most striking thing about his paintings is that the scenes depicted are not of artistic merit only, but have strong meaning and relationship to people. Though no persons may appear on the canvas, his houses, barns and roadways look lived in or used. His picturesque seas and rolling countrysides are places where men toil. Possessed of a fine sense of composition and atmosphere the artist has equal ability to portray a splendid panorama — such as he did of Blue Rocks with ships returning home before a rising storm — or focus down on a humble corner of a fisherman's cottage, with a lamp in the window awaiting his return." In 1971 Joe and Tela opened the Purcell Family Gallery. His work has been presented in shows at the following galleries: Granville Galleries, Halifax, N.S. (1947, 1951, 1952, 1967, —); Zwicker's Art Gallery, Halifax, N.S. (1969 April, 1969 Nov., 1970, 1972); Dartmouth Heritage Museum, Dartmouth, N.S. (1970); Robertson Galleries, Ottawa, Ont. ("Painters of Nova Scotia", 1972); Nova Scotia Fisheries Exhibition, Lunenburg, N.S. (1975) and others also many travelling shows in Montreal, Ottawa, New York and London (Eng.). Through his oils and water colours, places like Blue Rock, Peggy's Cove, Lunenburg and Herring Cove have become known throughout the world. Murals by Purcell (including those already mentioned) can be found at the following places: Place Ville Marie, Mtl.; and in Nova Scotia at the Lord Nelson Hotel, Halifax; Maritime Telegraph & Telephone Co., Halifax; Roy Building, Halifax; Eastern Trust Company, Halifax; St. Paul's Church, Halifax; Dartmouth Heritage Museum, Dartmouth; Fishermen's Memorial Room, Lunenburg. A collection of his water colours is housed in the Silver Dart in Baddeck, Cape Breton. He met Tela Monaghan when they were both attending scholarship courses at the Nova Scotia College of Art and after graduation they married. The Purcells have held a number of shows together. They have five children: Anthony Purcell (holds Doctorate & Post Doctorate degrees in Physics); Christopher (Master's Degree in Physics, teaches and researches); Julia (Honours Graduate in Arts); Stephen (Physics, Dalhousie Univ.); Tara (youngest who was attending Lunenburg Regional High School in 1977). Joseph Purcell's awards include: Second Prize, O'Keefe Art Awards (1950); *Saturday Night* Award for his painting reproduced on Bank of Montreal Calendar (1952); Second Award, Seagram Cities of Canada (1953); "Picture of the Month" *The Winnipeg*

PURCELL, Joseph Douglas (Cont'd)

Tribune (July 1953) and others. He is represented in the DesBrisay Museum, Bridgewater, N.S. and elsewhere.

References

Halifax Mail, N.S., July 5, 1947 "Young Artist Exhibits Work"

Halifax Mail-Star, N.S., Mar. 3, 1951 "Talented City Artist Has Two Exhibits"

The Gazette, Mtl., Dec. 29, 1951 "Bank of Montreal's Calendar Attractive — Painting Done at Chester, N.S., by Joseph Purcell Is Colorful"

Halifax Mail-Star, N.S., Mar. 20, 1952 "Critic Says Halifax Artist Makes Painting Look Easy"

Le Madawaska, Edmundston, N.B., Dec. 12, 1957 "Peinture du pont de Hartland"

Halifax Chronicle-Herald, N.S., Apr. 28, 1959 "Ship Pictures Work Of Halifax Artist"

Halifax Mail-Star, N.S., Apr. 28, 1967 "Joseph Purcell Exhibit Concludes On Saturday" by Marion Moore

Ibid, Apr. 1, 1969 "Artists Capture Spirit of N.S." by Gretchen Pierce"

Ibid, Nov. 13, 1969 "Brush Wave Makes Waves" by Gretchen Pierce"

Ibid, Mar. 17, 1970 "Another stormy opening for Joe Purcell" (bad weather hinders opening)

Halifax Chronicle Herald, N.S., Mar. 23, 1970 "Premiere set for Mar. 26" (second premiere because of bad weather on Mar. 17)

Ibid, May 7, 1974 "Purcell painting given to museum"

Halifax Mail-Star, N.S., Sept. 19, 1975 "The Purcells find Lunenburg ideal for painting seascapes" by Ivan Shortliffe

The Progress-Enterprise, Lunenburg, N.S., Apr. 20, 1977 "The Purcells — Maritime Artists" by Lucine Toomey

Halifax Mail-Star, N.S., Sept. 1, 1978 "Lunenburg's Most Famous Artist" (photo of Joe Purcell discussing craft and art displays with Marilyn Congdon for Nova Scotia Fisheries Exhibition)

Royal Canadian Academy of Arts, Exhibitions and Members, 1880-1979 by Evelyn de R. McMann, Univ. Tor. Press, Tor., 1981, P. 334

PURCELL, Tela

b.(c) 1932

Born in Halifax, N.S., the daughter of Mr. & Mrs. James Monoghan. At the age of seven she began her art studies in drawing, charcoal and water colour with a private teacher. She attended the Children's Art Classes at the Nova Scotia College of Art as well, under Miss E.F. Nutt, David Whitzman and Donald MacKay. At her regular school at Mount St. Vincent Academy she was encouraged to pursue many interests including drama and music. She graduated first in her class from Mount St. Vincent at the age of sixteen. She then had to choose between academic studies and art. A compromise was provided for her by Donald MacKay who allowed her to study at the Nova Scotia College of Art on a full-time basis while also allowing her time to study part-time at Dalhousie University. At the College she studied water colour in the American style with Bruce Hunter, and oil technique with Donald Holden. It was at the College that she met fellow art student Joseph Purcell. After graduation they married and became full-time painters. Tela took time off to raise her five children. But painting being an occupation one can pursue at home she was able to get back to her easel at the first opportunity. When their children were still growing up the Purcells took them on painting expeditions which resulted later in their interest too in painting and photography. Viewing her work in 1971 Gretchen Pierce in the *Halifax Mail Star* noted, "She paints

PURCELL, Tela (Cont'd)

prolifically and always out-of-doors because 'the elements are exhilarating, '. . .And unlike many artists who roam the country looking for suitable subject matter, she has only to stroll yards from her home in the small south shore town of Lunenburg to be 'turned on' by the inspiring scenery. If she ventures further along the rocky coast to Blue Rock or Mahone Bay it is in a huge weatherbeaten van large enough to contain the painting Purcell family and camping equipment for overnight excursions. Driving through heavy traffic the petite blue-eyed brunette manages to manoeuvre the van yet concentrate on her favorite subject, art. . . .These 41 watercolors on view weekdays until July 12 are the recent products of a busy winter and spring. . . .The landscapes run the gamut of the seasons depicting the scarlets of late autumn to the snowy banks of winter and the first signs of spring — tiny swallows which perch on fragile branches, her hallmark. Some of them have unusual effects achieved naturally when the cold froze the paints on the paper. Exposure to wind, rain and sun are part of the artist's affection for painting." Her shows include: dual show, Zwicker's Art Gallery, N.S. (1969); group show, "Maritime Women Artists", Zwickers Gallery, N.S. (1970); solo show, Neptune Theatre, Halifax, N.S. (1970); solo show, Dartmouth Heritage Museum, Dartmouth, N.S. (1971); group show, "Painters of Nova Scotia", Robertson Galleries, Ottawa (1972); group show, O'Keefe Centre, Tor. (1976); solo show, DesBrisay Museum, Bridgewater, N.S. (1977); solo show, Rosaria Gallery, Mount St. Vincent University, Halifax, N.S. (1979) and others.

References

> *Dartmouth Free Press*, N.S., Apr. 2, 1969 (show with husband Joe at Zwicker's Art Gallery)
> *The Progress-Enterprise*, Lunenburg, N.S., Apr. 29, 1970 "Maritime Women Artists to hold exhibition"
> *Halifax Mail Star*, N.S., July 4, 1970 "Lunenburg subject for exhibit" by Gretchen Pierce
> Ibid, June 24, 1971 "Artist finds inspiration within yards of her home" by Gretchen Pierce
> *Painters of Nova Scotia*, Robertson Galleries, Ottawa, June 1-17, 1972
> *Halifax Mail Star*, N.S., July 25, 1977 "Canadian artists making their home in Lunenburg" by Linda Mason
> Ibid, Apr. 26, 1979 "Entertainment — Tela Purcell to exhibit works at Rosaria Hall"

PURDY, Henry Carl
b. 1937

Born in Wolfville, Nova Scotia, after attending high school in Armdale, he entered the Nova Scotia College of Art on a scholarship in 1954. There he studied under Donald MacKay, Marion Bond, Ellen Lindsay and Hilery Morse. While still a student he won the Lieutenant-Governor's Medal in 1957 and was elected to the Nova Scotia Society of Artists when only a second year student at the College. He graduated from the College in 1948 with his Art Teacher's Certificate and Commercial Art Diploma. He worked that summer as an art teacher then joined CFCY-TV Charlottetown as staff artist. In 1963 he began teaching the art course at the Provincial Vocational Institute which he himself established. He was appointed Instructor in Commercial Art at the Holland College Charlottetown Centre in 1969 and later became Director of the School of Visual Arts there. In his own personal art he has worked in many fields including: painting, print-making, drawing, photography, calligraphy, com-

PURDY, Henry Carl (Cont'd)

mercial design and pottery. Viewing his work in 1978 in the *Truro Daily News* a reviewer noted, "Exploring virtually every popular visual artistic mode known today, Mr. Purdy unveils approximately 120 of his finest works from the past 10 years in the exhibition, 'Henry Purdy, A Personal Decade.' A highlight of the exhibition is a varied selection of Purdy's metal sculptures, one of his best known art forms. The large steel sculpture, Centennial Dimensions, was created by Purdy and was permanently installed on the main plaza of Confederation Centre of the Arts in 1973, becoming a noteworthy landmark of the Confederation block area. But there are no restraints concerning theme or subject matter in this new exhibition, as Purdy also presents his expertise in ink, acrylics, oils, silkscreen prints, etching and sketches. Some of his paintings depict well-known Prince Edward Islanders, including Father Adrien Arsenault, businessman Alan Holman, former Charlottetown mayor Elmer MacRae, and University of P.E.I. Professor David Morrison. Attempts by Purdy at self-portraiture are remarkably true-to-form, and paintings of family members seem to relate his consciousness of the family as a closely knit unit. As though there exists no way to confine Purdy, he also delves into illustration of the human anatomy through etchings, prints and drawings. . . .Of his sculpturing, Purdy says he achieves a 'glorious feeling of abandonment attached to the creation of assemblages. Texture, materials, and the ever-exciting third dimension, keep drawing me back to the welding shop." Purdy has been interested in dramatics for a number of years. He took "Best Actor's Award" for two years running in the Nova Scotia Competitions. He has also written several books of poetry. A few of his shows include: Group Show: Fifth Annual Calgary Graphics Exhibit (1965); 3-Man, Confederation Centre Art Gallery, Charlottetown, P.E.I. (1969); Solo, Charlottetown's Gallery On Demand, Charlottetown, P.E.I. (1976); Group, Arts Sacra '77, St. Mary's University art gallery, Halifax, N.S. (1977); 3-Man, Albert, Dumas, Purdy at Moncton, N.B. (1977); Solo, "A Personal Decade," Confederation Centre Art Gallery & Museum, Charlottetown, P.E.I. (1978); 2-Man, Irving, Purdy, Morrison Art Gallery, Saint John, N.B. (1979); Group Show Travelling, "Island Images" circulated by Confederation Centre, Charlottetown, P.E.I.; Group Show, "Arts East Exhibition," Maritime Art Association (1979); Solo, Painting & Sculpture, Rothman's Gallery, Moncton, N.B. (1980) also solo shows at St. Dunstan's University; The Playhouse, Fredericton, N.B.; Isle St. Jean Gallery, Charlottetown, P.E.I. and elsewhere. His commissions include: Sculpture, 22 ft. high modern image of polished steel for Confederation Centre Art Gallery & Museum (1972); Sculptural Fountain, Village of Parkdale, Charlottetown, P.E.I. (1972) and many others. Member of the Royal Canadian Academy and on the Executive (1980); Maritime Art Association (former Vice-Pres.); Nova Scotia Society of Artists (1957). Married, he and his wife Gertie have three children, Danny, Scott and Sharon.

References

Charlottetown Guardian, P.E.I., Feb. 12, 1965 "Fifty Artists' Work Accepted For Exhibit"

Ibid, Sept. 6, 1969 "Commercial Art Instructor Named"

Charlottetown Patriot, P.E.I., Dec. 3, 1969 "Local art show opens at centre"

Charlottetown Guardian, P.E.I., Apr. 14, 1972 "Local Artist Has Painting Purchased"

Charlottetown Patriot, P.E.I., Mar. 23, 1972 "Confederation Centre commissions sculpture" (photo of Purdy with scale model)

Ibid, Apr. 22, 1972 "Sculpture fountain for Parkdale park" by Philip Rodgers

PURDY, Henry Carol (Cont'd)

Ibid, Dec. 1, 1972 "Centre Wants A Name For Sculpture" (photo of sculpture)

Summerside Journal Pioneer, P.E.I., Dec. 1, 1972 "Centennial Project — Metal Sculpture Erected At Centre"

Charlottetown Guardian, P.E.I., Dec. 4, 1972 "Sculpture By Island Artist Erected In Charlottetown"

Charlottetown Patriot, P.E.I., Feb. 3, 1975 "Henry Purdy develops style through personal space, time" by Jill Birtwistle (photos and detailed article)

Charlottetown Guardian, P.E.I., Oct. 20, 1976 "Control, Discipline Mark Henry Purdy Work" by Janice Outcalt (Gallery On Demand showing)

Charlottetown Patriot, P.E.I., Aug. 31, 1977 "City artist chosen to exhibit works"

Moncton Transcript, N.B., Feb. 26, 1977 "Art Exhibition" (photo and caption about 3-Man show in Moncton)

Truro Daily News, N.S., Sept. 14, 1978 "Exhibition Features 'Purdy' Works" (solo at Confederation Centre Art Gallery)

Charlottetown Patriot, P.E.I., Dec. 23, 1978 "Island artists members of national academy" (becomes member of R.C.A.)

Evening Times Globe, Saint John, N.B., Oct. 11, 1979 "P.E.I. Artists Featured At Morrison Art Gallery"

Charlottetown Guardian, P.E.I., Nov. 30, 1979 "Purdy Painting Draws Attention" (photo of Purdy's painting "Clam Chowder")

Moncton Transcript, N.B., Feb. 16, 1980 "Henry Purdy art exhibit" (Rothman's Gallery)

Charlottetown Guardian, P.E.I., May 31, 1980 "First To Academy In Over 100 Years" by Julie Watson

NGC Info. Form

Royal Canadian Academy of Arts, Exhibitions and Members 1880-1979 by Evelyn de R. McMann, Univ. Tor. Press, Tor., 1981, P. 334

PURDY, Rena

Born in Ottawa, Ontario, her grandfather Purdy emigrated from Ireland to work in the lumbering industry in the Bancroft area and gave his name to Purdy Lake. Her father at one time worked on one of the last square-timer rafts (booms) to navigate the Ottawa River to Quebec City. Being the only crewman who could read and write he became bookkeeper, clerk-storekeeper for the journey. At an early age Rena's family moved to Toronto. In later years she worked with the Red Cross and during the War served with the Army Medical Corps overseas at Clochester, Essex and after two years as Messing Officer for the Nursing Sisters and Medical Officers she returned to Canada. With the assistance of the Department of Veterans' Affairs she attended the Ontario College of Art and worked as a summer student at Simpsons and following graduation from the College she became full-time display artist with this company. Interested in stained glass she left Simpsons to apprentice for two years in a stained glass studio. She free-lanced as a stained glass artist for a time then moved to Winnipeg where she became Art Director for the YWCA, a multi-faceted position which she held for five years. She moved to Deep River, Ontario, in 1960 and became Matron of the AECL hotels. During her free hours she developed her interest in sketching old mills, bridges, farm buildings and landscapes of the Ottawa Valley in oils and water colours. She taught an art course at night school at Deep River. She is a member of the Canadian Society of Painters in Water Colour and has exhibited with this Society in

PURDY, Rena (Cont'd)

travelling shows in both Canada and the United States. Viewing her work in 1965 Lesley Lyn for the *North Renfrew Times* noted, "The seventeen water-colours and two crayon drawings are the work of a sensitive artist in full command of an exacting medium. In this current showing of her work Miss Purdy displays herself as an artist of no mean order and it is not surprising that she is becoming well-known in other parts of Canada." She has exhibited at Forest Hall, Deep River, Ont. (1965); the Public Library, North Bay, Ont. (1974) and elsewhere.

References
> *Deep River North Renfrew Times*, Deep River, Ont., Nov. 24, 1965 "Rena Purdy exhibition in Forest Hall" by Lesley Lyn
> Ibid, Dec. 15, 1971 "Rena Purdy — daughter of the Valley comes home"
> *North Bay Nugget*, Ont., May 11, 1974 (exhibit of paintings at North Bay Public Library)

PURDY, Richard
b.(c) 1953

An Ottawa, Ontario artist he studied art at the High School of Commerce; the Ontario College of Art, Toronto; Mount Allison University, Sackville, N.B. and the Nova Scotia College of Art, Halifax, N.S. He held his first exhibition (two-man) in 1975 at the Anna Leonowen's Gallery, Halifax with artist Carmelo Arnoldin. In 1976 Purdy travelled to Florence, on a post-graduate scholarship from the Italian government, where he completed a master's thesis on musical sources in Raphael's Stanze della Segnatura in the Vatican (architecture's relation to music). Describing his activity Rosalie Smith McCrea in the *Ottawa Journal* explained, "An artist, dancer and papermaker, Purdy wrote a 1977 master's thesis in Florence about architecture's relation to music. The experience may have been the catalyst. In Kalamata, Greece, he discovered an old amphitheatre whose proportions could be expressed in other ways. Ways such as geometry, music and dance movements. Travelling by rail from Europe to Asia in 1979, over a 10-month period with a large sketchbook, the experience at Kalamata was to be adopted at every site approached. The entire project was supported by grants from the Italian Government and the Canada Council. Purdy became interested in the evolution of religious architecture moving west to east. The cross of the Christian Church and the O (urobus) of Greek and of Buddhist Temples. Taking the ground plans of selected temples, earthworks or natural formations, he made measured blueprints of them. . . .These sites were measured and mapped into large blueprints as mentioned above. Purdy then conceptually reduced the shapes of these religious sites into essential shapes. Many assumed 'archetypal' forms. Those seen were circles, spirals and rotating cubes. These 'archetypal' forms were then drawn onto a second plan — the whiteprint. It is the whiteprints which became the pattern for a series of ritualized movements and dances connected to six sites during the performance work. Those present had a chance to preview the photographs, blue and white prints, maps and historical information all related to the dances and sites that they evoked." This particular exhibition took place at the SAW Gallery, Ottawa, in April of 1980. His papermaking was described by Robert Smythe as follows, "In these paperworks he deals with the honesty of the materials.

PURDY, Richard (Cont'd)

They stand alone. Those materials may be drawn from any source; his own life, a friend's or his surroundings. The paper portrait is a romantic Purdy invention — 'I have followed people over a period of time, collecting every single piece of paper that they have used; notes, kleenex, letters.' all combined and broken down in the pulp vat, before it re-emerges as a sheet of paper built from biographical fibres." Purdy has continued to explore new avenues in his art, a recent area being doctrines in the face of death, judgement or the future state, referred to by the term Eschatology. He believes one should meld the arts with science and was once described by Kathleen Walker as, "a 'renaissance man' who is searching for knowledge by studying language, history, music and art." Active in the Ottawa area Purdy has made props for the National Arts Centre; lectured for the Education Services of the National Gallery of Canada; taught at the Ottawa School of Art in several courses; taught as a supply art teacher in Ottawa high schools and was co-ordinator for the Department of Recreation and Parks, Ottawa. His shows include: Paintings, SAW Gallery, Ottawa (1976); Paperworks, Studios of Le Groupe de la Place Royale, Ottawa (1978); "Blueprints: The Sacred Circuit," Musée d'Art Vivant Vehicule, Montreal (Feb., 1980), SAW Gallery, Ottawa (Apr., 1980), Mercer Union, Toronto (May, 1980); Eschatology, 101 Gallery, Ottawa (1981).

References

Ottawa Journal, Ont., July 22, 1976 "Buddhist influence in one-man exhibit"

Ottawa Citizen, Ont., July 22, 1976 "Complicated simplicity subtle oriental blend" by Kathleen Walker

Ibid, Sept. 14, 1977 "Artist introduces course to help Ottawans appreciate their art" by Don Lajoie

Ibid, June 17, 1978 "Art — Art of the paper maker" by Robert Smythe

Ottawa Journal, Apr. 19, 1980 "Rare and sustained beauty — Conceptual artist Richard Purdy presents artistic pilgrimage at SAW Gallery" by Rosalie Smith McCrea

PURGINA, Emil

b. 1937

Born in Czechoslovakia, he studied at the University of Creative Arts in Bratislava where he graduated with his Master's degree. He came to Canada in the late 1960's and exhibited his drawings, oils and graphics in Ottawa at the Glebe Photo Gallery on Bank Street. Viewing his work W.Q. Ketchum noted, "The exhibition shows professional competence. All his works have a sense of unity. Vigor and a fine sense of color are exemplified in the oils".

References

The Saturday Citizen, Ottawa, Ont., Jan. 9, 1971 "First Ottawa exhibition for Czechoslavak artist" by Jenny Bergin

Ottawa Journal, Ont., Jan. 15, 1971 "Czech Artist's Works Show Originality" by W.Q. Ketchum

PURVITIS, Mentauts Dennis (MINTO)
b.(c) 1942

Born in Latvia, the son of Mr. & Mrs. Ernest Purvitis, he came to Canada with his family in 1950 and they lived in British Columbia for a year before settling in Sault Ste. Marie, Ontario. Purvitis, the son of a forester was employed in 1968 with the Algoma Central Railway as a cartographer and began sketching after hours. He did take an art course for five months mostly about commercial layouts and decided he was not interested in this field. For a period he worked in British Columbia and the Yukon as a guide, trapper and forest firefighter. All this time he was drawing scenes of life in the North country with the hope that he would someday become a full-time artist. His work was seen by a former advertising salesman John A. Carson who took some of it to the Canadian National Exhibition in Toronto. Purvitis in the meantime had adopted the professional name of Minto because it is the way his first name sounds in Latvian. His work was viewed by the CNE authorities and enthusiastically included in the exhibit. The Royal Ontario Museum became interested in his work as did Vincent Price, famous actor and art connoisseur, who acquired one of his drawings. Purvitis settled near Wawa, Ontario close to the country he depicts in his drawings and paintings. Early in his career he did prints in an issue of 500 after which he destroyed the plate. He established a company named DD & W with Carson for distributing his prints to branch stores across Canada including Eaton's but later continued to distribute on his own. Describing his work in the *Sault Ste. Marie Star* Rob Bostelaar wrote, "First he makes a rough pencil sketch, then uses a fine tip pen to place thousands of dots on the canvas. The technique is one he developed on his own. He's had little formal art training. Straight lines are used to illustrate wood grains and other linear subjects, but the dots are used everywhere else and bring out a fine subtle texture that would be impossible to see in any other medium. The drawings have the look of iron or stone cuts, a style he wants to stay close to." Purvitis has done several large paintings for the Rankin Arena in Sault Ste. Marie depicting wildlife, early Indian life and mythology. These panels are done in oils or oil pastels. His work can also be seen on the walls of local motels and coffee shops. A solo show of his original pen and ink sketches and seven prints was held at the Walz Gallery in Sault Ste. Marie in April of 1976. When Purvitis is not in the wilds he makes his base at his parents' home in Sault Ste. Marie. Much of his work is done on commission.

References
> *Toronto Telegram*, Ont., Aug. 28, 1969 "Minto 'genius' artist at CNE" by George Kidd
> *Sault Ste. Marie Star*, Ont., Sept. 24, 1969 "ACR map maker may be genius"
> Ibid, Oct. 23, 1969 "Sault's self-taught artist guides out of Wawa on the side" by Kathryn Johnson
> Ibid, July 13, 1970 "Artist Portrays North With His Drafting Pen" by Marianne White
> Ibid, Apr. 15, 1976 "Minto's art reflects his life" by Rob Bostelaar
> Ibid, Feb. 28, 1979 "Minto's work has been called 'genius'" by Robin Koivisto Waples

---

PUTMAN, Amy Elsie Violet
1893-

Born in Brockville, Ontario, she moved to Hamilton where she studied art at the Hamilton Technical School under Hortense Gordon. She was active with

PUTMAN, Amy Elsie Violet (Cont'd)

the Women's Art Club of Hamilton (Recording Secretary 1943-46; Treasurer 1950-51). She was a public school teacher in Hamilton.

References
>NGC Info. Form rec'd Sept. 11, 1951

PUTMAN, Gerry
b.(c) 1938

From Belleville, Ontario, he studied commercial art at the Ontario College of Art in Toronto for five years (1959-64) and for the next two years had a design studio in Belleville, working on layout and advertising. He returned to Toronto where he worked for Maclean-Hunter Limited as a creative designer while still free-lancing his design work in Belleville. He became head of the art department at Prince Edward Collegiate Institute in Picton in 1969 while developing his own personal art in his free hours. He has become known especially for his pen and ink sketches and water colours although he has painted in oils, egg tempera and dabbled in ceramics. Explaining how he works Ian Robertson of the *Kingston Whig Standard* wrote, "Armed with a battered old camera or a sketch pad, he will record a scene. On the pad, he will quickly outline what he wishes to later transfer on the canvas or paper. He jots down details of color and mood to assist him. A camera is particularly important, and while some artists frown on photography as an easy way to compose art, he finds it serves as merely a solid base for artistic impression. He can alter perspectives or record them faithfully, depending on how he 'sees' or 'feels' the subject at hand. Several years ago, he completed four country pen and ink sketches, which he had printed on good stock 'strictly as a commercial venture.' They proved so popular, he now has seven more — several of the ideas having been inspired by friends and customers." Up to 1978 Putman had estimated that he had completed between 300 and 400 works with 100 pen sketches done in the greater Kingston and Belleville areas, particularly Prince Edward County. His shows include: Tom Thomson Memorial Art Gallery, Owen Sound, Ont. (3-man, 1965); Prince Edward County Museum, Picton, Ont. (1974); Corby Gallery, Belleville, Ont. (1978). He was awarded the 10th annual "Artist of The Year" award by the Lake Ontario Cement Limited for his water colour painting of the lighthouse at Salmon Point, south of Picton. The painting is now in the permanent collection of Lake Ontario Cement Limited. He lives at Bloomfield near Picton.

References
>*Owen Sound Sun-Times*, Ont., Dec. 8, 1965 "Art Gallery Features Contemporary Art By Three Artists"
>*Kingston Whig Standard*, Ont., Sept. 4, 1974 "Museum features artwork"
>Ibid, Sept. 17, 1974 "Cement company honors artist"
>Ibid, Jan. 13, 1978 "He has designs on art" story & photos by Ian Robertson

PYLYPIUK, Taras
b.(c) 1948

A Hamilton, Ontario artist, he held a solo show of his water colours, acrylics and pencil sketches at the Alan Gallery, Hamilton, when reviewer John Bryden noted that his work was very good and very creative.

Reference
> *Hamilton Spectator*, Ont., Apr. 8, 1972 "Art" by John Bryden

PYM, Harold

A Vancouver, B.C. artist who uses a very old technique which he learned in England for painting murals. He works with a fine brush and dry oil, blended with modern media. He has done religious paintings for various institutions and organizations around Vancouver.

Reference
> *Vancouver Times*, Van., B.C., Feb. 26, 1965 "Harold Pym. . .in search of sanity — His aim: Christianity back in art" by Les Rimes

QARRUQ, Johnny Ashivak
19..-1974

An Eskimo of the North West Territories, he became known for his carvings which were exhibited in New York City in 1973 and elsewhere. He died in a fire with his wife Doris in 1974 in their two-room frame house at Spence Bay, about 550 miles northeast of Yellowknife.

Reference
> *Winnipeg Free Press*, Man., Oct. 22, 1974 (photo of artist with his work and caption)

QUACKENBUSH, Diane
b.(c) 1951

Born in California, U.S.A., she now lives in Montreal where she is known for her drawings, prints and paintings. Her work was described by Virginia Nixon in *The Gazette* during her solo show at the Powerhouse Gallery in 1980 as follows, "Diane Quackenbush paints the subjects her great-grandmother would have enjoyed painting — a bouquet of tulips, a begonia plant, a heap of red, green and yellow peppers piled in an ivory white Chinese bowl. But these charming acrylic and pencil works on rice and handmade paper, on view at the women's gallery Powerhouse, are not revivals of Victorian parlor art. Quackenbush has a contemporary eye and an original, slightly abrupt way of presenting things, not to mention technical facility and a superb eye for color. The tulips for example, are ready for the waste-basket. But Quackenbush has captured them in a last unexpected moment of glory — crimson petals scattered symmetrically where they've dropped off the green stems. The. . .

QUACKENBUSH, Diane (Cont'd)

Montreal artist is also showing portraits of friends. These are interesting. . . Quackenbush's exhibition is a reminder that one of the very real accomplishments of the women's movement in art has been to give validity and a new lease on life to supposedly old-fashioned domestic subject matter." A few of her shows include: Anna Leonowens Gallery, Halifax, N.S. (1975); Powerhouse Gallery, Mtl., P.Q. (1976, 1978, 1980).

References
> The Gazette, Mtl., P.Q., Feb. 7, 1976 (review of show at Powerhouse)
> Ibid, June 21, 1980 "Diane's acrylics display a bouquet of color" (photo of one of her flower paintings)

QUADRI, Sohan

Born in India he received his formal education at Punjab University where he was awarded a diploma in art. He taught at a post-graduate college and worked as a professional photographer before coming to Canada. He exhibited his relief paintings at the Picture Loan Gallery, Toronto and at Gallery 93, Ottawa when Jenny Bergin of the *Ottawa Citizen* noted, "Physically, Quadri's relief paintings — repeated dialogues between fathomless areas of thin color and rock-like forms made of roughly-applied beeswax — are well presented and immaculately executed. I particularly liked White Whisper Unto Silence, a white-on-white painting which carries something of the dramatic, dictatorial quality of mountains rising from a plain, and the richly purple Hara Continuum III, with its strong foreground reiteration of distant, gilded vertical forms."

References
> Globe & Mail, Tor., Ont., April 15, 1972 (review of show at Picture Loan Gallery)
> Ottawa Citizen, Ont., July. 7, 1972 "Enigmatic art exhibition immaculately executed" by Jenny Bergin

QUAN, Elizabeth (Mrs.)

b. 1921

Born in Toronto, Ontario, she spent two years in China where painting was an accepted part of the teaching. Her father worked very hard to send five of his seven children to university. Although Elizabeth wanted to study at the Ontario College of Art she was guided instead to academic studies in university. Later, after she was married, she had the opportunity to study oriental philosophy which has influenced her art. She began to paint seriously when her three children were past their vulnerable early years. She has become known for her attractive linen banners, collages, mixed media paintings and her water colours in a style which she describes as "organic impressionism." Her work has been very well received. She teaches young people part-time in the education department of the Royal Ontario Museum. Her solo shows include: Pollock Gallery, Tor., Ont. (1966, 1967); Shaw-Rimmington Gallery, Tor., Ont. (1972, 1973, 1976). She is represented in the collection of the Bank of

QUAN, Elizabeth (Mrs.) (Cont'd)

Canada, Ottawa, by a wall hanging and in many private collections. She received an award from the Colour & Form Society in 1975.

References

Globe & Mail, Tor., Ont., Nov. 18, 1967 "Pollock Gallery"

Ibid, Nov. 4, 1969 "Art — Linen banners evoke moon and tides" by Kay Kritzwiser

Ibid, May 20, 1972 (review of show at Shaw-Rimmington Gallery)

The Index of Ontario Artists, Ed. Hennie Wolff, Vis. Arts Ont./Ont. Assoc. of Art Galleries, Tor., Ont., 1978, P. 224

QUINN, Hugh Summerville

(c) 1872-1948

Born in Ottawa, son of the late Hugh Quinn and Alice Barrett he studied art with Henry Harold Vickers and exhibited his paintings with the Royal Canadian Academy (1916, 1918, 1924) and also collected art. He was employed by Bate and Company and later the Department of National Defence until his retirement in 1928. He married Marie Alma Scantland in 1903 and they had four sons and three daughters. He died in Ottawa at the age of 76.

References

Ottawa Citizen, Ont., Aug. 26, 1948 "Hugh S. Quinn, Noted Artist, Passes At 76"

Royal Canadian Academy of Arts, Exhibitions and Members 1880-1979 by Evelyn de R. McMann, Univ. Tor. Press, Tor. 1981, P. 335

QUINN, John

He moved to Vancouver from London, Ontario in 1972 and first exhibited in the Vancouver Art Gallery exhibition "Alternative Space" (1975). He exhibited in a show at the Surrey Art Gallery in 1977 when David MacWilliam noted his work in the *Georgia Straight* as follows, "His paintings show a complete disregard for art history, yet he achieves what many trained artists strive to recapture — spontaneity. He paints with water-based acrylics which he mixes from powders giving him high color saturation. Rather than using canvas, Quinn paints on old doors, and found pieces of wood which he cuts to the shape he wants with his jig saw. . . .Overall Quinn's work gives one a sense of painting style, rather than content. It is the way he paints one remembers, rather than specific forms or what they might mean." Quinn was sponsored by a LIP grant in 1977 and is represented in the City of Vancouver's Artists Gallery.

Reference

Georgia Straight, Van., B.C., July 21, 1977 "Art — Sexplicit art for Surrey" by David MacWilliam

QUINN, Ken
b.(c) 1950

Born in Ottawa, he learned pottery from Wayne Cardinalli then proceeded on his own. He set up a studio in a basement of his Cobourg, Ontario apartment and later moved to his property at Lakeport, Ontario where he renovated an old barn into a studio-workshop and kiln room. There he makes his pottery. A writer for the *Cobourg Daily Star* in an article on Quinn noted, "Although he has had some training in the elements of visual design, his hands move instinctively by 'feel' as much as anything else. 'Throwing' a pot, as it is called in the trade, is only half the story. After the piece is dry, it has to be fired, then glazed and then finally fired again. The glazes are different blends of minerals and metal oxides that Quinn formulates himself. They have no more color than a mixture of flour and water, but once fired the glazes are transformed into the deep rich earth tones that Ken is building his reputation on." He markets his pottery through outlets in Cobourg, Port Hope and Toronto and also at Lakeport. His wife, Severina, is a weaver. When the Quinns are not working at their respective crafts they are with their children working together in their garden or fixing up their studio-workshop and kiln room.

Reference
Cobourg Daily Star, Ont., July 8, 1977 "Kenn Quinn — Lakeport potter"

QUINNEY, Gerrard Joseph
b. 1913

Born in Vancouver, B.C., he moved to Hamilton, Ontario, where he continued as a broadcaster. He studied painting for a brief period with Charles Playfair in 1950 but was mainly self-taught.

Reference
NGC Info. Form rec'd Feb. 5, 1952

QUINTAL, Dorothy
b. 1922

Born in Manitoba, she is a landscape painter in oils and acrylics and has exhibited her work in Watrous, Saskatchewan, where she lives. She has a lyrical quality to her paintings and was awarded a prize in the Watrous Art Salon (1968) and also participated in "A Summer Show."

Reference
Canadian artists in exhibition, 1972-73, Roundstone, Tor., 1974, P.173

QUINTANILLA, Guillermo

Born in San Salvador, El Salvador, he finished secondary schooling in Canada at Loyola College, Montreal. He travelled in Europe where he studied works of

QUINTANILLA, Guillermo (Cont'd)

the Great European Masters also the British, Flemish, Italian, French and Spanish Schools of painting. He returned to Canada and attended the University of Ottawa while spending summers studying art in El Salvador and in Mexico at San Miguel de Allende. Returning to Ottawa he finished his academic studies at Carleton University. In his painting he experimented in all kinds of mediums. After exploring various forms of expression he turned to non-representative painting using rich colours. In his work he reflects the passion of his Spanish-American ancestry and strives for depth and movement in his work. He held a solo show of his work at Robertson Galleries, Ottawa in 1962.

Reference
Biographical data (1962) in artist's file at NGC Library Documentation Centre.

QUIRK, Marilyn (Mrs. Keith Quirk)

A painter from the Owen Sound area, she exhibited her work in the *Sun-Times* lobby in 1966. Her work was mainly in oils and covered a wide range of subjects including landscapes, aquarium studies, abstracts inspired by poetry, portraits including character studies, figure compositions and scenes from the Bible. A subsequent show of her work at the *Sun-Times* displayed her sketches for the TV series "Living Faith" originating from CKNX Wingham produced by John Day and sponsored by the Owen Sound Association of Baptist Churches. Her papier-mâché puppets illustrating a mission in India were shown in this exhibit and other creative art aids for children's storytelling.

References
Sun-Times, Owen Sound, Ont., May 11, 1966 "Arresting Show Hanging on Lobby Walls"
Ibid, Apr. 20, 1967 "Artist Uses Visual Aids For TV Program"

QURESHI, Abdur Rehman
b. 1927

Born in Karachi, Pakistan, he attended the Sind University and the University of Karachi, Pakistan. He came to Canada and settled in Montreal where he attended McGill University and Sir George Williams University. He is known for his non-objective paintings which have been exhibited at the Colbert Gallery, Mtl. (1972) and the T. Eaton Company Limited, Mtl. (1972).

Reference
Canadian artists in exhibition, 1972-73, Roundstone, Tor., 1974, P. 173

RAAB, Ernest
b. 1926

Born in Komarno, Czechoslovakia, he studied ceramics at the Beaux-Arts, Paris with Professor Gimond and at the Académie de la Grande Chaumière,

RAAB, Ernest (Cont'd)

Paris with Professors Kretz and Martin. A specialist in ceramics he came to Toronto, Canada in 1953. A member of the Société des artistes indépendants, Paris, he revisited France periodically.

Reference

NGC Info. Form rec'd 1954

RAAB, George
b(c)1950

He spent his early years in Toronto and studied General Arts at the University of Toronto; Creative Arts (specializing in Printmaking) at Sheridan College and etching at Erindale College, Streetsville, Ontario. In 1970 he travelled in Africa, Europe, the Middle East and later in the Canadian Arctic on two occasions where he worked first as a bulk oil fuel pump man on the Mackenzie River and then as a geological explorer. In his art Raab attempts to capture the subtle mystique of wilderness areas and explains, "I look for haunting moments when everything seems to have a strong effect on all my senses — when a feeling is evoked that has a lasting impact on me." Raab has explored various mediums and found etching and aquatinting particularly well suited for his artistic expression. By 1978 he was living at Maynooth Station a few miles north of Bancroft, Ontario. There he set up a studio and by May of 1978 held his first solo show at the Downstairs Gallery, Bancroft. His work since then has become increasingly popular with collectors and has been exhibited in many important international shows and solo shows. He moved to Lakefield, Ontario, in 1980 to be nearer university activity at Peterborough. He became artist in residence in March, 1981, at Trent University's Otonabee College. Describing his work in 1981, Lydia Pawlenko in the *Peterborough Examiner* noted, "By studying small segments of landscapes, he picks up things that wouldn't be noticed otherwise. Whether it be in rocky reliefs, fields of delicate reeds, or an old wooden farmhouse, the artist is able to disclose illusions and ambiguities in each. His prints contain a timelessness that is ever-challenging to the observer. During his three canoe trips a year to the Madawaska Valley, in Algonquin Park, Raab captures images through drawings or photographs." His solo shows include: Downstairs Gallery, Bancroft, Ont. (1978); Georgian Woodlands Chalet, Collingwood, Ont. (1978); "Reflections", Bancroft, Ont. (1979); Corby Street Public Library, Belleville, Ont. (1979); Hawkers and Peddlers Gallery, Deep River, Ont. (1980); Hart House Gallery, U. of T., Tor. (1980); retrospective exhibition of etchings at Otonabee College, Peterborough (1981). His important group shows include: 7th International Miniature Print Exhibition, Pratt Graphics Center, New York, N.Y. (1979); Rockford Prints '79, International Print Exhibition, Rockford, Illinois (1979); 13th International Biennial of Graphic Art, Museum of Modern Art, Ljubljana, Yugoslavia (1979); 18th Toronto Outdoor Exhibition, Nathan Phillips Square, Tor., where he won Best Graphics Award (1979); The Boston Printmakers 32nd National Exhibition, Boston, Mass. (1979); Ontario Society of Artists Open Juried Exhibition "Image '79," where he was awarded two Collector's Choice Purchase Awards, Rodman Hall, St. Catharines, Ont. also travelling to the Market Gallery, Tor. and the Kitchener-Waterloo Gallery, Kitchener, Ont. (1980); 19th Toronto

RAAB, George (Cont'd)

Outdoor Exhibition, Nathan Phillips Square, Tor., Ont., where he received a Graphics Award (1980); 8th International Print Biennial, Krakow, Poland (1980); Premio Internazionale Biella 1979 Per L'Incisione, Biella, Italy (1980); Norwegian International Print Biennial, Fredrikstad, Norway (1980); 2nd Canadian Biennial of Prints & Drawings where he received an award at the Edmonton Art Gallery and touring major Canadian Galleries until March, 1982; Internationald Grafik Biennale, Kolping Hall, Freschen, West Germany (1980). Raab and his wife Evelyn were looking for a farm where they could raise some animals and where he could continue with his art. He is represented in the following collections: Art Gallery of Hamilton, the Oakville Centennial Gallery, the Toronto Dominion Bank Collection and Dofasco Incorporated as well as many private collections in major cities throughout Europe, Africa, United States and Canada.

References

The Bancroft Times, Ont., Feb. 7th, 1979 "George Raab Exhibits in New York"

Peterborough Examiner, Ont., Feb. 20, 1979 "Art Exhibit"

Sunday Star, Tor., Ont., June 17, 1979 "Art show winners"

The Bancroft Times, Ont., June 27, 1979 "Raab Takes Top Prize at Toronto Show"

Bowmanville Canadian Statesman, Ont., Sept. 19, 1979 "Etchings Featured At Margot Samuel Gallery Opening" by Carlene Kirby

The Bancroft Times, Ont., Apr. 23, 1980 "Raab Exhibits In International Exhibition In Europe"

Ibid, Aug. 13, 1980 "Artists' Works To Go On Display In West Germany"

Peterborough Examiner, Ont., Aug. 13, 1980 "Lakefield artist's stuck on realism" by Kerry White

Ibid, Mar. 14, 1981 "Artist George Raab — He sees things not noticed by others" by Lydia Pawlenko

Biographical sheet "George Raab, etchings"

RAADE, Wilhelm

b. 1893

Born in Norway, he went to sea in 1915 and served on three and four masted schooners travelling between the eastern shores of Canada and Norway. He spent his spare time painting seascapes and other subjects. By 1930, then aged 37, he decided to leave the sea and become an artist. In 1956 he arrived in Canada with his wife and settled in Port Arthur, Ontario. He exhibited his work at the Lakehead Exhibition in 1957. He worked for a time in the northern interior of British Columbia then made his home in Calgary, Alberta. Following his wife's death in 1970 he packed his belongings in two trucks and headed for Watson Lake to join a prospector friend. There he planned to hunt, fish, prospect, trap and capture the wilderness on canvas. Describing his work in 1970 Gloria Phillips in the Calgary Herald noted, "Vivid greens and yellows, rusts and oranges gave richness to his canvases, depicting mountains and meadows, fjords and islands of the old country. He also painted the sea. High rolling breakers and quiet translucent waters leaped from his agile brush. . . .Many of the scores of paintings finished by Mr. Raade have been sold through department stores in Canada. Many of his oils also hang in homes in Europe." One of his two daughters, Elizabeth Kitch, lives in Calgary.

RAADE, Wilhelm (Cont'd)

References

Fort William Times-Journal, Ont., July 31, 1957 "Copies Great Works of Art"
Ottawa Citizen, Ont., Aug. 20, 1957 "Oil Painting Artist Turns House Painter"
Calgary Herald, Alta., June 1, 1970 "Calgary Artist — Oldster Forsakes City Life For North" by Gloria Phillips

RABENA, Glen

Born in Wapato, Washington, U.S.A., he began carving in Seattle in 1970. In 1971 he moved to Quesnel, B.C., and studied at the Kitanmax School of Northwest Coast Art at Ksan. He is known for his carvings and has worked in gold, silver, wood and ivory also silkscreen prints which he produces in editions of 225. Titles of his subjects include: "Eagle", "Robin", "Cormorants", "Chickadee", "Sparrow", "Swans", and "Horned Grebe" which are available from Potlatch Arts Limited, Vancouver.

Reference

Potlatch Arts Limited, 100 - 8161 Main Street, Van., B.C., V5X 3L2 (flyer with reproduction of work)

RABINOWITCH, David
b. 1943

Born in Toronto, Ontario, the son of Joseph and Ruth Rabinowitch, he studied at the University of Western Ontario and the Ontario College of Art, Toronto. He has become known for his non-representational steel constructions made from cold and hot rolled steel. He has been living in New York City while actively exhibiting his work in Canada. His solo shows include: Bykert Gallery, N.Y.C. (1975); Heiner Friedrich Gallery, Munich, W. Germany (1975); Carmen Lamanna Gallery, Tor. (1975, 1976); Galerie Hetzler & Keller, W. Germany (1975). His awards include: Canada Council Grant (1968); Canada Council Art Bursary (1969, 1970, 1971, 1972, 1973); Canada Council Senior Grant (1974); Guggenheim Senior Fellowship (1975). He is represented in the following collections: National Gallery of Canada, Ottawa; Art Gallery of Ontario, Tor.; Mount Allison University, Sackville, N.B.; Art Bank, Ottawa; University of Western Ontario, London and in a number of private collections. Member: Royal Canadian Academy(e). Dealer: Carmen Lamanna Gallery, Toronto.

References

Canadian artists in exhibition, Roundstone, Tor., 1972-73, P.174
Ibid, 1974, P.182
The Index of Ontario Artists, Ed. Hennie Wolff, Vis. Arts Ont./Ont. Assoc. Art Galleries, Tor., 1978, P.224
Royal Canadian Academy of Arts, Exhibitions and Members, 1880-1979 by Evelyn de R. McMann, Univ. Tor. Press, Tor., 1981, P.335

RABINOWITCH, Joseph

His found object sculpture was exhibited at Ruthe Calverley's Gallery, Toronto (1968) and in the Automotive Building of the Canadian National Exhibition in Toronto (1968) when a reviewer for the *Richmond Hill Liberal* noted, "Found objects, including chrome bumpers, wheel discs, brake drums and various other parts of wrecked cars have been welded together by the local sculptor into imaginative and intriguing works of art." Rabinowitch, a lawyer, is also active in the theatre. Two of his sons are sculptors.

Reference

Richmond Hill Liberal, Ont., Aug. 15, 1968 "Local Sculptor Shows At 'Ex' "

Ibid, Sept. 5, 1968 (Joseph Rabinowitch appears in play)

RABINOWITCH, Royden

b. 1943

Born in Toronto, Ontario, the son of Joseph and Ruth Rabinowitch, he studied at the University of Western Ontario, London, and the Ontario College of Art, Toronto. He is known for his non-representational cold and hot rolled steel constructions. His solo shows include: O.K. Harris Gallery, N.Y.C. (1973); Forest City Gallery, London, Ont. (1974); Carmen Lamanna Gallery, Tor. (1975, 1976); and he participated in The First Dalhousie Drawing Exhibition, Dalhousie University, Halifax (1976). His awards include: Canada Council Grant (1967); Canada Council Art Bursary (1968, 1969, 1970, 1971, 1972); Canada Council Grant (1973); Canada Council Senior Grant (1975, 1976). He is represented in the following collections: National Gallery of Canada, Ottawa; Art Bank, Ottawa; Aldrich Museum of Contemporary Art, Ridgefield, Conn., and a number of private collections. Dealer, Carmen Lamanna Gallery, Toronto. He lives in New York City.

References

Canadian artists in exhibition, 1972-73, Roundstone, Tor., 1974, P.174

Ibid, 1974, P.182

Artscanada, Tor., Ont., April/May 1976 "The First Dalhousie Drawing Exhibition", P.51

The Index of Ontario Artists, Ed. Hennie Wolff, Vis. Arts Ont./Ont. Assoc. Art Galleries, Tor., 1978, P.225

RABY, Herman

Born in St-Jean, Port-Joli, Quebec, he does large impressive wood sculptures which have been exhibited in many shows including one at the Cultural Centre of Amqui (1968). He carved two gigantic wood sculptures in pine for permanent display outside "The Montreal Carver" store on the road near the Montreal River, Ontario, north of Sault Ste. Marie. He has also demonstrated his carving in bas-relief at an international fair in Louisville, Kentucky, of specialized machinery used for woodworking and furniture making. Forty Canadian manufacturers participated in the fair through the assistance of the Canadian Ministry of Trade and Commerce.

RABY, Herman (Cont'd)

References

Québec L'Action, Qué., Oct. 18, 1968 "Le sculpteur Herman Raby. . ." (photo and caption)
L'Avant-Poste Gaspésien, Amqui, Qué., Dec. 26, 1968 (photo and caption — showing Raby at work at the Amqui Cultural Centre)
Saguenay Le Quotidien, Chicoutimi, Qué., Apr. 20, 1978 "Art Dans L'Entrée" (photo and caption of two gigantic wood sculptures done by Raby for "The Montreal Carver" store)

RACEY, Arthur George
1870-1941

Born in Quebec City, the son of Dr. John Racey, M.D.E. who was largely responsible for the establishment of the Jeffrey Hale Hospital at Quebec. Arthur Racey's grandfather was also a doctor. His mother, Martha S. Ritchie had been born and educated in Scotland. He attended the Quebec High School, then St. Francis College where he was active in sports (was captain of the football team). He entered McGill University and during this period became interested in cartooning. He submitted a cartoon to John R. Dougall of *The Montreal Witness* who was so impressed with his work that he hired him as a full-fledged newspaper artist. Racey did both cartoons and illustrations during this period and was described by S. Morgan-Powell in these words, ". . .his lively wit, his shrewd survey of the daily scene, his ability to hit off the world situation from day to day, speedily gained for him widespread recognition, not only in his own field, but throughout the Dominion." He joined *The Montreal Star* in November of 1899 and in later years was described by Morgan-Powell as follows, "He reads everything that is likely to help him in his work. He keeps more than abreast of the news of the world. He has in many instances anticipated with astonishing vision the development of world affairs. He often sees through the beclouding miasma of conflicting news despatches right into the heart of an international situation. He has developed that invaluable faculty of reading between the lines which is, to the cartoonist, both inspiration, authority and finesse. With Racey, the idea is everything, as indeed it should be. . . .He says what he has to say outright, forcefully, vividly, dramatically; and he says it in such a manner as to leave you under no delusion. . . .He will submit half a dozen suggestions daily for a cartoon. Once he sets to work, he works more rapidly than any other artist I have ever known; and I have known many, in many lands. His work is broad in technique, bold in outline, and free from decorative drawbacks. . .Racey's humour is universal. It belongs to no particular school. That is why his cartoons are reproduced in newspapers and magazines round the world, in Europe, throughout the United States, in South America, in Australia, in India and in South Africa and Japan." He studied painting under William Brymner and many of his oils and water colours found their way into private collections. He was also a collector of antiques which included such items as French bayonets dug up from the Plains of Abraham; the sword belonging to the first Canadian officer under de Salaberry to cross the Chateauguay River in pursuit of the American forces (the officer was Captain Daley, great-grandfather of Racey's wife); relics from East Africa and other items. He was fond of friends, golf, curling and animals. He was a charitable person and helped many causes. During World War One he raised $50,000 for the Canadian Red Cross by touring Canada and showing lantern slides of

1900

RACEY, Arthur George (Cont'd)

his cartoons with a running commentary. He gave talks to various groups on many other occasions. He published two books of his cartoons entitled, *The Englishman in Canada* (1902) and *Canadian Men of Affairs in Cartoon*. Examples of his work were hung in the White House; office of the U.S. Secretary of the Navy; houses and offices of many U.S. Senators, Members of Congress, Consuls as well as homes of several Canadian Premiers and in libraries across Canada. A collection of his work was donated to McGill University Library and Morin College, Quebec. Some of his work also appeared in *Grip*, *Life* (N.Y.), *Punch* (Lond., Eng.) and other publications. Nearly 200 of his original sketches were presented to the Library of Trent University in 1968 by John R. Dickinson, a grandson of Racey and resident of Peterborough. At the time of his death Racey was survived by his wife the former Isabel Julia Daley; one daughter, Mrs. A.G. Dickinson (Trail, B.C.); five brothers: John (Lennoxville, P.Q.); Kenneth (Vancouver, B.C.); Robert (Paris, Ont.); Herbert (Westmount, P.Q.); Percy (Oakland, Cal., U.S.A.); three sisters: Miss Harriet Racey (Quebec City); Miss Daisy Racey (Lennoxville, P.Q.); Mrs. C.B. Washer (New Carlisle, P.Q.) two grandchildren: John and Anne Dickinson (Trail, B.C.).

References

Canadian Men and Women Of The Time by H.J. Morgan, Briggs, Tor., 1912, P.924

The McGill News, McGill University, Mtl., Vol.XVI, Autumn, 1935, No.4 "Racey," by S. Morgan-Powell, P.9-15

The Gazette, Mtl., Dec. 22, 1941 "Noted Cartoonist A.G. Racey, Is Dead"

Montreal Star, Mtl., Dec. 22, 1941 "Cartoonist Was World Famous"

Quebec Chronicle-Telegraph, Quebec City, Dec. 23, 1941 "Arthur Racey A Gifted Quebecer"

Peterboro Review, Ont. May 2, 1968 "Sketches Given to Trent"

RACICOT, Camille
b. 1935

Born in Valcourt, Quebec, he took classical studies at the Séminaire de Sherbrooke, then travelled to Paris, France, to attend drawing courses at the A.B.C. School. He returned to Canada and studied for five years at the École des Beaux-Arts, Montreal (1955-60). A sculptor, painter, ceramist and potter he opened his first studio and workshop in Lachine where he conducted research into ceramics, plastics and fibreglass then began his first productions integrated with architecture which included ceramic murals, hammered brass murals, concrete bas-reliefs, sculpture in stone, granite, bronze and ceramics. He did mainly figurative work up to 1961. He began his evening courses in painting, sculpture and ceramics for adults and children. By 1965 he had out-grown his Lachine studio and built a new three storey structure in Kirkland Industrial Park, Montreal, which opened in 1966. Ninety students attended his classes including sixty adults and thirty children. In his own work he soon developed a reputation for his advanced concepts in art. Between 1972 and 1974 he also did cultural animation and in 1975 and 1976 did the same type of anima-tion for the Ministry of Cultural Affairs regional office in Sherbrooke. He opened a store for artists' supplies and ceramic products in 1972. In 1974 he sold his Kirkland workshop and moved to the mountain area at Melbourne, Quebec, where he built himself a workshop in the forest and painted a series of pictures which he called "Return to my youth." In 1976 he spent some time on

RACICOT, Camille (Cont'd)

the Île d'Orléans. During the same year he completed a life-sized wood sculpture for the St-Laurent Art Centre. He also gave lectures on the history of painting using transparencies and lectured as well on picture composition. In 1980 he was still residing at Melbourne, Quebec. He held his first solo show in 1965 and subsequent shows as follows: Le Boutique Vic Karo, Quebec City (1965); Kirkland studio (1968); Maison Rothmans, Sherbrooke, Que. (1975); Expo Hall du CHU, Sherbrooke (1975); Galerie Artistique, Sherbrooke (1976); Valcourt Cultural Centre, Valcourt, Que. (1977); Beaulne Museum, Coaticook, Que. (1980); Sherbrooke University Centre, Sherbrooke, Que. (1980). His ceramic murals can be seen at l'École Dalbé-Viau, Lachine, Que.; St-Grégoire-le-Loyola, Mtl. West, Que.; Caisse Populaire, St-Grégoire-le-Grand, Mtl.; Chapel St-Charles Seminary, Sherbrooke, Que.; Bombardier Museum, Valcourt, Que.; mural on facade of St-Ignace-de-Loyola, Mtl. West, Que.; mural in hammered brass for a Windsor, Ont. bank; Central Theological College, Mtl., Que.; in Parc Octogonal, Ville St-Michel, Mtl.; University of Sherbrooke, Sherbrooke, Que.; sculpture in Carrara marble on side of altar for Saint-Pierre-aux-Liens Church, Ville Saint-Pierre, Mtl. Island, Que. and elsewhere. In his spare time Racicot makes decorative and utilitarian objects out of ceramics and from pottery clay. He collects old furniture, tools, vases and earthenware pots from all over Quebec and Acadia country in the Maritimes.

References

La Tribune, Sherbrooke, Que., undated clipping "Camille Racicot a livré une mural au Séminaire"

Le Messager de Lachine, Lachine, Que., April 30, 1964 "Deux murales intérieures à l'École Dalbé Viau"

Le Soleil, Quebec City, April 6, 1965 "Exposition du sculpteur et céramiste Camille Racicot, chez 'Le Boutiquier' " par Gaston L'Heureux

Le Messager de Lachine, Que., Dec. 1, 1966 "Atelier de sculpture et céramique ouvert par Camille Racicot"

La Patrie, Mtl., Que., Dec. 4, 1966 "Sculpteur, peintre et céramiste, Camille Racicot" par M. Maitre

Messenger, Lachine, Que., Nov. 28, 1968 (show at his workshop in Kirkland).

Pointe Claire Lakeshore News & Chronicle, Que., June 19, 1969 "Artist to open new gallery"

Equipment Journal, Tor., Ont., Nov. 2, 1972 "Pneumatic Equipment Is An Aid To Artist"

La Tribune, Sherbrooke, Que., Aug. 26, 1975 "L'exposition de Camille Racicot: des tableaux où le peintre est absent" par Pierre Francoeur

Ibid, Dec. 11, 1975 "Racicot expose à la Maison Rothmans"

Ibid, Apr. 28, 1976 "Sur les ailes de la peinture"

Ibid, Nov. 24, 1976 "Racicot expose"

La Voix de l'Est, Granby, Que., Apr. 28, 1976 "Un cours d'histoire de l'art avec Racicot. . ."

Ibid, Apr. 15, 1976 " 'Les gens de mon village' vus par Camille Racicot"

La Tribune, Sherbrooke, Que., Oct. 6, 1977 "Racicot de retour à Valcourt avec l'automne"

Ibid, May 22, 1980 "Racicot expose au Musée Beaulne"

RACICOT, Dan
b.(c) 1943

The son of Mr. & Mrs. Stanley Racicot, he attended Sudbury High School where he became particularly interested in English Literature and the poets Wordsworth, Shelley and Coleridge. His own poems were described as having the metre of Shelley with a modernist view and staccato flair symbolic of the

RACICOT, Dan (Cont'd)

age of space. It is his poetry and literature which has inspired many of his paintings. Two large murals were painted by him in his Sudbury home, one a landscape described by E.J. Meakes of *The Sudbury Star* as follows, "The mural, which decorates one wall of the recreation room. . .was inspired by a poem entitled Birnham Wood, appearing in a book of poems Dan Racicot hopes to have published this year. . .The 12-foot long mural brings the wood into the recreation room, and the stringent limits of the four walls achieve a certain airiness. The gnarled tree trunk with its twisting branches demands to be touched, to be incised with names and lovers' hearts. 'I like painting big,' says Dan Racicot. 'It is so satisfying.' The small figure in the middle background is the artist's version of Tom Jones and is the key to the theme of the picture: 'The world is beautiful but it needs man to make it alive.' " Many of Racicot's other sketches and paintings are on a variety of subjects. He was writing a classical tragedy for the stage in the Shakespearean idiom but modernized, also a Canadian novel, a romantic allegory. He auditioned with the National Theatre School, Montreal in 1965. He also intended to study drama for his M.A. He was a teacher at Sudbury High School in 1965.

Reference

    The Sudbury Star, Ont., July 30, 1965 " 'Painting big is satisfying' says talented city teacher" by E.J. Meakes

RACICOT, Denyse
b. 1937

Born in Montreal, Quebec, she showed early artistic talent and later attended the École des Beaux-Arts, Montreal for five years. A painter and muralist she is known for her water colours, drawings and wood construction murals. She exhibited her work at the following places: Comité Paritaire de la Construction, Sorel, Que. (1965); Press Club Mtl.; Municipal Library, Sorel, Que.; Cultural Centre, Tracey, Que. (1968). Her commissions include: Wood mural for Centre d'Apprentissage des Métiers de la Construction, Sorel, Qué.; mural at the Cultural Centre, Tracey, Que. She was teaching drawing and painting for first year students at the Cultural Centre in Tracy in 1968.

References

    Courrier Riviera, Sorel, Que., Feb. 6, 1968 "Expositions de peintures au Centre Culturel de Tracy"

    Courrier Riviera, Sorel, Que., Dec. 23, 1969 "Denise Racicot: Artiste De Son Temps"

RACICOT, Georges
b.(c) 1943

He started carving in 1977 and is a self-taught artist. The National Museum of Man became interested in his work after reading about him in *Le Droit*. Subsequently the Museum purchased twelve of his sculptures and exhibited his work in a show of folk art. He is married to Thérèse Clermont of Hawkesbury. They have three sons and live in Calumet, Quebec.

RACICOT, Georges (Cont'd)

Reference

Le Droit, Ottawa, Ont., Aug. 1, 1979 "Le sculpteur Georges Racicot — Un reportage le mène au musée" par Edmond Laughren

---

RACINE, Cecile s.c.o.

Born in Casselman, Ontario, she received her primary education from local schools and graduated with her Superior Diploma, Class "A" Certificate in Arts and Education from the Scolasticat Notre-Dame-de-Grâce which is affiliated with Laval University. For ten years she studied painting, sculpture, modelling, ceramics, frescoes, weaving, theatre decor, history of art and music and also graduated in Fine Arts from the Catholic University of America. For a number of years she taught in several schools in Quebec. In her own art she has done a wide range of work. Her collages-montages covering the history of music from the 16th to 20th Centuries were shown in 1971 in a retrospective exhibition at the National Arts Centre, Ottawa. These particular works were done as part of her requirements for her Master's Thesis. The exhibition was also shown at the Stanton Residence by the Centre d'animation culturel de l'Université d'Ottawa. The National Arts Centre bought her musical history works for its permanent audio-visual collection. She has been art coordinator for the Outaouais regional school board. She taught art at the École poly-valente, Cité des Jeunes, l'école St-Jean-Baptiste, Hull, Que.; Collège Marguerite d'Youville, Hull. Que. Was teaching art and art history at St-Joseph Secondary School, Hull, in 1971.

References

Le Droit, Ottawa, Ont., Feb. 10, 1971 "Une artiste qui est aussi une expérimentatrice" (photo of artist with her work)

Le guide des artisans créateurs du Québec par Jean-Pierre Payette, la Presse, Mtl., 1974, P.280

RACINE, Guy

Born in Ayersville near Lachute, Quebec, he graduated from the École des Beaux-Arts, Montreal and also studied two years with Janine Leroux. A painter he took part in a two-man show at the Centre d'Art d'Argenteuil, Lachute (1965) and participated in several group shows at Granby, Sherbrooke and Lachute. Was teacher of plastic arts for schools in the C.E.C.M. and also for classes at the Argenteuil Art Centre in 1965.

References

Montreal Metro-Express, Mtl., Que., Apr. 28, 1965 (notice of show at Argenteuil Art Centre)

Hawkesbury Le Carillon, Hawkesbury, Ont., Apr. 29, 1965 "Exposition de deux jeunes peintres"

RACINE, Jacques

Born in Montreal, he studied drawing and sculpture at the Montreal Museum of Fine Arts and at the Academy of Commercial Art at the New England School of Art, Boston. A wood sculptor, film producer and graphic artist he is known for his audio-visual conceptions, sculpture reliefs, drawings and other works. He produced a film on children's Saturday Workshops also a film on bilingualism and biculturalism. He carried out studies in Haiti on graphic expression of children's faces. He has worked for thirty-eight years in publicity in audio-visual communications. His drawings for biological illustrations have appeared in publications of Boston University. He is also a concepteur-graphiste for the Unemployment Insurance Commission in Quebec. Racine teaches Saturday Workshops for children, adolescents and adults at the parish of St. Pierre Chanel, Hull. He held a two-man show with potter Jean Aubry at his workshop in Hull in 1972. He has been an inventor for over thirty years and has about thirty letters of patent.

Reference

Le Droit, Ottawa, Ont., May 23, 1972 "Une exposition où l'originalité brille de mille et un feux" par Darquise Timmerman

RACINE, Marie

Originally from Granby, Quebec, she studied at the École des Beaux-Arts, Montreal with Jacques de Tonnancour and Gordon Webber. She is known for her paintings which show the influence of the automatists. She has participated in a two-person show with Paul Lussier at Galerie les 2B, Saint-Antoine-sur-Richelieu, Quebec (1977); three-person show at the Centre Culturel de Shawinigan, Que. (1979). She is also known for her activity in radio and television and is the author of a T.V. series.

References

Exhibition notice with biographical sketch, La Galerie les 2B, 948 rue du Rivage, Saint-Antoine-sur-Richelieu, Que., 1977

La Voix de l'Est, Granby, Qué., Aug. 31, 1977 "Une concitoyenne expose pour la première fois!"

Le Nouvelliste, Trois Rivières, Qué., May 4, 1979 "Le Salon du printemps"

RACINE, Raymonde

She is known for her sculpture in wood, soapstone and sandstone and gave a demonstration of sculpture at the Centre des arts visuels, Montreal, Quebec (1977).

Reference

La Presse, Mtl., Qué., Mar. 12, 1977 "Au Centre des arts visuels" (photo of artist with work)

RACKUS, George Kestutis
b. 1927

Born in Lithuania, he came to Canada at an early age and spent most of his childhood in a small town near Toronto. He studied Fine Arts at Wayne University, Detroit (1949-50); Drawing and Painting at the Ontario College of Art, Toronto (1952-53); Figure Painting and Composition at the Académie André Lhote, Paris (1953-54) (1955-56) and at the École Nationale Supérieure des Beaux-Arts, Paris (1953-54) (1955-57). During his summers he travelled in Europe and Spain and on the Balearic Islands. After returning home he sailed on a fifty-foot sloop in 1955 with two writers and two other painters. Heading for South America they managed to sail a good way down the eastern seaboard before returning home. Later that year Rackus visited Mexico on a painting trip. While studying in Paris Rackus lived on the left bank. His early work was strongly influenced by Cubists since Lhote, his mentor, had been part of the Cubist movement around 1907. He assisted Lhote in the production of murals (1955-56). It was Lhote that brought Rackus's work to the attention of Agnès Lefort in Montreal. By 1957 he was exhibiting his work at Galerie Agnès Lefort and in 1960 held his first solo Canadian exhibition there. By now he had moved from Cubism to a freer form of painting and was noted by Robert Ayre in *The Montreal Star* as follows, "He paints in synthetics and oils, mostly on board, and he works large. But his paintings are bigger than their actual dimensions. His concepts are big. You have a feeling of weight, of tremendous displacement, of power and intense conviction. Waldemar George has felt his work to be Canadian, the work of a man of the north. You will not find the Canadian landscape in it, unless implicitly. But if vigor and amplitude and a profound seriousness are Canadian, then he is intensively a Canadian. The painting Miss Lefort has called 'The Black Sun' may suggest the Arctic, with its shapes like the bleached bones of a lost ship and the sun, an immense presence without heat, brooding over the wintry waste. But it is a landscape drawn by the imagination out of the depths of the unconscious and composed by the conscious mind. Rackus uses a great deal of black, which he has discovered to be in accord with the fundamental gravity of his spirit, and this, with the powerful movement of his portentous forms, impresses you with a sense, sometimes, of foreboding. I found his painting a profoundly stirring and enlarging experience." By 1960 Rackus was conducting art classes at the Clarkson Artists' Centre near Toronto in the summers, a school which he himself founded to provide a wide range of learning opportunities for the young and old alike. Students from as far away as Brantford attended. From 1961 to about 1964 he worked on a series of lithographic prints "Terre et Ciel" (Earth and Sky). And in 1962 he also presented for the first time water colours. Viewing his water colours and monotypes at the Alice Peck Gallery in Burlington a writer for the *Port Credit Weekly* noted, "There is in the works of Rackus, a fine feeling for subtle relations of color and lyric movement. Each painting creates within a non-objective sphere, moods of infinite variety. In both media Rackus evokes spontaneity and freshness that characterize his work. With this there is a strong sense of construction that does not over-impose." In 1962 he also became administrator of the Glenhyrst Arts Council and Glenhyrst Gardens, Brantford. He was invited as art instructor to the Six Nations Indian Reserve in Ontario in 1962 and was instrumental in founding the Six Nations Indian Arts Council. He became director of the Picture Loan Gallery, Toronto. In his own work he pioneered the development of painting with dyes on aluminum sheets. He started his first research of painting on metal in 1961. From 1964-67 he experimented with anodizing techniques and developed a direct dye application for anodized aluminum. His experiments were done in his Clarkson studio where he received the help of Dave Burry, then technical advisor for Alcan Aluminum Limited. He tried out colour applications for various metal alloys in his search for maximum colour intensity. He experimented to achieve colour control. His search for proper processing facilities ended in Brussels, Belgium, where work was being done along the lines he had in mind. There he found an anodizing plant that met the needs of the artist. He made arrangements with the firm to process a set number of panels each year from special grade high-purity aluminum which would be ready for him to work on during the summers. The finished panels were then shipped back to Canada. The process was highly successful and the colourful luminous works were selected by the Belgium government to be included in their exhibit, "Art and Technology" at "Man and His World" in Montreal in 1968. He exhibited a collection of his aluminum paintings along with his prints in Toronto and then they were circulated in the Maritimes (1972-73) through the sponsorship of the Art Department of The New Brunswick Museum for the Atlantic Provinces Art Circuit. Accompanying the exhibition was a documentary film on the anodizing technique, and a catalogue of works with introduction by Robert Percival. A selection of his aluminum works was shown in the Oakville Centennial Gallery in 1974 when they were described by the *Oakville Daily Journal* in these words, "The large panels glitter and the colors, in a variety of abstract renditions, are usually rich and vibrant. The colors seem to be not so much on the material as in it. Viewers are intrigued and wonder how the effect is achieved. At the opening of the Oakville exhibit Rackus showed a film explaining the process." On the larger aluminum panels he uses a pointillistic technique of multiple colours to arrive at a coloured area. Some of the individual panels come as large as 40 by 82 inches and can be assembled to cover any given area. Because of the light weight of aluminum, large works can be easily installed. By 1979 he was also making tapestry designs. In this work he prepared sketches, chose colours and textures of the materials and then worked closely with the artisans who produce the finished pieces. His solo shows include: Galerie Foyer des Artistes, Paris, France (1954); British Institute, Barcelona, Spain (1956); Galeria Corcarijo, Ibiza, Spain (1956); Two-man show, Hart House, Tor. (1957); Galerie Foyer des Artistes, Paris (1959); Galerie Agnès Lefort, Mtl. (1960); Picture Loan Society, Tor. (1960, 1963, 1969, 1972, 1973); New Vision Centre Gallery, Lond., Eng. (1961); Galerie des Beaux-Arts, Paris (1961); Gallery Moos, Tor. (1962); Alice Peck Gallery, Burlington, Ont. (1962); Ciurlionis Gallery, Chicago, Ill. (1964); Glenhyrst Arts Council Gallery, Brantford, Ont. (1964); Galerie Horn, Luxembourg, Lux. (1964); Galerie Wildanger, Brussels, Belgium (1964); Lofthouse Galleries Ltd., Ottawa (1968); McMaster University, Hamilton (1970); travelling exhibit in the Maritimes (1972-73); Centennial Gallery, Oakville (1974); Picture Loan Gallery, Hamilton Place, Mississauga (1975); Canadian Embassy, Brussels, Belgium (1976); Harbourfront Community Gallery, Tor. (1979); Studio 3, Hamilton (1979); Clarkson-Lorne Park Library, Mississauga (1979). He has participated in many group shows in Paris, London, Chicago, New York, Mexico and Canada. He is represented in the following collections: Sarnia Public Library & Art Gallery, Sarnia, Ont.; Univ. of Western Ontario, Lond., Ont.; Art Gallery of Ontario, Tor.; York Univ., Tor.; Alcan Aluminum Ltd., Tor.; Shell Canada Ltd., Oakville, Ont.; National Gallery of

RACKUS, George Kestutis (Cont'd)

Canada, Ottawa; Memorial University, St. John's, Nfld.; New York Central Library, N.Y.C.; Ciurlionis Art Gallery, Chicago, Ill.; Victoria and Albert Museum, Lond., Eng.; Misarachi Collection, Mexico. Rackus lives on an old farm in Cayuga, Ontario with his wife Denise and their two children. He owns a 23-foot fibreglass sailboat "Matilda" in which he travels to summer activity centres and makes other trips as well. One of his hobbies which he took up in the early 1960's was skin diving, an experience which has no doubt added concepts for him in his art. Rackus speaks four languages and has been instrumental in bringing Lithuanian art to Canada and arranging Canadian art to be shown in Lithuania.

References

Globe & Mail, Tor., Oct. 12, 1957 "Current Displays" (Rackus & Coates at Hart House)

La Presse, Mtl., Mar. 10, 1959 "Expo d'un peintre canadien à Paris"

The Gazette, Mtl., Jan. 23, 1960 "One-Man Show of Abstracts" D.Y.P.

Le Petit Journal, Mtl., Jan. 24, 1960 "Un interprète de notre siècle" par Paul Gladu

Le Devoir, Mtl., Jan. 25, 1960 "La Peinture de Rackus"

The Montreal Star, Mtl., Jan. 30, 1960 (review by Robert Ayre)

N.D.G. Monitor, Mtl., Feb. 25, 1960 "Writer puts foot into own mouth when interviewing artist Rackus" by Wanda Boytscha

Oakville Journal, June 1, 1961 "Artists' Centre Starting Junior Classes In June"

Burlington Gazette, Ont., June 1, 1961 "Artists' Centre For Area Painters To Open In June For Second Summer" (photo and article)

The Toronto Star, Ont., Jan. 27, 1962 "A Painter Speaks Up" (Rackus answers Fulford)

Globe & Mail, Tor., Ont., Apr. 14, 1962 "Pick Rackus to Head Arts Council, Centre"

Brantford Expositor, Ont., May 15, 1962 "Glenhyrst Cultural Showcase Of Province-Wide Importance"

Port Credit Weekly, Ont., June 28, 1962 "Abstract Watercolors, Monotypes Exhibited By George Rackus"

Ibid, Mar. 12, 1964 "Art Gallery Home — Murphy Family In The Picture" (Dr. and Mrs. Gordon Murphy hang paintings & prints by George Rackus)

Canadian Water Colours, Drawings and Prints 1966, NGC, Ottawa, No. 104

Ottawa Journal, Ont., Sept. 10, 1968 "Aluchromes — New-Look Art On View in City" by W.Q. Ketchum

Globe & Mail,Tor., Ont., Feb. 1, 1969 (about his Aluchromes)

Hamilton Spectator, Ont., Dec. 19, 1970 "Art — Fascinating contrast at McMaster Gallery" by John Bryden

Toronto Daily Star, Ont., Mar. 12, 1971 "Gallery director trailblazes extraordinary new medium" by Peter Wilson

Chatham News, Ont., Jan. 22, 1972 "Art Of Canadian Indian Gallery Lecture Topic"

Welland-Port Colborne Tribune, Ont., Mar. 23, 1971 "A Cultural Experience — Art Gallery Gives New Dimension To Living" by Ted Thurston

Gift from the Douglas M. Duncan Collection and the Milne-Duncan Bequest by P. Théberge, NGC, Ottawa, 1971, No. 246

Art Gallery of Ontario, the Canadian collection by Helen Pepall Bradfield, McGraw-Hill, Tor., P.381

Art Magazine, Tor., Summer, 1971 "Anodized Aluminum As An Art Media" by George Rackus

Globe & Mail, Tor., Ont., Oct. 28, 1972 "Other Galleries"

George Rackus, Anodized Aluminum Works & Prints with introduction by Robert Percival, New Brunswick Museum, 1972 (catalogue with biographical notes)

Halifax Mail Star, N.S., Apr. 9, 1973 "George Rackus anodizes aluminum into works of art" by Gretchen Pierce

Oakville Daily Journal Record, Ont., Jan. 9, 1974 "George Rackus puts a new shine on art"

Hamilton Spectator, Ont., Mar. 14, 1975 "Practical plan puts an artist in the classroom"

RACKUS, George Kestutis (Cont'd)

St. Catharines Standard, Ont., June 2, 1977 "Visiting artist lives aboard boat in Port Dalhousie basin"
Hamilton Spectator, Ont., Feb. 3, 1979 "Aluminum is not a light medium"
Ibid, Nov. 15, 1980 "International artist makes Cayuga home" by Cheryl MacDonald

RADFORD, Ed

He studied art in Vancouver and Toronto and held a solo show at the Isaacs Gallery, Toronto in 1981 when John Bentley Mays noted his work as follows, "Radford's images generally depict real, recognizable things and people. There are dads and moms and prom-dates, Naugahyded lounge chairs, fast cars, sailboats — visual quotes, picked out of the suburban and cottage-country environments just like ones Ed Radford grew up in, and served up fast and dumb all over large black and blue fields of heavily shoved and dragged paint. His colored-pencil drawings, as well, feature the same scraps of subject-matter scattered like sketchbook doodles over the page. . . .Whether the subject is a new Canadian immigrant, surrounded by glittering status-symbols, or the Junes, loons and moons of Cottage Country (1980), compassion pervades these pictures, and gives them unexpected strength. It is true that Radford denies us elegant Renaissance perspective — his objects have no necessary spatial relation to each other, any more than things in a supermarket do — and he doesn't give us a shred of Matisse-like pictorial prettiness. But he does these things, not to show what a bad boy he can be, but in order to rivet attention on his rather affecting sermons."

Reference

Globe & Mail, Tor., Ont., June 2, 1981 "Ed Radford's style Rec Room Realism?" by John Bentley Mays

RADFORD, Gary Charles

b. 1952

Born in St. Thomas, Ontario, he is known for his work in acrylic, ink, pencil, water colour, serigraph, sculpture and creative photography. He exhibited his photography at the Trajectory Gallery, London, Ontario, in 1976 when Judy Malone noted his work as follows, "The Windowed Walls, a collection of 300 slides technically treated to produce some stunning results, operates on one level as an absorbing visual experience. The St. Thomas artist has transformed ordinary camera studies of landscapes or figures into extraordinary abstracted expressions, with tricks including scratching the surface of the slide or coloring it with food dye." He is represented in the collections of the St. Thomas Psychiatric Hospital and the Elgin County Museum, St. Thomas.

References

London Evening Free Press, Ont., Oct. 28, 1976 "Widowed Walls at Trajectory — Slide projections sometimes stunning" by Judy Malone
The Index of Ontario Artists, Ed. Hennie Wolff, Vis. Arts Ont./Ont. Assoc. of Art Galleries, Tor., 1978

RADFORD, John A.
1860-1940

Born in Devonport, Devenshire, England, he studied drawing in the Mechanics Institute (a branch of the South Kensington School of Art) and came to Montreal, Canada, where he continued his studies at the Montreal School of Design and completed his mechanical education with honours. He practiced architecture for a number of years. Later he moved to Toronto where he worked with the firm of Edwards and Webster and other architects. He designed the "Ice Palace" in Montreal in 1897 and did designs for the Toronto Opera House and The Forum Building, Yonge Street. He became a member of the Ontario Society of Artists (1890), the Architectural Club and he exhibited his paintings with the Royal Canadian Academy. He painted in oils and water colours but worked mainly in water colours. He did architectural work in Winnipeg and finally he moved to Vancouver in 1911 where he continued his interest in art. He wrote an art column for the *Vancouver Sun*. Viewing his paintings in 1933 when he was seventy-three years old, the *Vancouver Province* noted, "An interesting display of water colors is to be found in the quarters of the Vancouver Sketch Club, 163 West Hastings. John Radford is the artist, and those who know the calibre of this painter's work need no introduction to his sketches. The group at present on exhibit is composed of landscapes, little bits chosen by an artist's eye here and there in Ontario and British Columbia. There are bits of farm land, seen from a hill, which offer an intriguing vista of autumn colorings; there are wintry woodland scenes where the new fallen snow lies lightly between bare-branches of trees and there are lilting notes in the spring as it falls across green meadow-lands. Clear color and balanced composition lend interest to this work, while the artist displays his excellent grasp of draughtsmanship." Many of Radford's paintings included scenes of the Pacific Coast. One of his activities was writing short stories. Radford died at the age of eighty in Vancouver and was active in writing and painting until the end.

References

Vancouver Province, Aug. 23, 1931 (note of Radford's work as a painter)
Ibid, Oct. 18, 1933 "Fine Group of Water Colors On Display At Vancouver Sketch Club"
Vancouver Sun, B.C., Sept. 24, 1938 "John Radford Noted Artist, 78 Next Week"
Ibid, Dec. 4, 1939 "Radford to Hold 1-Man Art Display"
Vancouver Province, B.C., Dec. 13, 1939 "Radford Paintings Are On Exhibition"
Vancouver Sun, B.C., May 25, 1940 "John Radford, Dean of City Artists, Dies — Architect Who Turned to The Brush"
Toronto Telegram, Ont., June 8, 1940 "John Radford Dead At Coast Familiar Here — Architect, Artist and Short Story Writer, Designed Old Toronto Opera House and Forum Building"
Early Painters and Engravers in Canada by J. Russell Harper, Univ. Tor. Press, Tor., 1970, P.258
Royal Canadian Academy of Arts, Exhibitions and Members 1880-1979 by Evelyn de R. McMann, Univ. Tor. Press, Tor., 1981, P.335

RAE, George

A wildlife artist who produced stamps in 1973 for the Zoological Society of Montreal for its campaign against abuses practiced on Canadian wildlife. The stamps included scenes of a lynx held in a leg-hold trap, a baby seal being clubbed, the shooting of a polar bear and a deer being chased by a snowmobile.

RAE, George (Cont'd)

References

    Toronto Star, Ont., July 20, 1973 (wildlife stamps reproduced with caption)
    Sarnia Observer, Ont., July 21, 1973 (wildlife stamps reproduced with caption)

RAE, Jim (James D. Rae)

Born in Ontario, he received his basic training at Toronto's Danforth Technical School and the Ontario College of Art. A painter of landscapes, portraits, nude studies, still life, abstracts and non-figurative works. He held solo shows at the Commonwealth Savings and Loan Corporation on Sparks Street, Ottawa, Ont. (1964); Orchard Park Mall, Kelowna, B.C. (1973).

References

    Ottawa Citizen, Nov. 13, 1964 "Rae's playful search exercises many media" by Carl Weiselberger
    Kelowna Courier, B.C., Dec. 31, 1973 "Rae Works On Display"

RAE, Dr. John

A family doctor who lives in Moose Creek, Ontario, who came to Canada from England in 1968. During his free hours he has done some remarkably fine oil and water colour paintings which include portraits, landscapes and other subjects. He held shows of his paintings at Gallery Colber and Place Ville Marie, Montreal; Simon Fraser Centennial Library, Cornwall (1977).

Reference

    Cornwall Standard Freeholder, Ont., Jan. 29, 1977 "Water Color Display" (photo of paintings and caption)

RAE, Leah (Rose Greenberg)

She attended the Central Technical School and Ontario College of Art night courses in Toronto and over the years has worked in painting, enamel work, wood-carving, mosaics, sculpture, ceramics, and dolls. Her dolls include world known celebrities and historical figures. She has exhibited her work at the Canadian National Exhibition in Toronto and has a wide range of creative interests. Lives in Toronto.

References

    The Toronto Star, Ont., June 15, 1959 "Took Flier in Arts When She Was Forty"
    Globe & Mail, Tor., Ont., June 28, 1973 "Dollmaker's apartment scattered with heads — Searching for Sir Winston among the apples"

RAE, Nina

A painter from Cranbrook, B.C., who has done a variety of subjects including portrait painting and has demonstrated her fine skills in that centre.

Reference

The Daily Townsman, Cranbrook, B.C., Mar. 6, 1979 "Cranbrook Artist Nina Rae" (photo of artist at work)

RAECHER, Stan

A sculptor from Calgary, Alta., who works in steel. His work is modern and pleasing. He is represented in the collection of the Calgary Planetarium. Raecher works for the Glenbow Foundation.

References

Calgary Albertan, Alta., Nov. 14, 1967 (article on one of his sculptures)
Calgary Herald, Alta. (clipping undated, article by John Francis)

RAEGELE, Mabel (Mrs.)

A Moncton, N.B. artist she is known for her enameling and batik work. Each piece she makes is an original as she doesn't believe in producing assembly line products. Her designs come from her imagination or from magazines or books which she then adapts to her own personal statement. In some of her batiks Mrs. Raegele has combined tie-dyeing to create interesting effects. Her works are on display at the Tourism New Brunswick Information and Handicrafts Shop in Moncton.

Reference

Moncton Transcript, N.B., Feb. 2, 1974 "She's The Artist's Artist" by Anne Leslie

RAICUS, Ethel

Born in Toronto, Ontario, she graduated from the Central Technical School in Commercial Art and was a scholarship student at the Ontario College of Art graduating with her Industrial Design Certificate. She worked in industrial design and commercial art and has been painting on a part-time basis for twenty-two years. Known for her work in water colour, acrylic, oil and gouache she has painted mainly in non-representational style. Kay Kritzwiser noted her work for the Holy Blossom Temple, Toronto, as follows, ". . .the dynamic, disciplined paintings by Ethel Raicus at Holy Blossom Temple. . .are big, open, serene with a kind of gathering force at the centre of each. The furious vitality which often seemed trapped in her watercolors sorts itself out into disciplined paint areas. The emotion is still there, her colors are firm and the work becomes a statement of self, made with this new conviction. She has a warm, wide smile

RAICUS, Ethel (Cont'd)

for everything on the walls. 'What I'm saying is on these walls. That's all paint, all brushwork, no spray; just brush, paint and me. And I feel great about it. I feel mature. An artist has peaks and low points. He can't push. He must wait out the low period and be ready for the peak period when it comes'. . . .Her previous work — watercolors, beautiful but full of driving fury — sold well and were well-liked." Ethel Raicus has been a staff member of Holy Blossom Religious School for over twenty years. She is director of the Hebrew department, which includes a language department for adults as well as children. She also taught evening art classes for the Etobicoke Community Art Group. Her solo shows include: Pollock Gallery, Tor. (1973, 1974, 1975, 1976). She has exhibited as well with the Royal Canadian Academy (1963); the Ontario Society of Artists and the Canadian Society of Painters in Water Colour. She was awarded "Best in Show" prize at the Canadian Society of Painters in Water Colour Annual Show. Member: C.S.P.W.C. and O.S.A. Lives in Toronto.

References

Advertiser-Guardian, Etobicoke, Ont., Apr. 14, 1966 "New Experiences In Painting Goal Of Etobicoke Art Group"

Globe & Mail, Tor., Ont., Jan. 25, 1969 "Art At The Galleries — Art That Bears No Name" by Kay Kritzwiser

Fifty Years The Canadian Society of Painters in Water Colour 1925-1975, by Katherine A. Jordan, A.G.O., Tor., 1976, P.33

The Index of Ontario Artists, Ed. Hennie Wolff, Vis. Arts. Ont./Ont. Assoc. of Art Galleries, Tor., 1978, P.225-6

Royal Canadian Academy of Arts, Exhibitions and Members 1880-1979 by Evelyn de R. McMann, Univ. Tor. Press, Tor., P.335

RAILLARD, Michel

Born in Paris, France, he attended the École des Beaux-Arts where he studied drawing and painting for two years. He came to Canada and lived in Kitimat, B.C., in 1955, where he was an aluminum plant employee. Later he went to Vancouver where he opened a painting and sketching club. He did other jobs on the coast including making an industrial film at Bridge River for a French firm. Later he acted as cameraman for the Lew Perry Studio in Capilano, B.C. then moved to California in 1962. He was back in Victoria, B.C. in 1972. He is represented in Canadian collections by paintings in pastel and oils also by wood carvings.

References

Kitimat Northern Sentinel, B.C., Feb. 6, 1958 "Youthful Artist Gives Exhibition Here"

Victoria Colonist, B.C., Oct. 15, 1972 "Parisian's Story — Each New Task Just a Breeze" by Dorothy Wrotnowski

RAINE, Herbert
1875-1951

He was born in Sunderland, Durham County, England. As a boy he won many prizes for drawing. At the age of 17 he was articled to Frank Caws, F.R.I.B.A., architect. Evenings he studied at the Sunderland School of Art and received high marks in the South Kensington Art examinations. He won the annual prize from the Northern Architectural Association for his work on Gothic Architecture which he studied through the Oxford and Cambridge extension lectures. At 21 he entered the office of W.J. Gilliland in Belfast while he attended evening classes in art. He won the Sir Charles Lanyon Prize for measured drawings. He left Belfast to take a tour of France to make sketches of important cathedrals. He returned to England and entered the office of Sir Aston Webb, P.R.A. and was admitted as a student at the Royal Academy Schools where he studied for five years in the evenings. After leaving Webb's office he took a sketching trip to Italy for fourteen weeks, visiting Florence, Siena, Genoa, Verona, Venice, Milan, Vicenza and other places then returned to London to practice architecture. He came to Canada in 1907 and settled in Montreal to work as an architect. Around 1914 he began etching and made a series of plates of Old Montreal, some of which were made into a book which was published in 1921. He was elected A.R.C.A. in 1919 as architect, and R.C.A. as an etcher in 1926. Viewing his work in 1920 for *The Montreal Star*, S. Morgan-Powell noted, "Mr. Herbert Raine, the leading exponent in Canada of the art of architectural etching, has elected to place on record a number of the best known — as well as some of the least known — old landmarks in this city in the form of etchings which constitute a veritable historic panorama. . . .Mr. Raine has the keen eye of the artist for perceiving that upon which the average individual may gaze day after day with unseeing eyes. . . .One does not need to look very closely to discern a profound knowledge of architectural design in Mr. Raine's work. But this, although it is of immense significance, does not obtrude itself in his work, nor does it rob that work of a vestige of its intrinsic artistic value or charm. There are among these etchings gems of art. . . ." Raine also exhibited his water colours with his etchings over the years. His solo shows include: W.H. Scott & Sons, Mtl. (1920, 1934, 1936, 1942) and over 100 original paintings were exhibited at the Quebec Provincial Museum in 1950 when Raine presented them to the Museum. He died in Montreal in May of 1951 and was survived at that time by his three sisters, Edith Raine (Sunderland, England); Mrs. Leonard Kinimonth (Milnathort, Scotland); Mrs. D. Pickering (Penaemore, Wales) and a sister-in-law Miss Ada Bolton (Montreal). He was predeceased by his wife Maud Mary Bolton. He is represented in the following collections: National Gallery of Canada, Ottawa; Art Gallery of Ontario, Toronto; Art Gallery of Hamilton, Hamilton; Quebec Provincial Museum, Quebec City and in many private collections.

References

The Gazette, Mtl., Dec. 13, 1920 "Etcher Preserves Vanishing Scenes — Mr. Herbert Raine Finds Sympathetic Subjects in Oldest Montreal"

Montreal Star, Mtl., Dec. 17, 1920 "Old Montreal Perpetuated in Notable Etchings"

The Gazette, Mtl., Dec. 3, 1936 "Raine Water Colors, Etchings at Scott's"

Ibid, July 4, 1942 "Raine's Artistic 'Find' Same After 21 Years — Old Buildings on St. Paul Street East Were Subject of Etching" (reproductions of his etchings)

Quebec Chronicle-Telegraph, Que., Feb. 9, 1950 "Art Exhibition Opened At Museum"

The Gazette, Mtl., May 26, 1951 "Herbert Raine, 75, Noted Artist, Dies"

Art Gallery of Ontario by Helen Pepall Bradfield, McGraw-Hill, Tor., 1970, P.381

RAINE, Herbert (Cont'd)

Royal Canadian Academy of Arts, Exhibitions and Members 1880-1979 by Evelyn de R. McMann, Univ. Tor. Press, Tor., 1980, P.335-337
NGC Info. Form July 9, 1915; May 3, 1920
NGC Catalogue, Volume 3, Canadian School by R.H. Hubbard, NGC, Ottawa, 1960, P.409

RAINE, Michael
b. 1932

He studied at the École des Beaux-Arts, Montreal, where he met Mary and following their marriage they travelled to Paris where Michael studied at the Académie Julian. He took his Grade 13 examinations in the Canadian Embassy there and after his return to Canada entered the University of Western Ontario where he studied psychology. He then turned to painting and first became known for his variety of styles. He took his work to the public rather than waiting for the public to discover his work in galleries. He allowed the paintings to sell themselves and soon his patrons included nurses, doctors, physiotherapists, lawyers, scientists, teachers, students, news writers, artists, musicians, housewives and salesmen. He next moved into sculpture using the medium of fibreglass. Viewing his work in 1973 the *Globe & Mail* noted, "Michael Raine's fibreglass and resin sculptures appear to be lighted from within. His women in the garden at the Shaw-Rimmington Gallery have torsos of rough-cast fibreglass but their faces are beautifully smooth and clear. The translucent clarity draws attention away from their naked torsos and concentrates it on their faces which are all thrust upward with eyes closed. Their apparent tranquility invites contemplation, especially because one can look literally into their faces to a depth of several inches through the clear resin. With their faces tilted up the women look as though they might be standing under a shower. This impression is reinforced by the technique used to create the ladies' long flowing hair. Liquid resin has been poured over loose fibreglass strands and allowed to harden into droplets like water permanently on the point of falling from the ends of strands of hair. The three sculptures done in this manner are entitled Maria, Ellen and Vivian. They are all beautiful women although Vivian is, perhaps, a little sad." Raine has also exhibited his work at Gallery House Sol, Georgetown, Ontario (1972) with Joan Willsher-Martel.

References
Toronto Telegram, Ont., Feb. 2, 1967 "Art a la cart" by Elizabeth Kimball
Toronto Daily Star, Ont., June 26, 1972 "In Touch With Art"
Globe & Mail, Tor., Ont., Sept. 29, 1973 (review of Toronto shows)
Canadian Artists in Exhibition, 1972-1973, Roundstone, Tor., Ont., P.174

RAINEY, Paul
b. 1949

Born in Winnipeg, Manitoba, his family moved east to Oakville, Ontario, where he attended Gordon E. Perdue High School. Subsequently he began painting on a free lance basis and in 1971 was exploring the use of colour and its spatial relationship using acrylics on canvas. His drawings caught the attention of the

RAINEY, Paul (Cont'd)

Oakville Journal-Record who reproduced one of them for a Christmas issue. By 1973 he was working in hard-edge, other modern modes as well as traditional concepts. His exhibitions include: Oakville Centennial Gallery, Oakville, Ont. (3-man, 1968); Kitchener-Waterloo Gallery, Kitchener, Ont. (solo prior to 1971); Erindale College, Mississauga, Ont. (solo, 1971); Gallery House Sol, Georgetown, Ont. (solo, 1972); Oakville Art Society, Oakville, Ont. (group shows).

References

Oakville Beaver, Ont., Oct. 10, 1968 "The first of three at gallery"
Brampton Daily Times, Ont., Oct. 23, 1971 "Erindale Shows Artist's Work"
Oakville Journal-Record, Ont., Sept. 13, 1972 "Georgetown gallery exhibits works of two town artists" by Suzanne Morrison
Ibid, clipping, December, 1974 "Christmas memories can be frightening"

RAINEY, Tim
b. 1946

Born in Winnipeg, Manitoba, his family moved east to Oakville, Ontario where he attended the Gordon E. Perdue High School and then studied four years at the Ontario College of Art, Toronto. A painter and ceramist he has been interested in ceramic high relief murals. He completed one of these murals for the new Pottery Supply House on Speers Road opposite Proctor, in Oakville. He made plaster of Paris molds for the mural pieces then filled the molds with clay and let the clay set. He then removed the clay pieces to dry. Each clay piece was then fired by Rainey at Sheridan College and returned for final assembly at the Pottery Supply House. The mural measures 17 feet by 11 feet. Tim was planning to move to Bracebridge where he and his brother Paul, also a painter, would erect a studio to their own specifications

References

Oakville Beaver, Ont., Sept. 26, 1968 "Do not disturb — Mural maker at work" by Robert Blans (article with photos)
Ibid, Apr. 24, 1969 "It's like a giant jigsaw puzzle" by Barbara Scott (article with photo)
Hamilton Spectator, Ont., Aug. 23, 1969 "Fancy wall" (photo of ceramic mural by Rainey with caption)
Orangeville Banner, Ont., Sept. 4, 1969 (photo of ceramic mural by Rainey with caption)
Oakville Beaver, Ont., Sept. 25, 1969 "What ever happened to Tim's sculpture?" (photo of mural with Tim Rainey alongside)

RAINFORD, Ken

He won a design contest in 1972 for the Canada Summer Games logo while he was an employee of the *Vancouver Sun*. The design appeared on promotional material and was created in the form of a giant mosaic on the floor of the plaza built atop Mount Burnaby to commemorate the 1973 Canada Summer Games.

Reference

Vancouver Sun, B.C., Nov. 23, 1972 "Sun Artist" (photo of Ken Rainford with his winning design)

RAINNIE, Hedley Graham Jones
1914-1961

Born in London, England, he studied at the West Ham Municipal College (School of Art) London East; Royal Academy School, Burlington House, Piccadilly, London with Sir Walter Russell, R.A. He completed his studies in 1936 and for the next two years painted portraits in England. He left England in 1938 on a tour visiting Australia (6 months) where he painted, entertained (sang in a nightclub) and acted on radio, and New Zealand (12 months) where he travelled and taught life drawing in the Wellington Art School. His tour was cut short at the outbreak of the Second World War. He arrived in Vancouver, Canada in 1940 and moved on to Toronto where he became a radio actor, illustrator for a number of Canadian magazines and a portrait painter. Rainnie was good at voice imitation and played the 'Digger,' an Australian gunnery officer in the CBC serial "Fighting Navy." He also played the part of Prime Minister Winston Churchill in the series "Mr. Churchill of England." In painting he did oils, water colours and pastels and became known for his portrait and figure studies. He exhibited with the Ontario Society of Artists and the Royal Canadian Academy and became a member of both (O.S.A., 1944-1953; A.R.C.A., 1945-1953). In 1944 he spent six weeks on the frigate H.M.C.S. St. Catharines, to make drawings and paintings of Naval personnel in action. He later did larger paintings from some of his on-the-spot sketches. His Canadian Naval War paintings were exhibited in the Avon Galleries of the Robert Simpson Company Limited, Toronto (January 5 to 20th, 1945) with half the proceeds of the show going to The Navy League of Canada. His war paintings were also exhibited in Hamilton later that year. By 1947 Rainnie was living in New York City. He died in England in 1961. He is represented in the Canadian War Collection by an oil painting.

References

Globe & Mail, Tor., Ont., Aug. 24, 1944 "To paint the Royal Canadian Navy" (photo of Rainnie and caption)

Aylmer Express, Ont., Sept., 1944 "Newfoundland Accent Stumps Impersonator" (article on Rainnie's ability to imitate different accents)

The Evening Telegram, Tor., Ont., Dec. 30, 1944 "Rainnie Naval Paintings" (exhibited at Simpsons under the auspices of the Navy League of Canada)

Press Release — From Frances Turner, The Robert Simpson Company Limited, January 5, 1945 (re: exhibition and biographical notes)

The Evening Telegram, Tor., Ont., Jan. 6, 1945 "At The Galleries — Action Of Sea Captured In Navy League Exhibit"

Globe & Mail, Tor., Ont., Jan. 6, 1945 "Exhibit of Naval Paintings Opened at Robert Simpson Co."

Mayfair, Tor., Ont., March, 1945 "The Draftiest Studio In The World" (photo of Rainnie at work on board ship — also reproduction of his painting "Is Your Loud-Hailer Working?"

Saturday Night, Tor., Ont., Sept. 29, 1945 (photo of "Torps" a painting by Rainnie of a torpedo officer)

Hamilton Spectator, Ont., Oct. 17, 1945 "Art Exhibition Opens; Proceeds To Navy League"

Check List of The War Collections by R.F. Wodehouse, NGC, Ottawa, 1968, P.187

A History of the Royal Canadian Academy of Arts, by Rebecca Sisler, Clarke, Irwin & Company Ltd., Tor., 1980, P.287

Royal Canadian Academy of Arts, Exhibitions and Members 1880-1979 by Evelyn de R. McMann, Univ. Tor. Press, Tor., 1981, P.337

NGC Info. Form rec'd Dec. 10, 1941

RAINS, Malcolm
b. 1947

Born in Bristol, England, he emigrated to Canada in 1955 and studied Architecture at the University of Detroit (1967-69); Architecture at the University of Toronto (1969-70); Art at the Ontario College of Art (1971-74) graduating in 1974. A sculptor and painter, his 1979 work was noted by the *Globe & Mail* as follows, "Rains is a sculptor with roots in the Minimalist tradition. He is showing a group of wall pieces cast in plaster. Each is marked with a cross or a single chiselled incision, colored with the subtlest of pigments and glazed with wax. These works, Rains says, have made themselves under his direction. Some have been cracked or chipped by his chisel or the curing process and such accidents are incorporated into the work, which is elegant and hushed in the manner of a musical tone poem. The work evolved from Rains' earlier work with plaster to be translated into bronze. 'One day I heard the plaster,' he says, 'I heard the plaster and I began to listen.' " His solo shows include: Recent Sculpture, Sable-Castelli Gallery, Tor. (1979); Recent Drawings, Sable-Castelli Gallery, Tor. (1979) and he has participated in the following group shows: 2 plus 5, Gallery Pascal, Tor. (1973); A Space Gallery, Tor. (1974); Aspects of Sculpture, Ontario College of Art (1978); Performance, Harbourfront Art Gallery, Tor. (1978); Toronto Alternatives Exhibition, Etobicoke Civic Centre Art Gallery, Etobicoke (1978); From A to Z, Sable-Castelli Gallery, Tor. (1979); Small Sculpture, Harbourfront Art Gallery, Tor. (1979); Beyond Color, The Gallery, York University's Glendon Campus, Tor. (1980); Ewart, Menzies, Rains, Art Gallery of Ontario Members' Lounge, Tor. (1981). His awards include: Ont. Assoc. of Architects Scholarship (1972); Ontario Art Council Grants (1977, 1978); Canada Council Short-term Grant (1978); Canada Council Arts Grant 'B' (1979). He is represented in the Canada Council Art Bank, Ottawa.

References

    Vie des Arts, Automne, 1978

    Artmagazine, November/December, 1978 "A Look Back at Sculpture during the Sculpture Conference" by Badanna Zack, P.48

    Performance, An Exhibition of Sculpture, Harbourfront Art Gallery, Tor., 1978, P.8 (No.85)

    Globe & Mail, Tor., Ont., Jan. 27, 1979 "Gallery Reviews"

    Ibid, Nov. 3, 1979

    Artscanada, Tor., August/September, 1979

RAINVILLE, Jacques   see JARAIN Volume 3

RAINVILLE, Kenneth

A self-taught artist he exhibited his landscapes at Gallery 93, Ottawa, when W.Q. Ketchum of the *Ottawa Journal* noted, "This viewer particularly liked Revival, exemplifying spring. Trilliums are in the foreground against a backdrop of trees. Rainville is an artist for all seasons. Autumn Glow shows the trees with their leaves in the 'sere and yellow' stages. They have a connotation of sadness. Last Snow shows the snow-encrusted trees. Rainville's display highlights a significant and natural talent."

RAINVILLE, Kenneth (Cont'd)

Reference

Ottawa Journal, Ont., Nov. 10, 1975 "An artist for all seasons" by W.Q. Ketchum

---

RAINVILLE, Réal
b. 1949

Born in Berthierville, Quebec, he studied at Collège André Grasset, Montreal and Visual Arts at the University of Ottawa. He studied Occidental Art at the Prado Museum, Spain and 20th Century Art in Provence, France. He taught ceramics to classes at the Rockland Cultural Centre, Rockland, Ontario. He lives at Berthierville, Quebec. Has exhibited his work at the Centre Culturel de Berthierville (1966) and Collège André Grasset in a group show (1971).

References

NGC Info.Form undated

Dictionnaire Biographique des Créateurs de la Région de Joliette par Réjean Olivier, Musée du Québec, Québec, P.81

RAJOTTE, Yves
b. 1932

Born in Montreal, Quebec, he studied five years at the École des Beaux-Arts, Montreal, under Picard, Cosgrove and de Tonnancour and completed his studies in 1956. A painter mainly in the abstract working in a variety of mediums including acrylic with which he has achieved effective results. He has exhibited his work at Galerie Libre, Mtl. (1960); Musée d'art contemporain, Mtl. (1965); Centre d'art du Mont-Royal, Mtl. (1967); Galerie Bernard Desroches, Mtl. (1976), and elsewhere. He is represented in the collections of the Musée d'art contemporain, Mtl., and Musée du Québec, Que. He has taught Plastic Arts for C.E.C.M. for a number of years. Lives in Montreal.

References

L'enseignement, Mtl., November, 1960 "M. Yves Rajotte" (photo of artist and caption)

La Presse, Mtl.,Nov. 26, 1960 "Yves Rajotte" (photo of painting and review of Galerie Libre show)

Dimanche-Matin, Mtl., Nov. 19, 1967 "Exposition d'Yves Rajotte" (notes on Rajotte during showing at Centre d'art du Mont-Royal)

NGC Info. Form undated

RAKINE, Boris
b. 1905

Born in Russia, he studied sculpture in the Royal Academy of Bucharest, Romania, then received a Romanian government scholarship to study in Paris where he remained for over twenty years. He studied under Bourdelle; at the Académie Ranson under Charles Despiau and painting at the Académie de la Grande Chaumière with Othon Friesz. He did a memorial at the French-American Museum in France. He came to Toronto in 1949 to join his artist wife, Marthe Rakine. He had a framing shop in Toronto. Probably returned to Paris in 1958.

RAKINE, Boris (Cont'd)

References
> *NGC Info. Form rec'd 1954*
> *Mayfair*, Montreal, February, 1957 "Rakine: the happy compromise" by Robert Fulford

RAKINE, Marthe
b.(c) 1906

Born in Moscow, Russia, she lived there only a few years before making her home in Paris. Her father was a Swiss construction engineer and her mother came from Provence in southern France. During her early years she travelled with her father to many countries. It was her travel that stimulated her interest in painting. She worked initially in water colours and painted a wide range of subject matter. Her artistic education began in the heart of the Latin Quarter of Paris in 1926 at the School of Decorative Arts where she took painting courses. She also attended the Sorbonne for other courses. She frequented the Luxembourg Gardens and the Louvre Museum and there visited the art book-shops. It was in this setting that she developed her painting skills. She studied painting at the Académie de la Grande Chaumière under Othon Friesz (c.1937) under whom her husband Boris also took studies (they probably met there first). She began exhibiting her work in 1932 and her sensitivity to colours was noted by the art critic Jacques Guenne, director of *L'Art Vivant*. Her work was later written about by Guy Weelen in an intimate book *Marthe Rakine* (1949) covering her background, development, influences, philosophy and analysis of her work. During World War II painting was difficult and exhibiting was thought to be a type of collaboration. One painting she showed "Arc de Triomphe", was purchased by a German general so she decided to abstain from further showings. She turned instead to iconography which she worked on for the next four years and exhibited her icons in a Paris cathedral. Boris and Marthe lived in joint studios in the southwest section of Paris near Porte de Versailles in a cottage hidden beneath a wild grape arbor with its bay windows opening onto a quiet street. By 1945 she was painting reclining women described by Weelen as follows, "Marthe Rakine preferred to paint reclining women, lying near vast windows opening onto a garden or overlooking the sea, in an atmosphere of blissful calm." But the Rakines found Europe tired and uninspiring after the war so they decided to seek new horizons in the Americas. With a Swiss citizenship, money to support herself and a place to study, Marthe was accepted by Canada late in 1948 and enrolled at the Ontario College of Art where she studied ceramics (1949-50). In 1949 she was joined by her husband Boris. In 1950 she received the "Form and Design" prize awarded by the Drakenfeld Company of New York for her ceramics at the Canadian National Exhibition. She participated in many group shows in Toronto and in 1951 held a solo show at Hart House which roused immediate enthusiasm. In 1952 she was invited to participate in the Canadian section of the Pittsburgh International Exhibition and chose her painting "The Daffodils." Subsequently she exhibited at the Eaton Fine Art Galleries when Pearl McCarthy noted, "While everything from still life to figures held attention, the recent Canadian landscapes were most surprising. Here was Algonquin Park, done as one had never seen it before, and yet true in spirit to that typical Canadian land. Apparently this artist is a valuable addition to the Toronto art circles." In 1954 a review of her work appeared in the *Montreal Herald*, "Mlle. Rakine's paintings make such direct sensuous appeal that objective comment is difficult. She impresses me as one of the most competent colorists exhibiting in Canada

RAKINE, Marthe (Cont'd)

today. Each individual painting is a feast of color presented in the impressionist manner, yet there is not a single discord in the entire display. . .the picture looked at quickly organizes itself, revealing the sound composition that is essential to any form of art." A three column article in *Mayfair* by Robert Fulford covered biographical details and noted her painting as follows, "Not surprisingly, the paintings give very little importance to the subjects but emphasize the quality. Her surfaces are exciting and vibrant, full of the piercing tension that can be seen in some of the best non-objective painting. Still, she believes the subjects are important; she thinks total non-objective art is limiting in its emotional scope. 'It is hard to paint that way with love,' she says, 'I think it is quite important that a painter paint with love." Her paintings were quickly acquired by collectors and public galleries. She returned to Paris in 1958. She was a member of the Ontario Society of Artists (1953) and the Canadian Group of Painters (1956). Her solo shows include: Hart House, Tor. (1951); Eaton Fine Art Galleries, Tor. (1951); Picture Loan Society, Tor. (1952); Laing Galleries, Tor. (1953); Gallery XII, M.M.F.A., Mtl. (1954); Waddington Galleries, Mtl. (1957). She is represented in the following collections: Hart House, Univ. Tor., Tor.; Art Gallery of Ontario, Tor.; Agnes Etherington Art Centre, Kingston; Art Gallery of Cobourg, Cobourg; National Gallery of Canada, Ottawa and elsewhere.

References

Globe & Mail, Tor., Ont., Feb. 24, 1951 "Marthe Rakine's Exhibition Among Best New Displays" by Pearl McCarthy

Ibid, Dec. 6, 1952 "Marthe Rakine" (show at Picture Loan Society)

Ibid, Nov. 28, 1953 "Art and Artists — Joyousness, the Keynote For This Week's Openings" by Pearl McCarthy

Montreal Gazette, Mtl., Dec. 4, 1954 "Paintings Are Shown By Marthe Rakine"

La Presse, Mtl., Dec. 10, 1954 "L'art de Marthe Rakine doué d'un rare prestige" par R. de Repentigny

Montreal Herald, Mtl., Dec. 17, 1954 (review of Gallery XII show)

Toronto Star, Tor., Oct. 31, 1956 "Nearly Wasn't Admitted Now Successful Artist"

Mayfair, Mtl., February, 1957 "Rakine: the happy compromise" by Robert Fulford

Canadian Paintings In Hart House by J. Russell Harper, H.H./Univ. of Tor. Press, Tor., 1955, P.81

Art Gallery of Ontario, the Canadian Collection by Helen Pepall Bradfield, McGraw Hill, Tor., 1970, P.382

Second Biennial of Canadian Art, N.G.C., 1957, No.27

The Arts in Canada, Ed. Malcolm Ross, "Painting" by Robert Ayre, MacMillan, Tor., 1958, P.14

Marthe Rakine par Guy Weelen, Éditions Les Presses Littéraires de France, Paris, 1949

National Gallery of Canada Catalogue, Volume III by R.H. Hubbard, N.G.C., Ottawa, P.253

Cobourg Sentinel-Star, Ont., Sept. 19, 1962 "Six Original Paintings In Art Gallery"

Canadian Group of Painters Exhibition, 1962, Art Gallery of Toronto/N.G.C., 1963, No.50

Agnes Etherington Art Centre Permanent Collection 1968 by Frances K. Smith, Queen's Univ., Kingston, 1968, No.114

Hart House Collection of Canadian Paintings, H.H./Univ. Tor. Press, Tor., 1969, No.121

Canadian Art At Auction, 1968-1975 by Geoffrey Joyner, Sotheby, Tor., 1975, P.161

Permanent Collection, 1977, Art Gallery of Cobourg by Shirley M. O'Neil, Cobourg, Ont., 1977

Canadian Art Auctions, Sales and Prices, 1976-1978 by Harry Campbell, General Publishing, Don Mills, Ont., P.200

Royal Canadian Academy of Arts, Exhibitions and Members, 1880-1979 by Evelyn de R. McMann, Univ. Tor. Press, Tor., 1981, P.337

NGC Info. Form rec'd Feb. 25, 1952

A note on the proposed site of the National Gallery

There have been proposals to establish a ring of national cultural institutions around Parliament Hill on the Ontario and Quebec sides of the Ottawa River. The choice of such a site for the relocation of the National Gallery of Canada would not be in the best interests of the many thousands of Canadians and citizens from other countries who visit and use our Gallery.

Since 1957 the National Gallery of Canada has been housed in temporary quarters in the Lorne Building — an inadequate, converted office block, which has only one virtue — its location on Elgin Street in the cultural heart of our capital, near the National Arts Centre, Confederation Park, the Rideau Canal and CARTIER SQUARE. It is a friendly, busy area, where office and government workers, visitors and strollers pass by and mingle at all seasons of the year.

CARTIER SQUARE (bounded by Laurier, Elgin, Lisgar and the Canal), named after Georges-Étienne Cartier, one of the Fathers of Confederation, is the last significant piece of land in the centre of the national capital still owned by the federal government. It is on this site that many people believe the new National Gallery should be located.

The National Gallery of London is on Trafalgar Square, the Louvre is in the centre of Paris, the Uffizzi in the centre of Florence, the American National Gallery is in the centre of Washington, the Art Gallery of Ontario is in downtown Toronto, like the Centre Pompidou in Paris. Shouldn't the National Gallery of Canada be located in the heart of Ottawa?

If you think our National Gallery should be placed in the living, breathing heart of your capital, express your views by writing to the Prime Minister and/or your own MP. Send a copy of your letter to your local newspaper.

For further information write to:

Chairman B. Kay,
Cartier Square Advisory Committee,
248 Elgin Street, Suite 3,
OTTAWA, Canada
K2P 1L9